Best Vacation Rentals

Europe

Produced by The Philip Lief Group, Inc.

Managing Editor, Richard Eastman

Edited by Constance Jones

Written and Researched by:

Julia Banks
Scott Corngold
Luz Cruz
Loren Elmaleh
Josh Eppinger
Robyn Feller
Fiona Gilsenan
Catherine Henningsen
Robert Hernandez
Robin Hohman
Mitsy Campbell Kovacs
Lisa Schwartzburg
Willy Spain
Paula Stelzner
Susan Wells
Denise Wydra

Design by Margaret Davis
Maps by Myra Klockenbrink and Charlie Williams

Best Vacation Rentals

Europe

A Traveler's Guide to Cottages, Condos, and Castles

Prentice Hall Press
New York

The information in this book is the most up-to-date available at the time of publication. However, specifics can change and we recommend that you confirm all details before making reservations. In addition, many states are currently reviewing and changing policies on the right of accommodations to refuse children as guests, and if a child-free environment is important, you should check with the establishment about its current policy.

 Published by Prentice Hall Press
A division of Simon & Schuster Inc.
15 Columbus Circle
New York, NY 10023

Produced by The Philip Lief Group, Inc.
6 West 20th Street
New York, NY 10011

ISBN 0-13-928-219-X

ISSN 1054-9765

Manufactured in the United States of America

First Edition   10 9 8 7 6 5 4 3 2 1

Contents

Introduction:
A World of Homes Away from Home

Picture yourself at the window seat of the Venetian townhouse you've rented for a week. Tucked away on a warm and quiet sun-filled canal, the waters gently lap against the stone foundation as they have for hundreds of years. Passing gondoliers serenade you, and this most romantic of Italian cities seems to come alive just for you.

Perhaps you'd rather imagine a cozy stone cottage in Provence. Outside your door, meadow grasses and wild flowers sway in the mild breezes of spring. Filling your canteen from the old hand pump in the yard, you watch your children wheel bicycles out of the barn where they've been playing. Together you peddle off to the village to buy provisions for the day's picnic.

Or envision a sleek modern flat in Austria. The weekend's jaunt to Vienna—filled with music, coffeehouses, and carriage rides—is still fresh in your mind. With the snow-covered Alps as a backdrop, you prepare a hearty breakfast for your companion, who lounges in the featherbed. Then grab your skis and head out the door for a day on the slopes.

Each of these vacation fantasies can come true once the secrets of the self-catered getaway are revealed. People seeking an extra element of privacy, comfort, adventure and economy on vacation have begun to discover the advantages of renting houses, cabins and apartments when they travel. Instead of settling for a cramped, nondescript room in a hotel or an inn and paying for three expensive restaurant meals a day, you can enjoy the convenience and independence of homes away from home. Today, a whole world of vacation rental options—from fully staffed mansions to compact studios, from lavish resort bungalows to rustic lodges—lies open to the savvy, adventurous traveler.

A traveler's guide to cottages, condos, and castles, *Best Vacation Rentals: Europe* introduces you to the unique pleasures of self-sufficient travel. The properties presented in the pages that follow offer stunning locales and delightful features unavailable in traditional lodgings to create an exciting and intimate environment seemingly designed just for you. Gardens, Jacuzzis or balconies; historic surroundings, breathtaking views or fireplaces; a taste for local color or seclusion off the beaten path—a uniquely suited vacation rental lets you choose the best setting for your next trip.

The personalized touch you can get in planning a vacation of this kind allows you to indulge all of your specific needs and interests more completely than simply registering at the best local hotel. For instance, couples can enjoy the privacy, peace and solitude offered by a romantic and secluded place of their own while senior citizens may appreciate the services, comfort and convenience of self-contained units at full-staffed resort condos. Families appreciate the extra indoor and outdoor space, savings on food and lodging and access to kitchen and laundry room facilities.

Best Vacation Rentals: Europe lists in its pages vacation rental properties scattered throughout every region of Europe—from a charming houseboat on the Adriatic to a working farm in the center of the Loire's chateau country to the tumultuous Berlin cityscape—to suit every desire and budget. An astonishing array of self-sufficient lodgings is available through several types of businesses and organizations:

- Vacation rental agencies that rent vacation houses, apartments and condominiums owned by individuals who use them only during certain seasons.

- Hotel and resort complexes that include bungalows and apartments.

- Private owners who offer their homes for rent at certain times of the year.

- Historical societies and government agencies that manage unusual properties maintained by foundations or municipalities.

This diverse combination of sources gives you access to every type of vacation rental accommodation—whether you seek a restored castle, a contemporary holiday home or a simple cottage—and to every vacation destination, from the most popular to the most secluded. An appendix at the end of the book directs you to national tourism boards that can provide you with further information on self-catered travel in Europe.

Before you turn to the listings, take a moment to read "Travel Tips." It covers the nuts and bolts of self-sufficient travel and outlines exactly what to look for and what to expect when planning a self-catered vacation. As you read, you will find valuable information on selecting the appropriate type of lodging, making reservations and determining what to bring. You'll learn how to research the differences among rentals, such as frequency of housekeeping service, provision of kitchen equipment and linens and requirements for minimum stays. Specific suggestions relating to European travel are featured in a special section. A short "How to Use This Guide" follows and describes how the book is organized and how to read the listings. A quick glance at these guides will help you make the most of this invaluable source book, no matter which kind of getaway you choose.

Welcome to the exciting world of *Best Vacation Rentals: A Traveler's Guide to Cottages, Condos, and Castles*—and have a great European trip!

Travel Tips:
Making Yourself at Home

Congratulations on selecting a travel option that will make your trip more fascinating, relaxing and fun! Experienced vacation renters have found that a little preparation can go a long way toward making your vacation rental a smashing success. And with that in mind, this section shows you both what to look for and what to expect when renting a vacation home. A little research will help you get the most out of your home away from home.

What kind of vacation home is right for me?

Although many American travelers are new to self-catering vacations —those where you make a rental home your own for the length of your stay—a dizzying array of possibilities lies open to the traveler who knows where to look, especially in Europe. Travel-hungry Europeans have been vacationing this way for decades, and the incredible abundance of vacation rentals available in every area of Europe will astound you: Fishing shacks along Norwegian fjords, storybook castles in Ireland—whatever your dream destination, you can find a European vacation home there. Many different sources are available. Each has distinct advantages, and all are represented in this guide.

Vacation rental agencies based in North America and Europe often represent dozens, hundreds or even thousands of rental homes and apartments in one or more countries, giving you an almost endless selection of properties to choose from. Many of the listings that appear in this book are handled by such agencies, most of which also offer scores more rentals than could be listed here—so when you call or write to request information on a property, inquire as well about other rentals that might be of interest. Leasing through an agency can make the job a lot easier: This arrangement ensures that your selection has met stringent quality requirements, and they handle all the financial and scheduling arrangements and any problems that may arise during your stay. You may find dealing with a North American-based agency the easiest solution to selecting a European vacation rental, because differences in language, currency and time zones are eliminated. But most European agencies are accustomed to servicing American clients and do everything they can to make renting through them as easy as possible.

Hotel and resort complexes with bungalows or condominiums on the grounds offer less variety in lodging type but provide all of the amenities expected from a standard hotel or motel. Swimming pools, complimentary breakfasts, housekeeping/linen service and child care are only a few comforts offered in this category. And because self-catering suites or apartments in such establishments may cost no more than an ordinary hotel room, they represent a real bargain. The level of luxury often far exceeds what you might expect for the price, so resorts are guaranteed to appeal to vacationers who want to be pampered. Generally located near the action—in downtown areas or popular tourist destinations—resort condos have the added advantage of easy access to all the local attractions.

Private owners provide wonderfully personal vacation lodgings— where personal libraries, video collections, gourmet kitchens or even cars or boats are often at your disposal. And because owners may have only one property for rent, they can give undivided attention to your questions, requests and needs. Ask the owners for advice on shopping, dining, sightseeing and local traditions, or have them put you in touch with neighbors who can ease you into a foreign setting. Private owners may not be equipped to accept your credit cards, but they'll often leave a trail of personal touches and amenities seldom found in more formal arrangements.

Historical societies and government agencies offer unique vacation rental possibilities. If you are looking for a perfectly preserved sea captain's home on the coast of Brittany or a cleverly converted landmark Dutch windmill, these sources are for you. Maintained through private donations or public funds, historic properties frequently rent for absurdly low rates. (In fact, many agencies are interested only in covering the cost of your stay, not in making a profit.) Time spent in this truly special kind of setting could prove unforgettable, and make your vacation stay a lifelong treasured memory.

Regardless of the self-catering alternative you select, you are guaranteed to derive tremendous benefits from this kind of vacation. If you managed to locate comparable accommodations in a traditional hotel, they would likely be far more expensive. While squeezing into a good London hotel room for a week strains the finances of many families, a spacious two-bedroom self-catered flat—with a kitchen and maybe a fireplace or washing machine—can be quite affordable. Self-caterers save even more by eating some meals (particularly breakfasts, which are often light but expensive) at "home" instead of in restaurants.

Even when money is not an issue, the extra space and increased privacy of a house or apartment makes any vacation more pleasurable. Good-bye paper-thin walls and postage-stamp rooms! These become a thing of the past when you leave hotels behind for rentals. The freedom to whip up a midnight snack or a secret family recipe for finicky children can also be a boon to weary tourists. A place to keep your beer cold, a machine to wash your socks, or a grassy yard to nap in removes that great stress of traveling: the need to compromise on comfort.

But it's up to *you* to tap the potential of your vacation rental to the fullest. Maybe you prefer to travel with friends, and need separate bedrooms at night in addition to common areas for group activities. Perhaps your family can't live without at least two bathrooms. A private yard for your children to play in, a secluded haven miles away from the next neighbor, a wide porch to view spectacular sunsets: Renting a vacation home can secure any creature comforts you require while traveling. Even if no one in your party wants to be the cook, self-catering still makes sense: You'll save money while enjoying more space, greater privacy and personalized comforts not found in traditional inns or hotels.

Be sure to reserve far in advance, because the demand for these appealing properties is high among travel aficionados. Many travelers return again and again to a favorite rental, sometimes booking their time slot a year in advance. Don't worry, however, that you won't be able to find something you like: The sheer number of vacation rentals on the market almost ensures a suitable property will be available wherever you're going—and whenever you're going there. But remember that the most attractive lodgings and those that represent the best value go quickly, especially in peak seasons.

The various rental sources offer a wide array of vacation homes, from compact studio apartments to modern condominiums and from rustic cottages to lavish estates. When deciding among these vacation rental options, consider your traveling needs, desires and budget and make sure your lodging meets them. The location, setting, design and decor should satisfy your tastes and enhance your vacation experience. For instance: Do health problems preclude an isolated setting far from town? Would you prefer the excitement of the city? Do A-frame chalets make you feel claustrophobic? Have you always wanted to live in an eighteenth-century chateau?

The Comforts of Home—and More

Each traveler has a unique notion of the ideal vacation lodging. (Indeed, self-catering is not for everyone.) But travelers who appreciate the advantages of renting a home away from home can expect their vacation rentals to offer certain amenities. The rentals included in this book all have kitchen facilities, living areas and at least one comfortable bed, but beyond that vary widely. As you set out to find your dream flat or cottage from among the listings that follow, keep these few pointers in mind to help you determine how potential rentals rate.

Each listing includes information on the special features most important to travelers. Look for a mention of balconies, decks, porches or patios if you like to lounge outdoors, or of yards, gardens or extensive acreage if you long to stretch out. Imagine the perfect setting, then scour the listings for properties with water frontage, views or unusual architectural or design features.

Indoors, you'll make decisions about telephones, televisions, VCRs, fireplaces, Jacuzzis, hot tubs and saunas. Many rentals come complete with barbecues, while others offer swimming pools or private beaches. Decide which items will make your vacation complete and mark the listings that meet your requirements.

Basic services are at least as important to a rental's appeal as its location is, and the listings present comprehensive information that will help you narrow your selection of possibilities. Is heat or air conditioning important to you? Will you need a parking space? Are linens and blankets provided, and are they changed on a daily or weekly basis? Is housekeeping service included? Is it offered daily, weekly or between tenants only? Will you have the assistance of a full- or part-time maid or other staff member? Among the other diverse services available: complimentary breakfast, lunch, dinner or cocktails and babysitting or other child care services.

You can expect the kitchen to come equipped with a refrigerator, stove, cooking and eating utensils, plates and glassware (listings generally do not make specific mention of these items). Look for references to items you require in addition to the basics—such as a microwave—to help narrow your field of choices. For those who want to rent but don't plan to cook, many listings mention bars or restaurants on the premises or close by. Some rentals offer private cooks who can prepare your favorite meals without your having to lift a finger.

Having established this basic information, the listings go on to describe a colorful array of optional amenities. You'll come across everything from stereos, pianos and wet bars to security systems, valet service and meeting rooms. Some listings mention free use of bicycles, docking facilities or country club privileges, while others make note of playgrounds, tennis courts or skiing in the area. Don't despair if your dream rental seems to be missing one key element: It might be there; we just couldn't fit it all in. If a rental sounds tempting, investigate it further by calling or writing the contact listed to learn more.

Clearly, *Best Vacation Rentals: Europe* is only meant to be a starting point—the variety of features offered in vacation rental homes couldn't be contained in these pages. But the abundance of features described in the listings proves that, whatever your travel desires, self-catering can fulfill them.

Check It Out

Once you've targeted some possible properties, take the first step in planning a self-catered trip: Request brochures with photographs of those that interest you; and ask for local maps and any other available materials. If you're contacting an agency, ask for information on its rules and regulations and inquire about other properties in the area you will visit. Agencies publish extensive catalogues containing data on many more vacation rentals than *Best Vacation Rentals: Europe* could accommodate, and their listings change periodically.

The agents, resorts, private owners and historical societies will pro vide complete details, in writing, about the properties listed in this book and let you know if anything has changed since publication. Additionally, we recommend that you speak with someone by telephone to confirm everything. As you review the material and prepare to make your final choice, be sure none of your questions are left unanswered.

Take the time to formulate a complete picture of your potential rental. If something you require is not mentioned—fax service, for example, or a kitchen with an automatic coffee maker—ask if it is available. A kennel to make it easier to tour around without an enthusiastic Fido in tow, an on-site owner or manager to set your mind at ease or a game room to help keep the kids busy while you sunbathe are other considerations that may apply to your individual travel situation. The athletic vacationer might ask if there's a gym on the premises, or if golf, boating, fishing, hiking or riding are available nearby.

Confirm that the property is open and available on the dates you plan to visit. Find out if your visit will fall in peak season, and if the proprietor will book a reservation as far in advance as is practical to avoid disappointment. If a minimum stay is required (many vacation rentals are offered by the week only), see if it applies to your off-season stay. When you are not renting an individual house, you may want to find out how many units the building, resort or restoration you've chosen encompasses. Some travelers prefer the security of large complexes; others like the intimacy of smaller establishments.

Ascertain that the unit you want to rent is the right size. Make sure it can accommodate at least the number of guests in your party, and determine if the number of bedrooms included provides adequate privacy. You may wish to confirm that the beds are the size you prefer. (If you and your mate like to share a double bed, for instance, don't risk ending up with two twins.) Get a sense of the overall size of the unit, including any common areas, the kitchen and outdoor space.

Ask about any restrictions placed on guests: Are pets allowed? What about St. Bernards? Can you smoke indoors? Even if you smoke a pipe or cigar? Is the unit accessible to the handicapped? Are there steep stairs or a wheelchair ramp? Some older rentals—reached by rugged footpaths, equipped with steep stairs or built with narrow doorways—may be particularly problematic for the infirm.

Request precise rate information on the dates of your intended stay. Most rates fluctuate on a seasonal or even a weekly basis. Find out what is included in the rate quoted and what sorts of extra charges might apply. You may or may not, for instance, be charged extra for heat, for the use of certain resort facilities, for daily instead of weekly housekeeping or linen service, for extra guests or for a pet.

On the other hand, some establishments offer discounts to senior citizens, groups or guests who pay in advance. Check to see if you can take advantage of any price breaks. You may also discover tantalizing package deals, in which extra amenities or privileges are included at cut rates. Historic restorations sometimes offer packages that include the price of a unit rental plus golf or fishing privileges, tours of historic sites, cocktail parties and other bonuses.

Confirm the forms of payment accepted, and determine what kind of deposit is required to guarantee a reservation. Many properties ask for a deposit equal to one night's charge; others may request half or even all of the total rental fee up front. In some cases, the deposit may be charged by phone to a credit card, but most renters require a bank draft in the currency of the country in which the rental is located, and will hold your reservation for seven days to receive it. Agencies and individuals will also often ask you to sign a rental agreement (like a short-term lease agreement) and pay a security deposit against possible damage. The deposit is refunded to you after your stay, when it is determined you have not damaged the property.

Finally, check to see if check-in and check-out times fit your itinerary and if you must follow any special procedures when arriving or departing.

Make sure you understand the renter's cancellation policy before putting down a deposit: You can lose the entire amount if you need to cancel and don't give enough notice. This is also a good time to find out who is responsible for assisting you if something goes wrong with your rental while you are on vacation. And read any contracts carefully before you sign. Then, once you are satisfied with the details, go ahead and make your reservation. When you do, ask for a receipt or other confirmation that your deposit has been received and your reservation finalized.

Some carefree travelers, of course, can't be tied down by reservations, or prefer to experiment with new locations once their trip is well underway. Upon arrival in some irresistibly tempting locale, adventurers can usually find self-catering accommodations through local travel information bureaus, newspaper or real estate agents. In popular tourist destinations, rentals are sometimes found simply by walking or driving around with an eye out for "vacancy" or "for rent" signs. When a charming vacant property is spied, rent it on the spot—often for a favorable rate and no minimum stay requirement. Using this method, savvy self-caterers who don't require the security of advance planning can find wonderful lodgings at great rates. *But if you're traveling on-season, reservations are strongly recommended.*

Be Prepared

Do you need to pack any differently for a self-catered vacation than you would for a traditional one? Not really. If the unit, especially the kitchen, does not provide some item or convenience you absolutely require, think about bringing it along. Of course, if you must pack light and the missing element—a television or microwave—is not easily transportable, you might consider either doing without or renting a different property.

Those whose rentals include access to laundry facilities may choose to pack fewer clothes than usual. You may want to add a flashlight or some candles to your luggage if it will help you feel safer in a strange house. Or if you have a favorite cook's knife or corkscrew, toss it in with your toothbrush and swimsuit.

Some self-caterers pack a few nonperishable necessities—herbal tea, a pound of their favorite coffee, a special spice—if they suspect the items might be difficult to find in local stores. Others surrender entirely to their destination, savoring the adventure of shopping and eating like a local resident. Experienced international self-caterers agree it is impractical and unnecessary to carry more than the smallest food items with you.

Beyond these few minor points, making arrangements for your self-catered trip should be no different from preparing for a traditional vacation. Pack as you normally would, and get ready to have a great time!

At Home on the Road

The travel experience is distinctly different when you choose a home away from home instead of lodging in a hotel. The extra space, comfort, independence and privacy are a luxury, but those who are first-timers may wonder if it involves more work. After all, who wants to do housework on vacation? A little planning goes a long way toward making your self-catered trip carefree.

The most obvious difference between self-catered and hotel accommodations is access to a kitchen. But remember: You can make as much or as little use of it as you like. Some self-caterers prepare every meal, but others only enter the kitchen to enjoy a midnight snack in their pajamas. Whatever your preference, a few simple rules will help you minimize shopping and cooking time.

Plan your basic weekly menu before leaving home. Find out from guidebooks, your property's management or neighbors what kinds of foods and shopping facilities are available. Take into account the number of meals you are likely to eat out, and design a menu based on as few ingredients as possible to avoid wasted staples and uneaten leftovers at departure time.

You'll find breakfast will be the time when you make best use of your rented kitchen, and you'll love the freedom of having your morning coffee and croissant in your bathrobe and slippers. So shop to make your vacation breakfasts special. Go ahead and buy the kinds of foods you normally don't indulge in.

For lunch and dinner, simple dishes requiring little advance preparation are best. Cooks who love to experiment with regional cuisines, however, have an exciting opportunity to cut loose when they travel the self-catered way—prowling the farmers' markets, fishermen's stalls and specialty shops in search of delectable local ingredients to bring home and cook up to their heart's delight.

Don't despair if you want to self-cater and can't stand the prospect of doing even minimal housework on vacation. As the listings in *Best Vacation Rentals* show, plenty of European vacation rentals include daily or weekly housekeeping service (this may or may not include dishwashing)—or even a full-time staff. And for those that do not include maid service during your stay, we've found that a small amount of housework on a daily basis goes a long way toward saving you from a laborious clean-up on the day of departure. It's all in choosing your dream rental and taking the time to make the simple preparations and inquiries about services necessary to ensure your comfort and happiness.

On the Continent: Special Tips for European Travel

Keep the following suggestions and tips in mind as you plan your self-catered vacation in Europe:

- Renting a vacation home in Europe involves only slight adjustments for visitors from North America. Various differences in currency, language and culture face all American and Canadian travelers in Europe, and individuals must observe proper customs and immigration procedures when crossing international borders. A travel agent or guidebook should provide answers to most of your questions, but for additional information, contact a branch of the national tourist office of the country you are visiting—there will almost always be one in major cities such as New York—or call the country's consulate in Washington, DC.

- Because travelers to Europe have more details to attend to than those who stay in North America, many self-caterers, especially first-time renters, find it easiest to locate and reserve a European vacation home through a U.S.-based agency. Many such agencies now serve American travelers, usually representing European agencies that in turn represent property owners. Going through an agency can simplify the process of arranging a self-catered trip to Europe, eliminating language barriers and the difficulty of trans-Atlantic contact. In addition, a single agency may offer you a selection of hundreds of properties, so one phone call can open up all kinds of rental possibilities. It may also be easier to obtain help from an agency in the U.S. if you should experience problems with your rental. Be aware, however, that agencies generally charge a commission; you must decide if the convenience is worth the expense.

- Do not expect European vacation homes to have exactly the same features as U.S. accommodations. European culture is less consumer-oriented, so you may find that the items you are used to seeing in abundance at home—such as soaps, paper products and other conveniences—are not as lavishly displayed there. This is not to say that European rentals are any less comfortable: They are just *different*.

- One such difference frequently encountered in European rentals: Towels, sheets and blankets might not be included in the price. Tenants must bring along their own linens or pay extra to have them supplied. Because these items are bulky, most American visitors elect to pay the extra charge rather than lug bedding overseas. When researching your vacation rental, be sure to check about linen service.

- Heat, electricity or other utilities may not be included in the base cost of your European rental, although they generally are figured into North American rentals. Find out if utilities are separate, and if so, how much they cost.

- In contrast with hotel travel, self-catering in Europe will sometimes require renting a car. Many vacation rentals are located near the excellent public transportation facilities available throughout Europe, but many appealing properties are not. Be prepared to check out car rental possibilities if you select a more remote locale. Consult your guidebook or ask your self-catering contact to find out how and where to rent a car.

- Be cautious about drinking water in southern Europe. Stick with hot, distilled, bottled and carbonated beverages. Make ice with purified water only.

- Europe uses the metric system. Bring your metric conversion table and be prepared to do a little arithmetic in the market.

- Except in large cities, food is sold in specialty shops (bakeries, butcher shops, fish markets, etc.) rather than supermarkets, so you'll have to make several stops to get everything you need. Europeans—concerned with conserving natural resources years before it was fashionable in the States—often bring a fishnet or canvas bag to carry their purchases home. These are sold locally. To really blend in, you may want to do the same. Otherwise, paper grocery bags are usually available at an additional price.

- Like all your new neighbors, you'll find yourself buying fresh bread on a daily basis. Since Europeans depend on local bakeries that do not use preservatives in their products, anything left over becomes stale by the end of the day. (The good news, of course, is that the mouthwatering taste of each morning's freshly baked goods will remain a pleasant memory long after you've returned home.)

- Wine is sometimes sold from huge casks. Avoid the cheapest offerings and taste the wine before you buy it. You can bring your own bottle or buy one from the wine seller for a small charge.

- Europe uses 220 volts, 50 amps DC electricity instead of the 110 volts, 60 amps AC current used in the United States. Pack an adapter if you plan to bring any American appliances.

- In general, transporting pets across international borders involves an array of immunization and quarantine (six months in England!) procedures that may make taking your pet on vacation impractical. If you're still determined to bring Rover or Fluffy along, check to see which requirements your pet must meet in order to enter the country you plan to visit.

- Peak season for travel in Europe is the summertime, except in skiing regions, where travel is heavy all year. Reserve your rental well in advance—six months or so—if you plan to visit during popular months.

- Enjoy!

How to Use This Guide

The listings in this guide appear alphabetically by country, region, city and lodging name, in that order. A list of tourist boards appears at the end of the book; contact them as a valuable source of information and ideas to enhance your self-catered vacation.

Each listing contains the following information:

Rates
Instead of quoting actual figures, prices are divided into categories. Rates change too often to be quoted exactly, but the price range provided in the listings will give you a reliable impression of the cost of a unit. More than one rate category in a listing generally reflects the difference between on-season and off-season rents. Be sure to ask specific questions about rate changes when planning your vacation to get the best possible deal. Prices are quoted per unit, not per person, and reflect conversion into American dollars. The categories are as follows:

budget	up to $75/night or $600/week
inexpensive	$76-125/night or $601-850/week
moderate	$126-175/night or $851-1,200/week
expensive	$176-250/night or $1,201-1,750/week
deluxe	$251 and up/night or $1,751 and up/week

Open
Indicates the dates when the property is open.

Minimum Stay
Information on the length of stay required is provided here. Minimum stay requirements may differ between the high and low tourist seasons.

Description
This paragraph describes the highlights of the property. Outstanding features and furnishings of the unit, amenities and services available on the premises, and characteristics of the surrounding region are touched on. If something is not mentioned in this paragraph, do not assume it is not available: The description is not comprehensive and provides only an introduction to the property. For your convenience, agency listings often include a reference number for particular rentals. Use this number when you contact the agency to find out more.

Children (Yes or No)
Indicates if children are permitted.

Pets (Yes or No)
Indicates if pets are permitted. In some countries, such as the United Kingdom, visitors must arrange to quarantine their pets for up to six months before the pets are allowed to join them. In such cases, we have listed "no" pets.

Be sure to check the quarantine policies of your particular destination well in advance.

Smoking (Yes or No)
Indicates if cigarette smoking is permitted. Restrictions on pipes and cigars should be confirmed with the rental proprietor.

Handicap Access (Yes or No)
Some properties, such as ground-floor units, represent themselves as partially accessible to the handicapped. Unless it has been determined, however, that the property is fully accessible, we have indicated "no" accessibility.

Payment
Indicates the forms of payment accepted:

C	Cash
P	Personal check
T	Travelers check
A	American Express
V	Visa
M	MasterCard
O	Other credit cards
EC	International Money Order
All	All forms of payment

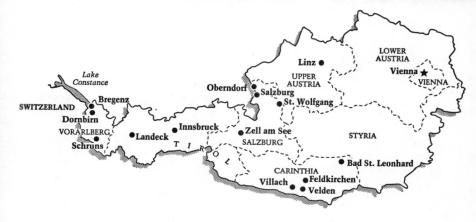

Austria

Bad Kleinkirchheim

SKIER'S HOLIDAY FLAT   *Rates: moderate*
Open: year-round   *Minimum Stay: one week*

Modern and centrally located, this two-to-four-person flat is ideal for those who chose not to rent a car. Convenient to the ski center, cable runway and ski courses, it's also close to Roman baths, heated indoor-outdoor pools and saunas, tennis, cross-country ski tracks and hiking trails. The flat features an anteroom, a living room with a convertible couch, a large terrace, a modern kitchen, a bath and one double bedroom. Contact: Europa-Let, PO Box 3537, Ashland, OR 97520. Call 1-800-462-4486 or 503-482-1442.

Children: Y   Pets: Y   Smoking: Y   Handicap Access: N   Payment: C, P, T

Bad St. Leonhard

LOG CABIN   *Rates: budget*
Open: year-round   *Minimum Stay: one week*

Whether you're drawn to Bad St. Leonhard for its sulphur baths, its skiing or the relaxing country atmosphere, you won't be disappointed. And what could be more "country" than a one-room log chalet on a hillside at the edge of the woods? This cozy, rustic cabin with a breathtaking view of the valley consists of a large living/dining room with a double sofa bed, a kitchenette, a bath with a shower and a separate toilet. A restaurant, a ski lift and a ski school are just minutes away. The resort community itself lies just nine miles away and offers concert evenings, folklore festivals, dancing, dining, shops, historical attractions and an indoor pool. In the summer there is tennis, hiking, riding and much more. Contact: Interhome Inc., 124 Little Falls Road, Fairfield, NJ 07004. Call 201-882-6864. Ref. A9462/80.

Children: Y   Pets: Y   Smoking: Y   Handicap Access: N   Payment: P, V, M

Feldkirchen

ONE-ROOM CHALET   *Rates: budget*
Open: year-round   *Minimum Stay: one week*

Feldkirchen, a peaceful country town in the heart of the Austrian pasture and lakes region, is home to this charming wooden chalet. The surrounding countryside is nothing short of magnificent, a perfect getaway when you need to relax and commune with nature. With room for three, the chalet encompasses a double bedroom with a shower and a pull-out bed in the kitchen/living area. A TV is included among the simple furnishings; outside, garden furniture is available on the lawn and patio. The nearby lakes present nearly endless opportunities for recreation. For the stout of heart, a glider airport offers a unique way to see the countryside. Contact: Interhome Inc., 124 Little Falls Road, Fairfield, NJ 07004. Call 201-882-6864. Ref. A9560/7.

Children: Y   Pets: Y   Smoking: Y   Handicap Access: N   Payment: P, V, M

Velden

EXCELSIOR BUNGALOWS   *Rates: deluxe*
Open: year-round   *Minimum Stay: one week*

The Excelsior Bungalows occupy a quiet, sunny spot on the southern shore of Lake Woerth. One of the comfortably furnished cottages, a three-bedroom unit, can house six guests and has plenty of amenities to make everyone feel at home, including a TV and a phone, a terrace and a lawn with garden furniture. The living room is spacious and homey, and the kitchen has a stove, a grill and a dishwasher. You'll enjoy access to a private beach with moorings; the town center is just over a mile away. Also close by is a restaurant, a cross-country ski trail, an indoor pool, a grocery store, an ice rink and a bus stop. Contact: Interhome Inc., 124 Little Falls Road, Fairfield, NJ 07004. Call 201-882-6864. Ref. A9220/100.

Children: Y   Pets: Y   Smoking: Y   Handicap Access: N   Payment: P, V, M

Velden

HOLIDAY HOUSE AM TEICH   *Rates: budget-inexpensive*
Open: year-round   *Minimum Stay: one week*

Velden is a stylish spa and resort on the sheltered, sunny west bay of Lake Woerth. Centrally located at the edge of the forest, the Holiday House am Teich commands a splendid view of the water. The ground-floor apartment sleeps three in a twin and a single bedroom, but there is also a sofa bed in the living room for overflow. In the flat, guests have a TV and a kitchen with a stove; you can share a washing machine with other tenants. When you're not soaking up sun on the terrace, you may want to take advantage of some of the area's recreational offerings, such as boat trips, dances, all kinds of water sports, horseback riding, mountaineering and cycling. Contact: Interhome Inc., 124 Little Falls Road, Fairfield, NJ 07004. Call 201-882-6864. Ref. A9220/8A.

Children: Y   Pets: Y   Smoking: Y   Handicap Access: N   Payment: P, V, M

Villach

BLUEWATER RETREAT *Rates: inexpensive*
Open: year-round *Minimum Stay: one week*
This chalet directly above the shores of glacier-fed Lake Magdalensnse offers a wonderful lake and mountain view. Though not far from the village center, with its lakeside promenade, tennis and other amusements, you can relax in complete solitude, barbecue on your terrace and enjoy your own pine garden, bathing jetty and sun terrace. This furnished chalet accommodates two persons and features an anteroom, a cozy living room with a dining niche, a kitchen, a double bedroom and a bath. Contact: Europa-Let, PO Box 3537, Ashland, OR 97520. Call 1-800-462-4486 or 503-482-1442.

Children: Y Pets: Y Smoking: Y Handicap Access: N Payment: C, P, T

LOWER AUSTRIA

Schwarzenbach

COUNTRY STAY *Rates: inexpensive*
Open: year-round *Minimum Stay: one week*
Peaceful, sunny and deep in the countryside, this first-rate double bungalow has a swimming pool, a double shower and a sauna. A large hall leads to a spacious living room with an open fireplace, a kitchenette and a dining room. Outside, a terrace features a fireplace for cookouts. A sofa sleeps one adult or two children; two adjoining double rooms sleep four to six. You'll love the garden, lawns and children's playground, but will want to visit the nearby ski slopes, historic villages, castles and lakes, too. Contact: Europa-Let, PO Box 3537, Ashland, OR 97520. Call 1-800-462-4486 or 503-482-1442.

Children: Y Pets: Y Smoking: Y Handicap Access: N Payment: C, P, T

SALZBURG

Flachu

SNOW CREST LODGE *Rates: expensive*
Open: year-round *Minimum Stay: one week*
Built in 1870, this renovated hunting lodge is located at the end of a valley at the foot of the Nieder Tavern, one of the most majestic Alps in Austria. Its rustic charm intact, the lodge has its own sauna and is finished inside with natural wood. The lodge can accommodate four to ten guests and features a living room with traditional tiled stove, a hunters' room with four bunk beds, one double bedroom and one bedroom/sitting room with four bunk beds. The tavern motorway, cross-country ski routes, three downhill skiing areas and shopping are within easy reach. Contact: Europa-Let, PO Box 3537, Ashland, OR 97520. Call 1-800-462-4486 or 503-482-1442.

Children: Y Pets: Y Smoking: Y Handicap Access: N Payment: C, P, T

Leogang

FRESH PLEASURE LODGE
Open: year-round

Rates: budget-inexpensive
Minimum Stay: one week

Steep cliffs and granite mountains form the backdrop for this traditional lodge that offers three flats for four to six guests each. Located just outside the village on a sunny southern slope, the lodge is perfect for skiers, since a chair lift and the circular ski route between Leogang and Saalbach are nearby. Each flat includes a living room with a double bed-settee, a kitchenette, a dining alcove, two double bedrooms, a bath and a balcony. Contact: Europa-Let, PO Box 3537, Ashland, OR 97520. Call 1-800-462-4486 or 503-482-1442.

Children: Y   Pets: Y   Smoking: Y   Handicap Access: N   Payment: C, P, T

Lungau

CASTLE LODGE
Open: year-round

Rates: moderate
Minimum Stay: one week

With medieval Maunterndorf Castle as a backdrop, this former hunting lodge on the castle grounds puts you in the middle of a historical setting. Completely renovated, this lodge can be rented as a whole to accommodate ten persons or divided into two flats for four to five. The lodge is close to the castle restaurant, ski bus service, cross-country ski track, tennis facilities, horseback riding and swimming. Each flat includes two double bedrooms, a modern kitchen, a large living room, a dining area, a tiled stove and a bath; upstairs guests enjoy a private terrace. Contact: Europa-Let, PO Box 3537, Ashland, OR 97520. Call 1-800-462-4486 or 503-482-1442.

Children: Y   Pets: Y   Smoking: Y   Handicap Access: N   Payment: C, P, T

Mariapfarr

CHALET IRENE
Open: year-round

Rates: inexpensive-moderate
Minimum Stay: one week

A snow-lover's paradise awaits you at this chalet in the quiet, remote village of Mariapfarr. There's plenty to attract non-skiers, too, especially in the summer months. Bring the gang, because this house sleeps ten in three twin bedrooms, one triple and one single—and there are two full bathrooms. In addition, you'll find a living room, an eat-in kitchen with a stove and a large balcony. What to do when you're not lazing around the house gazing at the spectacular mountain views? In winter, you can cross-country or downhill ski or do some snowmobiling. In summer, take lovely mountain hikes, play tennis, swim or go cycling. Year-round attractions include shops, restaurants, dances, folklore evenings and historical attractions. Contact: Interhome Inc., 124 Little Falls Road, Fairfield, NJ 07004. Call 201-882-6864. Ref. A5571/1.

Children: Y   Pets: Y   Smoking: Y   Handicap Access: N   Payment: P, V, M

Saalbach-Hinterglemm

HILLSIDE APARTMENT *Rates: budget*
Open: year-round *Minimum Stay: one week*

A quiet, sunny slope is the setting for this lovely apartment house on the outskirts of town. One unit sleeps five in a triple bedroom and a double sofa bed; outside, lounge in the grassy yard. Further afield, enjoy skiing, skating, curling, tennis, golf, swimming and all manner of water sports. In summer, take in the woodland and meadow festivals. Year-round pleasures include cozy restaurants and shops, dance halls, folklore evenings and mountain train rides to scenic wonders. Contact: Interhome Inc., 124 Little Falls Road, Fairfield, NJ 07004. Call 201-882-6864. Ref. A5753/10A.

Children: **Y** Pets: **Y** Smoking: **Y** Handicap Access: **N** Payment: **P, V, M**

Salzburg

SUNNY FLAT *Rates: inexpensive*
Open: year-round *Minimum Stay: one week*

Unforgettable countryside beckons you to Salzburg and its surroundings. Make this sunny, first-floor studio apartment, convenient to bus stops, grocery stores, restaurants and the Festival Theater, your home base. Everything you need for a comfortable stay is here—a living room with a double sofa bed, a kitchen with a stove and a full bath. Your only decision is what to do first. How about a cable car ride to see the view from Hohensalzburg Fortress? Or you may prefer a visit to the casino, museum, zoo or spa baths. For the athletic, there's swimming and tennis nearby and beautiful gardens and parks for strolling. Contact: Interhome Inc., 124 Little Falls Road, Fairfield, NJ 07004. Call 201-882-6864. Ref. A5020/100B.

Children: **Y** Pets: **Y** Smoking: **Y** Handicap Access: **N** Payment: **P, V, M**

St. Gilgen

ALPENLAND AM SEE *Rates: budget*
Open: year-round *Minimum Stay: one week*

Quietly situated at the edge of a village on the shore of Wolfgang Lake, this rustic apartment house lies about twenty miles east of Salzburg. The cozy third-floor, two-room apartment sleeps four in one twin-bedded room and a living-room double sofa bed. A kitchen, a bath with shower and a balcony with lake and mountain views round out the accommodations. On the grounds, guests share laundry facilities, lounge, patio and garden. The lakeside resort community abounds with activities, including concerts, folklore events, hiking, tennis, swimming, boating, fishing, cycling, lido and miniature golf. You can also take a cable railway up 3,500 feet to what seems like the top of the world. Contact: Interhome Inc., 124 Little Falls Road, Fairfield, NJ 07004. Call 201-882-6864. Ref. A5340/61D.

Children: **Y** Pets: **Y** Smoking: **Y** Handicap Access: **N** Payment: **P, V, M**

Zell am See
CHALET APARTMENT
Open: year-round

Rates: moderate-expensive
Minimum Stay: one week

Located on a quiet side street of an alpine resort town, this tree-ringed chalet has the secluded look of a country hideaway. In a lovely apartment that takes up the entire first floor of the house, there are three bedrooms, each with its own shower. With the additional sofa bed, a total of eight guests can be accommodated in comfort. A well-equipped kitchen and all towels, linens and final cleaning are included. Only a brief walk from the Zeller Bergbahn ski lift, the chalet stands near a public indoor swimming pool and sauna. Make the most of the fresh air with a stroll to the lake or go ice skating. In summer the lake is beautifully warm for swimming, and there are many excursions to choose from to scenic local spots. Contact: Rent A Home International, Inc., 7200 34th Avenue N.W., Seattle, WA 98117. Call 206-545-6963.

Children: **Y** Pets: **N** Smoking: **Y** Handicap Access: **N** Payment: **C, P, V, M**

Zell am See
POET'S RETREAT
Open: year-round

Rates: moderate-expensive
Minimum Stay: one week

This guest cottage on the grounds of a small castle offers access to immaculate grounds, wonderful mountain views and secluded meadows. A three-minute walk takes you to tennis courts, riding stables and a lake where you can sail, wind surf or just rest. Varied activities such as golf, shopping, dining and even glider flying are close by. The seven-room cottage can accommodate seven guests and features a living room with a tiled stove, a kitchen parlor with a dining niche, two double bedrooms and one single bedroom with a balcony. All bedrooms have adjoining baths and are located on the upper floor. Contact: Europa-Let, PO Box 3537, Ashland, OR 97520. Call 1-800-462-4486 or 503-482-1442.

Children: **Y** Pets: **Y** Smoking: **Y** Handicap Access: **N** Payment: **C, P, T**

Zell am See
WIESENGUETL I
Open: year-round

Rates: budget-inexpensive
Minimum Stay: one week

Zell am See, on Lake Zell, is an international tourist resort, the heart of "Europa Sportregion." Although the area is particularly well suited to sports-minded individuals, the picturesque old town, with its twisting streets, verdant parks, lively dance halls, fascinating museum and more, offers plenty for others as well. Located just outside town near a 27-hole golf course, this sunny first-floor studio sleeps two in the living/dining room and includes a kitchenette, bathroom, phone and TV; laundry facilities are on the premises. Winter sports include cross-country and downhill skiing, indoor riding, tennis, squash and swimming. Summer offers all types of water sports, hiking, cycling and, yes, skiing, too. The year-round ski region Kitzsteinhorn/Kaprun is only five miles away. Contact: Interhome Inc., 124 Little Falls Road, Fairfield, NJ 07004. Call 201-882-6864. Ref. A5700/601B.

Children: Y   Pets: Y   Smoking: Y   Handicap Access: N   Payment: P, V, M

TIROL

Baumkirchen

BROADLAWN LODGE   *Rates: budget*
Open: year-round   *Minimum Stay: one week*
Sandwiched between a flower-covered meadow and a forest, this lodge has two large apartments for eight to twelve guests. The larger unit sleeps up to twelve in two double and two triple bedrooms; its lovely kitchen-parlor, anteroom, large dining area, kitchen and two baths offer spacious comfort. The smaller unit offers a living room with a balcony, a kitchen, a dining area and two double, one triple and one single bedroom. Savor beautiful views or hike the trails through the surrounding countryside. Tennis, riding and swimming facilities are located nearby, as are tobogganing and ice skating. In the villages, experience everything from a museum of Tryolean folk art to open-air concerts to tours of local castles. Contact: Europa-Let, PO Box 3537, Ashland, OR 97520. Call 1-800-462-4486 or 503-482-1442.

Children: Y   Pets: Y   Smoking: Y   Handicap Access: N   Payment: C, P, T

Fiss/Serfaus

ROYAL SPRING LODGE AND SPA   *Rates: budget-moderate*
Open: year-round   *Minimum Stay: one week*
Members of the royal family once enjoyed the charms of this beautiful lodge with spa and mineral springs. Indeed, people have delighted in the natural restorative qualities of the spring since the year 1212, but you'll also enjoy the mountain views, the quiet, sunny beauty of the nearby woods and the easy walks to mountain summits and pastures. The lodge features five flats for two to six and has both a restaurant and cafe. A broad sun terrace stretches the length of the lodge; there's also a large lawn for children. The flats include separate sleeping, living and dining areas, kitchens, private baths and balconies. Contact: Europa-Let, PO Box 3537, Ashland, OR 97520. Call 1-800-462-4486 or 503-482-1442.

Children: Y   Pets: Y   Smoking: Y   Handicap Access: N   Payment: C, P, T

Kitzbuhel

CHALET DR. SCHERER   *Rates: budget-moderate*
Open: year-round   *Minimum Stay: one week*
It's no wonder that VIPs from all over the world converge on this little Alpine town—winter or summer, it's a vacationer's paradise. Best of all, this adorable chalet in a quiet, residential area allows you to get away from the hubbub without missing the attractions of a popular resort. Enjoy your privacy in a cozy four-room apartment with a living room, an eat-in kitchen with a stove, one twin and two single bed-

rooms, a bath and a half and a large balcony with gorgeous views. When you're ready to step out, there are plenty of activities to choose from—indoor and outdoor swimming and tennis, skiing, skating, golf (both miniature and standard), squash, as well as complete spa facilities. Less physical pursuits include a casino, clubs and dance halls, a museum and entertainment in the pleasant theater. Contact: Interhome Inc., 124 Little Falls Road, Fairfield, NJ 07004. Call 201-882-6864. Ref. A6370/160B.

Children: Y   Pets: N   Smoking: Y   Handicap Access: N   Payment: P, V, M

Kufstein

STILL HAVEN HOUSE   *Rates: budget*
Open: year-round   *Minimum Stay: one week*
This private country home located on a quiet residential street of a small village has its own heated pool and sauna as well as sweeping views. Each of the two flats is comfortably furnished and has a living room with a double sofa bed, a dining room, a balcony or terrace facing south, a kitchenette and one bedroom sleeping three. Hiking trails into the forest start a stone's throw away; the village also offers fine skiing and ice skating in winter, riding and tennis in summer. Contact: Europa-Let, PO Box 3537, Ashland, OR 97520. Call 1-800-462-4486 or 503-482-1442.

Children: Y   Pets: Y   Smoking: Y   Handicap Access: N   Payment: C, P, T

Landeck

MAIR HOUSE   *Rates: budget*
Open: year-round   *Minimum Stay: one week*
Landeck nestles in the mountains at the junction of the rivers Inn and Sanna, at the crossroads of the main north-south and east-west routes through Tirol. On the outskirts of town, bordering the woods, stands a lovely house in a quiet, sunny location. Here you'll find a delightful apartment with a magnificent view, whose interior features one double and one triple bedroom and a living room/kitchen. There's also a balcony with deck chairs for warm-weather relaxing. The town's highlights include a restaurant, shops, hikes starting right from the house, an indoor pool, ski lifts, a ski school, a toboggan run, tennis, an ice rink, concerts, Tyrolean evenings and a museum. Contact: Interhome Inc., 124 Little Falls Road, Fairfield, NJ 07004. Call 201-882-6864. Ref. A6500/1B.

Children: Y   Pets: Y   Smoking: Y   Handicap Access: N   Payment: P, V, M

Leutasch

MAJESTIC VISTA LODGE   *Rates: budget-expensive*
Open: year-round   *Minimum Stay: one week*
Located in the romantic village of Leutasch, this lodge puts you within walking distance of everything from fine dining to hiking paths. In summer, guests enjoy golf, fishing, hiking and swimming; in winter, they can take a horse-drawn sleigh ride, ski the Olympic cross-country course or shoot down a natural toboggan run. The flats housed in the

lodge can accommodate four to six guests. Each includes a living room suite with double bed settee, a kitchenette, a dining niche and a bath. The larger units offer one or two double bedrooms; some suites have balconies as well. Contact: Europa-Let, PO Box 3537, Ashland, OR 97520. Call 1-800-462-4486 or 503-482-1442.

Children: Y Pets: Dogs only Smoking: Y Handicap Access: N Payment: C, P, T

Navis

MOUNTAIN INN EXTENSION   *Rates: budget*
Open: year-round   *Minimum Stay: one week*

From the terrace of this hillside inn, you can gaze across a valley where an ancient church stands framed by a spectacular mountain range. Two apartments, separate from the inn, are located on a southern slope on the edge of a mountain meadow. From the inn, hike to any number of pastures and peaks, or enjoy nearby shopping, swimming or tennis courts. In the winter, you can ski, toboggan or ice skate. Both the ground floor and the upstairs apartment accommodate four to six guests. Each has a living room with a double sofa bed, a dining area, a kitchenette, a bath, a living room suite with a convertible couch, a dining room and a bedroom with bunk beds for four; the downstairs unit also contains a double bedroom. Contact: Europa-Let, PO Box 3537, Ashland, OR 97520. Call 1-800-462-4486 or 503-482-1442.

Children: Y Pets: Y Smoking: Y Handicap Access: N Payment: C, P, T

Oberndorf, near Kitzbuhel

TIROLEAN CHALET   *Rates: inexpensive-moderate*
Open: year-round   *Minimum Stay: one week*

With a wide, sloping roof and a spacious second-floor balcony from which to soak up the sunshine, this modern house is a Tirolean classic. Up to eight visitors can stay in three double bedrooms with washbasins, and use one and a half bathrooms. On a quiet day, you may wish to picnic in the garden, gazing up at the magnificent Kitzbuheler Alps. The large living room provides a gathering place for visitors after skiing or exploring the many historic and scenic treasures. A unique seasonal treat is Christmas mass, since Oberndorf is the birthplace of "Silent Night." Contact: Rent A Home International, Inc., 7200 34th Avenue N.W., Seattle, WA 98117. Call 206-545-6963.

Children: Y Pets: N Smoking: N Handicap Access: N Payment: C, P, V, M

Pettne

ALPINE APARTMENTS   *Rates: budget-moderate*
Open: year-round   *Minimum Stay: one week*

Rambling and rustic, this house comprises four apartments, each filled with light and boasting excellent mountain views. All have kitchens with a dining niche. The apartment for two includes a living room, a double bedroom and a bath; the apartment for three has one triple bedroom, a living room and a bath. Two apartments for five are available as well, both with a south-facing balcony, an anteroom, a living room, a dining alcove, a bath and one triple plus one double bedroom.

The village offers shopping, indoor pools and saunas, but nature lovers will enjoy the pathways leading along the valley floor past ice-blue streams and unspoiled forest meadows. Many visitors enjoy touring the glacier-fed lakes and waterfalls or discovering mountain spots where wild goats and marmot graze on flowers. Contact: Europa-Let, PO Box 3537, Ashland, OR 97520. Call 1-800-462-4486 or 503-482-1442.

Children: **Y**   Pets: **Y**   Smoking: **Y**   Handicap Access: **N**   Payment: **C, P, T**

Seefeld

SEEFELD SPA AND LODGE   *Rates: budget-moderate*
Open: year-round   *Minimum Stay: one week*

With its own indoor swimming pool, sauna, fitness room and solarium, this lodge caters to your every desire. Here, you can rent a variety of suites, many with fireplaces, accommodating four to seven people. Sweeping views and proximity to restaurants, the Olympic Center and walking trails make this a wonderful place to holiday. The apartments offer living rooms with dining alcoves and convertible double divans, kitchens, private baths and sunny balconies. Except for the studio accommodations for two, each has separate bedrooms. Contact: Europa-Let, PO Box 3537, Ashland, OR 97520. Call 1-800-462-4486 or 503-482-1442.

Children: **Y**   Pets: **Dogs only**   Smoking: **Y**   Handicap: **N**   Payment: **C, P, T**

Soll

TWO-ROOM APARTMENT   *Rates: budget*
Open: year-round   *Minimum Stay: one week*

An old-fashioned country house on the edge of a Tyrolean village houses this sunny two-room apartment, which sleeps four. It comes complete with breathtaking views, a balcony, a kitchenette, a double bedroom and living/dining room with a sofa bed. There is a pleasant lawn supplied with garden furniture for shared use. The mountains and lake, surrounded by fir and pine woods, provide myriad opportunities for recreation. Complete summer and winter sports facilities can be found in the area, as well as dance halls and nightclubs for evening entertainment. Contact: Interhome Inc., 124 Little Falls Road, Fairfield, NJ 07004. Call 201-882-6864. Ref. A6306/20C.

Children: **Y**   Pets: **Y**   Smoking: **Y**   Handicap Access: **N**   Payment: **P, V, M**

Zirl

CASTLE STAR   *Rates: moderate*
Open: year-round   *Minimum Stay: one week*

Part of a small castle built in 1200, this five-room annex in the wooded countryside offers beauty, charm and romance for four to eight persons. A private entrance opens onto a comfortably furnished apartment featuring a large living room, a dining area, a tiled stove and kitchen. One double bedroom includes a bath, while another is connected to a bedroom with two single beds and two bunks. For fun, hike on the trails that ramble through meadows and mountains or venture to the casino and nightlife of Seefeld. Zirl, home to two winter Olympics, offers varied winter sports facilities and accessibility to Innsbruck. Contact: Europa-Let, PO Box 3537, Ashland, OR 97520. Call 1-800-462-4486 or 503-482-1442.

Children: Y Pets: Y Smoking: Y Handicap Access: N Payment: C, P, T

UPPER AUSTRIA

Altenhof/Hofkirchen

PALACE DANUBE   *Rates: budget*
Open: year-round   *Minimum Stay: one week*
This 17th-century palace stands on a gentle hill above the Danube, surrounded by wooded hills and wide meadows. Guests staying in the three apartments enjoy private tennis courts, a pond for fishing, hunting facilities and acres of surrounding park, lawn and meadows. Outside the estate, you'll find summer and winter activities ranging from folk dancing in the local villages to superior downhill-ski runs. The beautifully furnished apartments feature spacious common areas, fireplaces, modern kitchens and baths, plus sleeping accommodations for four to six. All have access to the garden and recreational meadow. Contact: Europa-Let, PO Box 3537, Ashland, OR 97520. Call 1-800-462-4486 or 503-482-1442.

Children: Y Pets: Y Smoking: Y Handicap Access: N Payment: C, P, T

St. Wolfgang

LAKE'S EDGE VILLA   *Rates: expensive*
Open: year-round   *Minimum Stay: one week*
On the banks of a fine Alpine lake bordered by a delightful promenade, this lovely villa owned by a world-champion skier contains an apartment large enough for four to eight people. A separate entrance ensures privacy; the living area, dining niche, modern kitchen, two baths and four double bedrooms offer spacious comfort. Guests can enjoy a sunbathing jetty, two fenced meadows and walking trails from the house to pastures, meadows, woods and mountains. Contact: Europa-Let, PO Box 3537, Ashland, OR 97520. Call 1-800-462-4486 or 503-482-1442.

Children: Y Pets: N Smoking: Y Handicap Access: N Payment: C, P, T

VIENNA

Vienna

12TH DISTRICT APARTMENT   *Rates: budget*
Open: year-round   *Minimum Stay: one week*
Recently renovated and located in Vienna's 12th district, this apartment house stands near the magnificent Schonbrunn Palace. An elevated ground-floor unit inside offers a twin bedroom as well as a double sofa bed in the living room by the TV. In the kitchen you'll find a stove and washing machine. The downtown location puts you near shops and restaurants; the building is right on the bus line for easy accessibility to the rest of Vienna's historical landmarks, to theaters and

concerts—not to mention pastries. Contact: Interhome Inc., 124 Little Falls Road, Fairfield, NJ 07004. Call 201-882-6864. Ref. A1010/20A

Children: Y Pets: Y Smoking: Y Handicap Access: N Payment: P, V, M

Vienna
COZY STUDIO
Open: year-round
Rates: budget
Minimum Stay: one week

You'll find this cozy apartment on a quiet, tree-lined street not too far from the Zoological Gardens, less than two miles from Vienna's center. Homey and neat, the second-floor apartment consists of a living/dining room with two pull-out beds and a TV, plus a kitchen and a bath with shower. There's plenty to keep you busy in Vienna, a city famed for its numerous cultural activities. Whether you prefer to take in concerts in the park, admire the horses at the Spanish Riding School or just explore the city at random, this flat puts all of Vienna within easy reach, only a short walk or bus ride away. Contact: Interhome Inc., 124 Little Falls Road, Fairfield, NJ 07004. Call 201-882-6864. Ref. A1010/30C.

Children: Y Pets: Y Smoking: Y Handicap Access: N Payment: P, V, M

Vienna
FOUR STAR APARTMENTS
Open: year-round
Rates: budget-expensive
Minimum Stay: one week

This residence in one of Vienna's most historic districts offers a wide choice of apartments to call home while visiting one of the great cultural centers of Europe. For those who plan to be out all day museum-hopping and sightseeing, a studio with a kitchenette might suffice; for families or those who wish to relax at home and take advantage of the many amenities provided, one- and two-bedroom units (some with balconies and lofts) and even penthouses are available. Each apartment comes with modern furnishings, TV, phone, weekly maid service and laundry facilities. The residence also contains a sports center in which to stretch tired muscles, a library for rainy days and such extras as a soothing sauna. Downtown Vienna is only fifteen minutes away, with its wealth of parks, restaurants, museums and historic sites. Contact: Rent A Home International, Inc., 7200 34th Avenue N.W., Seattle, WA 98117. Call 206-545-6963.

Children: Y Pets: N Smoking: Y Handicap Access: N Payment: C, P, V, M

Vienna
GREEN IVY HOUSE
Open: year-round
Rates: budget-inexpensive
Minimum Stay: one week

This old-world Viennese manor house covered with ivy stands near a lovely park with a swimming pool. Inside is an apartment accommodating four to six people. Located in the 19th District and well furnished in the Baroque/Biedermeir style, it features a living room with a convertible couch, a simple kitchen, a breakfast room, a bath, a garden terrace and a bedroom with a double and a fold-away bed. Nearby are beautiful walking paths winding through the Vienna

Woods and Kahlenburg. You'll also want to visit the local vineyards and sample some of the wine at one of the many fine taverns nearby. Contact: Europa-Let, PO Box 3537, Ashland, OR 97520. Call 1-800-462-4486 or 503-482-1442.

Children: Y   Pets: N   Smoking: Y   Handicap Access: N   Payment: C, P, T

Vienna

HEART OF VIENNA APARTMENTS   *Rates: inexpensive-moderate*
Open: year-round   *Minimum Stay: one week*
Large French windows overlooking Stephen's Square, the Archbishop's Palace and Rothen Square show you the very heart of Vienna. Located on Graben-Karntner Street in the 1st District, these apartments offer easy access to the underground, restaurants, coffeehouses, concert halls and all the sophistication and elegance that is Vienna. The two apartments—one for two guests, one for three—include comfortable living, dining and sleeping areas with all the amenities of home. Contact: Europa-Let, PO Box 3537, Ashland, OR 97520. Call 1-800-462-4486 or 503-482-1442.

Children: N   Pets: Y   Smoking: Y   Handicap Access: N   Payment: C, P, T

Vienna

HERITAGE   *Rates: budget*
Open: year-round   *Minimum Stay: one week*
Located in the 8th District, this romantic apartment for two to four is furnished with antiques and features a sitting room with a convertible couch, a dining room, a double bedroom, a kitchen and a bath. Convenient to the historic 1st District, with its opera house, congress, theater and restaurants, the building even has a pizzeria on the ground floor. Contact: Europa-Let, PO Box 3537, Ashland, OR 97520. Call 1-800-462-4486 or 503-482-1442.

Children: Y   Pets: Y   Smoking: Y   Handicap Access: N   Payment: C, P, T

Vienna

THE VIENNA WOODS   *Rates: inexpensive*
Open: year-round   *Minimum Stay: one week*
Located on a quiet street on the edge of the Vienna Woods and vineyards, this elegant, vine-covered home offers accommodations for four to five. Lovely views and walks are right outside your door. Stroll to a wine bar and listen to Viennese music or shop or dine in the nearby boutiques and restaurants. A 30-minute bus ride takes you to the city center. This well-furnished apartment features a garden terrace, a living room with a convertible couch, a dining room, a kitchen, a shower and one double and one single bedroom. Contact: Europa-Let, PO Box 3537, Ashland, OR 97520. Call 1-800-462-4486 or 503-482-1442.

Children: Y   Pets: Y   Smoking: Y   Handicap Access: N   Payment: C, P, T

VORARLBERG

Alberschwende

WOODS EDGE COTTAGE   *Rates: budget*
Open: year-round   *Minimum Stay: one week*

Set in an open meadow on the edge of a wood, this five-room cottage offers four to six people comfortable accommodations and wonderful mountain and meadow views. The ground floor features a living room suite opening onto a large terrace and garden, a dining area, a full bathroom and a kitchen. Three double bedrooms, two adjoining each other, can be found upstairs. Wood paneled walls and ceilings impart a warm rustic look. There's also a small sauna for relaxing after a day of hiking the routes that start from your door and lead to the high mountains overlooking Lake Constance. Sailing, swimming and indoor and outdoor tennis are also nearby. In winter, extensive ski runs offer superior courses for the new and seasoned skier. Contact: Europa-Let, PO Box 3537, Ashland, OR 97520. Call 1-800-462-4486 or 503-482-1442.

Children: Y   Pets: Y   Smoking: Y   Handicap Access: N   Payment: C, P, T

Au

SERENITY CHALET   *Rates: moderate*
Open: year-round   *Minimum Stay: one week*

Charming and secluded, this five-room renovated chalet offers lovely mountain views and the pure mountain air of the pristine countryside. Equipped with a farmstyle living room, a modern kitchen, a wood-burning stove, an anteroom and full bathroom, the house can accommodate four to six. Bedrooms include one double, one single room and one room featuring a single and two bunk beds. Relax on the large lawn and recreational meadow or fish for mountain trout, go white-water rafting or venture into the nearby village. Excellent ski areas famous for reliable snow conditions are nearby. Contact: Europa-Let, PO Box 3537, Ashland, OR 97520. Call 1-800-462-4486 or 503-482-1442.

Children: Y   Pets: Y   Smoking: Y   Handicap Access: N   Payment: C, P, T

Bartholomaberg

FRESH VIEW HOUSE   *Rates: moderate-expensive*
Open: year-round   *Minimum Stay: one week*

With the valley below and the mountains above, this seven-room house is ideal for six to twelve nature lovers. Finished in wood paneling, the cozy living room with tiled stove leads to a lovely kitchen parlour. There's also a large dining area, a bath and one double bedroom on the ground floor. Upstairs is another bath, two triple bedrooms that share a balcony facing south, another triple room and one single. On the terrace you can enjoy the sun as you grill on the barbecue or watch your children play in the large meadow. The winter season features plenty of snow for winter sports and sunshine no less than six hours a day. Contact: Europa-Let, PO Box 3537, Ashland, OR 97520. Call 1-800-462-4486 or 503-482-1442.

Children: Y   Pets: Y   Smoking: Y   Handicap Access: N   Payment: C, P, T

Fontanella

MOUNTAIN LODGE   *Rates: inexpensive*
Open: year-round   *Minimum Stay: one week*

Perched on a sunny slope, this seven-room lodge offers seclusion along with admirable mountain views. Modern and comfortable, the house features a living room, a terrace and a kitchen, plus three double bedrooms (two with a shower and a balcony), one single and one room with bunk beds. Nearby are well-marked paths across green pastures, foaming mountain rivers, deep canyons and waterfalls. The nearby villages offer a wide range of entertainment and sporting activities. Choose from cross-country or downhill skiing, or hike on the cleared walking paths. Contact: Europa-Let, PO Box 3537, Ashland, OR 97520. Call 1-800-462-4486 or 503-482-1442.

Children: **Y** Pets: **N** Smoking: **Y** Handicap Access: **N** Payment: **C, P, T**

Frastanz/Gurtis

EAGLE'S NEST   *Rates: inexpensive*
Open: year-round   *Minimum Stay: one week*

By day, the view from your own private mountain cabin is of imposing peaks. At night, the soft lights of villages glow like stars sprinkled across the valley floor. This cozy and comfortable four-room cabin has an anteroom, a living room with dining niche, a terrace, a full bath and kitchen. Two double bedrooms, two sleeping niches in the anteroom and a fold-out couch accommodate four to six persons. You can cross-country ski from your front door across your own private pasture and into untouched trails, or downhill from any number of nearby lifts. A full array of summer and winter activities, from tennis and swimming to dancing and sightseeing, are a short drive away. Contact: Europa-Let, PO Box 3537, Ashland, OR 97520. Call 1-800-462-4486 or 503-482-1442.

Children: **Y** Pets: **Y** Smoking: **Y** Handicap Access: **N** Payment: **C, P, T**

Gaschurn

OUR SECRET CHALET   *Rates: deluxe*
Open: year-round   *Minimum Stay: one week*

Surrounded by dark green forests and lush meadows and close to Piz Buin, the highest mountain in Vorarlberg, this six-room chalet is a favorite of hikers and mountaineers. A covered porch spanning the length of the chalet overlooks a large meadow complete with a bench and deck chairs. Relax in the sauna, by the tiled stove in the cozy living room or around the table in the eat-in kitchen. On the upper floor are two large bedrooms; one sleeps four, the other three. The lower floor features one bedroom with two bunks and another with six bunks. Wooden paneling adds rustic beauty throughout. The chalet stands very close to the Silvretta Nova chair lift, making visits to the valley quick and easy. Contact: Europa-Let, PO Box 3537, Ashland, OR 97520. Call 1-800-462-4486 or 503-482-1442.

Children: **Y** Pets: **Y** Smoking: **Y** Handicap Access: **N** Payment: **C, P, T**

Gaschurn

SILVERETTA-NOVA LODGE   *Rates: deluxe*
Open: year-round   *Minimum Stay: one week*
Above the village, near the woods and surrounded by meadows created
by ancient glaciers, this ten-room lodge is perfect for skiers because
it's next door to the Silveretta-Nova downhill ski run. Large and well
furnished, the lodge can accommodate eight to sixteen guests and
features a spacious living room with a TV and a tiled oven, two kitchen
parlors with dining niches and wood-burning stoves, plus two bathrooms. Enjoy the view from either the balcony or the small terrace, or
relax in your own sauna. Sleeping accommodations include two single
bedrooms, one twin and four triples. Cleared trails make for excellent
hiking; the village offers shopping, tennis and swimming. Come to
this international winter playground to ski, toboggan or ice skate.
Contact: Europa-Let, PO Box 3537, Ashland, OR 97520. Call 1-800-
462-4486 or 503-482-1442.

Children: Y   Pets: Y   Smoking: Y   Handicap Access: N   Payment: C, P, T

Hittisau

SUNNY VIEW HOUSE   *Rates: inexpensive*
Open: year-round   *Minimum Stay: one week*
High above the village of Hittisau, with its Baroque church and rural
town square, this seven-room house built on a sundrenched slope
commands magnificent views of the mountains, valley and Lake Constance. With room enough for four to ten, the house is well furnished,
complete with wood paneling and ceiling. The ground floor features
two double bedrooms, a living room with a sun terrace, a dining niche
with corner seating, a full bathroom and an eat-in kitchen. Upstairs is
one triple bedroom, one twin, one small single and a terrace. Year-
round activities range from hiking and skiing to fishing and water
sports. Contact: Europa-Let, PO Box 3537, Ashland, OR 97520. Call
1-800-462-4486 or 503-482-1442.

Children: Y   Pets: Y   Smoking: Y   Handicap Access: N   Payment: C, P, T

Lech Am Arlberg

VILLAGE HAVEN   *Rates: moderate*
Open: year-round   *Minimum Stay: one week*
This six-room chalet located in a resort area is both charming and
convenient. Alpine-style furnishings and wood paneling add character
to the comfortable lodge that features a living room, a dining niche, a
breakfast bar, an anteroom, a terrace, a small kitchen and two baths.
Five double bedrooms can accommodate eight to ten guests. Located
next to a hotel that offers swimming, sauna and dining, the house is
also a stop on the free ski bus. Fish in one of the six area lakes or
wander the vast network of mountain trails leading to high peaks and
crystal-clear lakes. The village itself has several pools, sports fields,
tennis courts and riding centers. Contact: Europa-Let, PO Box 3537,
Ashland, OR 97520. Call 1-800-462-4486 or 503-482-1442.

Children: Y   Pets: Y   Smoking: Y   Handicap Access: N   Payment: C, P, T

Mellau

HILLSIDE CHALET   *Rates: moderate*
Open: year-round   *Minimum Stay: one week*

As you stand on the terrace of this five-room chalet, your gaze takes in the surrounding mountains, a village and the valley below. Built on the southern slope of the flower-covered meadow, this nicely furnished house features an anteroom, a living room with a dining niche, a tiled stove, an open kitchen and a bathroom. On the ground floor, you'll find two bedrooms with double beds and another room with bunk beds. Two of the bedrooms open onto covered balconies facing south. Perfect for children, the chalet has a playground complete with wading pool, swing and slide. Adults will enjoy the many mountain trails and the charming village of Mellau, where you'll find restaurants and shops. Contact: Europa-Let, PO Box 3537, Ashland, OR 97520. Call 1-800-462-4486 or 503-482-1442.

Children: **Y**   Pets: **Y**   Smoking: **Y**   Handicap Access: **N**   Payment: **C, P, T**

Schruns

ANGEL'S VIEW CHALET   *Rates: budget*
Open: year-round   *Minimum Stay: one week*

Built on the edge of a high mountain ridge, this three-room chalet offers amazing views of mountain peaks, the valley floor and the villages of Schruns and Tschaggus. Wood paneled throughout and nicely furnished, the chalet sleeps four persons in two double bedrooms and features a living room with dining alcove and a kitchenette. A short drive takes you to the village center, the cable railway, indoor pools and village amusements. Enjoy cross-country skiing, downhill skiing, hiking and a view so beautiful it hardly seems real. Contact: Europa-Let, PO Box 3537, Ashland, OR 97520. Call 1-800-462-4486 or 503-482-1442.

Children: **Y**   Pets: **Y**   Smoking: **Y**   Handicap Access: **N**   Payment: **C, P, T**

Schruns

VILLAGE REST   *Rates: inexpensive*
Open: year-round   *Minimum Stay: one week*

Hemingway loved Schruns, and you'll love this five-room flat located in the heart of the famous spa and winter resort. Situated on a quiet residential street, it's seconds from sidewalk cafes, parks, shopping, dining and the riverside promenade. The second-floor flat accommodates four and features an anteroom, a large living room furnished in Alpine style, two lovely double bedrooms, a dining niche, complete video/stereo equipment, a color TV, and an eat-in kitchen. Contact: Europa-Let, PO Box 3537, Ashland, OR 97520. Call 1-800-462-4486 or 503-482-1442.

Children: **Y**   Pets: **N**   Smoking: **Y**   Handicap Access: **N**   Payment: **C, P, T**

North Sea

De Haan
Bredene
Bruges
Nieuwpoort
WEST FLANDERS

Ghent

Antwerp

Hechtel
Houthalen
LIMBURG

★ Brussels

BRABANT

Belgium

BRABANT

Brussels

EURO-FLAT HOTEL   *Rates: moderate-expensive*
Open: year-round   *Minimum Stay: none*

With a wonderful location in the heart of Brussels, the Euro-Flat Hotel offers sleek, modern apartments for up to four people. Each room has a convenient kitchenette; a friendly restaurant and bar are located in the hotel. A buffet breakfast and daily maid service are provided and child care is available for that romantic night on the town. The sauna, TV, gym, solarium and a delightful garden will keep you amused at your hotel, but who can stay home when the excitement of this international capital beckons? If you begin to tire of the elegant museums and exquisite guild halls, walk over to the Mannekin Pis, the city's most intriguing fountain. Contact: Katarina Zikmundova, 50 Boulevard Charlemagne, 1040 Brussels, Belgium. Call 32-2-23000-10.

Children: **Y**   Pets: **N**   Smoking: **Y**   Handicap Access: **Y**   Payment: **A**

LIMBURG

Hechtel-Eksel

DE LAGE KEMPEN BUNGALOWS   *Rates: budget*
Open: March-October   *Minimum Stay: three nights*

This convenient bungalow for four is found in a friendly family vacation paradise in the bucolic countryside of eastern Belgium. The central attraction here is the enormous outdoor swimming pool heated with solar power and featuring a terrific slide. There is also a playground for the kids and a nice restaurant for the whole family. The bungalows are compact but comfy, with a living/dining room, a modern kitchen, a bathroom and two bedrooms—one with a bunk bed. Outside, there is a small terrace where you can relax after a day of fun in the sun. This area boasts some of the most beautiful scenery in Belgium; the rolling foothills of the nearby Ardennes are the perfect place for a hike and picnic. Contact: De Lage Kempen, Kiefhoekstraat 19, 3588 Hechtel-Eksel, Belgium. Call 32-11-402243.

Children: **Y**   Pets: **Y**   Smoking: **Y**   Handicap Access: **N**   Payment: **C, T**

Houthalen-Helchteren

DOMAIN KELCHTERHOEF   *Rates: budget-inexpensive*
Open: year-round   *Minimum Stay: one week*

The Domain Kelchterhoef is a small vacation village in the verdant countryside of Limburg near the popular holiday town of Houthalen-Helchteren. The pleasantly situated bungalows can accommodate between four and six guests in simple convenience. The recreational options here are diverse and plentiful: Tennis, golf and bicycling facilities cater to athletic types; boating and fishing will please water enthusiasts; the gentle waters at the beach will delight those who have dreamed all year of quiet swims beneath a warm sun. Contact: Domain Kelchterhoef, Kelchterhoefstraat 9, 3530 Houthalen-Helchteren, Belgium. Call 32-11-38-32-33.

Children: **Y**   Pets: **Y**   Smoking: **Y**   Handicap Access: **N**   Payment: **C, P**

Houthalen-Helchteren

MOLENHEIDE DELTA COTTAGE   *Rates: budget-inexpensive*
Open: year-round   *Minimum Stay: two days*

Set in the beautiful green countryside of the Kempen in eastern Belgium, Molenheide is a paradise for those who seek a bucolic, outdoorsy holiday. In addition to the fine countryside laced with canals, there are fish for anglers and seaworthy craft for boaters here. After a peaceful day outside, you can return to the comfy lodgings of your cottage. There's a color TV/VCR with a full range of video options in the living room; the kitchen and bathroom are fully modern. You may want to enjoy your supper out on the terrace, shaded by the handsome trees surrounding your secluded abode. And after a pleasing repast topped off with a glass of rich Belgian beer, you can retire to one of the two cozy bedrooms you'll find inside (the cottage sleeps six people). Contact: Mr. Vanherk, Molenheidestraat 7, 3538 Houthalen-Helchteren, Belgium. Call 32-11-52-10-44.

Children: **Y**   Pets: **Y**   Smoking: **Y**   Handicap Access: **N**   Payment: **C, P, T**

Houthalen-Helchteren

MOLENHEIDE RELAX COTTAGE   *Rates: budget-inexpensive*
Open: year-round   *Minimum Stay: two days*

Every convenience of a large modern resort is waiting for you at Mo lenheide. The Jacuzzi and sauna soothe away the aches and pains of modern life, while the several eateries cater to your every culinary need. For those who prefer to whip up a little something at home, there's a supermarket on the grounds and a full kitchen in your cottage. The recreational facilities are outstanding, the color TV and VCR provide other entertainment options and child care is available for couples who'd like to spend a few hours alone. All these amenities are found in the lovely green countryside of eastern Belgium. The Relax Cottage is an ideal rental for four people who want to get away from it all but still have everything at their fingertips. Contact: Mr. Vanherk, Molenheidestraat 7, 3538 Houthalen-Helchteren, Belgium. Call 32-11-52-10-44.

Children: Y Pets: N Smoking: Y Handicap Access: N Payment: C, P, T

WEST FLANDERS

Bredene Klemskerke

HOUSE EIGHT ON THE DUNES   *Rates: budget*
Open: year-round   *Minimum Stay: one week*

Larger groups traveling together will appreciate this roomy apartment near the sea. The area around Bredene offers abundant diversions: In addition to swimming and sunning, the horseback riding, cycling, picnics on the dunes and pleasant walks through the countryside should keep you busy. There's also the large resort town of Ostende just a little to the south, where you'll find facilities for wind surfing, sailing, water skiing and all your other favorite aquatic activities. The sunny apartment includes a kitchenette, a living/dining room with a double divan bed and two bedrooms. Contact: Interhome Inc., 124 Little Falls Road, Fairfield, NJ 07004. Call 201-882-6864. Ref. B1500/17M.

Children: Y Pets: Y Smoking: Y Handicap Access: N Payment: P, V, M

Bredene Klemskerke

HOUSE TWO ON THE DUNES   *Rates: budget*
Open: year-round   *Minimum Stay: one week*

Rolling dunes, quiet countryside and wind-swept beaches—this is the stuff romantic getaways are made of. This pleasant little apartment is ideal for couples who want to escape from it all but still not be too far away. The area boasts some charming shops where you can while away the hours, friendly pubs for midafternoon refreshment and excellent seafood restaurants for intimate interludes. The cozy apartment includes a kitchenette and one bedroom, and there's a convertible bed in the living/dining area for an extra guest. Contact: Interhome Inc., 124 Little Falls Road, Fairfield, NJ 07004. Call 201-882-6864. Ref. B1500/30M.

Children: Y Pets: Y Smoking: Y Handicap Access: N Payment: P, V, M

Bruges

ACACIA   *Rates: moderate*
Open: year-round   *Minimum Stay: one week*

With picturesque canals, narrow streets, dainty bridges and ancient buildings, Bruges is rightfully known as the Venice of the North. The Acacia is ideally situated right in the center of the old town, only a few feet from the beautiful facades of the market. Although the apartment building's environs are old, the Acacia itself is absolutely modern. After working out in the gym or swimming a few laps in the indoor pool, you can relax in the sauna before enjoying your complimentary breakfast. When your day of sightseeing is over, just park the car in the underground garage and stop by the friendly bar for a nightcap, then return to your one-bedroom apartment (which has been cleaned by the staff in your absence) and stretch out in front of the color TV. Contact: Interhome Inc., 124 Little Falls Road, Fairfield, NJ 07004. Call 201-882-6864. Ref. B8000/120M.

Children: Y   Pets: N   Smoking: Y   Handicap Access: N   Payment: P, V, M

Bruges

ELODEA CRUISER   *Rates: expensive-deluxe*
Open: year-round   *Minimum Stay: one week*

With the elegant Elodea, you never have to worry about finding someplace to sleep when you pull into a new town late at night: You'll bring your familiar, cozy accommodations with you. This six-person cruiser lets you see Belgium from one of its most picturesque venues, the thousands of miles of tranquil canals that weave throughout the countryside and glide through towns. Medieval houses and guild halls line the waterfront in ancient ports such as Bruges and Gent; charming waterfront cafes and tree-lined boulevards will greet you in other towns. And in the verdant countryside of the lowlands, you can sleep under the stars, lulled by the hush of the farmlands but surrounded by all the modern conveniences of a hotel room. Contact: Blakes Vacations, 4918 Dempster Street, Skokie, IL 60077. Call 1-800-628-8118 (in Illinois, 708-982-0561).

Children: Y   Pets: N   Smoking: Y   Handicap Access: N   Payment: V, M

Bruges

GOEZEPUTSTRAAT HOMES   *Rates: budget-inexpensive*
Open: year-round   *Minimum Stay: four nights*

On a quiet cobblestone street in the heart of picturesque Bruges, you'll find these handsome old buildings contain fully modernized guest apartments. The apartments can accommodate between two and seven people, and each one has its own special character. Some boast bright colors and sleek, modern furnishings; others feature arched doorways, tiled floors and exposed brick and stonework. All include fully equipped kitchens, color TVs and private parking spaces. These are wonderful bases for couples, families or small groups who have come to explore the ancient venues and charming canals of this historic town. Contact: Holiday City Center, Goezeputstraat 5, 8000 Brugge, Belgium. Call 32-50-331282.

Children: Y Pets: N Smoking: N Handicap Access: N Payment: C, T, A, V, M

Bruges

SAGITTARIA CRUISER *Rates: moderate-expensive*
Open: year-round *Minimum Stay: one week*

Can't decide between Bruges, Gent or Antwerp, but don't want to change hotel rooms every night? You'd like to see the houses of Ieper and the cathedral at Tournai, but you dread traveling back to your distant apartment after an exhausting day trip? Why not take advantage of the low countries' unique system of canals, and charter a private boat by which to see Belgium? Based in Bruges, the Sagittaria is an elegant 31-foot cruiser that has been fully outfitted as a home-away-from-home. The two double berths will comfortably sleep four; a galley, salon, bathroom with shower and roomy wheelhouse complete the accommodations. There's even a stereo system aboard, plus two bikes for doing the shopping on shore. Contact: Blakes Vacations, 4918 Dempster Street, Skokie, IL 60077. Call 1-800-628-8118 (in Illinois, 708-982-0561).

Children: Y   Pets: N   Smoking: Y   Handicap Access: N   Payment: V, M

De Haan

PARK ATLANTIS APARTMENTS *Rates: budget-moderate*
Open: year-round *Minimum Stay: three nights*

The Park Atlantis is a modern resort offering hundreds of comfortable apartments right on the water's edge. The tastefully furnished rooms include a kitchen complete with coffee maker, a living room with a color TV and sleeping quarters for two to eight people. Each apartment also has its own sunny terrace with garden furniture where you can stretch out after a day at the beach. De Haan is a lively seaside town with all the expected water-sports facilities. It also boasts a convivial social life, with fine seafood restaurants, charming outdoor cafes, energetic discos and plenty of bars where you can sample Belgian beer. Contact: Park Atlantis, Torenhoefstraat 2, 8420 De Haan, Belgium. Call 32-59-233-622.

Children: Y Pets: Y Smoking: Y Handicap Access: N Payment: C, P, A, V, M

Nieuwpoort

YSERMONDE COTTAGES *Rates: inexpensive-moderate*
Open: year-round *Minimum Stay: none*

Ysermonde is a beautiful holiday village set in the verdant countryside near Nieuwpoort. Flemish hospitality and charm are everywhere in evidence here, from the picturesque architecture and furnishings of the individually designed cottages to the quiet walks your hosts have planned throughout the scenic area. Although each cottage is different, every one of them comes with central heating, a color TV and a private terrace with garden furniture. The tranquil beauty at Ysermonde makes this the perfect spot for a peaceful holiday in the country; the historic town of Veurne is within a short distance for touring. Contact: Ysermonde, Victorlaan 1, 8620 Nieuwpoort, Belgium. Call 32-5823-65-44.

Children: Y Pets: Y Smoking: Y Handicap Access: N Payment: C, P, T, A, V

Westende-Bad

BUNGALOW FOR FOUR

Open: year-round

Rates: budget-inexpensive

Minimum Stay: one week

Westende-Bad is a large modern resort that takes full advantage of its marvelous situation on the coast of the North Sea. A lovely promenade wends its way along the fine, sandy beach and the restaurants and cafes do a brisk business catering to bronzed visitors. This bungalow is part of a guest complex found in a quiet spot just behind the dunes and still near the water. The terrace houses are clustered together in small groups, and each house is uniquely furnished. The four-person bungalow comprises a living room with a double divan bed, a kitchenette and a double bedroom. There's also a pleasant terrace for relaxing outside and a TV for watching inside. Contact: Interhome Inc., 124 Little Falls Road, Fairfield, NJ 07004. Call 201-882-6864. Ref. B2300/1.

Children: Y   Pets: Y   Smoking: Y   Handicap Access: N   Payment: P, V, M

Westende-Bad

BUNGALOW FOR SIX

Open: year-round

Rates: budget-inexpensive

Minimum Stay: one week

This large bungalow near the sea is an ideal holiday home for families. Up to six people can find accommodations in the comfy rooms; the two sets of bunk beds in one of the bedrooms are sure to be a hit with the kids. The complex also caters to younger visitors by providing several playgrounds and by prohibiting cars on the grounds (parking spaces are provided at the edge of the complex). The bungalow also has access to a pleasant terrace with garden furniture and a large grassy area. Shops, restaurants and tennis courts are a short walk away and the inviting sands of the beach are just a bit further. Contact: Interhome Inc., 124 Little Falls Road, Fairfield, NJ 07004. Call 201-882-6864. Ref. B2300/10.

Children: Y   Pets: Y   Smoking: Y   Handicap Access: N   Payment: P, V, M

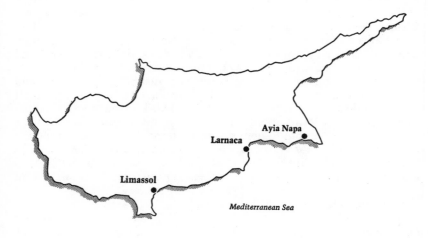

Cyprus

Ayia Napa

ANTHEA APARTHOTEL *Rates: budget*

Open: year-round *Minimum Stay: none*

This lovely two-story resort has been attracting an ever-growing crowd of international business people and vacationers since it opened its doors in the summer of 1985. Ideally situated with easy access to the island's diverse offerings, the Anthea is close to the picturesque harbor of Ayia Napa and only a short walk from the inviting sands of Grecian Bay beach. 125 units range from studios to two-bedroom apartments, all of an ultra-modern design and featuring a fully equipped kitchenette, a bath and shower, a balcony, central air conditioning and heat and five days/week of maid service. Additional amenities include a cafeteria, indoor and outdoor bars, a swimming pool, a restaurant and a supermarket. Contact: Mrs. Zacharoulla, Reservations Dept., H & C Hotels and Catering Col Ltd., PO Box 40, Ayia Napa, Cyprus. Call (011-357-3) 721-450.

Children: Y Pets: N Smoking: Y Handicap Access: N Payment: C, T, A, V, M

Ayia Napa

KAROUSOS APARTHOTEL *Rates: budget*

Open: year-round *Minimum Stay: none*

Its convenient location near the center of town belies the Karousos Aparthotel's luxurious proximity to the soft sands of the Grecian Bay and Sandy Bay beaches. Close to the harbor as well, this modern two-story building of studios, one- and twobedroom apartments (sleeping two to five) has a full view of Ayia Napa's ruggedly beautiful coastline.

All units feature convertible sofas in the livingroom; a modern and well-equipped kitchen; a balcony; a full bathroom with a tub and shower; and maid service five times/week. A lounge, cafeteria, bar, restaurant and supermarket are also on the grounds, ensuring that your stay is comfortable and your needs are met. Bicycles—a popular way to see the island's sights—are available for hire. Contact: Mrs. Zacharoulla, H & C Hotels and Catering Co. Ltd., PO Box 40, Ayia Napa, Cyprus. Call (011-357-3) 721-450.

Children: Y Pets: N Smoking: Y Handicap Access: N Payment: C, T, A, V, M

Ayia Napa

KERMIA BEACH BUNGALOWS *Rates: budget*
Open: year-round *Minimum Stay: none*

These pleasant little beachside bungalows enjoy a splendid setting on one of Cyprus's most delightful shores. Charming villages cluster around ancient churches, and the rugged countryside transforms abruptly into wide, sandy beaches. Devoted sightseers will want to visit Ayia Napa's monastery, a stately edifice built in 1500. The bungalows vary in size from studios to two-bedroom apartments; all receive maid service daily. The complex conveniently includes a restaurant and laundry facilities, and there is a large swimming pool for the guests' use. If you tire of swimming, sunning and the usual water sports, there are tennis courts, playgrounds and bike trails nearby. Contact: Kermia Beach Bungalows Hotel, Cavo Greco Avenue, Ayia Napa, Cyprus. Call 357-3-721401.

Children: Y Pets: N Smoking: Y Handicap Access: N Payment: C, V, M

Larnaca

ADONIS BEACH APARTMENTS *Rates: budget*
Open: year-round *Minimum Stay: none*

Larnaca is a vibrant port, the big city of Cyprus where international trade bustles and nightlife hustles. In addition to the popular beach, the town boasts a surprisingly extensive museum and a handsome medieval fortress. Practically on the water's edge, these studio, one- and two-bedroom apartments offer all the amenities of a resort hotel. The restaurant, daily maid service and laundry facilities ensure that all your needs are met quickly and conveniently; there's even a babysitter available to watch the kids when you want to enjoy a romantic night on the town. Contact: Photis Adonis, Piale Pasha 300, P.O. Box 231, Larnaca, Cyprus. Call 357-4-656644.

Children: Y Pets: N Smoking: Y Handicap Access: N Payment: C, T, A, V, M

Limassol

PIER BEACH APARTMENTS *Rates: budget-inexpensive*
Open: year-round *Minimum Stay: three nights*

Limassol is a splendid base for exploring the island of Cyprus: The mysterious Troodos Mountains loom in the north, elegant and ancient Paphos awaits you in the west, while the lovely area around Ayia Napa lies in the east. If you prefer to stay put, try some Cypriot delicacies in a neighborhood restaurant and take an afternoon to explore the 700-year-old Limassol Castle. The Pier Beach Hotel offers air-conditioned apartments for between two and eight people. The complex is wonderfully close to the water, and there's a swimming pool and gym for the use of the guests. Tennis, boating, fishing and water skiing can also be enjoyed nearby. Contact: Lazaros Lazaron, P.O. Box 221, Limassol, Cyprus. Call 357-5-361414.

Children: **Y**   Pets: **N**   Smoking: **Y**   Handicap Access: **N**   Payment: **C, V**

Protaras

PROTARAS SEA VIEW APARTMENTS   *Rates: budget*
Open: year-round   *Minimum Stay: none*

Enjoy a morning coffee from your balcony overlooking Fig Tree Bay Beach — or step outside for a quick ocean dip as you start your day as a resident of the delightful, oceanfront Protaras Sea View Apartments. Here, in units that range from studios to three-bedrooms, the whole family is catered to whether indoors or out, at the minimarket or in the restaurant, at the pool or in the playground. Apartments all feature a well-equipped kitchenette, a full bathroom with a tub and shower, central air conditioning and maid service five times/week. Contact: Mrs. Zacharoulla, Reservations Department, H & C Hotels and Catering Co. Ltd., PO Box 40, Ayia Napa, Cyprus. Call (011-357-3) 721450.

Children: **Y** Pets: **N** Smoking: **Y** Handicap Access: **N** Payment: **C, T, A, V, M**

North
Sea

Liseleje

★ Copenhagen

ZEALAND

Baltic
Sea

Denmark

NORTH ZEALAND

Frederiksvaerk

BITTENS HOUSE   *Rates: budget*
Open: April 1-October 1   *Minimum Stay: one week*

Set in a sunny clearing among dense, fragrant woods, this two-bedroom, one-bathroom (hand shower only) cottage for five features a spacious, semi-enclosed front terrace ideal for outdoor cooking and dining (a barbecue is provided). Five bikes provide ready transportation to the nearby shops (less than a mile away) or the beach (one-and-a-half miles). So jump on your bike and let your impulses be your guide. The price includes the Danish VAT but does not cover linens and towels (visitors must bring their own). There's an additional charge for electric heating. Contact: Lise Christiansen, at Liseleje Ejendomskontor, Liselejevej 60, 3360 Liseleje, Denmark. Call: (011-45) 42-34-6334. Ref. 75 M2.

Children: **Y**   Pets: **N**   Smoking: **Y**   Handicap Access: **N**   Payment: **C, EC**

Frederiksvaerk

FJORD COTTAGE   *Rates: budget*
Open: April 1-October 1   *Minimum Stay: one week*

On a direct path to the sea, the shore is a mere six miles down the road
from this serene two-bedroom, one-bathroom cottage suitable for four
people. The cozy living room contains a wood-burning stove, a color
TV and an old-fashioned fireplace. Guests can use the property's three
bicycles for short trips to the local shops—less than two miles away—
or to tour highlights of the area's natural beauty—including the largest
lake in Denmark. Don't miss this opportunity to experience the real
Denmark. Prices include the Danish VAT but do not cover linens and
towels (visitors must bring their own). There's an additional charge for
electric heating. Contact: Lise Christiansen at Liseleje Ejendomskontor, Liselejevej 60, 3360 Liseleje, Denmark. Call: (011-45) 42-34-63-
34. Ref. 65 M2.

Children: Y   Pets: N   Smoking: Y   Handicap Access: N   Payment: C, EC

Frederiksvaerk

RANCH HOUSE   *Rates: budget-inexpensive*
Open: April 1-October 1   *Minimum Stay: one week*

This three-bedroom, one-bathroom ranch house accommodates six
people in a particularly spacious living area that features a fireplace in
the living room (which can supplement the electric heating), a family
room with a color TV, a kitchen equipped with a dishwasher, and a
sauna. A delightful swimming pool and a children's playhouse are star
attractions in a yard enclosed by a large, Ponderosa-like fence. Three
bicycles are available for the short trips to the local shops or beach.
The price includes the Danish VAT but does not cover linens and
towels (visitors must bring their own). There's an extra charge for
electricity also. Contact: Palle Knudsen at Liseleje Ejendomskontor,
Liselejevej 60, 3360 Liseleje, Denmark. Call: (011-45) 42-34-6334. Ref.
105 M2.

Children: Y   Pets: N   Smoking: Y   Handicap Access: N   Payment: C, EC

Frederiksvaerk

WOODEN COTTAGE   *Rates: budget*
Open: April 1-October 1   *Minimum Stay: one week*

This two-bedroom, one-bathroom wooden cottage for four offers a
rustic, tranquil retreat only 35 miles from Copenhagen. A wood-
burning stove can supplement the electric heating or simply add extra
coziness to cool evenings. Ride the two bikes to the local shops. Check
out the nearby beach (one of the country's best), the large lake, tennis
court or golf course. Additionally, this is an area famous for its idyllic
fishing villages, local museums and good restaurants in every price
range. The price includes the Danish VAT but does not cover linens
and towels (visitors must bring their own); electricity is an extra
charge. Contact: Palle Knudsen at Liseleje Ejendomskontor, Lisele-

jevej 60, 3360 Liseleje, Denmark. Call: (011-45) 42-34-63-34. Ref. 40
M2.

Children: Y   Pets: N   Smoking: Y   Handicap Access: N   Payment: C, EC

Liseleje

BEACH COTTAGE   *Rates: budget*
Open: April 1-October 1   *Minimum Stay: one week*
Exploring Danish culture can be your top priority in this typically
lovely Scandinavian setting or just relax and watch the time go by. A
large patio surrounds this three-bedroom, one-bathroom cottage ideal
for six people and set on a particularly unspoiled plot of tree-filled
land. A cozy, L-shaped living room offers a fireplace and TV; and an
open kitchen contains both a dishwasher and a washing machine.
Denmark's most beautiful beach is a short block away, and local shops
are a mile down the road. The price includes the Danish VAT but does
not cover linens and towels (visitors must bring their own). There's an
additional charge for electric heating. Contact: Palle Knudsen at
Liseleje Ejendomskontor, Liselejevej 60, 3360 Liseleje, Denmark.
Call: (011-45) 42-34-63-34. Ref. 70 M2

Children: Y   Pets: Y   Smoking: Y   Handicap Access: N   Payment: C, EC

Liseleje

ROSENBERG COTTAGE   *Rates: budget*
Open: April 1-October 1   *Minimum Stay: one week*
In this lovely setting you can enjoy the serenity of the country and the
quaintness of a typical fishing village. This two-bedroom, one-
bathroom cottage suitable for five people features two terraces ideal
for outdoor dining (a barbecue is provided), a carport and an inviting
fireplace in an L-shaped living room. The beach and local shops are a
short half-mile away in an area well-known for its restaurants, museums, and fishing. The price includes the Danish VAT but does not
cover linens and towels (visitors must bring their own). There's an
additional charge for electric heating. Contact: Palle Knudsen at
Liseleje Ejendomskontor, Liselejevej 60, 3360 Liseleje, Denmark.
Call: (011-45) 42-34-63-34. Ref. 55 M2.

Children: Y   Pets: N   Smoking: Y   Handicap Access: N   Payment: C, EC

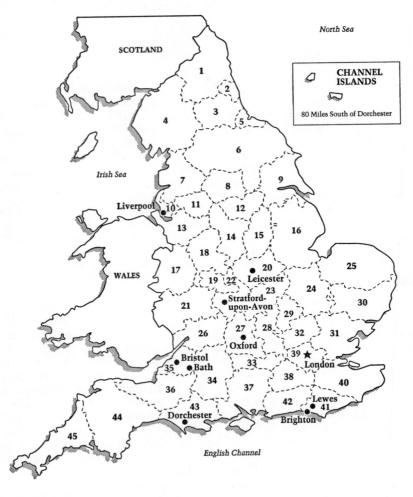

CHANNEL ISLANDS

80 Miles South of Dorchester

North Sea

SCOTLAND

Irish Sea

Liverpool

WALES

Bristol
Bath

Dorchester

English Channel

Leicester

Stratford-
upon-Avon

Oxford

London

Lewes

Brighton

1. NORTHUMBERLAND
2. TYNE AND WEAR
3. DURHAM
4. CUMBRIA
5. CLEVELAND
6. NORTH YORKSHIRE
7. LANCASHIRE
8. WEST YORKSHIRE
9. HUMBERSIDE
10. MERSEYSIDE
11. GREATER MANCHESTER
12. SOUTH YORKSHIRE
13. CHESHIRE
14. DERBYSHIRE
15. NOTTINGHAMSHIRE

16. LINCOLNSHIRE
17. SHROPSHIRE
18. STAFFORDSHIRE
19. WEST MIDLANDS
20. LEICESTERSHIRE
21. HEREFORD AND WORCESTER
22. WARWICKSHIRE
23. NORTHAMPTONSHIRE
24. CAMBRIDGESHIRE
25. NORFOLK
26. GLOUCESTERSHIRE
27. OXFORDSHIRE
28. BUCKINGHAMSHIRE
29. BEDFORDSHIRE
30. SUFFOLK

31. ESSEX
32. HERTFORDSHIRE
33. BERKSHIRE
34. WILTSHIRE
35. AVON
36. SOMERSET
37. HAMPSHIRE
38. SURREY
39. GREATER LONDON
40. KENT
41. EAST SUSSEX
42. WEST SUSSEX
43. DORSET
44. DEVON
45. CORNWALL

England

AVON

Bath

GEORGIAN HOUSE *Rates: budget-inexpensive*
Open: year-round *Minimum Stay: one week*
This house stands a short walk from the center of a city that's a testament to the beauty of Georgian architecture. One newly renovated wing of the house is available for rent and provides well-furnished accommodations for two adults. The kitchen is brand new, the bathroom has marble fixtures and there's one twin bedroom and a double sofa bed in the living room. No children under 14 are permitted. Contact: British Travel Associates, P.O. Box 299, Elkton, VA 22827. Call 1-800-327-6097 (in Virginia, 703-298-2232). Ref. F95.
Children: N   Pets: N   Smoking: Y   Handicap Access: N   Payment: All

Bath

MARSHAL WADE'S HOUSE *Rates: budget-moderate*
Open: year-round *Minimum Stay: three nights*
Situated over a shop run by the National Trust, this two-bedroom apartment is at the center of one of England's most historic and beautiful cities. The view from the second floor encompasses the Abbey Church yard and the elaborately carved entrance to the Bath Cathedral. Two bedrooms (one twin and one double) are on the third floor, while on the second floor is a living room and a large kitchen/dining room with a charming octagonal kitchen "island." The rooms are wood paneled and the long windows allow in plenty of light. It is hard to imagine a better situation from which to visit the Roman baths that give this town its name. Contact: The Landmark Trust, Shottesbrooke, Maidenhead, Berks, England SL6 3SW. Call 011-44-628-82-5925.
Children: Y Pets: N Smoking: Y Handicap Access: N Payment: C, P, T, V, M

BERKSHIRE

Lambourne

CLEEVE COTTAGE *Rates: inexpensive-expensive*
Open: year-round *Minimum Stay: one week*
A magnificent garden setting with croquet, badminton, a tree swing and outdoor furniture make Cleeve Cottage a unique find. Surrounded by twelve acres of rolling woodlands, the four-bedroom house (two doubles, a twin and a single) provides sleeping accommodations for eight. A large, beamed living room has a wood-burning stove for warmth, and a small study contains a Ping-Pong table and other games as well as books about the wildlife and flowers in the area. The Nature

Conservancy Council has classified part of the downs as a site of special interest because rare flowers, birds, deer and fox inhabit the area. Racing stables, shops, restaurants, riverside walks, boating and fishing all lie within five miles. Contact: British Travel Associates, P.O. Box 299, Elkton, VA 22827. Call 1-800-327-6097 (in Virginia, 703-298-2232). Ref. NMP.

Children: Y   Pets: N   Smoking: Y   Handicap Access: N   Payment: All

BUCKINGHAMSHIRE

Amersham

HIGH STREET HOUSE
Open: year-round

Rates: inexpensive
Minimum Stay: one week

Imagine the grace and elegance of a 300-year-old terraced cottage only 35 minutes from London! This fastidiously restored home features a beamed living room and the best of furnishings and also enjoys a lovely setting in the historic section of a charming town with cobbled courtyards and Georgian homes. The walled patio garden, which looks onto a field and stream to the rear of the house, offers that special opportunity to linger at the end of a perfect day. The home for five includes a kitchen, a living/dining room with a color TV and three bedrooms. Frequent tube and BritRail service to central London as well as the whole of central England only a short drive away make this an ideal center for an English holiday. Contact: British Travel Associates, P.O. Box 299, Elkton, VA 22827. Call 1-800-327-6097 (In Virginia 703-298-2232). Ref. 022143.

Children: Y   Pets: N   Smoking: Y   Handicap Access: N   Payment: P

Beaconsfield

OAK BEAM COTTAGE
Open: year-round

Rates: inexpensive
Minimum Stay: one week

This elegant whitewashed cottage offers the comfort and convenience of a modern restoration while retaining some charming original features. The handsomely furnished home includes a wealth of heavy oak beams and old-style windows. Set in the historic district of this lively town, the house also includes its own charming patio garden and a private garage. Accommodations for four consist of a living room, a dining room, a kitchen and two bedrooms. Located ideally for trips into the city—the trip takes 35 minutes by car or BritRail—or the surrounding Buckinghamshire countryside, this house offers an opportunity to sample England at its best. Contact: British Travel Associates, P.O. Box 299, Elkton, VA 22827. Call 1-800-327-6097 (In Virginia 703-298-2232). Ref. 020141.

Children: Y   Pets: N   Smoking: Y   Handicap Access: N   Payment: P

Windsor

WINDSOR APARTMENT
Open: year-round

Rates: budget
Minimum Stay: one week

Situated in the heart of royal Windsor only a half hour by BritRail from

London, this luxurious modern apartment enjoys the especially pleasant setting of a quiet courtyard just off Windsor High Street. From here, a short walk will bring you to the magnificent Windsor castle, Madame Tussot's Royalty and Empire exhibit and the many fashionable shops, restaurants and pubs of this beautiful town. Car excursions promise the many delights of the lovely countryside west of London, and for horselovers, Ascot Racecourse is only a short drive away. The carefully appointed apartment for four includes a living/dining room, a galley kitchen and two bedrooms, and offers the much valued conveniences of a color TV and a washing machine. Contact: British Travel Associates, P.O. Box 299, Elkton, VA 22827. Call 1-800-327-6097 (In Virginia 703-298-2232). Ref. 020005.

Children: Y   Pets: N   Smoking: Y   Handicap Access: N   Payment: P

CHANNEL ISLANDS

Alderney

FORT CLONQUE   *Rates: inexpensive-expensive*
Open: year-round   *Minimum Stay: three nights*

This low-lying fortress on a rocky tip of Alderney has a checkered past—it was originally built by the Duke of Wellington, left empty for sixty years and then renovated by the Germans during World War II. Now it is a unique accommodation able to house up to twelve guests. The bedrooms are in various places throughout the fort, and there are three bathrooms and a kitchen large enough to contain two long tables. The two living rooms have open fireplaces. Located on one of the Channel Islands, the fort is connected to Alderney at low tide by a causeway. The island is well worth exploring, since it's covered with wildflowers and a wealth of tide pools. It also boasts the pretty little town of St. Anne, which has a distinctive French-English air. Contact: The Landmark Trust, Shottesbrooke, Maidenhead, Berks, England SL6 3SW. Call 011-44-628-82-5925.

Children: Y Pets: N Smoking: Y Handicap Access: N Payment: C, P, T, V, M

St. Clements

THE NICOLLE TOWER   *Rates: budget-moderate*
Open: year-round   *Minimum Stay: three nights*

This 160-foot tower is situated on a field named "Le Clos de Hercanty" and has a fascinating past that includes German occupation during World War II. It has now been carefully converted to a three-story accommodation for two, with cozy rooms and high-peaked windows on each side. The ground floor contains an eat-in kitchen, the first floor has a living room (whose hexagonal rug and table reflect the tower's shape) and the bedroom is on the third floor. Jersey is one of the prettiest and liveliest islands in the channel and puts you close to the coast of France. There are ample opportunities for recreation, since Jersey has good beaches and is a popular vacation spot. Contact: The Landmark Trust, Shottesbrooke, Maidenhead, Berks, England SL6 3SW. Call 011-44-628-82-5925.

Children: Y Pets: N Smoking: Y Handicap Access: N Payment: C, P, T, V, M

CHESHIRE

Astbury

BLACK AND WHITE COTTAGE *Rates: budget*
Open: year-round *Minimum Stay: one week*

The 13th-century church of St. Mary stands close by this cozy little cottage, built around 1580 and extensively renovated since then. A sitting/dining room, a large corner fireplace, a small kitchenette and a large double bedroom with an extra cot provide plenty of room for two to three people. North Wales, the Peak District and Little Moreton Hall (the famous National Trust Tudor house) are nearby. Contact: British Travel Associates, P.O. Box 299, Elkton, VA 22827. Call 1-800-327-6097 (in Virginia, 703-298-2232). Ref. QAA.

Children: **Y** Pets: **N** Smoking: **Y** Handicap Access: **N** Payment: All

Nantwich

CANAL COTTAGE *Rates: budget-moderate*
Open: year-round *Minimum Stay: one week*

Use the rowboat that comes with this two-bedroom house to explore the picturesque river that rolls right outside your door. Or instead, hire an all-weather day boat, stroll along one of the riverside walks to see an abundance of wildlife or enjoy the quaint market town of Nantwich, with its many excellent dining and recreational options. The house features central heating and modern kitchen, an open fireplace and elegant French windows looking out onto a splendid private walled courtyard and gardens. Contact: British Travel Associates, P.O. Box 299, Elkton, VA 22827. Call 1-800-327-6097 (in Virginia, 703-298-2232).

Children: **Y** Pets: **Y** Smoking: **Y** Handicap Access: **N** Payment: All

CLEVELAND

Yarm

BEECH TREE APARTMENT *Rates: budget-inexpensive*
Open: year-round *Minimum Stay: one week*

This exquisitely decorated and furnished second-floor apartment for four offers the finest appointments imaginable, including such niceties as guest bathrobes. Located in the romantic Georgian town of Yarm by the River Trees, the apartment includes two bedrooms, a living room, a dining room and a kitchen with a microwave and washer/dryer. From here, the whole of North England opens up to you—from the soft and rolling dales to the wild beauty of the moors—for walking, cycling or car excursions. Contact: Castles, Cottages & Flats in Ireland and U.K. Ltd., Box 261, Westwood, MA 02090. Call 617-329-4680. Ref. 1053.

Children: **Y** Pets: **N** Smoking: **N** Handicap Access: **N** Payment: P

CORNWALL

Callington

WHITEFORD TEMPLE *Rates: budget*
Open: year-round *Minimum Stay: three nights*

This unusual structure has been converted into a charming studio apartment with a separate kitchen and bathroom. Three floor-length arched windows offer a view that stretches all the way to the estuary of the Tamar River. Attractive rugs have been placed on the equally attractive polished wood floors, and there is a round dining table for four. Before the fireplace are a large armchair, a couch and two single beds that can be pushed together. Within easy reach of both Dartmoor National Park and Bodmin Moor, the location offers opportunities for hiking through scenery that varies from gentle to rugged. The coast and the maritime town of Plymouth are within driving distance. Contact: The Landmark Trust, Shottesbrooke, Maidenhead, Berks, England SL6 3SW. Call 011-44-628-82-5925.

Children: Y Pets: N Smoking: Y Handicap Access: N Payment: C, P, T, V, M

Coombe, near Morwenstow

HAWKERS COTTAGES *Rates: budget-moderate*
Open: year-round *Minimum Stay: three nights*

A charming little crooked gate opens to reveal a quiet, pretty garden with a pathway leading up to this pair of thatched cottages named after a famous vicar in the parish. Both have open fireplaces and consist of a living room, kitchen and three bedrooms. Number 2 is slightly larger and has the added attraction of a small sitting room and some notable pieces of furniture, including a lovely old cupboard. An old water mill sits intact beside the hamlet's little stream, where you can try your hand at catching trout for supper. It is only a short walk to the lovely north Cornish coast, and though the Atlantic Ocean is brisk, there is a sandy beach nearby. All along this stretch of the coast are magnificent views and ancient lighthouses, castles and churches. Contact: The Landmark Trust, Shottesbrooke, Maidenhead, Berks, England SL6 3SW. Call 011-44-628-82-5925.

Children: Y Pets: Y Smoking: Y Handicap Access: N Payment: C, P, T, V, M

Coombe, near Morwenstow

THE CARPENTER'S SHOP *Rates: budget-moderate*
Open: year-round *Minimum Stay: three nights*

Reflecting its original purpose, this small cottage has simple furnishings, clean detailing and a fireplace that once served as a forge. A large window lets sunlight stream into the downstairs living/dining area, which is open to the second floor. A spiral staircase leads to a gallery on the second level, at either end of which is a bedroom, one with twin beds and the other with a set of bunk beds. The doors lead to an old orchard bordered by the trout-stocked stream that runs through the hamlet of Coombe. It is just a half-mile walk to a sandy beach and access to this magnificent coastline, which has many fine viewpoints along the coastal path. The hamlet itself and the surrounding area have many interesting sites, ranging from the old mill situated in Coombe to a selection of fine museums and old churches. Contact: The Landmark Trust, Shottesbrooke, Maidenhead, Berks, England SL6 3SW. Call 011-44-628-82-5925.

Children: Y Pets: Y Smoking: Y Handicap Access: N Payment: C, P, T, V, M

Garker

SUN COTTAGE   *Rates: budget*
Open: year-round   *Minimum Stay: one week*

Sun Cottage's light and airy sun room gives this attractive cottage its name. Filled with interesting decorative features throughout, it includes a ceramic-tiled floor in the sun room, an open pine staircase, beamed ceilings and a wood-burning stove. A living room, a kitchen/dining area and one double bedroom make this a cozy cottage for two. The quarry town of St. Austell and Carlyon Bay (with a mile-long sandy beach, sports and entertainment complexes, and a golf course) are within three miles. Contact: British Travel Associates, P.O. Box 299, Elkton, VA 22827. Call 1-800-327-6097 (in Virginia, 703-298-2232). Ref. F1171.

Children: Y   Pets: N   Smoking: Y   Handicap Access: N   Payment: All

Helford

FRENCHMAN'S CREEK COTTAGE   *Rates: budget-inexpensive*
Open: year-round   *Minimum Stay: none*

This hidden granite cottage is perfect for a romantic hideaway or a solitary vacation. Surrounded by dense thickets and located on a tidal basin, the cottage was described in the novel The Helford River. Inside, there is one twin and one double bedroom, and the whole building has been recently renovated and winterized. The garden makes a pleasant place to sit and picnic. Nearby are the towns of Penzance and Falmouth, and there are many ancient sites throughout the local countryside—some of the stone circles and cairns date back thousands of years. The turquoise sea at Lizard Point, just a few miles away, makes it one of Cornwall's best-loved spots. Contact: The Landmark Trust, Shottesbrooke, Maidenhead, Berks, England SL6 3SW. Call 011-44-628-82-5925.

Children: Y Pets: Y Smoking: Y Handicap Access: N Payment: C, P, T, V, M

Helford

ROSEMULLION COTTAGE   *Rates: inexpensive-expensive*
Open: year-round   *Minimum Stay: one week*

This picturesque 17th-century thatched cottage has been in the same seafaring family for generations. It's privately situated in a wooded area by the River Helford. There's room for six in a sunny living room facing the garden, a dining room with a corner fireplace, a kitchen, two double bedrooms and two small singles. Frenchman's Creek, pubs, restaurants, fishing and shopping lie within walking distance. For golf, take the ferry half a mile; sailing and horseback riding can be found within eight miles. Contact: British Travel Associates, P.O. Box 299, Elkton, VA 22827. Call 1-800-327-6097 (in Virginia, 703-298-2232). Ref. GEW.

Children: Y   Pets: N   Smoking: Y   Handicap Access: N   Payment: All

Helston

BOCHYM MANOR COTTAGES   *Rates: budget-inexpensive*
Open: year-round   *Minimum Stay: one week*
Nestled contentedly amidst 16 lush acres of private garden, six rental units—a rustic cottage, two converted houses, a manor house, a stable block and clock tower—form a lordly group around a cobbled courtyard. Central heating, color TV and a washer/dryer add extra convenience and comfort to your holiday. The cottages include a charming living room/eat-in kitchen and one double bedroom. From here, you can enjoy a countless number of natural and historic pleasures. On foot or by car, you can explore the coast and countryside, the castles and ancient remains of the West Country. Contact: Castles, Cottages & Flats in Ireland and U.K. Ltd., Box 261, Westwood, MA 02090. Call 617-329-4680. Ref. 123940.

Children: Y   Pets: N   Smoking: Y   Handicap Access: N   Payment: P

Penzance

THE EGYPTIAN HOUSE   *Rates: budget*
Open: year-round   *Minimum Stay: three nights*
Built in a style briefly popular in the late 18th century following Napolean's Egyptian campaign, this accommodation consists of three completely renovated and fully equipped apartments on Chapel Street. The first-floor apartment, which was once a shop stocking geological specimens from the area, has one single and one twin bedroom; the second- and third-floor apartments both have one twin and one double bedroom each. The top floor provides a view over the town to St. Michael's mount, a huge mansion in the middle of Mount's Bay and accessible only by foot at low tide. Penzance is a busy seaside resort and fishing town, whose waters are warmed by the Gulf Stream— some hardy residents swim in the town harbor year-round. There are many shops, pubs and good restaurants that serve fresh local seafood. Contact: The Landmark Trust, Shottesbrooke, Maidenhead, Berks, England SL6 3SW. Call 011-44-628-82-5925.

Children: Y Pets: N Smoking: Y Handicap Access: N Payment: C, P, T, V, M

Perranporth

REEN MANOR FARM   *Rates: budget-moderate*
Open: year-round   *Minimum Stay: one week*
There are three separate rentals available at Reen Manor Farm, set on a south-facing hillside and offering a panoramic view of the town, the sand dunes and the sea. Reen Cottage, which sleeps five, dates from the 17th century and has a large living room with exposed beams, stone walls and leaded windows. Little Reen, part of a wing of the farmhouse, is small but airy and sleeps two in a living room with a sofa

bed. The Manor Barn dates from medieval times and has a very large, heavy-beamed living room with a wood-burning stove, a galley kitchen and a grand piano. Its four bedrooms—two doubles, one twin and one bunk—sleep eight. Fifteen minutes by foot from the farm, the resort town of Perranporth has three miles of sandy beaches; golf, riding and walking along the Cornish Coastal Footpath are all available nearby as well. Contact: British Travel Associates, P.O. Box 299, Elkton, VA 22827. Call 1-800-327-6097 (in Virginia, 703-298-2232). Ref. GFR/ GFS/GFT.

Children: Y   Pets: N   Smoking: Y   Handicap Access: N   Payment: All

Shutta, near Looe

COBWALLS
Rates: budget-inexpensive
Open: year-round
Minimum Stay: one week

Perfectly situated for a delightful coastal holiday, Cobwalls is a charming 17th-century cob cottage located in the restful village of Shutta, a quarter mile upstream from the popular seaside town of Looe. Sandy beaches, boating, fishing, golf and tennis are all nearby, as are the matchless scenic hamlets of the south Cornish coast. The two-floor house features a spacious, slate-flagged living/dining room with beamed ceilings and carpeted floors, a contemporary kitchen and two bedrooms (one double and one with bunk beds), along with a snug and sunny terrace overlooking the picturesque grounds. Contact: British Travel Associates, P.O. Box 299, Elkton, VA 22827. Call 1-800-327-6097 (in Virginia, 703-298-2232).

Children: Y   Pets: N   Smoking: Y   Handicap Access: N   Payment: All

Tintagel

CORNISH COTTAGE
Rates: budget-inexpensive
Open: year-round
Minimum Stay: one week

This delightful Cornish cottage commands superb, panoramic views from 500 feet above sea level across the valley to the resort town at Tintagel. The cottage's location offers both privacy and seclusion and proximity to the sea (one and a half miles) and the popular tourist spots at Boscastle and Bossiney Cove. With room for six people, the cottage has a living room, a kitchen/dining room, a utility room and four bedrooms (one double, one twin and two singles). Good walking, riding and fishing can be had on the coast and along nearby rivers. Contact: British Travel Associates, P.O. Box 299, Elkton, VA 22827. Call 1-800-327-6097 (in Virginia, 703-298-2232). Ref. F1614.

Children: Y   Pets: N   Smoking: Y   Handicap Access: N   Payment: All

Week St. Mary

THE COLLEGE
Rates: inexpensive-moderate
Open: year-round
Minimum Stay: three nights

This two-story house of exceptional historical interest is located near the Tamar River, which runs along the border between Cornwall and Devon. It was discovered that unusual elements in the building's construction—such as Tudor windows and a carved granite doorway—

once belonged to a school founded by a remarkable woman on this site in 1506. The current building is an old stone house with a flagstone courtyard and several outbuildings. Three bedrooms, a bath, a good-sized kitchen and a living/dining room with a large open fireplace make five guests comfy. A sloping meadow stretches out behind the house to farmland beyond and, in the far distance, the black mountains of Dartmoor National Park. Contact: The Landmark Trust, Shottesbrooke, Maidenhead, Berks, England SL6 3SW. Call 011-44-628-82-5925.

Children: Y Pets: Y Smoking: Y Handicap Access: N Payment: C, P, T, V, M

West Pentire

MANOR HOUSE *Rates: inexpensive-moderate*
Open: year-round *Minimum Stay: one week*

An ideal Cornish residence for large groups seeking luxury, this lavishly furnished and restored 15th-century manor house stands by the village green of West Pentire. The impeccable green, accented with shrubs and flowers, lies only yards away from the golden sands of the Cornish coast. Enjoy some of the finest walking country and most diverse landscape in England, ranging from caves and rock pools to cliffs and beaches, with sporting activities including fishing and pony trekking along the shore. The vast manor house contains seven bedrooms—several with breathtaking seaward views—which together sleep thirteen comfortably. Extra fold-out beds accommodate even more. Contact: British Travel Associates, P.O. Box 299, Elkton VA 22827. Call 1-800-327-6097 (in Virginia, 703-298-2232).

Children: Y   Pets: Y   Smoking: Y   Handicap Access: N   Payment: All

Zennor

ARRA VENTON HOUSE *Rates: budget-moderate*
Open: year-round *Minimum Stay: three nights*

A jumble of architectural styles give this three-bedroom house its charm. Originally three separate buildings (a blacksmith shop, chapel and cottage), the house has been joined together to create a pleasant if eccentric residence. The living room contains a fireplace and a lovely, elongated bay window that lets in the sun and provides a view. Through a little corridor is the eat-in kitchen, from where you enter into a double bedroom and a bathroom. A staircase leads up to two bedrooms and another half bathroom. Outside, hike through a flower-strewn valley to reach a sandy cove, one of many along this shoreline, and follow the coastal path for spectacular views over the headlands, cliffs and sea. Contact: The Landmark Trust, Shottesbrooke, Maidenhead, Berks, England SL6 3SW. Call 011-44-628-82-5925.

Children: Y Pets: Y Smoking: Y Handicap Access: N Payment: C, P, T, V, M

Zennor

LOWER PORTHMEOR, THE FARMHOUSE *Rates: budget-moderate*
Open: year-round *Minimum Stay: three nights*

The Farmhouse is a two-story stone house surrounded by 400-year-old outbuildings and low stone walls. Though Porthmeor is a farming hamlet, the word means "great cove," and a valley runs from the buildings down to a sandy cove by the sea. The house has three bedrooms and there are fireplaces in one bedroom and the kitchen. From the windows or the gardens, there are good views over the landscape of high moors and rocky walls. The busy fishing town of Penzance is a few miles away, where there are many opportunities for entertainment, dining and sports facilities. Contact: The Landmark Trust, Shottesbrooke, Maidenhead, Berks, England SL6 3SW. Call 011-44-628-82-5925.

Children: Y Pets: Y Smoking: Y Handicap Access: N Payment: C, P, T, V, M

CUMBRIA

Catterlen

BLACKSMITH'S SHOP   *Rates: budget*
Open: year-round   *Minimum Stay: one week*

This attractively renovated 19th-century cottage was once a blacksmith's shop. Today, it provides a cozy base for exploring the northern Lake District, which includes Lake Windermere and Scafell Pike, the large lake and highest peak in England. The smith's large hand bellows remain in place, but the raised furnace recess that once ventilated the shop is now a fireplace and the stone walls are painted white. The living/dining room has an alcove with a double bed and a single chair/bed, to sleep two to three. Explore the medieval castle and St. Andrews Church at Penrith, three and a half miles away, or walk the nearby Pennine Way footpaths. Contact: British Travel Associates, P.O. Box 299, Elkton, VA 22827. Call 1-800-327-6097 (in Virginia, 703-298-2232). Ref. A707.

Children: Y   Pets: N   Smoking: Y   Handicap Access: N   Payment: All

Grasmere

HOWTHWAITE HOUSE   *Rates: moderate-expensive*
Open: year-round   *Minimum Stay: three nights*

Beautifully situated on a hill looking out over the mountains and vales of the Lake District stands this four-bedroom family house. The area was immortalized by the poet Wordsworth, whose famous home, Dove Cottage, is just below Howthwaite. Howthwaite has two floors containing a living room with a working fireplace, sitting room, kitchen, spacious dining room, two baths and two double, one twin and one single bedroom. A charming little summer house stands in the garden. Many visitors consider this to be the loveliest part of England, and you'll probably agree as you wander through the lakeland paths surrounded by daffodils, butterflies and perfect scenery. Contact: The Landmark Trust, Shottesbrooke, Maidenhead, Berks, England SL6 3SW. Call 011-44-628-82-5925.

Children: Y Pets: Y Smoking: Y Handicap Access: N Payment: C, P, T, V, M

Greystoke

RECTORY WING
Open: year-round

Rates: budget-inexpensive
Minimum Stay: one week

This red sandstone wing of an old rectory has its own courtyard and private front door. There's room for five to six people in three bedrooms (one double, one twin and one single) and an extra cot. Greystoke offers sweeping views of the open Cumbrian countryside and proximity to the border city of Carlisle. Swim in the village pool or drive five miles to horseback ride or play golf. Hadrian's Wall stands 20 miles away; visitors can also tour the Lake District and Eden Valley. Contact: British Travel Associates, P.O. Box 299, Elkton, VA 22827. Call 1-800-327-6097 (in Virginia, 703-298-2232). Ref. A6057.

Children: Y   Pets: N   Smoking: Y   Handicap Access: N   Payment: All

Kirkby Lonsdale

HIPPING HALL
Open: year-round

Rates: budget-inexpensive
Minimum Stay: one week

The Bronte sisters attended the Clergy Daughters' School in nearby Cowan Bridge, hence the names of these two cottages, which flank Hipping Hall and share the estate's four acres of well-manicured lawn and garden. Built in the 17th century, the cottages have been beautifully renovated with modern conveniences. Charlotte's Cottage is the smaller of the two and has a small kitchen and sitting room and a Victorian spiral staircase to the upper floor, which holds a double bedroom furnished in old cottage pine. Emily's Cottage is nearly identical but slightly larger. The Yorkshire Dales are a mile away, Lake District National Park, 20 minutes, and the Northwest coast, 14 miles. Contact: British Travel Associates, P.O. Box 299, Elkton, VA 22827. Call 1-800-327-6097 (in Virginia, 703-298-2232). Ref. LFS/LFR.

Children: Y   Pets: N   Smoking: Y   Handicap Access: N   Payment: All

Pardshaw

YEW TREE BARN
Open: year-round

Rates: budget-moderate
Minimum Stay: one week

A luxurious renovation has made this 400-year-old barn a warm and wonderful vacation home for six. Full of original character, with exposed wood beams and pitched roof, the accommodations include three bedrooms, a spacious living room with a wood-burning stove, a dining room and a kitchen with the added conveniences of a microwave, a dishwasher and a washer/dryer. A splendid private and fully furnished garden with a barbecue will surely enhance the warmer months of the year. Located in the North Lakes district, this spot will offer endless pleasures to hikers, since the scenery here is beyond compare. Contact: Castles, Cottages & Flats in Ireland and U.K. Ltd., Box 261, Westwood, MA 02090. Call 617-329-4680. Ref. 1311.

Children: Y   Pets: N   Smoking: Y   Handicap Access: N   Payment: P

Penrith

MONKS BRIDGE

Rates: budget-inexpensive

Open: year-round

Minimum Stay: one week

This former 18th-century school boasts a walled garden and terrace beside a stream, and sits a hundred yards from its nearest neighbor in the upper Lyvennet Valley. Just four miles away is the Lake District National Park, home of England's largest lake (Lake Windermere) and highest peak (Scafell Pike). There's plenty more to see and do at Ullswater Sailing Club and Lowther Wildlife Park nearby. Two twin bedrooms and two singles sleep six in the schoolhouse. You can prepare meals in the fully equipped kitchen or eat at pubs within walking distance. Contact: British Travel Associates, P.O. Box 299, Elkton, VA 22827. Call 1-800-327-6097 (in Virginia, 703-298-2232). Ref. LEU.

Children: Y   Pets: N   Smoking: Y   Handicap Access: N   Payment: All

DERBYSHIRE

Lea Bridge

GARDEN COTTAGE

Rates: budget

Open: year-round

Minimum Stay: one week

Florence Nightingale's family built this cottage in the 18th century near a waterfall, which once fed a waterwheel, about 20 yards from the bottom of the garden. The house still retains its original oak beams and stone-mullioned windows, but modern features, such as a microwave oven in the kitchen, have been added. There's room for four here, with two bedrooms (one double and one bunk). The former spa town of Matlock is four and a half miles away; Arkwright's Mill, a tramway museum, and the Riber Fauna Reserve are within two miles. Visit the many historic houses and sites in the area, including Nottingham, where the English Civil War began in 1642. Contact: British Travel Associates, P.O. Box 299, Elkton, VA 22827. Call 1-800-327-6097 (in Virginia, 703-298-2232). Ref. A5704.

Children: Y   Pets: N   Smoking: Y   Handicap Access: N   Payment: All

Taddington, Buxton

STAR HOUSE

Rates: budget-moderate

Open: year-round

Minimum Stay: one week

This newly renovated pub has been refurnished to accommodate up to eight people in style and comfort. The walled garden behind the house adjoins open fields and lush valleys dotted with silver birch, ash and goat willow trees and highlighted by waterfalls, moorlands and craggy summits. Two large bedrooms—one with three single beds, the other with one single and one double bed—plus two cots sleep up to eight. Open fireplaces make the sitting and dining rooms warm and cozy, but electric heaters throughout take the edge off exceptionally raw days. A color TV is provided. Contact: British Travel Associates, P.O. Box 299, Elkton, VA, 22827. Call 1-800-327-6097 (in Virginia, 703-298-2232). Ref. QED.

Children: Y   Pets: N   Smoking: Y   Handicap Access: N   Payment: All

Tideswell

THE OLD TOFFEE SHOP *Rates: budget-inexpensive*
Open: year-round *Minimum Stay: one week*

Standing in the main square of the Peakland village of Tideswell, the Old Toffee Shop was once just that. The sitting/dining room still has the original meat hooks and fireplace with a gas fire; the kitchen has modern conveniences and a breakfast area. Two bedrooms—one large double and one with full-size bunk beds—plus a cot sleep five. Babysitting is available by arrangement. This is good walking country, where you can hike the dales and gorges of the National Park. Horseback riding, fishing, golf and cycling are also nearby. Contact: British Travel Associates, P.O. Box 299, Elkton, VA 22827. Call 1-800-327-6097 (in Virginia, 703-298-2232). Ref. QNS.

Children: Y   Pets: N   Smoking: Y   Handicap Access: N   Payment: All

Wheston

VICARAGE FARM *Rates: budget-inexpensive*
Open: year-round *Minimum Stay: one week*

Bonnie Prince Charlie, the pretender to the English throne, sought shelter in these old stone buildings in 1744. Long since converted into three cottages, they offer glorious views of the uplands, woodlands, moorlands and crags of Peak District National Park. The Prince's Seat has a large sitting room with an open fireplace, a large kitchen/dining room, and it sleeps six to seven in three bedrooms. The Verger's End offers a sitting room with a fireplace and a modern kitchen/dining room, and it sleeps four in two bedrooms. The Gods is a first-floor apartment, with a sitting/dining room, a small kitchen, a double bedroom and a bedroom with bunk beds. View the stately homes at Chatsworth and Haddon Hall and the many museums, caverns and mines within easy reach. Contact: British Travel Associates, P.O. Box 299, Elkton, VA 22827. Call 1-800-327-6097 (in Virginia, 703-298-2232). Ref. QNL/QNN/QNM.

Children: Y   Pets: N   Smoking: Y   Handicap Access: N   Payment: All

DEVON

Axminster

SHUTE GATEHOUSE *Rates: budget-inexpensive*
Open: year-round *Minimum Stay: three nights*

Straddling the road that once led to a major medieval and Tudor home is a 16th-century former gatehouse—now a guest house of unique properties. A spiral staircase climbs up to two second-floor bedrooms, then upward to a large living/dining room and small kitchenette. A pathway leads to one of the two smaller wings, where there are two bunks—in total, there is room for five guests. The furnishings are comfortable, and among the delightful decorative touches is an elaborate 17th-century plaster ceiling. The windows of the gatehouse look out in one direction toward the estate's old deer park, and in the other, toward the hamlet of Shute. Axminster is just a few miles from the south Devon shore and the maritime town of Exeter. Contact: The Landmark Trust, Shottesbrooke, Maidenhead, Berks, England SL6 3SW. Call 011-44-628-82-5925.

Children: Y Pets: Y Smoking: Y Handicap Access: N Payment: C, P, T, V, M

Bideford

BRIDGE COTTAGE, PEPPERCOMBE *Rates: inexpensive-moderate*
Open: year-round *Minimum Stay: three nights*

This thatched cottage sits in a wooded valley that cradles a flower-decked meadow perched forty feet from a beach. A stream runs through the valley before cascading down the bright red cliffs to the sea. This wonderful setting enhances the charm of the newly renovated 18th-century stone dwelling. The ground floor contains a living area, a kitchen with a round table and a bathroom. Upstairs are two small but comfortable bedrooms, one single and one twin. The cottage once belonged to the Portledge estate, now owned by a historical preservation society. A path leads to the beach; further along the dramatic coastline is well worth exploring, as are the many sites of interest in the region. Contact: The Landmark Trust, Shottesbrooke, Maidenhead, Berks, England SL6 3SW. Call 011-44-628-82-5925.

Children: Y Pets: Y Smoking: Y Handicap Access: N Payment: C, P, T, V, M

Bigbury

HIGHER CUMERY HOUSE *Rates: budget-moderate*
Open: year-round *Minimum Stay: one week*

Guests drive through a working farm to reach the seclusion of this 17th-century stone farmhouse, which lies amid a lovely garden by a large pond. The house is comfortable and spacious enough for a family of eight or nine, with three double bedrooms, one twin, and one small single—all with curved ceilings. The large sitting and dining rooms overlook the garden, and the kitchen comes complete with a high chair. Shops are two miles away, the beach is four miles, and golfers can take a seven-mile trip to Thurlestone golf course. The owner's phone is available, and babysitting arrangements can be made. Contact: British Travel Associates, P.O. Box 299, Elkton, VA, 22827. Call 1-800-327-6097 (in Virginia, 703-298-2232). Ref. FAX.

Children: Y Pets: N Smoking: Y Handicap Access: N Payment: All

Broadwood Kelly, near Winkleigh

COB COTTAGE *Rates: budget-inexpensive*
Open: year-round *Minimum Stay: one week*

This 14th-century house sits among a cluster of old-world cottages that form the secluded and utterly charming hamlet of Broadwood Kelly. Here in the rustic heartland of Devon, panoramic views over miles of unspoiled countryside can be seen from the cottage windows; the beaches of North Devon are only an hour away. The house contains one bedroom, a living room, a modern kitchen with breakfast bar, plus a warm sun lounge/dining room and a delightful small garden. Contact: British Travel Associates, P.O. Box 299, Elkton VA 22827. Call 1-800-327-6097 (in Virginia, 703-298-2232).

Children: Over 10 years Pets: N Smoking: Y Handicap Access: N Payment: All

Chagford

EASTON COTTAGE   *Rates: budget-inexpensive*
Open: year-round   *Minimum Stay: one week*
This 15th-century cottage, which lies within Dartmoor National Park, features stone walls and low doorways that belie the modern-day comfort provided by a microwave oven, color TV and VCR. Spend a quiet afternoon lounging in the garden, or step inside to the rugged comfort of a beamed farmhouse kitchen and beamed living room with an open fireplace. The cottage sleeps five; one bedroom with three single beds connects to a master bedroom with a private bath. Shop in the nearby village of Chagford, take a walk on the moors, or fish in the Fernworthy reservoir, take a horseback ride or play some golf. Contact: British Travel Associates, P.O. Box 299, Elkton, VA, 22827. Call 1-800-327-6097 (in Virginia, 703-298-2232). Ref. FIK.

Children: Y   Pets: N   Smoking: Y   Handicap Access: N   Payment: All

Christow

MILL HOUSE COTTAGE   *Rates: budget-moderate*
Open: year-round   *Minimum Stay: one week*
This converted 17th-century mill, located on the edge of beautiful Dartmoor National Park in the village of Christow, makes a home of true distinction. The top floor opens out onto a sunny patio garden by the mill pond, which is populated by a family of geese. Garden furniture and a barbecue make for delightful meals al fresco. Two comfortable bedrooms lie downstairs; the rolling mill stream flows swiftly behind the cottage. Only nine miles from Exeter, the area offers recreational activities such as excellent fishing, tennis, riding and golf. Contact: British Travel Associates, P.O. Box 299, Elkton VA 22827. Call 1-800-327-6097 (in Virginia, 703-298-2232).

Children: Over 5 years Pets: Y Smoking: Y Handicap Access: N Payment: All

Dittisham

THE OLD BAKEHOUSE   *Rates: inexpensive-expensive*
Open: year-round   *Minimum Stay: one week*
Fishing and sailing on the River Dart are available just fifty yards away from the Old Bakehouse, which was once the village shop of Dittisham. The house has been renovated to accommodate eight, with one twin bedroom on the main floor and another twin with an extra single bed, a single bedroom and a double bedroom on the first floor. The living room is carpeted, the kitchen/dining area has a dishwasher and freezer, and there's a separate play area for children. Some of the rooms have views of the river, and shopping is within walking distance. Contact: British Travel Associates, P.O. Box 299, Elkton, VA, 22827. Call 1-800-327-6097 (in Virginia, 703-298-2232). Ref. FZQ.

Children: Y   Pets: N   Smoking: Y   Handicap Access: N   Payment: All

Eggesford

WATERMILL LODGE   *Rates: moderate-deluxe*
Open: year-round   *Minimum Stay: one week*

Watermill Lodge, originally a sawmill, has been creatively converted into a spacious vacation home that retains much of its original character. There's even a timber bridge spanning the mill stream (guests with young children take note). A groundfloor game room with billiards and darts and a living room that opens onto a balcony make this a unique and enjoyable resting spot. The lodge sleeps ten in three twin bedrooms, a double and a room with bunk beds. Dartmoor and Exmoor national parks lie within easy reach, Devon's north coast is about 40 minutes away and historic Eggesford can be reached in about a half-hour's drive. Contact: British Travel Associates, P.O. Box 299, Elkton, VA 22827. Call 1-800-327-6097 (in Virginia, 703-298-2232). Ref. FCJ.

Children: Y   Pets: N   Smoking: N   Handicap Access: N   Payment: All

Ipplepen

IPPLEPEN COTTAGE   *Rates: budget*
Open: year-round   *Minimum Stay: one week*

American fans of the BBC television series "Fawlty Towers" might recognize Torquay, a resort town on the southern coast known for its excellent sailing and August regatta. This semi-detached cottage stands six miles from Torquay and also provides a good touring base for Dartmoor National Park. Five can sleep here in three bedrooms (one small double, one twin and one large single). Take in its uninterrupted views of rolling farmland during the day, and at night, settle in front of the color television for some British entertainment. Beautiful beaches at South Ham, historic touring at Totnes Castle, Dartington Cider Press and boat trips down to Dartmouth will tempt you away when you're ready for some fun. Contact: British Travel Associates, P.O. Box 299, Elkton, VA 22827. Call 1-800-327-6097 (in Virginia, 703-298-2232). Ref. F3777.

Children: Y   Pets: N   Smoking: Y   Handicap Access: N   Payment: All

Kings Nympton

BREWERS COTTAGE   *Rates: budget-inexpensive*
Open: year-round   *Minimum Stay: one week*

The rolling Devon countryside provides a peaceful backdrop for this attractive thatched cottage. The low-beamed, sloping ceilings in many of the rooms convey a cozy, timeless atmosphere, as does the living room with its corner fireplace and baker's oven, the modern kitchen with a wood-burning stove and the dining area. Two bedrooms—one double and one twin—plus an extra cot provide sleeping accommodations for four to five. Exmoor National Park lies 12 miles away; sandy beaches on the Devon coast are within 25 miles. Contact: British Travel Associates, P.O. Box 299, Elkton, VA 22827. Call 1-800-327-6097 (in Virginia, 703-298-2232). Ref. FRV.

Children: Y   Pets: N   Smoking: Y   Handicap Access: N   Payment: All

Kingston

THE OLD FORGE   *Rates: budget-moderate*
Open: year-round   *Minimum Stay: one week*

Old-world charm pervades this 17th-century cottage located a mile from a sandy beach and near the village of Kingston in South Devon. A huge stone fireplace punctuates the large beamed living room/dining room, and the farmhouse kitchen has an open fire, electric stove and dishwasher. A fold-out bed in the living room and two bedrooms (one with two twin beds and the other with two small single beds) provide sleeping quarters for four to six people. Two excellent golf courses, charming shops and convivial pubs are all within five miles. Contact: British Travel Associates, P.O. Box 299, Elkton, VA 22827. Call 1-800-327-6097 (in Virginia, 703-298-2232). Ref. FLL.

Children: Y   Pets: N   Smoking: Y   Handicap Access: N   Payment: All

Lundy Island

CASTLE KEEP   *Rates: budget-inexpensive*
Open: year-round   *Minimum Stay: three nights*

The "keep," or inner part, of this 700-year-old castle contains three connected apartments, surprisingly snug and cozy given their unusual location. The original castle was built by Henry III and paid for by the sale of rabbits. Castle Keep East and Castle Keep North have one twin bedroom each; Castle Keep South has two twin bedrooms. The north and south sections have wood-burning stoves. All three have showers in the bathroom and open onto a cobbled inner courtyard. There are plenty of places to picnic and wander about on this three-mile-long island, which can be reached only by boat (the crossing takes two hours). Lundy Island is a true retreat, a nature-lover's paradise that only about twenty people call their permanent home. Contact: The Landmark Trust, Shottesbrooke, Maidenhead, Berks, England SL6 3SW. Call 011-44-628-82-5925.

Children: Y Pets: N Smoking: Y Handicap Access: N Payment: C, P, T, V, M

Lundy Island

HANMERS COTTAGE   *Rates: budget*
Open: year-round   *Minimum Stay: three nights*

This little wooden cottage with a garden was built by a fisherman many years ago. One can imagine him looking out over the sea to the mainland, snug in his sheltered home with a blazing fire in the fireplace. There are two bedrooms (one twin and one with a set of bunk beds), an eat-in kitchen, separate bathroom and shower and a living room. In one direction is the beach; in the other is the island's castle, built by Henry III in the 13th century. Though the island has been occupied for a long time, it is very quiet and secluded, with a working farm and only a few permanent residents. Contact: The Landmark Trust, Shottesbrooke, Maidenhead, Berks, England SL6 3SW. Call 011-44-628-82-5925.

Children: Y Pets: N Smoking: Y Handicap Access: N Payment: C, P, T, V, M

Lundy Island

OLD LIGHT EAST *Rates: budget*
Open: year-round *Minimum Stay: three nights*

This accommodation for one stands near the old lighthouse up on the island's highest point. Its living/dining/kitchen area has a fold-out couch and the bathroom has a shower. The views in each direction are fabulous. A store/tavern on the island provides groceries and companionship should you wish to break your reverie. A two-hour boat trip made daily from the mainland brings visitors who come to the island to appreciate its avian and marine treasures, try their skill at rock climbing or diving, or just walk along the shoreline to admire the view. Contact: The Landmark Trust, Shottesbrooke, Maidenhead, Berks, England SL6 3SW. Call 011-44-628-82-5925.

Children: N Pets: N Smoking: Y Handicap Access: N Payment: C, P, T, V, M

Lundy Island

ST. JOHN'S BIG AND SMALL *Rates: budget*
Open: year-round *Minimum Stay: three nights*

These cottages command a fine view of St. John's valley and across the sea to the north Devon shore. Snug and cozy, St. John's Small has a combined living/kitchen/dining room, a bedroom and a bath, perfect for a couple. St. John's Big is so named because it contains a separate kitchen and a living/dining room in which there is a fold-out couch in addition to the twin bedroom. The island of Lundy is only three miles long and is reached by a two-hour boat trip. With only twenty permanent residents, the island is quiet, but a steady stream of visitors come to sample its natural pleasures. Savor marvelous views across the ocean, over secluded coves and looming cliffs. Contact: The Landmark Trust, Shottesbrooke, Maidenhead, Berks, England SL6 3SW. Call 011-44-628-82-5925.

Children: Y Pets: N Smoking: Y Handicap Access: N Payment: C, P, T, V, M

Lundy Island

THE OLD HOUSE *Rates: budget-moderate*
Open: year-round *Minimum Stay: three nights*

This building is the pride of the island, architecturally speaking. Constructed of island granite, it has been recently restored and renovated into two separate apartments. Old House South is the larger of the two, with three bedrooms, a bathroom and a half, an eat-in kitchen and a spacious, comfortable living room with an open fireplace. The living/dining area in Old House North also contains a fireplace, but the kitchen is smaller and fully equipped, and there is a twin bedroom and a bathroom upstairs. Behind the house is a garden, also recently restored. Nature-lovers will find plenty to do here; both bird watching and diving are popular pastimes for visitors. There is a local store and tavern where you can purchase groceries and supplies. Contact: The Landmark Trust, Shottesbrooke, Maidenhead, Berks, England SL6 3SW. Call 011-44-628-82-5925.

Children: Y Pets: N Smoking: Y Handicap Access: N Payment: C, P, T, V, M

Lundy Island

THE OLD LIGHTHOUSE _Rates: budget-moderate_
Open: year-round _Minimum Stay: three nights_

This genuine lighthouse is over 170 years old and retains its original design if not its purpose. The lighthouse tower and two attached apartments are constructed of the island's indigenous pale granite. The apartments are essentially the same in design and layout, each with three bedrooms, a kitchenette, a bath with shower and a living room with a wood-burning stove. The upper apartment has fine views of the northern end of this three-mile-long island. This is an island for those who love the outdoors, solitude and nature, since there are few permanent residents and the land is largely undeveloped. There are ample sites for rock climbing, hiking, bird watching and diving. Contact: The Landmark Trust, Shottesbrooke, Maidenhead, Berks, England SL6 3SW. Call 011-44-628-82-5925.

Children: Y Pets: N Smoking: Y Handicap Access: N Payment: C, P, T, V, M

Lundy Island

THE RADIO ROOM _Rates: budget_
Open: year-round _Minimum Stay: three nights_

For years, the only contact that secluded Lundy Island had with the mainland was from this little building and the flashing lighthouses. This stone cottage is suitable for one person; it has a fold-out couch in the living area, a kitchenette and a bathroom with shower. Built of indigenous granite like most of the buildings on the island, it is located immediately behind another rental property known as the Old House. Lovers of nature and the outdoors take the two-hour boat trip out to Lundy in search of seclusion and an unspoiled way of life. Solitary travelers will find a uniquely meditative retreat here. Contact: The Landmark Trust, Shottesbrooke, Maidenhead, Berks, England SL6 3SW. Call 011-44-628-82-5925.

Children: N Pets: N Smoking: Y Handicap Access: N Payment: C, P, T, V, M

Lundy Island

TIBBETTS COTTAGE _Rates: budget_
Open: year-round _Minimum Stay: three nights_

It is said that from this simple cottage, fourteen mainland lighthouses can be seen on a clear night. Designed as a lookout at the turn of the century, the cottage is of sturdy pale granite with interior wood paneling. A small bedroom contains two sets of bunk beds, and the living/dining area has a sofa bed and a pair of armchairs arranged around the fireplace. There is a kitchenette and bathroom, but no tub or shower. The cottage is as remote as could be on this secluded island, which hosts nature-lovers and hikers alike. Contact: The Landmark Trust, Shottesbrooke, Maidenhead, Berks, England SL6 3SW. Call 011-44-628-82-5925.

Children: Y Pets: N Smoking: Y Handicap Access: N Payment: C, P, T, V, M

Paignton

PEPPERPOT COTTAGE *Rates: budget-inexpensive*
Open: year-round *Minimum Stay: one week*

This 200-year-old octagonal cottage in a residential area of a popular resort town makes an unusual vacation base. Two bedrooms—one double and one with bunk beds—offer accommodations for four, and a cot and high chair are provided for babies under two. Within a mile's distance, guests find beaches, shops and restaurants, along with a sports complex and the local zoo. The Torbay/Dartmouth railway offers a diversion for steam train enthusiasts, and golfing and riding are available nearby. Contact: British Travel Associates, P.O. Box 299, Elkton, VA 22827. Call 1-800-327-6097 (in Virginia, 703-298-2232). Ref. FUR.

Children: **Y** Pets: **N** Smoking: **Y** Handicap Access: **N** Payment: **All**

Roborough

FARMHOUSE WING *Rates: budget*
Open: year-round *Minimum Stay: one week*

This newly constructed wing of an old farmhouse offers easy access to the rugged north Devon coast and Dartmoor National Park, known for its beautifully eroded granite rocks and footpaths. There's plenty of room for two to three people in one double bedroom and a single convertible bed, plus a living room, a modern kitchen and a dining room. Many historic houses and gardens are located nearby; guests will savor long walks in the Exmoor National Park. Good surfing can be found on the northern coast. Contact: British Travel Associates, P.O. Box 299, Elkton, VA 22827. Call 1-800-327-6097 (in Virginia, 703-298-2232). Ref. F4080.

Children: **Y** Pets: **N** Smoking: **Y** Handicap Access: **N** Payment: **All**

Sherford

STANCOMBE *Rates: budget-deluxe*
Open: year-round *Minimum Stay: one week*

This magnificent and altogether grand holiday retreat offers a wealth of pleasures and comforts in a number of charming cottages for small families or couples. Or rent the grand manor house, which sleeps eight and includes a luxurious private garden with a veranda. The superb location of this country estate offers easy access to numerous fine beaches, glorious walks and nature preserves. You will certainly want to explore the unique Lizard Peninsula, a haven of wildflowers and wildlife. But the manor's many sporting opportunities right at home may persuade you never to leave. A heated indoor pool, a badminton court, a game room with table tennis, darts and pool—these are just a few of the many diversions available. Contact: Castles, Cottages & Flats in Ireland and U.K. Ltd., Box 261, Westwood, MA 02090. Call 617-329-4680. Ref. 1211-18.

Children: **Y** Pets: **N** Smoking: **Y** Handicap Access: **N** Payment: **P**

Stevenstone, near Great Torrington

THE LIBRARY   *Rates: budget-moderate*
Open: year-round   *Minimum Stay: three nights*

The Library conjures up visions of high ceilings, wooden moldings, gracious furniture and portraits of learned personages—and this is exactly what you'll find not far from the north Devon coast. The impressive library building and its smaller companion, the Orangery, have been painstakingly renovated to accommodate four guests in two twin bedrooms. The main room of the library building serves as a dining/living room and is most pleasant, with huge windows and a fireplace with a classical mantelpiece. Surrounding the building are the remains of an arboretum and formal gardens. Devon itself is a fascinating county, where picturesque valleys lead up to the forbidding mountains of Dartmoor National Park. Contact: The Landmark Trust, Shottesbrooke, Maidenhead, Berks, England SL6 3SW. Call 011-44-628-82-5925.

Children: Y Pets: Y Smoking: Y Handicap Access: N Payment: C, P, T, V, M

Stoke-in-Teignhead

LOWER ROCOMBE COTTAGE   *Rates: budget-inexpensive*
Open: year-round   *Minimum Stay: one week*

Rural charm permeates this 16th-century thatched cottage located three miles from Tobay on the South Devon coast. Guests can rent one self-contained wing of the house and enjoy access to private gardens and the owner's two-acre lot. A double bedroom, twin bedroom and extra cot sleep a total of five; the heavy-beamed living room features an open fireplace and the kitchen has modern appliances. Guests can arrange for babysitting services, while nearby they can find golf and riding facilities. A quick trip to Torbay promises good shopping as well as theater and cinema entertainment. Contact: British Travel Associates, P.O. Box 299, Elkton, VA 22827. Call 1-800-327-6097 (in Virginia, 703-298-2232). Ref. FNS.

Children: Y   Pets: N   Smoking: Y   Handicap Access: N   Payment: All

Waddeton

WADDETON BOATHOUSE   *Rates: budget-moderate*
Open: year-round   *Minimum Stay: one week*

The only way to reach this converted Victorian boathouse is by walking a hundred yards in from the road along a steep woodland path or by boating along the tranquil River Dart. Rent a boat from the many nearby boat yards and motor upstream for freshwater fishing, or drop a pole from your doorstep and take the catch of the day from the river's estuary. The living room and balcony overlook the river; the riverview master bedroom plus one single and one twin bedroom offer comfortable sleeping accommodations for five. The cottage's woodland setting makes TV reception difficult, but provides peaceful walking territory with an abundance of wildlife. Contact: British Travel

Associates, P.O. Box 299, Elkton, VA 22827. Call 1-800-327-6097 (in Virginia, 703-298-2232). Ref. FBU.

Children: Y   Pets: N   Smoking: Y   Handicap Access: N   Payment: All

Welcombe, near Hartland

WELCOMBE HOUSE   *Rates: budget*
Open: year-round   *Minimum Stay: one week*

Originally built for the "Johnnie Walker" whiskey family, the stately Welcombe house has been refurbished to include two self-contained, perfectly private apartment units on the second floor. One of the flats, with three bedrooms, features a sublime view of the craggy Bristol Channel; the other, containing two bedrooms, looks out over a splendid wooded valley. Both units have fully equipped kitchens, spacious sitting rooms and wall-to-wall carpeting. They share use of the extensive estate grounds, which include a small working farm, game room with exercise equipment and lovely footpaths leading to exhilarating walks along the Devon coast. Contact: British Travel Associates, P.O. Box 299, Elkton VA 22827. Call 1-800-327-6097 (in Virginia, 703-298-2232).

Children: Y   Pets: N   Smoking: Y   Handicap Access: N   Payment: All

DORSET

Bridport

YORK COTTAGE   *Rates: inexpensive-expensive*
Open: year-round   *Minimum Stay: one week*

York Cottage stands on the grounds of Chideock Manor, an historic country house that was once home to the Duke and Duchess of York. It's a spacious, lavishly furnished vacation house, completely peaceful yet only one mile from the coast. The modern kitchen/dining room has a pantry; the drawing room opens onto a terrace and walled garden. Six can sleep comfortably in three bedrooms—two double and one twin. Explore the rural Dorset countryside, with its gentle hills and dramatic coastline, from this base. Children under 12 are not permitted. Contact: British Travel Associates, P.O. Box 299, Elkton, VA 22827. Call 1-800-327-6097 (in Virginia, 703-298-2232). Ref. DEE.

Children: N   Pets: N   Smoking: Y   Handicap Access: N   Payment: All

Dorchester

CAME COTTAGE   *Rates: inexpensive-expensive*
Open: year-round   *Minimum Stay: one week*

The spectacular Dorset coastline is only six miles from the very comfortable Came Cottage, an enchanting building set on a large country estate. The cottage has an elegant drawing room with a fireplace, a dining area and a kitchen and sleeps six to seven in three bedrooms and an extra cot. There are an abundance of historic houses, castles and gardens nearby. Dorchester, two miles away, offers shops, inns, a weekly market and the Dorset County and Military museums and the Thomas Hardy Festival in August. Contact: British Travel Associates,

P.O. Box 299, Elkton, VA 22827. Call 1-800-327-6097 (in Virginia, 703-298-2232). Ref. DEM.

Children: Y   Pets: N   Smoking: Y   Handicap Access: N   Payment: All

Higher Moorbath

THE EAGLES NEST   *Rates: inexpensive-deluxe*
Open: year-round   *Minimum Stay: one week*

Old meets new in this modernized 15th-century thatched house in the rural Dorset countryside, minutes away from the market town of Bridport and the beach at Eype. A wood-burning stove warms the comfortable beamed living room and the large kitchen/dining area, equipped with a dishwasher, microwave and small freezer, opens onto the terrace and garden. One master and two double bedrooms, plus a cot and a chair bed, sleep eight. A color TV and VCR are provided; riding, golf and tennis are available nearby. Contact: British Travel Associates, P.O. Box 299, Elkton, VA 22827. Call 1-800-327-6097 (in Virginia, 703-298-2232). Ref. DCS.

Children: Y   Pets: N   Smoking: Y   Handicap Access: N   Payment: All

Piddlehinton

GROOM'S QUARTERS   *Rates: budget*
Open: year-round   *Minimum Stay: one week*

Thomas Hardy described the rolling, heather-laden moors of Dorset in his novels, and today's visitors will surely recognize the forested hills and chalk downs he praised. This cozy 18th-century cottage, creatively converted from a groom's quarters, is set on the outskirts of the small, scenic village of Piddlehinton, overlooking the lovely Piddle Valley. It's an ideal vacation house for two, with one double bedroom on the main floor and a living room, a dining room and a modern kitchen on the upper floor. The county market town of Dorchester is five miles away and the resort town of Weymouth just a few more, as are the ferries to the Channel Islands and to France. Contact: British Travel Associates, P.O. Box 299, Elkton, VA 22827. Call 1-800-327-6097 (in Virginia, 703-298-2232). Ref. F4216.

Children: Y   Pets: N   Smoking: Y   Handicap Access: N   Payment: All

Shroton

PRE-WAR HOUSE   *Rates: budget-inexpensive*
Open: year-round   *Minimum Stay: one week*

Set on the western edge of Cranbourne Chase, once a royal hunting forest, the farmland of Shroton lies close to the hill forts of Hambledon Hill and Hod Hill. This 1930 house is centrally heated and comfortably furnished, ideal for a family of up to six, with plenty of toys for the children. A living room, a dining room, a breakfast room, a kitchen, a utility room and three bedrooms (one double, one single, one bunk bed with an extra single) accommodate six. Visit the market towns of Blandford, Shaftesbury and Sturminster Newton, explore the medieval cathedral at Salisbury and wonder at the megaliths of Stonehenge on Salisbury Plain. Contact: British Travel Associates, P.O. Box 299, Elkton, VA 22827. Call 1-800-327-6097 (in Virginia, 703-298-2232). Ref. F4061.

Children: **Y**   Pets: **N**   Smoking: **Y**   Handicap Access: **N**   Payment: **All**

DURHAM

High Shipley

SHOOTING LODGE   *Rates: budget-moderate*
Open: year-round   *Minimum Stay: one week*

Built in 1670, this building was used by King James II as a shooting lodge, from which he hunted the wild boar which were once plentiful in the area. It looks much the same now as it did then, with a large inglenook fireplace, oak-paneled lounge, stone-flagged floors, original oak beams and period pieces. The three-story building overlooks a peaceful valley and is reached via a private tree-lined driveway. There's room for eight to nine in four bedrooms and the small kitchen has modern conveniences. The Yorkshire Dales, North Pennines, the Roman Wall, Northumberland and the Lake District all lie within easy reach. Contact: British Travel Associates, P.O. Box 299, Elkton, VA 22827. Call 1-800-327-6097 (in Virginia, 703-298-2232). Ref. A312.

Children: **Y**   Pets: **N**   Smoking: **Y**   Handicap Access: **N**   Payment: **All**

EAST SUSSEX

Crowborough

FRIAR'S GATE   *Rates: budget-inexpensive*
Open: year-round   *Minimum Stay: one week*

This delightful cottage with dark timber beams and rafters stands on the fringe of Ashdown Forest, which offers visitors a rare animal farm, picturesque villages and miles of walking and bridle paths. Small but comfortable, the house has a living room with a dining area, a kitchen and two bedrooms that sleep four adults and one child. Shop or go to the movies or pubs of nearby Tunbridge Wells, or travel just 40 miles to London. An artificial ski slope and climbing school, Scotney Castle Gardens, Bewl Water recreational area and Sheffield Park lie within a half-hour car ride. For a change of scenery, board the ferry at New Haven for a day trip to France. Contact: British Travel Associates, P.O. Box 299, Elkton, VA 22827. Call 1-800-327-6097 (in Virginia, 703-298-2232). Ref. F3683.

Children: **Y**   Pets: **N**   Smoking: **Y**   Handicap Access: **N**   Payment: **All**

Eastbourne

EDWARDIAN HOUSE   *Rates: budget-moderate*
Open: year-round   *Minimum Stay: one week*

Set in a residential area of a seafront town, this three-floor Edwardian house has room for ten people in a living room, a dining room, a kitchen and five bedrooms (two double and three twin). Eastbourne offers theaters, restaurants, shops and varied sports facilities to visitors, making this house an ideal base for touring the historic attractions of Kent and Sussex. Many charming towns, castles, cathedrals, vineyards and bird sanctuaries lie within easy reach. Contact: British Travel Associates, P.O. Box 299, Elkton, VA 22827. Call 1-800-327-6097 (in Virginia, 703-298-2232). Ref. F5331.

Children: **Y**   Pets: **N**   Smoking: **Y**   Handicap Access: **N**   Payment: All

Eastbourne

TERRACE HOUSE   *Rates: budget*
Open: year-round   *Minimum Stay: one week*

Whether you're looking for a seaside holiday or want to explore the many historic houses, cathedrals, towns and sites of East Sussex and Kent, Terrace House offers a convenient and comfortable place to stay. A living room, a dining room, a kitchen and two bedrooms (one double with an extra single and one twin) accommodate four or five guests. Battle, Rye and Hastings are waiting to be explored; cross the English Channel from Hastings for a day trip to France. Golf, sea fishing, sailing and wind surfing are all available nearby. Contact: British Travel Associates, P.O. Box 299, Elkton, VA 22827. Call 1-800-327-6097 (in Virginia, 703-298-2232). Ref. F5330.

Children: **Y**   Pets: **N**   Smoking: **Y**   Handicap Access: **N**   Payment: All

Hartfield

BOLEBROKE CASTLE GATEHOUSE   *Rates: budget*
Open: year-round   *Minimum Stay: one week*

Henry VIII used this 15th-century gatehouse on the grounds of Bolebroke Castle as a lodge when hunting in Ashdown Forest. Since modernized, the house still has its steep, solid-oak spiral staircase (possibly hazardous to the very young or infirm) and leaded windows. There's room for four in one double bedroom and one twin. Shops and a pub lie within one mile; many monuments and landmarks, including Hever Castle and Penshurst Place, can be found within five miles. Contact: British Travel Associates, P.O. Box 299, Elkton, VA 22827. Call 1-800-327-6097 (in Virginia, 703-298-2232). Ref. E6833.

Children: **Y**   Pets: **N**   Smoking: **Y**   Handicap Access: **N**   Payment: All

Rye

TERRACE HOUSE   *Rates: budget-inexpensive*
Open: year-round   *Minimum Stay: one week*

This 15th-century terraced house stands on a cobbled street in the storybook setting of Rye and includes many of its original beams and part of the wall of a monastery. Spacious enough for six, it has an eat-in kitchen with a microwave oven and a dishwasher, three bedrooms (two double and one twin), a living room and a TV room. Go shopping or dine at Battle and Winchelsea, or visit Canterbury Cathedral or the Channel ports a little further away. Contact: British Travel Associates, P.O. Box 299, Elkton, VA 22827. Call 1-800-327-6097 (in Virginia, 703-298-2232). Ref. A5534.

Children: **Y**   Pets: **N**   Smoking: **Y**   Handicap Access: **N**   Payment: All

Sedlescombe

VILLAGE HOUSE   *Rates: budget*
Open: year-round   *Minimum Stay: one week*

The charming village of Sedlescombe has been named the best-kept village in Sussex several times, and it offers easy access to the many attractions of Sussex and Kent. The white cliffs of Dover and Folkestone, a seaport resort, are nearby and offer ferry service to France. This cottage for three features a dining/living room area, a kitchen and one double and one single bedroom. Shops and a pub lie within 100 yards, and visitors can enjoy the miniature passenger railway at Hythe. You'll find fishing and sailing in Rye and sandy beaches at Camber. Contact: British Travel Associates, P.O. Box 299, Elkton, VA 22827. Call 1-800-327-6097 (in Virginia, 703-298-2232). Ref. F4656.

Children: Y   Pets: N   Smoking: Y   Handicap Access: N   Payment: All

Whydown

LITTLE COMMON   *Rates: budget-moderate*
Open: year-round   *Minimum Stay: one week*

The Normans began their invasion of England in 1066 on the battlefields of Hastings. Today, you can launch a visit to France via one of the many East Sussex ferries. Little Common is a renovated 17th-century barn that still retains all its original oak timbers and beams. Five to six find comfortable lodgings in a dining room, a fully equipped kitchen, a living room and three bedrooms (one double, one twin and one single or bunk as required). A horseback-riding school and a golf course are located close to the house, and many castles, abbeys, stately homes and gardens lie within a short drive. Guests can obtain babysitting service by arrangement. Contact: British Travel Associates, P.O. Box 299, Elkton, VA 22827. Call 1-800-327-6097 (in Virginia, 703-298-2232). Ref. F1492.

Children: Y   Pets: N   Smoking: Y   Handicap Access: N   Payment: All

ESSEX

Braintree

TUDOR COTTAGE   *Rates: budget*
Open: year-round   *Minimum Stay: one week*

When this thatched cottage was built in the early 14th century, Edward II's unpopular reign was nearly over. Its narrow stairways, low doors, sloping floors and leaded-glass windows bring that time to life for guests, but modern amenities make life a little easier than it was for the original owner. Five to six people can stay comfortably here in a living room, a dining room, a kitchen and three bedrooms (two twin, one single). There's a single bed in the curtained-off alcove of the sitting room. Central London is an hour's drive and the coast is 40 miles away. You can also visit nearby Colchester, which claims to be the oldest town in England. Contact: British Travel Associates, P.O.

Box 299, Elkton, VA 22827. Call 1-800-327-6097 (in Virginia, 703-298-2232). Ref. F5007.

Children: Y   Pets: N   Smoking: N   Handicap Access: N   Payment: All

GLOUCESTERSHIRE

Bledington

THE THATCHED COTTAGE   *Rates: budget-inexpensive*
Open: year-round   *Minimum Stay: one week*

True to its name, this well preserved 16th-century cottage features a steep thatched roof and all the rustic charm that goes with it. Situated in a traditional rural village where the waters of the Severn River, the village green and a flock of white ducks paint an idyllic picture, the cottage offers an ideal base from which to travel through the surrounding Wolds by car, foot or on bicycle. And excursions to Stratford-on-Avon, the sweeping hills of Shropshire and Oxford will round out any holiday. The accommodations for up to five include one double bedroom with extra double futon, one single bedroom, a charming entrance hall, a living room and an eat-in kitchen. The special grace of an enclosed garden finishes this pretty picture. Contact: Castles, Cottages & Flats in Ireland and U.K. Ltd., Box 261, Westwood, MA 02090. Call 617-329-4680. Ref. 2072.

Children: Y   Pets: N   Smoking: Y   Handicap Access: N   Payment: P

Bourton-on-the-Water

MAGNOLIA COTTAGE   *Rates: budget-inexpensive*
Open: year-round   *Minimum Stay: one week*

Your rooms in this tastefully furnished apartment are perched on the second floor above the owner's flower shop in this famous and picturesque Cotswold village. The cheery and fully heated apartment sleeps four in two twin bedrooms and also includes a living room with a TV and a VCR—you even get free membership at the video library across the street! The kitchen is equipped with many valuable conveniences including a microwave, a dishwasher and a washer/dryer. Excursions from this spot are too plentiful to list, but you will not want to miss a day at Oxford, famous for its cathedral and college buildings but equally appealing for its shops, restaurants and pubs. Contact: Castles, Cottages & Flats in Ireland and U.K. Ltd., Box 261, Westwood, MA 02090. Call 617-329-4680. Ref. 2048.

Children: N   Pets: N   Smoking: Y   Handicap Access: N   Payment: P

Chalford

LITTLE SKAITESHILL   *Rates: budget-inexpensive*
Open: year-round   *Minimum Stay: one week*

This sunny cottage sits on the grounds of a 17th-century manor with which vacationers share the use of a croquet lawn, six acres of woodland and an outdoor heated swimming pool. The cottage sleeps four to five and has a comfortable living room with a gas fire, a kitchen/dining room and two charming bedrooms (one double and one twin). For excellent shops and restaurants, visit Cirencester and Stroud. Horse-back riding, golf, polo and water sports are available within a few miles; the ancient Roman city of Bath is 25 miles away. Contact: British Travel Associates, P.O. Box 299, Elkton, VA 22827. Call 1-800-327-6097 (in Virginia, 703-298-2232). Ref. NMT.

Children: **Y**   Pets: **N**   Smoking: **Y**   Handicap Access: **N**   Payment: **All**

Cheltenham

REGENCY COURT   *Rates: inexpensive-expensive*

Open: year-round   *Minimum Stay: one week*

Cheltenham may be one of England's finest and most elegant towns, rich with antique shops, restaurants, inns, wine bars, an art gallery and a museum. Pittville Park, near the Regency Court townhouse, has acres of carefully tended lawns and trees, an ornamental lake, public tennis court and a children's play area. The house has a large L-shaped dining room with a fireplace and a three-quarter-size billiard table, a modern kitchen with a microwave and a dishwasher and a spacious drawing room. Four bedrooms (two double and two twin) plus an extra cot make room for eight or nine. Contact: British Travel Associates, P.O. Box 299, Elkton, VA 22827. Call 1-800-327-6097 (in Virginia, 703-298-2232). Ref. NLH.

Children: **Y**   Pets: **N**   Smoking: **Y**   Handicap Access: **N**   Payment: **All**

Dowdeswell

ROSSLEY MANOR FLAT   *Rates: budget*

Open: year-round   *Minimum Stay: one week*

A cozy and comfortable one-bedroom apartment is available on the first floor of the majestic Elizabethan Rossley Manor. The estate rests on high ground in the delightful Cotswolds, surrounded by forty acres of magnificent gardens, orchards, woodland and pasture. The grounds also offer trout fishing, a tennis and squash court and a heated swimming pool. Reached by a separate outdoor staircase entrance, the flat features wall-to-wall carpeting, sitting room, coal fire and stone-mullion windows looking out onto the impeccable manor gardens. Contact: British Travel Associates, P.O. Box 299, Elkton, VA 22827. Call 1-800-327-6097 (in Virginia, 703-298-2232).

Children: **Y**   Pets: **Y**   Smoking: **Y**   Handicap Access: **N**   Payment: **All**

Fairford

FAIRFORD MILL HOUSE   *Rates: budget-moderate*

Open: year-round   *Minimum Stay: one week*

Situated right next to the Severn River and close to the charming village of Fairford, this converted Cotswold water mill will charm you with its warmth and character. The generous features of this home for seven include a welcoming entrance hall, a rustic eat-in kitchen, four bedrooms and a living room with a stone fireplace. Lazy days pass quietly in the garden, but in time you may stir yourself to a game of tennis or an exploration of the upper Thames Valley and the roads that ramble through the many delightful villages of Cotswold. Contact:

Castles, Cottages & Flats in Ireland and U.K. Ltd., Box 261, Westwood, MA 02090. Call 617-329-4680. Ref. 2025.

Children: **N**   Pets: **N**   Smoking: **Y**   Handicap Access: **N**   Payment: **P**

Filkins

FILKINS FARMHOUSE   *Rates: budget*
Open: year-round   *Minimum Stay: one week*
This 17th-century farmhouse built of local stone sits in the open countryside bordering the Cotswold Hills. Secluded and picturesque, the house puts you near the upper reaches of the Thames. Four people can stay in one wing of the farmhouse, which has a living room, a kitchen/dining area and two bedrooms (one with three single beds). There's a high chair and a cot for a child (people with young children should note that the stairs are rather steep). Babysitting service is available by arrangement. The Cotswold Wildlife Park is two miles away. Contact: British Travel Associates, P.O. Box 299, Elkton, VA 22827. Call 1-800-327-6097 (in Virginia, 703-298-2232). Ref. F2630.

Children: **Y**   Pets: **N**   Smoking: **Y**   Handicap Access: **N**   Payment: All

Frampton-on-Severn

THE ORANGERY   *Rates: inexpensive-moderate*
Open: year-round   *Minimum Stay: one week*
Your imagination will whirl at the thought of a holiday in this beautifully converted 18th-century Gothic orangerie, furnished today with carefully selected period and antique furniture. Situated in the lordly grounds of wonderful Frampton Court and overlooking the ornamental Dutch canal and surrounding park land, this lovely home includes a living room with a fireplace, a dining room and kitchen, as well as sleeping accommodations for eight in two twin and two double bedrooms. Take advantage of the excellent nearby fishing and golf, and at only a little greater distance explore the Cotswold and Welsh border. Contact: Castles, Cottages & Flats in Ireland and U.K. Ltd., Box 261, Westwood, MA 02090. Call 617-329-4680. Ref. 2058.

Children: **N**   Pets: **N**   Smoking: **Y**   Handicap Access: **N**   Payment: P

Hawling

WALNUT TREE COTTAGE   *Rates: budget-inexpensive*
Open: year-round   *Minimum Stay: one week*
The Cotswold Hills form a scenic backdrop for this attractive cottage, which is surrounded by a large garden in the peaceful hamlet of Hawling. There's room for four to five people in a comfortable living room with a fireplace, a dining room, a kitchen with a microwave, a double bedroom and twin-bedded room with a cot. Picturesque villages, stately homes and good pubs stand nearby; Stratford-upon-Avon is 20 miles away. Come in July for the Cheltenham National Hunt steeplechases, held in the neighborhood. Contact: British Travel Associates, P.O. Box 299, Elkton, VA 22827. Call 1-800-327-6097 (in Virginia, 703-298-2232). Ref. NMZ.

Children: **Y**   Pets: **N**   Smoking: **Y**   Handicap Access: **N**   Payment: All

Highnam

HIGHNAM HOUSE
Open: year-round

Rates: budget-inexpensive
Minimum Stay: one week

This beautifully restored 17th-century cottage was once the schoolhouse for a country estate near the heart of Gloucester. Set in a large garden in a quiet village, it's close to the Cotswolds, Cheltenham and the Wye Valley. A dining/kitchen area and three bedrooms (one double, one twin, one with bunks beds), with extra cot and high chair on request, provide room for up to six adults and one child. The Forest of Dean and Westbury Court, the only remaining Dutch water garden in England, are nearby. Contact: British Travel Associates, P.O. Box 299, Elkton, VA 22827. Call 1-800-327-6097 (in Virginia, 703-298-2232). Ref. F2779.

Children: **Y**   Pets: **N**   Smoking: **Y**   Handicap Access: **N**   Payment: **All**

Leonard Stanley

YEW TREE COTTAGE
Open: year-round

Rates: budget-inexpensive
Minimum Stay: one week

A stay in this 300-year-old cottage of Cotswold stone, from which you can tour Coventry and Stratford-on-Avon as well as many cities that saw the birth of the Industrial Revolution, guarantees a balm to the heart and the mind. With its exposed beams and stonework, the centrally heated four-bedroom cottage for six offers something in winter, when the large living room with its stone fireplace is at its coziest. Summer days can be enjoyed in the furnished patio garden or at nearby Alderly Edge, home of the "witches," or in the Black Mountains to the west. Contact: Castles, Cottages & Flats in Ireland and U.K. Ltd., Box 261, Westwood, MA 02090. Call 617-329-4680. Ref. 1180.

Children: **Y**   Pets: **N**   Smoking: **Y**   Handicap Access: **N**   Payment: **P**

May Hill

VICTORIAN COTTAGE
Open: year-round

Rates: budget
Minimum Stay: one week

Experience Victorian England in this quaint cottage decorated with brass beds, lace, patchwork quilts, exposed beams and stone walls. A profusion of dried flowers inside, an abundance of clematis and ivy outside and a fruit orchard nearby complete the tasteful effect. Every window has breathtaking views of the Cotswold Hills, the woods or the Severn Valley. Two bedrooms (one double, one twin) and a single bed on the landing sleep four to five. Ross-on-Wye, Gloucester, the Royal Forest of Dean and the Wye Valley lie within ten miles. Lovely walks, fishing, golf and riding are all nearby, too. Contact: British Travel Associates, P.O. Box 299, Elkton, VA 22827. Call 1-800-327-6097 (in Virginia, 703-298-2232). Ref. A2397

Children: **Y**   Pets: **N**   Smoking: **Y**   Handicap Access: **N**   Payment: **All**

Norton

NORTON COTTAGE
Open: year-round

Rates: budget
Minimum Stay: one week

As you come upon this picturesque little cottage opposite the village green and duck pond, you get a taste of the way people lived in the 16th century. The cottage sleeps two to three in one twin bedroom and a bed settee on the landing. Walking, horseback riding and fishing in the nearby Cotswolds and the Forest of Dean are within easy reach. Historic sites in Tewkesbury (where the bitter fight for the English crown ended in the final battle of the War of the Roses), Gloucester and Malvern lie nearby. Contact: British Travel Associates, P.O. Box 299, Elkton, VA 22827. Call 1-800-327-6097 (in Virginia, 703-298-2232). Ref. A4660.

Children: Y   Pets: N   Smoking: Y   Handicap Access: N   Payment: All

Painswick

CAPP MILL   *Rates: budget-moderate*
Open: year-round   *Minimum Stay: one week*

Overlooking a trout-filled stream, the converted 17th-century Capp Mill is nestled in a serene valley below the historic Cotswold town of Painswick. This most uncommon two-floor, two-bedroom residence is filled with distinctive features, including open stonework walls, pitched elm-beamed ceilings and a sitting area with an inglenook and coal stove. Guests may enjoy the private garden, fishing and nature walks on the grounds; essential visitor attractions like Bath and Stratford are within close reach. Contact: British Travel Associates, P.O. Box 299, Elkton, VA 22827. Call 1-800-327-6097 (in Virginia, 703-298-2232).

Children: Y   Pets: Y   Smoking: Y   Handicap Access: N   Payment: All

Randwick

WEAVERS COTTAGE   *Rates: budget-inexpensive*
Open: year-round   *Minimum Stay: one week*

This converted 17th-century cottage, built of traditional Cotswold stone, retains much of its original character in its double-turreted spiral staircase and heavy oak beams. Large and airy, with carpeting throughout, the house has a living room, a dining room, a modern kitchen and four bedrooms (one double, three twin)—and even has a playroom with toys. Shops and pubs are very close by. This is good walking country, and you can start in the woods behind the cottage, which is owned by the National Trust. For bird watchers, Slimbridge Wild Fowl Trust lies 12 miles away. Contact: British Travel Associates, P.O. Box 299, Elkton, VA 22827. Call 1-800-327-6097 (in Virginia, 703-298-2232). Ref. F1368.

Children: Y   Pets: N   Smoking: Y   Handicap Access: N   Payment: All

Temple Guiting

COLLEGE BARN COTTAGE   *Rates: budget-inexpensive*
Open: year-round   *Minimum Stay: one week*

The charming village of Temple Guiting is one of the most remote of the Cotswold hamlets, nestled in a wooded, almost secret, valley near the mouth of the River Windrush. Built in the 17th century, this cottage has a dining room with a fireplace and a farmhouse kitchen. Two double bedrooms are on the first floor, and up fairly steep steps, the spacious attic/sitting room has a fireplace and a sleeping area with twin beds. An extra cot can sleep a seventh person. Cinema, theater, shops and museums are located at Cheltenham, 14 miles away. Contact: British Travel Associates, P.O. Box 299, Elkton, VA 22827. Call 1-800-327-6097 (in Virginia, 703-298-2232). Ref. NJD.

Children: Y   Pets: N   Smoking: Y   Handicap Access: N   Payment: All

Tetbury

TETBURY COTTAGE   *Rates: budget*
Open: year-round   *Minimum Stay: one week*

A long, sunny herb garden sets this spacious three-floor cottage apart from the bustling and lively town of Tetbury. The cottage has a living room, a dining room, a kitchen and a basement with laundry facilities, plus two bedrooms (one double, one twin) and a sofa bed, to sleep up to six. From this touring base, you can visit the ancient city of Bath, known for its Roman baths, 15th-century museum, abbey church and notable Georgian architecture. Contact: British Travel Associates, P.O. Box 299, Elkton, VA 22827. Call 1-800-327-6097 (in Virginia, 703-298-2232). Ref. F2897.

Children: Y   Pets: N   Smoking: Y   Handicap Access: N   Payment: All

Trellech

TRELLECH HOUSE   *Rates: budget-inexpensive*
Open: year-round   *Minimum Stay: one week*

This self-contained wing of a 17th-century house is located in the village center. Guests enter through a conservatory that fronts the main house. The stone construction dates from 1686 and includes a "secret" bedroom; it plus two others sleep six to seven people. French doors open from the living room onto a paved patio with a stone bench in a secluded front garden. Good walks and historic sites, such as Tintern, Llandogo, Monmouth and the Forest of Dean, beckon visitors to the countryside. Contact: British Travel Associates, P.O. Box 299, Elkton, VA 22827. Call 1-800-327-6097 (in Virginia, 703-298-2232). Ref. E7510.

Children: Y   Pets: N   Smoking: Y   Handicap Access: N   Payment: All

Weston Subedge

THREE STANLEY COTTAGES   *Rates: budget*
Open: year-round   *Minimum Stay: one week*

"A cottage for two" perfectly describes this traditionally rustic home warmly appointed with old oak beams and comfortable period furniture. Situated in its own south-facing garden, the cottage includes a small living/dining room with a color TV, a kitchen and one double bedroom. You can feed the romance by reciting Shakespeare's sonnets on the way to Stratford-on-Avon only eleven miles away, or head west to the Forest of Dean and its many lush acres. Contact: Castles, Cottages & Flats in Ireland and U.K. Ltd., Box 261, Westwood, MA 02090. Call 617-329-4680. Ref. 2070.

Children: **Y**   Pets: **N**   Smoking: **Y**   Handicap Access: **N**   Payment: **P**

GREATER LONDON

Croydon

LONDON COUNTRY APARTMENTS   *Rates: budget-moderate*
Open: year-round   *Minimum Stay: one week*

These apartments are located in Croydon, a pleasant garden suburb less than fifteen minutes' train ride from London. A variety of apartments are offered, ranging from studios to two-bedroom units, all with separate bath, kitchen and laundry facilities. Some apartments have gardens or patios where children can play or grown-ups can sip a quiet cup of tea. Other features that will make your stay more convenient are color TV, parking, weekly maid service, baby furniture and extra sofa beds. Some apartments also have a microwave oven and dishwasher in the kitchen. London Country Apartments prides itself on comfortable beds—and after a busy day in the bustle of London, you'll also appreciate the quiet of these residential streets. Contact: London Country Apartments Ltd., 161 Brighton Road, Purley, Surrey CR8 4HE. Call 011-44-1-660-8167.

Children: **Y** Pets: **N** Smoking: **Y** Handicap Access: **N** Payment: **C, P, T, A, V, M**

London

27B BURTON STREET, WC1   *Rates: budget*
Open: year-round   *Minimum Stay: one week*

This one-bedroom apartment, on the first floor of a stately Georgian house, sleeps two in compact but charming quarters just a short walk from the British Museum. The quiet residential street is near the Russel Square, Kings Cross and Euston underground stations, and only a slightly longer distance from the main lines. Restaurants, shops and theaters are also close by. Recently redecorated, there is a washing machine, bathroom with bath and hand-held shower, and a TV. Contact: Christine Ayling, Apartment Services Ltd., 2 Sandwich Street, London WC1H 9PL. Call: (011-44-71) 388-3558 or Fax: (011-44-71) 383-7255.

Children: **Y**   Pets: **N**   Smoking: **Y**   Handicap Access: **N**   Payment: All

London

35 RIVER COURT, SE1   *Rates: budget*
Open: year-round   *Minimum Stay: one week*

This one-bedroom, fifth-floor apartment sleeps two—and an optional third on a living room sofa-bed—in spacious, sun-filled quarters whose large living room windows open onto a balcony. The apartment, in a doorman building on a luxury block at the foot of the south side of the Thames, is stylishly and appealingly furnished with carpeting throughout. The well-equipped kitchen has a microwave oven and a washing machine; and a garage space is available below the building at extra cost. Additionally, guests have access to two communal garden areas, one overlooking the river. Contact: Christine Ayling, Apartment Services Ltd., 2 Sandwich Street, London WC1H 9PL. Call: (01144-71) 388-3558 or Fax: (011-44-71) 383-7255.

Children: Y   Pets: N   Smoking: Y   Handicap Access: N   Payment: All

London

37 DOUGHTY STREET, WC1   *Rates: budget-inexpensive*
Open: year-round   *Minimum Stay: one week*

Several studio and one-bedroom ground- and first-floor apartments are available at 37 Doughty Street, a few doors away from where Charles Dickens did some of his greatest writing and where his former house has now been restored as a museum. The apartments—each pleasantly furnished with wall-to-wall carpeting, the occasional antique, a color TV and a pay phone—offer a serene retreat on this quiet and lovely block of terraced Georgian houses. Well-located in London's fashionable Bloomsbury section, you are within walking distance of the Kings Cross, St. Pancras and Euston underground stations and just a short trip to Covent Garden, the West End theaters and the British Museum. Car parking is metered, and public lots are close by. Contact: Christine Ayling, Apartment Services Ltd., 2 Sandwich Street, London WC1H 9PL. Call: (011-44-71) 388-3558 or Fax: (011-44-71) 383-7255.

Children: Y   Pets: N   Smoking: Y   Handicap Access: N   Payment: All

London

ALLEN STREET, W8   *Rates: expensive-deluxe*
Open: year-round   *Minimum Stay: one week*

This period-style property in a lovely part of Kensington, off fashionable Kensington High Street, is just a few minute's walk from Kensington Palace and Holland Park. Here you can luxuriate in elegantly furnished one-, two- and three-bedroom apartments (most with two bathrooms) and enjoy a full array of amenities, including: five days/week of maid service (fresh towels and linens are supplied twice a week); a 24-hour doorman; an intercom system; private telephones; and a passenger elevator. Laundry service is available by special arrangement. Contact: Europa-Let Inc., P.O. Box 3537, Ashland, Oregon 97520. Call: 503-482-1442 or 1-800-462-4486.

Children: Y   Pets: N   Smoking: Y   Handicap Access: N   Payment: P, T

London

BEDFORD AVENUE, WC1   *Rates: expensive-deluxe*
Open: year-round   *Minimum Stay: one week*

These one- and three-bedroom apartments on a tree-lined street in the heart of London's Bloomsbury district provide a luxurious base for all discerning travellers. Here you are within easy walking distance of Oxford Street, the British Museum, and the restaurants and theaters of the West End; and the underground at Tottenham Court Road provides easy access to virtually all else. The high-ceilinged, spacious

rooms are graced by oil paintings and the ultra-modern kitchens ;
outfitted with microwaves and washing machines. Maid service is
available five days per week; linen and towels are changed upon request; and a car is available by special arrangement. We daresay that
all your needs will be met! Contact: Europa-Let Inc., P.O. Box 3537,
Ashland, Oregon 97520. Call: 503-482-1442 or 1-800-462-4486.

Children: Y   Pets: N   Smoking: Y   Handicap Access: N   Payment: P,T

London

BEDFORD COURT   *Rates: moderate*
Open: year-round   *Minimum Stay: one week*

Whether you are traveling with a large or small family or a group of
friends, you're sure to find the right apartment for you in this elegant
converted mansion on a quiet street in the very heart of Bloomsbury.
One- to three-bedroom accommodations for two to six feature beautifully furnished rooms appointed with oil paintings. A kitchen and a
living room with color TV and telephone complete the apartments;
those on the upper floors are serviced by an elevator. Nearby attractions, such as the British Museum and the West End theater district,
as well as Westminster Abbey, the Houses of Parliament and all the
many "must-see" places in London are only a short bus or subway ride
away. Contact: British Travel Associates, P.O. Box 299, Elkton, VA
22827. Call 1-800-327-6097 (In Virginia, 703-298-2232). Ref. 011222.

Children: Y   Pets: N   Smoking: Y   Handicap Access: N   Payment: P

London

CHARLES STREET APARTMENTS, W1   *Rates: moderate-deluxe*
Open: year-round   *Minimum Stay: one week*

Three period-style properties on Charles Street—the residential area of
London's Mayfair district, once a part of Lord Berkeley's estate—offer
simple but elegant studios and one-, two- and three-bedroom apartments (some with two bathrooms). Here you will live on the block
where Beau Brummel, the Duke of Clarence (later King William IV),
Admiral Codrington and Prime Minister Lord Rosebery once made
their homes, close to Green Park and Hyde Park and within short
walking distance of Bond Street and Piccadilly. The apartments, close
to the Green Park underground station and within easy reach of the
West End, offer maid service, an intercom system, private telephones,
weekly towel/linen service and, in many cases, a washing machine
and dishwasher. Contact: Europa-Let Inc., P.O. Box 3537, Ashland,
Oregon 97520. Call: 503-482-1442 or 1-800-462-4486.

Children: Y   Pets: N   Smoking: Y   Handicap Access: N   Payment: P, T

London

CHARTERHOUSE SQUARE   *Rates: moderate-expensive*
Open: year-round   *Minimum Stay: one week*

Used as a set during the filming of the Hercule Poirot TV series, this
luxurious ground-floor flat for two is beautifully furnished in the 1930s
art deco style. It overlooks Charterhouse Square and has a living/

...m, a kitchen and one double bedroom. Visitors have the use ...artment's swimming pool, sauna, gymnasium and laundry ...gnificent St. Paul's Cathedral, with its mixture of Palladian, ...d Italian Baroque features, is only five minutes away. Bus and rail transportation to central London and the West End are within walking distance. Contact: British Travel Associates, P.O. Box 299, Elkton, VA 22827. Call 1-800-327-6097 (in Virginia, 703-298-2232). Ref. CB7074.

Children: **Y** Pets: **N** Smoking: **Y** Handicap Access: **N** Payment: **All**

London

CHELSEA COTTAGE
Open: year-round

Rates: budget
Minimum Stay: one week

This lovingly furnished home for four is really a country cottage in the heart of London's popular Chelsea district. From this fashionable address on a quiet residential street off Fulham Road, you'll be able to explore the great shopping and dining on Kings Road, a five-minute walk away. And of course, the whole of London—Kensington, Knightsbridge, the West End theater district—is only a short bus or tube ride away. The two-story home features a living room, a dining room and a kitchen on the first floor. A spiral staircase ascends to the two double bedrooms and bath above. Contact: British Travel Associates, P.O. Box 299, Elkton, VA 22827. Call 1-800-327-6097 (In Virginia, 703-298-2232). Ref. 019888.

Children: **Y** Pets: **N** Smoking: **Y** Handicap Access: **N** Payment: **P**

London

CHELSEA GARDEN FLAT
Open: year-round

Rates: moderate
Minimum Stay: one week

This pleasant modern apartment in the heart of London's fashionable Chelsea area overlooks a peaceful garden square, to which guests hold a key. You can find diversion nearby in Kings Road, with its wealth of fashionable shops and restaurants. Lovers of the good life will also enjoy a leisurely stroll around the neighborhood for a look at many exquisite homes. An easy bus or tube ride takes you to all the sights of the city. The apartment for two features a sunny living/dining room with a color TV, a kitchen loaded with conveniences such as a dishwasher and a washer/dryer and one double bedroom. Contact: British Travel Associates, P.O. Box 299, Elkton, VA 22827. Call 1-800-327-6097 (In Virginia, 703-298-2232). Ref. 016751

Children: **Y** Pets: **N** Smoking: **Y** Handicap Access: **N** Payment: **P**

London

CLOTH FAIR APARTMENTS
Open: year-round

Rates: inexpensive-moderate
Minimum Stay: three nights

These are among the few residential apartments available to rent in the oldest part of London, known as "the City." The two units are part of a joined row of 18th-century buildings known as a "terrace." The terrace has stores on the ground floor, so each apartment is reached by a staircase. Number 43 has one bedroom with two twin beds and an outside sitting area; number 45A can sleep four guests in the two bedrooms (one double and two singles). Both apartments have baths and kitchens. This is a fascinating area of London—number 41 Cloth Fair is the only house in the city to have survived the infamous fire of 1666, and across the street is the graveyard of St. Bartholomew the Great, one of the city's most ancient churches. Contact: The Landmark Trust, Shottesbrooke, Maidenhead, Berks, England SL6 3SW. Call 011-44-628-82-5925.

Children: Y Pets: N Smoking: Y Handicap Access: N Payment: C, P, T, V, M

London

COLLINGHAM GARDENS, SW5   *Rates: moderate-deluxe*
Open: year-round   *Minimum Stay: one week*

Collingham Gardens, a period-style property situated in a quiet Kensington Square, features a number of recently redecorated one-, two- and three-bedroom apartments (some with two bathrooms) all equipped to a high standard. Located near the Earls Court and Gloucester Road underground stations, the tranquil setting belies its proximity to the bustle of the West End. A capable and helpful staff provide a luxurious degree of personal attention; and amenities include daily maid service, a 24-hour doorman, direct line telephones and a passenger lift. Fresh towels and linens are supplied once a week; and laundry service is available by special arrangement. Contact: Europa-Let Inc., P.O. Box 3537, Ashland, Oregon 97520. Call: 503-482-1442 or 1-800-462-4486.

Children: Y   Pets: N   Smoking: Y   Handicap Access: N   Payment: P, T

London

HAMPSTEAD HOUSES   *Rates: budget*
Open: year-round   *Minimum Stay: one week*

Your holiday in one of two modern townhouses in the middle of prestigious Hampstead will be gracious indeed. Set on a quiet cul-de-sac only 200 yards from the south end of picturesque Hampstead Heath, an 800-acre park overlooking the city, this address offers easy access to the endless wonders of the city of London as well as the great pleasure of a quiet walk in the park. Each house sleeps two to six in up to three bedrooms and features a living room with a color TV, a dining room and a thoroughly modern kitchen with a dishwasher, a microwave, a washer and dryer and a high chair. Extras such as a garage and a furnished patio can turn your good vacation into a great one. Contact: British Travel Associates, P.O. Box 299, Elkton, VA 22827. Call 1-800-327-6097 (In Virginia, 703-298-2232). Ref. 010455.

Children: Y   Pets: N   Smoking: Y   Handicap Access: N   Payment: P

London

HARINGEY PARK HOUSES   *Rates: budget*
Open: year-round   *Minimum Stay: five days*

Ideally suited to large families or groups, these six attractively furnished townhouses provide the perfect accomodations for those traveling on a tight budget. The pleasant residential area offers a good selection of shops, pubs and restaurants. The houses, built in 1989 and located east of Hampstead just a twelve-minute tube ride from downtown London, are convenient for those dependent on public transportation, with easy access to a BritRail station and Heathrow Airport. Guests with a car will enjoy the carport. Accommodations for six include a kitchen with a washing machine, a living/dining room with a color TV, three bedrooms and a private balcony. Contact: British Travel Associates, P.O. Box 299, Elkton, VA 22827. Call 1-800-327-6097 (In Virginia, 703-298-2232). Ref. 019005.

Children: Y   Pets: N   Smoking: Y   Handicap Access: N   Payment: P

London

HYDE PARK APARTMENTS   *Rates: moderate-deluxe*
Open: year-round   *Minimum Stay: one week*

Several quiet and privately owned studio, one-, two- and three-bedroom apartments (some with two bathrooms) around Hyde Park are offered here through the Europa-Let international apartment agency. These high-ceilinged luxury units are scrumptiously decorated and feature designer kitchens and bathrooms, comfortable and elegantly furnished living rooms, and a high level of personalized service. Conveniently located with easy access to Bond Street, Oxford Street and Piccadilly Circus, visitors will also find a fine selection of good restaurants and elegant boutiques nearby. Preference for an apartment with an elevator must be indicated when making a reservation. Contact: Europa-Let Inc., P.O. Box 3537, Ashland, Oregon 97520. Call: 503-482-1442 or 1-800-462-4486.

Children: Y   Pets: N   Smoking: Y   Handicap Access: N   Payment: P, T

London

KENSINGTON COURT AND SURROUNDINGS, W8   *Rates: moderate-deluxe*
Open: year-round   *Minimum Stay: one week*

Once owned by the late Aga Khan, this Edwardian mansion has been renovated and converted into individually designed studios and one-, two- and three-bedroom apartments (some with two bathrooms). Located within a quiet and picturesque square, it's hard to believe you're just a minute away from bustling Kensington High Street and within easy reach of Harrod's, Kensington Gardens, Kensington Palace, Hyde Park and the Royal Albert Hall. A complete package of amenities includes five days/week of maid service (fresh towels and linen are supplied twice a week); use of a passenger elevator; a lobby intercom; and a private telephone. Laundry service is available by special arrangement, and laundry room facilities are available at no extra charge. Contact: Europa-Let Inc., P.O. Box 3537, Ashland, Oregon 97520. Call: 503-482-1442 or 1-800-462-4486.

Children: Y   Pets: N   Smoking: Y   Handicap Access: N   Payment: P, T

London

KNIGHTSBRIDGE STUDIOS   *Rates: moderate*
Open: year-round   *Minimum Stay: one week*
Set on elegant and quiet Ennismore Garden, one of these dozen studio apartments can be the perfect base for your London holiday. With Hyde Park only a three-minute walk away, you can wind down from your busy days of sightseeing and touring with a stroll in the woods. Nearby is some of the city's best shopping (you can easily spend one whole day in Harrod's) and London's West End only three tube stops away. The studios are in a building serviced by an elevator and offer a kitchen and a living room with twin sleep sofas, as well as telephone and color TV. Contact: British Travel Associates, P.O. Box 299, Elkton, VA 22827. Call 1-800-327-6097 (In Virginia, 703-298-2232). Ref. 010900.

Children: Y   Pets: N   Smoking: Y   Handicap Access: N   Payment: P

London

MAYFAIR SUITES   *Rates: deluxe*
Open: year-round   *Minimum Stay: five days*
This beautifully remodeled old residence in elegant Mayfair offers a variety of spacious accommodations ranging from studios to two-bedroom apartments. Set on well-cared-for Hertford Street, the home provides the nearby pleasures of Green and Hyde Parks, where the English like to take long and thoughtful strolls. You'll also enjoy Shepherd Market, with its charming alleyway shops, restaurants and pubs. You can even do your marketing at Fortnum & Mason, the Queen's grocer! The apartments, which sleep from one to four people each, include a kitchen and a living room with telephone and TV. Contact: British Travel Associates, P.O. Box 299, Elkton, VA 22827. Call 1-800-327-6097 (In Virginia, 703-298-2232). Ref. 010022.

Children: Y   Pets: N   Smoking: Y   Handicap Access: N   Payment: P

London

PEMBRIDGE CRESCENT, W11   *Rates: moderate-deluxe*
Open: year-round   *Minimum Stay: one week*
Pembridge Crescent, a period-style property within easy reach of Kensington Gardens, Hyde Park, Marble Arch and Holland Park is comprised of several individually designed one- and two-bedroom modern, well-equipped apartments. From here you can walk to nearby Portobello Road to browse in the famous antiques market or use the Notting Hill Gate underground station for quick transportation to the center of town. Amenities include five days/week of maid service, an intercom system, a private telephone and towel/linen service twice a week—all supervised by a capable and friendly staff. Contact: Europa-Let Inc., P.O. Box 3537, Ashland, Oregon 97520. Call: 503-482-1442 or 1-800-462-4486.

Children: Y   Pets: N   Smoking: Y   Handicap Access: N   Payment: P, T

London

PRINCE OF WALES STUDIOS   *Rates: inexpensive*
Open: year-round   *Minimum Stay: one week*

A London vacation in one of these pleasant apartments in a former private home will assure you the best of times. You can enjoy a peaceful walk in the wooded areas of Hyde Park right across the road or the lively bustle of the West End theater district only a short bus or tube ride away. Other neighborhood attractions only a few steps away include Kensington Palace, the Royal Albert Hall and the Victoria and Albert Museum. All floors are served by an elevator; amenities such as laundry service and a bar on the premises offer additional comfort and convenience. Each apartment features a kitchen area and a studio living room with both telephone and TV. Contact: British Travel Associates, P.O. Box 299, Elkton, VA 22827. Call 1-800-327-6097 (In Virginia, 703-298-2232). Ref. 010019.

Children: Y   Pets: N   Smoking: Y   Handicap Access: N   Payment: P

London

QUEEN ALEXANDRA MANSIONS, JUDD STREET, WC1   *Rates: budget*
Open: year-round   *Minimum Stay: one week*

This charming one-bedroom apartment is on the second floor of an elevator building that comprises one section of a private "Edwardian mansion block," entered from the street through a lock-and-key entrance. The sunny apartment is beautifully decorated and features a sofa bed in the living room for an optional third guest; a color TV; a pay phone; and a kitchen equipped with electric stovetop burners and a microwave (but no standard) oven. Close to the West End theaters and shops, restaurants and museums, the apartment is convenient to both underground and bus stations. Contact: Christine Ayling, Apartment Services Ltd., 2 Sandwich Street, London WC1H 9PL. Call: (011-44-71) 388-3558 or Fax: (011-44-71) 383-7255.

Children: Y   Pets: N   Smoking: Y   Handicap Access: N   Payment: All

London

QUEEN'S GATE, SW7   *Rates: deluxe*
Open: year-round   *Minimum Stay: one week*

This delightful and fastidiously maintained period-style property in London's elegant South Kensington section features spacious, luxuriously furnished two-bedroom/two-bathroom and three-bedroom/two-bathroom apartments (some with a separate cloakroom). Amenities—supervised by an experienced husband and wife team—include: six days/week of maid service; 24-hour doorman service; color TV; an intercom system; direct-dial telephones; and a washing machine and dryer in each apartment. And (for those who can tear themselves away!), you are within easy walking distance of some of London's most popular sights, including the Victoria and Albert Museum, the Natural History Museum, Harrod's, the Royal Albert Hall and Hyde Park. Contact: Europa-Let Inc., P.O. Box 3537, Ashland, Oregon 97520.

Call: 503-482-1442 or 1-800-462-4486.

Children: **Y**   Pets: **N**   Smoking: **Y**   Handicap Access· **N**   Payment: **P, T**

London

SEVINGTON STREET, W9 *Rates: moderate*
Open: year-round *Minimum Stay: one week*

This two-bedroom, one-bathroom luxury duplex apartment for four—and an optional fifth on a sofa bed in the living room—was recently fashioned from part of a charming Victorian house on a quiet residential street in this popular area of London. Newly designed, furnished and decorated, here is the ideal combination of the comforts of a rambling private home and the convenience of a modern apartment. The large living room contains an abundance of hidden storage space and the spacious kitchen has a dishwasher and washer/dryer. Contact: Christine Ayling, Apartment Services Ltd., 2 Sandwich Street, London WC1H 9PL. Call: (011-44-71) 388-3558 or Fax: (011-44-71) 383-7255.

Children: **Y**   Pets: **N**   Smoking: **Y**   Handicap Access: **N**   Payment: **All**

London

SLOANE SQUARE APARTMENTS *Rates: moderate-expensive*
Open: year-round *Minimum Stay: one week*

This handsome building in central London contains eight luxury apartments accommodating from two to five guests. The elegantly appointed flats feature either stylish modern furnishings or more traditional surroundings. All are fully carpeted, and many boast beautiful open fireplaces and exquisite architectural details. Full sets of utensils are provided in the modern kitchens, and the tiled bathrooms offer a constant supply of hot water—a bonus not to be overlooked on the British Isles. Other modern amenities include a color TV and direct-dial telephones; you can even arrange to use the telex and fax machines. The building is ideally located whether you prefer the bucolic pleasures of Kensington Gardens, the fascination of the Victoria and Albert Museum, or the challenge of Harrods. Contact: Rent a Home International, Inc., 7200 34th Avenue, N.W., Seattle, WA 98117. Call 206-545-6963. Ref. E/R005.

Children: **Y** Pets: **N** Smoking: **N** Handicap Access: **N** Payment: **C, P, V, M**

London

SUSSEX GARDENS APARTMENTS *Rates: moderate-deluxe*
Open: year-round *Minimum Stay: one week*

These plush apartments can accommodate up to ten guests and are designed to make your stay in the heart of London as pleasant as possible. The modern furnishings are comfortable yet stylish; the bathrooms are sleek and convenient. The well-equipped kitchens include electric appliances and complete sets of china and glassware. Daily maid service, color TV, central heating, and a round-the-clock switchboard all conspire to make your sojourn trouble-free. The splendid location is a boon to dedicated sightseers: Hyde Park, Buckingham Palace, Madame Tussaud's, and Piccadilly Circus are all within easy walking distance. Contact: Rent a Home International, Inc., 7200 34th Avenue N.W., Seattle, WA 98117. Call 206-545-6963. Ref. E/R005.

Children: Y Pets: N Smoking: N Handicap Access: N Payment: C, P, V, M

London

TAVISTOCK COURT, TAVISTOCK SQUARE, WC1   *Rates: budget*
Open: year-round   *Minimum Stay: one week*
This enchanting studio for two is owned by an opera singer who has lovingly and elegantly furnished it with a combination of antique and modern pieces, a grand piano and (to fulfill more pedestrian cravings) a color TV and pay phone. The apartment, a tranquil haven from city noise, faces a courtyard garden through which sun streams in from a northerly direction. Every modern amenity is offered in a well-equipped kitchen and the bathroom is fully outfitted with both a bath-tub and shower. Bus and underground transportation are nearby. Contact: Christine Ayling, Apartment Services Ltd., 2 Sandwich Street, London WC1H 9PL. Call: (011-44-71) 388-3558 or Fax: (011-44-71) 383-7255.

Children: Y   Pets: N   Smoking: Y   Handicap Access: N   Payment: All

London

THEATER APARTMENTS   *Rates: inexpensive*
Open: year-round   *Minimum Stay: one week*
Choose from one of these three carefully appointed and handsomely furnished apartments for two, and you can be sure you have situated yourself well. Located in the very heart of London's West End theater district, the apartments are only a short walk to many theaters, the Royal Opera House, Covent Garden Market and the National Gallery. Alive with the people, commerce and the street life which are the pulse of any great city, this is a neighbordhood filled with fine shops, market stalls, pubs and restaurants. Each apartment includes a living room, a kitchen and a double bedroom; a single sofa bed is available as well. Your own metered telephone and color TV add to the convenience and comfort of these accommodations. Contact: British Travel Associates, P.O. Box 299, Elkton, VA 22827. Call 1-800-327-6097 (In Virginia, 703-298-2232). Ref. 010999.

Children: Y   Pets: N   Smoking: Y   Handicap Access: N   Payment: P

London

VICTORIAN FLAT   *Rates: inexpensive*
Open: year-round   *Minimum Stay: one week*
Truly a home away from home, this warm and comfortable apartment for two features tasteful appointments, such as a period gas-lit fire-place. Situated in a well-preserved historic Victorian terrace on one of London's lovely residential squares, the apartment also enjoys the use of a large private garden across the street. With all of London only a short tube ride away, the neighborhood offers its own pleasant shops, pubs and restaurants. Portobello Road, with its celebrated open mar-ket and connecting small streets, as well as the old village of Clarne-

don Cross are only a short walk away. The apartment includes a kitchen, a living room, and a double bedroom, and also shares a small garden right on the property. Contact: British Travel Associates, P.O. Box 299, Elkton, VA 22827. Call 1-800-327-6097 (In Virginia, 703-298-2232). Ref. 010002.

Children: Y   Pets: N   Smoking: Y   Handicap Access: N   Payment: P

London

WHITFIELD STREET WC1   *Rates: inexpensive*
Open: year-round   *Minimum Stay: one week*

This two-bedroom, two-bathroom recently redecorated groundfloor apartment accommodates four in the very center of the city, close to the theaters and within walking distance of many shops, restaurants and museums. Despite its central location the apartment is well-sheltered from traffic noise, thanks in large part to a sunroom and a tiny landscaped courtyard that provide a serene and beautiful retreat. The well-equipped kitchen resembles an atrium in style; a washing machine is being installed as this book goes to press; and a color TV and pay phone are provided. Contact: Christine Ayling, Apartment Services Ltd., 2 Sandwich Street, London WC1H 9PL. Call: (01144-71) 388-3558 or Fax: (011-44-71) 383-7255.

Children: Y   Pets: N   Smoking: Y   Handicap Access: N   Payment: All

HAMPSHIRE

Amport

7 SARSON COTTAGES   *Rates: budget-inexpensive*
Open: year-round   *Minimum Stay: one week*

Situated only 15 miles from the cathedral cities of Salisbury and Winchester, this lovely 15th-century cottage offers access to England's South East and West Country districts. Retaining much of its original rustic character, the centrally heated house for four includes a living room with an open fireplace, an eat-in kitchen, a sunny conservatory and a colorful furnished garden. Day trips to Cambridge, with its many colleges, pubs and shops, or to the beaches, parks and forests of south England will assure endless days of pleasure to your whole family. Contact: Castles, Cottages & Flats in Ireland and U.K. Ltd., Box 261, Westwood, MA 02090. Call 617-329-4680. Ref. 4011.

Children: Y   Pets: N   Smoking: Y   Handicap Access: N   Payment: P

Eaglehurst

LUTTRELL'S TOWER   *Rates: inexpensive-expensive*
Open: year-round   *Minimum Stay: three nights*

Built by a politician and reputed smuggler, this 18th-century architectural folly sits by the water's edge overlooking the Solent, the narrow passage of water between the mainland and the Isle of Wight. The design is that of a three-story castelated tower and features many delightful oddities such as the feet of an Egyptian statue, enormous gates giving access to the beach and a secret tunnel running from the basement to the beach. The two lower floors are occupied by twin bedrooms. The upper floor, whose bay windows provide splendid views, is a living/dining area with a kitchenette, where a dining table nestles in a sunny alcove. The towns of Southampton and Portsmouth are close by, as are a number of castles and abbeys. Those who appreciate nature will want to visit nearby New Forest. Contact: The Landmark Trust, Shottesbrooke, Maidenhead, Berks, England SL6 3SW. Call 011-44-628-82-5925.

Children: Y Pets: Y Smoking: Y Handicap Access: N Payment: C, P, T, V, M

Exbury

LIME TREE COTTAGE   *Rates: budget-moderate*
Open: year-round   *Minimum Stay: one week*

Situated in the peaceful hamlet of Exbury, this gracious cottage retains much of its original character in fine old furnishings and exposed beams throughout. The grounds feature an ample garden with a furnished terrace and barbecue for outdoor dining. The wonderful old house sleeps six in two double and one twin bedroom and includes a living room, a dining room, a study and a kitchen with a utility room, as well as the modern conveniences of central heat, a dishwasher, a washing machine and a color TV. Many nearby historic sites and the beauty of Exbury Gardens, Buckler's Hard and Beaulieu provide distraction enough for many days. Contact: Castles, Cottages & Flats in Ireland and U.K. Ltd., Box 261, Westwood, MA 02090. Call 617-329-4680. Ref. 4009.

Children: Y   Pets: N   Smoking: Y   Handicap Access: N   Payment: P

Lymington

SEA COTTAGE   *Rates: budget-inexpensive*
Open: year-round   *Minimum Stay: one week*

Situated in a quiet residential lane only a short distance from the town quay and the Royal Lymington Yacht Club, this fisherman's cottage offers an ideal holiday home for those whose passion is boating. Plentiful rentals at the nearby marinas will lure those who like to "mess around," and for those who just like to look, the lively harbor is sure to delight. The cottage sleeps four in one twin and one double and includes a living/dining room with a fireplace, a galley kitchen and a roof terrace, from which views of the quaint neighborhood will enchant you. Many conveniences—central heat, a washer and dryer, a microwave, a stereo and a color TV—make this truly a home away from home. Contact: Castles, Cottages & Flats in Ireland and U.K. Ltd., Box 261, Westwood, MA 02090. Call 617-329-4680. Ref. 4053.

Children: Y   Pets: N   Smoking: Y   Handicap Access: N   Payment: P

Lymington

THE COURT HOUSE   *Rates: budget-inexpensive*
Open: year-round   *Minimum Stay: one week*

Magnificent sailing ships used to crowd Lymington's harbor, their captains quartered along Captain's Row in town. Today the harbor is filled with all types of recreational vessels and Captain's Row houses accommodate only amateur sailors. This delightful three-story house looks across the harbor past an irregular range of chalk hills to the Isle of Wight, long associated with the poets Longfellow, Keats, Tennyson and Swinburne. There's room for four adults and one child in a living room, a dining room, a garden room and a kitchen, two double bedrooms and two bed settees. Lymington is on the edge of the New Forest, once the royal hunting grounds of William the Conqueror. Contact: British Travel Associates, P.O. Box 299, Elkton, VA 22827. Call 1-800-327-6097 (in Virginia, 703-298-2232). Ref. F3040.

Children: **Y**   Pets: **N**   Smoking: **Y**   Handicap Access: **N**   Payment: **All**

Steep

TUDOR COTTAGE   *Rates: budget*
Open: year-round   *Minimum Stay: one week*

The Tudor style of this very old cottage is obvious both inside and out—its exposed beams, tiny rooms, low doors and not-quite-modern, but charming, amenities. Two bedrooms (one twin, one single) sleep three; there's also a living room, a dining room and kitchen. The main A3 London/Portsmouth road is two miles away and the resort cities of Bournemouth and Portsmouth are not far. Also nearby is New Forest, which has ninety thousand acres inhabited by wild ponies, donkeys and deer. Contact: British Travel Associates, P.O. Box 299, Elkton, VA 22827. Call 1-800-327-6097 (in Virginia, 703-298-2232). Ref. F1542.

Children: **Y**   Pets: **N**   Smoking: **Y**   Handicap Access: **N**   Payment: **All**

HEREFORD AND WORCESTER

Bredwardine

OLD COURT FARM   *Rates: budget-inexpensive*
Open: year-round   *Minimum Stay: one week*

Three English kings have visited this 14th-century manor set regally on the banks of the Wye—Henry V went so far as to knight the establishment's owner. The house has been carefully restored, and great care has been taken to preserve the original beams. The sitting room has a decorative range and a wood-burning stove; adjacent to it there's a large kitchen/dining room. Two four-poster beds, three singles and an extra cot provide room for eight guests. The private gardens offer a stone barbecue and good views of the river. Visit the nearby Black Mountains and Brecon Beacons, or fish, canoe and ride in the area. Contact: British Travel Associates, P.O. Box 299, Elkton, VA 22827. Call 1-800-327-6097 (in Virginia, 703-298-2232). Ref. QDM.

Children: **Y**   Pets: **N**   Smoking: **Y**   Handicap Access: **N**   Payment: **All**

Bretforton

COTSWOLDS COTTAGE   *Rates: budget-inexpensive*
Open: year-round   *Minimum Stay: one week*

This charming thatched-roof cottage is set in the heart of the Vale of Evesham, known for its tasty fruits and vegetables. The cottage has modern conveniences and includes a secluded and sunny patio with a table and chairs. There's room for five in three bedrooms (one double, one twin and one single). In the vicinity, guests will find the Cotswold and Malvern Hills. Chipping Campden, Evesham, Stratford and Warwick Castle are also nearby. Contact: British Travel Associates, P.O. Box 299, Elkton, VA 22827. Call 1-800-327-6097 (in Virginia, 703-298-2232). Ref. F4043.

Children: Y   Pets: N   Smoking: Y   Handicap Access: N   Payment: All

Broadway

HALFPENNY COTTAGE   *Rates: budget-moderate*
Open: year-round   *Minimum Stay: one week*
Located on the main road in the graceful Cotswold village of Broadway, Halfpenny Cottage is an exquisitely restored residence for up to six. Four antique-filled bedrooms radiate warmth and taste, as does a living room with stone inglenook. The three-floor house also features a fully equipped modern kitchen with separate breakfast nook, plus a rear garden with patio furniture. Fine shopping and dining, as well as excellent sporting facilities, lie across the street. Contact: British Travel Associates, P.O. Box 299, Elkton, VA 22827. Call 1-800-327-6097 (in Virginia, 703-298-2232).

Children: Y   Pets: Y   Smoking: Y   Handicap Access: N   Payment: All

Broadway

THE OLD APPLE STORE   *Rates: budget-inexpensive*
Open: year-round   *Minimum Stay: one week*
This original 17th-century building offers an architect-designed second-floor apartment for two, which features beautiful views of the surrounding hills and the famous Broadway Tower. Just outside the main village, the owner of the house shares a tidy garden with the apartment. Accommodations include a kitchen, a dining area, a small living room and one twin bedroom. And if you find that you have slept too late and are anxious to be off exploring the neighboring Cotswold villages, or if you discover that your day in Oxford has left you exhausted, breakfasts and country suppers are available upon request. Contact: Castles, Cottages & Flats in Ireland and U.K. Ltd., Box 261, Westwood, MA 02090. Call 617-329-4680. Ref. 2099.

Children: N   Pets: N   Smoking: Y   Handicap Access: N   Payment: P

Byford

LOWER HOUSE   *Rates: budget-inexpensive*
Open: year-round   *Minimum Stay: one week*
When this farmhouse was built near the Welsh border in 1520, Wales was an independent principality 16 years away from formal union with England. One can only imagine how much its first owner, a yeoman farmer, depended on the River Wye, only a few yards from the house. Lower House has been updated with modern conveniences since then, but the countryside remains just as peaceful. The house is close to many places of historical interest in England and Wales.

There's room for six, with a large, beamed sitting room, a dining room, a kitchen and three bedrooms (one double with an extra single bed, one large twin and one single). Children under 12 are not permitted. Contact: British Travel Associates, P.O. Box 299, Elkton, VA 22827. Call 1-800-327-6097 (in Virginia, 703-298-2232). Ref. AQN.

Children: N   Pets: N   Smoking: Y   Handicap Access: N   Payment: All

St. Michael's

BROOK COTTAGE   *Rates: budget*
Open: year-round   *Minimum Stay: one week*

What a perfect vacation hideaway for keen botanists, naturalists and plain old nature lovers! The grounds of this delightful small cottage set in a large woodland garden feature the bubbling waters of a trout stream. The attractively furnished rooms accommodate three in one double and one single bedroom and include an entrance hall, a living/ dining room with a cozy open fireplace, a kitchen and the additional joy of a large furnished garden for afternoon repose. Here, you can't help but roam through countryside where farmlands and woods meet. Nearby opportunities for sailing and fishing are also plentiful. Contact: Castles, Cottages & Flats in Ireland and U.K. Ltd., Box 261, Westwood, MA 02090. Call 617-329-4680. Ref. 2010.

Children: Y   Pets: N   Smoking: Y   Handicap Access: N   Payment: P

HERTFORDSHIRE

St. Albans

ST. ALBANS MEWS   *Rates: budget-inexpensive*
Open: year-round   *Minimum Stay: one week*

The ancient cathedral city of St. Albans offers easy access to London and the rolling hills of the Cotswolds. Located within walking distance of a shopping mall and close to three sports complexes, theaters and music halls, these townhouse apartments provide modern comfort to guests. The smallest flat has room for two to four in one twin bedroom and a double bed-settee in the living room. Two other flats are larger, sleeping four to six in one double and one twin bedroom and a double bed settee in the living room. London is only 20 minutes away by rail. Contact: British Travel Associates, P.O. Box 299, Elkton, VA 22827. Call 1-800-327-6097 (in Virginia, 703-298-2232). Ref. F3657/3655/3656.

Children: Y   Pets: N   Smoking: Y   Handicap Access: N   Payment: All

HUMBERSIDE

Boynton

BOYNTON HALL DAIRY   *Rates: budget*
Open: year-round   *Minimum Stay: one week*

This unusual rental was once the dairy of the Boynton Hall estate, and it still has many of its late 18th-century elements. The original stone-flagged floor, stone slab shelves, Gothic arched doors and windows and gallery lounge overlooking the dining room send you back to the country living of more than two centuries ago. The huge double bedroom for two has been designed with the roof timbers in place; a walled garden with patio provides peace and seclusion. The resort town of Bridlington is two miles away, and York, site of the first-century Roman capital in Britannia, about a half an hour by car. Contact: British Travel Associates, P.O. Box 299, Elkton, VA 22827. Call 1-800-327-6097 (in Virginia, 703-298-2232). Ref. A1889.

Children: Y   Pets: N   Smoking: Y   Handicap Access: N   Payment: All

KENT

Boughton Aluph

WARREN FARM   *Rates: budget-inexpensive*
Open: year-round   *Minimum Stay: one week*

The tranquility of rural England permeates this 130-acre sheep farm surrounded by Forestry Commission woodlands. Enjoy the serenity of country life or visit nearby Canterbury, Leeds and Chilham Castle. The farmhouse has a living room, a kitchen and a dining room and sleeps six in four bedrooms (a double, a twin and two singles). Shops and a pub are located less than two miles away. Golf, horseback riding and fishing are also available nearby. Contact: British Travel Associates, P.O. Box 299, Elkton, VA 22827. Call 1-800-327-6097 (in Virginia, 703-298-2232). Ref. F4407.

Children: Y   Pets: N   Smoking: Y   Handicap Access: N   Payment: All

Cowden

HOLE COTTAGE   *Rates: inexpensive-moderate*
Open: year-round   *Minimum Stay: three nights*

You'll find this two-bedroom dwelling by a babbling brook in a pretty woodland clearing. Just a ten-minute walk from the town of Cowden, Hole Cottage is actually the surviving wing of a very fine medieval hall. The leaded-glass windows, beamed ceiling and open fireplace are all suggestive of the cottage's origins and add to its charm. Upstairs is a large double bedroom, a smaller bedroom with two bunk beds and a bath; downstairs is a kitchen and a living/dining area furnished in a traditional yet cozy style. Accessible both by train and by car, Hole Cottage is central to many historical sites and places of interest, including a number of the fine public gardens so popular in the south of England. Contact: The Landmark Trust, Shottesbrooke, Maidenhead, Berks, England SL6 3SW. Call 011-44-628-82-5925.

Children: Y Pets: Y Smoking: Y Handicap Access: N Payment: C, P, T, V, M

Elham

KENT COTTAGE   *Rates: budget*
Open: year-round   *Minimum Stay: one week*

Gently rolling hills and twisting lanes make for some of the prettiest scenery in southeast Kent, where this 15th-century cottage is set on the edge of an orchard. Inside, a sunny living room provides a comfy haven, while one twin bedroom and an extra cot sleeps two adults and one child. A short drive takes you to Canterbury, destination of Chaucer's famous pilgrims and scene of some the most notable events in English history. The cathedral there recalls England's conversion to Christianity in the 6th century, which began in Canterbury. Folkestone, from which travelers crossing the English Channel to France by boat and hovercraft, is also nearby. Contact: British Travel Associates, P.O. Box 299, Elkton, VA 22827. Call 1-800-327-6097 (in Virginia, 703-298-2232). Ref. F1338.

Children: Y   Pets: N   Smoking: Y   Handicap Access: N   Payment: All

Sellindge

SELLINDGE HOUSE   *Rates: budget-inexpensive*
Open: year-round   *Minimum Stay: one week*

Rent one wing of this attractively decorated and refurbished 18th-century house situated at the end of a private drive. The wing accommodates six comfortably in a living room, a dining room, a kitchen, a utility room and three bedrooms (one double and two twin). Within walking distance, you'll find shops and a pub. Further afield, you can enjoy touring, golf, horseback riding, tennis, boating and sea fishing—or even a day trip to France. Contact: British Travel Associates, P.O. Box 299, Elkton, VA 22827. Call 1-800-327-6097 (in Virginia, 703-298-2232). Ref. F1285.

Children: Y   Pets: N   Smoking: Y   Handicap Access: N   Payment: All

West Peckham, Maidstone

THE OAST   *Rates: inexpensive-deluxe*
Open: year-round   *Minimum Stay: one week*

This twin oasthouse, which once served as a kiln for drying grain, is part of a complex of Victorian farmhouses that date from the mid 1900s. The circular building has been renovated to include a dining room, kitchen/breakfast room and large living room that opens onto the garden. Cook for yourself in the modern kitchen, equipped with a microwave and coffee maker, or take the 50-yard walk to a pub for your meals. One master bedroom and three twins sleep a total of eight, and a gallery bedroom (unsuitable for children under five) sleeps two more. A tennis court and play area are available by arrangement with the owner. Contact: British Travel Associates, P.O. Box 299, Elkton, VA 22827. Call 1-800-327-6097 (in Virginia, 703-298-2232). Ref. PEE.

Children: Y   Pets: N   Smoking: Y   Handicap Access: Y   Payment: All

LEICESTERSHIRE

Corby

STREET HOUSE OF ROCKINGHAM CASTLE   *Rates: inexpensive-expensive*
Open: April to September   *Minimum Stay: one week*

This hilltop castle was built 900 years ago by William the Conqueror, acquired by Henry VIII in the 16th century, and has been owned by his descendants ever since. Street House, a private apartment in the castle, is available for rent and sleeps seven in three spacious bedrooms (one double and two twin) plus a cot. The kitchen is old-fashioned yet modern, and has a dishwasher. You can walk the castle grounds, which has acres of beautiful gardens and lawns, take in the panoramic view across the River Welland Valley, looking towards Stamford and the Fens, or take a dip in the outdoor swimming pool. Contact: British Travel Associates, P.O. Box 299, Elkton, VA 22827. Call 1-800-327-6097 (in Virginia, 703-298-2232). Ref. QFV.

Children: **Y** Pets: **N** Smoking: **Y** Handicap Access: **N** Payment: **All**

Rockingham

PASTURES HOUSE

Open: year-round

Rates: inexpensive-expensive

Minimum Stay: one week

Situated between Oxford and Cambridge some 90 miles from central London, Pastures House is the epitome of English rural affluence. Great care has been taken in maintaining the property's walled garden and croquet lawn outside and the well-appointed drawing room (with a large fireplace), dining room and study inside. Four bedrooms (a large double, two twins and a single) sleep seven. The surrounding countryside is just as lush, with fine trout fishing three miles away at Eyebrook Reservoir and a bird-watching paradise ten miles away at Rutland Water. Contact: British Travel Associates, P.O. Box 299, Elkton, VA 22827. Call 1-800-327-6097 (in Virginia, 703-298-2232). Ref. QPT.

Children: **Y** Pets: **N** Smoking: **Y** Handicap Access: **N** Payment: **All**

LINCOLNSHIRE

Folkingham

THE HOUSE OF CORRECTION

Open: year-round

Rates: budget-inexpensive

Minimum Stay: three nights

Despite its forbidding name, this converted jail makes a very pleasant and elegant apartment for four. Actually, the building was the grand entrance to grounds that once housed an important medieval castle and then a succession of jails. Inside, the rooms are spacious, airy and beautifully furnished. The ground floor has an eat-in kitchen and a living room with an open fireplace. Reached by two staircases, the second level contains a twin bedroom and a bathroom. The top floor is a bedroom with a brass double bed and a large window that gives the best views over the grounds. A small town with many fine buildings, Folkingham lies within a short driving distance of the protected bay known as the "Wash" on the east Midland coast. Contact: The Landmark Trust, Shottesbrooke, Maidenhead, Berks, England SL6 3SW. Call 011-44-628-82-5925.

Children: **Y** Pets: **Y** Smoking: **Y** Handicap Access: **N** Payment: **C, P, T, V, M**

Brancaster Staithe

NORTH NORFOLK COTTAGE
Open: year-round

Rates: budget
Minimum Stay: one week

The Norfolk Broads are an area of outstanding beauty, a land of interconnected waterways thought to have been created by extensive peat cutting in Saxon times. The Broads and the nearby North Sea coast offer many opportunities for wind surfing, sailing, swimming, and several bird reserves, golf courses and preserved areas make this superb country for vacationing. The cottage sleeps four in one double and one twin bedroom; the living room with its open fireplace, the color TV, the garden and the eat-in kitchen offer country comfort to guests. Sandringham Estate, Holkham Hall and many attractive villages and market towns are nearby. Contact: British Travel Associates, P.O. Box 299, Elkton, VA 22827. Call 1-800-327-6097 (in Virginia, 703-298-2232). Ref. F3287.

Children: **Y**   Pets: **N**   Smoking: **Y**   Handicap Access: **N**   Payment: **All**

Northrepps

NORTHREPPS COTTAGE
Open: year-round

Rates: budget
Minimum Stay: one week

This pretty flint cottage stands only half a mile from the coast and offers good budget accommodations about 25 miles from the resort town of Great Yarmouth. Guests enjoy private quarters surrounded by farmland just outside the village of Northrepps. The large living room has a heavy-beamed ceiling; the double and twin bedrooms sleep four. Take time to visit the 12th-century church of St. Nicholas and the Elizabethan Museum in Great Yarmouth, or play some golf at one of the four courses that lie within five miles of the cottage. Contact: British Travel Associates, P.O. Box 299, Elkton, VA 22827. Call 1-800-327-6097 (in Virginia, 703-298-2232). Ref. F2928.

Children: **Y**   Pets: **N**   Smoking: **Y**   Handicap Access: **N**   Payment: **All**

Salthouse

CLEY COTTAGE
Open: year-round

Rates: budget-inexpensive
Minimum Stay: one week

The North Sea coast is only a quarter mile from this comfortable family cottage, whose front bedroom has a good view across the marshes of the Cley Bird Sanctuary. The cottage has room for six to seven people in a living room, a dining room, a kitchen and three bedrooms (one double, one twin, one with three singles). Inland or along the coast, beautiful scenery beckons walkers, who will also admire the many historic houses along the way. Several golf courses are nearby, and the North Norfolk Steam Railway, based in Sheringham, travels along the coast. Contact: British Travel Associates, P.O. Box 299, Elkton, VA 22827. Call 1-800-327-6097 (in Virginia, 703-298-2232). Ref. F3572.

Children: **Y**   Pets: **N**   Smoking: **Y**   Handicap Access: **N**   Payment: **All**

Rates: budget-inexpensive
Minimum Stay: one week

...h, you'll find no better place to stay than this cottage ...rm that's close to a river and to the sea. The cottage has ...th modern conveniences and offers a living room with a a... ...nd kitchen, plus room for four to sleep in two bedrooms (one dou.. and one twin). Nearby shops and pubs meet your daily needs, and the resort city of Great Yarmouth, the Norfolk Broads and the cathedral city of Norwich offer abundant sightseeing opportunities. Contact: British Travel Associates, P.O. Box 299, Elkton, VA 22827. Call 1-800-327-6097 (in Virginia, 703-298-2232). Ref. F5052.
Children: Y   Pets: N   Smoking: Y   Handicap Access: N   Payment: All

Upper Tasburgh
DORMER COTTAGE   *Rates: budget*
Open: year-round   *Minimum Stay: one week*
Ah, Norfolk, where green and gray fens and broads meet the beautiful coastline and all the world seems devoted to beauty! This semi-detached cottage adjoining a traditional farmhouse in a quiet country village provides just the right rural setting from which to explore this wonderful corner of England. Centrally heated accommodations for four (one double, one twin bedroom) also include a living room and an eat-in kitchen, and guests are invited to share the beautiful landscaped gardens with the farm owner. Walks in the nearby forests of Rockingham and Sherwood or lunch at a friendly village pub are just the beginnings of all the wonder and pleasure a vacation at Dormer Cottage assures. Contact: Castles, Cottages & Flats in Ireland and U.K. Ltd., Box 261, Westwood, MA 02090. Call 617-329-4680. Ref. 1487.
Children: Y   Pets: N   Smoking: Y   Handicap Access: N   Payment: P

NORTH YORKSHIRE

Airton
CORN MILL FLAT   *Rates: budget*
Open: year-round   *Minimum Stay: one week*
Trout fishing and rock climbing are only steps away from this flat, part of a 12th-century corn mill in the town of Airton, which lies along the Pennine Way. The flat itself has been renovated with modern amenities, including electric heaters in every room, a heated towel rail in the bathroom and a coffee maker in the kitchen. Two bedrooms—one double and one small bunk—sleep three to four. The nearby historic market town of Skipton draws visitors to its 14th-century Holy Trinity Church, where the Earls of Cumberland are buried. Malham, three miles away, offers magnificent limestone outcroppings. Contact: British Travel Associates, P.O. Box 299, Elkton, VA 22827. Call 1-800-327-6097 (in Virginia, 703-298-2232). Ref. E7494.
Children: Y   Pets: N   Smoking: Y   Handicap Access: N   Payment: All

Cayton

KILLERBY OLD HALL   *Rates: budget-deluxe*
Open: year-round   *Minimum Stay: one week*

The ancient manor of Killerby Old Hall is mentioned in the "Domesday Book," the remarkable 11th-century census of English country life. Since then, the manor has added an indoor swimming pool open year-round and heated to a constant 84 degrees. The old stables have been converted into two separate cottages for six, with a sitting/dining/kitchen area, a twin bedroom and a large double with an extra single and a cot in each. The 16th-century manor house boasts early paneling and wainscoting and a fine inglenook fireplace. Its many luxurious modern features include a sauna, a double sunken bath with a solarium and a large kitchen. The master bedroom has a four-poster bed; three double bedrooms, a twin and an extra cot sleep nine more. Babysitting and maid service are available by arrangement. Contact: British Travel Associates, P.O. Box 299, Elkton, VA 22827. Call 1-800-327-6097 (in Virginia, 703-298-2232). Ref. KKW/KKV/KKU.

Children: Y   Pets: N   Smoking: Y   Handicap Access: N   Payment: All

Cragg Vale

GATEHOUSE LODGE   *Rates: budget-inexpensive*
Open: year-round   *Minimum Stay: one week*

Much of this 17th-century gatehouse lodge was rebuilt in the 1890s Arts and Crafts style by Richard Norman Shaw, the architect of New Scotland Yard. He created a fine mixture of old and new in the traditional box gutters, stone-roofed turrets, leaded windows, chimney pieces and superb woodwork throughout. Set on half an acre of gardens and woodland, Gatehouse Lodge is attractively decorated with antique furniture and period pieces, including a still-functioning gas range that once belonged to the actor Charles Laughton. Seven to eight can stay in this large house, which includes three bedrooms (two doubles, one twin) and a sofa bed in the lounge. Guests can use the private tennis courts by arrangement. Contact: British Travel Associates, P.O. Box 299, Elkton, VA 22827. Call 1-800-327-6097 (in Virginia, 703-298-2232). Ref. E7104.

Children: Y   Pets: N   Smoking: Y   Handicap Access: N   Payment: All

Helmsley

CASTLE COTTAGES   *Rates: budget-moderate*
Open: year-round   *Minimum Stay: one week*

You can look out from either of these two cottages and see Helmsley's Castle. Orchard Cottage is set among fruit trees and sleeps five in one bunk bedroom, one double and an extra cot. There's also a kitchen/dining room and a large sitting room with a fireplace. Osbourne Cottage, which overlooks a stream, is the larger of the two and has a sitting room with an open oak-beam ceiling, a large stone fireplace and a piano. Two twin bedrooms, one double and an extra cot sleep seven. The cottages share a patio and barbecue. Horseback riding and sightseeing are easily accessible. Contact: British Travel Associates, P.O.

Box 299, Elkton, VA 22827. Call 1-800-327-6097 (in Virginia, 703-298-2232). Ref. KMC/KMD.

Children: **Y**   Pets: **N**   Smoking: **Y**   Handicap Access: **N**   Payment: All

Hessay
ROSE COTTAGE

Rates: budget-moderate
Minimum Stay: one week

Open: year-round

You will find this luxurious and lovingly appointed cottage on the very edge of a small village in the beautiful open countryside. The colorful market towns of the region and the forested National Trust properties lie nearby. Only a short drive will bring you to the historic richness of York and Scarborough, Homsee and other traditional resorts of the east coast. The three-bedroom home features many comforts, including an entrance lobby, a utility room, an eat-in kitchen, three sitting/living rooms and two color TVs. The garden that surrounds the house includes a pond and a barbecue and is generously furnished for outdoor living. Contact: Castles, Cottages & Flats in Ireland and U.K. Ltd., Box 261, Westwood, MA 02090. Call 617-329-4680. Ref. 1100.

Children: **Y**   Pets: **N**   Smoking: **Y**   Handicap Access: **N**   Payment: P

Middleham
BEEVOR COTTAGE

Rates: budget-inexpensive
Minimum Stay: one week

Open: year-round

You might recognize the scenery in and around Middleham from its many appearances in the BBC television series "All Creatures Great and Small." Horses from a nearby racing stable trot past this stone cottage each morning on their way to workouts at nearby Middleham Moor. The adjacent cobbled market square and nearby Middleham Castle are equally appealing; shops are just 50 yards away. Beevor Cottage, whose sitting/dining room features a fireplace, sleeps four to five in two bedrooms. Contact: British Travel Associates, P.O. Box 299, Elkton, VA 22827. Call 1-800-327-6097 (in Virginia, 703-298-2232). Ref. KRK.

Children: **Y**   Pets: **N**   Smoking: **Y**   Handicap Access: **N**   Payment: All

Sleights
STATION HOUSES

Rates: budget-inexpensive
Minimum Stay: one week

Open: year-round

The stone station master's house and converted village train station typify the architecture that developed along the Victorian North Eastern Railway when it was built. Cars of the Esk Valley Railway still make 14 stops daily in Sleights. At the trains' next stop in Grosmont, passengers can connect to sightseeing trips on the scenic North Yorkshire Moors' steam railway. There are two houses for rent here: The station master's house, which sleeps five to seven, has one double bedroom with two extra singles, one bunk and one cot. The converted village station sleeps five to six in one double bedroom with an extra single, one twin and one single. The shop and pub are 50 yards away. Salmon fishing, boating, croquet and riding facilities are nearby, as is the North Yorkshire Moors National Park. Contact: British Travel Associates, P.O. Box 299, Elkton, VA 22827. Call 1-800-327-6097 (in Virginia, 703-298-2232). Ref. A2147/A2148.

Children: Y   Pets: N   Smoking: Y   Handicap Access: N   Payment: All

Thoralby

THORALBY FARMHOUSE   *Rates: budget-moderate*
Open: year-round   *Minimum Stay: one week*

The natural beauty of England surrounds this self-contained wing of a 17th-century farmhouse on a working farm in the center of Yorkshire Dales National Park. Stone-mullioned windows, oak paneling and several fireplaces lend it period charm, but many modern conveniences have been installed during renovations. Four bedrooms (two double, one twin and three singles) will accommodate eight to nine visitors. Bishopdale and the moors, offering fabulous walks, riding and fishing, are nearby. Contact: British Travel Associates, P.O. Box 299, Elkton, VA 22827. Call 1-800-327-6097 (in Virginia, 703-298-2232). Ref. E125.

Children: Y   Pets: N   Smoking: Y   Handicap Access: N   Payment: All

York City

FEVERSHAM HOUSE   *Rates: budget-inexpensive*
Open: year-round   *Minimum Stay: one week*

For a special look at the city of York, this handsome apartment in the Jewbury/Monkgate area overlooks the walls of this ancient town. Many of the city's attractions—the Minister, the Shambles and Jorvik Centre—are only a short walk away. Enter the apartment through a private lobby with the benefit of an entry intercom system. On the second floor you'll find a living/dining room with a TV and a double bed settee, a kitchen and one double bedroom. Outside the city but only a short drive away, the wild beauty of the North Yorkshire moors brings a change of scenery. Castle Howard, the scene of "Brideshead Revisited," and the Flamingoland Zoo and Fun Park suggest the great variety of amusements also available in this open north country. Contact: Castles, Cottages & Flats in Ireland and U.K. Ltd., Box 261, Westwood, MA 02090. Call 617-329-4680. Ref. 1321.

Children: Y   Pets: N   Smoking: Y   Handicap Access: N   Payment: P

NORTHUMBERLAND

Alnmouth

WATCHTOWER   *Rates: budget*
Open: year-round   *Minimum Stay: one week*

In Georgian times, harbor masters scanned the sea and Alnmouth Harbor for incoming ships from this watchtower. The view is still unobstructed, and the building is the oldest in Alnmouth. Its Georgian roots show up in the decorative plasterwork, classically designed fireplace, enclosed sun patio and the stone entrance. Upstairs, relax in the open-plan sitting/dining/kitchen area, or take the spiral staircase to the double bedroom on the ground floor. Shops and pubs are within 50 yards and the market town of Alnwick, on the River Aln, is nearby. The Scottish border lies about 20 miles away. Contact: British Travel Associates, P.O. Box 299, Elkton, VA 22827. Call 1-800-327-6097 (in Virginia, 703-298-2232). Ref. A172.

Children: **Y**   Pets: **N**   Smoking: **Y**   Handicap Access: **N**   Payment: **All**

Belford

WEST LODGE   *Rates: budget-inexpensive*
Open: year-round   *Minimum Stay: one week*

When Northumberland was the Anglo-Saxon kingdom of Northumbria, its hard-working monks made it the cultural center of England. The famous castles at Bamburgh and Lindisfarne still stand only four miles from West Lodge, one of 16 apartments in Belford Hall. The apartment for two people has a small galley kitchen, a dining area, a double bedroom and a sitting room with a sofa bed. Fifteen miles to the north lies the Scottish border; there's good bird-watching on the Farne Islands; and horseback riding is available in the Cheviot Hills nearby. Contact: British Travel Associates, P.O. Box 299, Elkton, VA 22827. Call 1-800-327-6097 (in Virginia, 703-298-2232). Ref. MCL.

Children: **Y**   Pets: **N**   Smoking: **Y**   Handicap Access: **N**   Payment: **All**

Craster

GEORGIAN HOUSE   *Rates: budget-inexpensive*
Open: year-round   *Minimum Stay: one week*

The south wing of this beautiful Georgian country house, which has been in the same family for centuries, is attached to a tower built in 1129 and rebuilt in 1432. Surrounded by six acres of gardens and woods, the house has a sweeping hallway, classically designed fireplaces and magnificent stairways. The wing is large enough for eight, with a drawing room, a library, a kitchen/dining room and four bedrooms (one double and three twins). Shop or dine a half mile away, or take a short walk to the coastal fishing village of Craster. Contact: British Travel Associates, P.O. Box 299, Elkton, VA 22827. Call 1-800-327-6097 (in Virginia, 703-298-2232). Ref. A3165

Children: **Y**   Pets: **N**   Smoking: **Y**   Handicap Access: **N**   Payment: **All**

OXFORDSHIRE

East Lockinge

SMITHY COTTAGE   *Rates: budget-inexpensive*
Open: year-round   *Minimum Stay: one week*

Deep in the beautiful English countryside lies a privately owned village of cottages boasting superb views over the park land and lakes of East Lockinge. The tastefully decorated Smithy Cottage has a sitting room and a dining room with large fireplaces, a modern kitchen with a dishwasher, a playroom with many toys and a pretty garden. The playroom also serves as a single bedroom; another single, a double and a twin, plus an extra cot, sleep a total of six to seven. Walk through the Lambourn Downs, the Cotswolds or the Thames Valley, all nearby.

Rent boats at Goring or visit Oxford and Newbury. Contact: British Travel Associates, P.O. Box 299, Elkton, VA 22827. Call 1-800-327-6097 (in Virginia, 703-298-2232). Ref. NCM.

Children: **Y**   Pets: **N**   Smoking: **Y**   Handicap Access: **N**   Payment: All

Headington

HEADINGTON FLAT   *Rates: budget*
Open: year-round   *Minimum Stay: one week*

This sunny second-floor apartment is only two miles from the center of Oxford, close enough to walk to the town's famous university, theaters, the Bodleian Library and the Ashmolean Museum. If that's not enough for you, there's regular bus service to London and "Nipper" buses every few minutes to Oxford's center. The roomy apartment has an open-plan living room with dining and kitchen areas and a shared garden. One double bedroom and one twin provide sleeping accommodations for four. It's only a short ride to the Cotswolds, the Chilterns, the Thames Valley and Blenheim Palace. Contact: British Travel Associates, P.O. Box 299, Elkton, VA 22827. Call 1-800-327-6097 (in Virginia, 703-298-2232). Ref. F4027.

Children: **Y**   Pets: **N**   Smoking: **Y**   Handicap Access: **N**   Payment: All

Henley-on-Thames

TUDOR COTTAGE   *Rates: budget-inexpensive*
Open: year-round   *Minimum Stay: one week*

This Tudor house was built in 1450, the year Cade's Rebellion threatened King Henry VI's reign. It stands now as the oldest house in Henley, providing an excellent starting point for touring the Thames Valley. The kitchen, dining room, spacious living room and double bedroom offer comfort for two. Phyllis Court is within walking distance, as is the site of the Royal Regatta, which takes place on the Thames in the last week of July. There are numerous pubs, shops and restaurants in the neighborhood. Contact: British Travel Associates, P.O. Box 299, Elkton, VA 22827. Call 1-800-327-6097 (in Virginia, 703-298-2232). Ref. PLL.

Children: **N**   Pets: **N**   Smoking: **Y**   Handicap Access: **N**   Payment: All

Iffley

THE OLD PARSONAGE   *Rates: inexpensive-moderate*
Open: year-round   *Minimum Stay: three nights*

Behind this house, a long garden stretches back to the sleepy Thames; at its front is Mill Lane, one of the many streets lined with high stone walls in this university town. Inside is a three-bedroom apartment that dates back to the 15th century, containing three bedrooms, a bathroom and a kitchen. The living room is wood paneled and has a fine open fireplace. A staircase in a separate tower leads to the upstairs rooms, one of which is in the attic. The house is full of unique decorative touches, such as stained-glass windows, molded ceilings and a unique Latin inscription running along one wall. Nearby Oxford offers fine restaurants, entertainment and sporting facilities. Not far away are the pretty villages of the Cotswolds district. Contact: The Landmark Trust, Shottesbrooke, Maidenhead, Berks, England SL6 3SW. Call 011-44-628-82-5925.

Children: Y Pets: Y Smoking: Y Handicap Access: N Payment: C, P, T, V, M

Little Rollright, near Chipping Norton

THE OLD RECTORY
Open: year-round

Rates: budget-inexpensive
Minimum Stay: one week

This elegantly furnished 17th-century house is set amid a sweeping garden in the ancient hamlet of Little Rollright in the heart of the Oxfordshire countryside. The two-story, three-bedroom residence, accommodating up to six, includes wall-to-wall carpeting, a spacious and sunny dining/sitting room, both a main and a galley kitchen and a barbecue outside. Oxford, Stratford-Upon-Avon and Blenheim Palace are all a short hop away; the area also features fine riding and golf. Access to private tennis courts and fishing grounds can be arranged. Contact: British Travel Associates, P.O. Box 299, Elkton, VA 22827. Call 1-800-327-6097 (in Virginia, 703-298-2232).

Children: Y   Pets: N   Smoking: Y   Handicap Access: N   Payment: All

Oxford

7 ST. MICHAEL'S STREET
Open: year-round

Rates: budget-inexpensive
Minimum Stay: three nights

If you can imagine sitting in a book-lined study while the sun streams in through a bay window, then you can imagine yourself in this marvelous set of rooms in the heart of Oxford. Tasteful decor and some fine paintings complete the gracious Edwardian feeling of these upstairs rooms. There is one twin bedroom, a small kitchen and a bathroom. The building is owned by the Oxford Union Society, formed in the last century as a debating society. It is an architectural treat—its window bays were painted by the young D.G. Rossetti, among other artists. From here the whole of Oxford is at your feet—whether strolling along the river, eating in one of the many lively restaurants or just wandering the streets is your desire. Contact: The Landmark Trust, Shottesbrooke, Maidenhead, Berks, England SL6 3SW. Call 011-44-628-82-5925.

Children: Y Pets: N Smoking: Y Handicap Access: N Payment: C, P, T, V, M

SOMERSET

Cricket St. Thomas

WEST LODGE
Open: year-round

Rates: inexpensive-moderate
Minimum Stay: one week

This Victorian lodge served as Penelope Keith's home in the popular British TV series, "To the Manor Born!" The house sits on the edge of the Cricket St. Thomas Wildlife Park and is ten miles from the Dorset coast. Inside, a beamed entrance hall gives way to a spacious living room, which opens onto the furnished patio and garden. The main floor has a small study, a compact modern kitchen, and a twin bedroom; climb the oak stairs to reach one double and one twin bedroom. During the day, shop in the market town of Chard, two miles away, then golf, sail or ride, all within 20 minutes of the lodge. Contact: British Travel Associates, P.O. Box 299, Elkton, VA 22827. Call 1-800-327-6097 (in Virginia, 703-298-2232). Ref. EGT.

Children: Y   Pets: N   Smoking: Y   Handicap Access: N   Payment: All

North Curry

CURRY COTTAGE   *Rates: budget*
Open: year-round   *Minimum Stay: one week*

A quaint cottage and a garden flat flank a magnificent Georgian house and offer views of the beautifully landscaped walled garden. The cottage sleeps four in one double bedroom and one twin, and has a living room and a kitchen. The upstairs flat has a large living room/dining area, a kitchen and two twin bedrooms. Visit historic Taunton, which was founded by the Saxons in 705. There, the Duke of Monmouth initiated an unsuccessful challenge to James II in 1685; he was later beheaded in Sedgemoor. For active people, superb horseback riding and nature paths abound in Exmoor National Park and the Quantocks. Contact: British Travel Associates, P.O. Box 299, Elkton, VA 22827. Call 1-800-327-6097 (in Virginia, 703-298-2232). Ref. F4059/F4060.

Children: Y   Pets: N   Smoking: Y   Handicap Access: N   Payment: All

Old Cleeve

MAY'S COTTAGE   *Rates: budget-inexpensive*
Open: year-round   *Minimum Stay: one week*

This beautifully restored thatched cottage situated in a charming village offers an ideal base for a seaside holiday, with nearby beaches and the gorgeous rambling countryside in every direction. Complete with its own cottage garden, the three-bedroom house sleeps four (and a baby!) and includes a kitchen and living room, as well as the convenience of a washing machine and the delight of a wood-burning stove. From here, you can wander the rolling chalk hills of Dorset or marvel at the magnificent moorlands and sandstone cliffs of Devon, then have your fill of the famous Somerset cider. Contact: Castles, Cottages & Flats in Ireland and U.K. Ltd., Box 261, Westwood, MA 02090. Call 617-329-4680. Ref. 4003.

Children: Y   Pets: N   Smoking: Y   Handicap Access: N   Payment: P

Tintinhull

STABLE COTTAGE   *Rates: budget*
Open: year-round   *Minimum Stay: one week*

Recently renovated to include a modern kitchen, a living room/dining room and two bedrooms (one double, one twin), this converted stable cottage accommodates four. The cottage provides a cozy base from which to tour the many historic houses and gardens nearby. In the market town of Yeovil, visit the 14th-century church of St. John the Baptist and explore Cadbury Castle. The resort city of Weymouth, about 40 minutes south of Tintinhull, offers shops, boating, swimming and ferries to the Channel Islands and to France. Contact: British Travel Associates, P.O. Box 299, Elkton, VA 22827. Call 1-800-327-6097 (in Virginia, 703-298-2232). Ref. F3405.

Children: **Y**   Pets: **N**   Smoking: **Y**   Handicap Access: **N**   Payment: **All**

Wellington

FARM COTTAGE   *Rates: budget*
Open: year-round   *Minimum Stay: one week*

This cottage is set on a working dairy and sheep farm of 80 acres. Located within easy walking distance of the bustling market town of Wellington, it accommodates four to six in a living room, a dining room, a kitchen and two bedrooms (one double and one twin). There's a double sofa bed in the living room. The town lies equidistant from both coasts, where you can fish, swim and sail in the Bristol and English channels. Walk or ride through the Exmoor National Park or visit the historic town of Exeter, established by the Romans nearly 2,000 years ago and site of a 12th-century cathedral and guild hall, plus a maritime museum. Contact: British Travel Associates, P.O. Box 299, Elkton, VA 22827. Call 1-800-327-6097 (in Virginia, 703-298-2232). Ref. F4773.

Children: **Y**   Pets: **N**   Smoking: **Y**   Handicap Access: **N**   Payment: **All**

SUSSEX

Lewes

LAUGHTON PLACE   *Rates: budget-moderate*
Open: year-round   *Minimum Stay: three nights*

Imagine living in a tall castle tower looking out over the rolling landscape of the Sussex Downs, and you can picture Laughton Place. Once part of a much larger house, the tower has been cleverly converted into an unusual four-story apartment. On the ground floor is an eat-in kitchen and a bathroom with a shower. A stone staircase spirals to the upper floors, providing glimpses of the countryside through window slits recessed into the massive walls. On the second floor is a living room with floor-to-ceiling leaded-glass windows. The third floor contains a double bedroom and the fourth, a twin. Be sure to visit the southern "holiday coast" of England, including the seaside resort of Brighton, with its famous piers, hotels and pebble beaches. Contact: The Landmark Trust, Shottesbrooke, Maidenhead, Berks, England SL6 3SW. Call 011-44-628-82-5925.

Children: **Y** Pets: **Y** Smoking: **Y** Handicap Access: **N** Payment: **C, P, T, V, M**

WARWICKSHIRE

Alcester

WOOD BEVINGTON MANOR   *Rates: budget*
Open: year-round   *Minimum Stay: one week*

This ancient manor house dates back to the reign of King Edward III—about six hundred years ago—and is located in a tiny country hamlet. Four bedrooms accommodate eight and the house includes a large entrance hall, a dining room, a spacious and thoughtfully furnished living room and a kitchen with a dishwasher and washing machine. Open fireplaces and central heat as well as a high chair and a cot make this home ideal for a family with a small child. From this gracious home, you can fill your days with country rambles and cross-country rides to the Cotswolds, the rivers and the historic sites of central England. Contact: Castles, Cottages & Flats in Ireland and U.K. Ltd., Box 261, Westwood, MA 02090. Call 617-329-4680. Ref. 2064.

Children: **Y**   Pets: **N**   Smoking: **Y**   Handicap Access: **N**   Payment: **P**

Ettington

THE CHANTRY   *Rates: budget-inexpensive*
Open: year-round   *Minimum Stay: one week*
Renovated and furnished for comfort and warmth, the Chantry dates from 1276. Authentic details distinguish the stone-flagged living room with superb beamed ceiling, stud walls and wood-burning stove, but modern amenities, such as a microwave oven, offer convenience in the dining room and kitchen. Two double bedrooms are furnished in oak and pine, one with a four-poster bed and a separate dressing area, the other with twin beds. Guests can find horseback riding and a pub/restaurant in the neighborhood; Stratford, Warwick, Oxford, Cheltenham and the Cotswolds are nearby. Contact: British Travel Associates, P.O. Box 299, Elkton, VA 22827. Call 1-800-327-6097 (in Virginia, 703-298-2232). Ref. QGF.

Children: **Y**   Pets: **N**   Smoking: **Y**   Handicap Access: **N**   Payment: **All**

Pebworth

PEBWORTH COTTAGE   *Rates: budget*
Open: year-round   *Minimum Stay: one week*
This cottage for four is situated next to a working farm and surrounded by the fertile lands of the Vale of Evesham. The setting is ideal for those who enjoy walking along quiet country lanes. Two bedrooms (one double and one twin) sleep four; a living room and a kitchen are also included. The Cotswolds and Stratford-upon-Avon, home of the Royal Shakespeare Theatre (whose season runs from April to January), are nearby. Contact: British Travel Associates, P.O. Box 299, Elkton, VA 22827. Call 1-800-327-6097 (in Virginia, 703-298-2232). Ref. F1810.

Children: **Y**   Pets: **N**   Smoking: **Y**   Handicap Access: **N**   Payment: **All**

Preston-on-Stour

PRIEST'S HOUSE   *Rates: budget-inexpensive*
Open: year-round   *Minimum Stay: one week*
Built around 1450, the Priest's House was once part of a monastery, a fact revealed in Spartan features such as low doorways, sloping walls and floors and steep staircases. Now, however, the house is located in a privately owned village of Tudor cottages, with modern conveniences close at hand. A nearby country club, where you can enjoy

squash, tennis, a Jacuzzi and swimming, offers daily and half-daily rates. The house has a modern kitchen, an oak-beamed sitting/dining room and a corner fireplace with a log-burning stove for added warmth. On the upper floor, a double and twin bedroom plus an extra cot sleep five. Historic Stratford-upon-Avon is just four miles away. Contact: British Travel Associates, P.O. Box 299, Elkton, VA 22827. Call 1-800-327-6097 (in Virginia, 703-298-2232). Ref. QAZ.

Children: Y   Pets: N   Smoking: Y   Handicap Access: N   Payment: All

Stratford-on-Avon

4 CHERRY STREET   *Rates: budget-inexpensive*
Open: year-round   *Minimum Stay: one week*

This handsomely renovated cottage built in 1852 is a relative new-comer to this town, surrounded as it is by Shakespeare's spirit within a short drive of ancient Cotswold villages. The carefully appointed and centrally heated rooms of this home for five include a particularly comfortable living room with an open fireplace and a number of well-used books and games, a dining room, a kitchen and three bedrooms. There's even a walled and fenced garden complete with barbecue. Devotees of the bard will find endless delight in exploring this town and attending performances of his work at the theaters of the Royal Shakespeare Company. Contact: Castles, Cottages & Flats in Ireland and U.K. Ltd., Box 261, Westwood, MA 02090. Call 617-329-4680. Ref. 2015.

Children: Y   Pets: N   Smoking: Y   Handicap Access: N   Payment: P

Stratford-upon-Avon

HATHAWAY HAMLETS   *Rates: budget*
Open: year-round   *Minimum Stay: one week*

This cottage sits just 300 yards from the family home of William Shakespeare's wife, Anne Hathaway, and just two miles from the center of historic Stratford-upon-Avon. The little house offers easy access to the sights, yet provides a quiet retreat in the village of Shottery. The beamed living/dining room with its large stone fireplace and the sloping ceilings and floors of the large double bedroom bespeak the cottage's 17th-century origins. Nonetheless, the kitchen contains all the modern conveniences. Warwick, Birmingham, Evesham and the Cotswolds are within easy touring distance. Contact: British Travel Associates, P.O. Box 299, Elkton, VA 22827. Call 1-800-327-6097 (in Virginia, 703-298-2232). Ref. QNX.

Children: Y   Pets: N   Smoking: Y   Handicap Access: N   Payment: All

WEST SUSSEX

Bedham

FOWLERS COTTAGE   *Rates: budget-inexpensive*
Open: year-round   *Minimum Stay: one week*

English composer Sir Edward Elgar drew inspiration for his cello concertos from the wooded hills at Bedham. Today, the peaceful English countryside inspires guests in this renovated 15th-century cottage attached to the owner's country house. The large living room with a corner fireplace, kitchen with a breakfast area and three bedrooms (one double, two single, plus an extra cot) accommodate four to five. There are many places of interest nearby, including the Bignor Roman Villa, Singleton Open Air Museum and Chichester, founded by the Romans and now home to the Chichester Festival Theatre, which runs from August to September. Contact: British Travel Associates, P.O. Box 299, Elkton, VA 22827. Call 1-800-327-6097 (in Virginia, 703-298-2232). Ref. PJS.

Children: Y   Pets: N   Smoking: Y   Handicap Access: N   Payment: All

Lyminster

COACH HOUSE   *Rates: budget-inexpensive*
Open: year-round   *Minimum Stay: one week*

This delightful 19th-century coach house is set on a two-acre estate and enjoys views of the South Downs, a range of low-lying chalk hills that turn into the white cliffs of Dover further north. Renovated to include modern conveniences, the house accommodates four people in a living room, a dining room, a kitchen and a double and a twin bedroom. Visit the lovely Norman cathedral at historic Chichester just ten miles away, or the many old houses and scenic villages in the area. Athletes can enjoy golf, fishing, horseback riding, sailing, wind surfing and fine sandy beaches within easy reach. Contact: British Travel Associates, P.O. Box 299, Elkton, VA 22827. Call 1-800-327-6097 (in Virginia, 703-298-2232). Ref. F2812.

Children: Y   Pets: N   Smoking: Y   Handicap Access: N   Payment: All

Petworth

FLORIST'S COTTAGE   *Rates: budget-inexpensive*
Open: year-round   *Minimum Stay: one week*

The small country town of Petworth features narrow streets, tea rooms, antique shops and a market square surrounded by 200- and 300-year-old houses. In the heart of town, this cottage wing of a fine florist's shop features old beams and support timbers throughout. There's room for four in a living room, a dining room, a kitchen and one double and one twin bedroom. People with small children should note the staircase to the upper floor is steep. Golf, polo, fishing, gardens, beautiful walks and bridle paths are all nearby on the South Downs. Contact: British Travel Associates, P.O. Box 299, Elkton, VA 22827. Call 1-800-327-6097 (in Virginia, 703-298-2232). Ref. F2800.

Children: Y   Pets: N   Smoking: Y   Handicap Access: N   Payment: All

Selsey

MAISONNETTE   *Rates: budget-inexpensive*
Open: year-round   *Minimum Stay: one week*

This maisonnette is 75 yards from the beach and offers outstanding views along the coast. Four can enjoy all the comforts of home in this traditional house with a living room, a dining area, a kitchen and two bedrooms (one double and one twin). Three-quarters of a mile from the town center, the house stands within easy reach of Pagham Harbor, a nature reserve and bird sanctuary. The Roman town of Chichester, which also has a medieval cathedral and a fairy-tale castle, is 20 minutes away by car. Contact: British Travel Associates, P.O. Box 299, Elkton, VA 22827. Call 1-800-327-6097 (in Virginia, 703-298-2232). Ref. F657.

Children: Y   Pets: N   Smoking: Y   Handicap Access: N   Payment: All

WILTSHIRE

Broughton Gifford

LENTON FARMHOUSE
Open: year-round

Rates: budget-inexpensive
Minimum Stay: one week

If a secure garden and a playroom with a good selection of toys isn't enough to lure your children to this 600-acre farm, then a multitude of friendly farm animals certainly will. The farmhouse has a comfortable sitting room with a fireplace, a dining room, a large modern kitchen and three bedrooms—one double, two twins, plus an extra cot—to sleep six or seven. The ancient Roman city of Bath, superb gardens at Bowood and medieval cathedrals are all nearby. Bicycles and babysitting are available by arrangement. Contact: British Travel Associates, P.O. Box 299, Elkton, VA 22827. Call 1-800-327-6097 (in Virginia, 703-298-2232). Ref. NKT.

Children: Y   Pets: N   Smoking: Y   Handicap Access: N   Payment: All

Fonthill Gifford, Tisbury

BECKFORD LODGE
Open: year-round

Rates: inexpensive-deluxe
Minimum Stay: one week

Modern conveniences have supplemented the faithful restoration of this 18th-century thatched house adjacent to the ancient royal forest of Cranborne Chase. Poachers, farmers, villagers and the keepers of royal hunting grounds once fought bitterly over game rights to the forest. Now, bucolic calm fills the large, farmhouse-style kitchen with its pine furnishings and dishwasher; the cozy study/television room and the elegantly furnished drawing room, which opens onto the patio area. Eight can sleep comfortably in three twin bedrooms and a master bedroom, and a ninth person can bed down on a cot. Fish, ride or play golf nearby, or travel to the seaside resort of Weymouth. A must is the half-hour car trip to Salisbury Plain, which holds the mysterious ruins at Stonehenge. Contact: British Travel Associates, P.O. Box 299, Elkton, VA, 22827. Call 1-800-327-6097 (in Virginia, 703-298-2232). Ref. PRS.

Children: Y   Pets: N   Smoking: Y   Handicap Access: N   Payment: All

Lower Woodford

HATCH COTTAGE
Open: year-round

Rates: budget-moderate
Minimum Stay: one week

Truly a rural paradise, this comely flint and brick cottage provides an ideal retreat for the vacationing family. Located a short distance from the lovely city of Salisbury and its Gothic cathedral, this charming home offers the added pleasures of a nearby riding school and stable as well as the golf course at High Post. Accommodations for six (one double and two twin bedrooms) include an eat-in kitchen, a living room with a fireplace and a large garden with lovely views of the surrounding farmland. The special attractions of the West Country— Stonehenge, Exeter and miles of country road—will fill as many days as you have, and then some. Contact: Castles, Cottages & Flats in Ireland and U.K. Ltd., Box 261, Westwood, MA 02090. Call 617-329-4680. Ref. 1044.

Children: Y   Pets: N   Smoking: Y   Handicap Access: N   Payment: P

Malmesbury

MALMESBURY COTTAGE   *Rates: budget-inexpensive*
Open: year-round   *Minimum Stay: one week*

Malmesbury Cottage has been renovated to modern standards but still retains its 17th-century character. Its cozy yet spacious interior accommodates five in a living room with a dining area, a kitchen and three bedrooms (one double, one twin and one small single). Visit the Norman abbey in Malmesbury, the Cotswolds, Bath, the Mendip Hills, the Wye Valley and Wales, or drive 45 minutes to the Salisbury Plain, home to the ancient megaliths of Stonehenge. Contact: British Travel Associates, P.O. Box 299, Elkton, VA 22827. Call 1-800-327-6097 (in Virginia, 703-298-2232). Ref. F4841.

Children: Y   Pets: N   Smoking: Y   Handicap Access: N   Payment: All

Salisbury

CRANE STREET   *Rates: budget-inexpensive*
Open: year-round   *Minimum Stay: one week*

This charming second-floor apartment occupies part of a fine old Georgian building. Situated in the historic district of town, the centrally heated flat sleeps two and features a living/dining room with a color TV and a kitchen with a rotisserie, as well as a small, secluded garden. From your windows, you will enjoy superb views of the tallest cathedral spire in all of England as well as the Cathedral Close. From Salisbury, you can plan excursions throughout the West Country, traveling to the elegant spa of Bath and to King Arthur's Winchester castle. There is no better countryside for the simple pleasures of a quiet walk, a stop at a pub for a draft or an inn for a cup of tea. Contact: Castles, Cottages & Flats in Ireland and U.K. Ltd., Box 261, Westwood, MA 02090. Call 617-329-4680. Ref. 4031.

Children: Y   Pets: N   Smoking: Y   Handicap Access: N   Payment: P

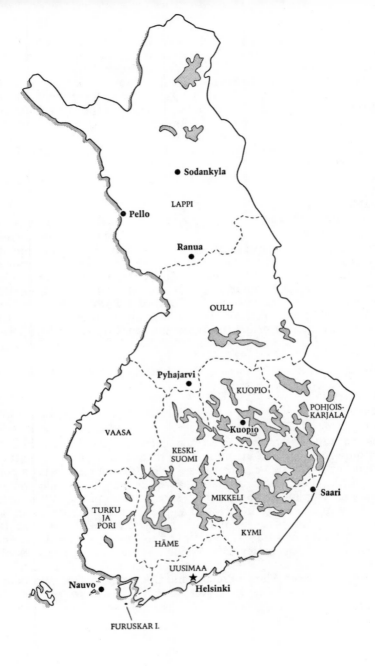

Sodankyla

LAPPI

Pello

Ranua

OULU

Pyhajarvi

KUOPIO

POHJOIS-
KARJALA

VAASA

Kuopio

KESKI-
SUOMI

Saari

TURKU
JA
PORI

MIKKELI

KYMI

HÄME

UUSIMAA

Nauvo

Helsinki

FURUSKAR I.

Finland

FURUSKAR ISLAND

Nauvo

JANSSON'S HOLIDAY COTTAGES *Rates: budget*
Open: year-round *Minimum Stay: one week*

Welcome to fishing paradise! A specially arranged trip brings you to the island of Furuskar, about four miles from the mainland in the Baltic Sea. This log cabin comes with its own boat and fishing nets; you can obtain licenses from the owner. One person can sleep in the living room and four more in two twin bedrooms; the lighting is by oil, the stove is gas and the fireplace provides extra warmth and coziness. The owner will bring extra supplies, and a sauna is shared with the other two cabins nearby. When you return to the mainland, stop to visit Turku (Abo), an hour north of the island—it's the oldest city in Finland. Contact: Lomarengas—The Holiday Chain, Museokatu 3, SF-00100 Helsinki, Finland. Call 011-358-0-441346. Ref. 314.

Children: **Y** Pets: **N** Smoking: **Y** Handicap Access: **N** Payment: **C, EC**

HAME

Asikkala

PATIALA MANOR HOLIDAY COTTAGES *Rates: inexpensive*
Open: year-round *Minimum Stay: one week*

Ten minutes from the village of Vaaksy, where you can dine or shop for local produce, this winterized log cabin is well built and cozy. Inside you'll find two bedrooms (both twins, one with an extra bed) and a living room/kitchenette; the cabin is heated and lit with electricity, and there is a well for water. From the porch, enjoy the view through the pine trees to Lake Paijanne, Finland's second-largest lake. On the lake you can use your own boat to fish for rainbow trout, and in the nearby woods are trails for hiking, horseback riding and cross-country skiing. The cabin is located on the peaceful grounds of a fifteenth-century manor, giving it historic appeal as well. Contact: Lomarengas—The Holiday Chain, Museokatu 3, SF-00100 Helsinki, Finland. Call 011-358-0-441346. Ref. 1953.

Children: **Y** Pets: **N** Smoking: **Y** Handicap Access: **N** Payment: **C, EC**

Padasjoki

WOODLAND COTTAGE *Rates: inexpensive*
Open: year-round *Minimum Stay: one week*

This vast, deeply forested area north of Lahti boasts the freshest of air and deep lakes such as Lake Saarijarvi, on which this cabin is situated. Of wooden construction, with a long balcony and large windows facing the lake, the cabin has a sleeping loft for three and a twin bedroom, plus a living room, kitchenette and shower room. Only seven years old, the cabin has electricity and hot and cold running water as well as a traditional-style fireplace and sauna. There are miles of cross-country ski trails through the woods; within driving distance are stores, restaurants and tennis courts. Contact: Lomarengas—The Holiday Chain, Museokatu 3, SF-00100 Helsinki, Finland. Call 011-358-0-441346. Ref. 3293.

Children: Y   Pets: N   Smoking: Y   Handicap Access: N   Payment: C, EC

KESKI-SUOMI

Hankasalmi

PINECONE CABIN   *Rates: budget*
Open: year-round   *Minimum Stay: one week*

The shallow waters of Lake Armisvesi hold the reflection of this little log cabin and the slim trees that surround it. Salmon fishing can be arranged here, and if you have good luck, you can cook up a mouth-watering feast on the outdoor grill and enjoy it on the private garden furniture or porch. Inside is a kitchen, living room with four beds, twin bedroom, bath and a sauna with shower. Electricity heats and lights the house, but a fireplace casts a rosy glow after a day of cross-country or downhill skiing. Although this area is secluded, there is a nearby store, restaurants, and facilities for horseback riding, all within a twenty-minute drive. Contact: Lomarengas—The Holiday Chain, Museokatu 3, SF-00100 Helsinki, Finland. Call 011-358-0-441346. Ref. 503.

Children: Y   Pets: N   Smoking: Y   Handicap Access: N   Payment: C, EC

KYMI

Saari

KIIVERI HOLIDAY COTTAGE   *Rates: budget*
Open: year-round   *Minimum Stay: one week*

Concentrated in this region about fifty miles southeast of Savonlinna is some of Finland's most striking scenery. Nestled in the woods is a simple log cabin, in harmony with the surrounding trees and glades. Lake Suur-Rautjarvi lies a few steps away, where you can take out your own boat for some fishing, or just go for a swim in its shallow waters. There are six beds altogether—two in the living room, two in the dressing room and two in the bedroom. Electric lights and heat are provided, and there is also an open fireplace that adds to the charm and warms up the winter days. There is cold running water and a sauna, without which no Finnish cabin would be complete. Contact: Lomarengas—The Holiday Chain, Museokatu 3, SF-00100 Helsinki, Finland. Call 011-358-0-441346. Ref. 3176.

Children: Y   Pets: N   Smoking: Y   Handicap Access: N   Payment: C, EC

Uukuneimi

FISHERMAN'S RETREAT   *Rates: budget*
Open: year-round   *Minimum Stay: one week*

A short flight of steps leads up to the wide veranda of this log cabin built just six years ago. Hot and cold running water, electric lights and heat, a well with drinking water and a freezer are among the modern amenities it has to offer. Two bedrooms each sleep two guests and the living room/kitchen has room for two more. In addition to the regular sauna, there is a smoke sauna nearby. The cabin is directly on the shoreline of Lake Pyhajarvi, which is shallow with a rocky bottom. A boat is provided for your use and fishing equipment and an outboard motor can be rented. A wood-burning stove and a fireplace help provide a nice welcome home from the winter sports scene, which includes downhill skiing less than two miles away. Contact: Lomarengas—The Holiday Chain, Museokatu 3, SF-00100 Helsinki, Finland. Call 011-358-0-441346. Ref. 3360.

Children: Y   Pets: N   Smoking: Y   Handicap Access: N   Payment: C, EC

LAPPI

Inari/Ivalo

PIILO CABIN   *Rates: budget*
Open: year-round   *Minimum Stay: one week*
The Arctic Road leads from Rovaniemi to Ivalo, truly the heart of this northern land of reindeer and endless summer twilight. Piilo is situated by the River Ivalojok (known as an excellent canoeing river), where you can fish from the boat provided for your use. Up to four people can stay here comfortably as long as they are prepared to "rough it" a little. Light is provided by oil and gas, the water is drawn from a pump and heating comes from the fireplace. Prepare your own sauna for a true Finnish experience. A store and restaurant are located ten minutes away; your parking spot is across the river. Excursions up the river for hunting and fishing can be arranged in advance. Contact: Lapland Travel Ltd., Maakuntakatu 10, 96 100 Rovaniemi, Finland. Call 011-358-60-16052. Ref. 121204.

Children: Y   Pets: N   Smoking: Y   Handicap Access: N   Payment: C, EC

Kuopio

VAIKON CABIN   *Rates: budget*
Open: year-round   *Minimum Stay: one week*
In summer this location is a canoeist's dream come true; in winter, a skier's, making this log cabin a year-round residence. About fifty miles from the lively town of Kuopio, the cabin stands by Lake Vihtajarvi, which has deep waters and wooded shores. The cabin is about seven years old and has a twin bedroom plus two extra beds in the living room, kitchenette, electric heat and lights, hot and cold running water, a shower and a toilet. A TV and a cozy fireplace complete the picture. A boat is available for fishing on the lake, or guests can shoot the rapids of the Vaikkojoki River with a professional guide. Contact: Lomarengas—The Holiday Chain, Museokatu 3, SF-00100 Helsinki, Finland. Call 011-358-0-441346. Ref. 2899.

Children: Y   Pets: N   Smoking: Y   Handicap Access: N   Payment: C, EC

Pello

TOP OF THE WORLD CABIN   *Rates: budget*
Open: year-round   *Minimum Stay: one week*

Pello lies quite high above the Arctic Circle close to the Swedish border. Located on rocky Lake Ylinen/Alinen, this wooden cabin is just two years old and exceptionally well equipped. In the kitchen you'll find an electric stove and microwave oven and hot and cold running water. The bathroom has a shower, and there is a color TV and electric heat. If you visit during the winter months to experience the splendor of the midnight sun and do cross-country skiing, you'll be grateful for the fireplace that warms the whole cabin. A sleeping loft contains three beds, and in the living room are two more. A sauna is on the ground floor. Explore the lake's shores and inlets and find the best fishing grounds in your own boat. Contact: Lomarengas—The Holiday Chain, Museokatu 3, SF-00100 Helsinki, Finland. Call 011-358-0-441346. Ref. 4418/4419.

Children: Y   Pets: N   Smoking: Y   Handicap Access: N   Payment: C, EC

Salla

HARJUNSYRJA CABIN   *Rates: inexpensive*
Open: October-mid-May   *Minimum Stay: one week*

East of Kemijarvi and close to the Russian border lies Lake Onkamo-jarvi, where you'll find this little community on the shore. Salla is a log cabin with two bedrooms and two sleeping balconies, and heated and lit with electricity and made cozy by a fireplace. A caretaker brings fresh drinking water, and water from the lake can be used for washing as well. There is a store about a mile away for supplies and a ski area about fifteen minutes by car. The rivers, lakes and fells in this remote area provide spectacular scenery matched only by the northern lights that flicker across the darkened sky. Fishing and hunting trips with qualified guides can be arranged by the agency. Contact: Lapland Travel Ltd., Maakuntakatu 10, 96 100 Rovaniemi, Finland. Call 011-358-60-16052. Ref. M261706.

Children: Y   Pets: N   Smoking: Y   Handicap Access: N   Payment: C, EC

MIKKELI

Enonkoski

FOREST PERCH CABIN   *Rates: budget*
Open: year-round   *Minimum Stay: one week*

Well shaded by trees, this little wooden cabin for four has its own dock on Lake Havujarvi, complete with a boat for its guests. The lake is good for fishing and swimming. The living room of the cabin contains two beds, two more occupy the twin bedroom, and a separate little cabin contains two beds ideal for kids. The sauna has a separate dressing room and there is cold running water; the well is a short walk away. Electrically lit and heated, the cabin features an open fireplace, another traditional Finnish touch. Just over a half-hour drive south is Savonlinna, an interesting city with a medieval past, many present-day cultural attractions and natural healing baths. Contact:

Lomarengas—The Holiday Chain, Museokatu 3, SF-00100 Helsinki, Finland. Call 011-358-0-441346. Ref. 1044.

Children: **Y**   Pets: **N**   Smoking: **Y**   Handicap Access: **N**   Payment: **C, EC**

Puumala

LOG HOUSE   *Rates: budget*
Open: year-round   *Minimum Stay: one week*
This renovated 19th-century log building has an interesting design and an upstairs balcony. It also has plenty of room, with two downstairs and two upstairs twin bedrooms, sleeping a total of eight guests. The kitchen is separate and there is a sauna with its own dressing room; water is provided by a tap in summer and also by a nearby well. Stores and restaurants are about fifteen minutes away by car, and local produce is available nearby. Lake Malonen-jarvi lies at the end of a short walkway, where you'll find a boat provided for your use. Both cross-country and downhill skiing facilities operate in the area, and the woods are full of trails for hiking. Contact: Lomarengas—The Holiday Chain, Museokatu 3, SF-00100 Helsinki, Finland. Call 011-358-0-441346. Ref. 3150.

Children: **Y**   Pets: **N**   Smoking: **Y**   Handicap Access: **N**   Payment: **C, EC**

OULU

Pyhajarvi

COZY HAVEN CABIN   *Rates: budget*
Open: year-round   *Minimum Stay: one week*
The province of Oulu is known for its rich history and wide-open spaces. Like the rest of Finland, Oulu does not lack for lakes, and on one of these, Lake Parkkimajarvi, you'll find this little log cabin. With three beds in a sleeping loft, two in the living room/kitchen and one in the sauna dressing room, it can sleep a maximum of six guests—but three is probably a more comfortable complement. Unlike many cabins of this type, it does have all modern conveniences—electric heat and lights, hot and cold running water, shower room, toilet and, of course, the traditional sauna. The shallow lake provides good fishing and guests have use of a boat. Contact: Lomarengas—The Holiday Chain, Museokatu 3, SF-00100 Helsinki, Finland. Call 011-358-0-441346. Ref. 4266/4267.

Children: **Y**   Pets: **N**   Smoking: **Y**   Handicap Access: **N**   Payment: **C, EC**

TURKU JA PORI

Ikaalinen

MODERN LOG CABIN   *Rates: budget*
Open: year-round   *Minimum Stay: one week*
Close to the Ikaalinen health resort and beside Lake Kyrosjarvi, this winterized wooden cottage sits on a slight rise of open ground. On the barbecue, you can cook up some fish fresh from the lake—there is a boat available for private use and fishing equipment can be rented.

Within driving distance are miles of cross-country ski trails, riding stables and a downhill ski area. Fresh produce is available locally. The combined kitchen and dining room contains two beds; there's also a twin bedroom. Cold water can be drawn from the well, and the house's electric heat is aided by a wood-burning fireplace. Contact: Lomarengas—The Holiday Chain, Museokatu 3, SF-00100 Helsinki, Finland. Call 011-358-0-441346. Ref. 3404.

Children: Y   Pets: N   Smoking: Y   Handicap Access: N   Payment: C, EC

UUSIMAA

Helsinki

ART TRAVEL APARTMENTS   *Rates: budget-moderate*
Open: year-round   *Minimum Stay: five nights*

Art Travel offers a selection of rental apartments located throughout downtown Helsinki, all furnished and equipped to feel like home— right down to the Scandinavian coffee maker and the bedside lamps. Some apartments have balconies overlooking the port area, others are close to a park or garden, while still others are in fashionable residential areas. You can choose from studio, one- or two-bedroom flats, depending on your needs. All have excellent kitchens with microwave ovens, color TV, shower, phone and radio; a cleaning service tidies up for you weekly. Be sure to ask about extras—some apartments have VCRs or a washing machine and dryer, or are in buildings with doormen. Contact: Mr. Heikki Artman, Art-Travel Oy, Paarynapolku 3, 02710 Espoo Puhelin, Finland. Call 011-358-0-592-916.

Children: Y   Pets: Y   Smoking: Y   Handicap Access: N   Payment: C, V, M

Helsinki

DOMINA RENTALS   *Rates: moderate-inexpensive*
Open: year-round   *Minimum Stay: one week*

Domina Rental service lists a number of apartments in and around the center of Helsinki, providing a uniform standard of comfort and service. Each apartment contains a completely equipped kitchen with microwave oven, toaster, coffee maker, fridge and stove; many have a washing machine and dryer. The apartments are cleaned weekly and one even has its own sauna—considered a daily necessity by many Finns. A warm, cozy look pervades these studio and one-bedroom units, many of which face south to draw in the sun. All of Helsinki lies at your feet, for the city's trams and metro cover most of the sites and attractions. Contact: Paivi Lahtela, Lahtela Trading Oy Ltd., P.O. Box 286, Uudenmaankatu 4-6 G, 00120 Helsinki, Finland. Call 011-358-0-601-501.

Children: Y Pets: N Smoking: Y Handicap Access: N Payment: C, T, V, M, A, O

Helsinki

FENNO APARTMENTS   *Rates: budget-moderate*
Open: year-round   *Minimum Stay: none*

Fenno Apartments are conveniently located close to Helsinki's number 3B and 3T tram lines, which draw a figure eight around the city center. The mid-sized, contemporary apartment building stands near notable sites such as the Exhibition Center and the Olympic Stadium. Choose between studio apartments for one or two guests, which are completely self-contained, or a room in a "shared apartment" with eight bedrooms, a living room, two shower rooms, two toilets and a kitchen. Compact and modern with sleek, Scandinavian decor, the studios have color TV, phone and a sparkling kitchenette where you can cook up fresh fish and other delights found at the open-air market in the South Harbor. Daily maid service, a cafeteria and a sauna make your stay a little easier. Contact: Kirsi Kontiokoski, Franzeninkatu 26, Helsinki, Finland. Call 011-358-0-773-1661.

Children: Y Pets: Y Smoking: Y Handicap Access: Y Payment: C, T, V, M, A, O

Lohja

LAKE HIIDENVESI VILLAS   *Rates: inexpensive*
Open: year-round   *Minimum Stay: one week*
Close enough to Helsinki for day trips, yet far enough to feel like a country resort, this house has its own boat on the shore of Lake Hiidenvesi. Built fifteen years ago, the house has modern amenities including electricity, hot and cold running water, a bathroom and an equipped kitchen. The long, covered porch is a pleasant place to sit and listen to the wind rustling through the pine trees, and the sauna is private. Inside are two twin bedrooms and a living room with full-length windows that let in plenty of light. Restaurants and stores are less than two miles away, or you can catch and cook your own fish from the lake. Contact: Lomarengas—The Holiday Chain, Museokatu 3, SF-00100 Helsinki, Finland. Call 011-358-0-441346. Ref. 3171.

Children: Y   Pets: N   Smoking: Y   Handicap Access: N   Payment: C, EC

France

AQUITAINE

Aquitaine
LAKESIDE HOUSE
Open: year-round

Rates: budget
Minimum Stay: one week

Do you dream of getting away from it all? You can do it here, in a secluded, modern house on its own lake among eight acres of garden and woodland about thirteen miles from the town of Perigueux. This centrally heated house for up to eight people consists of an open-plan kitchen/living/dining room with a double sofa bed, three bedrooms, a three-quarter bath and a washing machine. There is also a furnished patio and a stone-built barbecue. When you tire of swimming and fishing in the lake or loafing in front of the fireplace, take a drive to some of the famous medieval castles and prehistoric caves. Contact: Chez Nous Travel Service, 85 Dobb Top Road, Holmbridge, Huddersfield, HD7 1QP, England. Call 011-44-1-0484-684075. Ref. 18D.

Children: Y   Pets: N   Smoking: Y   Handicap Access: N   Payment: P, V, M

Aurignac

PAGANEL HOUSE AND BARN   *Rates: expensive-deluxe*
Open: year-round   *Minimum Stay: one week*

Paganel has it all: elegant furnishings, modern facilities and plenty of space, with a resident guardian/chef to boot. Built of limestone with tile roofs, the traditional-style buildings offer views of the rolling countryside. The old farmhouse sleeps six to eight in three bedrooms (the master bedroom boasts a king-size bed); nine people can sleep in the barn. In addition to bedrooms, the barn includes a large recreational area with weights, gym equipment and table tennis. Cooking, cleaning and babysitting can be negotiated. A swimming pool is sheltered within the walls of an old cottage. In July and August, the house and barn are rented together; at other times they're rented individually, with the other building kept empty to ensure privacy. Contact: Blakes Vacations, 4918 Dempster Street, Skokie, IL, 60077. Call 1-800-628-8118. Ref. AGP.

Children: Y   Pets: N   Smoking: Y   Handicap Access: N   Payment: P, T

Bertic Buree

FARM COTTAGE   *Rates: budget*
Open: April-October   *Minimum Stay: one week*

Nestled in the French countryside, this quaint farm cottage enjoys an idyllic rural setting only two and a half miles from Verteillac. The bright one-bedroom bungalow has been tastefully renovated to high standards and includes a modern bathroom and central heating (extra charge). Lounge in the open-plan kitchen/living room or on your own private patio with garden furniture and a barbecue. Your neighbors are the resident British owners, who are available at any time for help and information. When you've had your fill of peace and quiet, the nearby towns of Verteillac and Riberac provide swimming, horseback riding, tennis, shops and restaurants. Contact: Chez Nous Travel Service, 85 Dobb Top Road, Holmbridge, Huddersfield, HD7 1QP, England. Call 011-44-1-0484-684075. Ref. 20A.

Children: Y   Pets: N   Smoking: Y   Handicap Access: N   Payment: P, V, M

Boison

LA POUJADE   *Rates: deluxe*
Open: year-round   *Minimum Stay: one week*

This 17th-century chateau rests on a hillside high above the small village of Urval, which is known for its 12th-century architecture and medieval church. Today descendants of the chateau's original buil ers, the Count and Countess Commarque, offer guests a choice two wings. Each wing accommodates eight guests; the tw rented together or separately. Furnished with antiques, th dations boast such fine architectural details as bay windows, vaulted ceilings and crystal chandeliers. Both the Greenwall Wing and the Marie Wing contain a living and dining room, a fully equipped modern kitchen, two bedrooms and a bath. Outside, guests can walk the paths winding through the fifty acres of grounds, cultivated fields and woodlands or enjoy the parks, terraces and private gardens of the estate. Contact: Rent A Home International, Inc., 7200 34th Avenue N.W., Seattle, WA 98117. Call 206-545-6963.

Children: **Y** Pets: **N** Smoking: **Y** Handicap Access: **N** Payment: **C, V, P, M**

Castelnau-sur-l'Auvignon

STONE COTTAGE

Rates: budget

Open: year-round

Minimum Stay: one week

Surrounded by hills and vineyards, this secluded 18th-century stone cottage near the town of Condom has its own garden and a shady terrace for lounging and enjoying the view. It has been renovated to offer all modern facilities, including a washing machine. The cottage has two double bedrooms plus a sofa bed, a cavernous living room with a big open fireplace, a thoroughly equipped kitchen/dining room and an extra-large bathroom. The area abounds with interesting market towns and warm lakes for swimming and fishing. Horseback riding is another great way to take in the scenery. Contact: Chez Nous Travel Service, 85 Dobb Top Road, Holmbridge, Huddersfield, HD7 1QP, England. Call 011-44-1-0484-684075. Ref. 34G.

Children: **N** Pets: **N** Smoking: **Y** Handicap Access: **N** Payment: **P, V, M**

Catuffe

MANOR HOUSE

Rates: budget-inexpensive

Open: April-October

Minimum Stay: one week

This unique manor house sits on twenty beautifully landscaped acres with glorious views over the valley, its own small river and a lake. Suitable for two families or groups of up to ten people, the house consists of a magnificent master suite with a bath, four double bedrooms, a separate shower and two toilets. The new kitchen, finished in chestnut, has a dishwasher and washing machine and adjoins a large exposed stone dining area with a huge open fireplace. Two more downstairs salons overlook the terrace, with a barbecue and garden furniture provided. Close by lies the ancient town of Monflanquin and its fine local market, its swimming pool and its tennis courts. Also nearby is a new international golf course, lakes for water sports and horseback riding. Contact: Chez Nous Travel Service, 85 Dobb Top Road, Holmbridge, Huddersfield, HD7 1QP, England. Call 011-44-1-0484-684075. Ref.

ts: **N** Smoking: **Y** Handicap Access: **N** Payment: **P, V, M**

ugie

Rates: budget

Minimum Stay: one week

l hamlet just two miles from the Dordogne River is

this old cottage, which has recently been restored. The cozy living room with exposed beams and an open fireplace is simply yet comfortably furnished. French doors open onto a sunny terrace with views of the rolling countryside. Upstairs is a charming double bedroom and a bath with a shower. The area is well known for its fine restaurants; recreational facilities include swimming, water sports, fishing, horseback riding and tennis. Day trips to the ancient towns of Dromme, Sarlat and Rocamadour as well as the Les Eyzies caves and the chateaux of the Dordogne Valley are all possible as well. Contact: Chez Nous Travel Service, 85 Dobb Top Road, Holmbridge, Huddersfield, HD7 1QP, England. Call 011-44-1-0484-684075. Ref. 35C.

Children: Y   Pets: N   Smoking: Y   Handicap Access: N   Payment: P, V, M

Duras

VILLAGE APARTMENT   *Rates: budget*
Open: year-round   *Minimum Stay: one week*
The picturesque village of Duras is the setting for this lovely apartment in a charming old oak-beamed house with private grounds. Recently converted and furnished, the apartment consists of a kitchen/living room with a sofa bed and, upstairs, a double bedroom. Outside are a covered terrace ideal for dining and another, larger terrace with both sunny and shaded areas. Nearby is a recreational lake for swimming, boating, wind surfing, fishing, tennis and horseback riding. Despite its peaceful country setting, the apartment is only a few minutes' walk from several restaurants, good shopping and an historic chateau. Contact: Chez Nous Travel Service, 85 Dobb Top Road, Holmbridge, Huddersfield, HD7 1QP, England. Call 011-44-1-0484-684075. Ref. 28E.

Children: Y   Pets: N   Smoking: Y   Handicap Access: N   Payment: P, V, M

La Courberie

STONE FARMHOUSE   *Rates: budget*
Open: year-round   *Minimum Stay: one week*
In a little hamlet on the River Dronne, on an acre of grass, fruit trees and shade trees surrounded by vineyards and fields, stands this completely renovated stone farmhouse with a fantastic view. The large, fully equipped kitchen/dining room with the original open fireplace makes for cozy mealtimes. Glass doors lead to the terrace from the big, sunny living room, which has a loft above with two single beds. Two other twin-bedded rooms bring the sleeping total to six in all. There is a full-sized bath, a shower room and separate toilet all with sinks. Southwest France is famous for its chateaux and medieval villages; rivers and lakes provide plenty of recreational opportunities. Contact: Chez Nous Travel Service, 85 Dobb Top Road, Holmbridge, Huddersfield, HD7 1QP, England. Call 011-44-1-0484-684075. Ref. 22C.

Children: Y   Pets: N   Smoking: Y   Handicap Access: N   Payment: P, V, M

Langon
BERTRANON

Rates: budget

Open: year-round

Minimum Stay: one week

When Henry II married Eleanor, Duchess of Aquitaine, in 1152, this vast region of rolling pine forests, rivers and lakes came under English rule. It took the French 300 years to win it back, and it's easy to see why they fought so hard once you experience the long, mild summers, southern sunshine and golden beaches. Converted from an outbuilding of an old chateau, Bertranon has been refurbished with modern conveniences and set in a hillside among vineyards. The kitchen/living/dining room features an open fireplace; one double and one twin bedroom sleep a total of four. In the uninhabited chateau, wine is processed and stored—taste some for yourself. Sporting activities and shops are within walking distance; golf is a half-hour drive away. Contact: Blakes Vacations, 4918 Dempster Street, Skokie, IL, 60077. Call 1-800-628-8118. Ref. AOX.

Children: **Y**   Pets: **N**   Smoking: **Y**   Handicap Access: **N**   Payment: **P, T**

Laudibertie
RESTORED FARMHOUSE

Rates: budget

Open: year-round

Minimum Stay: one week

Real country living can be yours in this farmhouse surrounded by a lawn and garden in a tiny hamlet near the town of Riberac. The house, which accommodates eight people, has been beautifully restored to preserve the charm of tiled floors downstairs, polished wood floors upstairs and beamed ceilings throughout. On the lower level, the spacious living room with comfortable seating, a large dining table and an open fireplace is inviting; the kitchen is outfitted with a stove, a refrigerator and a dishwasher. There is also a full bath with a washing machine. Upstairs are two more baths and five sizable bedrooms. A swimming pool, tennis courts and a small lake with wind surfing and pedal boats all lie within easy reach. Contact: Chez Nous Travel Service, 85 Dobb Top Road, Holmbridge, Huddersfield, HD7 1QP, England. Call 011-44-1-0484-684075. Ref. 28B.

Children: **Y**   Pets: **N**   Smoking: **Y**   Handicap Access: **N**   Payment: **P, V, M**

Les Mondains
STONE HOUSE

Rates: budget

Open: May-September

Minimum Stay: one week

Set in seclusion amidst vineyards, orchards and woodlands, this quiet apartment occupies the ground floor of a fine old stone building. It consists of a spacious kitchen/dining room, a double bedroom/sitting room, a twin bedroom and a full bath. In addition, a wide veranda faces south and west over a terrace and grassy yard beyond—the perfect spot for unwinding after a day of sightseeing. Located in a hamlet halfway between the towns of Ste. Foy-la-Grande and Duras, this makes an ideal base from which to visit the wine districts of Bordeaux, Bergerac and Duras as well as many other places of interest in this picturesque region of France. Contact: Chez Nous Travel Service, 85 Dobb Top

Road, Holmbridge, Huddersfield, HD7 1QP, England. Call 011-44-1-0484-684075. Ref. 23B.

Children: Y   Pets: N   Smoking: Y   Handicap Access: N   Payment: P, V, M

Riberac

CHATEAU DE FONGRENON   *Rates: Budget*
Open: June-September   *Minimum Stay: one week*
Rent your own wing of an authentic chateau situated on a 250-acre estate with green lawns, a shady park, a beautiful boxwood garden and its own tennis courts. The ground floor has a cloakroom, a living room with an open fireplace, a completely equipped kitchen and a spacious, elegant bedroom with two twin beds. Upstairs is an attractively furnished double bedroom and modern bathroom. Two cots are available for children; garden furniture, a barbecue and two bicycles are provided as well. For recreation, swimming pools, rivers with bathing beaches and horseback riding are plentiful, or you may want to visit some of the nearby historical sites and vineyards. Contact: Chez Nous Travel Service, 85 Dobb Top Road, Holmbridge, Huddersfield, HD7 1QP, England. Call 011-44-1-0484-684075. Ref 22D.

Children: Y   Pets: N   Smoking: Y   Handicap Access: N   Payment: P, V, M

Riberac

STONE FARMHOUSE   *Rates: budget*
Open: year-round   *Minimum Stay: one week*
This restored 17th-century stone farmhouse on the edge of a hamlet stands near footpaths into the forest of La Double. It has a large sitting room with a fireplace, which leads to a terrace with garden furniture, a modern kitchen with a spacious dining area, two baths and a washing machine. Sleeping accommodations for up to nine people include a double, a triple and two twin bedrooms. The sizable yard with shade trees and pleasant views is a great place for the kids to play. Riberac, just over four miles away, holds a weekly outdoor market; swimming, boating, wind surfing, excellent restaurants and the region's castles and caves are all easily accessible. Contact: Chez Nous Travel Service, 85 Dobb Top Road, Holmbridge, Huddersfield, HD7 1QP, England. Call 011-44-1-0484-684075. Ref. 24C.

Children: Y   Pets: N   Smoking: Y   Handicap Access: N   Payment: P, V, M

Seyches

RESTORED FARMHOUSE   *Rates: budget*
Open: March-November   *Minimum Stay: one week*
Situated on an acre of grounds with large shade trees and a panoramic view of the rolling countryside, this farmhouse has been fully restored for your comfort. The living/dining area retains its rustic charm with exposed beams and an open fireplace; the kitchen includes a stove, a refrigerator and a dishwasher. There are two terraces—one open, one covered—as well as a closed sun porch with its own fireplace. Nine can sleep in two doubles, a twin and a triple bedroom. The house is close to lakes that offer swimming, sailing and wind surfing; tennis

courts and a swimming pool are five minutes away and a golf course is within a half hour's drive. Contact: Chez Nous Travel Service, 85 Dobb Top Road, Holmbridge, Huddersfield, HD7 1QP, England. Call 011-44-1-0484-684075. Ref. 25F.

Children: **Y**   Pets: **N**   Smoking: **Y**   Handicap Access: **N**   Payment: **P, V, M**

Souillac

STONE COTTAGE   *Rates: budget*
Open: May-September   *Minimum Stay: one week*

What a perfect spot for a romantic getaway for two. This traditional, one-story stone cottage sits peacefully on a half acre of grounds dotted with fruit trees, near a fantastic overlook of the Dordogne Valley. The living room is cozy with its large stone fireplace; the dining room has French doors that lead to a pleasant garden. There's also a double bedroom, a kitchen and a bath. For recreation, swimming, canoeing, riding and woodland walks are all available nearby. The attractions of the Dordogne Valley, including medieval villages, castles, caves and wineries are all within easy reach. Contact: Chez Nous Travel Service, 85 Dobb Top Road, Holmbridge, Huddersfield, HD7 1QP, England. Call 011-44-1-0484-684075. Ref. 26F.

Children: **Y**   Pets: **N**   Smoking: **Y**   Handicap Access: **N**   Payment: **P, V, M**

St. Cyprien

STONE COTTAGES   *Rates: budget-inexpensive*
Open: year-round   *Minimum Stay: three days*

A private sunny courtyard with a garden is the magnificent rural setting for these two fully equipped dwellings in the Dordogne Valley. The layout is ideal for two families vacationing together, but is equally suitable for one, in which case special pricing may be arranged. Each cottage sleeps four in two bedrooms; one also includes a sofa bed. There is table tennis, garden furniture and a barbecue for the guests' use. Just a short walk away is a farm where fresh milk, cheese and yogurt may be purchased. This is an ideal spot for touring the Dordogne castles, fortified towns and prehistoric caves, or for swimming, fishing, canoeing, horseback riding, tennis, walking or just relaxing and enjoying the superb food and wines. Contact: Chez Nous Travel Service, 85 Dobb Top Road, Holmbridge, Huddersfield, HD7 1QP, England. Call 011-44-1-0484-684075. Ref. 17D.

Children: **Y**   Pets: **N**   Smoking: **Y**   Handicap Access: **N**   Payment: **P, V, M**

St. Felix de Reilhac

LE PRESBYTERE   *Rates: budget*
Open: year-round   *Minimum Stay: one week*

This ancient Presbytery in the little hamlet of St. Felix has been completely and carefully restored to retain many of the original features, such as exposed beams, fireplaces and tiled floors. The kitchen is fully equipped with a refrigerator, a stove, a dishwasher and a washing machine, and the roomy and well-furnished dining and sitting rooms have open fireplaces and doors to the garden. Four bedrooms sleep up to eight people; three baths make the lodgings especially comfortable. Outside, the grounds include a barbecue and garden furniture. The house is within easy reach of Les Eyzies, Sarlat and the Dordogne and Vezere valleys for touring and sightseeing. Contact: Chez Nous Travel Service, 85 Dobb Top Road, Holmbridge, Huddersfield, HD7 1QP, England. Call 011-44-1-0484-684075. Ref. 25C.

Children: Y   Pets: N   Smoking: Y   Handicap Access: N   Payment: P, V, M

Thenon

CONVERTED COTTAGE   *Rates: budget*
Open: May-October   *Minimum Stay: one week*
Surrounded by ancient walnut trees, open fields and woodlands, this converted cottage was once used to dry walnuts, and it's now an ideal spot for a restful vacation. There is a kitchen/sitting room, a twin bedroom with space for a third bed if need be and a fully equipped bathroom. In addition, extra accommodations for up to four more people can be arranged on site for a small additional charge. Two little towns close by offer a full range of services, including a restaurant/bar, a street market and small shops. Swimming is available during July and August; the prehistoric sites of Lescaux and Les Eyzies, medieval Sarlat, Hautefort Chateau and other interesting locales are all easily accessible. Contact: Chez Nous Travel Service, 85 Dobb Top Road, Holmbridge, Huddersfield, HD7 1QP, England. Call 011-44-1-0484-684075. Ref. 30E.

Children: Y   Pets: N   Smoking: Y   Handicap Access: N   Payment: P, V, M

Verteillac

LES GARENNES MANOIR   *Rates: budget*
Open: year-round   *Minimum Stay: one week*
Three separate houses, each with its own unique character and charm, make up this 200-year-old manor situated on a hilltop with superb views of the Dordogne countryside. The extensive grounds provide a tranquil atmosphere and a safe environment for children to play. Garden furniture and a barbecue are provided, as are badminton and volleyball equipment, swings, indoor games and laundry facilities. Two houses sleep ten people each, and the third sleeps eleven; all have modern bathrooms. Some features include a garden-view veranda, a delightful kitchen with an old bread oven and a magnificent sitting room with French doors leading to a garden. Guests have easy access to shops, restaurants, a swimming pool, tennis and horseback riding, as well as a lake with sandy beaches, fishing, boating and wind surfing. Contact: Chez Nous Travel Service, 85 Dobb Top Road, Holmbridge, Huddersfield, HD7 1QP, England. Call 011-44-1-0484-684075. Ref. 17A.

Children: Y   Pets: N   Smoking: Y   Handicap Access: N   Payment: P, V, M

AUVERGNE

Le Chambon sur Lignon

CHEZ PANEL   *Rates: budget-moderate*
Open: year-round   *Minimum Stay: one week*

A string of extinct volcanoes give the Auvergne region in south central France its famous plateaus, rolling hills and many scenic rivers and lakes. Visitors to the region can stay in this ground-floor apartment, which sleeps seven and shares a swimming pool and tennis court with the house next door. The kitchen is equipped with a dishwasher and washing machine; the terrace has a barbecue. To keep warm, guests have their choice of central heating and an open fireplace in the living/ dining room. Take advantage of the many outdoor sporting activities available here in the summer, including sailing, wind-surfing, fishing, water-skiing and cycling. Contact: Blakes Vacations, 4918 Dempster Street, Skokie, IL 60077. Call 1-800-628-8118. Ref. ADB.

Children: Y   Pets: N   Smoking: Y   Handicap Access: N   Payment: P, T

Sedaiges

BAROQUE CHATEAU   *Rates: deluxe*
Open: April-September, week of December 25   *Minimum Stay: one week*

This magnificent 17th-century chateau is elegantly appointed yet feels comfortably lived-in. If you've always longed to ramble through the grand chambers of a fairy-tale castle, this is the place for you. A gorgeous great hall, two sumptuous living rooms and two dining rooms are furnished with splendid antiques; the kitchen and laundry room have full complements of modern appliances. Ten can sleep comfortably in six commodious bedrooms; smaller rooms for five more guests are available. Daily maid service and the nearby caretaker ensure that your stay will be relaxing. The chateau has its own pool and game room for the amusement of its guests. Nearby St. Etienne Lake offers swimming and sailing, or try a bit of riding for a truly royal experience. Contact: Villas and Apartments Abroad, Ltd., 420 Madison Avenue, New York, NY 10017. Call 1-800-433-3020.

Children: Y   Pets: Y   Smoking: Y   Handicap Access: N   Payment: C, P, T

Yssingeaux

CHEZ PANEL   *Rates: budget-inexpensive*
Open: year-round   *Minimum Stay: one week*

The Auvergne region is famous for its ten thermal spa resorts, where you can take health treatments or just taste some of the spa waters while you soak in the sun and fresh air. Chez Panel is built on a slope, giving this upstairs apartment a ground-floor entrance. Eight sleep comfortably here in one twin bedroom and two chambers with both a double and a single bed. All bedrooms have a separate bathroom or shower room, the kitchen/dining area includes a dishwasher and washing machine and the apartment shares a large swimming pool and tennis court with the next-door neighbors. Contact: Blakes Vacations,

4918 Dempster Street, Skokie, IL 60077. Call 1-800-628-8118. Ref. ADG.

Children: Y   Pets: N   Smoking: Y   Handicap Access: N   Payment: P, T

BRITTANY

Bannalec

CHALET DES ARTISTES   *Rates: moderate-expensive*
Open: year-round   *Minimum Stay: one week*

This cluster of Breton cottages stands on a 15th-century estate built on the site of a medieval fort. Charmingly renovated, the estate has spacious grounds to explore and wonderful facilities to pamper its guests, including a heated pool, hot tub, sauna, solarium, fitness center and indoor and outdoor games. Individually named after French painters, each cottage sleeps from four to six guests and has such special features as large stone fireplaces, sofa beds and private terraces overlooking the amber fields and dense woods surrounding the estate. Nearby are long, white beaches, ancient harbor towns and fishing villages, rolling farm country and woodland valleys. Contact: Rhoda and Joseph Kafer, Riviera Holidays, 31 Georgian Lane, Great Neck, NY 11024. Call 516-487-8094. Ref. SB153-6.

Children: Y Pets: Y Smoking: Y Handicap Access: N Payment: P, V, M, A

Benodet

VOIZEL   *Rates: inexpensive-moderate*
Open: June 30-August 31   *Minimum Stay: two weeks*

A comfortable, well-furnished house a quarter-mile from the sea offers easy access to a sandy beach a mile away. The living/dining room features an open fireplace and easy chairs for cozy evenings, while the kitchen area offers a dishwasher to save you work. Well groomed and equipped with garden furniture, the garden includes a barbecue. A washing machine and dryer are located in the cellar. Seven can sleep comfortably here, with a double bedroom on the main floor, and two doubles and a single on the upper floor. Contact: Blakes Vacations, 4918 Dempster Street, Skokie, IL 60077. Call 1-800-628-8118. Ref. ABR.

Children: Y   Pets: N   Smoking: Y   Handicap Access: N   Payment: P, T

Cancale

RENOVATED COTTAGE   *Rates: budget*
Open: year-round   *Minimum Stay: one week*

If you're looking for a quiet vacation spot on the beach, this may be just the place. In a small hamlet at the edge of Cancale, just eight miles to the east of the ancient city of Saint Malo and its ferry port, sits this 18th-century cottage. The exposed beams and stonework have been carefully renovated to maintain the original character of the place. There is a large sitting/dining room, a kitchen equipped with a stove and a refrigerator, and a full bath in addition to sleeping accommodations for up to eight—two double and two single bedrooms, plus a sofa bed. The cottage, which has easy access to numerous sandy beaches and the coastal path, also features a game room on the third floor, as well as a garage and a lovely garden. Contact: Chez Nous Travel Service, 85 Dobb Top Road, Holmbridge, Huddersfield, HD7 1QP, England. Call 011-44-1-0484-684075. Ref. 8G.

Children: **Y**   Pets: **N**   Smoking: **Y**   Handicap Access: **N**   Payment: **P, V, M**

Fouesnant

KERARIS

Rates: budget-inexpensive

Open: year-round

Minimum Stay: one week

A faithful restoration of this 18th-century Breton farmhouse, cottage and barn on two acres of grounds integrates new and old architectural styles in each two- and three-bedroom suite. Barbecue and laundry facilities are available, as well as easy access to idyllic beaches, excellent restaurants, tennis, squash, golf, sailing and wind surfing, to name just a few recreational options. You may also want to explore the town of Fouesnant, with its many tempting shops and its colorful Friday-morning market. The owners call Keraris "a haven for children" and welcome the kids to visit the ponies at the sister site of Kervoal. Contact: Chez Nous Travel Service, 85 Dobb Top Road, Holmbridge, Huddersfield, HD7 1QP, England. Call 011-44-1-0484-684075. Ref. 9A.

Children: **Y**   Pets: **N**   Smoking: **Y**   Handicap: **Y** (cottage only)   Payment: **P, V, M**

Kerroch

KERROCH COTTAGE

Rates: budget-inexpensive

Open: year-round

Minimum Stay: one week

This completely restored fisherman's cottage has a fine view of the Bay of Biscay, facing the Ile de Groix. Just minutes away are the Kerroch beach, port and shops; a nearby ferry takes you the port city of Lorient in 45 minutes. The cottage offers a modern kitchen with dishwasher and washing machine and a living/dining room. Both bedrooms have a double and a single bed, sleeping a total of six. Sail, fish and play tennis nearby or drive a half hour to the golf course. Contact: Blakes Vacations, 4918 Dempster Street, Skokie, IL 60077. Call 1-800-628-8118. Ref. ANQ.

Children: **Y**   Pets: **N**   Smoking: **Y**   Handicap Access: **N**   Payment: **P, T**

Lannion

POUL AR BELEC COTTAGE

Rates: budget-inexpensive

Open: year-round

Minimum Stay: one week

Use this quiet, countryside house less than three miles from the sea as a base to explore the rugged cliffs, fishing villages and isolated coves of Brittany. The house has a modern kitchen, dining room and sitting room, plus a large enclosed garden with table, chairs and barbecue. One double bedroom and three singles accommodate five in comfort. On the nearby beaches, you can try your hand at sailing and windsurfing. Contact: Blakes Vacations, 4918 Dempster Street, Skokie, IL 60077. Call 1-800-628-8118. Ref. ABT.

Children: **Y**   Pets: **N**   Smoking: **Y**   Handicap Access: **N**   Payment: **P, T**

Lasne en St. Armel

MAISON LASNE   *Rates: budget-moderate*
Open: year-round   *Minimum Stay: one week*

The quiet hamlet of Lasne en St. Armel lies three miles north of the city of Vannes on the southwest coast of Brittany. One small beach lies a quarter-mile away; four miles further are several others near the town of Sarzeau. The house has a large kitchen with a tiled floor and a beamed ceiling, a living/dining area with an open fireplace and color TV, two double bedrooms and a twin. A small folding single bed and a single divan in the living room boost the capacity of the house to seven guests. Fishing, sailing, riding and tennis are all available nearby. Contact: Blakes Vacations, 4918 Dempster Street, Skokie, IL 60077. Call 1-800-628-8118. Ref. ANL.

Children: Y   Pets: N   Smoking: Y   Handicap Access: N   Payment: P, T

Paimpol

L'ISLANDAIS   *Rates: budget-inexpensive*
Open: May 26-September 28   *Minimum Stay: one week*

Endowed with a rich and interesting history, the fishing village of Paimpol on the English Channel boasts its own maritime museum. Nearby, this traditional country house offers spacious lodgings, featuring a living/dining area that opens onto the garden, which is equipped with lawn furniture and a barbecue. The open fireplace, color TV and easy chairs make this house comfortable as well, with room enough for six to eight in two double bedrooms, two singles, plus a cot and a child's bed. Visit the ruined abbey at Beaufort, sail, fish and play tennis, or drive to the golf course a half-hour away. Contact: Blakes Vacations, 4918 Dempster Street, Skokie, IL 60077. Call 1-800-628-8118. Ref. AMH.

Children: Y   Pets: N   Smoking: Y   Handicap Access: N   Payment: P, T

Perros Guirec

GUERADUR   *Rates: budget-moderate*
Open: year-round   *Minimum Stay: one week*

Enjoy roomy comfort in this secluded country house near the lively resort town of Perros Guirec British. Located less than two miles from the coast, the cottage boasts all the modern amenities, including a dishwasher, telephone, washing machine, garage and television with British reception. The living/dining room features an open stone fireplace; outdoors, guests can relax in a garden complete with furniture and swings. Eight people can sleep comfortably in two double bedrooms and two twins. Two bicycles provide quick transportation to the beach. Contact: Blakes Vacations, 4918 Dempster Street, Skokie, IL 60077. Call 1-800-628-8118. Ref. AMZ.

Children: Y   Pets: N   Smoking: Y   Handicap Access: N   Payment: P, T

Pont l'Abbe

PEN HADOR APARTMENT
Open: year-round

Rates: budget-inexpensive
Minimum Stay: one week

This second-story apartment in a traditional stone house gives vacationers complete privacy because the ground floor is usually unoccupied. Situated on a quiet road, the house makes a peaceful seaside retreat but stands only thirteen miles from the bustling town of Quimper. Six people can sleep in the apartment's three bedrooms (two double and one twin), which open onto a kitchen/living/dining room. Outside, enjoy the large enclosed garden or venture to the beach only a short distance away. Contact: Blakes Vacations, 4918 Dempster Street, Skokie, IL 60077. Call 1-800-628-8118. Ref. ABK.

Children: **Y**   Pets: **N**   Smoking: **Y**   Handicap Access: **N**   Payment: **P, T**

Quatrevaux

SEAVIEW STONE COTTAGE
Open: year-round

Rates: budget-moderate
Minimum Stay: one week

Just a few minutes from a sheltered cove with a fine beach, this white-shuttered stone lodge stands on the grounds of a chateau. It has its own private garden in which guests can have a late brunch or supper while admiring the white-capped surf. The waves are ideal for wind surfing and sailing; golf, horseback riding and bicycling are also available. This northern coast of Normandy has a rich history over the centuries, which makes for fascinating explorations. The lodge has room for four adults and two children in one single and one double bedroom, a comfy sitting room with an open fireplace, laundry facilities and a small kitchen. Contact: Rhoda and Joseph Kafer, Riviera Holidays, 31 Georgian Lane, Great Neck, NY 11024. Call 516-487-8094. Ref. NB56.

Children: **Y** Pets: **Y** Smoking: **Y** Handicap Access: **N** Payment: **P, V, M, A**

Quimper

MAISON ADRIEN
Open: year-round

Rates: deluxe
Minimum Stay: none

This amazing 16th-century manor house of stone has ancient shuttered windows that open up to reveal tranquil, leafy surroundings. There are three bedrooms and two and a half baths, and the kitchen/dining room has the old-fashioned charm of a sprawling country estate with a fireplace in every room. One of the two living rooms is ideally suited to the long, lazy days of summer. The nearest town is Quimper, about a ten-minute drive away, and the beautiful Brittany coast is just three miles away, offering attractive beaches and numerous recreational activities. Fresh seafood is available in abundance, made more enjoyable when tried with the local wines. Drives and walks through the area will reveal a seemingly endless array of charming medieval villages, old stone chapels and attractive scenery. Contact: Overseas Connection, 70 West 71st Street, #1C, New York, NY 10023. Call 212-769-1170. Ref. F30.

Children: **Y**   Pets: **N**   Smoking: **Y**   Handicap Access: **N**   Payment: **C, P**

BURGUNDY

Remilly-en-Montagne

DOMAINE DE LA SOURCE
Rates: budget-inexpensive
Open: year-round
Minimum Stay: one week

When a wine grower built this house in 1654, Louis XIV ruled France, but it's been updated and refurbished to include modern conveniences while retaining its historic character. The large kitchen/living/dining room is furnished with many antiques, an open fireplace, easy chairs and color TV. In an elegantly furnished double bedroom and one twin, four people can rest peacefully at night. During the day, share the enclosed garden and fishpond with the owner or venture into the cellar to see the ancient wine presses and storage areas. Guests have use of a washing machine and dishwasher in the kitchen area and enjoy easy access to sailing, tennis, fishing, riding and, of course, many vineyards where you can taste and buy the region's famous wines. Contact: Blakes Vacations, 4918 Dempster Street, Skokie, IL 60077. Call 1-800-628-8118. Ref. APZ.

Children: Y   Pets: N   Smoking: Y   Handicap Access: N   Payment: P, T

CENTRE

Chartres

MODERN FLAT
Rates: budget
Open: year-round
Minimum Stay: one week

On the elevated ground floor of a modern block of apartments situated on the edge of town, this roomy flat for up to four comes with a garden and private tennis courts. Make yourself at home in this well-furnished, balconied apartment that includes two twin-bedded rooms, a modern bathroom, an ample kitchen with a table for four and a living/dining room. Within walking distance, you'll find two swimming pools, shops and a supermarket. In addition to sightseeing and shopping in Chartres itself, you can take many intriguing excursions to area attractions, such as Paris, Versailles and the Loire castles. Contact: Chez Nous Travel Service, 85 Dobb Top Road, Holmbridge, Huddersfield, HD7 1QP, England. Call 011-44-1-0484-684075. Ref. 7A.

Children: Y   Pets: N   Smoking: Y   Handicap Access: N   Payment: P, V, M

La Guerche

RIVERSIDE HOUSE
Rates: budget-moderate
Open: year-round
Minimum Stay: one week

On the banks of the River Creuse sits this recently modernized 300-year-old house, which can accommodate up to eight people. Cozy up to the stone fireplace or step down through the private garden to the river, where a rowboat is provided for fishing or just drifting with the current. The house has three large bedrooms, one with its own shower, plus a full bath upstairs. Downstairs, the kitchen is well equipped and there is a utility room with an automatic washer. In addition, full central heating means year-round comfort. La Guerche, with its own chateau, is a quaint, friendly village set in rolling countryside. Horse-back riding, tennis, canoeing and swimming facilities can be found nearby. Contact: Chez Nous Travel Service, 85 Dobb Top Road, Holmbridge, Huddersfield, HD7 1QP, England. Call 011-44-1-0484-684075. Ref. 4D.

Children: Y   Pets: N   Smoking: Y   Handicap Access: N   Payment: P, V, M

Ligueil

STONE COTTAGE   *Rates: budget*
Open: year-round   *Minimum Stay: one week*

Situated on the outskirts of the small farming community of Ligueil, this delightful cottage loaded with country charm offers accommodations for four. Two rooms with twin beds, a bath with a shower, a kitchenette and a combination sitting/dining room with patio doors opening onto a lovely garden and small vineyard make this a comfortable home base for touring. English-speaking babysitters are available as well. Ligueil, dating back to medieval times, has a weekly market, excellent restaurants and reliable bus service. Swimming, tennis and horseback or bike riding are only some of the activities that might fill your days here. Contact: Chez Nous Travel Service, 85 Dobb Top Road, Holmbridge, Huddersfield, HD7 1QP, England. Call 011-44-1-0484-684075. Ref. 4A.

Children: Y   Pets: N   Smoking: Y   Handicap Access: N   Payment: P, V, M

CORSICA

Calvi

CALVI HOUSE   *Rates: moderate-deluxe*
Open: late April-late September   *Minimum Stay: one week*

The open-air atmosphere of this hillside traditional house is accentuated by its high ceilings and large terrace. Make your way down the hill to swim off the rocks of the Golfe de la Revellata, or take the children to the sandy beach down the coast. Guests can also stay home and lounge by the pool, take in the views or stroll the bi-level gardens. Three twin bedrooms sleep six people. A word of caution for those traveling with young children: The pool is unfenced and has no shallow area and there are a few unguarded drops which could be hazardous. The bustling port of Calvi is a mile away. Contact: British Travel Associates, P.O. Box 299, Elkton, VA 22827. Call 1-800-327-6097 (in Virginia, 703-298-2232). Ref. Z19.

Children: Y   Pets: N   Smoking: Y   Handicap Access: N   Payment: All

Ile Rousse

ILE ROUSSE VILLA   *Rates: budget-moderate*
Open: September 1-June 30   *Minimum Stay: one week*

Corsica has a rich and varied history, from the Greek occupation in 565 B.C. to its union with France two centuries ago. But for many people, the sun, sand and mountains are its main attractions. Simply but tastefully furnished, this villa sits on the edge of a sandy beach.

The kitchen has be[en]
windows leading to a[...]
fortably in one bedroom [...]
bed. The airport at Calvi is i[...]
P.O. Box 299, Elkton, VA 22[...]
703-298-2232). Ref. Z5.
Children: Y   Pets: N   Smoking: Y

Marine de Davia
DAVIA HOUSE
Open: late April-late September

Accessed by a rough, steep path, this house is diffic[ult...]
the end of the climb, magnificent views of the Medi[terranean...]
Solitude and a rocky shoreline surround the property, w[...]
a sitting room, kitchen and dining room. A double sofa bed[...]
ble bedrooms and a folding bed sleep four to six, plus a child. R[elax on]
the large terrace or in the garden, or take the path down to the[...]
Contact: British Travel Associates, P.O. Box 299, Elkton, VA 2282[7.]
Call 1-800-327-6097 (in Virginia, 703-298-2232). Ref. Z11.
Children: Y   Pets: N   Smoking: Y   Handicap Access: N   Payment: All

Solenzara
CHATEAU SOLENZARA   *Rates: expensive-deluxe*
Open: late April-late September   *Minimum Stay: two weeks*

More luxurious than many of the simple seashore cottages Corsica offers, Chateau Solenzara boasts breathtaking views, well-manicured gardens and a tastefully appointed interior. Most of the rooms look out toward the Mediterranean Sea, including the master bedroom, which is luxuriously furnished and has a private balcony. Strikingly designed with mezzanine levels, the two other bedrooms sleep three apiece, with one bed reached by ladder. A fourth, simpler bedroom contains a single bed and double sofa bed, bringing the total sleeping accommodations to eight adults and two children. The sandy beach at Canella is less than a mile away; Solenzara is three miles away. Contact: British Travel Associates, P.O. Box 299, Elkton, VA 22827. Call 1-800-327-6097 (in Virginia, 703-298-2232). Ref. Z35.
Children: Y, over 10 Pets: N Smoking: Y Handicap Access: N Payment: All

DORDOGNE

Augignac
LA BEAUFARIE   *Rates: budget*
Open: year-round   *Minimum Stay: one week*

This small house is set on extensive grounds by its own private lake, which guests can view from French windows in the living room. Swim, fish or paddle around in the small boat that comes with the rental, or just relax on the terrace and fire up the barbecue. Four to six sleep comfortably here in a double sofa bed in the living room and two double bedrooms. This house may not be suitable for very young children because the lake is easily accessed. If you like tennis, you can find

Payment: P, T

expensive-deluxe
Stay: one week
...thout Bergerac
...r living/dining
...ough the gently
...ake the rowboat
...'s room for eight
...he historic towns
...arby, as are shops,
Dempster Street,

: N   Payment: P, T

renovated and the living/dining
large terrace. Three to four people sleep com-
with three beds plus a convertible single sofa
nearby. Contact: British Travel Associates,
...27. Call 1-800-327-6097 (in Virginia,

Handicap Access: N   Payment: All

FRANCE 119

Rates: inexpensive-expensive
Minimum Stay: one week
...ilt to reach, but at
...rranean await.
...ich includes
...two dou-
...relax on
...sea.
...7.

Rates: moderate
Minimum Stay: three nights

Open: y...
The medieval villag... ...he hills of Dordogne that it can be seen for miles arou... like a fairy-tale town rising out of the luscious French countryside. These rental apartments are located in the priory of an ancient chateau. Each suite comprises two double bedrooms, a living room and two bathrooms. Almost every window in these airy rooms opens onto lovely view. A complimentary breakfast is provided and guests may use a shared kitchen. Guests find these quarters an excellent base for exploring the remarkable castles, abbeys and caves sprinkled throughout the neighborhood. Contact: Villas and Apartments Abroad, Ltd., 420 Madison Avenue, New York, NY 10017. Call 1-800-433-3020.

Children: Y   Pets: Y   Smoking: Y   Handicap Access: N   Payment: C, P, T

Blanc

LA GRANGE   *Rates: budget-expensive*
Open: year-round   *Minimum Stay: one week*
Set in the rural hamlet of Blanc, this medium-sized stone house has its own lake and swimming pool. The living/dining area exudes old-world charm from its exposed beams and open stone fireplace, while the well-equipped kitchen/dining room with washer and dryer bespeaks modern convenience. Four to six sleep comfortably in one double bedroom, one twin, one single and a double sofa bed. Enjoy a cookout in the garden or leave the property to play tennis, ride, fish and play golf. Steep, open stairs make this unsuitable for very young children or the infirm. Contact: Blakes Vacations, 4918 Dempster Street, Skokie, IL 60077. Call 1-800-628-8118. Ref. AGN.

Children: Y   Pets: N   Smoking: Y   Handicap Access: N   Payment: P, T

Ecuras

LE CHAT - LE FORSYTHIA   *Rates: budget-moderate*
Open: year-round   *Minimum Stay: one week*

Part of a vacation village set around a large lake on the Dordogne/ Charente border, Le Forsythia sleeps six to eight guests. The kitchen area includes a breakfast bar; the living/dining room has an open fireplace and French windows that lead onto the terrace. On the village grounds, guests can find a swimming pool, children's pool, tennis courts, volleyball court, miniature golf and a children's play area. You can wind-surf, canoe and fish on the lake. Contact: Blakes Vacations, 4918 Dempster Street, Skokie, IL 60077. Call 1-800-628-8118. Ref. AKH.

Children: **Y**   Pets: **N**   Smoking: **Y**   Handicap Access: **N**   Payment: **P, T**

Le Buisson

CHATEAU LE BUISSON   *Rates: deluxe*
Open: year-round   *Minimum Stay: one week*

When you step through a magnificent stone archway into the enchanting inner courtyard of this 14th-century chateau, you step into history. Descendants of the original owners still live in the chateau lovingly decorated with ancient tapestries and antiques; they still maintain the chateau's extensive grounds, quiet woodlands and cheerful meadows. You, too, can partake of the chateau's timeless splendor: The south wing, a completely private section of the house, welcomes nine guests. Two of the five bedrooms have en suite bathrooms; one even boasts a four-poster bed. The living room features an open fireplace, the dining room boasts an exquisite crypted ceiling and the kitchen is fully equipped with dishwasher and washing machine. Contact: Villas and Apartments Abroad, Ltd., 420 Madison Avenue, New York, NY 10017. Call 1-800-433-3020.

Children: **Y**   Pets: **Y**   Smoking: **Y**   Handicap Access: **N**   Payment: **C, P, T**

Les Milandes

VILLAGE HOUSE   *Rates: moderate-luxury*
Open: year-round   *Minimum Stay: one week*

Josephine Baker, the renowned American jazz singer, fell in love with Les Milandes and you will too. Directly adjacent to the chateau once owned by Baker, this rental house features its own cheery garden and a large swimming pool. Inside, the airy living, dining and kitchen space welcomes you with a cozy fireplace. Upstairs are a comfortable master suite and two twin bedrooms. You'll want to sample some Gallic gastronomic delights at the enchanting little restaurant around the corner. Nearby Castelnaud offers shops and tennis, and the resplendent French countryside tempts you to explore. Contact: Villas and Apartments Abroad, Ltd., 420 Madison Avenue, New York, NY 10017. Call 1-800-433-3020.

Children: **Y**   Pets: **Y**   Smoking: **Y**   Handicap Access: **N**   Payment: **C, P, T**

Montagrier

LA ROUSSELIE   *Rates: budget*
Open: May 26-September 28   *Minimum Stay: one week*

Explore an area that abounds with caves and grottoes like the one at Lascaux, where prehistoric cave paintings were discovered. La Rousselie stands on a quiet country lane surrounded by farms and overlooking a beautiful valley. There's room for six to eight in two double bedrooms, a three-quarter single and twin. A large kitchen, a separate dining room and a large, enclosed garden with barbecue make for plenty of space. Sailing, riding, tennis, fishing and swimming are available nearby; golf is about twenty minutes away. Contact: Blakes Vacations, 4918 Dempster Street, Skokie, IL 60077. Call 1-800-628-8118. Ref. APJ.

Children: **Y**   Pets: **N**   Smoking: **Y**   Handicap Access: **N**   Payment: **P, T**

Urval

CHATEAU URVAL   *Rates: deluxe*
Open: year-round   *Minimum Stay: one week*

This marvelous 17th-century chateau overlooks the ancient village of Urval, whose Romanesque church and medieval buildings bespeak a rich history. Furnished throughout with exquisite antiques, the chateau retains its traditional ambience despite being fully modernized. The two wings can be rented separately or together: The right wing accommodates nine guests and the left wing seven. Each wing has its own secluded terraces and lush gardens; the more adventurous may be tempted to wander through the 50 acres of meadows and woodlands in the chateau's extensive grounds. Fishing, boating, tennis and riding are available nearby, as are refreshing swims in the area's pristine rivers. Contact: Villas and Apartments Abroad, Ltd., 420 Madison Avenue, New York, NY 10017. Call 1-800-433-3020.

Children: **Y**   Pets: **Y**   Smoking: **Y**   Handicap Access: **N**   Payment: **C, P, T**

ILE DE FRANCE

Paris

RESIDENCE ELYSEE   *Rates: expensive-deluxe*
Open: year-round   *Minimum Stay: one week*

Who hasn't pictured themselves strolling up the Champs Elysees? Well, picture staying there in a residential hotel that offers a relaxed atmosphere and a view of the world's greatest thoroughfares. The Residence Elysee has studio, one- and two-bedroom apartments grouped around a charming Parisian courtyard. It has been recently renovated and furnished with modern, cushioned couches and chairs and low tables that lend an air of elegance. All apartments have a full kitchen, color TV and telephone; the two-bedroom style offers an extra bath. For convenience, a receptionist is on the job around the clock and maid service is provided three days a week. The residence makes a fabulous starting point from which to explore the rest of Paris. Contact: Villas International, 71 West 23rd Street, New York, NY 10010. Call 212-929-7585.

Children: Y   Pets: N   Smoking: Y   Handicap Access: N   Payment: C, P, T, O

Paris

11 RUE ST. SAUVER   *Rates: expensive*
Open: year-round   *Minimum Stay: one week*

This extraordinary studio duplex in the Les Halles district features a living room with a balcony and a spiral staircase leading to the double bedroom. Modern and luxurious, the apartment is located on the fourth floor. A convertible couch makes room for two more guests. Nearby, the Forum, which opened in the early 1980s on the site of a 19th-century food market, offers some of the most exciting shops and cafes in Paris. The Forum also has a tropical garden and Olympic-size swimming pool. Contact: Overseas Connections, 70 West 71st Street, #1C, New York, NY 10023. Call 212-769-1170.

Children: Y   Pets: N   Smoking: Y   Handicap Access: N   Payment: C, P

Paris

14 RUE JULITTE   *Rates: expensive*
Open: year-round   *Minimum Stay: one week*

This classic Parisian apartment for six offers the quiet seclusion of one of the city's best residential neighborhoods along with the color and culture of the Champs Elysees, just a short walk away. In addition to commanding one of the most spectacular views in the city, it also lies close to fine dining and exclusive shopping. This third-floor apartment offers two double bedrooms, a living room with a convertible sofa, a full bathroom and a kitchen. Contact: Overseas Connections, 70 West 71st Street, #1C, New York, NY 10023. Call 212-769-1170.

Children: Y   Pets: N   Smoking: Y   Handicap Access: N   Payment: C, P

Paris

14 RUE QUINCAMPOIX   *Rates: expensive*
Open: year-round   *Minimum Stay: one week*

In a lovely 18th-century building on one of the oldest streets in Paris, you'll find this studio apartment offering quiet luxury for one. Located on the ground floor, it features a large living room, a modern separate kitchen and full bath. Experience the fine arts at nearby George Pompidou Center or take in the life and color of the Beauborug, with its acrobats, fire eaters, singers, break dancers, clowns and street performers. Contact: Overseas Connections, 70 West 71st Street, #1C, New York, NY 10023. Call 212-769-1170.

Children: Y   Pets: N   Smoking: Y   Handicap Access: N   Payment: C, P

Paris

14 RUE ST. GERMAIN L'AUXERROIS   *Rates: expensive*
Open: year-round   *Minimum Stay: one week*

Enjoy the splendor of the City of Light from the privacy of your very own 18th-century duplex. Modern conveniences include a full bathroom, a fully applianced kitchen, a TV, a stereo and a phone, but the fireplace and beamed ceiling preserve the flat's old-world charm. The second level houses two double bedrooms; the third bedroom, on the lower level, includes a small terrace. This centrally located apartment overlooks the Seine and lies close to the Chatelet Metro stop for easy access to all the delights of Paris—shopping, museums, cafes, nightclubs, art galleries and more. Contact: France Unlimited, 135 Isobella Street, #708, Ontario, Canada M4Y1P4. Call 416-920-6329.

Children: N   Pets: N   Smoking: Y   Handicap Access: N   Payment: C, P, T

Paris

15 RUE DE LILLE   *Rates: inexpensive*
Open: year-round   *Minimum Stay: one week*

Here's a charming third-floor studio apartment close to the Musee d'Orsay and the Seine. For budget-conscious travelers who don't need a lot of extra room, or for those who plan to spend most of their time out discovering the enchantments of Paris, the flat is an ideal choice. Comfortably appointed, it includes a phone, a TV and a stereo. The kitchen, though small, is modern and efficient. After you've explored the nearby environs, hop on the Metro at the Musee d'Orsay stop to reach any area in Paris. Contact: France Unlimited, 135 Isobella Street, #708, Ontario, Canada M4Y1P4. Call 416-920-6329.

Children: N   Pets: N   Smoking: Y   Handicap Access: N   Payment: C, P, T

Paris

15 RUE DES HALLES   *Rates: deluxe*
Open: year-round   *Minimum Stay: one week*

Located amidst the shops and restaurants of Les Halles near the Louvre, this bright, airy, three-room apartment is an ideal base for up to four people interested in exploring Paris. The apartment features two double bedrooms, a light-filled living room, a bath and a half and a fully equipped kitchen complete with washing machine. The apartment is located on the third floor of an elevator building. Contact: Overseas Connections, 70 West 71st Street, #1C, New York, NY 10023. Call 212-769-1170.

Children: Y   Pets: N   Smoking: Y   Handicap Access: N   Payment: C, P

Paris

15 RUE ST. HONORE   *Rates: budget*
Open: year-round   *Minimum Stay: one week*

Close to the Louvre and Chatelet, this studio for two is an ideal base from which to explore one of the most beautiful and historic areas in the city of Paris. Located in a handsome older building, the apartment faces the street and features a living room with a convertible couch for two, a kitchen and a bathroom with a shower. Venture outside to the Tuileries and enjoy a coffee at an open-air cafe, or walk along the banks of the Seine. Contact: Overseas Connections, 70 West 71st Street, #1C, New York, NY 10023. Call 212-769-1170.

Children: **Y**   Pets: **N**   Smoking: **Y**   Handicap Access: **N**   Payment: **C, P**

Paris

17 RUE DUPLEIX   *Rates: expensive*
Open: year-round   *Minimum Stay: one week*

Located in a classic Parisian building, this elegant apartment for two is close to the Eiffel Tower and the Champs de Mars. The third-floor flat in an elevator building features two luxuriously furnished rooms and a large kitchen with a dishwasher. Stroll down the broad avenues, or if you're feeling vigorous, climb the Eiffel Tower's 1,652 steps for a view that reaches, on a clear day, up to 42 miles. Contact: Overseas Connections, 70 West 71st Street, #1C, New York, NY 10023. Call 212-769-1170.

Children: **Y**   Pets: **N**   Smoking: **Y**   Handicap Access: **N**   Payment: **C, P**

Paris

2 RUE ST. GILLES   *Rates: expensive*
Open: year-round   *Minimum Stay: one week*

This two-room apartment for two offers a quiet refuge from the excitement and activity always found in the heart of the Marais district. Off the bedroom is a terrace overlooking a serene yard; inside, modern decor, a full bath and a separate kitchen provide all the convenience you'll need to make your stay a pleasant one. The Place des Vosgas, a haven of trees, arcades and elegant architecture dating from the 17th century, is also nearby. Contact: Overseas Connections, 70 West 71st Street, #1C, New York, NY 10023. Call 212-769-1170.

Children: **Y**   Pets: **N**   Smoking: **Y**   Handicap Access: **N**   Payment: **C, P**

Paris

21 RUE DU CIRQUE   *Rates: moderate*
Open: year-round   *Minimum Stay: one week*

Overlooking a courtyard filled with small shrubs and potted flowers, this two-bedroom apartment furnished with antiques has a double bedroom, a living room with a convertible couch for two and a kitchen. The third-floor apartment is located in a historic elevator building near the Palais de L'Elysees and the shopper's paradise of St. Honore. There, you'll find the fashions of St. Laurent, Hermes, Lanvin and Helena Rubenstein alongside art galleries and antique shops. Contact: Overseas Connections, 70 West 71st Street, #1C, New York, NY 10023. Call 212-769-1170.

Children: **Y**   Pets: **N**   Smoking: **Y**   Handicap Access: **N**   Payment: **C, P**

Paris

38 AVENUE GEORGE V   *Rates: expensive*
Open: year-round   *Minimum Stay: one week*

This two-bedroom apartment in a modern luxury building near the

Champs Elysees can accommodate four or five people. Located on the second floor of the elevator building, the apartment features a double bedroom and a living room with two single convertible sofas and a futon. You'll enjoy the close proximity to the most fashionable streets, where you can wander down broad paths, shop at stores featuring exclusive fashions, dine at elegant cafes or just watch some of the most interesting people in the City of Light. Contact: Overseas Connections, 70 West 71st Street, #1C, New York, NY 10023. Call 212-769-1170.

Children: Y   Pets: N   Smoking: Y   Handicap Access: N   Payment: C, P

Paris

45 RUE CAMBRONNE   *Rates: deluxe*
Open: year-round   *Minimum Stay: one week*

Near the Eiffel Tower and the Champs de Mars, this 1950 elevator building offers a roomy apartment for up to six guests. A sophisticated security system ensures safety, while the two bedrooms, living room, dining room and fully equipped kitchen offer luxury and comfort. Enjoy your view of the Eiffel Tower or visit one of the many nearby museums, including the Muse de Cinema, all just a short distance from this sixth-floor apartment. Contact: Overseas Connections, 70 West 71st Street, #1C, New York, NY 10023. Call 212-769-1170.

Children: Y   Pets: N   Smoking: Y   Handicap Access: N   Payment: C, P

Paris

5 BERNARD PALISSY   *Rates: inexpensive*
Open: year-round   *Minimum Stay: one week*

On a quiet street in a renovated older building, this studio for two is perfect for visitors wishing to discover places not listed in guide books. Adjacent to St. Germain des Pres, the apartment is close to clubs, art galleries and the market on the Rue de Seine. The area offers a charming blend of the chic and the shabby, with dozens of nooks and crannies you'll want to explore and claim for yourself. Stylish and unusual, the studio has fully mirrored walls and a small Japanese-style table at the foot of the double bed. The corner kitchen is fully equipped and the bathroom has a shower. Contact: Overseas Connections, 70 West 71st Street, #1C, New York, NY 10023. Call 212-769-1170.

Children: Y   Pets: N   Smoking: Y   Handicap Access: N   Payment: C, P

Paris

5 PLACE FELIX   *Rates: budget*
Open: year-round   *Minimum Stay: one week*

Near the Bois de Vincennes and built at the turn of the century, this building contains a charming studio for two. Guests reach the fifth-floor apartment via the building's elevator. The living area includes a convertible couch; a large kitchen offers cooking and eating facilities. Commissioned by Napoleon, who hoped to create a public space more beautiful than London's Hyde Park, the nearby park is a place of broad lawns and century-old trees. Restaurants and movie theaters also offer entertainment. Contact: Overseas Connections, 70 West 71st Street, #1C, New York, NY 10023. Call 212-769-1170.

Children: **Y**   Pets: **N**   Smoking: **Y**   Handicap Access: **N**   Payment: **C, P**

Paris

6 RUE BERTIN   *Rates: moderate*
Open: year-round   *Minimum Stay: one week*

Close to the Louvre and boasting a splendid view of the Seine as it winds through the city, this two-room apartment sleeps two people. The apartment features a beamed ceiling, a separate bath and a fully equipped kitchen. After conquering the Louvre, relax and enjoy an ice cream or a cool drink at one of the open-air cafes nearby. Contact: Overseas Connections, 70 West 71st Street, #1C, New York, NY 10023. Call 212-769-1170.

Children: **Y**   Pets: **N**   Smoking: **Y**   Handicap Access: **N**   Payment: **C, P**

Paris

6 RUE MANDAR   *Rates: deluxe*
Open: year-round   *Minimum Stay: one week*

Built in the early 19th century and located close to a ruin of the original Les Halles market, this one-bedroom apartment is close to excellent shops, cafes and restaurants. Nearby is the Center Georges Pomidau, an architectural wonder and home to one of the world's greatest collections of modern art. Located on the third floor, this apartment features a double bedroom opening onto a quiet internal courtyard, a kitchen and a full bath. A convertible couch provides additional sleeping for another person. Contact: Overseas Connections, 70 West 71st Street, #1C, New York, NY 10023. Call 212-769-1170.

Children: **Y**   Pets: **N**   Smoking: **Y**   Handicap Access: **N**   Payment: **C, P**

Paris

63 RUE DE BRIANCION   *Rates: expensive*
Open: year-round   *Minimum Stay: one week*

Overlooking the trees and flowers of Georges Brassens Park, this regal seven-story building offers four two-bedroom apartments accommodating six guests each. The apartments are located on the third and fifth floors of the elevator building. Each apartment features two bedrooms, a dining room, a living room and a fully equipped kitchen. In addition to the park, which lies fifty feet from your front door, you'll find dining and shopping within easy reach. Contact: Overseas Connections, 70 West 71st Street, #1C, New York, NY 10023. Call 212-769-1170.

Children: **Y**   Pets: **N**   Smoking: **Y**   Handicap Access: **N**   Payment: **C, P**

Paris

74 RUE DE SEVRES   *Rates: moderate*
Open: year-round   *Minimum Stay: one week*

The famous Left Bank—no place elicits more bohemian fantasies than this artist's haunt. Imagine staying in a cozy two-room apartment close to the cafes, bookstores, cinemas and art galleries of the colorful boulevard St. Germain. The bedroom overlooks a quiet courtyard; the living room's sofa bed provides extra sleeping accommodations. A TV, stereo and phone are provided for your convenience. There's a full bathroom and the kitchen is modern and well equipped for whipping up your favorite meal—if you can tear yourself away from the local bistros. For a day of museum browsing or boutique hopping, the Vaneau and Duroc Metro stops are nearby to take you anywhere in the city. Contact: France Unlimited, 135 Isobella Street, #708, Ontario, Canada M4Y1P4. Call 416-920-6329.

Children: N   Pets: N   Smoking: Y   Handicap Access: N   Payment: C, P, T

Paris

74 RUE SEVRES   *Rates: expensive*
Open: year-round   *Minimum Stay: one week*
Stroll from the Boulevard St. Germain past bookstores and cafes to this two-room Left Bank apartment, which accommodates two people. Located on the fifth floor of an elevator building, the apartment features a full bath, a modern kitchen and a bedroom opening onto a quiet courtyard. Wander along the neighborhood's streets and browse at unique shops offering everything from antiques to designer fashions. The Musee De Cluny, a museum famous for its medieval art and tapestry collection, is also nearby and worth seeing. Contact: Overseas Connections, 70 West 71st Street, #1C, New York, NY 10023. Call 212-769-1170.

Children: Y   Pets: N   Smoking: Y   Handicap Access: N   Payment: C, P

Paris

8 RUE DES LOMBARDS   *Rates: deluxe*
Open: year-round   *Minimum Stay: one week*
In the heart of the Marais district, amidst outdoor cafes, restaurants and shops, this two-bedroom apartment featuring wooden ceiling beams and a fully equipped kitchen offers both serenity and comfort. Able to accommodate four people, the apartment has a modern bath and even a washing machine. Contact: Overseas Connections, 70 West 71st Street, #1C, New York, NY 10023. Call 212-769-1170.

Children: Y   Pets: N   Smoking: Y   Handicap Access: N   Payment: C, P

Paris

AVENUE DE SUFFREN   *Rates: expensive*
Open: year-round   *Minimum Stay: three nights*
This small house is the perfect getaway for a couple visiting Paris, whether for the first time or the fifteenth. Tucked away in a tranquil neighborhood, the two-story house has a charming little garden of its very own. Downstairs is a tastefully furnished living room with kitchenette; the cozy bedroom and bathroom are upstairs. The peaceful retreat lies within walking distance of the Eiffel Tower and other

Parisian delights. Contact: Villas and Apartments Abroad, Ltd., 420 Madison Avenue, New York, NY 10017. Call 1-800-433-3020.

Children: Y   Pets: Y   Smoking: Y   Handicap Access: N   Payment: C, P, T

Paris

BOULEVARD GRENELLE   *Rates: deluxe*
Open: year-round   *Minimum Stay: one week*

Molded ceilings and hardwood floors are just a few of the elegant architectural elements that make this apartment in a lovely old stone building a pleasure for six guests. Protected by a modern security system, the second-floor apartment features two bedrooms, a dining room, a living room and a fully equipped kitchen. Located in an especially charming area in an established residential neighborhood, the flat puts you close to the Eiffel Tower, several parks and some extremely fine museums. Contact: Overseas Connections, 70 West 71st Street, #1C, New York, NY 10023. Call 212-769-1170.

Children: Y   Pets: N   Smoking: Y   Handicap Access: N   Payment: C, P

Paris

FLATOTEL INTERNATIONAL: EIFFEL TOWER   *Rates: inexpensive-deluxe*
Open: year-round   *Minimum Stay: none*

The Flatotel Eiffel Tower, a 32-floor hi-rise of 300 fully furnished apartments just steps away from the Eiffel Tower in the 15th arrondissement, offers vacation renters studios, five-room duplexes and everything in between. Flatotel visitors may choose from three price options: The economy plan, which requires a minimum seven-day commitment, offers cleaning and linen change once a week; and the residence and hotel plans, each progressively more expensive, offer twice-weekly and daily maid service respectively. The unusually low rates include the service charge but not the 6% French tax. Contact: Hometours International, Inc., 1170 Broadway, New York, NY 10001. Call: 212-689-0851 or 1-800-367-4668.

Children: Y   Pets: N   Smoking: Y   Handicap Access: N   Payment: C, P

Paris

FRANKLIN APARTMENTS   *Rates: expensive*
Open: year-round   *Minimum Stay: one week*

These elegantly furnished one-bedroom apartments stand in a residential Parisian neighborhood convenient to the metro and within walking distance of the chic cafes and the heavenly Trocadero Gardens. The apartment building is small and the service is excellent—daily maid service, elevator, TV and telephone are all included. Up to four guests can stay with comfort, since the living room has a pull-out couch for two and the bedroom has a double bed. The dining area sits four with ease and the kitchen has tasteful service for up to six people if you choose to entertain. It will be a pleasure to return to your apartment after sampling the finest of art, food, wine and music in Paris. The building has received a rating equivalent to four stars by the French Tourist Board. Contact: Rhoda and Joseph Kafer, Riviera Hol-

idays, 31 Georgian Lane, Great Neck, NY 11024. Call 516-487-8094.
Children: **Y**   Pets: **Y**   Smoking: **Y**   Handicap Access: **N**   Payment: **P**

Paris

ILE ST. LOUIS   *Rates: deluxe*
Open: year-round   *Minimum Stay: two weeks*

Located in the hub of Paris, this elegant first-floor apartment for six overlooks the ever-marvelous river Seine. The large living room and the beautiful oval dining room both enjoy unobstructed views of the river, with its colorful barges and sparkling play of lights. Three comfortable bedrooms (two with en suite bathrooms) and a large kitchen round out the accommodations. The stupendous location allows guests to go sightseeing all day and still get home early enough to enjoy the pleasures of their own home away from home. Contact: Villas and Apartments Abroad, Ltd., 420 Madison Avenue, New York, NY 10017. Call 1-800-433-3020.

Children: **Y**   Pets: **Y**   Smoking: **Y**   Handicap Access: **N**   Payment: **C, P, T**

Paris

MONT ST. GENEVIEVE   *Rates: budget*
Open: year-round   *Minimum Stay: one week*

This cozy studio apartment in a delightful older building stands near the St. Germain area, a haunt of artists, intellectuals and writers. Busy, colorful and cosmopolitan, this area has everything from hip cafes and bars to high-fashion shops to elegant buildings. Two famous churches, the St. Germain des Pres—the only Romanesque church in the city— and the St. Sulpice, famous for its Delacroix murals, are also nearby and worth seeing. The studio contains two single beds, a bathroom and a kitchenette. Contact: Overseas Connections, 70 West 71st Street, #1C, New York, NY 10023. Call 212-769-1170.

Children: **Y**   Pets: **N**   Smoking: **Y**   Handicap Access: **N**   Payment: **C, P**

Paris

RESIDENCE MONTPARNASSE   *Rates: moderate-expensive*
Open: year-round   *Minimum Stay: one week*

The Left Bank evokes images of sidewalk cafes, book stalls and colorful fashions. You can stay in the center of all this at a contemporary residence centrally located near the Montparnasse-Gaite metro, the tranquil Montparnasse Cemetery and the timeless Luxembourg Gardens. Studio apartments in the residence can sleep two guests; the one-bedroom apartments can sleep up to four. The wonderful pastries, breads and cheeses for sale at nearby patisseries and boulangeries can be prepared in the apartment kitchen. Whenever you need a moment to relax, settle down to the comfort of your apartment with color TV, telephone and private bathroom. Contact: Villas International, 71 West 23rd Street, New York, NY 10010. Call 212-929-7585.

Children: **Y** Pets: **N** Smoking: **Y** Handicap Access: **N** Payment: **C, P, T, O**

Paris

RESIDENCE TROCADERO *Rates: moderate-expensive*
Open: year-round *Minimum Stay: one week*
Rising above the bustle of the streets below is the unique modern building that houses the Residence Trocadero. Situated in an exclusive residential district, it offers easy access to many of the must-sees of Paris—the soaring Eiffel Tower, the Arc de Triomphe, the Champs Elysees and more. Studio-style apartments sleep either two or three guests and the one-bedroom apartments can sleep two to four. A large balcony and reception lounges with room to socialize provide a spot to look out over this sparkling city. After touring the streets and sights of Paris, relax in the sauna or stretch your muscles in the fitness room at the end of the day. For added convenience, the residence contains laundry facilities, TV and a cafeteria. Contact: Villas International, 71 West 23rd Street, New York, NY 10010. Call 212-929-7585.

Children: Y Pets: Y Smoking: Y Handicap Access: N Payment: C, P, T, O

Paris

RESIDENCE ZOLA *Rates: moderate-expensive*
Open: year-round *Minimum Stay: one week*
Named after the writer Emile Zola, one of the great observers of Parisian life, this residence sits on the Left Bank of the Seine in the southwest part of the city. A metro is just a few yards away, ready to whisk you toward the sights and lights of the city. If you prefer, the Eiffel Tower is a fifteen-minute walk. Sunny, traditionally styled studio, one- and two-bedroom flats offer tasteful furnishings and pleasant touches such as chandeliers and wall prints. If you prefer not to prepare your own meals, you can order them from room service. TV, 24-hour reception and in-room telephone will help make your stay more convenient. The mid-sized residence is located on a tree-lined street with the scenic Seine visible from the windows. Contact: Villas International, 71 West 23rd Street, New York, NY 10010. Call 212-929-7585.

Children: Y Pets: N Smoking: Y Handicap Access: N Payment: C, P, T, O

Paris

RUE BOURSALUT *Rates: inexpensive*
Open: year-round *Minimum Stay: one week*
Discover Paris from this centrally located one-bedroom apartment near the St. Lazare train station. Close to the Metro as well as to restaurants, cafes and shops, the third-floor apartment accommodates four and overlooks the peaceful courtyard of a graceful old building. The apartment features a living room with a convertible couch for two, a double bedroom, a fully equipped kitchen and a full bath. Contact: Overseas Connections, 70 West 71st Street, #1C, New York, NY 10023. Call 212-769-1170.

Children: Y Pets: N Smoking: Y Handicap Access: N Payment: C, P

Paris

RUE DES SABLONS   *Rates: moderate*
Open: year-round   *Minimum Stay: one week*
This marvelous apartment for four puts one of the best districts of
Paris right at your feet. The Eiffel Tower and the Seine are a stone's
throw away, as are such sites as the beautiful dome of Les Invalides,
where Napoleon was buried. Nearby museums range from the Musee
Gromet, featuring extraordinary Cambodian and Tantric Buddhist art,
to the Musee d'Art Moderne, offering works by 20th-century artists.
Located on the seventh floor of a modern elevator building, this one-
bedroom apartment features a living room with a convertible couch
for two, a double bedroom, a bath and a fully equipped kitchen. Contact: Overseas Connections, 70 West 71st Street, #1C, New York, NY
10023. Call 212-769-1170.
Children: **Y**   Pets: **N**   Smoking: **Y**   Handicap Access: **N**   Payment: **C, P**

Paris

RUE FANTIN LA TOUR   *Rates: budget*
Open: year-round   *Minimum Stay: one week*
This engaging studio apartment located in a classic Parisian building
in the residential 16th district has been completely renovated.
Equipped to sleep two, the flat features a full kitchenette, a shower and
a convertible couch. Board the Metro at the Exelman stop to reach all
the attractions of Paris. Contact: Overseas Connections, 70 West 71st
Street, #1C, New York, NY 10023. Call 212-769-1170.
Children: **Y**   Pets: **N**   Smoking: **Y**   Handicap Access: **N**   Payment: **C, P**

Paris

RUE FRANKLIN   *Rates: expensive*
Open: year-round   *Minimum Stay: one week*
Wander down the Champs Elysees and stop at an outdoor cafe after
shopping, or stroll the gardens and grounds of the Eiffel Tower, all just
outside the door of this one-bedroom apartment for four. Located in a
beautiful older building with an elevator, the apartment features a
living room with a convertible sofa bed, a double bedroom, a kitchen
and a bath. Nicely furnished, the flat includes a color TV. Contact:
Overseas Connections, 70 West 71st Street, #1C, New York, NY
10023. Call 212-769-1170.
Children: **Y**   Pets: **N**   Smoking: **Y**   Handicap Access: **N**   Payment: **C, P**

Paris

RUE ILE ST. LOUIS   *Rates: moderate*
Open: year-round   *Minimum Stay: one week*
A quiet courtyard leads to this charming one-bedroom apartment located on the Ile St. Louis, the smaller of the Seine's two islands. Sleeping two people, the apartment features a double bedroom, a kitchen
and a separate full bath. You can walk along the quiet residential
streets and explore the quay along the river's edge, or shop and dine in
any number of boutiques and restaurants. Those with a sweet tooth

should not miss the best ice cream in the entire ⟨
Contact: Overseas Connections, 70 West 71st Street,
NY 10023. Call 212-769-1170.

Children: Y   Pets: N   Smoking: Y   Handicap Access: N

Paris

RUE LALO APARTMENT   Rate.   ⌐ve
Open: year-round   *Minimum Stay. ⌐ne week*

From the fifth-floor balcony of this apartment, you can observe the
City of Light's timeless appeal and colorful characters. The location is
superb—close to the Arc de Triomphe, the Champs Elysees and several beautiful public gardens—as is the setting in a quiet, exclusive
residential district known as the Trocadero. The rooms are comfortable, with stylish Swedish furniture, a brand-new kitchen and the
convenience of a washing machine, TV and telephone. One bedroom
contains a double bed, another has twin beds, and there is a comfortable sofa bed in the living room. The building is only thirty years old
and has an elevator. Contact: Rhoda and Joseph Kafer, Riviera Holidays, 31 Georgian Lane, Great Neck, NY 11024. Call 516-487-8094.

Children: Y   Pets: Y   Smoking: Y   Handicap Access: N   Payment: P

Paris

RUE MESNIL APARTMENTS   *Rates: expensive*
Open: year-round   *Minimum Stay: one week*

Paris offers the finest things in life, and nowhere is this more apparent
than in the exclusive residential district known as Trocadero, which
lies close to the Seine, several charming parks and the Arc de Triomphe. This apartment with two twin bedrooms is a blissfully quiet
retreat from the bustling streets and squares. An elevator takes you up
to the second floor, where there is plenty of room to relax—two bathrooms, living and dining rooms decorated in a modern style and a fully
equipped kitchen. If it rains for a day during your visit, the living room
fireplace will take away the chill as you sip a glass of fine French wine.
Contact: Rhoda and Joseph Kafer, Riviera Holidays, 31 Georgian Lane,
Great Neck, NY 11024. Call 516-487-8094.

Children: Y   Pets: Y   Smoking: Y   Handicap Access: N   Payment: P

Paris

ST. GERMAIN DES PRES   *Rates: inexpensive-expensive*
Open: year-round   *Minimum Stay: none*

The exciting Left Bank, near Place St. Sulpice, is the setting for this
completely remodeled 17th-century building, which houses two comfortably furnished studio apartments. Both include mini-kitchens fully
equipped with refrigerators, microwaves, hot plates and sinks, and
both provide TV, radio, phone and a bath with shower. One has a
double bed, and the other has three singles plus a separate bunk-bed
cabin; together, they sleep up to seven people. With proximity to the
Musee d'Orsay, Notre Dame, the Louvre and the Jardin du
Luxembourg—all within 20 minutes' walking distance—it's a great

base. Excellent restaurants and some of the most elegant shops ...ris are right at your doorstep. Contact: Chez Nous Travel Service, 85 Dobb Top Road, Holmbridge, Huddersfield, HD7 1QP, England. Call 011-44-1-0484-684075. Ref. 10C.

Children: **Y**   Pets: **N**   Smoking: **Y**   Handicap Access: **N**   Payment: **P, V, M**

Paris

ST. JULIAN LE PAUVRE   *Rates: expensive*
Open: year-round   *Minimum Stay: one week*

Commanding splendid views of the Cathedral of Notre Dame, this romantic studio located on the historic Left Bank comfortably accommodates two persons. Close to the quay, the fourth-floor apartment has a fully equipped kitchen and separate bath. Nature lovers might want to visit the extensive gardens of the Luxembourg Palace or the Jardin des Plantes. Others might walk to Montparnasse, the historic haunt of poets and painters, to enjoy the restaurants, cafes and nightlife. Contact: Overseas Connections, 70 West 71st Street, #1C, New York, NY 10023. Call 212-769-1170.

Children: **Y**   Pets: **N**   Smoking: **Y**   Handicap Access: **N**   Payment: **C, P**

LANGUEDOC-ROUSSILLON

Agde

16TH-CENTURY TOWNHOUSES   *Rates: budget*
Open: year-round   *Minimum Stay: one week*

Agde lies along miles of sandy beaches on the Cote d'Or, midway between the Spanish border and the Camargue; every year it receives thousands of cloudless hours of sunshine. This ancient fishing port was founded by the Greeks in the sixth century B.C., and rebuilt after the Crusades to look much as it does today. These newly modernized houses for two to five are located in the old town, a maze of picturesque streets full of shops and cafes. They range from a stone-arched shop where a craftsman once sold his goods, to the 16th-century courtyard home of the town magistrate. All have spacious, modern kitchens and comfortable bedrooms, and all but one have sunbathing terraces. Contact: Chez Nous Travel Service, 85 Dobb Top Road, Holmbridge, Huddersfield, HD7 1QP, England. Call 011-44-1-0484-684075. Ref. 42A.

Children: **Y**   Pets: **N**   Smoking: **Y**   Handicap Access: **N**   Payment: **P, V, M**

Banyuls-sur-Mer

VINTAGE CITY HOME   *Rates: budget*
Open: year-round   *Minimum Stay: one week*

Sunny Banyuls lures visitors with warm pebble beaches to the east, majestic Spanish mountains to the south, intriguing historic towns to the north and endless azure skies above. This house, one of the oldest in Banyuls, is a perfect base for swimming, sailing, sightseeing or just wandering through the town's sun-bleached streets and fragrant vineyards. Greet the southern sun on the windowed terrace off the master bedroom suite upstairs; settle two children in the smaller bedroom downstairs. The dining/sitting room is also endowed with a balcony for devoted sunbathers and people-watchers. Contact: Villas and Apartments Abroad, Ltd., 420 Madison Avenue, New York, NY 10017. Call 1-800-433-3020.

Children: Y   Pets: Y   Smoking: Y   Handicap Access: N   Payment: C, P, T

Ceret

MAS PALLARES   *Rates: budget-inexpensive*
Open: year-round   *Minimum Stay: one week*

Situated between the Pyrenees to the west and the Mediterranean to the east, this restored first-floor apartment makes an excellent home base for exploring a beautiful but lesser-known region of France. An exterior staircase leads into the self-contained apartment in this stone house. Overlooking the enclosed garden, complete with barbecue, it sleeps a total of three to five people in a double bed on the mezzanine level and a single sofa bed and three-quarter bed in the kitchen/living/dining room. The owners of the house, who occupy part of it, are happy to share their swimming pool and patio with you. A half-hour's drive away lies the beach at Argeles, or hike three miles to the Spanish border. Contact: Blakes Vacations, 4918 Dempster Street, Skokie, IL 60077. Call 1-800-628-8118. Ref. AJA.

Children: Y   Pets: N   Smoking: Y   Handicap Access: N   Payment: P, T

Cirque de Navacelles

VILLA CEVENNES   *Rates: budget-moderate*
Open: year-round   *Minimum Stay: one week*

Recently refurbished, this magnificent detached villa is set in the foothills of the Cevennes, in a fascinating medieval village. The area is a naturalist's paradise where many rare birds, butterflies and flowers flourish. Three double bedrooms—one with a balcony—two full baths, a new kitchen with all modern conveniences, a sitting room and a newly added living room with a fireplace and a terrace make the villa a comfortable vacation home for six. The grounds have a large garden through which the Vis River flows, offering excellent swimming. The area boasts trout fishing, a local inn with good French cuisine, superb walking trails and nearby market towns. Contact: Chez Nous Travel Service, 85 Dobb Top Road, Holmbridge, Huddersfield, HD7 1QP, England. Call 011-44-1-0484-684075. Ref. 42F.

Children: Y   Pets: N   Smoking: Y   Handicap Access: N   Payment: P, V, M

Port Vendres

MODERN APARTMENT   *Rates: budget-inexpensive*
Open: year-round   *Minimum Stay: one week*

Between Collioure and Port Vendres, where the Pyrenees sweep down to a sparkling bay, stands this comfy two-story apartment with access to a safe beach. The comfortably furnished living/dining room opens onto a furnished balcony with a magnificent view of the bay. In the kitchenette, guests have use of a refrigerator/freezer, a stove, a dishwasher and a washing machine. A double bedroom and two twins, one with a seaside balcony, house six people very nicely. Shops and restaurants are located within one-quarter mile. Visit the charming fishing village of Coulioure, where Matisse and Picasso once lived and painted, or the working port of Port Vendres, which has a yachting harbor for recreation. For touring, Perpignan and Spain lie within a half hour's drive. Contact: Chez Nous Travel Service, 85 Dobb Top Road, Holmbridge, Huddersfield, HD7 1QP, England. Call 011-44-1-0484-684075. Ref. 40A.

Children: Y Pets: N Smoking: Y Handicap Access: N Payment: P, V, M

Roquebrun

VILLAGE HOUSE *Rates: budget*
Open: year-round *Minimum Stay: one week*

This 300-year-old fortified house stands in a medieval village on the banks of the River Orb. Restored to provide all modern comforts, the fascinating house retains many of its unique period features. The kitchen has a stove, a microwave oven, a refrigerator/freezer and a washing machine. The living room, graced with a traditional open hearth, is spacious and bright and opens onto the terrace, which allows uninterrupted views of the river, vineyards and hills. A spiral stone stairway leads to two double bedrooms, one with en-suite shower and sink, and a large bathroom with separate toilet. A supermarket, a general store, a butcher's shop, a bakery, a post office, a wine cooperative, restaurants, river swimming, fishing and canoeing are all within five minutes' walk. Contact: Chez Nous Travel Service, 85 Dobb Top Road, Holmbridge, Huddersfield, HD7 1QP, England. Call 011-44-1-0484-684075. Ref. 41A.

Children: Y Pets: N Smoking: Y Handicap Access: N Payment: P, V, M

Village de Vacances

LE MOULIN *Rates: budget*
Open: year-round *Minimum Stay: one week*

This historic region of southern France takes its name from langue d'oc, the language derived from Latin and spoken in Provence. Here, a group of eighteen terraced chalets stands on a gentle slope overlooking a lake where you can swim and fish. Each chalet features a kitchen/living/dining room opening onto a furnished terrace facing south. Six guests can sleep in two bedrooms, one with a bunk bed and two stacking beds, another with a double bed on the mezzanine level. Meet your neighbors around the communal barbecue or at the converted mill house with game room and restaurant. Riding, cycling and tennis facilities are close by, as are shops, a bank and a post office. Contact: Blakes Vacations, 4918 Dempster Street, Skokie, IL 60077. Call 1-800-628-8118. Ref. AJC.

Children: Y Pets: N Smoking: Y Handicap Access: N Payment: P, T

LIMOUSIN

Beaulieu-sur-Dordogne

L'OUSTALOU *Rates: budget-expensive*
Open: year-round *Minimum Stay: one week*
This old fisherman's cottage built from local stone has been extended twice in this century and modernized as well. Perched on the banks of the Dordogne River in a heavily wooded valley, the cottage commands sweeping river views. A kitchen, living/dining room with open fireplace and two baths offer roomy comfort; four bedrooms plus a double sofa bed in the living room accommodate eight to ten. Outside, a terrace and front and back gardens extend to the river's edge, where guests can launch the double canoe and two single kayaks. The opposite river bank has been made into a children's beach, with a heated municipal swimming pool and tennis courts. Golf is half-hour's car ride away. Contact: Blakes Vacations, 4918 Dempster Street, Skokie, IL 60077. Call 1-800-628-8118. Ref. AHL.

Children: **Y** Pets: **N** Smoking: **Y** Handicap Access: **N** Payment: **P, T**

Benayes

FARDEIX *Rates: budget*
Open: year-round *Minimum Stay: one week*
West of the rugged Massif Central and east of the gently rolling Dordogne, the Limousin region remains mostly undiscovered by tourists. Hills, forests and lakes surround the village of Benayes, where this pretty stone cottage stands. Six adults and a child can sleep here comfortably in two double bedrooms and a twin. On the main floor, an open fireplace warms the living/dining room and a dishwasher and washing machine make the kitchen complete. Use the house as a base from which to explore the Correze, swim and fish Lake Meuzac or visit local cafes and shops. Contact: Blakes Vacations, 4918 Dempster Street, Skokie, IL 60077. Call 1-800-628-8118. Ref. AKZ.

Children: **Y** Pets: **N** Smoking: **Y** Handicap Access: **N** Payment: **P, T**

Rougnat

CHALET SOUS BOIS *Rates: budget*
Open: year-round *Minimum Stay: one week*
A modern A-frame chalet nestled in the woods offers picturesque views of the lake at Vergnes, which warms up nicely in summer to offer sailing, swimming, fishing and wind-surfing. Four people can sleep comfortably in one double bedroom and one twin on the mezzanine level. Dine on the front porch overlooking the lake or watch the moon's reflection from the balcony above. Shops and restaurants are within walking distance at Auzances. Contact: Blakes Vacations, 4918 Dempster Street, Skokie, IL 60077. Call 1-800-628-8118. Ref. AQP.

Children: **Y** Pets: **N** Smoking: **Y** Handicap Access: **N** Payment: **P, T**

LOWER NORMANDY

Barfleur

TOCQUEVILLE CHATEAU *Rates: inexpensive-expensive*
Open: year-round *Minimum Stay: one week*

Not far from Cherbourg and the Cape de la Hague lies a palatial 16th-century chateau of special significance to Americans—it once belonged to Alexis de Tocqueville. Up to nine guests can live like nobility in one entire wing of the chateau, while the resident family still occupies part of the house. The grounds are beautifully landscaped, with a tennis court, formal garden and small lake. There are five bedrooms furnished with period antiques collected over centuries; one bath, two toilets and a small kitchen with washing machine complete the conveniences. You'll probably spend a lot of time in the marble-tiled sitting room, perhaps lying on a rug in front of the blazing hearth. Three miles away at Barfleur are a full range of seaside activities and a quay where the days' catch is for sale. Contact: Rhoda and Joseph Kafer, Riviera Holidays, 31 Georgian Lane, Great Neck, NY 11024. Call 516-487-8094. Ref. J23W.

Children: Y Pets: Y Smoking: Y Handicap Access: N Payment: P, V, M, A

Deauville

HALF-TIMBERED HOUSE *Rates: deluxe*
Open: year-round *Minimum Stay: one week*

Located in the heart of a bustling seaside resort, this handsome half-timbered house is perfect for those who want to be near everything but still able to get away from it all. The main rooms are stylish yet cozy, featuring high ceilings and French doors that open to a lush, private garden. The many pleasant bedrooms, several with windows overlooking the garden, can sleep ten; one large room on the third floor has its own living area. Visitors rarely have time to sleep in Deauville, though—the beach, casino, pool and market entice even homebodies out for a bit of fun. Contact: Villas and Apartments Abroad, Ltd., 420 Madison Avenue, New York, NY 10017. Call 1-800-433-3020.

Children: Y Pets: Y Smoking: Y Handicap Access: N Payment: C, P, T

Fontenay sur Mer

FONTENAY *Rates: budget-inexpensive*
Open: year-round *Minimum Stay: one week*

This modest house stands within walking distance of the beautiful sandy beaches where Allied troops landed on D-Day. A double sofa bed in the living room/dining room, two double bedrooms and one twin bedroom sleep up to six comfortably. Well equipped for cooking, the kitchen also has a washing machine. In the enclosed garden, guests enjoy a terrace and garden furniture. Shops are close by at Quineville, less than two miles away. Contact: Blakes Vacations, 4918 Dempster Street, Skokie IL 60077. Call 1-800-628-8118. Ref. AEA.

Children: Y Pets: N Smoking: Y Handicap Access: N Payment: P, T

Le Creully

CHATEAU CREULLET

Open: year-round

Rates: deluxe

Minimum Stay: one week

Surrounded by a lovely garden and well-manicured parkland, this magnificent 18th-century chateau offers luxurious country accommodations for up to 11 people. The three salons and large dining room downstairs and the spacious bedrooms upstairs are exquisitely furnished with antiques and rich tapestries; the house is centrally heated. The epitome of gracious country living, this chateau also enjoys easy access to the sun and fun of Normandy's sandy beaches. Yacht hire, fishing, tennis and riding are available nearby. Round out your stay in this country mansion with a trip to one of the local polo matches. Contact: Villas and Apartments Abroad, Ltd., 420 Madison Avenue, New York, NY 10017. Call 1-800-433-3020.

Children: Y   Pets: Y   Smoking: Y   Handicap Access: N   Payment: C, P, T

Manneville-la-Raoult

LA CHARRIERE

Open: year-round

Rates: budget-inexpensive

Minimum Stay: one week

This thatched Norman cottage is set in rural surroundings a few miles east of Honfleur. Six people can sleep comfortably in three double bedrooms and enjoy the split-level living/dining room and well-equipped kitchen with dishwasher. The spacious enclosed grounds include a small pond, furnished garden and barbecue. Less than seven miles away lie the beaches of Normandy; the Seine Valley is also close by and Paris is a two-hour drive. Contact: Blakes Vacations, 4918 Dempster Street, Skokie, IL 60077. Call 1-800-628-8118. Ref. AJE.

Children: Y   Pets: N   Smoking: Y   Handicap Access: N   Payment: P, T

Milly

NORMAN MANOR

Open: year-round

Rates: budget

Minimum Stay: one week

The small village of Milly provides the peaceful, rural surroundings for this Norman-style house twenty minutes from the beach. A living/dining room with an open stone fireplace and double sofa bed, two double bedrooms and one twin bedroom provide sleeping accommodations for six to eight. The Calvados distillery, which is open to the public, operates nearby. Fresh milk, cheese and eggs are available at a neighboring farm. Contact: Blakes Vacations, 4918 Dempster Street, Skokie, IL 60077. Call 1-800-628-8118. Ref. AAH.

Children: Y   Pets: N   Smoking: Y   Handicap Access: N   Payment: P, T

St. Vaast

VICTORIA

Open: year-round

Rates: budget-inexpensive

Minimum Stay: one week

Sample seaside life in this fishing town, which is famous for its oysters. Victoria is a pre-World War II detached house with a living room, separate dining room, kitchen and enclosed greenhouse. There's room for seven in three double bedrooms and one single. French windows open onto a balcony overlooking gardens complete with garden furniture and a barbecue. Within walking distance, you'll find the beach and tennis courts; golf is also nearby. Contact: Blakes Vacations, 4918 Dempster Street, Skokie IL 60077. Call 1-800-628-8118. Ref. AAD.

Children: **Y**   Pets: **N**   Smoking: **Y**   Handicap Access: **N**   Payment: **P, T**

MIDI-PYRENEES

Castelmayran

RESTORED FARMHOUSE   *Rates: budget-inexpensive*
Open: year-round   *Minimum Stay: one week*

Set in beautiful countryside midway between Castelsarrasin and St. Nicholas de la Grave, this tastefully restored farmhouse offers three double bedrooms, each with its own connected bathroom. The suites may be rented singly or together, and they include the use of a large lounge/dining room with a television and patio area. There's plenty to do in the area: The village is a five-minute walk; and within seven miles are several lakes with beaches, water sports, fishing, tennis and golf. Most of the nearby towns have places of historical interest to visit; both the Atlantic and Mediterranean are only two and a half hours away. Contact: Chez Nous Travel Service, 85 Dobb Top Road, Holmbridge, Huddersfield, HD7 1QP, England. Call 011-44-1-0484-684075. Ref. 33E.

Children: **Y**   Pets: **N**   Smoking: **Y**   Handicap Access: **N**   Payment: **P, V, M**

Jegun

LE MOULIN DE LA BOURDETTE   *Rates: inexpensive-moderate*
Open: year-round   *Minimum Stay: one week*

This little, round stone building right from a fairy tale makes a perfect hideaway for a couple or small family. The reason for its unusual appearance is that it is a former "moulin a vent," or windmill. No longer equipped with sails, the building has been comfortably converted into two floors of living space. On the ground floor is a cozy area with a fireplace and two futon chairs that convert to single beds, plus a bathroom and kitchen. Doors open from the fully equipped kitchen onto a terrace that's perfect for outdoor dining. Upstairs is a bedroom with a luxurious king-size bed and windows that provide a view of the pretty surrounding scenery. The village of Jegun is where you'll do your shopping. Contact: Vacances Provencales, 792 Cutter Lane, Elk Grove, IL 60007. Call 708-893-9402. Ref. F202.

Children: **Y**   Pets: **Y**   Smoking: **Y**   Handicap Access: **N**   Payment: **P, T**

Masseube

MASSEUBE I   *Rates: inexpensive-expensive*
Open: late April-late September   *Minimum Stay: two weeks*

Enjoy tranquil views of the Pyrenees from this peaceful property, one of two that share use of a swimming pool, bicycles, barbecue, washing machine and table tennis facilities with their owners. Large shade trees provide protection from the afternoon heat of the long Gascony summers. Inside, Masseube I is comfortably furnished with country antiques; modern bathroom facilities are accessible by going to the other wing of the house. Eight people and a baby can sleep comfortably in three double and one twin bedroom; an extra cot is available. Water sports, a nine-hole "pitch and putt" course and shopping lie a few miles away. Masseube I and Masseube II rent together from June 27 to August 28 and the pool is available from the end of May through December. Contact: British Travel Associates, P.O. Box 299, Elkton, VA 22827. Call 1-800-327-6097 (in Virginia, 703-298-2232). Ref. H12.

Children: Y   Pets: N   Smoking: Y   Handicap Access: N   Payment: All

Masseube

MASSEUBE II   *Rates: budget-moderate*
Open: late April-late September   *Minimum Stay: one week*

Masseube II offers views of rolling countryside uncluttered by cities and unspoiled by heavy tourism. This former "bergerie" has been converted into a small cottage with its own kitchen/dining room and indoor bathroom. Four to six people can sleep in two double bedrooms, one of which has two additional bunk beds. The swimming pool (available from the end of May through December), bicycles, barbecue, washing machine and table tennis facilities are shared with guests of Masseube I and the property owners. Masseube I and Masseube II rent together from June 27 to August 28. Contact: British Travel Associates, P.O. Box 299, Elkton, VA 22827. Call 1-800-327-6097 (in Virginia, 703-298-2232). Ref. H13.

Children: Y   Pets: N   Smoking: Y   Handicap Access: N   Payment: All

Montaigu-de-Quercy

17TH-CENTURY COTTAGE   *Rates: budget*
Open: April-October   *Minimum Stay: one week*

This charming, fully restored 17th-century cottage overlooks the valley of the River Seoune and comfortably houses five people in two upstairs bedrooms. Downstairs is a sitting room, a bathroom and a fully equipped kitchen/dining room leading to a private terrace with a magnificent view of the valley below. A heated swimming pool and barbecue await outside. The friendly owners live nearby and can provide supplies or helpful information about the villages and valleys of this picturesque region. Contact: Chez Nous Travel Service, 85 Dobb Top Road, Holmbridge, Huddersfield, HD7 1QP, England. Call 011-44-1-0484-684075. Ref. 19G.

Children: Y   Pets: N   Smoking: Y   Handicap Access: N   Payment: P, V, M

Tillac

MIDI-PYRENEES APARTMENTS   *Rates: inexpensive*
Open: year-round   *Minimum Stay: one week*

In the center of a 14th-century village, in the heart of "forgotten rural France," stand two recently refurbished apartments that have retained the charm of the old village house that contains them. Each apartment, with views of a medieval tower, a church and countryside, consists of a spacious dining/living room with a sofa bed, a kitchen, a three-quarter bath, and a double and twin bedroom, sleeping six in all. The town boasts shops and tennis courts; nearby is a large lake for water sports and fishing. There is also easy access to Lourdes, the Pyrenees—with great skiing in winter—lovely chateaux and Spain. Contact: Chez Nous Travel Service, 85 Dobb Top Road, Holmbridge, Huddersfield, HD7 1QP, England. Call 011-44-1-0484-684075. Ref. 33A.

Children· Y   Pets: N   Smoking: Y   Handicap Access: N   Payment: P, V, M

PAYS DE LA LOIRE

Blois

LA CHARMOISE   *Rates: budget*
Open: year-round   *Minimum Stay: one week*

Along the Loire River lies a fertile region renowned for its wine. Guests at La Charmoise have the chance to see a vineyard up close, for the property's owners operate one nearby, where they sell wine, vegetables and cheese. The house has a modern kitchen with gas stove, a large living/dining room with open fireplace, and a small garden with a swing and a barbecue. One double bedroom and one twin bedroom sleep a total of four. Take a day trip to the Sologne region northeast of Blois, where you can stroll in forests rich with lakes and wildlife. Nearer the house, the tennis, fishing, golf and swimming is good; the food is even better. Contact: Blakes Vacations, 4918 Dempster Street, Skokie, IL 60077. Call 1-800-628-8118. Ref. AEN.

Children: Y   Pets: N   Smoking: Y   Handicap Access: N   Payment: P, T

Blois

MAISON AUBOURG   *Rates: budget*
Open: year-round   *Minimum Stay: one week*

This recently modernized house on the grounds of a working farm lies right in the center of the Loire's chateau country. Its large living/dining area has an open fireplace and a modern kitchen, while two double bedrooms and a twin provide sleeping accommodations for six. Guests can buy wine produced right on the farm, visit neighboring chateaux and vineyards or stroll the famed city of Tours, where the Moors were stopped as they made their way into France in 732 A.D. Closer to home, you can sail, ride, fish, swim or play tennis and golf. Contact: Blakes Vacations, 4918 Dempster Street, Skokie, IL 60077. Call 1-800-628-8118. Ref. AET.

Children: Y   Pets: N   Smoking: Y   Handicap Access: N   Payment: P, T

THIS PAGE SEVEN LINES SHORT ...GL

Chevilly

COUNTRY MANOR *Rates: deluxe*
Open: July-August *Minimum Stay: one week*
Chevilly is a wonderful base for exploring the elegant chateaux and vineyards of the Loire, not to mention glorious Orleans and scintillating Paris only an hour away by train. This country manor, large and newly refurbished, accommodates 11 people in six ample bedrooms. Two additional singles suitable for children are also available. Downstairs are the comfortable study, living and dining rooms, plus a modern kitchen with a full complement of up-to-date appliances. After a day full of sightseeing, sip a glass of wine out on the sunny terrace or take a refreshing dip in the sparkling pool. Contact: Villas and Apartments Abroad, Ltd., 420 Madison Avenue, New York, NY 10017. Call 1-800-433-3020.

Children: Y Pets: Y Smoking: Y Handicap Access: N Payment: C, P, T

Chevire le Rouge

CHATEAU LA ROCHE HUE *Rates: budget-inexpensive*
Open: year-round *Minimum Stay: one week*
Enjoy the gentle rhythm of life in the beautiful Loire Valley when you rent this magnificent chateau. The spacious apartments housed in the mansion all have splendid views and range in size from studios to three bedrooms. Each is fully equipped with a microwave oven and modern bath/shower facilities. The owners live on the premises to help make your stay as enjoyable as possible. Within short driving distance, you'll find the larger towns of Angers, Saumur and Tours, but you may never get around to touring the area with all that's available on this 60-acre site: tennis, fishing, swimming, walking trails, gym, game and TV room, and more. Contact: Chez Nous Travel Service, 85 Dobb Top Road, Holmbridge, Huddersfield, HD7 1QP, England. Call 011-44-1-0484-684075. Ref. 5A.

Children: Y Pets: N Smoking: Y Handicap Access: N Payment: P, V, M

Croix de Vie

GARDEN VILLA *Rates: moderate-expensive*
Open: year-round *Minimum Stay: two weeks*
This huge, beautiful home offers comfort and modern convenience forup to nine guests in its four bedrooms (two doubles, one with three singles and one child's single). As you sit in the landscaped garden, the sound of tall trees swaying in the breeze is all you'll hear, since the house is located on a small lane five minutes from the town of Croix de Vie. The house is well appointed, with a tiled roof, shuttered French doors, comfortable sitting room with open fireplace and a spacious patio perfect for a barbecue on a long summer evening. There are two bathrooms and the kitchen is fitted with quality appliances including a dishwasher; laundry facilities are shared with the owner, who lives next door. Contact: B & D de Vogue International Inc., 1830 S. Mooney Boulevard, Suite 203, Visalia, CA 93277. Call: 209-733-7119; 1-800-727-4748. Ref. A51.

Children: Y Pets: Y Smoking: Y Handicap Access: N Payment: P, V, M, A

La Bernerie en Retz

ETOILE D'OR
Open: year-round

Rates: budget
Minimum Stay: one week

More than 600 miles long, the Loire River, France's greatest waterway, gives both name and nourishment to this region noted for its fine wines and beautiful chateaux. Here, the cozy little cottage Etoile d'Or stands in the seaside town of La Bernerie en Retz, about thirty miles west of the port city of Nantes, where the Loire empties into the sea. Two adults and two children can vacation comfortably here, sleeping in a double bedroom and one small room with bunk beds. The kitchen is small but well equipped and includes a dishwasher. A sun room faces south, offering a fine view of the rear garden. Sailing, riding, golf and tennis are available nearby. Contact: Blakes Vacations, 4918 Dempster Street, Skokie, IL 60077. Call 1-800-628-8118. Ref. ACM.

Children: **Y**   Pets: **N**   Smoking: **Y**   Handicap Access: **N**   Payment: **P, T**

Longeville sur Mer

VILLA SOUS BOIS
Open: May 26-September 28

Rates: budget-inexpensive
Minimum Stay: one week

Charmingly refurbished, this house stands near the sandy beaches of the Loire Atlantique and the resort cities of Les Sables d'Olonne and Longeville-sur-Mer. A large kitchen/living/dining room opens onto a terrace; the enclosed, furnished garden includes a barbecue. Seven people can sleep in three double bedrooms. One has an extra single bed, another has French windows opening onto a balcony. Tennis, sailing, riding and fishing are within easy reach, and golfing is less than a half-hour car ride away. Contact: Blakes Vacations, 4918 Dempster Street, Skokie, IL 60077. Call 1-800-628-8118. Ref. ACG.

Children: **Y**   Pets: **N**   Smoking: **Y**   Handicap Access: **N**   Payment: **P, T**

POITOU-CHARENTES

Archignac-La Dordogne

LA BORIE
Open: year-round

Rates: moderate-expensive
Minimum Stay: one week

Located in the heart of the picturesque Dordogne River valley just outside the village of St. Genies, this renovated three-bedroom house can comfortably house up to six adults and one child. The countryside is dotted with farms that make and sell their own pate de foie gras, and nearby towns are full of fascinating medieval buildings. Sarlat holds a summer music festival and has varied recreation facilities for tennis and riding buffs. The house has a living/dining room with a fireplace, a full kitchen, two double bedrooms and one twin and ample bathroom facilities. Surrounded by leafy trees, the house also has a new swimming pool. Contact: Vacances Provencales, 792 Cutter Lane, Elk Grove, IL 60007. Call 708-893-9402. Ref. DMF504.

Children: **Y**   Pets: **Y**   Smoking: **Y**   Handicap Access: **N**   Payment: **P, T**

Aulnay

BREUILLAT DE PAILLE *Rates: budget*
Open: year-round *Minimum Stay: one week*

Bring your children—the more the merrier—to this large restored farm-house where you'll find something for everyone. The nearby town of Saintes boasts ruins from its Roman past, while in Cognac, birthplace of the famous eau de vie, visitors can tour a distillery. Sleeping eight to ten people plus a baby in four bedrooms, plus a double sofa bed in the living room, this house can easily accommodate one or two families. Swim, ride and play tennis at nearby Aulnay, or take a day trip to the beach fifty miles away. Contact: Blakes Vacations, 4918 Dempster Street, Skokie, IL 60077. Call 1-800-628-8118. Ref. ADC.

Children: **Y** Pets: **N** Smoking: **Y** Handicap Access: **N** Payment: **P, T**

Corme-Ecluse

MOULIN DE SOUBIRAT *Rates: budget-inexpensive*
Open: May 26-September 28 *Minimum Stay: one week*

This completely refurbished 17th-century windmill is located ten miles east of the resort town of Royan and just a short walk from a river. An unusual vacation rental, the unit encompasses three floors. The kitchen/dining room is on the main floor, complete with dish-washer and washing machine. On the first floor, one bedroom has a single and bunk beds, and on the second floor, two more can stay in the double bedroom. In the summer, the adjoining miller's house pro-vides a dining room that's open on two sides. Sailing, riding, tennis and the beach are nearby; golf is about ten miles away. Contact: Blakes Vacations, 4918 Dempster Street, Skokie, IL 60077. Call 1-800-628-8118. Ref. AOK.

Children: **Y** Pets: **N** Smoking: **Y** Handicap Access: **N** Payment: **P, T**

Echillais

LES ERRONNELLES *Rates: budget*
Open: year-round *Minimum Stay: one week*

Poitou-Charentes may be the sunniest region in all of France: a place where you can sunbathe, swim or wind-surf and then explore the many historic ports and towns. This modern house is simple yet ac-commodating, with a kitchen and a living/dining room whose French windows open onto a terrace. A double and a twin bedroom sleep four. Sandy beaches, fishing, biking and golf are all nearby. Contact: Blakes Vacations, 4918 Dempster Street, Skokie, IL 60077. Call 1-800-628-8118. Ref. ADJ.

Children: **Y** Pets: **N** Smoking: **Y** Handicap Access: **N** Payment: **P, T**

Foussais

FOUSSAIS MANOR HOUSE *Rates: inexpensive-expensive*
Open: year-round *Minimum Stay: one week*

Step into the France of old as you stroll through the manicured park, with its abundance of flowers and old trees, that surrounds this manor house. Cross the moat and pause to drink the cool, pure mountain spring water flowing from the fountain by the entrance. One side of the garden gives way to a densely wooded forest and open fields lay on the other side, but inside this house features all the creature comforts in its many spacious rooms. A drawing room, dining room, reading room and kitchen occupy the main floor; on the two upper floors a maximum of ten people and two babies can sleep comfortably in five bedrooms (one double, three twins, two with an extra cot and three singles). Basic shopping lies within walking distance, with canoeing, wind-surfing, sailing, fishing and riding very close by as well. Contact: British Travel Associates, P.O. Box 299, Elkton, VA 22827. Call 1-800-327-6097 (in Virginia, 703-298-2232). Ref. G60.

Children: **Y**   Pets: **N**   Smoking: **Y**   Handicap Access: **N**   Payment: All

Journiac

MAISON SANTRAN—LA MEGIE   *Rates: moderate-expensive*
Open: year-round   *Minimum Stay: one week*

Maison Santran, a large stone house overlooking rolling fields, contains four double bedrooms on the second floor and one with two singles on the ground floor. The ground floor also features a living/dining area with massive old beams, a fireplace and a large table that seats up to ten people. There is a modern, eat-in kitchen in which you can try your hand at preparing the local delicacy—truffles. In the garden is a barbecue for use on the long evenings of summer. The town of Le Bugue, located on the banks of the Dordogne River just ten minutes away, has facilities for tennis and swimming; the village of Journiac is just over a mile away and worth visiting just for the fresh rolls at the local bakery. Contact: Vacances Provencales, 792 Cutter Lane, Elk Grove, IL 60007. Call 708-893-9402. Ref. DR401.

Children: **Y**   Pets: **Y**   Smoking: **Y**   Handicap Access: **N**   Payment: P, T

L'Isle d'Etaule

LA COTE DE BEAUTE   *Rates: budget*
Open: year-round   *Minimum Stay: one week*

Close to the sandy beaches of La Cote Sauvage and La Palmyre, overlooking rolling vineyards and farmlands, this modernized farmhouse can sleep up to six people. The roomy ground-floor accommodation comprises a large kitchen, two ample double bedrooms, a sitting room/third bedroom and a separate laundry, toilet and shower room. Two bicycles come with the house for guests who'd like to tour the area and sample some of the local specialties, including wine and seafood. Tennis, golf, water sports and horseback riding are all available nearby. For day trips, you might visit Cognac or Bordeaux or take the ferry across the Gironde to visit the Medoc. Contact: Chez Nous Travel Service, 85 Dobb Top Road, Holmbridge, Huddersfield, HD7 1QP, England. Call 011-44-1-0484-684075. Ref. 16F.

Children: **Y**   Pets: **N**   Smoking: **Y**   Handicap Access: **N**   Payment: P, V, M

Landeronde

LANDERONDE FORT *Rates: expensive-deluxe*
Open: late April-late September *Minimum Stay: two weeks*

This small chateau "fort" was built about 1590, and the owners have retained the original rugged character while renovating for modern comfort. Delightfully set in the rolling Vendee countryside, the manor house is surrounded by a gravel terrace and large lawns. A maximum of eight people are permitted in the four bedrooms. The grounds offer table tennis, tennis and pool facilities, while a short drive takes you to the shops at La Roche, the resorts of La Roche-sur-Yon and the beaches at Les Sables d'Olonne. Contact: British Travel Associates, P.O. Box 299, Elkton, VA 22827. Call 1-800-327-6097 (in Virginia, 703-298-2232). Ref. G50.

Children: Y   Pets: N   Smoking: Y   Handicap Access: N   Payment: All

Machecoul

MACHECOUL MANOR HOUSE *Rates: moderate-expensive*
Open: late April-late September *Minimum Stay: one week*

This beautiful, small stone manor house fits in with the rugged Romanesque architecture throughout the region. Equipped with a large farmhouse kitchen, living room and dining room on the main floor, the house offers sleeping quarters on the upper floor for added privacy. Up to nine people plus a baby can sleep in the five bedrooms—one double, one twin, two singles and one bedroom with three single beds. Families with young children should note that the stairs are partly open-sided and the garden has a pond. For recreation, the beautiful sandy beaches at Nantes lie less than eleven miles to the north. Contact: British Travel Associates, P.O. Box 299, Elkton, VA 22827. Call 1-800-327-6097 (in Virginia, 703-298-2232). Ref. G40.

Children: Y   Pets: N   Smoking: Y   Handicap Access: N   Payment: All

Mansle

RESTORED FARMHOUSE *Rates: budget*
Open: year-round *Minimum Stay: one week*

French country life at its most refreshing means beautiful river valleys, fields of sunflowers and vines, ancient market towns, chateaux, Romanesque churches and a fine climate. All this awaits you in the hamlet of Monpaple, close to the Charente River, where this restored farmhouse and barn can be found in a secure and spacious courtyard. Each is a faithfully restored traditional stone house with open fireplaces and exposed beams; each has a large kitchen/dining room, a sitting room/bedroom and a modern bathroom. One has three large private bedrooms, the other, two. Swimming, tennis, canoeing, fishing, bike rentals, restaurants and shops can all be found locally. You may also want to venture to Brie, Cognac or La Rochelle for day trips. Contact: Chez Nous Travel Service, 85 Dobb Top Road, Holmbridge, Huddersfield, HD7 1QP, England. Call 011-44-1-0484-684075. Ref. 14B.

Children: Y   Pets: N   Smoking: Y   Handicap Access: N   Payment: P, V, M

Nadaillac

LES TERRASSES   *Rates: budget-inexpensive*
Open: April 28-October 28   *Minimum Stay: one week*

Perched on a naturally terraced hillside with splendid views of the surrounding countryside, this lovely farmhouse sleeps up to nine people. The extensive grounds contain landscaped gardens, barns, lawns and woodlands, making it an ideal environment for children to play and explore. Guests at Les Terrasses have the use of a private swimming pool, barbecue and laundry facilities, garden furniture, swings, badminton, volleyball and table tennis equipment. Close by, the town of La Rochebeaucourt offers shopping and dining; the attractions of the Perigord region are easily accessible as well. Contact: Chez Nous Travel Service, 85 Dobb Top Road, Holmbridge, Huddersfield, HD7 1QP, England. Call 011-44-1-0484-684075. Ref. 15F.

Children: Y   Pets: N   Smoking: Y   Handicap Access: N   Payment: P, V, M

Nere/Lepinoux

LA PIERRE BLANCHE   *Rates: budget*
Open: year-round   *Minimum Stay: one week*

Here in wine country is a group of 17th-century stone houses and open barns faithfully restored to retain the rustic charm of their magnificent roofing timbers, tiled floors and open fireplaces. The houses stand on acres of lawns and gardens bordered by tall trees, with plenty of play areas for children. Each house has sleeping accommodations for at least six people, some for more than eight. Laundry facilities and babysitting services are available on the premises. Angouleme, St. Jean D'Angely, Cognac and La Rochelle are close enough for day trips; the immediate vicinity boasts beautiful fields of sunflowers, grapevines and tobacco. Some of the local attractions include horseback riding and horse-drawn coach tours, swimming, tennis and visits to potteries, honey farms and wineries. Contact: Chez Nous Travel Service, 85 Dobb Top Road, Holmbridge, Huddersfield, HD7 1QP, England. Call 011-44-1-0484-684075. Ref. 15B.

Children: Y   Pets: N   Smoking: Y   Handicap Access: N   Payment: P, V, M

North Dordogne

ST. SAUD LACOUSSIERE   *Rates: budget*
Open: year-round   *Minimum Stay: one week*

Rolling countryside laced with numerous rivers and lakes distinguishes this unspoiled region. Set in its own garden, a cozy, detached stone cottage in the heart of Perigord Vert has marvelous views of the surrounding meadowland. Downstairs is a spacious kitchen/living room, a sitting room and a three-quarter bath. Upstairs, two double bedrooms provide simple but comfortable accommodations for up to four people. This charming cottage is an ideal home base for exploring this beautiful locale: Two lakes lie within seven minutes' drive, and there is a good choice of local shops and restaurants. Contact: Chez

Nous Travel Service, 85 Dobb Top Road, Holmbridge, Huddersfield, HD7 1QP, England. Call 011-44-1-0484-684075. Ref. 14F.

Children: Y   Pets: N   Smoking: Y   Handicap Access: N   Payment: P, V, M

Romazieres

FARM COTTAGE   *Rates: budget*
Open: year-round   *Minimum Stay: one week*

In a friendly village set deep in the pristine countryside of the Charente-Maritime, this farm cottage has been lovingly restored by its owners. They have polished the oak beams and floors, kept the stone walls and fireplaces intact and added modern plumbing and other services. Two double bedrooms plus a cot sleep up to five; a large kitchen/dining room, a full bathroom, a garden area with a barbecue and the use of bicycles complete these pleasant accommodations. The nearby beaches can be enjoyed as early as March or as late as November. Not to be missed is the huge variety of produce at the many local markets. Contact: Chez Nous Travel Service, 85 Dobb Top Road, Holmbridge, Huddersfield, HD7 1QP, England. Call 011-44-1-0484-684075. Ref. 16D.

Children: Y   Pets: N   Smoking: Y   Handicap Access: N   Payment: P, V, M

Royan

LA ROSERAIE   *Rates: budget-moderate*
Open: year-round   *Minimum Stay: one week*

Enjoy the festive resort towns of Royan and La Palmyre when you stay at La Roseraie, or retire at night to your quiet residential community just a short walk from the main beach. This traditional seaside villa has room enough for eight: one double bedroom has a small cot for a young child, and, on a separate floor, one single, one double and one twin bedroom sleep five more. An enclosed, furnished garden includes a barbecue; the living/dining room features a large bay window and a fireplace. Water sports, tennis, golf and the beach are within walking distance. Contact: Blakes Vacations, 4918 Dempster Street, Skokie, IL 60077. Call 1-800-628-8118. Ref. ADP.

Children: Y   Pets: N   Smoking: Y   Handicap Access: N   Payment: P, T

Salignac de Mirambeau

LA MOULANDE   *Rates: budget-inexpensive*
Open: year-round   *Minimum Stay: one week*

Two small families or a large group of up to seven adults and two children will find this attractive house in the beautiful countryside of Mirambeau cozy and comfortable. A living/dining room, kitchenette with washing machine, two bedrooms and a loft make up the interior of this attractive home. Central heating and a garage with a Ping-Pong table round out the amenities. Your party can sail, ride, fish and play tennis nearby; the beach is a little further, about twenty-two miles away. Contact: Blakes Vacations, 4918 Dempster Street, Skokie, IL 60077. Call 1-800-628-8118. Ref. ADL.

Children: Y   Pets: N   Smoking: Y   Handicap Access: N   Payment: P, T

Siorac

MAISON "LE VILLAGE"   *Rates: moderate-expensive*
Open: year-round   *Minimum Stay: one week*

This stunning house is located on ten acres of land not far from the Dordogne River. Surrounded by trees and bushes, it has a peaked roof, stone walls, pretty, gabled windows and secluded swimming pool. Inside are four bedrooms that sleep nine, a living room with a fireplace, a separate dining room, two and a half bathrooms and a convenient kitchen with dishwasher and washing machine. The garden has comfortable furniture in which to sit and enjoy the view of the hills and vales of this scenic region. Day trips can easily be made throughout the area—perhaps down the river to Siorac for swimming and canoeing or to the prehistoric caves of Les Eyzies, with their impressive wall paintings. Contact: Vacances Provencales, 792 Cutter Lane, Elk Grove, IL 60007. Call 708-893-9402. Ref. DMF505.

Children: Y   Pets: Y   Smoking: Y   Handicap Access: N   Payment: P, T

St. Germain de Princay

MANOIR DE LOUSIGNY   *Rates: moderate-deluxe*
Open: late April-late September   *Minimum Stay: two weeks*

The owners' ancestors built this large, rambling house in 1787, one of the few buildings to survive the ravages of the counter-revolutionary Wars of the Vendee in the late 18th century. A light, airy breakfast room looks out onto the garden and the pretty Poitou-Charentes countryside of hills and plains. Climb the enormous staircase one flight up to reach the six bedrooms (two doubles, two twins and two singles, with two extra cots for young children). A nearby lake provides water sports and an hour's drive takes you to St. Vincent-s-Jard or St. Gilles Croix-de-Vie on the coast. Contact: British Travel Associates, P.O. Box 299, Elkton, VA 22827. Call 1-800-327-6097 (in Virginia, 703-298-2232). Ref. G53.

Children: Y   Pets: N   Smoking: Y   Handicap Access: N   Payment: All

St. Hilaire de Chaleons

ST. HILAIRE CHATEAU   *Rates: expensive-deluxe*
Open: late April-late September   *Minimum Stay: two weeks*

A magnificent, well-appointed chateau set on 75 acres with two lakes affords you privacy, comfort and luxury in the countryside. Upon entering, guests find themselves in a stone-faced entrance hall that gives way to an elegantly furnished salon with carved paneling. A library, dining room, kitchen, scullery, and a double bedroom with enclosed bathroom complete the ground floor. On the next floor, two double bedrooms, one twin and four singles sleep up to ten; on the top floor, two small single bedrooms sleep two more, for a total of fourteen. The price includes three hours of maid service per week. If you choose to wander from the lovely grounds, the beaches at Pornic lie about ten miles north, and basic goods can be found at St. Pazanne, within walking distance. Contact: British Travel Associates, P.O. Box 299, Elkton,

Terrebourg

STONE COTTAGE *Rates: budget*
Open: year-round *Minimum Stay: one week*

In a peaceful hamlet close to Mansle and about twelve miles north of
Angouleme, this completely renovated cottage, replete with exposed
beams and stone walls, forms a self-contained part of the owner's
farmhouse. Downstairs is the roomy living area/kitchen, with flagstone floor, a magnificent open fireplace, a dining table and easy chairs,
plus a refrigerator, a stove and all necessary utensils. Upstairs are two
spacious twin bedrooms, both of which have French doors leading to
a pleasant balcony and both large enough to accommodate an extra
bed. There is also a full modern bathroom. The area is quiet, with a
lovely garden and good shopping close by, as well as fishing, swimming and walking. Contact: Chez Nous Travel Service, 85 Dobb Top
Road, Holmbridge, Huddersfield, HD7 1QP, England. Call 011-44-1-
0484-684075. Ref. 25D.

Children: Y   Pets: N   Smoking: Y   Handicap Access: N   Payment: P, V, M

Tremolat

LA CABANE *Rates: inexpensive-moderate*
Open: year-round *Minimum Stay: one week*

You can watch the lazy Dordogne River from the terrace of this pretty
three-bedroom cottage located just outside the town of Tremolat. Or
you can walk down to the private beach for a swim or a paddle in the
canoe. Another day, you may want to follow the river to nearby towns
to sample the world-renowned pates and wines in an outdoor cafe. The
cottage itself can accommodate up to six people in three bedrooms and
features one bathroom, a living/dining area filled with plants and an
eat-in kitchen with a dishwasher. Sights in the region include ancient
cave paintings, towering chateaux perched on cliffs and bustling old
market towns. Contact: Vacances Provencales, 792 Cutter Lane, Elk
Grove, IL 60007. Call 708-893-9402. Ref. DMF502.

Children: Y   Pets: Y   Smoking: Y   Handicap Access: N   Payment: P, T

Vaux-sur-Mer

BEACH APARTMENTS *Rates: budget*
Open: year-round *Minimum Stay: one week*

This modern apartment block just three miles west of Royan is ideally
set among landscaped gardens only 100 yards from a fine sandy beach.
The spacious apartment will sleep four or five comfortably; the studio,
two or three. Both have modern furnishings and fully equipped kitchens. In the picturesque bay the whole family can swim safely, while
the more adventurous may want to try wind surfing. For gentler pursuits, how about a walk along the coastline or a round of golf? Excellent inexpensive restaurants abound and there are many small shops
nearby. Bordeaux, Cognac and La Rochelle are close enough for side

E-ALPES MARITIMES-COTE D'AZUR

Aix-en-Provence

DOMAINE DE TURREL   *Rates: inexpensive*
Open: year-round   *Minimum Stay: one week*

This two-story house is located in a shady setting just a few miles from
Aix-en-Provence. On the spacious grounds is a private swimming pool
not far from the house. Three bedrooms (one double and two twin),
two bathrooms and a comfortable living/dining area with a color TV
accommodate six. The kitchen is equipped with a dishwasher and
washing machine. Aix-en-Provence, a beautiful town with much fine
architecture and peaceful fountains, offers ready access to many other
splendid areas in the region, each with its special character. This is
excellent country for touring, with a wide variety of scenery, towering
chateaus and tiny villages, plus the sparkling waters of the Cote
d'Azur. Contact: Vacances Provencales, 792 Cutter Lane, Elk Grove,
IL 60007. Call 708-893-9402. Ref. AEP203.

Children: Y   Pets: Y   Smoking: Y   Handicap Access: N   Payment: P, T

Aix-en-Provence

L'AURELIENNE MAISON   *Rates: expensive-deluxe*
Open: year-round   *Minimum Stay: one week*

Lofty ceilings, an open fireplace, two bedrooms, a swimming pool and
extensive, landscaped grounds make this a luxurious vacation home
for up to seven people. From the terrace, which runs the length of the
house, you can watch the sunset as you gaze over the treetops to
Mount St. Victoire. The surrounding area provides endless opportunities for exploring—history buffs, nature lovers and gourmets will all
find their tastes satisfied. Sun-lovers can easily take day trips to the
coast, with its endless vistas of deep blue and gold. You may even want
to venture into Monte Carlo or some of the exclusive Riviera resorts.
Contact: Vacances Provencales, 792 Cutter Lane, Elk Grove, IL 60007.
Call 708-893-9402. Ref. AEP208.

Children: Y   Pets: Y   Smoking: Y   Handicap Access: N   Payment: P, T

Antibes

PETITE VILLA   *Rates: deluxe*
Open: year-round   *Minimum Stay: none*

This "petite" villa is actually quite spacious, with two bedrooms and
one and a half baths. The kitchen is fully equipped and there is a
living/dining room complete with a fireplace, elegant dining table and
a TV. The garden is filled with exotic Mediterranean plants that provide shady comfort while you sit outside. Just a few minutes from the
center of glamorous Antibes, this villa is centrally located on the

coast. It's well worth doing some exploring by foot in the area: In addition to the splendid scenery, there are numerous little villages and resort towns for entertainment, shopping and people-watching. And, of course, there's always the beaches and the deep, blue waters of the splendid Mediterranean. Contact: Overseas Connection, 70 West 71st Street, #1C, New York, NY 10023. Call 212-769-1170.

Children: Y   Pets: N   Smoking: Y   Handicap Access: N   Payment: C, P

Bagnols-sur-Ceze

MAISON DES CHASSEURS   *Rates: inexpensive-moderate*
Open: year-round   *Minimum Stay: one week*

Situated on a 12th-century estate in the heart of the country, these two cottages are part of the extensive properties that make up the Chateau de Boussargues. Wandering along the many paths throughout the estate, you are likely to come across rows of the grapevines that produce the fabulous local Cotes du Rhone wines. The two "hunter's cottages" have a similar rustic charm, and each has its own garden and wood-burning fireplace. La Petite Maison has two double bedrooms with a connecting archway; la Grande Maison has two separate bedrooms (one double, one with two single beds). The chateau's swimming pool and tennis court are available for use. Contact: Vacances Provencales, 792 Cutter Lane, Elk Grove, IL 60007. Call 708-893-9402. Ref. P101A, P101B.

Children: Y   Pets: Y   Smoking: Y   Handicap Access: N   Payment: P, T

Cannes Marina

LUXURY APARTMENT   *Rates: budget-inexpensive*
Open: year round   *Minimum Stay: one week*

From the front balcony of this modern third-floor luxury apartment, guests enjoy a view of a large swimming pool, beautiful gardens, a marina and a river. The apartment is elegantly furnished and has marble floors, two large balconies with marvelous views, a living room, a fully equipped kitchen, a double bedroom and a full bath. Park in the building's underground garage and walk to the nearby sandy beaches, fantastic golf course and tennis club. There is also easy access to Cannes, Nice, Monte Carlo, Grasse and the entire Cote d'Azur. Contact: Chez Nous Travel Service, 85 Dobb Top Road, Holmbridge, Huddersfield, HD7 1QP, England. Call 011-44-1-0484-684075. Ref. 50F.

Children: N   Pets: N   Smoking: N   Handicap Access: N   Payment: P, V, M

Cannes/Miramar

VILLA APARTMENT   *Rates: budget*
Open: year-round   *Minimum Stay: one week*

Overlooking the shining harbor of Miramar only eight miles from Cannes, is this self-contained villa/apartment set in a small, private luxury development. Built in the traditional Provencal style, the apartment comprises a double bedroom, a living room with a sofa bed, a fully equipped kitchen/dining area and a full bath. French doors open from the living room onto a sizable terrace with breathtaking views of the sea and mountains; from the bedroom, a patio leads directly into the pine-covered foothills of the Esterel. Below the apartment is a private garage, and there is a swimming pool on the grounds for residents' use. All of the Cote d'Azur is accessible from this prime location. Contact: Chez Nous Travel Service, 85 Dobb Top Road, Holmbridge, Huddersfield, HD7 1QP, England. Call 011-44-1-0484-684075. Ref. 52A.

Children: Y   Pets: N   Smoking: Y   Handicap Access: N   Payment: P, V, M

Cannes

RESIDENCE DE FRANCE   *Rates: deluxe*
Open: year-round   *Minimum Stay: one week*

Overlooking beautiful gardens on the famous Croisette Boulevard, this luxurious two-bedroom apartment is 300 feet from the beach and Port Canto. Located on the second floor of a modern security building with elevators and a concierge, the suite sleeps up to three people in one queen and one single bed. The living room and dining room feature a TV and complete stereo system; there's also a full bath. A short walk takes you to pools, boating, shopping and the Palm Beach Casino, or drive to golf courses and tennis courts as well as some excellent hiking trails. If you're interested in discovering the Cote d'Azur, this is an excellent starting point. Contact: Rent A Home International, Inc., 7200 34th Avenue N.W., Seattle, WA 98117. Call 206-545-6963

Children: Y   Pets: N   Smoking: Y   Handicap Access: N   Payment: C, V, P, M

Cannes

VILLA DU PIC DE L'OURS   *Rates: expensive-deluxe*
Open: year-round   *Minimum Stay: one week*

This three-level house named after Bear's Peak is built on a terraced slope surrounded by magnificent views of the Massif de L'Esterel. You'll enjoy the breathtaking scenery and fresh air when sitting by the unique pool or on one of the two large balconies. The living/dining room features a sofa bed, dining room set with an open fireplace, and opens onto a covered balcony. Two bedrooms can sleep up to five, and one leads to an open second-floor balcony. Though fairly modern, the house has a classic look and is well equipped. From Cannes, a scenic ten-minute drive away, the towns and resorts of the Riviera are strung along the coast in both directions. Contact: Vacances Provencales, 792 Cutter Lane, Elk Grove, IL 60007. Call 708-893-9402. Ref. CDA212.

Children: Y   Pets: Y   Smoking: Y   Handicap Access: N   Payment: P, T

Cap Ferrat

AVENUE CLAUDE APARTMENTS   *Rates: budget-inexpensive*
Open: year-round   *Minimum Stay: one week*

Tucked away in a charming villa are four apartments, each a colorful mix of the old and the new. Studio and one-bedroom units with a separate living room are available, each with a kitchen and bath with shower. Request an apartment with a sunny balcony or patio—along with the garden, they make a fine place to sit and enjoy the sea breezes.

Two hundred yards away is the beach and village, an untouched treasure in the heart of this exclusive area. Though close to the glamor and bustle of larger towns such as Nice or Cannes, a stay here will also provide long days of tranquility and recreation by the water's edge, as well as a glimpse of the celebrities who frequent the area. Contact: Villas International, 71 West 23rd Street, New York, NY 10010. Call 212-929-7585.

Children: Y Pets: N Smoking: Y Handicap Access: N Payment: C, P, T, O

Cap Ferrat

CUT-STONE VILLA   *Rates: deluxe*
Open: year-round   *Minimum Stay: none*
On this carefully preserved peninsula stand many beautiful private homes, and this Provencal-style villa offers you the chance to live like French nobility. There are many vantage points from which to admire the blue Mediterranean bays below. The house features four bedrooms, three baths, a living room that faces a large dining terrace, a kitchen with dishwasher, microwave and ice maker and maid's quarters. A heated pool with its own house offers self-contained accommodations for four additional guests. Everything needed to make your stay convenient is at your fingertips, including a satellite dish and a stereo system. Step across the carefully tended grounds to the beach. Contact: Overseas Connection, 70 West 71st Street, #1C, New York, NY 10023. Call 212-769-1170. Ref. L1270.

Children: Y   Pets: N   Smoking: Y   Handicap Access: N   Payment: C, P

Cap Ferrat

MAS DE LA RUBA   *Rates: deluxe*
Open: July-September   *Minimum Stay: one month*
Secluded in one of St. Jean's most exclusive neighborhoods, this house is perfect for entertaining. The beautifully landscaped, walled grounds lead down to a rugged shoreline dotted with palm trees. On the ground floor, guests find an elegant living/dining room, a fully equipped kitchen and a master double bedroom, and on the second floor are four twin bedrooms. In addition, there are five bathrooms and a maid's room. Mas de la Ruba is exquisitely furnished in an elegant yet unpretentious style. A cleaning lady comes daily to the house. The town of Cap Ferrat is one of the pearls of the Riviera, a seaside resort that makes an excellent center from which to explore the coast. Contact: Vacances Provencal, 792 Cutter Lane, Elk Grove, IL 60007. Call 708-893-9402. Ref. CDA210.

Children: Y   Pets: Y   Smoking: Y   Handicap Access: N   Payment: P, T

Cap Ferrat

RESIDENCE ST. JEAN   *Rates: moderate-expensive*
Open: year-round   *Minimum Stay: one week*
Basking in the Mediterranean sun by the pool or wandering through the streets of this sleepy little village, you'll experience the best the Cote d'Azur has to offer. Studio and one-bedroom apartments can be

rented in the modern low-rise Residence St. Jean, each with its own balcony, kitchen and bathroom, and pleasantly furnished with such decorative touches such as tiled floors and wicker furniture. The location is unbeatable—next to the harbor and beach and within short driving distance of the well-known resort towns of Nice, Cannes and Monte Carlo. The selection of restaurants will tempt you away from the kitchen, but nearby stores carry everything you need to prepare meals at home. Contact: Villas International, 71 West 23rd Street, New York, NY 10010. Call 212-929-7585.

Children: Y   Pets: N   Smoking: Y   Handicap Access: N   Payment: C, P, T, O

Cap Ferrat

REX HARRISON'S VILLA   *Rates: deluxe*
Open: year-round   *Minimum Stay: two weeks*

Furnished with elegant antiques, beautiful rugs and a magnificent master bedroom suite, this classical villa was once owned by Rex Harrison. The villa enjoys a premier location in an exclusive residential district of Cap Ferrat. Views of the sea stretch out before your eyes, whether from the windows or the beautifully maintained garden. There are two reception rooms, two double bedrooms, one single and one twin bedroom and five baths in all, so the house is well appointed for entertaining. The kitchen is equipped with a dishwasher and washing machine and the maids help to make the house seem like your own. When not visiting the beaches, you can swim in the private pool or stroll to the center of the village just three minutes away. Excursions to the towns of the magical coastline are a must. Contact: Villas International, 71 West 23rd Street, New York, NY 10010. Call 212-929-7585.

Children: Y   Pets: N   Smoking: Y   Handicap Access: N   Payment: C, P, T, O

Collobrieres

VILLAGE HOUSE   *Rates: budget*
Open: year-round   *Minimum Stay: one week*

Collobrieres is a traditional Provencal village that lies in a beautiful wooded valley in the Massif des Maures, a naturally lovely area of Provence. This Provencal townhouse is located near the village center. Although it is nearly 400 years old, it has been carefully renovated to provide first-class accommodations for up to ten people, including modern kitchen and bath facilities. The best beaches and other attractions of the Cote d'Azur are all within easy reach. Contact: Chez Nous Travel Service, 85 Dobb Top Road, Holmbridge, Huddersfield, HD7 1QP, England. Call 011-44-1-0484-684075. Ref. 49b.

Children: Y   Pets: N   Smoking: Y   Handicap Access: N   Payment: P, V, M

Entrecasteaux Villa

LES BELIERS   *Rates: deluxe*
Open: year-round   *Minimum Stay: one week*

This magnificent villa features a wide porch and lovely garden terraces where you can relax on chaise longues. The luxurious home is surrounded by trees and caressed by breezes laden with the delicate scent of lavender from nearby fields. You'll want to relax in the huge living/ dining area in front of a crackling fire and let the dishwasher and washing machine in the kitchen do the work. Three baths, three bedrooms (all doubles, with one extra single) and a separate mini-apartment with two double beds and its own shower and terrace, house up to eleven in style. The grounds feature a tennis court, and the countryside is ideal for walking and touring. Contact: Vacances Provencales, 792 Cutter Lane, Elk Grove, IL 60007. Call 708-893-9402. Ref. CDA201.

Children: **Y**   Pets: **Y**   Smoking: **Y**   Handicap Access: **N**   Payment: **P, T**

Eze Village

MODERN APARTMENT   *Rates: budget*
Open: year-round   *Minimum Stay: one week*

Eze is a medieval village perched on a hillside with superb views of the surrounding countryside. This modern ground-floor apartment with its own garden is in a small, exclusive development overlooking Cap Ferrat between Nice and Monte Carlo. Two twin bedrooms each have an adjoining bath and the large living room provides a sofa bed, sleeping six in all. The kitchen is fully equipped, with a stove, a fridge/ freezer, a dishwasher and a washing machine. Savor the magnificent climate on the sizable lounging and dining patio. Eze offers good shops and restaurants; Nice and Monte Carlo lie only six miles away and the rest of the Cote d'Azur is quite accessible. Contact: Chez Nous Travel Service, 85 Dobb Top Road, Holmbridge, Huddersfield, HD7 1QP, England. Call 011-44-1-0484-684075. Ref. 53C.

Children: **Y**   Pets: **N**   Smoking: **Y**   Handicap Access: **N**   Payment: **P, V, M**

l'Auziere

DOMAINE DE L'AUZIERE   *Rates: deluxe*
Open: year-round   *Minimum Stay: one week*

Provence is known for its olive groves, orchards and woodlands, and you'll find all three on the grounds of this magnificent estate. The Main House is the most luxurious lodging here, featuring a sunken living room, game room with billiards and chess tables and a walled court with fountain. Two double bedrooms have large four-poster beds and open out to a covered terrace; four others offer a variety of single and double beds. For exercise, try the tennis court, the mosaic-tiled, heated swimming pool or the pool house with a fully equipped gym, sauna, shower room and barbecue. All linen is included and the house is maintained by a housekeeper, a cleaner and a gardener. Contact: British Travel Associates, P.O. Box 299, Elkton, VA 22827. Call 1-800-327-6097 (in Virginia, 703-298-2232). Ref. J50.

Children: **Y**   Pets: **N**   Smoking: **Y**   Handicap Access: **N**   Payment: **All**

La Ciotat

ESTATE VILLA
Rates: budget-expensive
Open: April-October
Minimum Stay: one week

Set in a private estate, this attractive villa in a half-acre of garden is located between St. Cyr sur Mer and Bandol on the bay of La Ciotat. A private beach lies just 500 yards from the villa, and there are three tennis courts, a swimming pool and a lawn-bowling area on the grounds. The house accommodates up to twelve people in five double bedrooms (one with en-suite bathroom) and a pull-out bed in the living room. There is also a second bathroom, a large kitchen and a dining room that opens onto a lovely terrace; the huge living room has a fireplace and a balcony overlooking the sea. The surrounding area has good shopping, villages, restaurants, beaches, beautiful walks and an aquatic park. Contact: Chez Nous Travel Service, 85 Dobb Top Road, Holmbridge, Huddersfield, HD7 1QP, England. Call 011-44-1-0484-684075. Ref. 47C.

Children: **Y**   Pets: **N**   Smoking: **Y**   Handicap Access: **N**   Payment: **P, V, M**

La Napoule

VILLA DANS LE VENT
Rates: deluxe
Open: year-round
Minimum Stay: one week

Perched on a hillside overlooking forested mountains that slope into the Mediterranean, Dans le Vent is both serene and well situated. Just five miles from Cannes, it is an ideal base from which to explore the coast at any time of year. The terrace is large and offers a terrific view; there are three bedrooms, three bathrooms, dining room, kitchen with microwave oven and dishwasher and a large living room for your comfort. Tasteful furnishings and special touches make the villa especially pleasant. The owners have lovingly created a traditional look with such features as exposed beams and stone walls. Contact: Vacances Provencales, 792 Cutter Lane, Elk Grove, IL 60007. Call 708-893-9402. Ref. CDA202.

Children: **Y**   Pets: **Y**   Smoking: **Y**   Handicap Access: **N**   Payment: **P, T**

Loube

FLATOTEL INTERNATIONAL: MARINA-COTE D'AZUR   *Rates: budget-expensive*
Open: year-round
Minimum Stay: none

The Flatotel Marina-Cote D'Azur, an elegant hi-rise dedicated to short-term vacation renters, is set in one of the most beautiful marinas in the world just outside Nice (and a short 20-minute drive from the Nice airport). Here, studios—many with balconies and sea or mountain views—and two-room apartments accommodate two-four people. Visitors may choose from three price options: The economy plan, which requires a minimum seven-day commitment, offers cleaning and linen change once a week; and the residence and hotel plans, each progressively more expensive, offer twice-weekly and daily maid service respectively. The eminently reasonable rates include the service charge but not the 6% French tax. Contact: Hometours International, Inc.,

1170 Broadway, New York, NY 10001. Call: 212-689-0851 or 1-800-367-4668.

Children: Y   Pets: N   Smoking: Y   Handicap Access: N   Payment: C, P

Menerbes

RUSTIC STONE HOUSE   *Rates: deluxe*
Open: year-round   *Minimum Stay: one week*

This rambling stone house commands breathtaking views of fertile Provencal valleys and pine-clad hills. Arriving guests are greeted by a courtyard full of flowers and an imposing stone archway before climbing the stone stairway to their rooms. Inside, the furnishings are a pleasing mix of the antique and the rustic, and almost every room has a gorgeous view. The living room boasts a magnificent fireplace and its own terrace; six charming bedrooms comfortably sleep 11 people. An inviting patio with a panoramic vista surrounds the swimming pool in back, where guests will also find a tennis court. Bikes for touring the countryside can be rented nearby. Contact: Villas and Apartments Abroad, Ltd., 420 Madison Avenue, New York, NY 10017. Call 1-800-433-3020.

Children: Y   Pets: Y   Smoking: Y   Handicap Access: N   Payment: C, P, T

Montgenevre

MOUNTAIN VIEW APARTMENTS   *Rates: budget*
Open: June-September   *Minimum Stay: one week*

Set in a quiet Alpine village near the ancient fortified town of Brianon by the Italian border, this modern apartment block commands gorgeous mountain views. Choose accommodations for two, four or six people. The studio and one-bedroom apartments have twin beds (plus bunks in the one-bedroom) and a fully fitted kitchenette, a bath, a balcony and a small garden on the mountainside. The largest apartments have balconies overlooking the slopes, spacious sitting rooms, two twin bedrooms with bunks, a double bedroom and a full bath with a separate toilet. Visitors to the area enjoy lovely walks, golf, riding, tennis and swimming as well as easy accessibility to a number of attractions. Contact: Chez Nous Travel Service, 85 Dobb Top Road, Holmbridge, Huddersfield, HD7 1QP, England. Call 011-44-1-0484-684075. Ref. 37A.

Children: Y   Pets: N   Smoking: Y   Handicap Access: N   Payment: P, V, M

Mougins

MAS DU GRAND VALLON   *Rates: deluxe*
Open: year-round   *Minimum Stay: one week*

This property and its surroundings are a gourmet's paradise: On the grounds are grapevines and fig, eucalyptus and olive trees, and nearby is Mougins, a favorite haunt of discriminating gourmands. The large house, or "mas" in the local dialect, has two double bedrooms, three bathrooms, a living room (complete with a luxurious Persian rug on which to lounge in front of the fire), dining room and kitchen with dishwasher. The guest house offers one double bedroom. All guests are welcome to use the swimming pool and the unique outdoor cooking fire, designed by the owner to cook "gigot," or lamb, a local specialty. The entire French Riviera is at your disposal, with Cannes just ten minutes away. Contact: Vacances Provencales, 792 Cutter Lane, Elk Grove, IL 60007. Call 708-893-9402. Ref. CDA208.

Children: Y   Pets: Y   Smoking: Y   Handicap Access: N   Payment: P, T

Nice

CORNICHE APARTMENT   *Rates: deluxe*
Open: year-round   *Minimum Stay: none*

A terraced building in true Provencal style, this two-bedroom apartment provides stunning views of the old harbor of Nice and beyond. Very luxurious, with marble floors and separate living, and dining rooms and kitchen, this regal residence will house you in comfort while you visit the many lovely towns dotted along this magnificent coastline. Electric shutters shelter you from the blazing Mediterranean sun; the large terrace makes a lovely place to sit and watch the white sailboats bobbing in the water below. Nearby is a private beach, and only a few minutes' walk takes you down to the winding streets of Nice. Contact: Overseas Connection, 70 West 71st Street, #1C, New York, NY 10023. Call 212-769-1170.

Children: Y   Pets: N   Smoking: Y   Handicap Access: N   Payment: C, P

Nice

VILLA D'AZUR   *Rates: expensive*
Open: year-round   *Minimum Stay: none*

A large villa with a trelliswork of plants lacing upward to a beautiful, shaded balcony, this house is extremely well situated in one of Nice's few residential areas. Public transportation can take you down to the busy hub of Nice and to the beaches that line the shore. The town of Nice is one of the Riviera's most popular vacation destinations, but don't neglect the other little towns dotted along this most famous of coastlines. The villa itself can sleep up to six guests in its three comfortable bedrooms, and it also has two bathrooms and separate living and dining rooms. Since the palatial residence is perched at the top of a hill, the large balcony and shuttered windows all provide panoramic views of the mountains and the town. Contact: Overseas Connection, 70 West 71st Street, #1C, New York, NY 10023. Call 212-769-1170.

Children: Y   Pets: N   Smoking: Y   Handicap Access: N   Payment: C, P

North Montauroux

CHATEAU DE CHRISTIAN DIOR   *Rates: deluxe*
Open: year-round   *Minimum Stay: one week*

A grand entrance hall designed by Christian Dior, complete with sweeping staircase and ancient tapestries, welcomes guests into this lavish chateau once owned by the internationally famous designer. This magnificent estate offers seven beautifully appointed bedroom suites, each with a small fridge/bar, and can accommodate 15 guests. Large terraces and graceful balconies look out over two pools, beautifully tended lawns, wooded hills and olive groves. The master bedroom suite with bath and dressing room feature Dior's canopied bed and a unique circular bathroom finished completely in marble. Downstairs, guests can congregate in the dining room, grand hall, library, drawing room with marble fireplace and grand piano and summer lounge, which opens onto a covered pergola terrace overlooking an ornamental pool. The large gourmet kitchen has everything a chef might need, with two refrigerators and a microwave oven. Contact: Rent A Home International, Inc., 7200 34th Avenue N.W., Seattle, WA 98117. Call 206-545-6963.

Children: Y Pets: N Smoking: Y Handicap Access: N Payment: C, V, P, M

Ribas

MOULIN DE RIBAS   *Rates: moderate-expensive*
Open: year-round   *Minimum Stay: one week*

This old water mill beside a bubbling waterfall has been converted into a unique four-bedroom holiday home that can accommodate up to nine guests. Both the house and the setting are unique: The house has such features as beamed ceilings, stone floors and an open fireplace, as well as a well-equipped kitchen with a dishwasher, washing machine and two baths. The little hamlet of Ribas has remained unchanged for centuries. This area is famous for its Cotes du Rhone wine, and visitors find many fine restaurants with traditional French cooking, plus a range of seasonal festivals and cultural events. The local scenery varies from serene fields and woods to wild river gorges and, of course, the fabulous Cote d'Azur. Contact: Vacances Provencales, 792 Cutter Lane, Elk Grove, IL 60007. Call 708-893-9402. Ref. P106

Children: Y   Pets: Y   Smoking: Y   Handicap Access: N   Payment: P, T

Rognes

HOUSE OF DREAMS   *Rates: moderate-deluxe*
Open: year-round   *Minimum Stay: one week*

A courtyard with a fountain forms the heart of this unique four-bedroom villa for eight. Terraces lead you into a house that features a large living area in which a pagoda-shaped fireplace separates the sitting area from the dining room. Furnished by the artist-owner with antiques and modern furniture, the house features a master double bedroom suite, one double room and two singles. There are also two baths, a modern kitchen and a swimming pool that features its own waterfall. Nearby is an equestrian center for riding, plus several tennis courts. Contact: Rent A Home International, Inc., 7200 34th Avenue NW, Seattle, WA 98117. Call 206-545-6963.

Children: Y Pets: N Smoking: Y Handicap Access: N Payment: C, V, P, M

Roquebrune-Sur-Argens

RESTORED APARTMENT   *Rates: budget*
Open: year-round   *Minimum Stay: one week*

Located in the conservation section of a charming Provencal village, this beautiful old apartment occupies the upper floor of a traditional stone building. A large, sunny terrace offers superb views of the surrounding mountains and countryside. Inside, the recently renovated apartment includes a roomy living room with a modern corner kitchen, plus a double bedroom. The neighborhood is tranquil and all amenities can be found nearby. In addition, many places of historical and cultural interest, as well as superb beaches, lie within easy reach by car. Contact: Chez Nous Travel Service, 85 Dobb Top Road, Holmbridge, Huddersfield, HD7 1QP, England. Call 011-44-1-0484-684075. Ref. 49D.

Children: Y   Pets: N   Smoking: Y   Handicap Access: N   Payment: P, V, M

Rousset
CHATEAU DE LA BEGUDE APARTMENT   *Rates: budget-moderate*
Open: year-round   *Minimum Stay: one week*

A paleontologist's treasure chest, La Begude is one of only five sites that have yielded dinosaur eggs. The chateau is set near the foot of Ste.-Victoire mountain, near a working vineyard where you can buy good wine. Guests who rent this first-floor apartment use their own separate entrance and enjoy a small private terrace area. In the kitchen you'll find all the modern conveniences, but elsewhere you can admire the antique furnishings. A convertible sofa bed in the living room and one double bedroom sleeps a total of four; also, a cot will be provided on request. Contact: British Travel Associates, P.O. Box 299, Elkton, VA 22827. Call 1-800-327-6097 (in Virginia, 703-298-2232). Ref. J60.

Children: Y   Pets: N   Smoking: Y   Handicap Access: N   Payment: All

Sigoyer
RESTORED FARMHOUSE   *Rates: budget*
Open: June-September   *Minimum Stay: one week*

Enjoy the Mediterranean climate, clean air and rural French life in this roomy, comfortable farmhouse with spectacular mountain views. The sunny sitting/dining room has a big bay window and the eat-in kitchen is spacious and fully equipped. Two bedrooms each have a double bed and one has an additional single bed and a vanity. Outside, garden furniture and a barbecue are provided so guests can take advantage of the fantastic weather. Sigoyer, a great place for walking and touring, has a bakery, a grocery, a post office and a hotel with a restaurant. A nearby lake provides fishing and wind surfing, while tennis, swimming and gliding facilities are all available close by. Provence and the Italian border are within easy reach for day trips. Contact: Chez Nous Travel Service, 85 Dobb Top Road, Holmbridge, Huddersfield, HD7 1QP, England. Call 011-44-1-0484-684075. Ref. 36F.

Children: Y   Pets: N   Smoking: Y   Handicap Access: N   Payment: P, V, M

St. Laurent de Carnols
MAS DE VEYRAC   *Rates: expensive-deluxe*
Open: year-round   *Minimum Stay: one week*

You'll find this large family home on the outskirts of a little village nestled in the valley of the Ceze River. Typically in Provencal style, with stone walls, shuttered windows and a tiled roof, the house has a large garden where you can hold barbecues or sip morning cafe au lait while comfortably seated on the garden chairs. A game room and swimming pool are located on the property. Fireplaces and wood-burning stoves warm the many rooms. The kitchen has a separate eating area and there is also a comfortable dining room, three bathrooms and six bedrooms to accommodate up to eight guests. Avignon, the ancient papal city, is just one of the many historic sites within driving distance. Contact: Vacances Provencales, 792 Cutter Lane, Elk Grove, IL 60007. Call 708-893-9402. Ref. P105

Children: Y   Pets: Y   Smoking: Y   Handicap Access: N   Payment: P, T

St. Maximin

MAISON DE L'AUBERGE   *Rates: inexpensive-moderate*
Open: year-round   *Minimum Stay: one week*

Surrounded by trees and bushes and designed in the traditional Provencal village style, the Maison de l'Auberge is an old stone house on several levels. Balconies and staircases add architectural interest, while hanging plants and comfortable furniture create a cozy look. You'll have plenty of room—the house has a large living room with fireplace, a kitchen/dining room with dishwasher and washing machine, a bathroom and two bedrooms. St. Maximin is a lovely little village in this region where historical sites abound. Of course, you wouldn't want to miss the long sandy beaches, warm waters and recreational opportunities offered on the coast, just ninety minutes away. Contact: Vacances Provencales, 792 Cutter Lane, Elk Grove, IL 60007. Call 708-893-9402. Ref. PO219.

Children: Y   Pets: Y   Smoking: Y   Handicap Access: N   Payment: P, T

St. Remy

THE BERGERIE   *Rates: moderate-deluxe*
Open: late April-late September   *Minimum Stay: two weeks*

In this area, made famous by Vincent van Gogh, Roman ruins are plentiful. In fact, a small pool at the Bergerie is still nourished by spring waters running through a Roman stone conduit. The Bergerie was part of a large old estate since divided by inheritance; the main house is now a small private hotel about 55 yards away. Your privacy is assured in this house with many large, well-appointed rooms. The spacious entryway houses a baby grand piano, the comfortable sitting area includes an open fireplace and stereo and the modern kitchen opens onto a vine-covered terrace. Endowed with a splendid view of gardens and hills through its French windows, the large master bedroom has two large twin beds. One twin and two single bedrooms provide sleeping accommodations for four more. Each week, two mornings of cleaning service are supplied. Contact: British Travel Associates, P.O. Box 299, Elkton, VA 22827. Call 1-800-327-6097 (in Virginia, 703-298-2232). Ref. J34.

Children: Y   Pets: N   Smoking: Y   Handicap Access: N   Payment: All

St. Saturnin d'Apt

STONE HOUSE

Rates: budget

Open: May-July; September

Minimum Stay: one week

Surrounded by rugged hills and gentle valleys, this is an ideal location for enjoying the Provencal countryside and its architecture, history and customs. The two-story house, situated in a charming hamlet, offers a double and a single bedroom, a kitchen, a living/dining room and a bathroom. Outside is a pleasant yard for dining and sunbathing. Cafes, bakeries, shops, restaurants, a post office, tennis courts and bowling allies are all less than two miles away. Just a little further, in Apt, there is a weekly market, supermarkets, banks, swimming, wind surfing and a wine cooperative. Contact: Chez Nous Travel Service, 85 Dobb Top Road, Holmbridge, Huddersfield, HD7 1QP, England. Call 011-44-1-0484-684075. Ref. 44K.

Children: **Y** Pets: **N** Smoking: **Y** Handicap Access: **N** Payment: P, V, M

St. Tropez

VILLAS BOUILLABAISSE

Rates: moderate-expensive

Open: year-round

Minimum Stay: one week

What could be more appropriate for a Mediterranean stay than your own villa built in a wooded glade in Provencal style, with a tiled roof and long, shuttered windows? Available with one to three bedrooms, separate living rooms, color TV, telephone, kitchen and bathroom, each unit offers complete independence. Your own furnished patio and secluded little garden provides a place to sit or perhaps to barbecue some fresh fish; if you prefer company, there is a pool for swimming and sunbathing. The sandy beach of Bouillabaisse is a short walk, where you can watch the sailboats and yachts out on the blue horizon. All of the night spots and marvelous stores and restaurants are just five minutes away from the villa. Contact: Villas International, 71 West 23rd Street, New York, NY 10010. Call 212-929-7585.

Children: **Y** Pets: **N** Smoking: **Y** Handicap Access: **N** Payment: C, P, T, O

Vaison la Romaine

COLLINE ST. CROIX

Rates: deluxe

Open: year-round

Minimum Stay: one week

Come to Vaison la Romaine to be fascinated by ancient Roman ruins and enchanted by a Provencal village. Venerable Colline St. Croix is tucked away in the hills north of town, set amid lush gardens and tranquil natural beauty. Persian carpets on old tiled floors give the living room (with rustic central fireplace) and dining room a mellow tone. The kitchen is also on the first floor. Three sets of elegant French doors lead from these rooms out to the partially shaded patio. Eleven people can occupy the five bedrooms upstairs—one of which has its own stairway down to the patio. Popular diversions in the area include tennis, riding and Vaison's summer festival, but you may decide to pass your days by the sparkling swimming pool. Contact: Villas and Apartments Abroad, Ltd., 420 Madison Avenue, New York, NY 10017.

Call 1-800-433-3020.

Children: Y   Pets: Y   Smoking: Y   Handicap Access: N   Payment: C, P, T

Valbonne

PROVENCAL VILLA *Rates: budget*
Open: year-round *Minimum Stay: one week*
This modern Provencal-style villa sits on wooded parkland in a private estate at the foothills of the Alps. Attractively furnished and well equipped, the villa has one double and one twin bedroom, a living area, a kitchen and a dining alcove. Telephone, a washing machine and wall heaters are provided to make life a little easier. French windows lead from the main bedroom, the sitting room and the kitchen to an ample terrace overlooking a pleasant garden. The estate has a large swimming pool and tennis courts; nearby is Antibes, while the coast is only 15 minutes away. The area also offers three golf courses, horseback riding and many good restaurants. Contact: Chez Nous Travel Service, 85 Dobb Top Road, Holmbridge, Huddersfield, HD7 1QP, England. Call 011-44-1-0484-684075. Ref. 52D.

Children: Y   Pets: N   Smoking: Y   Handicap Access: N   Payment: P, V, M

Vallabrix

MAISON CHEZ ANGELINE *Rates: deluxe*
Open: year-round *Minimum Stay: one week*
Imagine lounging on an ivy-covered terrace where you can step down to a swimming pool. This luxurious house has four bedrooms that sleep two guests each; the lower two bedrooms are at pool level. A spacious living room with large, shuttered windows provides a comfortable meeting place; the dining room has a huge table and the kitchen is fully equipped with a dishwasher for easy cleaning. Just a few minutes' drive from the busy market town of Uzes, this house is perfectly situated for touring the center of old Provence. Surrounded by lush vineyards, picture-perfect villages and farms, and within driving distance of the magnificent Mediterranean coast, the area is filled with history. Contact: Vacances Provencales, 792 Cutter Lane, Elk Grove, IL 60007. Call 708-893-9402. Ref. PO204

Children: Y   Pets: Y   Smoking: Y   Handicap Access: N   Payment: P, T

Vence

HILLTOP VILLA *Rates: deluxe*
Open: July-August *Minimum Stay: none*
A unique stone villa with a wonderful round turret and long balconies, this residence has many features. The hilltop location is close enough to the coast to command views of the sea, but it's just a short drive to Nice. Vence itself is an old Roman market town that's well worth exploring for such treasures as a chapel designed by Henri Matisse. The house has four bedrooms and sleeps up to six people. Guests of all ages will enjoy the sprawling swimming pool and the assortment of recreational diversions and games. The living room has a corner dining

area, and there is a little outdoor kitchen in the pool house, which is perfect for preparing summer meals to eat beside the pool or in the huge garden. Contact: Overseas Connection, 70 West 71st Street, #1C, New York, NY 10023. Call 212-769-1170. Ref. C3841.

Children: Y Pets: N Smoking: Y Handicap Access: N Payment: C, P

Villefranch sur Mer

MARINE RESIDENCE *Rates: inexpensive-expensive*
Open: year-round *Minimum Stay: one week*

As its name suggests, this apartment residence faces the harbor of a Mediterranean town, where entertainment can be had simply by watching the comings and goings of fabulous yachts and sailboats. All the sights and pleasures of the coast are within easy reach—Nice, Cannes, Monte Carlo and, of course, the unparalleled beaches. From the residence, the old town of Villefranche sur Mer and the beach are a short but pleasant walk along a promenade strung with lively boutiques and cafes. The residence offers apartments that sleep up to seven guests, all with contemporary decor, full kitchens and TV if desired. Some include loft-type bedrooms. Contact: Villas International, 71 West 23rd Street, New York, NY 10010. Call 212-929-7585.

Children: Y Pets: N Smoking: Y Handicap Access: N Payment: C, P, T, O

Villefranche sur Mer

VILLA CASTELET *Rates: deluxe*
Open: year-round *Minimum Stay: one week*

The owners of Villa Castelet like to think their beautiful house will spoil you for any other vacation accommodations. Indeed, both the location and the quality of the house are sublime. The villa consists of two floors with large rooms, an outdoor swimming pool and a beautiful patio perfect for dining outdoors while taking in the panorama of the lovely coast spread out before you. A tiled living room with fireplace, dining room, kitchen with all modern appliances, three bedrooms and three baths guarantee your comfort. The house is secluded and elegantly furnished with beautiful objects d'art, making it perfect for entertaining. The popular town of Nice is just a five-minute drive, and glamorous Monte Carlo is just a bit further. Contact: Villas International, 71 West 23rd Street, New York, NY 10010. Call 212-929-7585.

Children: N Pets: N Smoking: Y Handicap Access: N Payment: C, P, T, O

RHONE-ALPES

Argentiere

RESIDENCE BELLEVUE *Rates: expensive*
Open: year-round *Minimum Stay: one week*

This former hotel was converted in 1970 into fifteen spacious duplex apartments capable of accommodating up to six guests each. Glass doors that open onto a balcony offer a perfect view of the ski trails that snake down the snow-dusted mountains. The ski lifts of Les Grands

Montets are just a few minutes' walk from the residence. In the living/dining area are two single beds and simple, modern furnishings; on the same floor are two baths, plus a kitchenette in which to make hot chocolate or hearty soup. Up the stairs are two bedrooms, one with a double bed and another with two singles. Residence Bellevue is in the center of Argentiere; the larger town of Chamonix is just a ten-minute drive away and offers a good starting point for mountain hikes or excursions. Contact: Vacances Provencales, 792 Cutter Lane, Elk Grove, IL 60007. Call 708-893-9402. Ref. C108.

Children: Y   Pets: Y   Smoking: Y   Handicap Access: N   Payment: P, T

Chamonix

CHALET AIMONETTO   *Rates: budget-moderate*
Open: year-round   *Minimum Stay: one week*

From the three apartments in this chalet, you can see the mountains where so many mountaineers have tested their skill. Nearby Mount Blanc is Europe's highest peak, and the facilities in this town for skiing, hiking and mountain climbing are all excellent. The chalet is about ten minutes from the busy town center—just far enough to provide a little peace if you choose to step out into the garden. The three apartments, ranging from a studio to a two-bedroom unit, sleep two to six guests. All the apartments are fully equipped and comfortable. Contact: Vacances Provencales, 792 Cutter Lane, Elk Grove, IL 60007. Call 708-893-9402. Ref. C102.

Children: Y   Pets: Y   Smoking: Y   Handicap Access: N   Payment: P, T

Evian

EVIAN VILLAS AND APARTMENTS   *Rates: budget-moderate*
Open: year-round   *Minimum Stay: two weeks*

The restorative powers of mineral waters and thermal baths have soothed generations of Europeans at Evian, which lies on the French side of Lake Geneva. Lake Geneva offers many resorts, and you can explore the French Alps, only ten miles away, in summer and winter. A casino and many fashionable shops will entertain you as well. This residence complex offers a variety of apartments and villas ranging from studio to four-bedroom units. All are comfortably furnished and have a living room, dining room, fully equipped kitchen and one or more baths. Some have a balcony or terrace, and there is a heated community pool for guests, with areas nearby for golf, fishing and other sports, just outside the cosmopolitan city of Geneva. Contact: Villas International, 71 West 23rd Street, New York, NY 10010. Call 1-800-221-2260 (in New York, 212-929-7585).

Children: Y   Pets: N   Smoking: Y   Handicap Access: N   Payment: C, P, T

Germany

BADEN-WURTTEMBERG

Biberach-Burren

WOODSMAN'S HOUSE *Rates: inexpensive-moderate*
Open: April-November *Minimum Stay: one week*

Two centuries old, this three-story house was once used by woodsmen but is now a retreat surrounded by magnificent trees. Three floors feature plenty of space, including an impressive entrance hall with a fireplace, a gallery looking down on the hall and a sloped-ceiling living room. Three bedrooms sleep six in comfort. Laundry and barbecue facilities make your stay more convenient and enjoyable. In Biberach are swimming pools, tennis and an interesting old town center. Within driving distance is beautiful Lake Constance bordered by Switzerland and Austria, both well worth a day trip. Contact: Interhome Inc., 124 Little Falls Road, Fairfield, NJ 07004. Call 201-882-6864. Ref. D7950/11

Children: Y Pets: Y Smoking: Y Handicap Access: N Payment: V, P, M

Gorwihl

BISAM-PELZ HOUSE *Rates: budget*
Open: June-November *Minimum Stay: one week*

Considered an ideal region for nature-lovers, the southern Black Forest offers something to suit every taste. Just a five-minute drive from the health resort of Gorwihl stands this family-style house, the ground floor of which can be rented by up to four guests. It has a combined living/dining/kitchen area and two double bedrooms; guests are welcome to use the phone, TV and radio. In the back of the house is a big garden and furnished patio. In summer, the woods, fishing streams and jagged gorges can be explored on foot; in winter, cross-country ski trails abound. Nearby restaurants and local folklore provide a taste of the special culture of this region. Contact: Interhome Inc., 124 Little Falls Road, Fairfield, NJ 07004. Call 201-882-6864. Ref. D7883/120A.

Children: Y Pets: Y Smoking: Y Handicap Access: N Payment: V, P, M

Herrischried

NIEDERGEBISBACH HOLIDAY COMPLEX *Rates: budget*
Open: April-November *Minimum Stay: one week*

Sloped roofs, wide balconies and patios with a view characterize the accommodations offered at this homey resort. Situated along the Swiss border, it provides easy access to St. Blasien, sparkling Lake Titisee, the legendary Black Forest and other excursion destinations. One- to three-room apartments accommodate up to four guests in chalet-style houses or the hotel building. All units have either a full kitchen or kitchenette. A shopping center is less than two miles away and a restaurant and cafe are just down the road. Those seeking activity will find it at the nearby swimming pool, tennis court, or along the extensive network of paths leading through the surrounding forest and meadows. Contact: Interhome Inc., 124 Little Falls Road, Fairfield, NJ 07004. Call 201-882-6864. Ref. D7881/100A/110B/ 120M/130M.

Children: Y Pets: Y Smoking: Y Handicap Access: N Payment: V, P, M

Titisee

BLACK FOREST CONDO *Rates: budget-inexpensive*
Open: year-round *Minimum Stay: one week*

Of the many sparkling lakes that reflect the mighty trees of the Black Forest, Lake Titisee is a jewel dotted in summer with the sails of boats and wind-surfers. The apartment is set in the village of Titisee within view of the lake—and the large windows and balcony ensure that you take full advantage of the view. It is located on the upper floor of a charming duplex and has plenty of room in its large, wood-paneled living room, two bedrooms and a complete kitchen and bathroom. The eight-hundred-year-old town of Freiburg is just a half-hour drive, or you may want to take a day trip to Switzerland or France, both less than an hour's drive. Contact: Hilde Freeman, Rent A Home International, Inc., 7200 34th Avenue N.W., Seattle, WA 98117. Call 206-545-6963.

Children: Y Pets: N Smoking: N Handicap Access: N Payment: C, V, P, M

Todtmoos/Schwartzwald

TODTMOOS APARTMENTS

Rates: budget-inexpensive

Open: year-round

Minimum Stay: one week

You'll find this spa and leisure center on a hillside overlooking Todtmoos. The rustic-style complex offers two types of apartments overlooking the hillside to the south. "Zartener Stube," a studio with a kitchenette, is perfect for a couple. The "Gutacher Sube Galerie" has a separate bedroom. All apartments are carpeted and furnished with traditional Black Forest appointments, plus color TV and either a terrace or a balcony. During winter months, come here to cross-country and downhill ski, or to toboggan, take sleigh rides or even try dog sledding. Summer activities include tennis, fitness training, and horseback riding. Full spa treatment is available, incorporating massage, herbal baths and supervised diets. Contact: ADZ, German National Tourist Board-Service Department (German Hotel Reservation Service), Corneliusstr. 34, D-6000 Frankfurt, Germany. Call 011-49-69-740767.

Children: Y   Pets: N   Smoking: Y   Handicap Access: N   Payment: EC

Triberg/Schwarzwald

TANNENHOF APARTMENTS

Rates: budget-inexpensive

Open: March-October

Minimum Stay: one week

These apartments stand in a quiet location in the vacation area known as the "Geutsche." The units can sleep from two to five guests in a combination of living/bedroom and separate bedrooms. You can start the day by sipping coffee on your balcony, which overlooks the resort area of Triberg. If the prospect of a full treatment at the spa or baths doesn't tempt you, the residence itself has a fully equipped gymnasium, swimming pool, sauna, sun room and visiting masseur. Not far away are tennis courts, and you can take long walks along well-marked woodland trails. Winter sports opportunities abound here, and there is a babysitting service and a children's playground. Contact: ADZ, German National Tourist Board-Service Department (German Hotel Reservation Service), Corneliusstr. 34, D-6000 Frankfurt, Germany. Call 011-49-69-740767.

Children: Y   Pets: Y   Smoking: Y   Handicap Access: N   Payment: EC

Tuttlingen-Mohringen/Schwabische Alb

"AUF DER BURG" VILLAGE

Rates: budget

Open: March-October

Minimum Stay: one week

From this ideal location, you can visit magnificent Lake Constance, the romantic valley of the Danube and the legendary Black Forest. Built on a slight rise, the vacation village consists of small houses near the center of a health resort. The houses have upstairs bedrooms for either four or five guests; on the ground floor, they offer a living/dining area with color TV, a kitchenette and furnished outdoor patio. A park filled with graceful deer is nearby, as well as an astounding array of nature trails throughout the region, some of which can be taken with a guide. A full range of recreational activities is available. Contact:

ADZ, German National Tourist Board-Service Department (German Hotel Reservation Service), Corneliusstr. 34, D-6000 Frankfurt, Germany. Call 011-49-69-740767.

Children: Y   Pets: Y   Smoking: Y   Handicap Access: N   Payment: EC

Waldachtal

KUR-SPORTS HOTEL   *Rates: budget*
Open: April-November   *Minimum Stay: one week*

Two- and three-room apartments are available at this vacation complex at Salstetten, which is part of the vacation resort of Waldachtal. The hotel offers a range of facilities, including sauna, sun room, TV room and Ping-Pong tables; the resort town itself has tennis courts, a health club, bicycle rentals and a special playground for children. Apartments with living/dining room, bunk beds, a twin bedroom, kitchen and bath sleep four; larger units add another twin bedroom. All apartments have balconies. The region is a walker's paradise, with numerous lakes throughout the forests and meadows and tiny farming communities unchanged for centuries. Contact: Interhome Inc., 124 Little Falls Road, Fairfield, NJ 07004. Call 201-882-6864. Ref. D7244/60M/70M.

Children: Y   Pets: Y   Smoking: Y   Handicap Access: N   Payment: V, P, M

Wimberg

TWO-STORY FARMHOUSE   *Rates: budget-inexpensive*
Open: April-October   *Minimum Stay: one week*

Wimberg is one of the small resort towns that populate this picturesque region. Up to eight guests are welcome to stay in this two-story house, which sits on a gentle slope in the tiny village. A small convenience store occupies the basement, and larger shops and restaurants are a few miles away. Four twin bedrooms make up the sleeping quarters, and there are two bathrooms in addition to the kitchen and living room, which has a TV. Deck chairs will make you comfortable if you choose to sit out in the garden or on the patio. Nearby Nesselwang has skiing facilities in the winter. Since the border is so close, Austria is just one of the many places you may wish to visit for an excursion. Contact: Interhome Inc., 124 Little Falls Road, Fairfield, NJ 07004. Call 201-882-6864. Ref. D8951/10

Children: Y   Pets: Y   Smoking: Y   Handicap Access: N   Payment: V, P, M

BAVARIA

Bohmischbruck/Bayerischer Wald

MAXIMILIANSHOF BUNGALOWS   *Rates: budget*
Open: year-round   *Minimum Stay: one week*

Situated on a southern slope with maximum sun exposure, this complex of vacation bungalows and apartments stands only a few miles from a reservoir and swimming lake. The surrounding slopes offer skiing (there is a national training center here), and skating is popular on the lakes and rivers that dot the region. The bungalows are private and accommodate up to four guests in a living room with sofa bed, separate bedroom, kitchen or kitchenette, dining area and a furnished patio or balcony where guests can soak up the sun. Play squash or Ping-Pong or go bicycle, horseback or carriage riding. The complex also has an indoor swimming pool, sauna and sun room. Contact: ADZ, German National Tourist Board-Service Department (German Hotel Reservation Service), Corneliusstr. 34, D-6000 Frankfurt, Germany. Call 011-49-69-740767.

Children: Y   Pets: Y   Smoking: Y   Handicap Access: N   Payment: EC

Grafenwiesen

WILDGATTER CHALETS   *Rates: budget*
Open: year-round   *Minimum Stay: one week*

Each of the chalets in this vacation village is divided into two apartments with a dining nook in the living/bedroom, a separate double bedroom, kitchenette, bath and balcony or furnished patio. The village itself is very peaceful, but offers plenty of amenities such as laundry facilities, restaurants, beer garden and barbecue area and special events. Cross-country and downhill skiing are available in winter, as are skating, curling and special guided winter walks and carriage rides. The ponds by the village are ideal for boating, swimming or letting the children splash around in the summer. A babysitting service allows parents to take a sauna, work out in the health club or take a romantic walk along one of the woodland trails. Contact: ADZ, German National Tourist Board-Service Department (German Hotel Reservation Service), Corneliusstr. 34, D-6000 Frankfurt, Germany. Call 011-49-69-740767.

Children: Y   Pets: Y   Smoking: Y   Handicap Access: N   Payment: EC

Munich

MAXIMILLIAN APARTMENTS   *Rates: expensive-deluxe*
Open: year-round   *Minimum Stay: one week*

Maximillian offers a selection of studio, one- and two-bedroom apartments in a modern building just five minutes from the central Marienplatz. Close to museums, markets and theaters, you couldn't ask for a better location in Munich. All apartments have a living room, dining room, kitchen and bathroom and are tastefully furnished and decorated. For stays of two weeks or more, free breakfasts are supplied; otherwise, you can purchase everything you need at the nearby open-air Viktualienmarkt, a great source of German and international food. A short drive outside the city brings you to the Bavarian Alps and the legendary Black Forest. Contact: Villas International, 71 West 23rd Street, New York, NY 10010. Call 212-929-7585.

Children: Y   Pets: N   Smoking: Y   Handicap Access: N   Payment: C, P, T, O

Munich

WESTKREUZ APARTMENTS   *Rates: buget-inexpensive*
Open: year-round   *Minimum Stay: one week*

These studio and one-bedroom apartments are furnished with couches, bookcases and plants to create a homey atmosphere. The modern apartment building is located on the western edge of the city and just a short subway ride from downtown. All units have a living/dining room, kitchen, bathroom and color TV; laundry facilities and parking are available for added convenience. A small shopping center nearby will provide for your needs, but you might want to visit Munich's outdoor markets for local and international food. There are many sights in this popular town, including museums, historic sites and fine restaurants. The Westkreuz Apartments are also convenient for excursions outside the city—perhaps to the Black Forest or the mountains. Contact: Villas International, 71 West 23rd Street, New York, NY 10010. Call 212-929-7585.

Children: Y Pets: N Smoking: Y Handicap Access: N Payment: C, P, T, O

Ramsau

HINTERMUHLE HOUSE   *Rates: budget*
Open: year-round   *Minimum Stay: one week*
This large, renovated chalet has been divided into seventeen apartments around a swimming pool, lawn, sauna and barbecue area. The apartments have a living/bedroom, one double bedroom, kitchenette, bathroom with shower and a balcony or patio from which the German Alps can be viewed. In winter, the historic spa of Ramsau becomes a wonderland for skiing (both downhill and cross-country), bobsledding, tobogganing, curling and sleigh riding. In summer, the area can be explored on foot or bicycle, or from a mountain cable car high above the treetops. Contact: ADZ, German National Tourist Board-Service Department (German Hotel Reservation Service), Corneliusstr. 34, D-6000 Frankfurt, Germany. Call 011-49-69-740767.

Children: Y   Pets: Y   Smoking: Y   Handicap Access: N   Payment: EC

Solla

SOLLA HOLIDAY COMPLEX   *Rates: budget*
Open: April-November   *Minimum Stay: one week*
The Bayerischer Wald is an outstanding area of great beauty that is filled with health and vacation resorts such as this one, which lies between Regen and Passau. Day excursions can be taken easily from here to Prague or to Vienna, or to beautiful Passau, with its mixture of Romanesque, Gothic and Baroque architecture. The vacation complex offers a choice of apartments for three or four guests. A living/dining room, one or two twin bedrooms, kitchenette, bathroom with shower and a balcony or terrace provide plenty of room. The resort has lots of facilities for keeping fit—tennis, Ping-Pong, fitness equipment and both cross-country and downhill skiing in the winter. A short drive brings you to a swimming pool or a crystal-clear lake fed by mountain springs. Contact: Interhome Inc., 124 Little Falls Road, Fairfield, NJ 07004. Call 201-882-6864. Ref. D8391/200M/210B/220B/225A.

Children: Y Pets: Y Smoking: Y Handicap Access: N Payment: V, P, M

Vilshofen-Otterskirchen/Sudlich der Donau

OTTERSKIRCHEN CHALETS *Rates: budget*

Open: March-November *Minimum Stay: one week*

Just twenty minutes from the beautiful town of Passau at the foot of the Bavarian hills sits this vacation village. Its Swiss-style chalets overlook the Danube and are divided into apartments, each of which has a living room, one or two bedrooms, bath, kitchen or kitchenette and sometimes a balcony or patio. Nature paths wind all around this lovely area and recreational opportunities abound, such as a swimming pool, sauna, pony rides, evening barbecues and children's parties. Sightseeing plane trips from the nearby airfield can be arranged, or boating and fishing excursions can be also be planned. Baked goods are delivered to your door every morning, so all you have to do is make the coffee and relax. Contact: ADZ, German National Tourist Board-Service Department (German Hotel Reservation Service), Corneliusstr. 34, D-6000 Frankfurt, Germany. Call 011-49-69-740767.

Children: Y   Pets: Y   Smoking: Y   Handicap Access: N   Payment: EC

BERLIN

West Berlin

HOTEL BERLIN *Rates: inexpensive-deluxe*

Open: year-round *Minimum Stay: one week*

This low-lying block of modern apartments is nearby the Zoologischer Garten and Kurfurstendamn (the city's busiest shopping and dining street) and is central to several underground subway lines. The apartments consist of one or two rooms for up to four guests, all with shower or bath, phone, cable TV and kitchenette. Enjoy a welcoming sauna or relaxing massage after a day of touring the sights of Berlin. The hotel features a piano bar, restaurant and pub, or you can venture out to sample some of Berlin's fabulous nightlife. Contact: ADZ, German National Tourist Board-Service Department (German Hotel Reservation Service), Corneliusstr. 34, D-6000 Frankfurt, Germany. Call 011-49-69-740767.

Children: Y   Pets: Y   Smoking: Y   Handicap Access: N   Payment: EC

BREMEN

Muden/Orzte/Luneburger Heide

AUF DEM RIPKENHOF APARTMENTS *Rates: budget*

Open: March-October *Minimum Stay: one week*

This former farm is located in a small village between the Wietze and Ortze rivers and has been renovated to include a row of apartments. The ground floor of each apartment has a large living room with plenty of seating, a small bathroom and a kitchen; upstairs are two twin bedrooms and a full bathroom with shower. There are also laundry and barbecue facilities, a children's playground and, if desired, TVs can be rented. Visit the zoo, horseback-riding facilities, lakes, health club and tennis courts, or try fishing, golf and explore the nature trails over the moors. After a busy day, you'll be glad to sit outside on a private patio, enjoying the view of the lawn and the impressive old trees. Contact: ADZ, German National Tourist Board-Service Department (German Hotel Reservation Service), Corneliusstr. 34, D-6000 Frankfurt, Germany. Call 011-49-69-740767.

Children: Y   Pets: Y   Smoking: Y   Handicap Access: N   Payment: EC

HESSE

Frankenau

FRANKENAU HOLIDAY PARK   *Rates: budget-inexpensive*
Open: April-November   *Minimum Stay: one week*

A vacation land that combines relaxation and activity nestles amid tall trees on a southern slope about a ten-minute walk from Frankenau. The two-story chalets offered here can sleep up to six guests, and feature a living room with country-style furniture by a fireplace, dining alcove, kitchenette and three twin bedrooms (two with balcony). Resort activities include tennis, squash, outdoor chess, horseback riding, bicycle rental and water sports on the small lake. During summer months, there is a whirlpool, sauna, steam room, health club and paddling pool. There are cross-country trails for skiing in the winter. Contact: Interhome Inc., 124 Little Falls Road, Fairfield, NJ 07004. Call 201-882-6864. Ref. D3558/10.

Children: Y   Pets: Y   Smoking: Y   Handicap Access: N   Payment: V, P, M

LOWER SAXONY

Haren/Ems

FERIENZENTRUM COTTAGES   *Rates: budget*
Open: March-October   *Minimum Stay: one week*

This vacation center is located just over a mile from a port city on the Ems River. The area on the Dutch border is full of interesting historic sites and buildings, including an elaborate Baroque palace, public parks and gardens and gentle woodlands with nature trails. The rustic wooden cottages available for rent feature a living room with sofa bed, two children's bedrooms, kitchen facilities, a dining nook and bathroom. There's also convenient access to barbecue and laundry facilities. The sunny lawn is perfect for sunbathing, and nearby there's a lake with sandy shores and warm water for a swim. There's plenty to keep the kids—and the grown-ups—busy, including pony rides, rowing and canoeing, a children's playground and fishing. Contact: ADZ, German National Tourist Board-Service Department (German Hotel Reservation Service), Corneliusstr. 34, D-6000 Frankfurt, Germany. Call 011-49-69-740767.

Children: Y   Pets: Y   Smoking: Y   Handicap Access: N   Payment: EC

Uelsen/Emsland

FERIENPARK BUNGALOWS   *Rates: budget*
Open: year-round   *Minimum Stay: one week*

Set in the windmill-dotted German countryside close to Holland, these comfortable bungalows are decorated in Scandinavian style. This pretty border region will suit adventurers who want to try horseback riding, and the more sedate guest who'd prefer a tour in a horse-drawn carriage. A nearby recreation area offers golf, tennis, fishing, a woodland swimming pool with water slide, indoor pool and sauna, guided walks and clubs for children and teenagers. The apartment kitchenettes are fully equipped with a stove, fridge and coffee maker, but those who prefer may barbecue outdoors or visit the restaurant. The bungalows have two bedrooms (one with bunk beds), a living/dining area, TV and a covered patio with furniture. Contact: ADZ, German National Tourist Board-Service Department (German Hotel Reservation Service), Corneliusstr. 34, D-6000 Frankfurt, Germany. Call 011-49-69-740767.

Children: Y   Pets: Y   Smoking: Y   Handicap Access: N   Payment: EC

NORTH RHINE-WESTPHALIA

Braunlage/Harz

WANDERRESIDENZ APARTMENTS   *Rates: budget*
Open: March-October   *Minimum Stay: one week*

This spacious, whitewashed building houses a number of two-room apartments with balconies or patios that provide a view of the Hasselkopf ski area. The apartments are cheerfully decorated and have sofa beds in the living room, one separate bedroom, kitchenettes and a TV for your enjoyment. The building has a game room with table tennis and a sauna to help you relax after a day of skiing or sightseeing. In town is a treatment spa and recreational facilities that include horseback riding, bowling, indoor and outdoor swimming pools, golf and tennis. There are several skiing schools for adults and children, plus guided ski tours and night skiing. Contact: ADZ, German National Tourist Board-Service Department (German Hotel Reservation Service), Corneliusstr. 34, D-6000 Frankfurt, Germany. Call 011-49-69-740767.

Children: Y   Pets: Y   Smoking: Y   Handicap Access: N   Payment: EC

Kirchberg-Liederbach

KIRCHBERG HOLIDAY HOUSE   *Rates: budget-inexpensive*
Open: April-November   *Minimum Stay: one week*

This three-bedroom holiday house sits in a shady glade less than a mile outside Kirchberg, the oldest town in the region. Up to six guests can stay in three bedrooms and spread out in the living/dining room, kitchen and two bathrooms. Though visitors to this region are bound to spend a lot of time appreciating the beauty of its isolated valleys and woodland trails, they may be tempted to stay home to enjoy the color TV, piano and two covered patios with furniture. There are barbecue facilities at the house and stores to buy provisions in Kirchberg. Tour castles, cemeteries and impressive historic buildings. Contact: Interhome Inc., 124 Little Falls Road, Fairfield, NJ 07004. Call 201-882-6864. Ref. D6541/10.

Children: Y Pets: Y Smoking: Y Handicap Access: N Payment: V, P, M

Lage-Horste/Teutoburger Wald

HIDDENTRUP BUNGALOWS   *Rates: budget*
Open: March-October   *Minimum Stay: one week*

Known as the "Lipperland," this region is filled with historic monuments and medieval towns containing some of Germany's finest art treasures. These family-run bunglows are located in Hiddentrup, near an officially designated health-resort town at the edge of the Teutoburger Wald, an area of great nautural beauty. Among the facilities offered for children are tours of the working farm, bike rentals, playground areas, pony-riding ring and organized activities. Adults can choose from indoor and outdoor swimming pools, golf, skittles and tennis, or go hiking on nature trails, horseback riding and sightseeing galore. Up to four people can stay in each separate lodge or apartment, all fully equipped. Contact: ADZ, German National Tourist Board-Service Department (German Hotel Reservation Service), Corneliusstr. 34, D-6000 Frankfurt, Germany. Call 011-49-69-740767.

Children: **Y**   Pets: **Y**   Smoking: **Y**   Handicap Access: **N**   Payment: **EC**

Meschede/Sauerland

FERIENDORF CHALETS   *Rates: budget*
Open: March-October   *Minimum Stay: one week*

This collection of attractive chalets has full-length windows and shaded patios. Set on a wooded slope, the chalets provide a fine view of Lake Hennesee, dotted with the colorful sails of wind-surfers and sailboats. There is also a beach at the lake and a swimming pool and sauna nearby. The Homert nature reserve and surrounding countryside are ideal for walking; more energetic guests will enjoy a range of activities from tennis and horseback riding to hang-gliding. In the winter, try cross-country and downhill skiing. The chalets sleep four or six people and have all amenities including color TV and fully equipped kitchens or kitchenettes. Contact: ADZ, German National Tourist Board-Service Department (German Hotel Reservation Service), Corneliusstr. 34, D-6000 Frankfurt, Germany. Call 011-49-69-740767.

Children: **Y**   Pets: **Y**   Smoking: **Y**   Handicap Access: **N**   Payment: **EC**

Polle

NEPTUN HOUSE   *Rates: budget-inexpensive*
Open: April-November   *Minimum Stay: one week*

Neptun House is a pretty little structure that sits right on the sunny bank of the Weser River near the vacation resort of Polle. The house sleeps two in the living room and four more in the two twin bedrooms, plus there is a kitchen and a bathroom with shower. You can pick up supplies at the grocery and butcher shop just up the road; a supermarket is about a ten-minute drive. Garden furniture tempts guests to sit and admire the river view and breathe in the clean air. There is a Ping-Pong table in the house, and a boat is available for a jaunt down the river. You'll spend pleasant days exploring the nature reserves, woods, valleys and ancient castles of this picturesque region, or perhaps take a drive on the "Road of Fairytales." Contact: Interhome Inc., 124 Little Falls Road, Fairfield, NJ 07004. Call 201-882-6864. Ref. D3453/1.

Children: Y   Pets: Y   Smoking: Y   Handicap Access: N   Payment: V, P, M

Salzgitter/Salzgitter-Bad/Harz

HARZ MOUNTAIN RESORT *Rates: inexpensive*
Open: March-November *Minimum Stay: none*

This country-style complex is situated on the edge of a conservation area by the Harz Mountains, a nature-lovers' region of wooded valleys, rivers and open moors. A choice of houses and apartments sleep up to six guests. All the houses face south and have a patio on which you can soak up the sun; the apartments offer either a balcony or a patio. The houses also have fireplaces to keep you cozy, and all accommodations have color TVs and phones. The complex facilities include indoor tennis, squash, skittles, golf, bowling, horseback riding, a health club and some therapeutic spa facilities. The more adventurous may wish to try hang-gliding, wind-surfing, sailing or canoeing—all of which are locally available. Contact: ADZ, German National Tourist Board-Service Department (German Hotel Reservation Service), Corneliusstr. 34, D-6000 Frankfurt, Germany. Call 011-49-69-740767.

Children: Y   Pets: N   Smoking: Y   Handicap Access: N   Payment: EC

RHINELAND-PALATINATE

Cond

MOWE HOUSE *Rates: budget*
Open: March-October *Minimum Stay: one week*

From the balconies of this modern apartment building, guests can look out over the Mosel River and the floodlit vision of Cochem Castle. The building stands directly beside the yacht harbor and has private access to the river that gives its name to the wonderful white wines produced from the vineyards lining the surrounding valleys. The town of Cochem is full of historic buildings, parks, gardens, a pretty river promenade and even a chairlift in the summertime. The building has fourteen apartments, either studios with a double sofa bed or one-bedroom units capable of accommodating up to four guests. All have a dining area, kitchenette and bathroom with shower. Contact: ADZ, German National Tourist Board-Service Department (German Hotel Reservation Service), Corneliusstr. 34, D-6000 Frankfurt, Germany. Call 011-49-69-740767.

Children: Y   Pets: N   Smoking: Y   Handicap Access: N   Payment: EC

Dreifelden/Westerwald

FERIENWOHNUNG HOUSE *Rates: budget*
Open: year-round *Minimum Stay: one week*

This large house set just thirty feet from the lake contains seven apartments, each decorated in true country style. Some apartments are able to accommodate four people in two bedrooms and a living room with an open fireplace; the others have one bedroom and suit couples with one child. Each apartment has a dining alcove and kitchenette, bathroom with shower and a balcony from which to survey the expanse of lawn with its fountain below. The Westerwald region abounds with towns of historic interest interspersed with lush forests, rivers and open meadows. In fact, the apartment house is set in the center of a nature park full of walking trails. The lake offers wind surfing, and there is a beach resort on its shores. Contact: Tourist Information, Westerwald, Kirchstabe 48, 5430 Montabaur. Call 011-49-26-023001.

Children: Y   Pets: N   Smoking: Y   Handicap Access: N   Payment: EC

Kronenburg/Eifel

KRONENBURGER CHALETS   *Rates: budget-inexpensive*
Open: year-round   *Minimum Stay: three nights*
Two styles of wood-paneled, Scandinavian-style cottages are offered here to suit up to six guests. The larger design has one double and two twin bedrooms; the other has one double and one twin bedroom. Both have a living room with a dining area by an open kitchen, plus laundry facilities are available. Immediately outside is a covered patio where you can sit and enjoy the clear air of the volcanic Eifel region. The resort also runs a leisure center on nearby Lake Kronenburg that offers tennis, skating, bicycling, wind surfing, sailing, rowing and fishing. Closer to home are an indoor pool and a children's pool, sauna, sun room and a playground where the kids can make friends. Contact: ADZ, German National Tourist Board-Service Department (German Hotel Reservation Service), Corneliusstr. 34, D-6000 Frankfurt, Germany. Call 011-49-69-740767.

Children: Y   Pets: Y   Smoking: Y   Handicap Access: N   Payment: EC

Schonecken/Eifel

FERIENDORF CHALETS   *Rates: budget-inexpensive*
Open: year-round   *Minimum Stay: one week*
This pretty arrangement of six vacation chalets in the center of the North Eifel Nature Reserve can be enjoyed during any season. Each chalet features an upper apartment with two double bedrooms, living room with fireplace, kitchen, dining alcove and a spacious balcony; the lower apartment has one double bedroom, living room and kitchen and a patio. In the winter, the view consists of tall, snow-covered pines that put you in the mood for tobogganing or cross-country or downhill skiing. In summer, you can soak up the sun on the lawn, take a dip in the indoor or outdoor pools, play a game of tennis or catch some fish for the evening barbecue. Contact: ADZ, German National Tourist Board-Service Department (German Hotel Reservation Service), Corneliusstr. 34, D-6000 Frankfurt, Germany. Call 011-49-69-740767.

Children: Y   Pets: Y   Smoking: Y   Handicap Access: N   Payment: EC

Thalfung/Hunsruck

HIMMELBERG CABINS   *Rates: budget-inexpensive*
Open: year-round   *Minimum Stay: one week*
You're sure to enjoy a vacation in this village of log cabins and stone bungalows nestled amid tall trees near the health resort of Thalfang.

Choose from apartments and complete houses, all with a full kitchen, TV, bathroom with shower or bath and either a balcony or terrace. If visiting the nearby winter sports center at Erbeskopf, you might wish to choose a bungalow with a fireplace to warm you after skiing, skating, tobogganing or sleigh riding. The village has its own restaurant, laundry, sauna, and Ping-Pong, golf and tennis facilities. The area can be discovered on foot or by rented bicycle. Contact: ADZ, German National Tourist Board-Service Department (German Hotel Reservation Service), Corneliusstr. 34, D-6000 Frankfurt, Germany. Call 011-49-69-740767.

Children: Y   Pets: Y   Smoking: Y   Handicap Access: N   Payment: EC

Traben-Trarbach

PROMENADE HOUSE   *Rates: inexpensive-moderate*
Open: April-November   *Minimum Stay: one week*

The Mosel River flows beside this huge timber-framed house in the picture-perfect twin towns of Traben-Trarbach. A roaring fire greets guests in the first-floor reception area; the second floor contains another living room with a TV. In total, the three floors have six twin bedrooms and one single, plus two full and two half baths. Everything lies at your doorstep—supermarket, shops, restaurant, swimming pool and, of course, the river itself. The town is encircled by vineyards, and the local white wines are world-renowned. Nearby thermal springs and spa facilities will help you unwind after a day of sightseeing, boating or a visit to the Eifel National Park or other nearby attractions. Contact: Interhome Inc., 124 Little Falls Road, Fairfield, NJ 07004. Call 201-882-6864. Ref. D5580/1.

Children: Y   Pets: Y   Smoking: Y   Handicap Access: N   Payment: V, P, M

SAARLAND

Frielendorf/Kurhessisches Bergland

SILBERSEE COTTAGES   *Rates: budget-inexpensive*
Open: March-October   *Minimum Stay: one week*

Secluded and small, this resort offers a full range of activities centered around a spring-fed lake. The accommodations consist of individual cottages or apartments set on the south side of the lake, all with a balcony or terrace from which to view the surrounding mountains. The wooden gabled cottages have a large living room with fireplace, a kitchen and dining area, two baths and three bedrooms (one twin, two double). Apartments feature a living room with fireplace and dining area, a kitchen and two bedrooms. Nearby facilities include a laundromat, barbecue site, snack bar and restaurant. Enjoy boating and other water sports on the lake, plus an indoor pool, sauna, steam bath and health club. Contact: ADZ, German National Tourist Board-Service Department (German Hotel Reservation Service), Corneliusstr. 34, D-6000 Frankfurt, Germany. Call 011-49-69-740767.

Children: Y   Pets: N   Smoking: Y   Handicap Access: N   Payment: EC

SCHLESWIG-HOLSTEIN

Glucksburg

HOTEL GLUCKSBURG   *Rates: budget-inexpensive*
Open: March-October   *Minimum Stay: one week*
This resort offers numerous facilities for recreation and entertainment, as well as an off-the-beaten-path location on a northern fjord high up the Baltic coast. The apartments face a sandy beach that offers an extended view over the sea toward Denmark. Both studio and one-bedroom apartments can be rented, all with a kitchen and a balcony from which to feel the morning sea breezes. The resort itself is fully equipped, with numerous water sports available, including sailing, wind surfing and swimming, or sunbathing on the beach. There is also a spa treatment center, sauna, whirlpool, pool and health club. Contact: ADZ, German National Tourist Board-Service Department (German Hotel Reservation Service), Corneliusstr. 34, D-6000 Frankfurt, Germany. Call 011-49-69-740767.

Children: **Y**   Pets: **Y**   Smoking: **Y**   Handicap Access: **N**   Payment: **EC**

Ostsee

OSTSEE APARTMENTS/HOUSES   *Rates: budget-inexpensive*
Open: April-October   *Minimum Stay: three nights*
Approximately forty-five minutes by car from Schleswig, this is a popular sailing and seaside destination, particularly during the summer months. The accommodations range from apartments for couples and small families to individual guest houses, the largest of which has two upstairs bedrooms, a living room and a dining room. All residences are furnished in a modern style and are equipped with a radio or TV. The resort itself offers endless amusements—spa treatment center, sauna, solarium, health club, indoor and outdoor pools, bowling, golf—in short, something for everybody. Contact: ADZ, German National Tourist Board-Service Department (German Hotel Reservation Service), Corneliusstr. 34, D-6000 Frankfurt, Germany. Call 011-49-69-740767.

Children: **Y**   Pets: **Y**   Smoking: **Y**   Handicap Access: **N**   Payment: **EC**

Greece

CORFU

Acharavi

ALMYROS
Open: April 7-November 20

Rates: budget
Minimum Stay: one week

Located in a sunny area on the north coast of Corfu, boasting miles of golden sandy beaches, Almyros is minutes from the beautiful seaside village of Acharavi. Ten self-contained studio flats are available here for a budget Greek island vacation that doesn't skimp on privacy or comfort. The units, lodged in two small apartment houses sitting on a green lawn, contain a living room with two beds, a kitchenette and a private terrace, and are all only steps from the water. Contact: Interhome Inc., 124 Little Falls Road, Fairfield, NJ 07004. Call 201-882-6864. Ref. R3140/40A.

Children: Y   Pets: N   Smoking: Y   Handicap Access: N   Payment: P, V, M

Nissaki

BARBATI OLIVE PRESS AND ANNEX   *Rates: expensive-deluxe*
Open: year-round   *Minimum Stay: one week*

Poised on the edge of the crystalline water, this converted old olive press is a tranquil retreat from modern worries. The private beach is ideal for water-skiing or just splashing about. The rooms are simply but comfortably furnished, featuring exposed-beam ceilings and handsome stone floors. The press and annex can be let either separately or together. The press is staffed with a maid and cook, has three twin bedrooms and features a large partially covered terrace. The annex (sleeping up to four) has a charming walled garden and a private terrace with steps down to the water; maid service is included. Contact: Villas International, 71 W. 23rd St., New York, NY 10010. Call 212-929-7585.

Children: Y   Pets: N   Smoking: Y   Handicap Access: N   Payment: C, P, T

Nissaki

THE SAINTS   *Rates: budget-moderate*
Open: year-round   *Minimum Stay: one week*

Olive groves and fruit trees cling to the hillsides and crumbling Venetian fortresses dot the landscape of Corfu. The island's culture is a healthy and convivial mix of all those who have come to its luxuriant shores—Romans, Venetians, Britons, Greeks and now visitors from around the world. The Saints are a pretty cluster of terraced villas overlooking the coast and surrounding a magnificent swimming pool. They have either two or four beds and most feature private terraces. The local bakery and several jolly tavernas are around the corner and the sandy beaches are only a 10-minute walk away. Contact: Villas International, 71 W. 23rd St., New York, NY 10010. Call 212-929-7585.

Children: Y   Pets: N   Smoking: Y   Handicap Access: N   Payment: C, P, T

Roda

ACHARAVI APARTMENTS   *Rates: budget*
Open: April 7-November 20   *Minimum Stay: one week*

Several two-room apartments that sleep up to four are available at this enticing Corfu holiday settlement right by the beach and just outside the resort of Roda. With fishing, surfing and a water-skiing school, as well as several excellent restaurants available in town, the complex features a cafe of its own, snack bar, tavern and minimart, plus patio furniture, barbecues, and outdoor showers are provided on the lawn. The flats contain a bedroom, living/dining room with extra sleeping accommodations and a kitchenette. Contact: Interhome Inc., 124 Little Falls Road, Fairfield, NJ 07004. Call 201-882-6864. Ref. R3140/20M.

Children: **Y**   Pets: **N**   Smoking: **Y**   Handicap Access: **N**   Payment: **P, V, M**

Sidari

SIDARI HOMES   *Rates: budget-inexpensive*
Open: April 7-November 20   *Minimum Stay: one week*

This small community of seaside vacation houses and studios is located near Sidari, a tiny resort along a pristine bay offering both sandy beaches and picturesque rock formations. The houses include a living room/dining area, kitchen, and two bedrooms, while the detached single-room studios contain a kitchen area and double divan. Every unit comes with its own private terrace and patio furniture. Miles from the crowds, Sidari features gourmet restaurants, fine facilities for wind surfing, water skiing and sailing, as well as bike and moped rentals for exploring the enchanting roads of Corfu. Contact: Interhome Inc., 124 Little Falls Road, Fairfield, NJ 07004. Call 201-882-6864. Ref. R3130/2 (house), R3130/5M (studio).

Children: **Y**   Pets: **N**   Smoking: **Y**   Handicap Access: **N**   Payment: **P, V, M**

CRETE

Kalamaki

THE WINDMILL   *Rates: moderate*
Open: year-round   *Minimum Stay: one week*

The cozy rooms of The Windmill include only a living and dining room with convertible beds, a kitchenette complete with an oven and a bathroom with a shower. You won't be spending much time indoors, however, once you discover the stony Crow's Nest above: The house's location on a rocky coastal headland allows fabulous views of the sea and surrounding islands. The rocky shore directly behind the house affords private sunning and bathing, or you can take a short stroll to the local sandy beach. The nearby town of Canea is a popular spot with plenty of tavernas and interesting shops. Throngs of visitors are drawn to the area each year, but miles of unspoiled beaches are only a short hike away. Contact: Villas International, 71 W. 23rd St., New York, NY 10010. Call 212-929-7585. Ref. GV003.

Children: **N**   Pets: **N**   Smoking: **Y**   Handicap Access: **N**   Payment: **C, P, T**

Pythari

PYTHARI HOUSE　　　　　　　　　　　　　　*Rates: moderate*
Open: year-round　　　　　　　　　　　*Minimum Stay: one week*

The spectacular terraces of this secluded perch truly lay the wild and rugged scenery of Crete open to your view. The living and dining rooms, featuring exquisite traditional stonework and woodwork, open onto a large patio and a covered dining area. Another terrace is located off the second-story bedroom and the rooftop terrace (near another double bedroom) offers the most impressive views of all: sweeping vistas of Souda Bay and the White Mountains. The sleepy village of Pythari has retained much of its traditional character; neighborhood tavernas are good places to enjoy the mellow local wine while listening to haunting melodies played on the lyra. Contact: Villas International, 71 W. 23rd St., New York, NY 10010. Call 212-929-7585. Ref. GV028.

Children: **Y**　Pets: **N**　Smoking: **Y**　Handicap Access: **N**　Payment: **C, P, T**

HYDRA

Hydra

PAPACHRISTOU VILLA　　　　　　　　　　*Rates: expensive*
Open: year-round　　　　　　　　　　　*Minimum Stay: one week*

Dazzling white houses cling to steep hills as fishing boats and yachts glide lazily into the harbor of Hydra. The rest of the island is virtually unsettled, preserving a serene and gracious natural beauty. Small wonder that artists find a haven here, perhaps the best place on earth to court a genuine Muse. The villa vaunts excellent views and its luxurious rooms feature local art works. The main floor comprises a large living and dining room with a fireplace, a kitchen with marble counters and a dishwasher, a study with convertible bed and two courtyards shaded by vines. Downstairs are two more bedrooms and a kitchenette; these rooms open onto a fragrant garden. The impressive master suite is upstairs, with a handsome fireplace, a study and a private rooftop terrace. Contact: Villas International, 71 W. 23rd St., New York, NY 10010. Call 212-929-7585.

Children: **N**　Pets: **N**　Smoking: **Y**　Handicap Access: **N**　Payment: **C, P, T**

MACEDONIA

Malaki Beach

MALAKI BEACH APARTMENTS　　　　　　　*Rates: budget*
Open: April 7-November 20　　　　　　*Minimum Stay: one week*

This modern apartment complex featuring a supermarket, restaurant and disco is only steps away from the pebble beach on the gleaming Malaki Pelion coast. The quality studio flats sleep either three or four depending on the unit, and contain a kitchenette and balcony with panoramic views and outdoor furniture. Less than five miles from Volos, the superbly situated residence makes an excellent base for touring the Hellenic mainland, with Athens, Delphi, Meteora, and Thessoloniki all within easy reach. Contact: Interhome Inc., 124 Little

Falls Road, Fairfield, NJ 07004. Call 201-882-6864. Ref. R1510/20M, R1510-31M.

Children: Y   Pets: N   Smoking: Y   Handicap Access: N   Payment: P, V, M

MYKONOS

Mykonos

THE PIGEON HOUSE   *Rates: moderate*
Open: year-round   *Minimum Stay: one week*

Just a 15-minute walk from the chic, sophisticated resort town of Mykonos stands this unique house with its crenelated roof line and intricate stone carvings. The house overlooks the sparkling blue waters of the Aegean and is set in its own luxuriant garden. The tastefully furnished rooms feature a mixture of antique and modern pieces; the lodgings for two consist of a living room, a complete kitchen and a bathroom on the first floor and a bedroom up the rustic wooden stairway. Maid service will help make your stay trouble-free. The tavernas and night life of town are just around the corner and sun-drenched beaches beckon nearby. Contact: Villas International, 71 W. 23rd St., New York, NY 10010. Call 212-929-7585.

Children: Y   Pets: N   Smoking: Y   Handicap Access: N   Payment: C, P, T

Ornos Beach

NAZOS VILLAS   *Rates: budget-expensive*
Open: year-round   *Minimum Stay: one week*

Perhaps the most cosmopolitan of the islands, Mykonos witnesses an annual parade of elegant sun worshipers and sophisticated jet-setters who flock here to enjoy the chic social life of the town. These pleasant villas will add a welcome note of charm and rusticity to your stay, yet they are close enough to the throbbing hub that you won't feel left out. The simple whitewashed buildings are surrounded by rock gardens and flowering shrubs; inside, the two-, three- and four-room apartments include well-equipped kitchens and separate living and dining rooms. You may prefer to enjoy your repasts out on the sunny terrace—many offer panoramic views of the gulf. The sandy beach is a short walk away and a bus into town stops right outside. Contact: Villas International, 71 W. 23rd St., New York, NY 10010. Call 212-929-7585.

Children: Y   Pets: N   Smoking: Y   Handicap Access: N   Payment: C, P, T

NAXOS

Pyrgaki

PYRGAKI BUNGALOWS   *Rates: budget-moderate*
Open: April 7-November 20   *Minimum Stay: one week*

This quiet collection of bungalows is located on lofty Naxos, a gorgeous island looming three hundred yards above the Aegean and blanketed with glimmering beaches and breathtaking landscapes. One-, two- and three-room units are available, each with a kitchenette and its own terrace, and all within a short romp to the water. An excellent base for journeying to Paros and the other exquisite Cyclades Islands, the residence offers boundless opportunities for enjoying the lustrous blue sea in an area renowned for its superb surfing. Contact: Inter-home Inc., 124 Little Falls Road, Fairfield, NJ 07004. Call 201-882-6864. Ref. R7110/1 (one room), R7110/5 (two rooms), R7110/10 (three rooms).

Children: Y   Pets: N   Smoking: Y   Handicap Access: N   Payment: P, V, M

PAROS

Parikia

COZY VILLAGE APARTMENTS   *Rates: budget*
Open: year-round   *Minimum Stay: one week*

Paros gives you everything a Greek isle should: rugged mountains, sandy beaches, ancient ruins and an energetic night life. Next to the sea in the picturesque town of Parikia are this two-room apartment for three people and studio apartment for two. The rooms are lovingly decorated with antiques; the ambience is quaint and comfy. Both apartments feature enchanting views of the old town, with its charming little houses and flagstone streets. These accommodations are ex-cellent bases for enjoying the beaches and the town. Contact: Villas International, 71 W. 23rd St., New York, NY 10010. Call 212-929-7585.

Children: Y   Pets: N   Smoking: Y   Handicap Access: N   Payment: C, P, T

PELOPONNESE

Psathopyrgos

PSATHOPYRGOS APARTMENTS   *Rates: budget-inexpensive*
Open: April 7-November 20   *Minimum Stay: one week*

Less than a mile from Psathopyrgos, a picturesque fishing village on the northern Peloponnesian coast, this contemporary apartment com-plex is right on the beach and offers a variety of recreational and leisure facilities, including a swimming pool, tennis court, playground, restaurant, tavern and discotheque. The comfortable one-, two-, and three-room units sleep from two to six, and each features a fully equipped kitchen area and a balcony. With Corinth, Mycenae, Epidau-ros and Olympia close by, many of the country's most celebrated ruins are only a short car or bus trip away. Contact: Interhome Inc., 124 Little Falls Road, Fairfield, NJ 07004. Call 201-882-6864. Ref. R4110/1M, R4110-10M, R4110/30M.

Children: Y   Pets: N   Smoking: Y   Handicap Access: N   Payment: P, V, M

Trapeza

VILLA PAPADOPOULOS   *Rates: expensive*
Open: year-round   *Minimum Stay: two weeks*

Tucked away on a hillside on the western coast of the Peloponnese, this charming villa offers beautiful views of the blue sea and rugged mountains. The traditionally furnished living and dining room fea-tures a stereo and the four pleasant bedrooms will comfortably accom-modate up to eight guests. The delightful terraces and balconies are ideal places for dining or simply enjoying the marvelous scenery and there is an enchanting garden as well. Sacred Mount Olympus and the Oracle at Delphi are within driving distance and some of Greece's most impressive and revered ruins are scattered throughout the fertile countryside. Contact: Villas International, 71 W. 23rd St., New York, NY 10010. Call 212-929-7585.

Children: N   Pets: N   Smoking: Y   Handicap Access: N   Payment: C, P, T

RHODES

Lindos

MIMI   *Rates: inexpensive-moderate*
Open: year-round   *Minimum Stay: one week*

Around the corner from the neighborhood bakery and near the tavernas and cafes, this appealing villa is ideal for four guests who relish the friendly bustle of the town. Although centrally located, the house is completely private. Fragrant tendrils of bougainvillaea delightfully shade the small courtyard. The main room inside is decorated with traditional pieces and creamy walls and boasts an original fireplace. In addition to the beds at one end of this sala, there is a separate twin bedroom and a complete kitchen in the villa. So that you can fully enjoy the beaches and night life, the villa comes with maid service five times weekly. Contact: Villas International, 71 W. 23rd St., New York, NY 10010. Call 212-929-7585. Ref. RV29.

Children: Y   Pets: N   Smoking: Y   Handicap Access: N   Payment: C, P, T

Lindos

PHAEDRA   *Rates: expensive-deluxe*
Open: year-round   *Minimum Stay: one week*

On the fair island of Rhodes, not far from the warm sands and dazzling waters of the beach, stands this beautiful villa for eight. In the traditional style, the house is built around a large central courtyard. Its rooms are spacious and cool, their light walls and spare furnishings providing a welcome respite from the sun. In addition to the comfortable lounge and well-equipped kitchen, there are two pretty bedrooms downstairs. Separate stairways lead to two more bedrooms above and one of these opens onto the sun-filled rooftop terrace, where the light breeze makes your private basking all the more pleasurable. The villa includes frequent maid service and is near the energetic night life of Lindos. Contact: Villas International, 71 W. 23rd St., New York, NY 10010. Call 212-929-7585. Ref. RV28.

Children: Y   Pets: N   Smoking: Y   Handicap Access: N   Payment: C, P, T

Lindos

POLYXENI   *Rates: budget-inexpensive*
Open: year-round   *Minimum Stay: one week*

A private stone stairway off of a pretty courtyard will lead you to this pleasant second-story apartment. Large and sunny, the terrace affords lovely views of the surrounding countryside, and the comfortable interior features a handsome exposed-beam ceiling. Best of all, this apartment is right in the center of Lindos, a perfect base for exploring the town's sights and hot spots. Off the roomy kitchenette and dining area are two pleasant bedrooms; maid service is provided five times weekly. Contact: Villas International, 71 W. 23rd St., New York, NY 10010. Call 212-929-7585. Ref. RV27.

Children: Y   Pets: N   Smoking: Y   Handicap Access: N   Payment: C, P, T

SANTORINI

Imerovigli

AEOLOS VILLAS   *Rates: budget-deluxe*
Open: year-round   *Minimum Stay: three nights*

The small village of Imerovigli on the island of Santorini will charm you with its narrow streets, whitewashed buildings and dome-shaped roofs, all set between glowing red cliffs and the glorious blue waters of the Aegean. The Aeolos Villas are perched at the edge of the cliffs and range in size from simple studios to a very large two-bedroom apartment sleeping up to 10. All feature wide terraces with astounding views of the sea and many have cozy fireplaces. If the crashing waves and glorious sunsets whet your appetite for excitement of a more gregarious sort, the restaurants and nightclubs of Thira are only two miles away. Contact: Villas International, 71 W. 23rd St., New York, NY 10010. Call 212-929-7585.

Children: Y   Pets: N   Smoking: Y   Handicap Access: N   Payment: C, P, T

Oia

CLIFF HOUSES   *Rates: inexpensive-moderate*
Open: year-round   *Minimum Stay: one week*

These traditional cliff houses are carved into the volcanic rock of Santorini; they cling to their perches and gaze out at the sea like unblinking white sentinels. Every house features a magnificent view of the sea and the neighboring islands. The barrel-roofed rooms are cool and inviting, with tasteful furnishings in the typical Santorini style. The houses can accommodate from two to four people and are set around a private sea-water swimming pool. The local shops and tavernas of Oia are an easy walk away. Or, if speeding along a dusty road through the lovely countryside is more your style, cars and mopeds are easily hired. Contact: Villas International, 71 W. 23rd St., New York, NY 10010. Call 212-929-7585.

Children: Y   Pets: N   Smoking: Y   Handicap Access: N   Payment: C, P, T

Thira

THANOS VILLAS   *Rates: budget-expensive*
Open: year-round   *Minimum Stay: one week*

These quaint whitewashed houses cling to the hillsides far above Santorini's famous black beaches. They can accommodate between two and six people and their splendid location affords breathtaking views of the sea and surrounding islands. Inside, the cool white walls and tall, barrel-shaped ceilings lend an air of tranquil rusticity. The airy main rooms feature cozy sleeping nooks on raised platforms; the traditional furnishings are simple yet cheerful. Devoted sightseers will want to visit Akroteri, an ancient city buried beneath volcanic ash; the volcano's violent eruptions are believed by some to be the inspiration for the tale of Atlantis. Contact: Villas International, 71 W. 23rd St., New York, NY 10010. Call 212-929-7585.

Children: Y   Pets: N   Smoking: Y   Handicap Access: N   Payment: C, P, T

SPETSAI

Dapias

MANITA'S VILLA   *Rates: deluxe*
Open: year-round   *Minimum Stay: one week*

The pretty little island of Spetses entices visitors with pine-clad hills, extravagant flora, a picturesque harbor and amazingly peaceful streets (only official cars are allowed on the island). Manita's Villa is a luxurious modern residence with cool, spacious rooms and elegant furnishings. The expansive living room with its whitewashed walls and brilliant Moorish cushions opens onto a large terrace with a covered dining area, a barbecue, a sparkling swimming pool and a patio clad in bougainvillaea and hibiscus. This terrace enjoys marvelous views of the Old Harbor and the sea beyond. The main house has five bedrooms (two with en suite bathrooms) and there is a separate cottage for additional guests. Contact: Villas International, 71 W. 23rd St., New York, NY 10010. Call 212-929-7585.

Children: Y   Pets: N   Smoking: Y   Handicap Access: N   Payment: C, P, T

SYROS

Syros

FILI TOU ANEMOU   *Rates: deluxe*
Open: year-round   *Minimum Stay: one week*

The peaceful island of Syros remains pleasantly unscathed by tourism; quaint fishing villages dot the coastline and colorful markets enliven the stately town of Hermoupolis. Fili Tou Anemou ("Friends of the Wind") is a modern residence splendidly perched on a rocky promontory. The flagstone floors, white walls and exposed-beam ceilings make the capacious rooms cool and inviting. The five main bedrooms all have en suite bathrooms and the two children's rooms feature bunk beds. Grand archways lead to the covered dining terrace; a separate sun terrace, carved from the living rock, has steps leading down to a private swimming area. A jeep for traversing wild island roads, three windsurfers and a speedboat are provided for guests' use. Contact: Villas International, 71 W. 23rd St., New York, NY 10010. Call 212-929-7585.

Children: Y   Pets: N   Smoking: Y   Handicap Access: N   Payment: C, P, T

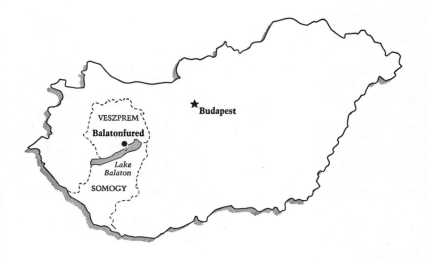

VESZPREM

Balatonfured

★Budapest

Lake
Balaton

SOMOGY

Hungary

SOMOGY

Balatonbereny

BALATONMARIAFURDO HOUSE   *Rates: budget-moderate*
Open: May 5-September 28   *Minimum Stay: one week*

This delightful home is near the old Hungarian town of Balatonbereny on the southwestern Balaton coast. While the lake has miles of wide and flat sandy beaches, this section of the shoreline has been left largely undeveloped, with some parts covered with reeds, offering a terrific opportunity for truly untouched nature walks. Moments away from the water, the house contains a living/dining room, well-equipped kitchen and two bedrooms, with a terrace and playground outside, making it a superb location for families with children. Daring adults, meanwhile, may opt to visit the nude beach that's not far away, while others will find sufficient challenge in the wind-surfing, tennis, sailing and horseback riding available in the area. Contact: Interhome Inc., 124 Little Falls Road, Fairfield, NJ 07004. Call 201-882-6864. Ref. H8647/109.

Children: Y   Pets: N   Smoking: Y   Handicap Access: N   Payment: P, V, M

Fenyves and Fonyod

BALATONFENYVES HOMES

Open: May 5-September 28

Rates: budget-moderate
Minimum Stay: one week

Several two-bedroom houses are available on the south side of Lake Balaton, near the friendly and active towns of Fonyod and Fenyves. All within walking distance of the lake, the two-story residences, sleeping up to six, feature a living room, kitchen and a balcony or terrace. A wide variety of activities are available in the area, from cycling and horseback riding to bowling and disco hopping, as well as the excellent water sports facilities. Visitors also won't want to miss a ride on the nearby railway that circles the entire lake, one of Hungary's premiere sightseeing opportunities. Contact: Interhome Inc., 124 Little Falls Road, Fairfield, NJ 07004. Call 201-882-6864. Ref. H8646/20.

Children: **Y**   Pets: **N**   Smoking: **Y**   Handicap Access: **N**   Payment: **P, V, M**

VESZPREM

Balatonalmadi

PLATTEN HOUSE

Open: May 5-September 28

Rates: budget-inexpensive
Minimum Stay: one week

This two-story house is located near the center of Balatonalmadi, a resort village on the northern shore of the lake renowned since the days of the Hapsburgs. The residence features a pleasant garden terrace and contains a living room/dining area, well-equipped kitchen and two comfortable bedrooms upstairs. Although your entire holiday can be spent swimming, boating, playing tennis and horseback riding all within walking distance, guests also won't want to miss excursions to Balatonfured, the Tihany peninsula and the puszta. Contact: Interhome Inc., 124 Little Falls Road, Fairfield, NJ 07004. Call 201-882-6864. Ref. H8220/4.

Children: **Y**   Pets: **N**   Smoking: **Y**   Handicap Access: **N**   Payment: **P, V, M**

Balatonfured

BALATONFURED APARTMENTS

Open: May 5-September 28

Rates: budget-inexpensive
Minimum Stay: one week

Close to the celebrated park lands of Balatonfured, this quality apartment building sits by Balaton, the largest lake in central Europe. Studio flats—each self-contained and with well-equipped kitchenettes—and one-bedroom units—also with a kitchenette as well as a living room and balcony offering scenic views—are available. The building is a short walk from the famous railway that runs along the entire shore of the lake. Numerous sports activities, including tennis, hiking, horseback riding, fishing, sailing, swimming and even surfing are nearby. Contact: Interhome Inc., 124 Little Falls Road, Fairfield, NJ 07004. Call 201-882-6864. Ref. H8230/11W (one room), H8230/20W (two rooms).

Children: **Y**   Pets: **N**   Smoking: **Y**   Handicap Access: **N**   Payment: **P, V, M**

Balatongyorok

BALATONGYOROK HOMES *Rates: budget-moderate*
Open: May 5-September 28 *Minimum Stay: one week*

These attractive cottages sit on peaceful sites close to Lake Balaton in the small resort of Balatongyorok. Topped by steeply pitched roofs, each two-story house is graced with a lovely view and contains two bedrooms, a living room/dining area with additional sleeping accommodations and a kitchen or kitchenette. Most offer a balcony or terrace plus a cozy garden area. Only six miles away is Keszthely, known as the unofficial capital of the Balaton. A leading center of culture with a colorful history, Keszthely features such impressive sights as the castle and town hall and offers a profusion of recreational activities. Contact: Interhome Inc., 124 Little Falls Road, Fairfield, NJ 07004. Call 201-882-6864. Ref. H8313/20.

Children: Y Pets: N Smoking: Y Handicap Access: N Payment: P, V, M

Boglarlelle

BOGLARLELLE HOMES *Rates: budget-inexpensive*
Open: May 5-September 28 *Minimum Stay: one week*

Only a short walk from the southern shore of Lake Platten, these comfortable two-story houses each sleep up to eight and contain a living room, kitchen or kitchenette, three bedrooms and a balcony or terrace. The residences are located in the charming resort of Boglarlelle, which features excellent restaurants, a modern harbor and miles of beaches punctuated with jetties that project far into the water. Swimming and a variety of aquatic sports are available on the lake, and the area also offers excellent hiking and numerous other recreational as well as cultural activities. Contact: Interhome Inc., 124 Little Falls Road, Fairfield, NJ 07004. Call 201-882-6864. Ref. H8638/30.

Children: Y Pets: N Smoking: Y Handicap Access: N Payment: P, V, M

Ireland

CARLOW

Borris

NEWTOWN FARMHOUSE

Open: year-round

Rates: budget

Minimum Stay: one week

This comfortable semi-detached farmhouse is graced by spacious gardens and a panoramic mountain view. It also features a charming and warm open-fire kitchen/dining room, with a living room and three bedrooms to accommodate five. Try some of the exceptional angling and canoeing on the nearby river Barrow, or perhaps a bracing hike in the foothills of Mount Leinster. Those with a passion for history won't want to miss the many renowned castles, houses and ancient settlements of the region. Contact: Mrs. C. Lennon, Newtown, Borris, Co. Carlow. Call 011-44-353503-24213.

Children: Y   Pets: N   Smoking: Y   Handicap Access: N   Payment: EC

Clonmore

18TH-CENTURY RECTORY   *Rates: deluxe*
Open: year-round   *Minimum Stay: two nights*

Ruined castles and ancient Celtic crosses stud the hills around Clonmore, which is where you'll find this stately 18th-century rectory. Intricate plasterwork, antique furniture, period paintings and a collection of old glass fill the newly restored rooms. Both of the bedrooms have en suite bathrooms, and the kitchen is spacious and convenient. Devoted sightseers should note that the historic medieval town of Kilkenny is only an hour away and the coast is within easy reach. Overnight guests enjoy the hospitality of the informative owners and receive a full Irish breakfast; there is a minimum rental of two months for those who wish have the entire house to themselves. Contact: Castles, Cottages & Flats, Box 201, Westwood, MA 02090. Call 617-329-4680. Ref. G 101.

Children: N   Pets: N   Smoking: Y   Handicap Access: N   Payment: P

Rathvilly

VICTORIAN COUNTRY HOUSE   *Rates: expensive*
Open: year-round   *Minimum Stay: two nights*

This grand Victorian country home has been in the same family since it was built a century and a half ago. The wooded grounds feature some lovely walking paths and a charming walled garden with a swimming pool. Time-honored country pursuits such as clay pigeon shooting, riding and hunting can be arranged. Inside you'll find an inviting paneled library, a stately drawing room, a more casual sitting room and a spacious formal dining room; fine furnishings and open fireplaces add to the air of genteel tranquillity. Two of the four double bedrooms boast four-poster beds. Curragh Racecourse, home of the Irish Derby, is within driving distance and enthusiasts will find a golf course only seven miles away. Contact: Castles, Cottages & Flats, Box 201, Westwood, MA 02090. Call 617-329-4680. Ref. G 100.

Children: Y   Pets: N   Smoking: Y   Handicap Access: N   Payment: P

CAVAN

Cavan Town

KILLYKEEN FOREST PARK   *Rates: budget-inexpensive*
Open: year-round   *Minimum Stay: one weekend*

Five elegant two-bedroom chalets and fifteen luxurious three-bedroom chalets are available in the splendid Killykeen Forest Park on the shores of Lough Outer. The lake is renowned for its coarse angling; the park and forest lands also offer fine opportunities for boating, cycling, horseback riding and woodland hikes. Guests are invited to take advantage of the complex's recreation center as well. Each of the two-bedroom residences accommodates up to five (one unit is adapted for use by disabled persons); the three-bedroom residences accommodate six to seven. Contact: Jim O'Reilly, Manager, Killykeen Forest Chalets, Killykeen Forest Park, Co. Cavan. Call 011-44-353-49-32541.

Children: Y Pets: N Smoking: Y Handicap Access: Y (one unit) Payment: EC

CLARE

Ballyvaughan

BURREN HOUSE *Rates: deluxe*
Open: year-round *Minimum Stay: one week*

Commanding marvelous views of the Burren, this large old house easily accommodates 12 guests. The lovely grounds boast a pleasant lawn and delightful garden; in the courtyard stand the mysterious remains of a 400-year-old tower. After passing through the tiled entrance hall, you can relax in the stylish drawing room before dining in front of a cheerful fire. The house is centrally heated and the TV, dishwasher and washing machine provide all the comforts of home. The location is splendid for those seeking active recreations: Fishing, sailing, windsurfing, rock climbing and hiking can all be enjoyed locally. Contact: Castles, Cottages & Flats, Box 201, Westwood, MA 02090. Call 617-329-4680. Ref. K 145.

Children: Y   Pets: N   Smoking: Y   Handicap Access: N   Payment: P

Ennis

THE COACH HOUSE *Rates: budget*
Open: April-September *Minimum Stay: one week*

This elegant 19th-century coach house, adjoining an august Victorian manor, is situated just off the Galway Road in the outskirts of Ennis, County Clare's choicest market town, within easy walking distance from the town center. Guests can enjoy the activities and recreational offerings along the River Shannon, the gleaming sandy beaches of the west coast and excursions throughout Clare, Limerick and Galway. The charmingly restored and utterly private residence sits on appealing, serene grounds and contains two bedrooms, with three twin beds and a double bed settee. Contact: Limerick Tourist Office, The Granary, Michael Street, Limerick, Co. Limerick. Call 011-44353-61-317522. Fax 011-44-353-61-315634. Ref. SR0148/1.

Children: Y   Pets: N   Smoking: Y   Handicap Access: N   Payment: A, V

Mountshannon

MOUNTSHANNON VILLAGE COTTAGES *Rates: budget*
Open: year-round *Minimum Stay: none*

These award-winning cottages were specially designed for vacationers and are ideally situated on carefully tended grounds between the village of Mountshannon and the harbor of Lough Derg, a sparkling lake. There are eight two-story cottages in all, offering two, three or four bedrooms, electric heat, open fireplaces, laundry facilities and TV. The area is a paradise for freshwater fishing, boating and swimming and boasts several championship golf courses. Offering a full range of activities from pony trekking to water skiing, Shannonside Activity Center is just fifteen minutes away by car. Visitors can also marvel at the centuries-old local castles, the gardens at Birr and the spectacular coastline. Contact: Tourist Information Office, 14 Upper O'Connell Street, Dublin, Ireland. Call 011-353-1-747733.

Children: Y   Pets: N   Smoking: Y   Handicap Access: N   Payment: T, V, M

Newmarket-on-Fergus

CHIEFTAIN'S HOUSE   *Rates: moderate*
Open: year-round   *Minimum Stay: two nights*

This welcoming home is only a few decades old, but it offers guests the style and grace of centuries past. The host is a genuine Irish chieftain, well renowned for his hospitality. Enjoy your complimentary pre-dinner drink before a roaring fire in the drawing room, dining room, or library; dinner and breakfast are both included as well. Each of the five tastefully decorated bedrooms has an adjoining bath and the house is centrally heated. The medieval castles of Bunratty and Knappogue are just a few miles away and the historic cities of Limerick and Galway are within driving distance. The locale also offers deer for hunters, wily salmon for anglers and championship links for golfers. Contact: Castles, Cottages & Flats, Box 201, Westwood, MA 02090. Call 617-329-4680. Ref. K 141.

Children: N   Pets: N   Smoking: Y   Handicap Access: N   Payment: P

Whitegate

GEORGIAN MEWS APARTMENTS   *Rates: budget*
Open: year-round   *Minimum Stay: three nights*

A peaceful and wooded lake, Lough Derg lies only thirty miles from Shannon Airport. This area seems to have been frozen in time, where cobbled streets wend through white-washed villages, crystalline lakes are stocked with fish and paths weave through open countryside. Two large apartments sleep up to five people in three bedrooms (one double, one twin and one single). The large open kitchen invites weary fishermen to sit up late telling tales of their trolling for trout; boats and dinghies can be rented at the nearby marina. Parking, linens, towels and extra heaters are supplied. Contact: Blakes Vacations, 4918 Dempster Street, Skokie, IL 60077. Call 1-800-628-8118. Ref. WBN.

Children: Y   Pets: N   Smoking: Y   Handicap Access: N   Payment: V, M, O

CORK

Bantry

BAUR NA GEARAGH BUNGALOW   *Rates: budget*
Open: April-September   *Minimum Stay: one week*

This splendidly situated bungalow is a quick walk from either the ocean shore or the fine shops, restaurants, pubs, great lawn and the other enticing attractions of the town of Ballylickey. It's also an excellent base for exploring the coves, inlets and islands of Cork's Atlantic coast. The comfortable house features three bedrooms (two with double beds, one with twin beds), fully equipped kitchen/dining room and living room with an inviting fireplace for cozy evenings. Contact: Cork Tourist Office, Tourist House, Grand Parade, Cork. Call 011-44-353-21-273251. Ref. SW0027/1.

Children: Y   Pets: N   Smoking: Y   Handicap Access: N   Payment: A, V

Bantry

TRAGARIFF HOUSE   *Rates: budget*
Open: year-round   *Minimum Stay: one week*

A secluded cottage in the woods reachable by a footpath from the garage overlooks Bantry Bay. This very private, very homey residence contains five bedrooms accommodating up to seven persons comfortably, a sitting room, dining room and fully equipped kitchen and has private access to a rock beach. The great houses and other historic landmarks of the region are only a short drive away; a journey through the coastal villages of County Cork or Kerry makes an easy—and unforgettable—day trip. Contact: Lady Haskard, Tragariff House, Snave, Bantry, Co. Cork. Call 011-44-353-27-50074.

Children: Y   Pets: N   Smoking: Y   Handicap Access: N   Payment: EC

Bere Island

HARBOUR VIEW   *Rates: budget*
Open: June-September   *Minimum Stay: one week*

Ten minutes by car ferry from the coastal town of Castletownbere, Bere Island is a picturesque vacation spot in Bantry Bay. This well-appointed four-bedroom house on the seashore gives guests unlimited opportunity to explore the island by foot, bike, or car and enjoy all of its attractions and recreational facilities. Rent a boat for superb sea fishing or simply cruise around the isle and scout the bay coves by sea. Or return to the mainland for mountain hikes and trips along the sublime Kerry and Cork coastline, plus a night on the town at one of the region's cosmopolitan clubs or quaint Gaelic pubs. Contact: Mr. P. Sullivan, Harbour View, Bere Island, Co. Cork. Call 011-44-353-27-75021.

Children: Y   Pets: N   Smoking: Y   Handicap Access: N   Payment: EC

Carrigrohane

TUDOR HOUSE   *Rates: deluxe*
Open: year-round   *Minimum Stay: two nights*

Only four miles from Cork stands this impressive Tudor castle and its tranquil emerald woodlands. The ornate dining room, drawing room, sitting room and library feature intricately carved stone fireplaces and the mellow tones of old polished wood. The second story offers peaceful views of the surrounding countryside through its tall arched windows. Welcoming bedrooms for six guests are found on the third and fourth floors; one has an en suite bathroom. The grounds include a lighted tennis court, and there is a game room complete with darts and Ping-Pong in the basement. Venture a bit farther to enjoy the excellent sailing at Crosshaven—home of the world's oldest yacht club—and fishing and hunting, in season. Ireland's miraculous Blarney Stone is only a stone's throw away, as are the restaurants and theaters of Cork. Contact: Castles, Cottages & Flats, Box 201, Westwood, MA 02090. Call 617-329-4680. Ref. EI 125.

Children: **Y**   Pets: **N**   Smoking: **Y**   Handicap Access: **N**   Payment: **P**

Castletownshend, near Skibbereen

FANNY'S LODGE, THE CASTLE   *Rates: budget*
Open: year-round   *Minimum Stay: one weekend*

The two-story detached gate lodge that once guarded the castle at Castletownshend has been smartly converted into a homey three-bedroom residence. Guests have use of the castle grounds, which include graceful gardens and a tennis court as well as inviting wooded footpaths and access to a golden sandy beach. Adjacent to the village and with an exceptional view of the sea, the two-story house features lofty pitched roofs and contains three bedrooms plus carpeted sitting room with an open fireplace. Contact: Mrs. R.M. Salter-Townshend, The Castle, Castletownshend, Nr. Skibbereen, Co. Cork. Call 011-44-353-2836100.

Children: **Y**   Pets: **N**   Smoking: **Y**   Handicap Access: **N**   Payment: **EC**

Courtmacsherry

THE OLD COASTGUARD   *Rates: budget*
Open: year-round   *Minimum Stay: one weekend*

This set of 19th-century stone cottages lies on a vast lawn overlooking Courtmacsherry Harbor. Built to provide the Cork coast guard with an unobstructed vantage point, these residences offer thrilling Atlantic views. From this vista, guests can spot the fine fishing, boating, swimming and other water-sports facilities the area offers in profusion. Inland, the legendary town of Blarney is only a short road trip away. Each house contains a spacious sitting room, kitchen, dining area and two bedrooms that can sleep up to six. Sunny terraces allow guests to better appreciate the extraordinary scenery. Contact: Cork Tourist Office, Tourist House, Grand Parade, Cork. Call 011-44-353-21-273251. Ref. SW0103/1.

Children: **Y**   Pets: **N**   Smoking: **Y**   Handicap Access: **N**   Payment: **A, V**

Fermoy

BLACKWATER RIVER HOUSE   *Rates: inexpensive-moderate*
Open: year-round   *Minimum Stay: none*

The warm welcome you'll receive at this handsome home on the river Blackwater cannot fail to persuade you that Celtic hospitality is alive and well. As you savor your complimentary toddy in front of the blazing fire in the elegant drawing room, you'll be charmed by your thoughtful hosts and their two friendly dogs. A delightful dinner is served in the Georgian dining room and five comfy bedrooms (sleeping six) await you upstairs. Hone your skill at billiards on the house's own table, or try your hand at the area's more outdoorsy sports: Opportunities for salmon and trout fishing, riding and golf abound. Novice anglers need not fear—an experienced gillie is available to show you the ropes. Contact: Castles, Cottages & Flats, Box 201, Westwood, MA 02090. Call 617-329-4680. Ref. ER 124.

Children: Y   Pets: N   Smoking: Y   Handicap Access: N   Payment: P

Fermoy

CASTLE HYDE
Open: year-round

Rates: deluxe
Minimum Stay: one week

Castle Hyde is a truly regal, fully staffed 18th-century Georgian mansion for groups of up to twelve who seek a first-class Irish holiday. Extravagantly decorated with one-of-a-kind period furnishings, the huge manor house is accented with such details as a cantilevered staircase. The castle contains six bedrooms—each with private fireplace—an opulent dining room (gourmet meal service is provided) and a grand reception hall. The manor estate, guarded by imposing gates, spreads over 150 acres highlighted by celebrated gardens, which are the third oldest in Ireland. Guests also have access to riding stables, orchards, woods stocked with wild game and castle ruins. The salmon- and trout-filled Blackwater River flows by the house and offers fishing right outside the door, while golf, boating and cycling are available as well. Contact: Richard Kroon, 172 Rumson Road, Rumson, NJ 07760. Call 212-504-3600 (day) and 201-741-5692 (evening).

Children: Y   Pets: N   Smoking: Y   Handicap Access: N   Payment: C, P

Goleen

HERONS COVE
Open: year-round

Rates: budget-inexpensive
Minimum Stay: one week

This isolated farmhouse-plus-cottage, located three miles off the main road, perches among the rocks in a serene farmland setting. Convenient to the beaches of Barley Cove, the location is superb for those who enjoy swimming, fishing, tennis and pastoral walks or horseback rides. The spacious renovated residence, with five bedrooms to accommodate ten or more, also boasts a rec room and stereo sound system. Comfortable and private, the cottage makes an ideal holiday home for a large family or group of vacationing friends seeking a chummy County Cork getaway. Contact: Sue Hill, Heron's Cove, Goleen, Co. Cork. Call 011-44-353-28-35225.

Children: Y   Pets: N   Smoking: Y   Handicap Access: N   Payment: EC

Grand Parade, near Kenmare

TOURIST HOUSE
Open: April-September

Rates: budget
Minimum Stay: one week

This traditional two-story house makes an excellent base for visitors yearning to drive—or bike—the celebrated Ring of Kerry. Other top historic and scenic highlights of Kerry and County Cork are also within easy reach; just off the mainland several islands beckon day-trip adventurers. The remodeled home sits behind a low stone gate and contains four bedrooms, each with double bed, as well as a spacious kitchen, a sitting room and a bright, sunny living room. Contact: Cork Tourist Office, Tourist House, Grand Parade, Cork. Call 011-44-353-21-273251. Ref. SW0378/1

Children: Y   Pets: N   Smoking: Y   Handicap Access: N   Payment: EC

Kinsale

GEORGIAN HOUSE   *Rates: inexpensive-moderate*
Open: May-September   *Minimum Stay: none*

On the outskirts of quaint Kinsale lies this idyllic old house for four. After enjoying the cheery fire glowing in the intimate sitting room, make friends with the resident Labrador and cat. A stroll through the pretty gardens around the house may lead you to the cows and mare who live here, too. Your gourmet hostess will serve a repast in the large dining room that features fresh vegetables from her own organic garden. The charming streets and rolling green hills of Kinsale await you beyond; the town is renowned for its gastronomic delights. Just a bit further away lie Blarney Castle, Bantry House, Garinish Island and Fota House, enough of Ireland's history to satisfy the most ardent sightseers. Contact: Castles, Cottages & Flats, Box 201, Westwood, MA 02090. Call 617-329-4680. Ref. E 129.

Children: N   Pets: N   Smoking: Y   Handicap Access: N   Payment: P

Mallow

AVENUE COTTAGE   *Rates: budget*
Open: year-round   *Minimum Stay: three nights*

This pretty cottage is ideally situated within driving distance of both the south and west coasts of Ireland and offers ample opportunities for recreation and touring. The cottage itself is charming, with a single bedroom that sleeps three (one double, one single) and an extra sleeping couch in front of the fireplace. It has its own peaceful garden with a barbecue, a color TV and a kitchen with a cozy breakfast nook. Freshwater fishing and golf are locally available, and much of this quiet and unspoiled area is ideal for exploring. The town of Mallow offers restaurants and shops; a little further afield are favorite destinations such as Blarney Castle, Mitchelstown Caves and the lovely Killarney lakeland. Contact: Blakes Vacations, 4918 Dempster Street, Skokie, IL 60077. Call 1-800-628-8118. Ref. WCM.

Children: Y   Pets: N   Smoking: Y   Handicap Access: N   Payment: V, M, O

Mallow

BAROQUE CASTLE   *Rates: deluxe*
Open: year-round   *Minimum Stay: one week*

This majestic 17th-century castle overlooks still older castle ruins; it was once the home of the Lord President of Munster. Whether browsing through the eclectic library, relaxing in the elm-paneled drawing room, or perambulating the extensive deer park, you will not fail to be impressed by the gentility and grace of this house. The main sleeping accommodations are found in two spacious suites, each with two double bedrooms; two additional bedrooms in the tower can sleep three more guests. A large staff cares for both the castle and its guests; the cordon bleu chef will prepare feasts of the finest local seafood and fresh produce from the castle's own gardens. The Blarney Stone and Lakes of Killarney are within a short drive and Dublin is only two hours away. Contact: Castles, Cottages & Flats, Box 201, Westwood, MA 02090. Call 617-329-4680. Ref. E 127.

Children: Y   Pets: N   Smoking: Y   Handicap Access: N   Payment: P

Mallow

GATE LODGE COTTAGE   Rates: budget
Open: year-round   Minimum Stay: three nights

Shaded by tall trees, this single-story cottage can sleep up to six people in its three bedrooms. There are open fireplaces in the sitting and dining rooms, color TV and a private garden in which to sit and listen to the leaves rustling in the breeze. Guests can roam Hazelwood Farm's emerald-hued fields dotted with sheep; the grounds also offer the use of a tennis court and swimming pool. There is never enough time to sample all of Cork's wonders, both scenic and historic—among them are ancient castles, coastlines both rugged and sandy, mysterious caves and countryside. Locally, enjoy freshwater fishing and golf; Mallow's shops and restaurants are less than five miles away. Contact: Blakes Vacations, 4918 Dempster Street, Skokie, IL 60077. Call 1-800-628-8118. Ref. WBG.

Children: Y Pets: N Smoking: Y Handicap Access: N Payment: V, M, O

Minane Bridge

RINGABELLA HOUSE   Rates: inexpensive
Open: year-round   Minimum Stay: one week

A farm road lined with trees and flowers leads to this 18th-century Georgian house offering spectacular views of Ringabella Bay and the Atlantic Ocean. Situated on four acres of grassland, this home has been converted to include an airy, spacious apartment with its own entrance. Guests enjoy use of a comfortable living room, two large bedrooms with bath en suite and a fully equipped kitchen stocked with everything required for a fine breakfast. A south-facing terrace overlooks a walled garden; the sea and sandy beach, as safe as it is beautiful, lies 150 yards away. Deep in the farming country, you're in easy reach of riding, golf, sailing, wind surfing and the popular resort of Kinsale. Contact: Michael Wynne-Wilson, Distinctive Country Rentals for Holidays, Box 261, Westwood, MA 02090. Call 617-329-4680.

Children: Y   Pets: N   Smoking: Y   Handicap Access: N   Payment: P

Schull

THE STANDING STONE   *Rates: budget*
Open: year-round   *Minimum Stay: one weekend*

Among the rental units available in the manor house of this grand seaside estate is a charming four-bedroom, ground-floor flat that overlooks the harbor of Schull, an enchanting County Cork fishing village. The grounds, sitting at the foot of Mount Gabriel, offer a sunny terrace, lovely gardens, library, a refreshing mountain stream that supplies pristine drinking water and a private beach steps away from the house. Boats can be chartered locally for a try at shark fishing in the Atlantic, while tamer water sports and other recreational activities are also plentiful. Fascinating archaeological sites provide yet another area highlight. Contact: C. Fenn, The Standing Stone, Schull, Co. Cork. Call 011-44-353-28-28201.

Children: **Y**   Pets: **N**   Smoking: **Y**   Handicap Access: **N**   Payment: **EC**

Skibbereen

BAROQUE MANOR   *Rates: deluxe*
Open: year-round   *Minimum Stay: one week*

This fine 17th-century house with its unique Teutonic furnishings is swathed in 100 acres of tranquil woods and farmland. Splendidly situated on a warm bay and sheltered by rolling hills, the estate is ideal for those who enjoy sailing, swimming, windsurfing or fishing. The house includes a large reception hall, two sitting rooms (one of which opens onto the lovely garden), a handsome dining room and a tiled kitchen complete with a dishwasher. Upstairs are charming accommodations for eight guests. For your pleasure, there's a sauna in the garden and a TV and video in the house; daily cleaning service adds to the comfort. The coastal villages nearby celebrate numerous festivals in late summer, or try one of the lively pubs of Skibbereen for a different kind of local flavor. Contact: Castles, Cottages & Flats, Box 201, Westwood, MA 02090. Call 617-329-4680. Ref. EI 128.

Children: **Y**   Pets: **N**   Smoking: **Y**   Handicap Access: **N**   Payment: **P**

Skibbereen

LOUGE INE, THE GATE LODGE   *Rates: budget*
Open: year-round   *Minimum Stay: one week*

Standing on the edge of Sea Loch, the authentic 18th-century gate house of Louge Ine makes a handsome two-bedroom residence. Guests are treated to splendid views from their windows and have use of the private beach only steps away. Other recreational opportunities nearby include golfing, fishing, hiking and horseback riding. The gate lodge contains a large living room with fireplace; a spiral staircase leads to two bedrooms with four single beds. Contact: Mr. & Mrs. R.W. Beard, 64 Elgin Crescent, London W11 2JJ, England. Call 011-44353-1-273129.

Children: **Y**   Pets: **N**   Smoking: **Y**   Handicap Access: **N**   Payment: **EC**

DONEGAL

Churchill

TIR ARGUS HOUSE *Rates: budget*
Open: April-September *Minimum Stay: one week*

This quaint Donegal country cottage overlooks picturesque lakes and makes a terrific home base for exploring the unforgettable sandy coves, towering cliffs and Gaeltacht communities of the northern coast. A wide selection of outdoor activities, including golf, swimming, cycling and nature hikes, is available nearby as well. The two-floor residence contains two bedrooms, a living room and a kitchen/dining room and features an open fireplace. Contact: Sligo Tourist Office, Aras Reddan, Temple Street, Sligo, Co. Sligo. Call 011-44-353-7161201.

Children: Y Pets: N Smoking: Y Handicap Access: N Payment: A, V

Cruit Island, Dungloe

DONEGAL THATCHED COTTAGES *Rates: budget*
Open: year-round *Minimum Stay: none*

These traditional thatched cottages can sleep up to seven guests and provide modern comfort off the beaten track. Situated on an flower-strewn island edged with rocky coves and sandy beaches, the cottages are centrally heated and have laundry facilities and TV. The mountains and seascape make a classic view for those who wish to sit in the garden and sketch, or for those who wish to admire the setting sun beyond the ocean's rim. Nearby are a full range of activities for walkers, golfers, pony-trekkers, bird-watchers and nature-lovers, including lovely Glenveigh National Park. Contact: Tourist Information Office, 14 Upper O'Connell Street, Dublin, Ireland. Call 011-353-1-747733.

Children: Y Pets: N Smoking: Y Handicap Access: N Payment: T, V, M

Dungloe

CONVERTED SCHOOLHOUSE *Rates: budget*
Open: April-September *Minimum Stay: one week*

A magnificently situated old schoolhouse on Trawenagh Bay has been smartly converted into a five-bedroom vacation house of distinction. Living rooms with open fireplaces are located on both of its two floors; the residence also features an airy sun room with spectacular views over the sea. Rosses fishery and the Portnoo golf course are two of the many notable recreational facilities in the area, while Glenveagh National Park and exquisite Aranmore Island represent two more top attractions. Contact: Paul & Catherine Sweeney, 97 Sandymount Avenue, Dublin 4. Call 011-44-353-1-6695462.

Children: Y Pets: N Smoking: Y Handicap Access: N Payment: EC

DUBLIN

Dublin

1 HERBERT PARK *Rates: budget-moderate*
Open: year-round *Minimum Stay: one week*

This handsome period house stands on one of Dublin's premiere residential streets less than a mile from the center of town and within easy reach of all the capital's top attractions. Recreational activities including tennis, golf and fishing are nearby as well, or rent a bike for a stimulating ride along the elegant city boulevards. The house contains two spacious, tastefully furnished three-bedroom apartments, both with modern kitchens and a balcony overlooking a quiet, private garden. Contact: Mrs. C. O'Connor, 1 Herbert Park, Dublin 4. Call 01144-353-1-93238. Fax 011-44-353-1-613409.

Children: **Y**   Pets: **N**   Smoking: **Y**   Handicap Access: **N**   Payment: **EC**

Dublin

MEWS HOUSE   *Rates: deluxe*
Open: year-round   *Minimum Stay: two nights*

In the heart of the fair city of Dublin, this converted mews house combines convenience with charm. Pubs, theaters, restaurants, shops and the enticing sights and sounds of Dublin are all around the corner. Yet guests need not sacrifice privacy or comfort—the house has its own entrance and courtyard and overlooks a lovely garden. The sunny living room boasts an open fireplace to ward off chills. The three bedrooms on the second story accommodate four guests; they are cheerfully decorated and all have en suite bathrooms. A butler, cook and cleaning staff can be hired to make your stay a bit more luxurious; guests receive a complimentary dinner and breakfast. Contact: Castles, Cottages & Flats, Box 201, Westwood, MA 02090. Call 617-329-4680. Ref. P 162.

Children: **Y**   Pets: **N**   Smoking: **Y**   Handicap Access: **N**   Payment: **P**

Dun Laoghaire

AYESHA CASTLE   *Rates: budget*
Open: year-round   *Minimum Stay: one week*

Noble Ayesha Castle, an expansive manor house dating from the Victorian era, offers its west wing to guests. Overlooking picturesque Killiney Bay, the estate consists of four and a half acres of meticulously kept grounds. The west wing apartment includes a spacious living/dining room, fully equipped kitchen with breakfast nook, utility room and three bedrooms sleeping a total of four. Cycling, golf, tennis, fishing, swimming and other water sports are all available, as is hiking along miles of lovely country and coastal trails. Contact: Mrs. Bridget Aylmer, Ayesha Castle, Killiney, Co. Dublin. Call 011-44-353-1852323.

Children: **Y**   Pets: **N**   Smoking: **Y**   Handicap Access: **N**   Payment: **EC**

GALWAY

Ballyconneely

THE BARN   *Rates: budget*
Open: April-September   *Minimum Stay: one week*

This beguiling traditional stone cottage sits beside a quiet, sandy lakeside beach, providing panoramic views of the Galway coast as well. A journey out to the Aran Islands, famed in film and folklore, or a trip inland to Joyce's Country and Loch Corrib are only two of the many pleasant excursions guests can make from this base. Located ten miles outside Cliften, the house includes two bedrooms and a quiet sitting/dining room with open fireplace. Contact: Mrs. Y.E. Phillpotts, The Barn, The Courtyard, Wonersh, Guildford, Surrey GU5 OPG, England. Call 011-44-483-893468.

Children: Y   Pets: N   Smoking: Y   Handicap Access: N   Payment: EC

Clifden

ARCHBISHOP'S RESIDENCE   *Rates: deluxe*
Open: year-round   *Minimum Stay: one week*

This former residence of the Archbishop of Tuam is splendidly situated on the very edge of Streamstown Bay, a sheltered inlet of the Atlantic. It boasts breathtaking views from every room and is a perfect base for enjoying deep-sea fishing and water sports; the lawn leads right down to the gently lapping waters of the bay. The handsome, commodious rooms of this newly refurbished house have a comfortable and informal ambience. A stereo, TV and VCR are found in the living room and the five spacious bedrooms sleep six. A full Irish breakfast is served to guests daily. The fee also includes household cleaning. Contact: Castles, Cottages & Flats, Box 201, Westwood, MA 02090. Call 617-329-4680. Ref. H 185.

Children: Y   Pets: N   Smoking: Y   Handicap Access: N   Payment: P

Clonbur

LAKESIDE HOUSE   *Rates: budget-inexpensive*
Open: year-round   *Minimum Stay: one weekend*

This sizable two-story house overlooks Lough Corrib, affording terrific views and easy access to all of the lake's fine recreational facilities. Lough Mask is also close by, and such top west-coast attractions as Joyce's Country, Sheefry Hills, the Maumturk Mountains and Killary Harbor are within easy reach as well. Not to be missed is an expedition to the accessible offshore islands of Innishbofin or Clare, where traditional Gaelic culture thrives and time seems to have stood still. Located three miles from Clonbur, the comfortable residence includes a spacious living room with open fireplace, plus four bedrooms for groups of up to eight. Contact: Mrs. Sheila Tynan, 23 Percy Place, Dublin 4. Call 011-44-353-1-684249.

Children: Y   Pets: N   Smoking: Y   Handicap Access: N   Payment: EC

Costelloe

COSTELLOE COTTAGE   *Rates: budget*
Open: April-September   *Minimum Stay: one week*

Sitting on the seashore, this luxury bungalow features charming well-tended gardens in both the front and rear. The residence consists of four bedrooms (each with a double bed), living room, dining room and fully equipped modern kitchen with automatic washer and dryer.

When not exploring the exquisite Galway coast or taking car trips to top area attractions like Connemara's majestic National Park, guests can fish off the pier at the rear of the bungalow or enjoy the nearby sandy beaches and hiking trails. Contact: Galway Tourist Office, Aras Failte, Galway, Co. Galway. Call 011-44-353-91-63081.

Children: Y   Pets: N   Smoking: Y   Handicap Access: N   Payment: A, V

Galway/Salthill

1 LENABOY PARK   *Rates: budget*
Open: June-September   *Minimum Stay: one week*

This handsome stone-built house contains two self-sufficient, fully equipped apartments, each with its own entrance for complete privacy. The carpeted lower flat contains two bedrooms, kitchen and sitting room and opens onto a large and sunny back garden; the upper unit holds three bedrooms and combined sitting room/dining room/ kitchen. Both apartments offer a fine chance to enjoy all the seaside attractions of Galway City and Salthill, west Ireland's top seaside resort areas. Contact: Mrs. Josephine Kelleher, 1 Lenaboy Park, Salthill, Galway, Co. Galway. Call 011-44-353-91-22418.

Children: Y   Pets: N   Smoking: Y   Handicap Access: N   Payment: EC

Gort

RAHALAY   *Rates: deluxe*
Open: year-round   *Minimum Stay: one week*

This ancient 13th-century tower house with its turrets and vaulted stone chambers combines an authentic ambience with modern amenities such as a TV, central heating and stylish furnishings. Off the traditional great hall are found a sitting room with an open fireplace, a small but well-equipped kitchen and a laundry room. One of the four large bedrooms (accommodating six guests) features a four-poster bed, and one has a crown bed. It is well located near the popular destinations of the Burren, the Cliffs of Moher and the Ailwee Cave; the lovely Aran islands can easily be reached by boat. The serene isolation of the castle obscures the fact that it is only 10 miles from Galway City. Contact: Castles, Cottages & Flats, Box 201, Westwood, MA 02090. Call 617-329-4680. Ref. H 181.

Children: Y   Pets: N   Smoking: Y   Handicap Access: N   Payment: P

Kilconnell

LAKESIDE FARMHOUSE   *Rates: budget*
Open: April-September   *Minimum Stay: one weekend*

Right in the heart of Galway, this fetching two-story, four-bedroom farmhouse overlooks the quiet waters of Loughacalla, celebrated for its rainbow trout. Excellent brown trout and coarse fishing are available within seven miles, along with golf, tennis and superb countryside hiking trails. Guests may also want to take an opportunity to tour along the Shannon River or the Galway Coast, both of which make fine day-trip excursions from this splendidly situated locale. Contact:

Galway Tourist Office, Aras Failte, Galway, Co. Galway. Call 011-44-353-9163081.

Children: Y   Pets: N   Smoking: Y   Handicap Access: N   Payment: A, V

Leenane

DELPHI COTTAGE   *Rates: budget*
Open: year-round   *Minimum Stay: one weekend*

The famous Delphi adventure center and fishery are only a five-minute stroll away from this traditional cottage overlooking beautiful Killary Harbor. Spectacular views surround the residence on all sides and a surfeit of activities, from riding and fishing to island jaunts and mountain hikes, are available to fill any vacationer's days. The cottage features a large kitchen and living room and two bedrooms plus an extra bunk bed to sleep up to six. Ample garden space allows guests to enjoy the fair Galway climate in private. Contact: Mrs. Deirdre Noone, Delphi Adventure Centre, Leenane, Co. Galway. Call 011-44-353-95-42208.

Children: Y   Pets: N   Smoking: Y   Handicap Access: N   Payment: EC

Moycullen

LAKESIDE MANSION   *Rates: deluxe*
Open: year-round   *Minimum Stay: one week*

On the bonny banks of Ross Lake lies this splendid 18th-century mansion. The grace of yesteryear is evident in the elegantly paneled library, the row boat on the lake and the two Connemara ponies; each of the handsome rooms boasts an open fireplace. More modern luxuries include a paved tennis court, a heated indoor swimming pool, a jacuzzi, completely tiled bathrooms with heated towel bars in each of the five large bedrooms and two Steinway pianos in the drawing room. The eat-in kitchen is paneled and includes a microwave; a cook and housekeeper will see after you. Located in Connemara, one of Ireland's most scenic locales, the house is also convenient to Galway City. Contact: Castles, Cottages & Flats, Box 201, Westwood, MA 02090. Call 617-329-4680. Ref. H 182.

Children: Y   Pets: N   Smoking: Y   Handicap Access: N   Payment: P

Oughterard

GORTDRISHAGH LAKEVIEW COTTAGE   *Rates: budget*
Open: April-September   *Minimum Stay: one week*

This secluded lakeside cabin rests in a verdant 25-acre park, lush with tropical shrubs, on the shores of Lough Corrib. The fertile grounds offer a private swimming area and jetty where a boat-for-hire awaits. An ideal location for enjoying the natural beauty of the Connemara district, it also offers access to trekking throughout the province of Connacht. The house features an open-plan living/dining room/kitchen area and two bedrooms. Contact: Galway Tourist Office, Aras Failte, Galway, Co. Galway. Call 011-44-353-91-63081. Ref. IW0382/1.

Children: Y   Pets: N   Smoking: Y   Handicap Access: N   Payment: A, V

Oughterard

RIVERSIDE HOUSE *Rates: budget*
Open: year-round *Minimum Stay: one weekend*

Guarded by an iron gate, Riverside House sits on the banks of the gently cascading River Owenriff. Inside the dignified two-story house are a comfortable sitting room with fireplace, a fully equipped kitchen plus breakfast room and four bedrooms, two with double beds. The friendly village of Oughterard is a short walk down the road; boats are available to navigate the waters of Lough Corrib. Guests can easily visit lofty Aughnanure Castle, Galway city and, via ferry, the popular Aran Islands. Contact: Mrs. Sheila Morley, Riverside House, Oughterard, Co. Galway. Call 011-44-353-91-82449.

Children: **Y** Pets: **N** Smoking: **Y** Handicap Access: **N** Payment: **EC**

Renvyle

SALRUCK COTTAGE *Rates: budget*
Open: year-round *Minimum Stay: one weekend*

This quality cottage is located in the lovely Connemara countryside very near the sea. Fine salmon and trout angling are available in the nearby lake. (Those renting the property in the months of May, June and September are treated to free use of a boat.) Perhaps even more than the ocean and the lake, visitors won't want to miss the district's sensational National Park. The house contains three bedrooms and a sitting room/kitchen area with open fireplace, plus a dishwasher. Contact: Mrs. Ruth Willoughby, Salruck, Renvyle, Co. Galway. Call 011-44-353-9543498.

Children: **Y** Pets: **N** Smoking: **Y** Handicap Access: **N** Payment: **EC**

KERRY

Annascaul

RECTORY FLAT *Rates: budget*
Open: year-round *Minimum Stay: one week*

This self-contained two-bedroom flat is located within a converted rectory attached to the owner's house. A comfortable and very private vacation residence of unusual character, the period building is surrounded by a burgeoning garden overlooking a peaceful mountain valley just outside the Kerry town of Annascaul. Here on the Dingle Peninsula, opportunities for nature walks abound and the many nearby bodies of water—rivers, lakes and bay—offer a deluge of fishing possibilities and other recreational opportunities. Contact: Monica Phelan, Ardrinane, Annascaul, Co. Kerry. Call 011-44-353-66-57186.

Children: **Y** Pets: **N** Smoking: **N** Handicap Access: **N** Payment: **EC**

Caragh Lake

COTTAGE AT LAKEFIELD HOUSE *Rates: budget-inexpensive*
Open: year-round *Minimum Stay: one week*

Nestled amid verdant woodlands and surrounded by mountains, the picturesque Lakefield House estate sits adjacent to the shore of Kerry's

Caragh Lake, with magnificent views as well of Dingle Bay. This old-world cottage on the estate grounds features modern amenities and contains two bedrooms, an open-plan living room and kitchen/dining area, plus an open fire. Hire a boat and enjoy the calm lake waters, play some Ping-Pong, take a sauna and wander the footpaths crisscrossing the idyllic setting. Contact: Richard & Annegret Holtkot, Lakefield House, Caragh Lake, Co. Kerry. Call 011-44-353-66-69138.

Children: **Y**   Pets: **N**   Smoking: **Y**   Handicap Access: **N**   Payment: EC

Glenbeigh
HIGH ROAD COTTAGE   *Rates: budget*
Open: year-round   *Minimum Stay: one week*

A marvelous setting overlooking the sea, forest lands and an ancient Gaelic castle surrounds this traditional cottage. The residence contains a living room, fully equipped kitchen, dining area and three bedrooms, each with double beds. Free fishing is available and golfing, scenic nature trails and the pure sandy beaches of Dingle Bay are nearby. Only a short distance away is celebrated Kilarney National Park, a must-see natural highlight for any visitor to County Kerry. Contact: Mr. John Falvey, High Road, Glenbeigh, Co. Kerry. Call 011-44-353-66-68238.

Children: **Y**   Pets: **N**   Smoking: **Y**   Handicap Access: **N**   Payment: EC

Kenmare
KILLEEN HOUSE   *Rates: budget*
Open: year-round   *Minimum Stay: one week*

This sizable 17th-century farmhouse is situated in the captivating Roughty Valley in the scenic heart of southwest Ireland. Guests can enjoy exceptional trout angling right on the premises or venture out to explore—by foot, bike, car, or horseback—the Kenmare River, which empties into a jagged Atlantic estuary. The two-story house contains four bedrooms, three with double beds and one with two twins plus an extra cot, to accommodate up to nine. Contact: Monica O'Sullivan, Killeen House, Cahaer East, Kenmare, Co. Kerry. Call 011-44-353-6441492.

Children: **Y**   Pets: **N**   Smoking: **Y**   Handicap Access: **N**   Payment: EC

Kenmare
TUBRID HOUSE   *Rates: budget*
Open: April-September   *Minimum Stay: one week*

The gabled Turbid House is a secluded residence on a twelve-acre farm whose grounds are accented by emerald pastures and orchards of aged trees. Over 150 years old, the renovated, completely modern three-bedroom home faces south, providing impressive far-reaching views of Kenmare Bay and the Caha Mountains. Visitors can enjoy bounteous hiking, riding and aquatic activities nearby. The charming town of Kenmare, whose restaurants and pubs overflow with Irish charm, is within two miles. After a day in the beguiling bucolic setting, guests can go into town for a little Gaelic socializing. Contact: Eileen Daly,

Tubrid, Kenmare, Co. Kerry. Call 011-44-353-21-273504 or 21-273251.

Children: Y   Pets: N   Smoking: Y   Handicap Access: N   Payment: EC

Kilflynn, near Tralee

LABURNUM COTTAGE   *Rates: budget*
Open: year-round   *Minimum Stay: one weekend*
This traditional cottage, surrounded by luminous yellow laburnum blossoms, is located midway between the renowned literary and entertainment centers of Tralee and Listowel. A fine location for traveling the Ring of Kerry and exploring Dingle Peninsula, it offers opportunities to enjoy such athletic pursuits as tennis, fishing, horseback riding and hiking. The appealing house features a completely modern kitchen and three bedrooms sleeping up to seven. Contact: Limerick Tourist Office, The Granary, Michael Street, Limerick, Co. Limerick. Call 011-44-353-61-317522. Fax 011-44-353-61-315634. Ref. SR0184/0

Children: Y   Pets: N   Smoking: Y   Handicap Access: N   Payment: EC

Killarney

COUNTESS ROAD FLAT   *Rates: budget*
Open: April-September   *Minimum Stay: one week*
This cozy, self-contained ground-floor flat attached to the owner's residence makes a superb budget hideaway for two travelers to Killarney. A mere three minutes outside the world-famous town, the residence (with separate entrance offering complete privacy) contains a bedroom, bath and living room with kitchen and features a large garden in the rear. For grander vistas, the National Park is a quick hop away, as are most of the top attractions that draw visitors from across the globe to this unforgettable corner of Ireland. Contact: Sean and Mary O'Callaghan, Countess Road, Killarney, Co. Kerry. Call 011-44-353-64-31465.

Children: Y   Pets: N   Smoking: Y   Handicap Access: N   Payment: EC

Kilshanning, near Castlegregory

ILLAUNE LEA BUNGALOW   *Rates: budget*
Open: year-round   *Minimum Stay: three nights*
Perched at the end of the Maharees, a sandy spit of land on the Dingle Peninsula, stands a valiant little bungalow with beamed ceilings. At low tide along the beaches and rocky coves, marine treasures are revealed by the retreating Atlantic. For those who wish to pursue the ocean's bounty, both deep-sea and inland fishing facilities are nearby. An astounding ten-mile surf beach, horseback riding and country walks will satisfy the tastes of active sports enthusiasts; the area also provides ample opportunity for bird watchers. At the local pub, guests can enjoy Irish songs; for quiet nights at home, a large stone fireplace keeps out the chill of crisp ocean air. Up to six guests sleep in three bedrooms and share two bathrooms, a kitchen and an open living/

dining area. Contact: Blakes Vacations, 4918 Dempster Street, Skokie, IL 60077. Call 1-800-628-8118. Ref. WAC.

Children: Y   Pets: N   Smoking: Y   Handicap Access: N   Payment: V, M, O

Lauragh

CREVEEN LODGE

Rates: budget

Open: April-September

Minimum Stay: one week

A refurbished dormer-style farmhouse, Creveen Lodge dates from the 1800s and offers both gracious living and modern comfort. The allure of this four-bedroom residence attached to the owner's home is further enhanced by glorious sweeping views of both the sea and the lush countryside. An inviting sunny porch is furnished for guests to take full advantage of the scenery. Perfect for mountain climbing and fishing, the area also offers fine facilities for golf, tennis and water sports. Contact: Mrs. Mary Moriarty, Creveen Lodge, Healy Pass Road, Lauragh, Co. Kerry. Call 011-44-353-64-83131.

Children: Y   Pets: N   Smoking: Y   Handicap Access: N   Payment: EC

Lehid Harbor

KENMARE RIVER HOLIDAY COTTAGES

Rates: budget

Open: year-round

Minimum Stay: two nights

Offering a choice of styles and sizes, from a charming two-bedroom restored house to a private villa, these cottages perch above the river surrounded by the magnificent Caha Mountains. The accommodations all contain full kitchens, open fireplaces, private half-acre gardens and patios, plus central heating. It's just a short walk to the harbor, where fishing expeditions, surfing, sailing and boat tours can all be arranged. Other local sports include tennis and golf. The scenery is accessible to walkers, bicyclists and drivers alike, and varies from low-lying rugged mountains to inland lakes to exotic gardens warmed by the tropical air of the Gulf Stream. Contact: Tourist Information Office, 14 Upper O'Connell Street, Dublin, Ireland. Call 011-353-1-747733.

Children: Y   Pets: N   Smoking: Y   Handicap Access: Y   Payment: T, V, M

Lispole

SEASIDE FARM BUNGALOW

Rates: budget

Open: year-round

Minimum Stay: three nights

The garden of this two-bedroom cottage looks out over the sandy bays and shores of the Dingle Peninsula. Suitable for four adults and a child and carpeted throughout, it has an eat-in kitchen and a wood-paneled living area with an open fireplace. A swimming beach is just fifteen minutes away and there are plenty of opportunities for fishing, surfing, boating or beachcombing the rocky bays and coves that ring the peninsula. Inland pleasures include golf, horseback riding and hillside rambles. The little village of Lispole offers local shopping and a pub in which to meet the locals, while Dingle, eight miles away, is a larger center for dining out. Contact: Blakes Vacations, 4918 Dempster Street, Skokie, IL 60077. Call 1-800-628-8118. Ref. WAD.

Children: **Y**   Pets: **N**   Smoking: **Y**   Handicap Access: **N**   Payment: **V, M, O**

Tralee

GERANDON   *Rates: budget*
Open: April-September   *Minimum Stay: one week*

Located near a tiny village, this expansive, converted 19th-century rectory offers authentic Victorian atmosphere. The fully carpeted house sits on its own flawlessly tended grounds along the banks of a gently flowing river. Footpaths winding into the woodlands invite exploration of the area's scenic highlights. The five elegantly furnished bedrooms (four with double beds) make this residence an ideal choice for two or three families seeking a group vacation. Contact: Limerick Tourist Office, The Granary, Michael Street, Limerick, Co. Limerick. Call 011-44-353-61-317522. Fax 011-44-353-61-315634. Ref. SR0169/1.

Children: **Y**   Pets: **N**   Smoking: **Y**   Handicap Access: **N**   Payment: **A, V**

Tralee

THE KERRIES   *Rates: budget*
Open: year-round   *Minimum Stay: one weekend*

A sunny garden apartment with its own private entrance is available in this charming Kerry farmhouse, which is surrounded by peaceful grounds. From here, explore the literary Tralee region and enjoy outdoor activities like golf, horseback riding, mountain climbing, angling and swimming in the bay. A well-equipped sports complex operates nearby and a trip up the coast to the mouth of the Shannon is rewarded by matchless sea views. The garden flat features a cozy sun room and contains two bedrooms. Mrs. Alice Dowling, The Kerries, Tralee, Co. Kerry. Call 011-44-353-66-21542.

Children: **Y**   Pets: **N**   Smoking: **Y**   Handicap Access: **N**   Payment: **EC**

KILDARE

Ballylinan

18TH-CENTURY LODGE   *Rates: budget*
Open: May-September   *Minimum Stay: one week*

This authentic lodge from the 1800s stands in shady Midlands woods. The residence includes two bedrooms—one with a double bed and one with two twins—and both the living room and kitchen feature open fireplaces. An inviting, timbered footpath awaits visitors to the grounds, while fishing and other lakeside recreational activities are nearby. Visit the region's distinguished historic landmarks, such as the Romanesque abbey at Durrow or the towering Rock of Dunamase, a spectacular pre-Viking hilltop fortress ruin. Contact: Mullingar Tourist Office, Dublin Road, Mullingar, Co. Westmeath. Call 011-44-353-44-48761.

Children: **Y**   Pets: **N**   Smoking: **Y**   Handicap Access: **N**   Payment: **A, V**

LEITRIM

Ballinamore

KEALADAVILLE

Open: year-round

Rates: budget

Minimum Stay: one week

Kealadaville is an elegantly restored Georgian house set in the heart of Leitrim, Ireland's lake country. From its windows, visitors can see an exquisite panoramic view of Fenagh Lake, plus majestic mountains and captivating ancient monasteries. Some of the country's finest coarse angling is found nearby; the area also offers top golf and tennis facilities as well as cycling and hiking trails. The house lies close to the amiable village of Fenagh, where friendly pubs and rollicking traditional Gaelic entertainment can be found. Contact: Sligo Tourist Office, Aras Reddan, Temple Street, Sligo, Co. Sligo. Call 011-44-353-7161201.

Children: Y   Pets: N   Smoking: Y   Handicap Access: N   Payment: A, V

Dromahair

DRUMLEASE

Open: year-round

Rates: inexpensive-deluxe

Minimum Stay: two nights

You'll find this large, handsome Georgian-style house located in the heart of Yeats country. Off the impressive entrance hall, the drawing and dining rooms feature elegant period furniture and open fireplaces to warm you after a brisk country stroll. The kitchen is attractive and convenient and a small library proffers audio and video tapes in addition to its eclectic book collection. The eight commodious bedrooms (most with en suite bathrooms) can comfortably accommodate up to 17 guests. The estate includes a refreshing outdoor swimming pool and some lovely shade trees; fishers will be pleased by the bountiful river Bonet, which runs through the grounds. A full staff will work to make your stay here comfortable and memorable. Contact: Castles, Cottages & Flats, Box 201, Westwood, MA 02090. Call 617-329-4680. Ref. D 500.

Children: Y   Pets: N   Smoking: Y   Handicap Access: N   Payment: P

Dromahair

THE LODGE

Open: year-round

Rates: budget

Minimum Stay: one week

A comfortable one-bedroom apartment accommodating three is available in this august country mansion. Set on twelve fertile acres of gardens, lawns and woodlands, it offers use of the estate's excellent salmon- and trout-angling facilities for fishing in solitude. The residence is close to the fine pubs and shops of Dromahair. Lough Gill and Sligo Bay are also nearby, with opportunities for tennis, boating, riding and terrific country hiking. Contact: Sligo Tourist Office, Aras Reddan, Temple Street, Sligo, Co. Sligo. Call 011-44-353-71-61201.

Children: Y   Pets: N   Smoking: Y   Handicap Access: Y   Payment: A, V

LIMERICK

Ballingarry

THE DOWER HOUSE *Rates: moderate-expensive*
Open: year-round *Minimum Stay: one week*

A secluded retreat in the glorious green hills of West Limerick, the Dower House is located on the grounds of lovely Glenwilliam Castle. This quaint cut-stone house is near Killarney, the Ring of Kerry and other scenic spots; the area also offers abundant opportunities for tennis, golf, shooting, hunting and fishing. The house is centrally heated, but wood fires in the drawing room, library and dining room add to the old-world charm. The spacious farmhouse kitchen will tempt you to whip up some hearty rural repasts before retiring to the comfy bedrooms that sleep six guests. A TV is available upon request, but you may prefer simply to escape from the modern world. Contact: Castles, Cottages & Flats, Box 201, Westwood, MA 02090. Call 617-329-4680. Ref. C 213.

Children: Y   Pets: N   Smoking: Y   Handicap Access: N   Payment: P

Cratloe

2 ASHBROOK PARK *Rates: budget*
Open: year-round *Minimum Stay: one weekend*

Standing adjacent to the rich Cratloe Woods, this authentic thatched farm cottage makes an ideal residence for a memorable Limerick holiday. The town of Limerick is less than five miles away, as is the truly majestic Bunratty Castle and folk park. And Shannon, Tipperary and the fruitful Golden Vale are not much further. Recreational opportunities, including golf, fishing, cycling, sailing, horseback riding and hiking, are plentiful. The comfortable house, which rests on peaceful, rustic grounds, contains three bedrooms (two with double beds) and a spacious living room and kitchen area. Contact: Mrs. M. McNamara, 2 Ashbrook Park, Ennis Road, Limerick, Co. Limerick. Call 011-44-353-61-54553/317522.

Children: Y   Pets: N   Smoking: Y   Handicap Access: N   Payment: EC

Croom

BANOGUE CROSS *Rates: budget*
Open: April-September *Minimum Stay: one week*

This traditional thatched farmhouse in a pastoral setting will take you back to a kinder, gentler era. Hire a horse-drawn carriage and trot along the local bucolic roads. Or bike into the legendary town of Adare, which maintains its authentic old Gaelic atmosphere with care and pride. When the mood calls for a more urban amusements, Limerick lies a 20-minute drive away. Or you can simply linger on the grounds and indulge in exceptional private fishing. Inside the house, you'll find a homey living room/sitting room with open fire, plus two bedrooms to accommodate six in old-world comfort. Contact: Limerick Tourist Office, The Granary, Michael Street, Limerick, Co. Limerick. Call 011-44-353-61-317522. Ref. SR0096/1.

Children: Y   Pets: N   Smoking: Y   Handicap Access: N   Payment: A, V

Drumcollogher

COUNTRY MANSION

Open: year-round

Rates: moderate-expensive

Minimum Stay: one week

A Maori-inspired gateway and zebra-skin rugs add exoticism to this lovely rural mansion. The grounds are lushly wooded and include fascinating castle ruins, a tennis court and a croquet lawn; you may also see some of the red and fallow deer that the owners raise here. The seven comfortable bedrooms (six with running water) provide tranquil accommodations for up to 12 guests. You can spend your days perambulating the grounds, honing your billiard and Ping-Pong skills, or just relaxing in front of an open fire. Those who wish to venture further will find plentiful fishing and hunting in the neighborhood, the beautiful Dingle peninsula nearby and the lively cities of Cork and Limerick just a short drive away. Contact: Castles, Cottages & Flats, Box 201, Westwood, MA 02090. Call 617-329-4680. Ref. C 213.

Children: Y   Pets: N   Smoking: Y   Handicap Access: N   Payment: P

Glin

FITZGERALD CASTLE

Open: year-round

Rates: expensive-deluxe

Minimum Stay: two nights

Splendidly situated amidst 500 acres of gardens, woods and farmlands, sits this enchanting white castle. The 18th-century edifice is opulently accoutered with antique Irish mahogany furniture, old family portraits and rich fabrics. Main rooms include a drawing room with a sublime neoclassical ceiling, a magnificent dining room, an extensive library and a delightful garden room. Walk up the majestic double flying stairway and you'll find a series of elegant bedrooms and baths for eight guests. Overnight guests enjoy the hospitality of the erudite Knight of Glin and his wife. Breathtaking scenery and ancient ruins in the vicinity please sightseers. The active crowd will appreciate the castle's tennis court and croquet lawn and the renowned golf courses nearby. Contact: Castles, Cottages & Flats, Box 201, Westwood, MA 02090. Call 617-329-4680. Ref. C 211.

Children: Y   Pets: N   Smoking: Y   Handicap Access: N   Payment: P

Kilmallock

GROOM'S COTTAGE AT FAIRYFIELD ESTATE

Open: year-round

Rates: budget

Minimum Stay: three nights

Located in the heart of Limerick's Golden Vale, the Fairyfield Estate contains a two-bedroom house tucked in a private corner of a courtyard. The estate offers lawn croquet, a tennis court, putting and horseback riding; tennis and riding lessons can also be arranged. In the area, guests can find indoor and outdoor swimming pools, golf, seasonal hunting and freshwater fishing. This historic region abounds with fascinating places to visit, including Castles Caher and Cashel and the fabled towns of Tipperary and Limerick. The bedrooms contain one double and two single beds, with a third single bed available. Guests who have spent the day walking through the picturesque local area will appreciate the open fire and deep cozy seating in the living room.

Contact: Blakes Vacations, 4918 Dempster Street, Skokie, IL 60077. Call 1-800-628-8118. Ref. WAY.

Children: Y   Pets: N   Smoking: Y   Handicap Access: N   Payment: V, M, O

Kilmallock

THE NEST AT FAIRYFIELD ESTATE   *Rates: budget*
Open: year-round   *Minimum Stay: three nights*

Picturesque Limerick is dotted with perfect villages and estates. Here, a quiet, whitewashed cottage for four overlooks the walled garden and orchard of an old Irish farm. One of the centrally heated bedrooms has a double bed; the other has two singles. There is a little kitchen with a lovely pine dresser and a living room with overstuffed chairs to sink into while an open fire blazes, as well as a color TV. Guests can sip tea in the garden, play tennis, croquet or putt on the grounds. If horseback riding, seasonal hunting and freshwater fishing are not enough to keep you busy, the Nest makes an ideal touring center for nearby historic towns, castles and natural wonders, such as the caves of Mitchelstown. Contact: Blakes Vacations, 4918 Dempster Street, Skokie, IL 60077. Call 1-800-628-8118. Ref. WCA.

Children: Y   Pets: N   Smoking: Y   Handicap Access: N   Payment: V, M, O

LONGFORD

Carrigglass

CARRIGGLASS MANOR   *Rates: budget*
Open: year-round   *Minimum Stay: one week*

A charming period guest cottage stands in a shady stable yard at the historic mansion of Carrigglass Manor. The very homey three-bedroom residence includes a comfortable living room, kitchen and pantry and has a private garden area. Surrounded by extensive forest lands, the manor itself is one of County Longford's main attractions. Guests can also venture to the region's other highlights, including the pristine village of Ardagh, recently proclaimed "Ireland's Tidiest Town" in a national competition. Contact: Mrs. J.G. Lefroy, Carrigglass Manor, Longford, Co. Longford. Call 011-44-353-43-45165.

Children: Y   Pets: N   Smoking: Y   Handicap Access: N   Payment: EC

Longford

VICTORIAN MANSION   *Rates: inexpensive-moderate*
Open: year-round   *Minimum Stay: two nights*

This Gothic Revival mansion with its showy towers and turrets was built in 1837 by one of Jane Austen's suitors, Thomas Lefroy. Lovingly restored by his great-great-great-grandson, the house now features ornate ceilings, fine paintings and furniture and a lovely formal garden. Downstairs are spacious entrance halls, formal dining and drawing rooms, an inviting library complete with TV and video and a cozy breakfast room for informal dining. These rooms have log fires and independent heating; portable heaters warm the five bedrooms above. The locale offers rough shooting (snipe, woodcock and pigeon) and excellent fishing. Others may prefer riding through the stunning countryside of Ireland's lake land. And of course, there are plenty of castles, gardens and parks nearby to keep any sightseer amused. Contact: Castles, Cottages & Flats, Box 201, Westwood, MA 02090. Call 617-329-4680. Ref. J 241.

Children: Y   Pets: N   Smoking: Y   Handicap Access: N   Payment: P

MAYO

Claremorris

HOUNDSWOOD CROSS
Open: April-September

Rates: budget
Minimum Stay: one week

Resting on the smooth shores of Laugh Corrib, this seductive farmhouse looks out over the water and the farm's private rustic grounds. The two-story residence contains four bedrooms, each with a double bed, plus an extra twin bed and cot to accommodate parties as large as ten in style. A boat is available for fishing or lake voyages and a bike or horse can be hired to meander down the lovely country paths of County Mayo. Leaving the immediate environs, the dynamic town of Galway and the enticements of the bay are a mere 20 miles away. Contact: Galway Tourist Office, Aras Failte, Galway, Co. Galway. Call 011-44-353-91-63081. Ref. IW0083/1.

Children: Y   Pets: N   Smoking: Y   Handicap Access: N   Payment: A, V

Cong

THE OLD RECTORY
Open: year-round

Rates: budget
Minimum Stay: one week

Two self-contained apartments—a one-bedroom and a two-bedroom unit—are available in this restored cut-stone coach house dating from 1817. The maisonette-style residences are superbly located between Lough Corrib and Lough Mask on the comely grounds of the Old Rectory of Cong, near local golf and fishing, tennis and cycling, riding and hiking facilities. Among the many historically significant locales in the area is one landmark truly not to be missed—Ashford Castle, one of the preeminent Gaelic fortresses. Contact: Mr. Robert Hall, The Old Rectory, Cong, Co. Mayo. Call 011-44-353-46087.

Children: Y   Pets: N   Smoking: Y   Handicap Access: N   Payment: EC

Crossmolina

ENNISCOE HOUSE
Open: year-round

Rates: budget
Minimum Stay: one weekend

An antiquated estate office has been cleverly converted and refurbished into a comfortable one-bedroom vacation residence, with an extra bed to accommodate a family of three. The unit features an open fireplace and winding staircase and has private access to Lough Conn. Boats are available for hire on the lake, and with scenic Killala Bay nearby as well, there's an array of recreational opportunities open to the water sports enthusiast. Land-bound visitors will enjoy the area's golf, tennis and cycling plus the many picturesque hikes for novice strollers and experienced trekkers alike. Contact: Mrs. Susan Kellett, Enniscoe House, Castlehill, near Crossmolina, Ballina, Co. Mayo. Call 011-44-353-96-31112.

Children: Y   Pets: N   Smoking: Y   Handicap Access: N   Payment: EC

Mulrany

BAY BUNGALOW   *Rates: budget*
Open: year-round   *Minimum Stay: one weekend*

This quality three-bedroom bungalow is located on peaceful farmland overlooking Clew Bay. The dramatic vista includes an unobstructed view of the peak of Crough Patrick looming majestically over the bay. Recreational activities of all sorts abound in this corner of western Ireland. Fishing, golf and walks, rides or bike trips along winding trails and paths provide ample opportunity for relaxation. Visitors may also want to journey offshore to savor sometimes overlooked but fascinating Achill Island. Contact: Galway Tourist Office, Aras, Failte, Galway, Co. Galway. Call 011-44-353-61-317522. Ref. IW0234/1.

Children: Y   Pets: N   Smoking: Y   Handicap Access: N   Payment: A, V

Mulrany

ROSTRUK CASTLE   *Rates: inexpensive-expensive*
Open: April-September   *Minimum Stay: one weekend*

Towering over the shores of Clew Bay, this grand castellated Victorian mansion is a available for parties seeking total immersion in noble Gaelic living. Here on a sublimely secluded estate, guests claim a private unspoiled beach and angling grounds for their own use, as well as sweeping sea views. The magnificent house contains six bedrooms and features a spacious drawing room, a dining room, a quiet study and several cozy fireplaces for intimate evenings. Contact: Mrs. Miriam Healy, 5 Claremont Villas, Glenageary, Co. Dublin. Call 011-44-353-1802230.

Children: Y   Pets: N   Smoking: Y   Handicap Access: Y   Payment: EC

OFFALY

Birr

BIRR CASTLE   *Rates: expensive-deluxe*
Open: year-round   *Minimum Stay: two nights*

This august 17th-century castle and its magnificent demesne allow one to partake today of the lavish elegance of yesteryear. The sumptuous residence has been graciously opened by the Earl and Countess of Rosse to small groups of up to four guests. Spacious and opulently appointed, the reception rooms feature exquisite ceilings and architectural details. The extensive gardens comprise a unique botanical collection that draws visitors from around the world: Thousands of species from all over the world are represented. The lush surrounding countryside will refresh your soul. Contact: Castles, Cottages & Flats, Box 201, Westwood, MA 02090. Call 617-329-4680. Ref. A 301.

Children: Y   Pets: N   Smoking: Y   Handicap Access: N   Payment: P

ROSCOMMON

Castlerea

CLONALIS
Rates: inexpensive-moderate
Open: September-October
Minimum Stay: none

Clonalis is the ancestral home of the O'Connors of Connacht; the lands on which it stands have been in the family's possession for 15 centuries. The current mansion was built in 1878 and is richly decorated in a mixture of styles. Clonalis possesses some famous archives dating back to the 16th century and an interesting collection of family portraits. In the autumn, the family graciously hosts up to six people for overnight stays. Guests stay in the four double bedrooms (one with a four-poster bed and two with adjoining baths) and are served a full Irish breakfast every morning. There is clay pigeon shooting on the estate and golf is available nearby. Contact: Castles, Cottages & Flats, Box 201, Westwood, MA 02090. Call 617-329-4680. Ref. Q 341.

Children: Y   Pets: N   Smoking: Y   Handicap Access: N   Payment: P

SLIGO

Bruckless

BRUCKLESS HOUSE COTTAGE
Rates: budget
Open: year-round
Minimum Stay: one week

This cozy cottage sits on its own tranquil grounds next to stately Bruckless House. Tucked beneath elegant aged trees on the shore of Bruckless Bay, the two-bedroom residence with open fireplace is graced with gorgeous Sligo coastal views and a peaceful, sheltered setting. From here, enjoy the area's fine recreational opportunities or explore the heart of Yeats country, including the Nobel laureate's final resting place at Drumcliffe. Contact: Sligo Tourist Office, Aras Reddan, Temple Street, Sligo, Co. Sligo. Call 011-44-353-71-61201.

Children: Y   Pets: N   Smoking: Y   Handicap Access: N   Payment: A, V

Carney

ARDTARMON COTTAGE
Rates: budget
Open: year-round
Minimum Stay: one week

This renovated thatched cottage adjoins an elegant country house on a fertile 75-acre farm. Set in a scenic coastal location, the grounds feature a tennis court and private beach for the guests' use. The area offers excellent opportunities for golf, fishing, horseback riding and cycling. Comfortable and roomy, the cottage contains two bedrooms (one with double bed and one with bunk beds) plus an extra cot to provide accommodations for up to five. Contact: Mr. Charles Henry, Ardtarmon, Ballinfull, Co. Sligo. Call 011-44-353-71-63156.

Children: Y   Pets: N   Smoking: Y   Handicap Access: N   Payment: EC

Sligo

BREEOGUE HOUSE
Rates: budget
Open: June-September
Minimum Stay: one week

Overlooking scenic Sligo Bay, this handsomely restored country house occupies lovingly tended grounds filled with gardens, lawns and a shady orchard. The spacious four-bedroom residence is tastefully decorated with antique furniture and contains a drawing room with open fireplace, kitchen/dining room and a seductive sun lounge. It's an excellent locale for hiking or cycling along the coast, as well as exploring the historic and scenic highlights of the north country. Contact: Mrs. Ena MacLoughlin, Breeogue House, Breeogue, Knocknahur, Co. Sligo. Call 011-44-353-71-68202.

Children: **Y**   Pets: **N**   Smoking: **Y**   Handicap Access: **N**   Payment: **EC**

TIPPERARY

Cahir

BALLYBRADO HOUSE   *Rates: budget*
Open: year-round   *Minimum Stay: one week*

This appealing Victorian-style lodge is located along the wooded belt of a working organic farm in the premier walking and riding country of south Tipperary. Within lies a quality two-bedroom unit with living/dining area suitable for four guests. The lodge grounds offer a splendid view of the Galtee Mountains, a mile of sandy beaches and private fishing on the river Suir. As an added attraction, delicious and wholesome organic food grown right on the premises is provided to guests. A visit to the great Castle of Cahir is the must-see attraction in this area full of historic and scenic highlights. Contact: Mr. J. Finke, Ballybrado House, Cahir, Co. Tipperary. Call 011-44-353-52-66206.

Children: **Y**   Pets: **N**   Smoking: **Y**   Handicap Access: **N**   Payment: **EC**

Carrick-on-Suir

COMERAGH HOUSE   *Rates: inexpensive-deluxe*
Open: year-round   *Minimum Stay: two nights*

This ivy-clad house set amidst gardens and parkland combines gracious living with a friendly air of informality. Everything is provided for your pleasure: Curl up in front of the open fire with a book from the galleried library, or try out the sauna. Several TVs, a microwave in the country-style kitchen and daily cleaning add to the comfort. A stunning collection of Peruvian paintings provides a touch of exotica amidst more traditional antiques. Luxurious bedrooms upstairs accommodate six people; many rooms have glorious views of the lovely Comeragh Mountains. The area proffers golf, fishing, riding and hunting; the city of Waterford with its famous crystal is only eight miles away. Contact: Castles, Cottages & Flats, Box 201, Westwood, MA 02090. Call 617-329-4680. Ref. B 601.

Children: **Y**   Pets: **N**   Smoking: **Y**   Handicap Access: **N**   Payment: **P**

Cashel

SUIR CASTLE   *Rates: budget*
Open: year-round   *Minimum Stay: one week*

A cozy two-bedroom detached bungalow stands on the grounds of Suir

Castle, making an excellent hideaway. From Cashel, it is not a "long way" at all to the heart of Tipperary or to its many attractions, including the legendary site of the Rock of Cashel and the historic Holy Cross Abbey. Among the plentiful recreational opportunities available here in the Golden Valley are golfing, tennis, riding, cycling and fishing and water sports on the Suir River. Contact: Mrs. Bridget McGrath, Suir Castle, Golden, Cashel, Co. Tipperary. Call 011-44-62-72247.

Children: **Y** Pets: **N** Smoking: **Y** Handicap Access: **N** Payment: **EC**

Newtown
GEORGIAN ESTATE

Rates: moderate

Open: *year-round*

Minimum Stay: one weekend

This sweeping Georgian estate extends more than a quarter of a mile to the shore of exquisite Lough Derg, carved out by the river Shannon in scenic north Tipperary. The huge manor house, lovingly restored, dates from 1738 and features a pine kitchen with dishwasher and deep freezer, four bedrooms and four reception rooms (with six bathrooms) making plenty of space for a large group seeking a luxury residence. Your party can enjoy the impeccably manicured estate grounds and lake-shore recreational enticements (including boat moorings), or play a bit of golf or tennis at the nearby facilities. Contact: Limerick Tourist Office, The Granary, Michael Street, Limerick, Co. Limerick. Call 011-44-353-61-317522. Ref. SR0110/1.

Children: **Y** Pets: **N** Smoking: **Y** Handicap Access: **N** Payment: **A, V**

Newtown
YOUGHAL HOUSE

Rates: budget

Open: *year-round*

Minimum Stay: one week

Set in a sedate woodland area, this traditional Tipperary farm cottage lies adjacent to graceful Lough Derg. A tennis court is moments away, as well as boating facilities for superb lake fishing or cruising along the Shannon River. The cheery cottage offers splendid views and contains a cozy sitting room with an old-fashioned wood-burning stove, modern kitchen and dining room. Three bedrooms plus an extra cot accommodate a total of seven. Contact: Limerick Tourist Office, The Granary, Michael Street, Limerick, Co. Limerick. Call 011-44-353-317522. Ref. SR0114/1.

Children: **Y** Pets: **N** Smoking: **Y** Handicap Access: **N** Payment: **A, V**

WATERFORD

Cappagh
CAPPAGH HOUSE

Rates: budget

Open: *year-round*

Minimum Stay: weekend

This spacious mews house has its own sheltered cobbled yard and is situated on a picturesque working farm. The three-bedroom residence (one bedroom with double bed, two with twin beds) comfortably accommodates six and is only seven miles from the sandy beaches and charming fishing villages of the Atlantic coast. Adventures in Cork, Tipperary and Limerick are each only a short excursion away as well, and closer to the house, fine fishing, tennis and cycling are available. Contact: Mrs. Claire Chavasse, Cappagh House, Cappagh, Co. Waterford. Call 011-44-353-58-68185.

Children: Y   Pets: N   Smoking: Y   Handicap Access: N   Payment: EC

Cappoquin

LITTLEBRIDGE INCHES   *Rates: budget*
Open: year-round   *Minimum Stay: one week*
A former stable has been cleverly converted into a distinctive and comfortable two-bedroom residence with its own secluded courtyard for absolute privacy and relaxation. This restful home base is ideally situated for recreational excursions, including swimming at the beaches of nearby coastal resorts, angling on the rivers Blackwater and Bride, sea fishing on the Atlantic and hiking, riding, or cycling in the serene Waterford countryside. Contact: Mrs. Mary Nicholson, Littlebridge Inches, Cappoquin, Co. Waterford. Call 011-44-353-58-54329 or 011-44-353-51-75823.

Children: Y   Pets: N   Smoking: Y   Handicap Access: N   Payment: EC

Glencairn

FORTWILLIAM ESTATE COTTAGE   *Rates: budget*
Open: year-round   *Minimum Stay: one week*
A comfortable semi-detached residence offers total privacy and an exceptional home base for a memorable Waterford holiday. Fortwilliam is close to the county's finest beaches; scenic Youghal Bay and superb golf, tennis and fishing facilities are within easy reach as well. There are miles of hiking, riding and cycling paths winding through the breathtaking countryside. The house contains two bedrooms (both with double beds, plus one cot), fully equipped kitchen/dining area, living room and a cozy fireplace. Contact: Waterford Tourist Office, 41 The Quay, Waterford. Call 011-44-353-51-75823 Ref. SE0136/0.

Children: Y   Pets: N   Smoking: Y   Handicap Access: N   Payment: A, V

Lismore

LISMORE CASTLE   *Rates: deluxe*
Open: year-round   *Minimum Stay: one week*
Secluded in the wooded hills of the scenic Blackwater Valley between Waterford and Cork is charming Lismore and its magnificent castle. The large, handsome rooms feature log fires and elegant accouterments. Six double bedrooms and four singles (six with en suite bathrooms) provide sumptuous accommodations for up to 12 guests. A full staff (butler, maids and cook) and all your meals are included here—take the opportunity to relish the life of luxury. The splendid grounds enjoy private access to the unspoiled river Blackwater; a tennis court and golf course are found here, too. Riding and fox hunting can be arranged for those dedicated to these genteel pursuits. Contact: Cas-

tles, Cottages & Flats, Box 201, Westwood, MA 02090. Call 617-329-4680. Ref. F 381.

Children: Y   Pets: N   Smoking: Y   Handicap Access: N   Payment: P

Tarr's Bridge, near Dungarvan

RIVERSIDE

Open: year-round

Rates: budget

Minimum Stay: one weekend

The town of Waterford, where artisans create world-famous crystal, is but one essential Emerald Isle attraction easily reachable from this cozy thatched cottage. Resort beaches, golf, fishing, riding and the engaging harbor town of Dungarvan are close by. Set amid tranquil grounds, the house, containing three bedrooms (one double, one single, one with bunk beds) and a living room/dining area, has plenty of room for five. On raw days, it may be kept warm by either a roaring fire or central heating. Contact: Mrs. P. Beresford, Riverside, Tarr's Bridge, Dungarvan, Co. Waterford. Call 011-44-353-58-41040.

Children: Y   Pets: N   Smoking: Y   Handicap Access: N   Payment: EC

WESTMEATH

Castlepollard

VICTORIAN CASTLE

Open: year-round

Rates: deluxe

Minimum Stay: one week

This enormous Gothic Revival castle might seem imposing, but it inevitably charms guests with its casual family atmosphere. The large, sunny rooms are comfortably furnished in the country-house style and cheery window seats overlook the beautiful landscape. The magnificently proportioned banquet hall even serves as a children's playroom. Eleven double bedrooms can easily accommodate a large party. Central heating and a helpful staff add comfort to your holiday. The extensive grounds feature a croquet lawn, a grass tennis court, formal gardens with ornamental ponds and verdant woodlands; guests may arrange to borrow the owner's ponies. Anglers will find Lough Derravargh well stocked with brown trout, and the rolling hills of County Westmeath satisfy all who seek a pleasant country stroll. Contact: Castles, Cottages & Flats, Box 201, Westwood, MA 02090. Call 617-329-4680. Ref. T 421.

Children: Y   Pets: N   Smoking: Y   Handicap Access: N   Payment: P

Tyrrellspass

TYRRELLSPASS CASTLE

Open: year-round

Rates: deluxe

Minimum Stay: one week

This venerable 15th-century castle will captivate you with its stony towers and crenelated battlements. Although the Norman edifice retains the character of its glorious history, the central heating, the TV, the washing machine and the elevator make drafty castle discomfort a thing of the past. In addition to the great hall, this castle features handsome living and dining rooms, a convenient kitchen and four comfortable bedrooms (one with an en suite bathroom). This area abounds in landmarks of Ireland's heritage—Tullynally Castle, Clonmacnois and Birr Castle are all within a short drive. Fishing and hunting can be enjoyed locally and the championship golf course at Mullingar is only eight miles away. Contact: Castles, Cottages & Flats, Box 201, Westwood, MA 02090. Call 617-329-4680. Ref. T 423.

Children: Y   Pets: N   Smoking: Y   Handicap Access: N   Payment: P

WEXFORD

Butlerstown

STONE COTTAGE   *Rates: budget*
Open: year-round   *Minimum Stay: one week*

A delightful architectural oddity, this adorable stone cottage is built right alongside a majestic 16th-century Norman castle. The comfortable residence includes two bedrooms (with five twin beds, plus a cot) and a combined living/dining room/kitchen area with fireplace. Guests will want plenty of time to take in the exquisite Wexford countryside by horseback, bike, or foot and to enjoy the ample athletic offerings of the region. Contact: Mrs. H. Skrine, Butlerstown, Killinick, Co. Wexford. Call 011-44-353-53-35107.

Children: Y   Pets: N   Smoking: Y   Handicap Access: N   Payment: EC

Drinagh

KILLIANE CASTLE APARTMENTS   *Rates: budget*
Open: year-round   *Minimum Stay: one weekend*

Several fully equipped, quality apartments are available in the main building of the dazzling Norman Killiane Castle. Set in a placid castle courtyard convenient to both town and the beach, the units each contain two bedrooms (one double bed, one bunk, one cot) and an open-plan living room with kitchen. A tennis court and lovely bucolic footpaths are available right on the grounds, but guests will also want to go exploring throughout the county of Wexford, a celebrated artistic center of Ireland that happens to be as well the ancestral land of the Kennedys. Contact: Waterford Tourist Office, 41 The Quay, Waterford. Call 011-44-353-51-75823. Ref. SE0102/1.

Children: Y   Pets: N   Smoking: Y   Handicap Access: N   Payment: A, V

Ferns

ITALIANATE MANSION   *Rates: deluxe*
Open: year-round   *Minimum Stay: one week*

At the foot of Mount Leinster near the rushing waters of the river Slaney stands this Italianate mansion with its working farm. The commodious rooms downstairs include two drawing rooms, a conservatory, a study and a large dining room, all handsomely decorated with 18th-century paintings and antique furniture. Each of the four double bedrooms (all with adjoining baths) have splendid views of the grounds or the river Slaney. The river's proximity makes this mansion a fisher's dream—only a short amble away are abundant salmon in springtime and a good run of sea trout in the summer. A full staff will look after you during your stay. Contact: Castles, Cottages & Flats, Box 201, Westwood, MA 02090. Call 617-329-4680. Ref. O 527.

Children: Y   Pets: N   Smoking: Y   Handicap Access: N   Payment: P

WICKLOW

Ashford

GEORGIAN MANSION

Open: year-round

Rates: deluxe

Minimum Stay: one week

Set in 300 acres of peaceful farmland, this refined Georgian mansion at the foot of the Wicklow hills has its own secluded beach. The keynote of this house is tranquil elegance: the main rooms are stylishly decorated with antique furniture and paintings. After strolling along the beach or through the pretty gardens, retire to one of the two impressive drawing rooms or pull up a chair before a cheerful open fire. Six guests will find pleasant sleeping quarters in the four charming bedrooms. The kitchen features a dishwasher, and maid service is included. The Ashford area boasts several excellent restaurants and tennis, riding and shooting can be arranged. Contact: Castles, Cottages & Flats, Box 201, Westwood, MA 02090. Call 617-329-4680. Ref. U443.

Children: Y   Pets: N   Smoking: Y   Handicap Access: N   Payment: P

Roundwood

CLARABEG

Open: year-round

Rates: moderate

Minimum Stay: two nights

This lovely old country house overlooks both the sea and the rolling green hills of beautiful County Wicklow. After riding through the countryside on horseback for a couple of hours (complimentary for guests), relax in front of the roaring fire in the spacious, rustic living room. An excellent dinner, breakfast and lunch prepared by your gourmet hostess and served in the quaint 200-year-old dining room are also included. One of the double bedrooms features a lovely private patio and en suite dressing room and bathroom; the other is a spacious timbered room overlooking the sea with its own sitting area and luxurious bathroom. Both suites have access to a living room where guests can curl up with a book from the library or relax in front of the TV. Contact: Castles, Cottages & Flats, Box 201, Westwood, MA 02090. Call 617-329-4680. Ref. U 446.

Children: N   Pets: N   Smoking: Y   Handicap Access: N   Payment: P

Italy

Apulia

Martina Franca

VALLEY HOUSE   *Rates: budget-inexpensive*
Open: year-round   *Minimum Stay: one week*

Poised between the Adriatic and the Ionian seas on the heel of Italy's boot, the medieval town of Martina Franca has been watching travelers come and go for centuries. Today the area is a quiet wine-growing district, with marvelous hunting and hiking opportunities in the pine forests outside of town. This sun-soaked house is a fine example of the Apulian architectural style, located in a quiet valley outside of town. The spacious lodgings include a handsome entrance hall, two large living rooms, a kitchen with a charming fireplace and two bedrooms. The house is simply furnished, but up to six people can be comfortably accommodated here. Contact: Interhome Inc., 124 Little Falls Rd., Fairfield, NJ 07004. Call 201-882-6864. Ref. I6866/8.

Children: **Y**   Pets: **Y**   Smoking: **Y**   Handicap Access: **N**   Payment: **P, V, M**

San Vito Dei Normanni

IL DESERTO

Rates: budget-moderate

Open: year-round

Minimum Stay: one week

Travelers to the heel of Italy's boot will take special pleasure in discovering the "trulli," local buildings with domed or conical roofs. Il Deserto is such a home—round, made of stone and standing in the center of a grove of arched trees—and sleeps three to four. Guests may also stay in the main house of this farm, a large, handsome residence with a dining room, a living room with a terrace, and sleeping accommodations for seven adults and two children. Far from the urban hub this region will introduce visitors to the timeless traditions of old Italy. Nearby beaches provide sunning and windsurfing diversions, and excursions through the countryside reveal the richness of this land, golden with fields of wheat and tangled with olive trees and vineyards. Contact: British Travel Associates, P. O. Box 299, Elkton, VA 22827. Call 1-800-327-8097 (in Virginia, 703-298-2232). Ref. IP1, IP2.

Children: **Y**   Pets: **N**   Smoking: **Y**   Handicap Access: **N**   Payment: **All**

CAMPANIA

Amalfi

VILLA SARACENO

Rates: deluxe

Open: June 1-September 30

Minimum Stay: one week

Situated at the end of a narrow street high above Fornillo beach, the moorish-style, whitewashed Villa Saraceno commands breathtaking views of the coastline and sea, with a steep path leading down to the water below. Furnished with antiques and accented with such singular features as a marble staircase with moorish columns at the base, the house is built around a gentle courtyard adorned with potted flowers and shrubs. The residence contains a living room, kitchen with breakfast area, library alcove and dining room downstairs, all with exits to the courtyard. Two bedrooms, both opening onto a terrace looking over the sea and one with a four-poster bed, are on the second floor, and a third bedroom plus kitchen corner is located on the third. Contact: Villas and Apartments Abroad Ltd, 420 Madison Ave, New York, NY 10017. Call 212-759-1025 or 1-800-433-3020.

Children: **Y**   Pets: **Y**   Smoking: **Y**   Handicap Access: **N**   Payment: **C, P, T**

Ischia

GARDEN CLUB VILLAS *Rates: moderate-deluxe*
Open: year-round *Minimum Stay: one week*

An oasis of tranquility, this cluster of whitewashed villas and apartments, each with its own patio-terrace, is set amidst 17 acres of subtropical vegetation in Lacco Ameno, a lively resort town on beautiful Ischia. Hidden within the lush grounds visitors will discover an indoor thermal pool, table tennis and a children's play park. Villa Camelia, a ground-floor, one-bedroom apartment, sleeps up to four and Villa Orchidea, a first-floor, one-bedroom apartment, also sleeps up to four. A bungalow villa divided into two one-bedroom apartments, Villa Oleandro sleeps up to three in each. Ulivi, a first-floor studio apartment, sleeps two. Contact: Hometours International, Inc., 1170 Broadway, New York, NY 10001. Call: 212-689-0851 or 1-800-367-4668. Ref. 3110/1, 3110/2, 3110/3, 3110/4.

Children: Y Pets: N Smoking: Y Handicap Access: N Payment: C, P, T

Sorrento

RESIDENZA MIRAMARE *Rates: inexpensive-expensive*
Open: year-round *Minimum Stay: one week*

The Residenza Miramare, a superb old villa set amid landscaped gardens a half mile above Sorrento, has recently been converted into spacious luxury apartments which overlook the Bay of Naples. Each apartment has a private patio or terrace and features daily maid service and—a fully equipped kitchen notwithstanding—a daily, complimentary continental breakfast in the breakfast/bar lounge. Aranci, a one-bedroom apartment, sleeps four in one double and two single divan beds. Large and airy, Miramare Studio sleeps two in a double bed. Vesuvio, a superb studio, accommodates two in a double bed. The spacious Amalfi studio sleeps up to three in a double bed and single divan. Contact: Hometours International, Inc., 1170 Broadway, New York, NY 10001. Call: 212-689-0851 or 1-800-367-4668. Ref. 3102/1, 3102/2, 3102/3, 3102/4.

Children: Y Pets: N Smoking: Y Handicap Access: N Payment: C, P, T

Termini

GOCCE DI CAPRI *Rates: inexpensive-moderate*
Open: year-round *Minimum Stay: one week*

These brand-new villa apartments set high on the hillside of Termini-Massalubrense offer breathtaking views of the isle of Capri and the Bay of Naples below. You will particularly enjoy the splendor of the panoramic scenery from the large pool, dramatically set within a spacious sun terrace. The one- and two-bedroom apartments, accommodating four to six, contain a living room with a double sofa bed, a kitchen and a bathroom. Comfortably furnished, each has a spacious terrace overlooking the sea and a rear patio with a barbecue. Private parking is available and there is regular bus service to nearby Sorrento, Massalubrense and the beach of Marina del Cantone. Contact: Hometours

International, Inc., 1170 Broadway, New York, NY 10001. Call: 212-689-0851 or 1-800-367-4668.

Children: **Y**   Pets: **N**   Smoking: **Y**   Handicap Access: **N**   Payment: **C, P, T**

Vietri

VILLA VIETRI   *Rates: deluxe*
Open: June 1-September 30   *Minimum Stay: one week*

This smashing contemporary villa sits perched above the Mediterranean 30 miles from Naples, commanding breathtaking views of the Amalfi coast. With a swimming pool built into the rocks overlooking the sea, the property also includes a garden containing a barbecue, volley ball court and bowling alley, plus a path leading down to the private rocky beach below. Inside, an entrance hall, superbly equipped kitchen, studio and large sitting room/dining area are located downstairs, while the second floor contains the master suite with a dressing room and oceanview terrace, plus four other bedrooms, one of which has a balcony. Contact: Villas and Apartments Abroad Ltd, 420 Madison Ave., New York, NY 10017. Call 212-759-1025 or 1-800-433-3020.

Children: **Y**   Pets: **Y**   Smoking: **Y**   Handicap Access: **N**   Payment: **C, P, T**

EMILIA-ROMAGNA

Cattolica

SUNNY APARTMENT   *Rates: budget*
Open: July-November   *Minimum Stay: one week*

This spacious apartment is located on the second floor of an attractive two-family house near the sea. The pleasant accommodations include a living room with a TV, an eat-in kitchen complete with an oven, three bedrooms and a sunny balcony. The delightful garden and patio outside are welcoming spots for relaxation, or take a short walk to the gently sloping beach. Cattolica maintains its ancient character as a fishing harbor but today offers visitors a plethora of amusements, from sailing, windsurfing and water skiing to its discos, cinemas and convivial restaurants. In addition, Rimini, Pesaro and San Marino are only a short drive away. Contact: Interhome Inc., 124 Little Falls Rd., Fairfield, NJ 07004. Call 201-882-6864. Ref. I4550/1C.

Children: **Y**   Pets: **N**   Smoking: **Y**   Handicap Access: **N**   Payment: **P, V, M**

Lido Adriano

CALANDRE   *Rates: budget-inexpensive*
Open: April-November   *Minimum Stay: one week*

Located right beside the sea on the outskirts of town, the Calandre features all the amenities of a large modern resort. When the crowds at the beach get to be too much, recline in a deck chair beneath a shady umbrella or take a refreshing plunge in the large pool. There is reserved parking in the guarded carport and a convenient elevator to whisk you to your room. The fourth-story apartment vaunts a balcony and can easily accommodate five people. The kitchenette comes complete with an oven and one of the two bedrooms features bunk beds. Restaurants and shops are just around the corner and the center of town is not too far away. Contact: Interhome Inc., 124 Little Falls Rd., Fairfield, NJ 07004. Call 201-882-6864. Ref. I4380/45E.

Children: Y Pets: N Smoking: Y Handicap Access: N Payment: P, V, M

Lido Spina

MANDRIOLE *Rates: budget-inexpensive*
Open: April-November *Minimum Stay: one week*

The Mandriole is a small, welcoming apartment house just a few yards from the lovely beaches of Lido Spina. The establishment offers its guests a large, well-landscaped swimming pool, a pleasant garden and reserved parking. Four guests can be comfortably accommodated in the airy second-floor apartment, which includes a living and dining room with a double divan bed, a kitchenette and a double bedroom. Soak up a few rays or catch up on your people-watching out on the private balcony. Spina is also a fine place to sample the culinary wonders of Emilia-Romagna and to squander a bit of loose change in the interesting boutiques; the Mandriole is near both shops and restaurants. Contact: Interhome Inc., 124 Little Falls Rd., Fairfield, NJ 07004. Call 201-882-6864. Ref. I4330/490B.

Children: Y Pets: Y Smoking: Y Handicap Access: N Payment: P, V, M

Rosolina Mare

SPORTING *Rates: budget-moderate*
Open: April-November *Minimum Stay: one week*

The Sporting lives up to its name, with a swimming pool on the grounds; a sandy beach just down the lane; and sailing, riding and tennis available in town. Pleasantly secluded by a verdant stand of pines, the residence also offers its guests a pretty garden and proximity to restaurants and shops. The first-floor apartment for five includes a living and dining room with a divan bed, a kitchenette and two bedrooms. The three-room apartment for four people is also on the ground floor and features bunk beds for the kids. This is an agreeable base for families enjoying seaside holidays. Contact: Interhome Inc., 124 Little Falls Rd., Fairfield, NJ 07004. Call 201-882-6864. Ref. I4250/220A, /222A.

Children: Y Pets: Y Smoking: Y Handicap Access: N Payment: P, V, M

FRIULI-VENEZIA GIULIA

Aprilia Marittima

APRILIA *Rates: budget-inexpensive*
Open: May-November *Minimum Stay: one week*

This holiday spot on a lagoon off the Adriatic Sea features long sandy beaches and warm maritime breezes. Surrounded by large, showy gardens and right next to the yacht harbor, the Aprilia is an impressive resort complex with splendid views of the lagoon from every room. The complex boasts its own swimming pool, tennis courts, restaurants, shops and newsstand; a private bus transports guests hourly to the sandy beaches nearby (gratis). Both the three-person and the five-person apartments feature modern furnishings and kitchenettes, and comfortable garden furniture on the seaward balconies allows you to enjoy a glass of vino as you watch the dazzling play of lights on the water. Contact: Interhome Inc., 124 Little Falls Rd., Fairfield, NJ 07004. Call 201-882-6864. Ref. I4070/100F, /150F.

Children: Y   Pets: Y   Smoking: Y   Handicap Access: N   Payment: P, V, M

Lignano

BORGO BIANCO   *Rates: budget*
Open: April-November   *Minimum Stay: one week*

Well located on Lignano's sandy peninsula, the Borgo Bianco is a pleasant Adriatic retreat. The nicely maintained apartment includes a tasteful living and dining room with a convertible double bed, a kitchenette and an additional bedroom with comfy twin beds. Outside is a pretty little garden open to the residence's guests. If your ideal summer consists primarily of fine sand, golden sun and crystalline water, the renowned beaches of Lignano are less than two miles away. More gregarious souls will appreciate the taverns, restaurants and nightspots just a few feet down the road. Contact: Interhome Inc., 124 Little Falls Rd., Fairfield, NJ 07004. Call 201-882-6864. Ref. I4071/160A.

Children: Y   Pets: Y   Smoking: Y   Handicap Access: N   Payment: P, V, M

Lignano

LE MIMOSE   *Rates: budget-moderate*
Open: April-November   *Minimum Stay: one week*

Lignano's fine, sandy beaches have made it a popular resort on the Adriatic; the thermal baths and tennis, riding and watersport facilities don't hurt either. Le Mimose is a complex of individual houses that caters to holiday visitors. It is conveniently located on a quiet street near the center of town and features a pleasant patio. The two-story house includes a tastefully furnished living and dining room and a kitchenette downstairs; up the spiral staircase you'll find two comfortable bedrooms (sleeping four). The two airy balconies provide the perfect place to unwind and reminisce after a day filled with sun and fun. Contact: Interhome Inc., 124 Little Falls Rd., Fairfield, NJ 07004. Call 201-882-6864. Ref. Il4071/10.

Children: Y   Pets: Y   Smoking: Y   Handicap Access: N   Payment: P, V, M

Lignano

VILLA ROSY   *Rates: budget*
Open: April-November   *Minimum Stay: one week*

Nestled in a quiet corner of the town near a cool, green pine forest, the Villa Rosy combines convenience with solitude. The second-story apartment can easily accommodate five guests in its four pleasant rooms (living and dining room, kitchenette and two bedrooms). A southern-facing balcony with comfortable furniture will please dedicated sunbathers. Those seeking a more public sunning will find the sandy beaches within walking distance. And the restaurants, shops and nightspots of Lignano are just around the corner. Contact: Interhome Inc., 124 Little Falls Rd., Fairfield, NJ 07004. Call 201-882-6864. Ref. I4071/130B.

Children: Y   Pets: Y   Smoking: Y   Handicap Access: N   Payment: P, V, M

LATIUM

Campagnano

VILLA IL SORBO   *Rates: deluxe*
Open: June 1-September 30   *Minimum Stay: one week*

Villa il Sorbo lies on 21 pristine acres of woods, meadows and fields. Dominating the extraordinary sweeping view is Santuario del Sorbo, an exquisite 12th-century romanesque church. The property is a half-an-hour drive from the center of Rome and offers quiet and seclusion, as well as many areas of interest nearby. With a swimming pool out front, the single-story house includes an entrance hall, two living rooms, large kitchen, dining room and five bedrooms, plus an additional bedroom tucked away in the villa's "Little Tower." Contact: Villas and Apartments Abroad Ltd, 420 Madison Ave, New York, NY 10017. Call 212-759-1025 or 1-800-433-3020.

Children: Y   Pets: Y   Smoking: Y   Handicap Access: N   Payment: C, P, T

Frascati

LA VACCHERIA   *Rates: deluxe*
Open: June 1-September 30   *Minimum Stay: one week*

Located in the flourishing countryside just outside Rome, La Vaccheria is a wonderful villa that sits on vast private parklands surrounded by woods and gardens. The legendary Castle Gondolfo and its Palace of the Popes is right nearby, and Rome itself is about 12 miles away. With a refreshing swimming pool on the property, the villa is a luxurious and restful vacation home containing an entrance hall, two large sitting rooms, a kitchen opening onto the garden and five bedrooms. It features such charming accents as a wood-beamed ceiling. Contact: Villas and Apartments Abroad Ltd, 420 Madison Ave, New York, NY 10017. Call 212-759-1025 or 1-800-433-3020.

Children: Y   Pets: Y   Smoking: Y   Handicap Access: N   Payment: C, P, T

Rome

APARTMENT NITTI   *Rates: inexpensive*
Open: year-round   *Minimum Stay: one week*

This simply furnished apartment near the Olympic Stadium brings to life the old saying, "when in Rome...." Only a twenty-minute bus ride from the historic center of the city, this apartment situates guests in the heart of one of Rome's colorfully characteristic residential centers. At the daily street market you can improve your Italian by haggling over tomatoes, or select just the right cheese for dinner. Take the elevator to the fourth floor of a large home, where a kitchen with a dining area, a living room with two sofa beds and one double bedroom accommodate two to four. Contact: British Travel Associates, P. O. Box 299, Elkton, VA 22827. Call 1-800-327-8097 (in Virginia, 703-298-2232). Ref. IR3.

Children: Y   Pets: N   Smoking: Y   Handicap Access: N   Payment: All

Rome

IL PALAZZO AL VELABRO

Open: year-round

Rates: moderate-expensive
Minimum Stay: one week

In a tranquil yet central setting convenient to all the major sights, Il Palazzo al Velabro faces the Piazza Bocca della Verita and its Temple of Vesta and Arch of Giano. These elegant and comfortable apartments—which have air conditioning, telephones, television and radios—are well-served by an efficient reception area which is open 24 hours a day. Studio apartments accommodate two people on a double divan and have concealed kitchenettes equipped with electric stove-top burners. The one-bedroom, one-bathroom apartments accommodate up to three in one double bed and a single divan in the living room. Here too, the concealed kitchenettes are equipped with electric stove-top burners. Contact: Hometours International, Inc., 1170 Broadway, New York, NY 10001. Call: 212-689-0851 or 1-800-367-4668. Ref. 3120/1, 3120/2.

Children: Y   Pets: N   Smoking: Y   Handicap Access: N   Payment: C, P, T

Rome

SAN GIOVANNI APARTMENT

Open: year-round

Rates: moderate
Minimum Stay: one week

Empires come and go, but Rome remains eternal. Twenty-five centuries of history have woven this city into an opulent and varied tapestry. This apartment near the magnificent Coliseum brings the heart of Rome practically to your door, but its quiet neighborhood ensures that you won't be deluged with urban sounds and traffic. The convenient kitchen includes a dishwasher and an oven, and five guests will find comfy lodgings in its three pretty bedrooms. The apartment is centrally heated and there is also a washing machine on the premises. Groceries and restaurants are around the corner, and the vital hub of Rome is only a 10-minute walk away. Contact: Interhome Inc., 124 Little Falls Rd., Fairfield, NJ 07004. Call 201-882-6864. Ref. I5700/15B.

Children: Y   Pets: N   Smoking: Y   Handicap Access: N   Payment: P, V, M

Rome

VATICAN CITY FLATS

Open: year-round

Rates: inexpensive-expensive
Minimum Stay: one week

Visitors to Rome can enjoy this astounding city from one of four attractive apartments in a newly renovated house situated only three minutes' walk from St. Peter's Cathedral and the Holy City. As near to the center of the city as they are, these flats also lie in an artisan district, where workshops and cafes abut one another in the narrow side streets. Handsomely finished, all four apartments feature exposed beams and handmade tile floors and sleep either two to four people.

The two rear apartments overlook the wall of the Vatican from their private terraces. Contact: British Travel Associates, P. O. Box 299, Elkton, VA 22827. Call 1-800-327-8097 (in Virginia, 703-298-2232). Ref. R01, R10-12.

Children: Y   Pets: N   Smoking: Y   Handicap Access: N   Payment: All

LIGURIA

Cipressa

SUNNY VILLA   *Rates: budget-inexpensive*
Open: year-round   *Minimum Stay: one week*

Outside the small village of Cipressa, surrounded by trees and quiet streets, is this private, sun-filled abode. A spacious living and dining room, a full kitchen and a bathroom with a shower are located on the first floor; upstairs are another bathroom (with a bath), three pretty bedrooms and a balcony with stunning views of the sea. The lush, fragrant garden will tempt you to laze about in idyllic seclusion, but don't miss the lovely pebble beaches and warm waters only a few miles away. There are some small shops and restaurants in the village and more gregarious souls find San Remo and Imperia conveniently close. Contact: Interhome Inc., 124 Little Falls Rd., Fairfield, NJ 07004. Call 201-882-6864. Ref. I1785/1.

Children: Y   Pets: Y   Smoking: Y   Handicap Access: N   Payment: P, V, M

Pietra Ligure

ALTAIR   *Rates: moderate*
Open: year-round   *Minimum Stay: one week*

Around Pietra Ligure, the Ligurian coastline becomes a bit rockier and more rugged; correspondingly, the scenery grows more breathtakingly beautiful. The Altair with its apartment for five occupies a tranquil, sunny spot on the outskirts of town. The kitchen is unusually spacious and includes an oven and a dining table; a living and dining room equipped with a TV and divan bed, a large bedroom and a bathroom with a bathtub round out the accommodations. The apartment boasts both a balcony and a small patio. Genoa is less than an hour away, but lively Pietra Ligure offers plenty of amusement; after a game of tennis or a few tries at water skiing, enjoy a cappuccino at one of the small cafes or take a stroll along the seaside promenade. Contact: Interhome Inc., 124 Little Falls Rd., Fairfield, NJ 07004. Call 201-882-6864. Ref. I1910/1A.

Children: Y   Pets: Y   Smoking: Y   Handicap Access: N   Payment: P, V, M

Rapallo

PEIRANO   *Rates: budget-inexpensive*
Open: year-round   *Minimum Stay: one week*

Protected from rough winds and stormy seas by its sheltered bay-side location, Rapallo is a friendly resort town with all the corresponding amenities. You can learn to sail or brush up on your tennis here, or maybe just enjoy a glass of vino and some local seafood in one of the many cheerful restaurants. The Peirano is set on a hill outside of town, with a lovely view of the bay. With both a generous balcony and a pretty terrace, the first-floor apartment (part of a two-family house) is a welcoming abode for four people. The furnishings are modern and comfortable and the kitchen is fully equipped with an oven. Outside you'll find a charming garden, and the town and beaches are a brisk walk away. Contact: Interhome Inc., 124 Little Falls Rd., Fairfield, NJ 07004. Call 201-882-6864. Ref. I5050/1B.

Children: Y   Pets: Y   Smoking: Y   Handicap Access: N   Payment: P, V, M

San Remo
PIAN DELLA CASTAGLIA   *Rates: budget*
Open: year-round   *Minimum Stay: one week*

Stately San Remo is one of the oldest resorts on the Italian Riviera, as its elegant old holiday houses and thriving tourist business attest. The town delights visitors with tennis, golf and cable car rides, not to mention its lovely beaches, warm weather and lush flora. Perched on a sunny hillside on the outskirts of town, the Pian della Castaglia is removed from the crowds but still convenient to the fun. Every apartment has a private terrace and enjoys a lovely view; many face the sea and San Remo. The well-equipped apartments can accommodate between two and four people and are centrally heated. Contact: Interhome Inc., 124 Little Falls Rd., Fairfield, NJ 07004. Call 201-882-6864. Ref. I1750/40A, /41A, /42A.

Children: Y   Pets: Y   Smoking: Y   Handicap Access: N   Payment: P, V, M

Ventimiglia
VILLA GRAZIA   *Rates: budget*
Open: year-round   *Minimum Stay: one week*

Gateway to the Italian Riviera, lovely Ventimiglia is only six miles from the French border. Cafes and charming restaurants abound on the friendly streets and the town boasts some interesting Roman ruins. Located in a quiet, sunny nook near a shady woods on the outskirts, the Villa Grazia enjoys fine views of the sea and town. The downstairs apartment is for three people. There is a divan bed in the simply furnished living and dining room, and the kitchen comes complete with an oven. French doors in the pleasant double bedroom open onto the splendid garden. The upstairs apartment for five has an additional bedroom and its generous terrace overlooks the garden. Contact: Interhome Inc., 124 Little Falls Rd., Fairfield, NJ 07004. Call 201-882-6864. Ref. I1710/10A, /11B

Children: Y   Pets: Y   Smoking: Y   Handicap Access: N   Payment: P, V, M

LOMBARDY

Brezzo di Bedero
TERRACE HOUSES   *Rates: budget*
Open: May-November   *Minimum Stay: one week*

Only a couple of miles from the beaches of Lago Maggiore, but splendidly placed on a hillside above the lake, these cozy houses for four people combine privacy with convenience. Each of the three independent houses on the outskirts of town includes a living/dining room with a convertible bed, a double bedroom, a kitchen and a balcony. The houses are wonderful bases for pleasant excursions around the lake and lovely hikes through the countryside. The area also offers water sports, tennis and riding, as well as festive diversions in nearby Luino. Contact: Interhome Inc., 124 Little Falls Rd., Fairfield, NJ 07004. Call 201-882-6864. Ref. I2084/4, /5, /6.

Children: Y   Pets: Y   Smoking: Y   Handicap Access: N   Payment: P, V, M

Como

MONTE OLIMPINO APARTMENT   *Rates: budget*
Open: year-round   *Minimum Stay: one week*

A cosmopolitan city placed between cool, deep waters and the soaring Alps, Como greets visitors with a lively array of holiday amusements. Theaters, restaurants, discos and shops all create a festive atmosphere. Sports enthusiasts esteem Como's tennis, golf and water sport opportunities. Or you can enjoy one of the pleasant hikes and excursions around lovely Lake Como, its shores adorned with olives and figs. Near to the action, but removed from the bustle, is this comfy apartment for two. The house is set on a quiet, sunny hillside by a small woods and enjoys a beautiful view of the mountains. The third-story apartment has a furnished balcony for enjoying the scenery and one of its three rooms is heated. Contact: Interhome Inc., 124 Little Falls Rd., Fairfield, NJ 07004. Call 201-882-6864. Ref. I2400/1C.

Children: Y   Pets: N   Smoking: Y   Handicap Access: N   Payment: P, V, M

Limone s/Garda

GARDA PANORAMA   *Rates: budget*
Open: April-November   *Minimum Stay: one week*

This charming house for five is part of a well-groomed holiday village with lovely views of Lake Garda and the valley. The village's facilities comprise two swimming pools, four tennis courts, a pretty garden and a wide-open lawn for sunning and games. The house includes a tastefully furnished living and dining room with a divan bed, two bedrooms, a kitchenette and a terrace. The old fishing village of Limone is found on the western shore of the lake and delights visitors with its mild climate, sunny beaches, abundant water sports and atmospheric taverns. Every summer the festivity is heightened when the amusement park opens its gates. Contact: Interhome Inc., 124 Little Falls Rd., Fairfield, NJ 07004. Call 201-882-6864. Ref. I2853/10.

Children: Y   Pets: Y   Smoking: Y   Handicap Access: N   Payment: P, V, M

Livigno

LA FONTE   *Rates: budget-inexpensive*
Open: year-round   *Minimum Stay: one week*

A lovely alpine village studded with quaint wooden houses, Livigno amuses active visitors with hiking, tennis, fishing and, of course, with skiing on the Diavolezza and the Stilfserjoch. Dedicated shoppers will be overwhelmed with the town's low prices, the product of its status as a free-trade region. La Fonte is located just outside of town on a sunny slope with a breathtaking mountain view. The two- and four-person apartments are tastefully furnished and centrally heated. Both feature balconies for enjoying the splendid scenery. Contact: Interhome Inc., 124 Little Falls Rd., Fairfield, NJ 07004. Call 201-882-6864. Ref. I3430/150B, /151C.

Children: Y   Pets: Y   Smoking: Y   Handicap Access: N   Payment: P, V, M

Luino

LAKESIDE APARTMENT   *Rates: budget-inexpensive*
Open: April-November   *Minimum Stay: one week*

Tucked away in a sun-drenched spot outside of town, this large apartment is half of a two-family house. The accommodations for six include separate living and dining rooms, an eat-in kitchen, two double bedrooms and an additional room with two wall trunk beds. Outside, the lawn, large garden and patio with furniture will tempt you to bask in the sun and enjoy the magnificent views of Lago Maggiore. But if you do wander into town, you'll find that Luino, a popular resort on the eastern shore of the lake, features opportunities for swimming, riding, tennis, water skiing and sailing, not to mention tempting shops and convivial restaurants. Contact: Interhome Inc., 124 Little Falls Rd., Fairfield, NJ 07004. Call 201-882-6864. Ref. I12088/1B

Children: Y   Pets: Y   Smoking: Y   Handicap Access: N   Payment: P, V, M

Malcesine

L'ERTA   *Rates: expensive-deluxe*
Open: year-round   *Minimum Stay: two weeks*

Situated in the lively town of Malcesine on the shore of Lake Garda, this beautiful villa boasts a quiet, residential address surrounded by other villas. Just a short walk from the historic center of town, the villa offers wonderful views of the lake and the small island "Di Sogna." Its grounds feature sprawling outdoor spaces, a barbecue and a large swimming pool with diving board and dressing room. In the open and luminous living/dining room, enjoy the handsome fireplace and long terrace overlooking the lake. Five will sleep comfortably in this carefully furnished and centrally heated home. From this location central to northern Italy, take car trips to the splendid cities of Mantua or Verona, or travel by ferry or hydrofoil to other cities along the lake. Contact: Posarelli Vacations (Cuendet Italia), 180 Kinderamack Road, Park Ridge, NJ 07656. Call 201-573-9558. Ref. 4.01.03.

Children: Y   Pets: N   Smoking: Y   Handicap Access: N   Payment: C, P, T

Mezzegra

VILLAGE HOUSE   *Rates: inexpensive-moderate*
Open: year-round   *Minimum Stay: one week*

Located in a bright, quiet spot on the outskirts of a small village, this pleasant house offers guests glorious views of Lake Como. Beneath the tiled roof you'll find a modern kitchen complete with a dishwasher, three bedrooms accommodating six people, a TV, two bathrooms and a cheery fireplace in the living and dining room (the house is heated). Outside is a partially covered terrace and a large private garden with a patio and furniture; household help can be hired. In town are ample opportunities for enjoying the warm waters of Lago di Como, from sunning and fishing to water skiing and wind-surfing. Contact: Interhome Inc., 124 Little Falls Rd., Fairfield, NJ 07004. Call 201-882-6864. Ref. I2427/3.

Children: Y   Pets: Y   Smoking: Y   Handicap Access: N   Payment: P, V, M

Porto Valtravaglia

MONTE SOLEIL   *Rates: budget*
Open: April-November   *Minimum Stay: one week*

A peaceful gem in Italy's stunning lake country, Lago Maggiore offers the same warm breezes, breathtaking landscape and crystalline waters that have lured visitors for centuries. The Monte Soleil lies on a quiet, sunny slope in a small village on the lake; it enjoys marvelous views and the lake's waters lap the shingle beach just a few yards away. The three or four people who stay in the complex's three-room houses will appreciate the roomy terraces complete with garden furniture for enjoying the surroundings; one unit even has a barbecue for a bit of outdoor grilling, Italian-style. Contact: Interhome Inc., 124 Little Falls Rd., Fairfield, NJ 07004. Call 201-882-6864. Ref. I2082/4, /5.

Children: Y   Pets: Y   Smoking: Y   Handicap Access: N   Payment: P, V, M

Sirmione

COLOMBARE APARTMENTS   *Rates: budget-inexpensive*
Open: April-November   *Minimum Stay: one week*

Romantic Sirmione is found on a lovely peninsula at the southern end of Lake Garda. The town's venerable pedigree—it's been a health resort since Roman times—has given it several interesting historic sites. The sports-minded crowd will appreciate the hiking, tennis, boating, water skiing, windsurfing, fishing and miniature golf that the town can provide. The two compact apartments (suitable for four people each) are located on a sunny side street near the shops, restaurants and beach. Each apartment has a living and dining room with a TV and a convertible bed, an additional twin bedroom and a kitchen with a dishwasher. Contact: Interhome Inc., 124 Little Falls Rd., Fairfield, NJ 07004. Call 201-882-6864. Ref. I2811/11A, /11B.

Children: Y   Pets: Y   Smoking: Y   Handicap Access: N   Payment: P, V, M

MARCHES

Urbania

CA' MANGANO   *Rates: deluxe*
Open: June 1-September 30   *Minimum Stay: one week*

Dating from 1500, this dignified villa rests amid a vast orchard of ancient oaks in an area steeped in history. Journeys to renowned villages in the region, like Urbino, Gubbio, Spello and Assisi, take visitors past gorgeous unspoiled countryside. With well-tended grounds highlighted by a garden swimming pool, the splendid three-story house includes a studio, dining room, sitting room and entrance hall on the ground floor; a library, four bedrooms and a grand hallway perfect for parties on the second; and two additional bedrooms on the third. Contact: Villas and Apartments Abroad Ltd, 420 Madison Ave, New York, NY 10017. Call 212-759-1025 or 1-800-433-3020.

Children: Y   Pets: Y   Smoking: Y   Handicap Access: N   Payment: C, P, T

PIEDMONT

Sestriere

GRANGESISES
Open: year-round

Rates: inexpensive
Minimum Stay: one week

Sestriere is an elegant, modern sports center near the French border, whose excellent location affords pleasant mountain hikes in summer and plenty of ski action in winter. In addition to over 70 miles of ski runs are a ski school and an ice rink. The Grangesises is just outside of town and conveniently contains a grocery store and a restaurant. The one-, two- and three-room apartments can sleep up to six in their cozy accommodations, and a picturesque mountain railway will carry you right into town. Contact: Interhome Inc., 124 Little Falls Rd., Fairfield, NJ 07004. Call 201-882-6864. Ref: I3250/10A, /12B, /13A.

Children: Y   Pets: N   Smoking: Y   Handicap Access: N   Payment: P, V, M

SARDINIA

Baia Sardinia

LILLA
Open: year-round

Rates: inexpensive-expensive
Minimum Stay: one week

Enjoy the rugged beauty of Sardinia from a splendid one-bedroom, one-bathroom apartment which accommodates a third guest on a single divan in the living room. This cluster of ground-floor apartments, each with a balcony, terrace, well-tended garden and spectacular view of the sea, is furnished in the high standard that has become a trademark of the area's style. Fine shops, restaurants and nightspots are nearby—although a car is essential since there is no public transportation. The main beach at the center of Baia Sardinia is a short half-mile away and a delightful sandy cove is a four-minute walk down the road. Contact: Hometours International, Inc., 1170 Broadway, New York, NY 10001. Call: 212-689-0851 or 1-800-367-4668. Ref: 3116.

Children: Y   Pets: N   Smoking: Y   Handicap Access: N   Payment: C, P, T

Baia Sardinia

VILLA CHRISTINA
Open: year-round

Rates: inexpensive-expensive
Minimum Stay: one week

This whitewashed, two-story villa comfortably accommodates up to five people in two bedrooms and the living room. The living/dining room features an open fireplace and direct access to both the kitchen—which contains a washing machine—and a spacious terrace facing the sea. Here you can enjoy gracious al fresco dining after a day at the beach just a few steps down the road. If you're more ambitious, visit the fine tennis club and wind-surfing facilities available during July and August. Contact: Hometours International, Inc., 1170 Broadway, New York, NY 10001. Call: 212-689-0851 or 1-800-367-4668. Ref. 3116/7.

Children: **Y** Pets: **N** Smoking: **Y** Handicap Access: **N** Payment: **C, P, T**

Porto Rafael

LA CONCA MAISONETTES *Rates: inexpensive-expensive*
Open: year-round *Minimum Stay: one week*

"Les Maisonettes" are delightfully terraced mini-villas located a half-mile down the road from the piazza of Porto Rafael. Set on elevated terrain amid a dense profusion of shrubs, plants and bougainvillaea, each one-bedroom, one-bathroom villa accommodates up to three in one double bed and a single divan in the living-dining room. A private terrace offers breathtaking views of Porto Rafael and the Mediterranean less than half a mile away. Although a highly regarded tennis club is just across the road, a car is virtually essential to enjoy the area to the fullest. Ask about special car rental discounts. Contact: Hometours International, Inc., 1170 Broadway, New York, NY 10001. Call: 212-689-0851 or 1-800-367-4668. Ref. 3117.

Children: **Y** Pets: **N** Smoking: **Y** Handicap Access: **N** Payment: **C, P, T**

Porto Rafael

VILLA FEDI *Rates: inexpensive-expensive*
Open: year-round *Minimum Stay: one week*

This superb bungalow villa—one of the area's loveliest—accommodates a maximum of five people in three bedrooms. The house is built at the water's edge and wide stone steps lead directly to a private mooring for a dinghy or a small boat. Beautifully furnished and decorated with great style, Villa Fedi features a lovely private terrace with views of the Mediterranean and the piazza of Porto Rafael. Sun worshippers can walk the four short blocks to the beach or luxuriate in the villa's rooftop solarium. The living room/dining room has direct access to both the terrace and the kitchen, which has a washing machine and a dishwasher. Contact: Hometours International, Inc., 1170 Broadway, New York, NY 10001. Call: 212-689-0851 or 1-800-367-4668. Ref. 3117/4.

Children: **Y** Pets: **N** Smoking: **Y** Handicap Access: **N** Payment: **C, P, T**

San Pantaleo

TERRACE HOUSE *Rates: moderate-expensive*
Open: year-round *Minimum Stay: one week*

The tiny resort of San Pantaleo offers its visitors the same lovely beaches as its larger cousins do, but without the crowds and noise. This charming terrace house, with its tiled roof and well-cultivated garden, is picturesquely located on a dusty road outside the village; many rooms enjoy stunning views of the sea. The main floor has a living room with a handsome fireplace, two bedrooms, a kitchen complete with an oven and a dishwasher and a lovely terrace. Upstairs is another living room and two more bedrooms; one of these opens onto a small sunny terrace. Another bedroom on the lower level means the house can easily lodge ten guests. A short walk will bring you to the town's shops, restaurants and nightspots, and the sandy beaches are only a little further. Contact: Interhome Inc., 124 Little Falls Rd., Fairfield, NJ 07004. Call 201-882-6864. Ref. I7170/1.

Children: Y   Pets: Y   Smoking: Y   Handicap Access: N   Payment: P, V, M

Vecchie Saline

SEA VIEW APARTMENTS   *Rates: inexpensive*
Open: year-round   *Minimum Stay: one week*

Only a few miles from the bustling port of Olbia, the holiday village of Vecchie Saline is both a splendid seaside haunt and a good base for exploring Sardinia's more rugged hinterland. The town boasts marvelous views of the surrounding bays and cliffs and long stretches of sandy and rocky beaches. The apartment house features a central location, lovely sea views and a bocce alley for a friendly game. Several three- and four-room apartments can accommodate either four or six guests in their cozy lodgings. Guests receive reserved parking spots. Just down the road a bit, pleasant little restaurants beckon. Contact: Interhome Inc., 124 Little Falls Rd., Fairfield, NJ 07004. Call 201-882-6864. Ref. I7200/1C, /5B, /8B, /15B.

Children: Y   Pets: Y   Smoking: Y   Handicap Access: N   Payment: P, V, M

SICILY

Cefalu

PLAIA   *Rates: budget-moderate*
Open: year-round   *Minimum Stay: two weeks*

From this charming hilltop retreat you can marvel at the views of sea and the surrounding countryside, thick with willowy trees and exotic cactus. The small house for six features a living/dining room and a tiled kitchen, plus one double and two twin bedrooms. The shady yard offers a barbecue and a table for outdoor dining. You will find small beaches about a mile from the house and the long sandy beaches of the seaside town of Cefalu four miles away. Here, you will enjoy access to a variety of water sports, views of the city's Arab, Norman and medieval architecture and a starting point for an excursion to Palermo. Contact: Posarelli Vacations (Cuendet Italia), 180 Kinderamack Road, Park Ridge, NJ 07656. Call 201-573-9558. Ref. 8.01.12.

Children: Y   Pets: Y   Smoking: Y   Handicap Access: N   Payment: C, P, T

Cefalu

SEACLIFF   *Rates: inexpensive-moderate*
Open: year-round   *Minimum Stay: two weeks*

A vacation in this simply furnished apartment may give you the feeling of having spent your time aboard a boat: The living room balcony and windows face the sea and offer an unobstructed view of the peaceful water. The third-floor apartment sleeps three in one divan bed and one double bedroom and features a cozy fireplace. In addition to the pleasures of the water and the sand, Cefalu mounts a lively summer music and dance festival; numerous outdoor discos make this an especially festive spot for a holiday. Contact: Posarelli Vacations (Cuendet Italia), 180 Kinderamack Road, Park Ridge, NJ 07656. Call 201-573-9558. Ref. 8.01.21.

Children: Y   Pets: Y   Smoking: Y   Handicap Access: N   Payment: C, P, T

Lampedusa

DUSA   *Rates: deluxe*
Open: year-round   *Minimum Stay: two weeks*

You can walk from this beautiful modern villa right onto the sandy and rocky beach at your doorstep and feel the sea kiss your bare feet. Located on a small bay on the Sicilian isle of Lampedusa, the home offers shimmering views of the sea and the bay from each of two terraces, which are made inviting with plenty of deck furniture. The house sleeps six in two twin bedrooms and two small sun beds and also features a large living/dining room with contemporary furniture and a TV. When you tire of the sound of the gentle waves washing over the rocks below, you can rent mopeds or a boat to explore the beauty of the interior or the coast of this beautiful island. Contact: Posarelli Vacations (Cuendet Italia), 180 Kinderamack Road, Park Ridge, NJ 07656. Call 201-573-9558. Ref. 8.01.01.

Children: Y   Pets: N   Smoking: Y   Handicap Access: N   Payment: C, P, T

Polizzi Generosa

SCANNALE   *Rates: deluxe*
Open: June 1-September 30   *Minimum Stay: one week*

Two thousand feet above sea level at the foot of the Madonie, the most famous mountains on the island, this 19th-century Sicilian baglio sits surrounded by trees and olive groves overlooking the fertile valley of Scillato. The residence features a beautiful Mediterranean garden with a swimming pool. The two-story house contains an entrance hall, kitchen, dining room, studio and six bedrooms to accommodate a large group in style. Parts of the film *The Sicilian* were shot here on this working farm, which produces vegetables, cheese and eggs that may be purchased by guests. Contact: Villas and Apartments Abroad Ltd, 420 Madison Ave, New York, NY 10017. Call 212-759-1025 or 1-800-433-3020.

Children: Y   Pets: Y   Smoking: Y   Handicap Access: N   Payment: C, P, T

Sciacca

CASA DE LA GRUYERE   *Rates: budget*
Open: year-round   *Minimum Stay: one week*

Sciacca is a small village with a big past. Like the rest of Sicily, there are abundant reminders here of the many empires—Greek, Roman, Saracen, Norman and Spanish—that have conquered the island and then faded away. Today Sciacca lures less violent visitors with its marvelous thermal spa, luxurious climate and sandy beaches. Tucked away on a quiet, private road outside of town, the Casa de la Gruyere is on the water's edge and enjoys lovely views of the sea. The four-room apartment for five occupies the first floor of a two-family house and features a large, shaded veranda. If a stroll through the garden doesn't sate your appetite for natural beauties, a hike through the countryside will. Contact: Interhome Inc., 124 Little Falls Rd., Fairfield, NJ 07004. Call 201-882-6864. Ref. I9250/1A.

Children: Y   Pets: Y   Smoking: Y   Handicap Access: N   Payment: P, V, M

Taormina

18TH-CENTURY HOUSE   *Rates: expensive-deluxe*
Open: year-round   *Minimum Stay: one week*

This handsome old house set among expansive gardens has been fully renovated to accommodate up to 12 guests. Upstairs you'll find a pleasant living room boasting an open fireplace and an attractive archway leading to the separate dining room. The fully equipped kitchen and two bedrooms are also found on this floor. Outside is a marvelous terrace framed by lush trees and featuring a nice stairway that leads downstairs. Four bedrooms are located on the ground floor. The house enjoys wonderful views of the sea and Taormina's famous Greco-Roman Theater. The rocky beaches of Sicily's glorious coastline are only a couple of miles away. Contact: Interhome Inc., 124 Little Falls Rd., Fairfield, NJ 07004. Call 201-882-6864. Ref. I9649/10.

Children: Y   Pets: Y   Smoking: Y   Handicap Access: N   Payment: P, V, M

Terasini

VENERE   *Rates: budget-inexpensive*
Open: year-round   *Minimum Stay: two weeks*

Situated at the eastern end of the graceful Gulf of Castelammare, these three vacation rentals enjoy great privacy while still being only minutes from the sea and the conveniences of a small town. Two villa apartments accommodate either three or six and feature breathtaking views of the gulf from several terraces. A small house for five also features a long terrace and shares the delights of beautifully landscaped gardens and pathways, two swimming pools (one for adults and one for children) and a small tennis court. From this location, you can enjoy excursions to Palermo, a city rich with history and famous for its Norman-Saracen architecture, as well as the popular beach town of Cefalu. Contact: Posarelli Vacations (Cuendet Italia), 180 Kinderamack Road, Park Ridge, NJ 07656. Call 201-573-9558. Ref. 8.01.2931.

Children: Y   Pets: Y   Smoking: Y   Handicap Access: N   Payment: C, P, T

Trabia

IBISCUS   *Rates: deluxe*
Open: June 1-September 30   *Minimum Stay: one week*

Ibiscus is a handsome, traditional Sicilian farmhouse located on a hill on the island's north coast. The village of Trabia with its famous castle lies below about two miles away. Other top attractions, including Bagheria and the capital city of Palermo, are also within easy reach. The residence is situated on the second floor of the house and features a sitting room/dining area, kitchen, four bedrooms and a huge terrace with a splendid view of the sea. In front of the house is an elegant courtyard with an antique fountain; beyond it, a swimming pool is nestled among the palm trees. Contact: Villas and Apartments Abroad Ltd, 420 Madison Avenue, New York, NY 10017. Call 212-759-1025 or 1-800-433-3020.

Children: Y Pets: Y Smoking: Y Handicap Access: N Payment: C, P, T

Vittoria

CAMARINA *Rates: budget-moderate*
Open: year-round (villa not available in August) *Minimum Stay: two weeks*
Situated on the southeastern coast of Sicily, this lovely villa and smaller house share a handsomely outfitted courtyard and large garden thick with Mediterranean vegetation. The villa sleeps eight comfortably and features several terraces, many with views of the sparkling sea. The small house sleeps three in one double bedroom and a divan in the study and is complemented by its own large, covered terrace. From this sunny spot with its own beach, you can make pleasant excursions to the nearby cities of Siracuse and Noto, or explore the surrounding archeological area of Kamarina with its scattering of digs and small museums. Contact: Posarelli Vacations (Cuendet Italia), 180 Kinderamack Road, Park Ridge, NJ 07656. Call 201-573-9558. Ref. 8.01.27-8.

Children: Y Pets: Y Smoking: Y Handicap Access: N Payment: C, P, T

TRENTINO-ALTO ADIGE

Marilleva

MARILLEVA 1400 *Rates: budget*
Open: year-round *Minimum Stay: one week*
In the summer, the mild climate and splendid countryside around this modern resort tempt visitors to gratify their eyes and lungs by hiking through the nearby Stelvio and Adamello national parks. In the winter, numerous ski lifts, a ski school on the premises and the opportunity to ski right from the front door make this a skier's paradise. The Marilleva 1400 enjoys lovely views of the mountains and features its own swimming pool, sauna, shops, restaurant, bar and even hairdresser. The cozy two-room apartment for four people is pleasantly furnished and has a pretty balcony; the central heating and fitted carpets will make your apres-ski hours comfy. Contact: Interhome Inc., 124 Little Falls Rd., Fairfield, NJ 07004. Call 201-882-6864. Ref. I3650/103E.

Children: Y Pets: Y Smoking: Y Handicap Access: N Payment: P, V, M

Riva del Garda

BERETTA
Open: year-round

Rates: budget-inexpensive
Minimum Stay: one week

Riva del Garda is a cosmopolitan holiday town on Lake Garda. Surrounding the picturesque harbor and waterside promenade are cinemas, restaurants and discos; the sheltered bay allows a plethora of water sports before a stunning backdrop of rocky cliffs. The newly renovated Beretta is located on a quiet, sunny street near the harbor in the historic center of Riva. Each of the apartments can accommodate five guests; all include a combined living and dining room (with a convertible bed), a kitchenette and two double bedrooms. Although the conveniences of town are just around the corner, the solitude of nature can also be found nearby in lovely woods with walking paths. Contact: Interhome Inc., 124 Little Falls Rd., Fairfield, NJ 07004. Call 201-882-6864. Ref. I2859/1B, /1C, /2B.

Children: Y   Pets: Y   Smoking: Y   Handicap Access: N   Payment: P, V, M

Riva del Garda

VILLA MONTE BRIONE
Open: year-round

Rates: budget-inexpensive
Minimum Stay: one week

High above Lake Garda's blue waters on the lush slopes of Monte Brione is this charming two-family house with marvelous views of the lake and the city of Riva. The pleasant ground-floor apartment features a stylishly furnished living and dining room, an eat-in kitchen complete with an oven, two bedrooms (sleeping four) and a very large, partially covered terrace with garden furniture. A TV, a washing machine and central heating add modern convenience to this resort getaway. If you tire of basking in the sun or wandering along the nature paths near the villa, the boat harbor and beach are just around the corner and the rest of Riva's attractions are only a couple of miles away. Contact: Interhome Inc., 124 Little Falls Rd., Fairfield, NJ 07004. Call 201-882-6864. Ref. I2859/3A, /15C, /15D, /16D.

Children: Y   Pets: Y   Smoking: Y   Handicap Access: N   Payment: P, V, M

Torbole s/Garda

AURELIA
Open: year-round

Rates: budget-inexpensive
Minimum Stay: one week

Torbole and its resplendent environs provide many lovely walks and hikes, a wide variety of water sports, angling opportunities, sunny beaches and the convivial atmosphere of a small resort town. Tucked away with the other villas in the wooded hills above Torbole, the Aurelia boasts its own swimming pool. The ground-floor apartment for four includes two bedrooms, a full kitchen complete with an oven and a tasteful living and dining room; both the living room and kitchen open onto a pleasant terrace. Torbole is about a mile away, but Aurelia's guests can reach it on foot in a few minutes by following a little footpath down the hill. Contact: Interhome Inc., 124 Little Falls Rd., Fairfield, NJ 07004. Call 201-882-6864. Ref. I2861/5A.

Children: Y   Pets: Y   Smoking: Y   Handicap Access: N   Payment: P, V, M

TUSCANY

Ancano, Lucignano

VILLA ANCANELLA *Rates: moderate-expensive*
Open: year-round *Minimum Stay: one week*

This beautifully renovated "casa colonia" lies midway between the splendors of Florence and Perugia only a short distance from Lake Trasimeno, where swimming, sailing and wind-surfing await you. Closer to home, a sunflower field in the front of the house and a restful garden behind the house offer welcome repose. Pass through a covered terrace into the ground floor of the house, which is dominated by a kitchen/dining room with an open fireplace and a living room with French windows opening onto the terrace. As you ascend to the second floor, pass a large landing with a fireplace and a terrace. Bedrooms on the second and third floors include two twin and one double. The house is centrally heated. Contact: British Travel Associates, P. O. Box 299, Elkton, VA 22827. Call 1-800-327-8097 (in Virginia, 703-298-2232). Ref. IT29

Children: N   Pets: N   Smoking: Y   Handicap Access: N   Payment: All

Anghiari

COUNTRY COTTAGE *Rates: inexpensive-expensive*
Open: year-round *Minimum Stay: one week*

Perched high in the hills with fantastic views of the rugged landscape of rocks, woods and pasture, this charming cottage has the added advantage of the cool, fresh air its altitude affords. Outside brick stairs lead to this simple, unpretentious home for four to six people adjoining the house of the tenant farmer, whose chickens, sheep and friendly Old English sheep dogs wander around freely. The country atmosphere continues in the eat-in kitchen, with its large open fireplace and living room with plenty of comfortable seating. Two bedrooms, a double and twin, along with living room sofa beds, provide ample accommodations for up to six people. Use the pool at the owners' castle or rent horses to explore the countryside. Contact: B & D de Vogue International, Inc., 1830 S. Mooney Blvd. Ste. 203, Visalia, CA 93277. Call 209-733-7119 or 1-800-727-4748. Ref. IT 73.

Children: Y Pets: N Smoking: Y Handicap Access: N Payment: P, A, V, M

Arezzo

CAPITELLO *Rates: moderate-expensive*
Open: year-round *Minimum Stay: two weeks*

Here at this spacious villa restored under the direction of a famous Italian artist, you can bask in the golden Tuscan sun on the wooden terrace, wade in the nearby river or stroll among the several gardens on the property. Inside, a spacious living/dining room with fireplace, two drawing rooms and sleeping accommodations for six afford the comfort and warmth of wood-beamed ceilings and whitewashed walls. A short drive will find you in the city of Arezzo, where Italy's largest Gothic cathedral stands and art collections include the works of Fra

Angelico and Signorelli. Recent area digs have unearthed many Etruscan wonders; for the collector, the antique fair is held in Arezzo on the first Sunday of every month. Contact: Posarelli Vacations (Cuendet Italia), 180 Kinderamack Road, Park Ridge, N.J. 07656. Call 201-573-9558. Ref. 1.20.02.

Children: Y   Pets: N   Smoking: Y   Handicap Access: N   Payment: C, P, T

Arezzo

IL MULINO   *Rates: inexpensive-moderate*
Open: year-round   *Minimum Stay: one week*

There could be nothing more romantic than this enchantingly isolated old water mill converted into a spacious studio apartment for two. Nestled in the hills east of the Chianti district and only twenty minutes north of the beautiful city of Arezzo, this charming hideaway borders a lake where you may swim and, with the owner's permission, pretend to fish while you count clouds or bird calls. Simply laid out on one level, the house includes a sitting area with a fireplace and a double convertible bed and a kitchen/dining area, both with lovely views of the lake. There can be no more private retreat than this, and yet, all the riches of Tuscany and her jewelled cities lie within easy reach. Contact: Vacances Provencales Vacations, 729 Cutter Lane, Elk Grove, IL 60007. Call 708-893-9402. Ref. 306.

Children: Y   Pets: Y   Smoking: Y   Handicap Access: N   Payment: P

Arezzo

VILLA DI COZZANO   *Rates: expensive-deluxe*
Open: April 28-September 28   *Minimum Stay: one week*

Rising from the middle of a lovely park and surrounded by its own private grounds, this peaceful villa is situated in Valdichiana, an area of great cultural interest and natural beauty. The villa's furnishings are typical of a Tuscan country home—functional, comfortable and in good taste. Inviting and restful, the spacious living room, with three arches, white walls and terra-cotta floors, constitutes the center of daily life. Also on the ground floor are an entrance hall, a kitchen/breakfast room and a dining room. Upstairs is another living room, a single and three double bedrooms, as well as two baths. Guests can use a large swimming pool on the grounds, and the villa's location offers the possibility of numerous excursions throughout central Italy. Contact: Europa-Let, PO Box 3537, Ashland, OR 97520. Call 1-800-462-4486 or 503-482-1442. Ref. Solemar C.10.

Children: Y   Pets: N   Smoking: Y   Handicap Access: N   Payment: C, P, T

Asciano/Siena

PODERUCCIO   *Rates: inexpensive-moderate*
Open: year-round   *Minimum Stay: one week*

This especially charming farm setting, entirely fenced to provide privacy, is set atop a hillside. The spacious, converted two-story farmhouse enjoys the rich surroundings of a small farm that cultivates both olive trees and vineyards. Views from many of the windows offer a spectacular look over the Crete Senesi. The owner visits from time to time to water the garden and offer his farm products to guests. The house offers accommodations for four in one double and one twin bedroom, as well as two living rooms and a dining room with three fireplaces. Guests will take special pleasure in the furnished stone-paved courtyard and garden. Less than an hour's drive to nearly every attraction Tuscany offers, this generous home in a beautiful country setting promises a holiday to remember. Contact: Rent A Home International, 7200 34th Avenue, N.W., Seattle, WA 98117. 1-206-545-6963. Ref. 11.16.01.

Children: Y Pets: N Smoking: Y Handicap Access: N Payment: C, P, V, M

Bacheretto

TUSCAN FATTORIA   *Rates: moderate-deluxe*
Open: year-round   *Minimum Stay: one week*

Situated in the heart of the Tuscan countryside amid rolling hills covered with olive groves and vineyards, this traditional fattoria, or farm, evokes a peaceful feeling that comes from being close to the land. A rambling complex of stuccoed buildings with tile roofs houses a range of uniquely charming rental units, from an apartment for two to four people to a detached farmhouse sleeping fifteen. The owners produce excellent wines and olive oil, as well as fragrant honey and wild fruit preserves, which can be enjoyed at breakfast in the enormous old kitchen of the villa. A superb restaurant located in an old mill that was once the home of Leonardo da Vinci's grandmother is one of the highlights of a visit here. Contact: B & D de Vogue International, Inc., 1830 S. Mooney Blvd. Ste. 203, Visalia, CA 93277. Call 209-733-7119 or 1-800-727-4748. Ref. IT 90, 91, 92, 93.

Children: Y Pets: N Smoking: Y Handicap Access: N Payment: P, A, V, M

Barberino Val d'Elsa

PALAZETTO COVONI   *Rates: inexpensive*
Open: year-round   *Minimum Stay: one week*

This handsomely furnished apartment occupies the second floor of a 14th-century house in the small village of Barberino Val d'Elsa, where the well-known Pasolini wines are produced. A large terrace and typically shuttered windows afford breathtaking views of the surrounding Chianti hills. Two twin bedrooms and one single, a kitchen and the living/dining room with an open fireplace and exposed beams make up this hillside rental. A short drive brings you to Siena, Florence or the 13 medieval towers of San Gimignano. A fine local trattoria is only a brisk twenty-minute walk from the apartment. Contact: British Travel Associates, P. O. Box 299, Elkton, VA 22827. Call 1-800-327-8097 (in Virginia, 703-298-2232). Ref. IT45.

Children: Y Pets: N Smoking: Y Handicap Access: N Payment: All

Barberino Val d'Elsa

SEMIFONTE   Rates: inexpensive-expensive
Open: year-round   Minimum Stay: one week

This ancient tower, partially renovated and divided into three apartments, sits peacefully amidst hills and cultivated fields. The owners have furnished the whole place with sculptures and paintings. Choose from a spacious three-bedroom apartment with a fireplace for up to seven, or a cozy one-bedroom unit that sleeps up to three. Both share a large, lovely garden with a barbecue and a built-in pool. The village is close by, as are tennis and riding facilities; Florence is just over 20 miles away. Contact: Europa-Let, PO Box 3537, Ashland, OR 97520. Call 1-800-462-4486 or 503-482-1442. Ref. Solemar 1.28.

Children: Y   Pets: N   Smoking: Y   Handicap Access: N   Payment: C, P, T

Bossi

FATTORIA DI BOSSI   Rates: budget-expensive
Open: year-round   Minimum Stay: one week

Situated in the Chianti hills and surrounded by vineyards and olive groves, this renovated stone farmhouse commands a wonderful view of Siena in the distance. The original character has been preserved in wooden ceilings, fireplaces and "cotto" floors, offering a rustic atmosphere. Simple and comfortable in the classic Tuscan country style, the furnishings in these eight modernized apartments for up to six create a relaxing atmosphere. Guests can enjoy the large swimming pool and the excellent wine produced in the Fattoria. The Tuscan countryside and the cities of Siena and Florence offer a wide range of touring opportunities. Contact: Europa-Let, PO Box 3537, Ashland, OR 97520. Call 1-800-462-4486 or 503-482-1442. Ref. Solemar 1.35.

Children: Y   Pets: N   Smoking: Y   Handicap Access: N   Payment: C, P, T

Camaiore

CASACCIA   Rates: budget-inexpensive
Open: April 28-November 2   Minimum Stay: one week

This stone farmhouse, surrounded by a large tract of private property, rests on the top of a hill overlooking the town of Camaiore on one side and the beaches of the Versilia coast on the other. Formerly the home of groundskeepers for the nearby villa, it is cozy and rustically furnished. The ground floor has an entrance hall, a kitchen/breakfast room with a fireplace, a living/dining room with a fireplace and a bath with a shower. Upstairs are a single and two double bedrooms. There is a small cobblestone courtyard at the front of the house, furnished with an umbrella table and chairs. Casaccia lies close to beaches and makes an excellent home base for touring the area. Contact: Europa-Let, PO Box 3537, Ashland, OR 97520. Call 1-800-462-4486 or 503-482-1442. Ref. Solemar 3.07.

Children: Y   Pets: N   Smoking: Y   Handicap Access: N   Payment: C, P, T

Canale/Porona

TRE QUERCE   *Rates: moderate-expensive*
Open: year-round   *Minimum Stay: one week*

Smack in the middle of Italy's luscious lake district, this recently renovated farmhouse assures guests a handsome vacation home within minutes of the Etruscan ruins of Ferentium and Bolsano, home of the famous Capidomnte porcelain, plus the ancient city of Orvieto. From its hilltop roost, the house offers sweeping views of the surrounding valleys. A comfortable vacation home for eight, the home features a large open living room with a fireplace, a study and a charming dining room with a characteristically warm stone wall. Romantic details of the master bedroom include a carved stone wash basin, a fireplace and a private terrace. Available to guests are maid service, central heating and firewood, all at extra charge. Contact: Rent A Home International, 7200 34th Avenue, N.W., Seattle, WA 98117. 1-206-545-6963. Ref. 14.03.01.

Children: Y Pets: N Smoking: Y Handicap Access: N Payment: C, P, V, M

Castagneto Carducci

VILLA MONTEPEREGOLI   *Rates: deluxe*
Open: year-round   *Minimum Stay: one week*

Grace and elegance mark this exquisite villa set in the Tuscan hills only a few miles from the coast. The nearby sandy beaches and Marina di Cecina, the several excellent area restaurants and even proximity to the attractions of Tuscany may not lure you away. Surrounded by landscaped grounds featuring an immense swimming pool and a large terrace overlooking the broad and sweeping valley below, this stunning house appeals to lovers of pleasure and beauty. Its two living rooms—one with a large television—and dining room are detailed with the finest furnishings and antiques. All five bedrooms offer fine views of the countryside amid comfort and luxury. Maid service and grounds care are included with the rental of this property. Contact: Vacances Provencales Vacations, 729 Cutter Lane, Elk Grove, IL 60007. Call 708-893-9402. Ref. 299.

Children: Y   Pets: Y   Smoking: Y   Handicap Access: N   Payment: P

Castellina in Chianti

CASALTA   *Rates: inexpensive-expensive*
Open: year-round   *Minimum Stay: one week*

Three sunny and spacious apartments occupy most of this newly restored farm building poised on a hillside and surrounded by rolling acres of vineyards. Handsomely appointed with the features traditional to Tuscan homes—whitewashed walls, terra-cotta floors and wood-beamed ceilings—the apartments for four to eight offer lovely furnishings and central heat as well as serene views of the beautiful Tuscan countryside. A new swimming pool built just below the house offers a sunning terrace where you can while away the days. Of course, with all of the Chianti district within minutes of your door and the cities of Siena, Florence and San Gimignano nearby, you may find yourself straying from home for a stroll in the gorgeous countryside or going on an excursion into medieval and Renaissance Italy. Contact: Vacances Provencales Vacations, 729 Cutter Lane, Elk Grove, IL 60007. Call 708-893-9402. Ref. 207-9.

Children: Y   Pets: Y   Smoking: Y   Handicap Access: N   Payment: P

Castellina in Chianti

CASTELLO DI TUOPINA   *Rates: deluxe*

Open: year-round   *Minimum Stay: one week*

Set atop a hill and surrounded by vineyards, this lordly country home features tended gardens and lawns, a swimming pool and a delightfully furnished gazebo. Details of the interior include a vaulted entrance with a splendid pietraserana staircase leading to the upper floors. The eat-in kitchen features a walk-in fireplace and the living/dining room is dramatically divided by three majestic arches. A master bedroom with heavy silk draperies and two other bedrooms sleep eight. Telephone and maid service are available, as well as central heating and firewood. Secluded down one of the many dirt roads that criss-cross the area yet convenient to the many cultural attractions the area boasts, this extraordinary home offers guests a heightened experience of comfort and indulgence. Contact: Rent A Home International, 7200 34th Avenue, N.W., Seattle, WA 98117. Call 1-206-545-6963. Ref. 6.01.01.

Children: Y Pets: N Smoking: Y Handicap Access: N Payment: C, P, V, M

Castellina in Chianti

RONDINELLA   *Rates: deluxe*

Open: May 24-September 27   *Minimum Stay: one week*

Though this excellent home offers easy access to the riches of Tuscany—you can be in Siena, Florence or San Gimignano in less than twenty minutes—you may never want to venture any further than the grounds and the Chianti hills that surround you. On a leisurely walk, you may pass the remains of an Etruscan well, or cross a running brook. Or you may while away the hours enjoying the stunning views from poolside. The rooms of this house, with their relaxed atmosphere and appointments, invite a family on vacation to feel genuinely at home. With sleeping accommodations for seven, the charm of a large dining room fireplace and a living room with a terrace, you may want to stir no further than the colorful and lively nearby village of Castellina in Chianti. Contact: British Travel Associates, P. O. Box 299, Elkton, VA 22827. Call 1-800-327-8097 (in Virginia, 703-298-2232). Ref. IT47.

Children: Y   Pets: N   Smoking: Y   Handicap Access: N   Payment: All

Castellina in Chianti

TRAMONTI   *Rates: budget-moderate*

Open: year-round   *Minimum Stay: one week*

Situated less than two miles from the small but lively town of Castellina in Chianti, this carefully restored apartment occupies part of the main farmhouse of a wine and olive-producing estate. Secluded down a private road surrounded by woodlands and vineyards, this remarkably quiet hilltop spot offers a panoramic view from Siena to San Gimignano. The house itself dates back to Roman times and features a section of original stone wall. The bedrooms (one double and one twin), dining room and living room with sofa bed are handsomely appointed with antiques in the Tuscan tradition. A short drive to Siena or Florence offers a world of natural and artistic riches, and your return home promises a barbecue in the garden or a cup of tea in the roomy eat-in kitchen. Contact: Rent A Home International, 7200 34th Avenue, N.W., Seattle, WA 98117. Call 1-206-545-6963. Ref. 6.07.01.

Children: Y Pets: N Smoking: Y Handicap Access: N Payment: C, P, V, M

Castelnuovo Berardenga

FARMHOUSE COTTAGES   *Rates: inexpensive-expensive*
Open: year-round   *Minimum Stay: two weeks preferred*

This romantic medieval castle perched high on a wooded promontory and commanding wide views of the countryside once harbored a viable community, including a one-room schoolhouse. Now, charming English-speaking owners live permanently in the main part of the castle and rent out the rest, some to permanent tenants, some to lucky vacationers like you. Four charming cottages are available, accommodating four to six people each, each with its own garden or terrace and all with access to the magnificent grounds, swimming pool and fishing stream. The owner sells wine, olive oil, eggs and fresh vegetables when available, and gives away fresh herbs to help add a country flavor to your cooking. Contact: B & D de Vogue International, Inc., 1830 S. Mooney Blvd. Ste. 203, Visalia, CA 93277. Call 209-733-7119 or 1-800-727-4748. Ref. IT 60, 61, 32, 34.

Children: Y Pets: N Smoking: Y Handicap Access: N Payment: P, A, V, M

Certaldo

LA CORTE DEI CAVALLI   *Rates: moderate*
Open: April-November   *Minimum Stay: one week*

Amidst vineyards and other greenery on a farm in the hills between Florence and Siena, this country house contains two apartments for four. The apartments share an entrance with a wood-burning oven and also enjoy access from the garden. Both apartments are quite rustic and simply furnished, but are very pleasant. Both have a kitchen/breakfast room with a fireplace, a twin and a double bedroom and a bathroom with a shower. In one, the double bedroom has an additional single bed. The farm has stables with ten horses for riding lessons or organized excursions, and its location makes it ideal for touring Tuscany, including Florence, Siena, San Gimignano and more. Contact: Europa-Let, PO Box 3537, Ashland, OR 97520. Call 1-800-462-4486 or 503-482-1442. Ref. Solemar 1.47.

Children: Y Pets: N Smoking: Y Handicap Access: N Payment: C, P, T

Certaldo

VILLA DI FONTI *Rates: deluxe*
Open: year-round *Minimum Stay: two weeks*

Once an active center of wine and olive oil production, Villa di Fonti is now a sumptuous residence for up to nine. Nestled among perfectly kept gardens in the heart of Tuscany, the building is over 300 years old but was recently remodeled and redecorated. An in-ground pool, a stereo system and a TV with a VCR guarantee guests' comfort. The spacious ground floor includes a large entrance hall with a fireplace, a dining room, living room, kitchen, twin bedroom and a full bath. Upstairs, guests find ample accommodations in a double, a single and two twin bedrooms, plus two baths. Maid service is included in the rental, and telephone is available upon request. The villa is located equidistant between Florence and Siena. Contact: Europa-Let, PO Box 3537, Ashland, OR 97520. Call 1-800-462-4486 or 503-482-1442. Ref. Solemar C.04.

Children: Y   Pets: N   Smoking: Y   Handicap Access: N   Payment: C, P, T

Chianti

IL FAGGETO *Rates: deluxe*
Open: June 30-September 1 *Minimum Stay: one week*

This immense stone farmhouse sits on a secluded hillside with sweeping views over the olive groves and vineyards of the valley below. The grounds include a vast lawn, graceful landscaped gardens and a swimming pool with a changing hut. Lavishly decorated with fine antique furniture and exceptional Italian artwork, the painstakingly restored three-floor house includes an extremely well-equipped kitchen, dining room and sitting room with a huge, commanding fireplace, plus a TV room, study and six bedrooms, making a posh vacation residence for large parties. Contact: Villas and Apartments Abroad Ltd, 420 Madison Ave, New York, NY 10017. Call 212-759-1025 or 1-800-433-3020.

Children: Y   Pets: Y   Smoking: Y   Handicap Access: N   Payment: C, P, T

Chiusdino

MONTALCINELLO *Rates: deluxe*
Open: June 1-September 30 *Minimum Stay: one week*

A converted 14th-century convent just outside a quiet medieval hamlet 20 miles from Siena, Villa Montalcinello offers accommodations that are anything but monastic. A wooden gate off a small piazza next to the village church marks the entrance to the grounds, which feature a lovely old walled garden, swimming pool and a long veranda. Set on a hillside giving uninterrupted views of cornfields and thick woods covering the countryside, the villa includes several huge sitting rooms—one opening onto the veranda and another with majestic high ceilings—a dining room, kitchen and eight bedrooms, making plenty of room for a party of up to 13. Contact: Villas and Apartments Abroad Ltd, 420 Madison Ave, New York, NY 10017. Call 212-759-1025 or 1-800-433-3020.

Children: Y   Pets: Y   Smoking: Y   Handicap Access: N   Payment: C, P, T

Chiusi

BELLAVISTA
Open: year-round

Rates: moderate-deluxe
Minimum Stay: one week

Three homes comprise this large estate situated near three of Italy's most beautiful lakes. The area, rich with Etruscan history, offers excursions to the nearby towns of Moiano and Paciano, where swimming pools and tennis courts are open to the public. The estate grounds provide spectacular lake views as well as a private lake for carp fishing. Guests at the villa enjoy the exclusive use of a swimming pool, billiard room, veranda with ivy-covered trellis and sleeping accommodations for six to eight. The hilltop hunting lodge for ten offers incredible views of the countryside and lakes as well as a fully furnished terrace. A restored farmhouse sits atop another hill and provides 360 degrees of vista. Panoramic windows in the living room and bedroom give the sensation that you are sitting on top of the world. Contact: Rent A Home International, 7200 34th Avenue, N.W., Seattle, WA 98117. Call 1-206-545-6963. Ref. 13.01.01-.03.

Children: Y   Pets: Smoking: Y   Handicap Access: N   Payment: C, P, V, M

Chuisi

VILLA POGGIO AL VENTO
Open: June 1-September 30

Rates: deluxe
Minimum Stay: one week

The exceptional and imposing Villa Poggio al Vento, accented with gothic arches, was built in the last century as a country residence for one of the most important families of the region. It sits amid hilly countryside and meadows in an area literally littered with Etruscan ruins. Approached by an august avenue of cypresses, the estate covers three acres of private park grounds that include a new swimming pool in the garden. The ground floor of the house contains a large entrance hall, traditional Mediterranean kitchen and spacious breakfast room, dining room, study and sitting room, all with frescoed ceilings. Upstairs are four bedrooms; the entire villa is handsomely furnished with family antique pieces. Contact: Villas and Apartments Abroad Ltd, 420 Madison Avenue, New York, NY 10017. Call 212-759-1025 or 1-800-433-3020.

Children: Y   Pets: Y   Smoking: Y   Handicap Access: N   Payment: C, P, T

Cortona

CASA FARINA
Open: May 15-October 15

Rates: budget
Minimum Stay: one week

High in the Tuscan hills above the walled medieval town of Cortona sits the Casa Farina. Here, magnificent views of the town below, Lake Trasimeno and the valley beyond are matched only by the heady fragrance of the surrounding pine trees. A spacious apartment with separate entrance sleeps five and provides such conveniences as a dishwasher and washing machine. A large living room with whitewashed walls and furnished in handsome, rough-hewn wood includes a cozy breakfast nook with a fireplace. Take a short drive down the side of the hill to Cortona, a stroll through narrow, winding streets and enjoy simple, good fare at one of the local restaurants. Contact: Mrs. Patricia Farina, Sant 'Egidio, 52044 Cortona, Italy. Call 011-39-575-603509.

Children: Y   Pets: N   Smoking: Y   Handicap Access: N   Payment: C, P, T

Cortona

COTTAGE METALLIANO   *Rates: moderate-expensive*
Open: year-round   *Minimum Stay: one week*

Situated only a short drive from the beautiful medieval city of Cortona, this handsome cottage offers architectural features such as arches, extraordinary large-beamed ceilings and a raised living room hearth. This vacation home for four includes exclusive use of the round swimming pool and free access to the 25 acres of private park that compose the estate. Take twilight walks engulfed in the scent of lemon trees, rose gardens and other flora that flourish on the grounds of the villa. The English-speaking owners will gladly direct you to the best routes through Tuscany and neighboring Umbria. Contact: Vacances Provencales Vacations, 729 Cutter Lane, Elk Grove, IL 60007. Call 708-893-9402. Ref. 3309.

Children: Y   Pets: Y   Smoking: Y   Handicap Access: N   Payment: P

Elba

ACQUARIO   *Rates: inexpensive-deluxe*
Open: year-round   *Minimum Stay: one-two weeks*

Four seaside apartments form this perfect summer beach retreat, which boasts the lapping water of the Mediterranean less than a hundred feet from the front door. Each apartment, alive with beautiful views and gentle sea air, sleeps two to six and includes a living/dining room, a patio and outdoor shower and barbecue. Elba, with its white beaches and colorful rocky cliffs, affords a seemingly endless array of diversions—swimming, skin-diving, golf and tennis for athletes, Romanesque churches, Roman and Etruscan ruins and fabulous boutiques for those whose passions are less strenuous. Contact: Posarelli Vacations (Cuendet Italia), 180 Kinderamack Road, Park Ridge, NJ 07656. Call 201-573-9558. Ref. 9.01.110-113.

Children: Y   Pets: N   Smoking: Y   Handicap Access: N   Payment: C, P, T

Elba

SERA MATTINA   *Rates: moderate-deluxe*
Open: year-round   *Minimum Stay: two weeks*

This modern villa sits only a short walk from the sandy beach of Naregno, but you may prefer to sit in the terraced garden and gaze out over the rocky cliffs and gorgeous vegetation which characterize this island. The spacious white-walled, tile-floored home sleeps six to seven in one double and two twin bedrooms plus an additional folding bed. It also includes a large living room and a dining room/kitchen. You can spend your days wandering among Etruscan and Roman ruins and visiting the monastery that once housed the exiled Napoleon. Sports lovers can take advantage of the tennis courts and a golf course, and beginners can learn sailing, skin-diving and water skiing here. Contact: Posarelli Vacations (Cuendet Italia), 180 Kinderamack Road, Park Ridge, NJ 07656. Call 201-573-9558. Ref. 9.01.75.

Children: Y Pets: N Smoking: Y Handicap Access: N Payment: C, P, T

Fiesole

SAN JACOBO HOUSE   *Rates: inexpensive-expensive*
Open: April-November   *Minimum Stay: one week*

Surrounded by well-tended parkland and a luxurious garden, this charming villa is an idyllic dwelling near some of Italy's most renowned sights—the ancient ruins, medieval edifices and Renaissance wonders of Fiesole and Florence are scarcely a couple miles down the road. The sunny, well-furnished rooms include a spacious living and dining room, a kitchen complete with an oven and a dishwasher and a bedroom on the first floor. These rooms open onto a large, shaded terrace and a sunny patio with deck chairs. Walk upstairs and you'll find yet another large terrace with a lovely view and two more comfy bedrooms (the house accommodates six). The house is centrally heated and there is a washing machine on the premises to add to your convenience. Contact: Interhome Inc., 124 Little Falls Rd., Fairfield, NJ 07004. Call 201-882-6864. Ref. I5217/1.

Children: Y Pets: Y Smoking: Y Handicap Access: N Payment: P, V, M

Fiesole

VILLA ROMENA   *Rates: deluxe*
Open: June 1-September 30   *Minimum Stay: one week*

This residence dating from the 16th century is one of the fine old villas of the Florentine area. Three miles away is the historic town of Fiesole, a chief city of Etruria until it was eclipsed by Florence in the late middle ages. The "pietra serena" quarries of Monte Ceceri, which first drew sculptors to the region, are also nearby. Villa Romena offers superb views of the Arno and the countryside adorned with olive groves and cypresses. A private chapel is located on the grounds, as well as a lovely traditional Italian-style garden with a terrace and swimming pool. Inside, the noble house contains an entrance hall, dining room, several sitting rooms and six bedrooms. Contact: Villas and Apartments Abroad Ltd, 420 Madison Avenue, New York, NY 10017. Call 212-759-1025 or 1-800-433-3020.

Children: Y Pets: Y Smoking: Y Handicap Access: N Payment: C, P, T

Florence

APARTMENT FAENZA   *Rates: expensive-deluxe*
Open: year-round   *Minimum Stay: one week*

If a week or two spent exploring the golden city has long been your dream, then this apartment on the third floor of an antique palazetto offers the perfect point of departure for your days in Florence. Located on a little side street right off the bustling San Lorenzo market and not more than a five-minute walk from the incomparable Duomo, this cheery and simply furnished apartment sleeps five in one twin and one

bedroom, plus a single sofa divan. Experiment with Italian
ng in your own kitchen, or visit the vast number of fine restau-
and neighborhood trattorias with which the city abounds. Contact: Vacances Provencales Vacations, 729 Cutter Lane, Elk Grove, IL
60007. Call 708-893-9402. Ref. 266.

Children: Y   Pets: Y   Smoking: Y   Handicap Access: N   Payment: P

Florence
LA RIPA   *Rates: expensive-deluxe*
Open: year-round   *Minimum Stay: one week*

Peacefully situated with a panoramic view, La Ripa is a large stone
farmhouse that has been carefully renovated and divided into three
apartments, one of which the owners occupy. Totally modern yet
retaining a rustic atmosphere, the apartments are spacious and beautifully furnished. The kitchens include dishwashers, and the bathrooms are equipped with shower-massage. Sleeping up to five in three
bedrooms, the larger apartment contains a Jacuzzi in an additional
bathroom and a fireplace in the living room. The smaller unit accommodates three in a double bedroom and a sofa bed. A large garden
offers a swimming pool and tennis court; nearby visitors can find golf
and riding facilities. Contact: Europa-Let, PO Box 3537, Ashland, OR
97520. Call 1-800-462-4486 or 503-482-1442. Ref. Solemar 1.46.

Children: Y   Pets: N   Smoking: Y   Handicap Access: N   Payment: C, P, T

Florence
LA TORRE   *Rates: moderate*
Open: year-round   *Minimum Stay: one week*

Only a few yards from the Piazza Signora and the Ponte Vecchio in the
historic center of the city, this three-level apartment occupies the
tower of the 14th-century "Palazzo Buondelmonti." The elegant tower
is still in great condition, and from the roof terrace you can enjoy an
incomparable view of the city, with its old palaces, red rooftops and
church spires. The third floor has a small kitchen, a living/dining
room and a bathroom; the mezzanine has a twin bedroom; the fourth
floor has a double bedroom with a toilet and enjoys unforgettable
views at sunrise and sunset. The museums and art treasures of the
city, as well as fashion, jewelry, leather goods and antiques shops are
all very close. Contact: Europa-Let, PO Box 3537, Ashland, OR 97520.
Call 1-800-462-4486 or 503-482-1442. Ref. Solemar 1.39.

Children: Y   Pets: N   Smoking: Y   Handicap Access: N   Payment: C, P, T

Florence
PALAZZO ANTELLESI   *Rates: deluxe*
Open: June 1-September 30   *Minimum Stay: one week*

Situated right in the center of Florence in Piazza Santa Croce, Palazzo
Antellesi has been recently renovated into a number of comfortable,
self-contained apartments. The palace itself was converted from several medieval towers in the 16th century. Its facade was painted by the
master Giovanni da San Giovanni around 1620 and some of the rooms

have frescoed ceilings dating from the 1600s. The apartments, each one nicely furnished and containing a fully equipped kitchen and bath, accommodate from two to five persons. Most have working fireplaces and many have access to the palazzo's formal garden or its roof terrace. Contact: Villas and Apartments Abroad Ltd, 420 Madison Avenue, New York, NY 10017. Call 212-759-1025 or 1-800-433-3020.

Children: Y   Pets: Y   Smoking: Y   Handicap Access: N   Payment: C, P, T

Florence

PALAZZO CAPPONI   *Rates: moderate*
Open: April-November   *Minimum Stay: one week*
In one of the most fascinating mansions in the historic center of Florence, just a stone's throw from the Piazzas Duomo and Santissima Annunziata, this gorgeous apartment for two is decorated with frescoes painted in the 1700s. Comfortable and elegantly furnished, the flat offers a great alternative to staying in a hotel during a visit to Florence: it even has its own parking space, hard to come by in this neighborhood. The apartment consists of a large frescoed living room with a loft above for the double bed, a dining room with a kitchen area and a bath with a shower. This is a marvelous way to get a feel for Florence between visits to museums, restaurants and shops. Contact: Europa-Let, PO Box 3537, Ashland, OR 97520. Call 1-800-462-4486 or 503-482-1442. Ref. Solemar 1.49.

Children: Y   Pets: N   Smoking: Y   Handicap Access: N   Payment: C, P, T

Florence

PALAZZO GUICCIARDINI   *Rates: moderate-deluxe*
Open: June 1-September 30   *Minimum Stay: one week*
Palazzo Guicciardini, a regal Renaissance building restored in the 16th century and located in the center of Florence between the Ponte Vecchio and the Pitti Palace, contains an elegant and spacious top-floor apartment for guests. Featuring a large roof terrace with a sensational panoramic view over the city, it offers the opportunity to enjoy all the area's matchless cultural and historic highlights from a residence that is itself a part of history. An elevator brings guests up to the tastefully furnished apartment, which contains an entrance hall, modern kitchen, dining room, sitting room and three bedrooms. Contact: Villas and Apartments Abroad Ltd, 420 Madison Avenue, New York, NY 10017. Call 212-759-1025 or 1-800-433-3020.

Children: Y   Pets: Y   Smoking: Y   Handicap Access: N   Payment: C, P, T

Florence

PALAZZO RICASOLI   *Rates: budget-inexpensive*
Open: year-round   *Minimum Stay: two weeks*
A palace and a convent in turn, this large, five-story apartment house with elevator is home to eight simple vacation accommodations in the center of glorious Florence. Many of the windows face the large sunny courtyard, where potted plants and Etruscan-style urns sit in repose. Apartments sleeping two to four include kitchen areas and color TV.

Central heat, air conditioning and maid service are available. From here, you will have no trouble immersing yourself in the magic and mystery of this city, so rich with the intrigue of the Medici, the art of da Vinci and Michelangelo, and the daily markets filled with the gastronomic richness for which this city is so famous. Contact: Posarolli Vacations (Cuendet Italia), 180 Kinderamack Road, Park Ridge, NJ 07656. Call 201-573-9558. Ref. 1.05.122-129.

Children: Y   Pets: N   Smoking: Y   Handicap Access: N   Payment: C, P, T

Florence

PIANISTA   *Rates: expensive*
Open: year-round   *Minimum Stay: two weeks*

This spacious and charmingly appointed apartment for eight boasts its own history. Here, in the small study, Dostoevsky wrote *The Idiot*. From five of the windows of this second-floor residence, views of the Pitti Palace evoke centuries of art and intrigue. Other features of the apartment include a living room with a fireplace and a grand piano, a large, modern bathroom with a round whirlpool and brick floors throughout. From here, you can wander the streets of the city to your heart's content. Central heating and telephone are available. Contact: Posarelli Vacations (Cuendet Italia), 180 Kinderamack Road, Park Ridge, NJ 07656. Call 201-573-9558. Ref. 1.05.130.

Children: Y   Pets: N   Smoking: Y   Handicap Access: N   Payment: C, P, T

Florence

POGGIO SECCO   *Rates: moderate-expensive*
Open: year-round   *Minimum Stay: one week*

Set on a rise just south of Florence, this typically Tuscan, totally renovated, stone farmhouse commands an incredible view of the entire city and the surrounding hills. Four of the apartments on the premises are occupied by long-term tenants; two roomy apartments bursting with rustic charm are available to vacationers. Each has a double bedroom, a bath with a shower, a living room and kitchen; both have their own private outdoor area. The beautiful, expansive grounds include a lighted tennis court and a large pool. In the barn, the owner produces ceramic tiles, restores furniture and works bronze and copper pieces. With Florence so close, you can enjoy the best of both worlds— a country vacation with trips to the city as often as you desire. Contact: Europa-Let, PO Box 3537, Ashland, OR 97520. Call 1-800-462-4486 or 503-482-1442. Ref. Solemar 1.40.

Children: Y   Pets: N   Smoking: Y   Handicap Access: N   Payment: C, P, T

Florence

TERGOLAIA   *Rates: inexpensive-moderate*
Open: year-round   *Minimum Stay: one week*

From this delightful and spacious apartment for two it's only a few minutes' walk to the colorful open-air market of Piazza Santo Spirito and the breath-taking art collection of the Pitti Palace. Beautifully furnished with both contemporary and antique pieces, this third-floor

home boasts the Tuscan charm of wooden beamed ceiling and white-washed walls. The open second floor includes the living room and kitchen with washing machine. From a sitting room corner, a flight of open wooden steps ascends to a cozy double bed loft. With the additional comforts of weekly maid service and telephone and the charm of a small balcony overlooking an internal courtyard, this apartment provides an ideal hide-away for painters and honeymooners right in the heart of the city. Contact: Rent A Home International, 7200 34th Avenue N.W., Seattle, WA 98117. Call 1-206-545-6963. Ref. 1.01.01.
Children: Y   Pets: N   Smoking: Y   Handicap Access: N   Payment: C,P,V,M

Florence

TIRATOIO   *Rates: budget*
Open: year-round   *Minimum Stay: two weeks*
Young couples will find this charming house the perfect spot for a Florentine stay. Located on a small square in the "old" part of the city, you will find the Arno River and one of its many bridges only a few feet from your door. Carefully restored, the house features the original brick floors and wood-beamed ceilings and offers a view of the small square of which it is a part. The ground-floor living/dining room includes a kitchen area, and the second-floor bedroom sleeps two in twin beds warmed by a wood-burning stove. With nearby parking available, you can easily take excursions to the hill towns and medieval cities that abound in Tuscany. Contact: Posarelli Vacations (Cuendet Italia), 180 Kinderamack Road, Park Ridge, NJ 07656. Call 201-573-9558. Ref. 1.05.147.
Children: Y   Pets: Y   Smoking: Y   Handicap Access: N   Payment: C, P, T

Florence

TOLOMEO   *Rates: budget-inexpensive*
Open: year-round   *Minimum Stay: two weeks*
You can make this cozy little third-floor apartment your Florentine headquarters. Ideally located in the heart of the city, this simply furnished apartment, one of five in the building, sleeps four in two double bedrooms and includes a homey living room/dining room as well as an entrance/sitting room. Only a few feet away, the Via Tornabuoni offers some of the world's most luxurious shopping, and nearby markets await. Contact: Posarelli Vacations (Cuendet Italia), 180 Kinderamack Road, Park Ridge, NJ 07656. Call 201-573-9558. Ref. 1.05.131.
Children: Y   Pets: N   Smoking: Y   Handicap Access: N   Payment: C, P, T

Florence

VILLA FONTALLERTA   *Rates: expensive*
Open: April 28-September 28   *Minimum Stay: one week*
This sumptuous rental invites guests to discover the "city of art" while enjoying the serenity and elegance of a stay in a 15th-century villa. Nestled on a vast estate on one of the hills that surround Florence, the house stands less than three miles from the city's historic center. Guests can stay behind the main villa in a tastefully furnished

apartment for four with its own section of garden complete with lawn furniture. A mezzanine-level living room, a kitchen/dining room with a washing machine and a dishwasher, twin and double bedrooms plus two baths make up the unit. In addition to manicured gardens, the grounds offer an enormous swimming pool and private tennis courts, complete with showers and dressing rooms. Contact: Europa-Let, PO Box 3537, Ashland, OR 97520. Call 1-800-462-4486 or 503-482-1442. Ref. Solemar C.02.

Children: **Y**   Pets: **N**   Smoking: **Y**   Handicap Access: **N**   Payment: **C, P, T**

Florence

VILLA PAOLA   *Rates: deluxe*
Open: June 1-September 30   *Minimum Stay: one week*

Only a five-minute drive from the center of Florence, Villa Paola is an attractive house sitting amid the tranquil garden of a 16th-century, high-Renaissance era residence. Out front is an elegant veranda offering exquisite views of the Florentine countryside. Luxuriously furnished, the two-story residence contains a hallway, fully equipped kitchen, dining room and sitting room with a fireplace on the ground floor. Three bedrooms, each with its own bathroom and sleeping up to six comfortably, are upstairs. Contact: Villas and Apartments Abroad Ltd, 420 Madison Avenue, New York, NY 10017. Call 212-759-1025 or 1-800-433-3020.

Children: **Y**   Pets: **Y**   Smoking: **Y**   Handicap Access: **N**   Payment: **C, P, T**

Fonterutoli

CASTELLO DI FONTERUTOLI   *Rates: moderate-expensive*
Open: year-round   *Minimum Stay: one week*

Perfectly situated for excursions throughout beautiful Tuscany, this small medieval village is peaceful and charming. Two apartments in the village have been created within ancient structures and furnished in the classic Tuscan country style. Sleeping up to six each, they share a huge swimming pool and have fireplaces and fully modernized kitchens and bathrooms. One also has a study that can sleep up to two more guests. The region, known for its olive groves and vineyards, offers wonderful touring possibilities; the cities of Siena and Florence are close enough for those interested in less pastoral pursuits. Contact: Europa-Let, PO Box 3537, Ashland, OR 97520. Call 1-800-462-4486 or 503-482-1442. Ref. Solemar 1.33.

Children: **Y**   Pets: **N**   Smoking: **Y**   Handicap Access: **N**   Payment: **C, P, T**

Gaiole in Chianti

CASTELLO DI TORNANO   *Rates: expensive-deluxe*
Open: year-round   *Minimum Stay: one week*

This imposing 11th-century castle offers two very different and utterly unique rental options. Find the larger unit in the castle tower, where appointments include a huge dining hall with a monumental fireplace and windows and stone walls original to the structure. Wooden steps and a spiral staircase lead to bedrooms for four to six, topped by a solarium terrace with the best views imaginable. The second unit, a perfectly renovated stone barn, provides an intimate holiday home for four to five. Hot days are the perfect opportunity to swim in the pool that has been created from the original moat and measures about thirteen by sixty-six feet. Contact: Rent A Home International, 7200 34th Avenue, N.W., Seattle, WA 98117. Call 206-545-6963. Ref. 10.01.01, 10.01.02.

Children: Y   Pets: N   Smoking: Y   Handicap Access: N   Payment: C, P, V, M

Gaiole in Chianti

VILLA VISTARENNI   *Rates: inexpensive-expensive*
Open: year-round   *Minimum Stay: one week*

This imposing palace with its 18th-century facade offers a truly regal holiday retreat, as it did when Queen Margherita took her repose here. Royal indeed are the spacious accommodations for seven in the second-floor apartment, where beautiful furnishings and antiques, central heat and bedrooms with en suite bathrooms provide the kind of features the aristocracy requires. The grounds also include a large swimming pool and barbecue terrace with outstanding views. If a change of venue is what you desire, you will find yourself ideally situated to explore the medieval villages of the Chianti valley as well as the artistic jewels of Tuscany, Florence, Siena and San Gimignano. Contact: Vacances Provencales Vacations, 729 Cutter Lane, Elk Grove, IL 60007. Call 708-893-9402. Ref. 240.

Children: Y   Pets: Y   Smoking: Y   Handicap Access: N   Payment: P

Gianella/Albinia

LE SALINE   *Rates: budget-expensive*
Open: year-round   *Minimum Stay: one week*

Rent a vacation home so close to the Mediterranean, you can see and hear it. This landscaped property offers an idyllic view of one of the bays along this exclusive stretch of Italian coastline. Ideal for families with children, the two apartments are assured privacy by a fence and enjoy access to the beach (especially quiet and uncrowded during the months of June and September) through a small gate. An apartment for four features a private pergola with garden furniture. Enter the other—which sleeps eight—through a large covered terrace with a view of the sea. Only a short drive away, the fashionable towns of Porto Santo Stefano and Porto Ercole offer fine restaurants and exclusive shops that draw a handsome crowd. Contact: British Travel Associates, P. O. Box 299, Elkton, VA 22827. Call 1-800-327-8097 (in Virginia, 703-298-2232). Ref. IM1, IM2.

Children: Y   Pets: N   Smoking: Y   Handicap Access: N   Payment: All

Greve in Chianti

CENNATOIO   *Rates: budget-inexpensive*
Open: year-round   *Minimum Stay: one week*

Happily situated in the very center of the Chianti Classico hills, this farmhouse apartment affords an ideal spot from which to explore the many wine cellars of the area. The estate owners themselves produce and sell wine as well as honey, olive oil and vinegar. They also take great care with the surrounding grounds, and their love of plants and cats is evident whenever a guest spots a tiny kitten curled up inside a flower pot. Enter the second-floor apartment from a private outside flight of stairs that leads into a spacious living/dining room with a TV. Sleeping accommodations include one double and one twin bedroom which offer beautiful views of the surrounding countryside, thick with vineyards. Contact: Rent A Home International, 7200 34th Avenue, N.W., Seattle, WA 98117. Call 206-545-6963. Ref. 9.02.01.

Children: Y   Pets: N   Smoking: Y   Handicap Access: N   Payment: C, P, V, M

Greve in Chianti

SANTA LUCIA A BARBIANO   *Rates: inexpensive-deluxe*
Open: year-round   *Minimum Stay: one week*

These several intimate and romantic apartments were originally part of a monastic community of the Middle Ages. Today, this cluster of charming houses surrounds an idyllic courtyard near an herb garden fragrant with rosemary, sage and mint. The warm and tastefully appointed apartments differ from each other in character, but share a common quality of homeyness imparted by details such as crossbeamed ceilings and fireplaces. Situated only a 10-minute drive from the enchanting medieval town of Greve, you can savor the local food and wine in one of the town's little restaurants, and in September, enjoy the annual wine fair. Contact: Vacances Provencales Vacations, 729 Cutter Lane, Elk Grove, IL 60007. Call 708-893-9402. Ref. 271-75.

Children: Y   Pets: Y   Smoking: Y   Handicap Access: N   Payment: P

Greve in Chianti

VILLA VITIGLIANO   *Rates: deluxe*
Open: year-round   *Minimum Stay: one week*

Within the rich Chianti hills, this 15th-century villa rises majestically from its own pine-topped promontory overlooking 300 wine and olive producing acres. Grounds both rustic and formal offer gardens, terraces and a swimming pool. The magnificent accommodations for eight to ten are lavishly furnished with period pieces and many interesting oil paintings. Architectural details, such as a bedroom with a restored mural, a dumb waiter from the ground-floor kitchen to the formal dining room above and a Great Hall dominated by a family crest, create an ambience of elegance and richness. Conveniences in this veritable palace include maid and cooking services, a TV and a laundry room. Contact: British Travel Associates, P. O. Box 299, Elkton, VA 22827. Call 1-800-327-8097 (in Virginia, 703-298-2232). Ref. IT100.

Children: Y   Pets: N   Smoking: Y   Handicap Access: N   Payment: All

Grosseto

TORRE CIVETTE   *Rates: budget-inexpensive*
Open: year-round   *Minimum Stay: one week*

This working farm, which produces excellent wines and olive oil, offers a unique opportunity for a combined seashore and countryside vacation. Located just over 500 yards from the beach of Punta Ala, the farm sits between thick underbrush and cultivated land. Four apartments are available, each sleeping four in twin bedrooms and sofa beds. Each has a cozy country atmosphere, including a fireplace in one living room and a garden furniture set out in the shade of a gigantic pine tree. Guests can rent beach chairs, umbrellas, tennis rackets, surfboards, sail boats, hobie-cats and pedal boats at nearby Puntala Campground. The campground also has a complete shopping center and restaurants. Contact: Europa-Let, PO Box 3537, Ashland, OR 97520. Call 1-800-462-4486 or 503-482-1442. Ref. Solemar 2.01.

Children: **Y**   Pets: **N**   Smoking: **Y**   Handicap Access: **N**   Payment: **C, P, T**

Lake Massaciuccoli

VILLA IL CAVALIERE   *Rates: deluxe*
Open: April 28-September 28   *Minimum Stay: one week*
Amid the green hills between Lucca and Lake Massaciuccoli stands this stately 17th-century villa surrounded by a park with a swimming pool and lovely gardens. The house is elegantly furnished, partly with fine antiques and partly with rustic Tuscan furniture. Central heating, two modern baths and a kitchen equipped with modern appliances make your stay comfortable. In keeping with the country atmosphere, there are three fireplaces downstairs, one each in the kitchen, living room and dining room. Upstairs are two double and two twin bedrooms. The rental fee includes cleaning service six days a week; for an extra charge, a cook will be provided if requested when reservations are made. Contact: Europa-Let, PO Box 3537, Ashland, OR 97520. Call 1-800-462-4486 or 503-482-1442. Ref. Solemar C.14.

Children: **Y**   Pets: **N**   Smoking: **Y**   Handicap Access: **N**   Payment: **C, P, T**

Lakes Orvieto and Bolsena

LA CARRAIA   *Rates: moderate-expensive*
Open: year-round   *Minimum Stay: one week*
Follow a private road bordered with cypress trees to this lovely restored farmhouse surrounded by the countryside of the lake district. The gracious grounds offer a barn used as a game room where a Ping-Pong table, a bread oven and a barbecue grill are provided. In one of two altogether private apartments, guests enter through a partially covered paved patio into a spacious dining room with fireplace. Other features of this apartment for eight include a living room with a fireplace, a panoramic window opening onto a rear patio and a stone staircase leading to the second floor bedrooms. Outings to nearby Lakes Bolsena and Orvieto or dining in one of the area's many fine restaurants make this farmhouse apartment an appealing holiday home. Contact: Rent A Home International, 7200 34th Avenue, N.W., Seattle, WA 98117. Call 206-545-6963. Ref. 14.01.01

Children: **Y**   Pets: **N**   Smoking: **Y**   Handicap Access: **N**   Payment: **C, P, V, M**

Lucca

BORROMEI

Rates: deluxe

Open: June 1-September 30 *Minimum Stay: one week*

Set in the foothills of the Apuan Alps, Borromei, a stately 18th-century manor house, stands 20 minutes from the historic Tuscan town of Lucca. Sections of the villa date from the 13th century. Many of the walls and ceilings feature the original frescoes and the entire residence is lovingly furnished with unique antique pieces. Downstairs is an elegant hall, kitchen and dining room with intricately carved wooden doors that open onto the garden, while the second floor includes six bedrooms, each with its own bathroom and a huge sitting room with sweeping views towards Pisa. Ancient urns and statues sit in the formal part of the garden, and an irresistible swimming pool, fed by mountain spring water, is located in the wooded area. Contact: Villas and Apartments Abroad Ltd, 420 Madison Avenue, New York, NY 10017. Call 212-759-1025 or 1-800-433-3020.

Children: Y   Pets: Y   Smoking: Y   Handicap Access: N   Payment: C, P, T

Lucca

FUBBIANO

Rates: deluxe

Open: June 1-September 30 *Minimum Stay: one week*

This 18th-century villa accented with palm trees and oleanders dominates the ancient "borgo" of Fubbiano, a captivating tiny wine- and oil-producing village. The house's first floor includes a large country kitchen with fireplace and a dining room opening onto a side garden, while a sitting room and four bedrooms, each with its own bath, are upstairs. Set on a panoramic hillside, the grounds feature gardens and terraces, with a private swimming pool overlooking the plain of Lucca. A footpath winding through the small oak wood just off the estate leads to an ancient fountain. Guests may also traipse through Fubbiano's vineyards, cellars, olive groves and mills and buy the fine wine and "extra virgin" oil produced here. Contact: Villas and Apartments Abroad Ltd, 420 Madison Avenue, New York, NY 10017. Call 212-759-1025 or 1-800-433-3020.

Children: Y   Pets: Y   Smoking: Y   Handicap Access: N   Payment: C, P, T

Lucca

MIMOSE

Rates: deluxe

Open: June 1-September 30 *Minimum Stay: one week*

This handsome, traditional Tuscan farmhouse is less than a mile outside the charming village of Segromigno Monte. Encircled by lawns and olive groves and offering a magnificent view of the countryside, the two-story main house contains a kitchen, dining room and living room on the ground floor, with three bedrooms and two baths upstairs. A few yards away is a hayloft that has been cleverly converted to hold two additional bedrooms and a bath, plus a second kitchen and sitting room. There's an enticing circular swimming pool in the garden and, for additional sports activities, riding stables and tennis courts are within three miles. Contact: Villas and Apartments Abroad Ltd, 420

Madison Avenue, New York, NY 10017. Call 212-759-1025 or 1-800-433-3020.

Children: Y   Pets: Y   Smoking: Y   Handicap Access: N   Payment: C, P, T

Lucca

PODERI LENZI   *Rates: budget-moderate*
Open: April 28-September 28   *Minimum Stay: one week*

These lovely accommodations—a house for eight and two apartments for four—stand on a large estate that enjoys a breathtaking view of the medieval city of Lucca. The units have all been completely remodeled and refurnished to maintain the simple, rustic ambience characteristic of this part of Italy. On the ground floor, the two apartments have a kitchen/breakfast room with a fireplace and a living room that opens onto a terrace with a view. Upstairs each has a double and twin bedroom and a bath with shower. The house offers similar accommodations downstairs, with a fireplace in the living room instead of a terrace. Its first floor has a twin and three double bedrooms, and two baths with showers. Tennis is available nearby and the beaches are about 12 miles away. Contact: Europa-Let, PO Box 3537, Ashland, OR 97520. Call 1-800-462-4486 or 503-482-1442. Ref. Solemar 3.19.

Children: Y   Pets: N   Smoking: Y   Handicap Access: N   Payment: C, P, T

Lucca

VILLA OLIVA-SAN PANCRAZIO   *Rates: budget-moderate*
Open: year-round   *Minimum Stay: one week*

Imagine a 16th-century town with its moat and original fortified walls intact. This is Lucca, a fascinating combination of old and new that, having no major tourist attractions, does not draw the crowds that Pisa and Florence do. Here, amid absolutely beautiful countryside, is a villa dating back to 1650. A long, winding road climbs through the estate's enormous park to the villa in its panoramic setting. Four apartments for four to six people are housed in the building next to the main villa. All look onto the splendid garden with its sculptured hedges, statues and fountains; one unit opens directly onto the huge pool. The site also includes a tennis court. Simply and comfortably furnished, the apartments have kitchens, at least one bath with a shower and some combination of twin, single and double bedrooms; two have fireplaces. Contact: Europa-Let, PO Box 3537, Ashland, OR 97520. Call 1-800-462-4486 or 503-482-1442. Ref. Solemar 3.11.

Children: Y   Pets: N   Smoking: Y   Handicap Access: N   Payment: C, P, T

Lucignano/Arezzo

VILLA SIGNANA   *Rates: budget-moderate*
Open: year-round   *Minimum Stay: one week*

This elegant second-floor apartment in a 16th-century villa boasts as neighbor the fortified town of Lucignano, where a small museum and highly regarded restaurant provide local diversion. The surrounding area of Valdichiana has yet to be discovered by tourists, making this a particularly unspoiled location. Restored in 1986, the villa offers a private garden furnished for pleasant lounging. The apartment accommodates three to five people in rooms exquisitely appointed with antiques, frescoed ceilings, a banquet hall-sized living room and a terrace. Central heat, firewood, maid service and electricity are available for an extra charge. The owner, an excellent cook, can sometimes be persuaded to prepare a meal from local produce. Contact: Rent A Home International, 7200 34th Avenue, N.W., Seattle, WA 98117. Call 206-545-6963.

Children: Y   Pets: N   Smoking: Y   Handicap Access: N   Payment: C, P, V, M

Lucignano

VILLA ALZATO   *Rates: moderate-deluxe*
Open: year-round   *Minimum Stay: one week*

In the rural Chianti hills just 15 miles from spectacular Florence, this ancient villa is quietly situated on a splendid estate. Three very large apartments are available for up to seven people each, two in the main part of the villa and one converted from the old stables. All have been carefully restored, retaining the classic, elegant furnishings of the Tuscan country villa. All apartments share a magnificent garden and a large, inviting built-in pool. Alzato's location lends itself to excursions throughout the region, but the beauty of the surroundings and the special charms and comforts of the house and gardens will tempt you to relax and stay put. Contact: Europa-Let, PO Box 3537, Ashland, OR 97520. Call 1-800-462-4486 or 503-482-1442. Ref. Solemar 1.06.

Children: Y   Pets: N   Smoking: Y   Handicap Access: N   Payment: C, P, T

Maiori

VILLA LA NAVE   *Rates: expensive-deluxe*
Open: year-round   *Minimum Stay: one week*

Overlooking the awe-inspiring Amalfi Coast from cliffs above the sea, these two modern villas are situated in a delightful residential area. The larger villa (for up to eight) has four bedrooms and four full bathrooms on two floors, with a small private terrace off each bedroom boasting a magnificent view of the bay below. It also has its own saltwater swimming pool and a path leading directly to the rocky beach. The smaller villa for five stands in an equally beautiful position and contains two twins and a single bedroom plus three baths; it also has a path that leads to the beaches underneath the cliff. Both have spacious living rooms and kitchens complete with dishwashers. Contact: Europa-Let, PO Box 3537, Ashland, OR 97520. Call 1-800-462-4486 or 503-482-1442. Ref. Solemar C.01.

Children: Y   Pets: N   Smoking: Y   Handicap Access: N   Payment: C, P, T

Marina di Pietrasanta

VILLA GRAZIA   *Rates: inexpensive-expensive*
Open: April 14-October 13   *Minimum Stay: one week*

At the very hub of the Italian Riviera, well known for its sandy beaches, pine woods and proximity to the mountains and countryside, Marina di Pietrasanta is a destination ideally suited to those who wish to relax completely. Villa Grazia, a modern duplex located in a quiet residential area within walking distance of the beach and town, affords guests the opportunity to experience life as the Italians lead it. With patios in the front and back, outdoor dining area and an inviting yard, the house invites guests to stay outdoors, yet the attractive and comfortable living/dining room will beckon as well. Guests may enjoy themselves without a care, as daily cleaning service is provided. Villa Grazia sleeps up to five people in two bedrooms. Contact: Beth Davies, Italian Villa Rentals, P.O. Box 1145, Bellevue, WA 98009. Call 206-827-3694.

Children: **Y**   Pets: **N**   Smoking: **Y**   Handicap Access: **N**   Payment: **C, P**

Massa Marittima

POGGIO AL GUARDIONE   *Rates: budget*
Open: year-round   *Minimum Stay: one week*

On the slope of a hill, surrounded by woods and a spacious garden, Poggio al Guardione invites you to enjoy complete peace. Extremely comfortable and tastefully furnished, this typically Tuscan farmhouse has a spacious living room with a fireplace, a dining area/kitchen, a twin bedroom and a bathroom on the ground floor. Upstairs is a small sitting area overlooking the main living room, two twin bedrooms (one with bunk beds) and a bath with a shower. The lovely grounds lend themselves equally well to walking or lounging; tennis and horseback riding facilities may be found within five miles. Poggio al Guardione stands at the center of a vast area of archeological interest as well as within reach of the coast. Contact: Europa-Let, PO Box 3537, Ashland, OR 97520. Call 1-800-462-4486 or 503-482-1442. Ref. Solemar 2.10.

Children: **Y**   Pets: **N**   Smoking: **Y**   Handicap Access: **N**   Payment: **C, P, T**

Mercatale

LA COLOMBA   *Rates: expensive-deluxe*
Open: year-round   *Minimum Stay: one week*

This splendid farmhouse on a peaceful slope lush with grape vines, olive trees and woods enjoys a breathtaking view of the valley below. The house for 12 has been renovated with extreme care and furnished with pieces in the classic Tuscan country style. On the ground floor, guests enter through a large furnished loggia, only one of many of the home's outdoor living areas. Also downstairs is a dining room, kitchen, laundry room and living/dining room with a fireplace. The upper floor has five double bedrooms with private baths, and in the tower is another double bedroom with its own bath. Florence lies a mere 151/2 miles away, a great destination for day trips. Contact: Europa-Let, PO Box 3537, Ashland, OR 97520. Call 1-800-462-4486 or 503-482-1442. Ref. Solemar C.12.

Children: **Y**   Pets: **N**   Smoking: **Y**   Handicap Access: **N**   Payment: **C, P, T**

Migliarino Pisano

FIUMACCINO   *Rates: expensive*
Open: April 28-November 2   *Minimum Stay: one week*

Situated in a peaceful position and surrounded by a spacious garden, this big farmhouse is a perfect starting point for excursions to Lucca and the entire Tuscan coast. Ideal for big families or groups of friends vacationing together, this house sleeps eight. The interior has been restored and furnished with antiques to give it a Tuscan country atmosphere. The ground-floor entrance, living room and dining room each have fireplaces, and a veranda leads to the garden. Two double and two twin bedrooms plus four bathrooms make this house especially comfortable for groups. It stands just two miles from the beach and about 12 miles from the coast of Versilia. When you tire of the beach, the city of Pisa is nearby, offering a wide range of activities, not to mention its leaning tower. Contact: Europa-Let, PO Box 3537, Ashland, OR 97520. Call 1-800-462-4486 or 503-482-1442. Ref. Solemar 3.01.

Children: Y   Pets: N   Smoking: Y   Handicap Access: N   Payment: C, P, T

Montaione

COLLEGALLI   *Rates: inexpensive-moderate*
Open: year-round   *Minimum Stay: one week*

You will find this impeccably furnished apartment on a lovely hilltop, down a long, typically unpaved country road. En route to your retreat, you may stop to use the large swimming pool, the tennis court or riding facilities available nearby. Or you may be content to take a dip in the small pool guests share with the owners of the house, and stir up a meal from local vegetables and wines. A sitting/dining room, small kitchen, and two twin bedrooms accommodate four in the heart of Tuscany, less than an hour's drive from San Gimignano and Florence. Contact: British Travel Associates, P. O. Box 299, Elkton, VA 22827. Call 1-800-327-8097 (in Virginia, 703-298-2232). Ref. IT1.

Children: Y   Pets: N   Smoking: Y   Handicap Access: N   Payment: All

Montaione

LA SCUDERIA   *Rates: inexpensive-moderate*
Open: year round   *Minimum Stay: one week*

Once part of the stables in a grand 17th-century villa about midway between Florence and Pisa, this cozy apartment has a warm, vaulted brick ceiling and opens onto a semi-private terrace. It shares extensive grounds, including swimming pool, laundry room, game room and bowling alley, with seven other apartments situated in and around the villa. Furnished comfortably with a nice mix of rustic and modern pieces throughout, the apartment is centrally heated. The double and twin bedrooms are semi-private, with walls that do not reach the ceiling, creating a partially open plan with the living room. To add a little Tuscan flavor to your cooking, the owner sells wine, oil and preserves; prepared dishes can be ordered in advance if you'd rather leave the work to someone else. Contact: B & D de Vogue Interna-

tional, Inc., 1830 S. Mooney Blvd. Ste. 203, Visalia, CA 93277. Call
209-733-7119 or 1-800-727-4748. Ref. IT 89.

Children: Y Pets: N Smoking: Y Handicap Access: N Payment: P, A, V, M

Montegemoli/Volterra

LA VOLPINAIA   *Rates: budget-inexpensive*
Open: year-round   *Minimum Stay: one week*
This charming and rustic Tuscan cottage built in the 17th century
stands on the grounds of a large villa estate and enjoys the ample and
gentle shade of numerous cypress trees. Every room in the house affords views of the ancient hilltop city of Volterra. Enjoy quiet walks or
welcome repose in the spacious garden. Three twin bedrooms, a
kitchen and a living/dining room with a large fireplace complete the
accommodations for six. For amusement, the nearby village of Ponte-
ginori offers a swimming pool, but more ambitious travellers will go
the distance—less than twenty miles—to swim and windsurf in the
Mediterranean. Contact: British Travel Associates, P. O. Box 299, Elkton, VA 22827. Call 1-800-327-8097 (in Virginia, 703-298-2232). Ref.
IT50.

Children: Y Pets: N Smoking: Y Handicap Access: N Payment: All

Monteriggioni/Siena

CASTEL PETRAIO   *Rates: inexpensive-expensive*
Open: year-round   *Minimum Stay: one week*
Located in a wing of a turreted stone castle, these three apartments are
entered from a serene internal courtyard. Simply appointed, light-filled
and peaceful, the apartments sleep four to seven and offer color TV.
Nearby facilities include public swimming pool and tennis courts.
Mountain bikes available for guest rental offer a special opportunity to
ride the mountain trails and enjoy the spectacular views of Montagnola Senese. A recent ordinance banned motorcars from the Montagnola, making these pathways all the more attractive. The castle's
delightful location in the heart of Tuscany gives guests easy passage to
the beauty of this province. Contact: Rent A Home International, 7200
34th Avenue, N.W., Seattle, WA 98117. Call 206-545-6963. Ref.
5.02.01, 5.02.02, 5.02.03.

Children: Y Pets: N Smoking: Y Handicap Access: N Payment: C, P, V, M

Monteriggioni

ABBADIA A ISOLA   *Rates: budget-expensive*
Open: year-round   *Minimum Stay: one week*
Originally a cloister surrounding a church built in the 12th century,
the tiny village of Abbadia a Isola probably dates back to the same
period. These apartments occupy one of the ancient houses, restored
with fastidious attention to the old structure and handsomely furnished with antiques. The larger apartment on the second floor offers
spacious sleeping accommodations for six to eight people, a luminous
hall with an arched doorway leading into a sitting room with a fireplace and a study in the tower that dominates the countryside of the

surrounding village. The ground floor apartment sleeps four and includes private access to a sunny terrace. In addition to the immense beauty travelers expect in this region, two recently discovered Etruscan tombs are sure to excite the imagination. Contact: Rent A Home International, 7200 34th Avenue, N.W., Seattle, WA 98117. Call 206-545-6963. Ref. 5.01.01, 5.01.02.

Children: Y Pets: N Smoking: Y Handicap Access: N Payment: C, P, V, M

Montevarchi/Arezzo

IL POGGIOLO   *Rates: budget-moderate*
Open: year-round   *Minimum Stay: one week*

The English-speaking owners of this 18th-century villa have divided this splendid home into two apartments that share a beautifully furnished hanging garden as well as a handsomely equipped terrace. Available for either four or six persons, each apartment features fireplaces in both the living room and dining room, along with an eat-in kitchen and "live-in" bathroom. A warm and rich mixture of traditional and contemporary furnishings combine handsomely with the traditional Tuscan ambience created by whitewashed walls and terracotta floors. Only a short drive to both Siena and Arezzo, this beautiful holiday home also offers beautiful views of the surrounding countryside from every window. Maid service is available and farm products can be bought locally. Contact: Rent A Home International, 7200 34th Avenue, N.W., Seattle, WA 98117. Call 206-545-6963. Ref. 12.04.01, 12.04.02.

Children: Y Pets: Y Smoking: Y Handicap Access: N Payment: C, P, V, M

Nocchi

AL TENENTE   *Rates: budget-inexpensive*
Open: year-round   *Minimum Stay: one week*

On a quiet estate with a splendid view of the tiny village, surrounded by hills covered with vineyards, three modern accommodations house up to four people apiece. One is an independent house and two are annexed apartments in a single building. They have been completely remodeled and furnished in the past year, yet have retained their country charm. All have a living/dining room with a fireplace and a kitchen on the ground floor. Upstairs, all have a double and a twin bedroom and a bath with shower. The house has a terrace off the double bedroom and the apartments share a garden. A tennis court is on the grounds for guests' use, and the beaches of Versilia are less than eight miles away. Contact: Europa-Let, PO Box 3537, Ashland, OR 97520. Call 1-800-462-4486 or 503-482-1442. Ref. Solemar 3.04.

Children: Y Pets: N Smoking: Y Handicap Access: N Payment: C, P, T

Panzano

CORBULO   *Rates: moderate-expensive*
Open: year-round   *Minimum Stay: one week*

In the oldest part of a village in the heart of Chianti Classico, this lovely, spacious apartment offers all the attractions of traditional village life. Guests enter the recently restored and refurbished gem from the piazzetta (village square); on the other side, the living room opens onto a terrace complete with a pool and a sweeping vista of the hills beyond. The dining room, the kitchen/breakfast area with a fireplace, the two twin bedrooms and the bathroom are all comfortably furnished in excellent taste. For recreation, tennis and horseback riding can be found within ten miles. The village itself offers shopping and services, including a very good restaurant just steps away from the house and bus service to Florence (21 miles) every hour on work days. Contact: Europa-Let, PO Box 3537, Ashland, OR 97520. Call 1-800-462-4486 or 503-482-1442. Ref. Solemar 1.41.

Children: N   Pets: N   Smoking: Y   Handicap Access: N   Payment: C, P, T

Passignano

CASTELROTTO   *Rates: inexpensive-moderate*
Open: year-round   *Minimum Stay: one week*

Commanding a panoramic view of vineyards, fields and the Badia castle, one of the most beautiful spots of the Chianti Classico is the quiet setting for this restored apartment in a country house. The huge living/dining room has beamed ceilings, a cooking area and large, open fireplace. A double bedroom and a walk-through single share a full bath. Tastefully furnished with nicely restored rustic pieces for a homey, country atmosphere, the house has a large garden with a gazebo. Locally produced wine, olive oil, poultry, vegetables and fruit are all available on the premises. Tennis and riding facilities are close by and the delights of Florence are a mere 16 miles away. Contact: Europa-Let, PO Box 3537, Ashland, OR 97520. Call 1-800-462-4486 or 503-482-1442. Ref. Solemar 1.02.

Children: Y   Pets: N   Smoking: Y   Handicap Access: N   Payment: C, P, T

Pieve Santo Stefano

14TH-CENTURY VILLA   *Rates: expensive-deluxe*
Open: May 19-September 29   *Minimum Stay: one week*

Amid rolling hills above the Tiber River valley, this former watchtower complete with its own enchanting chapel is loaded with character without skimping on modern comforts. Excellent for a large family or group, four bedrooms sleep up to nine people, and there are two bathrooms. You can pack lightly, since you'll probably spend a lot of time at the swimming pool in swimsuits; and the washing machine allows you to recycle your other clothes. Sit down for a meal in the unusual barrel-vaulted kitchen or on the shaded terrace, then let the dishwasher clean up. Afterward, relax in front of the big open fireplace in the living room; two other living areas lead off it, one with a TV. Contact: B & D de Vogue International, Inc., 1830 S. Mooney Blvd. Ste. 203, Visalia, CA 93277. Call 209-733-7119 or 1-800-727-4748. Ref. IT 75.

Children: Y   Pets: N   Smoking: Y   Handicap Access: N   Payment: P, A, V, M

Pievescola/Siena

TORRE DOGANIERA

Open: year-round

Rates: inexpensive-moderate
Minimum Stay: one week

Immersed in history, this completely restored and luxurious apartment occupies what was once the tower that regulated commerce over the lower Siena road. On the estate property, digs have uncovered an original stone-paved road that dates back to the time of the Romans. The proud tower and estate dominate the hills and countryside for miles around. From the ground-floor dining room and kitchen that includes a raised fireplace, a semi-circular flight of wooden stairs leads to the second floor, where traditional Tuscan features appoint a large, spacious living room. The apartment sleeps two to four and offers color TV, a private furnished garden, barbecue grill and laundry room as well as optional conveniences including central heat, air conditioning and maid service. Contact: Rent A Home International, 7200 34th Avenue, N.W., Seattle, WA 98117. Call 206-545-6963. Ref. 5.05.01.

Children: Y Pets: N Smoking: Y Handicap Access: N Payment: C, P, V, M

Pistoia

IL CASONE

Open: year-round

Rates: moderate-deluxe
Minimum Stay: one week

Situated at the end of the tiny village of Signorino, where several good restaurants and local produce ensure many memorable meals, this renovated farmhouse offers privacy and charm along with the rich color of the surrounding chestnut woods. The light-filled main floor of the house features an open living/dining room and a blue and white tile-accented kitchen equipped with a fireplace for grilling and a wood oven for baking bread and pizza. This simply but elegantly furnished house accommodates nine to ten people in the generous comfort of two double bedrooms, one twin and three singles, with the convenience of three bathrooms. Additional conveniences include telephone, optional maid service and central heating. Contact: Rent A Home International, 7200 34th Avenue, N.W., Seattle, WA 98117. Call 206-545-6963. Ref. 2.01.01

Children: Y Pets: Y Smoking: Y Handicap Access: N Payment: C,P,V, M

Pomino

MODERN VILLA

Open: May 19-September 29

Rates: inexpensive-expensive
Minimum Stay: one week

Pomino is a village set in steep, hilly countryside surrounded by the vineyards of one of the biggest Chianti producing families in Italy. On the outskirts of town, amid green lawns and red roses, stands this traditionally styled modern villa. French doors lead from the shaded terrace into the dining room and living room, comfortable and elegant with an open fire and antique furniture. The kitchen is fully equipped with a dishwasher, and other modern conveniences include a washing machine, television and, upon request, telephone and cleaning service. The villa sleeps six in three bedrooms, two bathrooms and a barbecue. Contact: B & D de Vogue International, Inc., 1830 S. Mooney Blvd. Ste.

203, Visalia, CA 93277. Call 209-733-7119 or 1-800-727-4748. Ref. IT 83.

Children: Y Pets: N Smoking: Y Handicap Access: N Payment: P, A, V, M

Pontedera

LE FERRINE   *Rates: deluxe*
Open: June 30-September 1   *Minimum Stay: one week*

Set in the rolling Tuscan hills, the beautiful villa of Le Ferrine over-looks an unspoiled valley blanketed with vineyards, olive groves and woods. This superbly situated residence is only a few miles from such charming villages as Montaione, Volterra and San Gimignano and within easy reach of Pisa and Florence. Featuring gothic-style vaulted ceilings, the villa contains a large living room with French doors open-ing onto the patio, a separate sitting room, spacious kitchen, master suite and three other bedrooms. The well-tended grounds offer an ap-pealing garden with a swimming pool surrounded by flowers and bushes. Contact: Villas and Apartments Abroad Ltd, 420 Madison Ave, New York, NY 10017. Call 212-759-1025 or 1-800-433-3020.

Children: Y Pets: Y Smoking: Y Handicap Access: N Payment: C, P, T

Pontremoli

PARESI   *Rates: deluxe*
Open: June 1-September 30   *Minimum Stay: one week*

This opulent villa featuring exquisite murals by the celebrated artist Natali was built in 1720 as the country home for the illustrious Paresi family. Situated in a lovely valley surrounded by Apeninninean peaks and lying near the meeting point of two rivers, it is near many of the medieval castles of the Lunigiana. It's also within easy reach of the "five terre" coast at La Spezia, made famous by the Romantic poets. The villa grounds offer beautiful gardens and a refreshing swimming pool. The guest accommodation itself is contained in the ground floor of the immense main house surrounding the courtyard and includes a sitting room, drawing room and dining room, a large kitchen and five comfortable bedrooms. Contact: Villas and Apartments Abroad Ltd, 420 Madison Avenue, New York, NY 10017. Call 212-759-1025 or 1-800-433-3020.

Children: Y Pets: Y Smoking: Y Handicap Access: N Payment: C, P, T

Poppiano

CASTELLO DI POPPIANO   *Rates: deluxe*
Open: year-round   *Minimum Stay: one week*

Set on a hill and dominating the medieval town that surrounds it, this majestic castle dates back to the 12th century. Its grounds encompass vineyards, olive groves, gardens, terraces and a large pool. Counts from the original owners' family still live in a wing of the villa, and some of the antique furniture is as old as the house. The apartment for nine housed in the castle features spacious rooms with high ceilings. On the ground floor, guests enjoy a vast entrance gallery, a living room with a fireplace, a dining room, a kitchen, a double bedroom and a full bath. Upstairs is another gallery, a studio, a bath and a single, a double and two twin bedrooms. With all the estate has to offer and Florence just over 15 miles away, there is something for everyone here. Contact: Europa-Let, PO Box 3537, Ashland, OR 97520. Call 1-800-462-4486 or 503-482-1442. Ref. Solemar C.06.

Children: Y Pets: N Smoking: Y Handicap Access: N Payment: C, P, T

Populonia

CASA NUOVA   *Rates: expensive-deluxe*
Open: April 28-November 2   *Minimum Stay: one week*

On a vast farm amid fields of grain less than a mile from the beach, this large remodeled farmhouse is surrounded by a huge enclosed garden. Furnished in excellent taste, the roomy house for up to nine is comfortable in any season. During the warmer months, the rooms on the ground floor—a living area, dining room, double bedroom and small walk-through bedroom with a sofa bed—are cool. Upstairs, the spacious living room with a fireplace offers warmth on the coldest nights. The upper floor also has a kitchen/breakfast room with a washing machine, two full bathrooms and a double, single and two twin bedrooms. The rental includes maid service for three hours a day, and guests have private beach access at Baratti. Contact: Europa-Let, PO Box 3537, Ashland, OR 97520. Call 1-800-462-4486 or 503-482-1442. Ref. Solemar 2.16.

Children: Y Pets: N Smoking: Y Handicap Access: N Payment: C, P, T

Porto Santo Stefano

CASA MARCHE   *Rates: budget-deluxe*
Open: year-round   *Minimum Stay: one week*

A small road leads from the port of this very fashionable seaside town out along a promontory jutting into the sea. Here stands one of the oldest villas in Porto Santo Stefano. It is positioned ideally in a private and stunning setting, which a locked gate and lush tropical foliage ensure. You can choose from three apartments for four that feature details such as balconies overlooking the port and the sea, and furnished terraces spilling into the garden. Shuttered windows and French doors admit light and cooling breezes from the sea. Afternoons pass quickly at one of the many fine restaurants near the port, or in meditation at the monastery in the hills overlooking the coast. You can also explore the vineyards of the nearby island of Giglio. Contact: British Travel Associates, P. O. Box 299, Elkton, VA 22827. Call 1-800-327-8097 (in Virginia, 703-298-2232). Ref. IA3-5.

Children: N Pets: N Smoking: Y Handicap Access: N Payment: All

Prato

GARDEN VILLA   *Rates: inexpensive-moderate*
Open: year-round   *Minimum Stay: one week*

The ancient town of Prato still retains the aura of its rich history amidst the bustle of modernity. Masterworks of Fra Filippo Lippi and Donatello can be found in the town as well as evocative remnants of the mysterious Etruscans. Set in a private park and flanked by a charming garden, this quiet house on the outskirts provides easy access to Prato and the neighboring towns. Although the house is centrally heated, a cheery fire in the living room's handsome fireplace evokes the cozy pleasures of yesteryear. There are also a separate dining room and a kitchen downstairs and a spacious bedroom is found upstairs (the house accommodates five). Contact: Interhome Inc., 124 Little Falls Rd., Fairfield, NJ 07004. Call 201-882-6864. Ref. I5287/1.

Children: Y   Pets: Y   Smoking: Y   Handicap Access: N   Payment: P, V, M

Quercegrossa

CASTELLO   *Rates: budget-expensive*
Open: year-round   *Minimum Stay: one week*

Amid lush greenery on a working farm that produces wine and olive oil, this faithfully restored castle offers an exquisite panorama of the Tuscan countryside. Maintained in the classic country style, with gleaming tile floors and polished wood furniture, the apartments and separate house feature exposed beams, stone arches and open fireplaces. Each offers charming accommodations for two to six people, and shares an in-ground pool, courtyard and garden (the house has its own private garden). This is a marvelous place for a peaceful country vacation, yet Siena lies just five miles away and Florence, 35 miles, so opportunities for touring abound. Contact: Europa-Let, PO Box 3537, Ashland, OR 97520. Call 1-800-462-4486 or 503-482-1442. Ref. Solemar 1.05.

Children: Y   Pets: N   Smoking: Y   Handicap Access: N   Payment: C, P, T

Radda in Chianti

CEPPETO   *Rates: expensive-deluxe*
Open: year-round   *Minimum Stay: two weeks*

Like a pair of handsome twins, these two nearly identical apartments issued from the careful conversion of a Tuscan farmhouse. Available individually or together—a corridor door can be opened to connect them—the apartments sleep seven each and feature spacious living and dining rooms. The two share a tile-roofed loggia, a second loggia and thoughtfully appointed grounds with an outdoor barbecue. To one side of a sloping lawn that spills gracefully from the lofty height of the house—about 1,800 feet above sea level—is the swimming pool, which offers a breathtaking view of Radda in Chianti. Country strolls or day trips to Siena, Florence or Castellina in Chianti enrich a stay at this majestically situated villa. Maid service is available. Contact: Rent A Home International, 7200 34th Avenue, N.W., Seattle, WA 98117. Call 206-545-6963. Ref. 7.02.01, 7.02.02.

Children: Y   Pets: N   Smoking: Y   Handicap Access: N   Payment: C, P, V, M

Radda in Chianti

FATTORIA DI CASTELVECCHI   *Rates: inexpensive-expensive*
Open: year-round   *Minimum Stay: one week*

Magnifico Castelvecchi! In the ancient vaults beneath this exquisite castle the finest Chianti Classico wines mature in oak casks, as they have done for centuries. The tranquil gardens of roses, dahlias and flowering cherry trees offer an exquisite haven from the outside world. Accommodations for two to six in either charming cottages or spacious apartments feature appointments such as open fireplaces, private gardens and central heating, and all share an immense swimming pool and tennis court. You will find yourself smack in the middle of the Chianti-producing district of Tuscany, which is ideal for wine tasting and collecting and happily situated only a short drive away from the astounding riches of Siena, Florence and San Gimignano. Contact: Vacances Provencales Vacations, 729 Cutter Lane, Elk Grove, IL 60007. Call 708-893-9402. Ref. 201-6.

Children: Y   Pets: Y   Smoking: Y   Handicap Access: N   Payment: P

Radda

FRONCOLE   *Rates: budget-expensive*
Open: year-round   *Minimum Stay: one week*

Surrounded by a lovely, well-kept garden, this distinctive farmhouse has been wonderfully remodeled into two apartments. Beautifully furnished in the classic Tuscan country style, it is equipped with every modern comfort, including a telephone, a TV, a washing machine and a dishwasher. Maid service is available as well. Both apartments, a studio for two and a two-bedroom for up to four, have separate entrances and share the large swimming pool with each other and the owners, who live in the villa next door. Tennis and horseback riding are available nearby and Florence, with its magnificent art and architecture, is less than 30 miles away. Contact: Europa-Let, PO Box 3537, Ashland, OR 97520. Call 1-800-462-4486 or 503-482-1442. Ref. Solemar 1.01.

Children: Y   Pets: N   Smoking: Y   Handicap Access: N   Payment: C, P, T

San Casciano

VILLA TENDA   *Rates: expensive*
Open: year-round   *Minimum Stay: one week*

On a ridge dominating the Greve Valley, surrounded by olive groves and woods, Villa Tenda offers an ideal blend of traditional and modern style. Outside, it has the look of an old Tuscan country home, yet inside it is filled with modern conveniences such as central heating, a refrigerator, a freezer, a dishwasher, a television and a telephone. The estate's old threshing floor has been paved in terra cotta and equipped with garden furniture; next to it is a covered loggia with a wood-burning oven perfect for cooking pizza or barbecuing in the cool evening air. The villa's upper floor, furnished in typical Tuscan style, contains three twin bedrooms and three baths. The ground floor, equally comfortable, has an entrance hall, a living room, a dining room, a TV room and a kitchen/breakfast room. Contact: Europa-Let, PO Box 3537, Ashland, OR 97520. Call 1-800-462-4486 or 503-482-1442. Ref. Solemar C.03.

Children: Y   Pets: N   Smoking: Y   Handicap Access: N   Payment: C, P, T

San Donato in Poppio

LE FILIGARE *Rates: budget-expensive*
Open: year-round *Minimum Stay: one week*

Three independent apartments in this perfectly restored hilltop farmhouse share spacious grounds graciously appointed with abundant garden furniture and a barbecue. Ideally located only 15 miles from Florence and Siena, the house offers views of rich Chianti valleys and woodlands, making this working farm a feast for the eyes. A tennis court and intimate outdoor chapel with rustic stone benches invite both athletic and meditative pursuits. Apartments appointed with the charm of traditional Tuscan touches accommodate four to six people. Guests will enjoy meals featuring produce and wine from the estate prepared in their own kitchens. Maid service is available, as is firewood. Contact: Rent A Home International, 7200 34th Avenue, N.W., Seattle, WA 98117. Call 206-545-6963. Ref. 3.08.01, 3.08.02, 3.08.03.

Children: Y Pets: Y Smoking: Y Handicap Access: N Payment: C,P, V, M

San Gimignano

LE TORRI *Rates: moderate*
Open: year-round *Minimum Stay: one week*

Located in the very heart of the medieval city of San Gimignano, this handsomely restored apartment is only a few feet away from the world-famous Piazza Della Cisterna. A quick drive through the Tuscan hillsides delivers visitors to Volterra, an Etruscan city know for its alabaster quarries and factories. A gated entrance leads to the grounds, where a huge hanging garden rises above the road. Follow a stone-paved path to the house rich with architectural features, such as barrel-vaulted ceilings and original stone steps. The two-story dwelling includes kitchen, living room with sofa bed and two bedrooms (one double, two twin). Contact: Rent A Home International, 7200 34th Avenue, N.W., Seattle, WA 98117. Call 206-545-6963. Ref. 4.01.01

Children: Y Pets: N Smoking: Y Handicap Access: N Payment: C, P, V, M

San Gimignano

PIETRASERENA *Rates: budget-inexpensive*
Open: year-round *Minimum Stay: one week*

The windows of this delightful apartment offer a glorious view of the walled city and sky-reaching medieval towers of San Gimignano less than a mile away. Situated on the second floor of a recently refurbished hilltop farmhouse, the apartment shares a spacious garden with the owners of the house, who, when they are present, offer guests the friendliest of welcomes. Open windows and doors at every turn bathe this luminous apartment in Tuscan sunshine. The apartment includes a spacious living room with two single sofa beds, a double bedroom with one extra bed, a separate dining room and kitchen equipped with washing machine. Contact: Rent A Home International, 7200 34th Avenue, N.W., Seattle, WA 98117. Call 206-545-6963. Ref. 4.03.01.

Children: Y Pets: N Smoking: Y Handicap Access: N Payment: C, P, V, M

San Gimignano
RUSTIC FARMHOUSE

Rates: moderate-expensive

Open: year-round

Minimum Stay: one week

This simple, rustic farmhouse above a cantina overlooks some of the prettiest countryside in Tuscany, with profiles of San Gimignano's towers on the skyline and rows of olive trees and grapevines below. This is a working vineyard, and the owner encourages guests to do some wine tasting and maybe buy a bottle or two. The large, old fashioned living room/kitchen, cozy with an open fire, invites guests to savor their vacation fully. Four bedrooms sleep up to six people, and for an additional charge, two more beds may be added. The swimming pool and its surrounding terrace are shared with the owner and one other apartment. When and if you can tear yourself away from here, the cultural, historic and artistic attractions of Pisa, Siena and Florence are all easily accessible. Contact: B & D de Vogue International, Inc., 1830 S. Mooney Blvd. Ste. 203, Visalia, CA 93277. Call 209-733-7119 or 1-800-727-4748. Ref. IT 88.

Children: Y Pets: N Smoking: Y Handicap Access: N Payment: P, A, V, M

Sansepolcro/Arezzo
VILLA LA CASTELLACCIA

Rates: inexpensive-moderate

Open: year-round

Minimum Stay: one week

Splendor and elegance define this large, two-story apartment in a 16th-century villa. Surrounded by a well-kept garden and centuries-old trees, this home less than an hour's drive from Perugia, Assisi and Lake Trasimeno, is ideal for those who want to explore central Italy. Enter the apartment through a furnished garden and step into a spacious hall with period furniture. Other ground-floor features include a furnished rear garden, a drawing room with TV and a rustically furnished dining room. The upper floor, which includes sleeping accommodations for six (including a French bed in a romantic 18th-century room), provides a dramatic living room with decorated walls and ceiling in perfect 18th-century style. Contact: Rent A Home International, 7200 34th Avenue, N.W., Seattle, WA 98117. Call 206-545-6963. Ref. 12.01.01.

Children: Y Pets: N Smoking: Y Handicap Access: N Payment: C, P, V, M

Sarteano
LO SCROGIO

Rates: deluxe

Open: June 1-September 30

Minimum Stay: one week

Set in the serene "Val di Chiana," Lo Scrogio is a striking 17th-century country house. Majestic Mount Cetona dominates this beautiful Tuscan valley, with alluring woods, rocky ravines and bewitching grottoes for the hardy hiker. Offering a secluded garden and swimming pool, the house includes two bedrooms and a kitchen/breakfast room on the first floor; three more bedrooms, a sitting room/dining area and a veranda on the second. It also features a tower containing a very private sixth bedroom, this one a hideaway master suite with a sumptuous French bed. Contact: Villas and Apartments Abroad Ltd, 420

Madison Avenue, New York, NY 10017. Call 212-759-1025 or 1-800-433-3020.

Children: Y   Pets: Y   Smoking: Y   Handicap Access: N   Payment: C, P, T

Scarlino

LA MACINA   *Rates: budget-inexpensive*
Open: year-round   *Minimum Stay: one week*

This vine-covered, tile-roofed house was once used to press olives. It is now a very comfortable dwelling for four, furnished in the Tuscan country style. Everything is on the ground floor; the entrance leads directly into a living room with a fireplace adjoining a kitchen/breakfast area, one charming double and one twin bedroom and a full bathroom. The house is surrounded by a large private yard with plenty of sunshine, grass and trees. The famous beach of Punta Ala lies about ten miles away, but the village and nearby beaches are less than four miles distant. Contact: Europa-Let, PO Box 3537, Ashland, OR 97520. Call 1-800-462-4486 or 503-482-1442. Ref. Solemar 2.19.

Children: Y   Pets: N   Smoking: Y   Handicap Access: N   Payment: C, P, T

Siena

AGRESTO   *Rates: Deluxe*
Open: April 28-September 28   *Minimum Stay: one week*

Within its own private garden on a knoll covered with vineyards, this ivy-covered farmhouse sleeps 11. The house enjoys a panoramic view of the rolling terrain typical of the "Lower Sienese," an area famous throughout the world for its excellent wines, olive oil and honey. Faithfully renovated and elegantly furnished, this home is often acclaimed as a classic example of Tuscan architecture. The ground floor has a large living room with a fireplace, two twin bedrooms, two full baths and a kitchen complete with a washing machine and a dishwasher. The upper floor has a loggia, another large living room with a fireplace, a single and three twin bedrooms, two full baths and a sitting room up in the tower. Outside, enjoy the view from the terrace beneath the loggia or take a dip in the large built-in pool. Contact: Europa-Let, PO Box 3537, Ashland, OR 97520. Call 1-800-462-4486 or 503-482-1442. Ref. Solemar C.09.

Children: Y   Pets: N   Smoking: Y   Handicap Access: N   Payment: C, P, T

Siena

CASON DEL BOSCO   *Rates: budget-inexpensive*
Open: year-round   *Minimum Stay: one week*

This traditional farmhouse apartment makes a happy holiday home, with the glorious city of Siena only minutes away and the Tuscan countryside outside your door. Closer yet, the village of Sovicille offers a full selection of shops and marketing, and walks in the Montagnola Senese afford splendid views of the countryside. Other apartments in this working farm complex are occupied by local people, but the court yard with garden furniture is for the exclusive use of guests. Features of the second-floor apartment include living room, dining room, eat-in kitchen and one double and one twin bed. Maid service is available. Contact: Rent A Home International, 7200 34th Avenue, N.W., Seattle, WA 98117. Call 206-545-6963. Ref. 11.10.01.

Children: Y Pets: Y Smoking: Y Handicap Access: N Payment: C, P, V, M

Siena

CASTELLO DI FROSINI   *Rates: inexpensive-expensive*
Open: year-round   *Minimum Stay: one week*

The turreted roof line of this castle rises dramatically above the surrounding treetops. The windows of this two-bedroom, two-bath apartment for four offer spectacular countryside views of the lower Siena valley. A fireplace and sitting area warm the large entrance hall that serves as living/dining room to this beautifully furnished apartment. An eat-in kitchen with washing machine adds extra convenience. Maid service is available, as are central heating and fireplace wood. Guests will find nearby tennis courts, swimming pool and swimming in the Merse River a welcome change from taking in the endless and splendid culture and art of Tuscany. Contact: Rent A Home International, 7200 34th Avenue, N.W., Seattle, WA 98117. Call 206-545-6963. Ref. 11.12.01.

Children: Y Pets: N Smoking: Y Handicap Access: N Payment: C, P, V, M

Siena

MONTALCINO   *Rates: budget-moderate*
Open: year-round   *Minimum Stay: one week*

For a breathtaking view of Montalcino and the beautiful surrounding countryside, you need only step out onto one of these apartment's three terraces, including a rooftop terrace reached by a pull-down ladder. The recently renovated apartment for four or five occupies the third floor of a very old house on the edge of this Tuscan city famous for its Brunello wine. You can take the chill off a cool night with a fire in the living room fireplace, or simply turn on the central heat. A short stroll will bring you down little winding streets to local shops and restaurants. A drive of under an hour will find you in Pisa, Florence or Siena. Contact: British Travel Associates, P. O. Box 299, Elkton, VA 22827. Call 1-800-327-8097 (in Virginia, 703-298-2232). Ref. IT18.

Children: Y Pets: N Smoking: Y Handicap Access: N Payment: All

Siena

VILLA ROSMARINO   *Rates: deluxe*
Open: year-round   *Minimum Stay: one week*

Situated only a short drive away from famed sights of Tuscany as well as the seaside town of Castiglione della Pescaia, this estate house offers especially grand grounds that include a tartan tennis court surrounded by olive, oak, and cypress trees. A walk through the rustic hillside garden scattered with stone terraces, or through rock gardens fragrant with local herbs appeals to every nature lover. The villa proper features not one but two living/dining rooms, one of which opens onto a large loggia covered with roses and wisteria. A second-floor living room adjoins the two double and three twin bedrooms. To one side of the villa, a little two-story barn contains a pair of guest suites as well as a bread oven and wood stack. Contact: Rent A Home International, 7200 34th Avenue, N.W., Seattle, WA 98117. Call 206-545-6963. Ref. 11.09.01.

Children: Y Pets: N Smoking: Y Handicap Access: N Payment: C, P, V, M

Sinalunga

VILLA BELLA   *Rates: expensive-deluxe*
Open: year-round   *Minimum Stay: one week*

A library filled with oft-read books, old prints and a ceramic collection, tastefully wall-papered bedrooms and French windows flooding the rooms with light: These are the touches that make this house feel especially homey. Three twin, two single and one double bedroom provide ample sleeping space for ten. A garden with weeping willows and pampas grass offers a romantic setting, and the old town of Sinalunga, only minutes away, has numerous fine restaurants for the cook's day off. With its views of the 15th-century Santuario del Rifugio and the surrounding mountains and valleys, this villa offers near-perfect repose. Car excursions can easily be planned throughout Tuscany and Umbria and to Lake Trasimeno, where swimming and water sports await you. Contact: Vacances Provencales Vacations, 729 Cutter Lane, Elk Grove, IL 60007. Call 708-893-9402. Ref. 222.

Children: Y Pets: Y Smoking: Y Handicap Access: N Payment: P

Starda

LA VALLE   *Rates: budget-inexpensive*
Open: year-round   *Minimum Stay: one week*

High on a hill in the heart of Chianti Classico stands the small stone village of Starda, surrounded by the woods of Monteluco. Here, nestled on a slope with a beautiful view, is La Valle, a house whose upper floor has been completely renovated to provide comfortable vacation living for four. This completely private house is nicely furnished with modern and traditional Tuscan pieces, and has a kitchen with a fireplace, a living/dining room, a double and a twin bedroom and a bath with a shower. If you want to enjoy the countryside but still have access to the Italian marvels of Siena and Florence, this may be just the place for you. Contact: Europa-Let, PO Box 3537, Ashland, OR 97520. Call 1-800-462-4486 or 503-482-1442. Ref. Solemar 1.11.

Children: Y Pets: N Smoking: Y Handicap Access: N Payment: C, P, T

Stigliano

LA PODERINA   *Rates: budget-moderate*
Open: year-round   *Minimum Stay: one week*

It is only about ten miles from this turreted castle to the glorious city of Siena, but you'll never know you're that close to an urban center. Surrounded by gracious grounds with the added delight of an ancient ornamental pool renovated into an enchanting swimming pool, this imposing and splendid stone building stands on the edge of the small village of Stigliano. Three very private third-floor apartments sleep two to four people each. Quiet walks in the countryside near the village or a game of billiards or Ping-Pong assure relaxation from the hard work of sightseeing. Contact: British Travel Associates, P. O. Box 299, Elkton, VA 22827. Call 1-800-327-8097 (in Virginia, 703-298-2232). Ref. IT35-37.

Children: Y   Pets: N   Smoking: Y   Handicap Access: N   Payment: All

Tavarnelle Val di Pesa

POGGIO FRANTOIO

Open: year-round

Rates: budget-deluxe

Minimum Stay: one week

Situated on a hilltop, the wine producing farm of Poggio Frantoio offers a large swimming pool, panoramic views, nearby public tennis courts and the valued privacy of a fenced estate. The estate comprises three farmhouses, one of which is reserved for the owner. The other two are divided into charming apartments that feature the warmth of traditional Tuscan appointments—whitewashed walls, terra-cotta floors and wood beamed ceilings. Apartments sleep two to eight people. Other features include kitchens and ready access to surrounding gardens and views of the sweeping countryside. Contact: Rent A Home International, 7200 34th Avenue, N.W., Seattle, WA 98117. Call 206-545-6963. Ref. 3.06.01, 3.06.02, 3.06.03.

Children: Y   Pets: N   Smoking: Y   Handicap Access: N   Payment: C,P, V, M

Tavarnelle

L'UGO

Open: year-round

Rates: inexpensive

Minimum Stay: one week

The "Fattoria dell'Ugo" is a majestic villa that dates back to the year 1600. Wine is still produced in the old cellars beneath the farm, which is surrounded by rolling hills covered with vineyards and olive groves. A wing of the villa contains a comfy apartment for four with an entrance directly from the garden. The cozy living/dining room has a cooking area with a stove; two twin bedrooms and a bathroom complete the accommodations. There are private tennis courts and a barbecue on the grounds and shopping nearby. Offering a myriad of cultural pursuits, Florence is less than 20 miles away. Contact: Europa-Let, PO Box 3537, Ashland, OR 97520. Call 1-800-462-4486 or 503-482-1442. Ref. Solemar 1.19.

Children: Y   Pets: N   Smoking: Y   Handicap Access: N   Payment: C, P, T

Torre Nuova

POGGIO AL MULINO

Open: April 28-November 2

Rates: inexpensive-expensive

Minimum Stay: one week

At the foot of the promontory that forms the northern limit of the Gulf of Baratti, one of the most striking and pristine parts of the Tuscan coast, stands an old villa divided into four apartments for up to six. The huge park in which the house is situated offers an incomparable view and extreme tranquility. Furnished comfortably with antique as well as modern pieces, the apartments have high, partly fresco, beamed ceilings. All share the garden with lawn furniture, from which a path leads directly to the cliffs and beach. Guests can drive about two miles to another beach on the gulf or take the ferry from nearby Piombino to the island of Elba. Contact: Europa-Let, PO Box 3537, Ashland, OR 97520. Call 1-800-462-4486 or 503-482-1442. Ref. Solemar 2.20.

Children: Y   Pets: N   Smoking: Y   Handicap Access: N   Payment: C, P, T

Trequanda

LA SELVA   *Rates: budget-moderate*
Open: April 28-November 2   *Minimum Stay: one week*
Absolute tranquility and a marvelous panorama of rolling hills are yours at this very large stone farmhouse, which has been divided into ten apartments accommodating up to six people each. A recent restoration retained original beamed ceilings, fireplaces, tile floors and stone archways. Each apartment is tastefully and comfortably furnished and each, with one exception, has its own terrace, veranda or courtyard. All guests have access to a barbecue, a Ping-Pong room, a wine "canteen" and a large pool on the grounds overlooking the valley. The owners live on site and usually serve a weekly dinner of regional specialties. Tourists will find the famous Abbey of Monte Oliveto Maggiore nearby; the highway is close enough for easy access to Florence and beyond. Contact: Europa-Let, PO Box 3537, Ashland, OR 97520. Call 1-800-462-4486 or 503-482-1442. Ref. Solemar 1.43.

Children: Y   Pets: N   Smoking: Y   Handicap Access: N   Payment: C, P, T

Troghi

STABLE COTTAGE   *Rates: inexpensive-moderate*
Open: year-round   *Minimum Stay: one week*
This charming old stable cottage, whose spectacular views stretch for miles across cypress covered hills and the valley below it, sits snugly beneath the walls of the owner's impressive villa. Furnished comfortably with a mixture of modern and period pieces, it sleeps six in a double and two twin bedrooms; a crib will be provided upon request. Guests will surely want to congregate in the living room whose fully equipped kitchen area keeps the cook from getting lonely. When the food is ready, you may choose to eat out on the large terrace with a shady area. Troghi is an especially good base from which to visit Florence, only 11 miles or a half hour bus ride away, but don't overlook the simple pleasures available close by, such as tennis, swimming, shops and restaurants. Contact: B & D de Vogue International, Inc., 1830 S. Mooney Blvd. Ste. 203, Visalia, CA 93277. Call 209-733-7119 or 1-800-727-4748. Ref. IT 63.

Children: Y   Pets: N   Smoking: Y   Handicap Access: N   Payment: P, A, V, M

Vagliagli

VILLA IL CAMPO   *Rates: deluxe*
Open: year-round   *Minimum Stay: two weeks*
The elegant entrance to this beautifully restored Tuscan villa sets the

tone for the entire home: Here, a gallery of rustic wooden pillars support the high roof of this gorgeous country estate house. Other exceptional features include panoramic living room doors opening onto a large patio, a piano in the master bedroom and a lavishly appointed kitchen with an original wood oven. Six sleep here in luxurious accommodations. Located in a natural amphitheater, the villa grounds offer a large swimming pool and one of the most desirable views in all of Tuscany, as well as an herb garden and a meadow heady with the scent of lavender. Both maid service and central heat are available for an extra charge. Contact: Rent A Home International, 7200 34th Avenue, N.W., Seattle, WA 98117. Call 206-545-6963. Ref. 8.02.01.

Children: Y Pets: N Smoking: Y Handicap Access: N Payment: C, P, V, M

Venturina

CASTELLO DI MAGONA   *Rates: Deluxe*
Open: year-round   *Minimum Stay: one week*

For anyone who has ever imagined living in a fairy-tale castle, this rental could be a dream come true. Sitting atop a ridge overlooking the Tyrrhenian Sea on one side and a wide expanse of the Tuscan countryside on the other, this magnificent residence is surrounded by a verdant garden with a lovely pool. The antique furnishings and spacious rooms and halls create royal comfort in an atmosphere of refined elegance. There is a kitchen and a living/dining room downstairs, as well as an entrance hall, a double bedroom and full bath. Upstairs, a second living room features a fireplace; one double and one twin bedroom plus a bath and a half complete the accommodations. On the premises is a playroom for children, with Ping-Pong and other games. Nearby are beaches, tennis and riding facilities as well as a world-class golf course. Contact: Europa-Let, PO Box 3537, Ashland, OR 97520. Call 1-800-462-4486 or 503-482-1442. Ref. Solemar C.15.

Children: Y Pets: N Smoking: Y Handicap Access: N Payment: C, P, T

Viareggio

ESPLANADE   *Rates: budget-deluxe*
Open: year-round   *Minimum Stay: one week*

Viareggio has long been a popular Ligurian resort, first for fashionable Florentines and now for foreign visitors. During the annual Carnivale di Viareggio in the early spring, the city comes alive with gaudy celebrations and festive parades. Even if you miss the carnival, there's plenty to do: play tennis, fish and engage in assorted aquatic pursuits to name just a few possibilities. You'll find the handsome Esplanade in the center of town, practically on the water's edge. The luxury residence features a bar, a restaurant and a lounge right in the building; a garage eliminates parking-space blues. Each of the air-conditioned apartments boasts a pleasant balcony and a TV and can accommodate up to four guests in its nicely decorated rooms. Contact: Interhome

Inc., 124 Little Falls Rd., Fairfield, NJ 07004. Call 201-882-6864. Ref. I5200/1M, /5M, /7M.

Children: Y   Pets: Y   Smoking: Y   Handicap Access: N   Payment: P, V, M

Viareggio

GRACE   *Rates: inexpensive-moderate*
Open: year-round   *Minimum Stay: one week*

This magnificent 18th-century villa, in which guests can rent a gorgeous apartment for six, stands on a hill surrounded by tall pines. It has been perfectly remodeled to combine the house's original characteristics with modern amenities. Located on an upper floor of the villa, the apartment has a spacious living/dining room and cooking area with a fireplace, a double and a twin bedroom and a full bath. A staircase leads from the living room to an "attic" with another double bedroom and a bath with shower. There is a private garden for relaxation, or guests can visit nearby beaches, tennis and riding facilities. Pisa is also close enough for a day trip. Contact: Europa-Let, PO Box 3537, Ashland, OR 97520. Call 1-800-462-4486 or 503-482-1442. Ref. Solemar 3.06.

Children: Y   Pets: N   Smoking: Y   Handicap Access: N   Payment: C, P, T

Viareggio

VILLA L'OLIVETO   *Rates: deluxe*
Open: April 28-September 28   *Minimum Stay: one week*

Villa L'Oliveto stands on a hill overlooking the coast of Versilia, and on clear days you can see the island of Capraia and the entire coastline from Livorno to La Spezia. The magnificent grounds feature a gorgeous pool, two outdoor dining tables (one in the cool shade of the loggia), a barbecue and an orchard. The villa sleeps 11 in six bedrooms on three floors, and has a number of terraces offering panoramic views. In addition, there are two living rooms with fireplaces, a study, a kitchen/breakfast room and five bathrooms, some with tubs, some with showers. The villa's location in a private residential area assures peacefulness and privacy and is an ideal spot from which to visit the beaches of the coast as well as many interesting destinations nearby. Contact: Europa-Let, PO Box 3537, Ashland, OR 97520. Call 1-800-462-4486 or 503-482-1442. Ref. Solemar C.13.

Children: Y   Pets: N   Smoking: Y   Handicap Access: N   Payment: C, P, T

Vignale

FARMHOUSE TRIPLEX   *Rates: moderate-expensive*
Open: year-round   *Minimum Stay: one week*

Quietly situated by the side of a little lane, this large farmhouse and stable hold three apartments. They range from a unit complete with exposed stone walls, brick arches and vaulted ceiling, which sleeps four plus a baby; to a large two-level apartment for up to seven plus a baby, with an open fireplace in the spacious living room. The furnishings are an attractive mix of old country antiques and modern pieces. The large swimming pool, grassy yard and shaded gazebo offer ample opportunity for relaxation and recreation. The medieval town of Arezzo, with its magnificent churches and palaces, is just a ten-minute drive. Contact: B & D de Vogue International, Inc., 1830 S. Mooney Blvd. Ste. 203, Visalia, CA 93277. Call 209-733-7119 or 1-800-727-4748. Ref. IT 55, 56, 57.

Children: Y Pets: N Smoking: Y Handicap Access: N Payment: P, A, V, M

UMBRIA

Agello

PLATANI/IL TIGLIO *Rates: inexpensive-expensive*
Open: year-round *Minimum Stay: one week*

What lovelier way to pass an afternoon than to take a stroll in this estate's beautiful formal gardens and dip in the large swimming pool? This pair of handsome apartments—one in the annex of the splendid villa, the other in a nearby estate building—share both with the usually absent owner of the estate. Fragrant lemon trees and bougainvillaea surround the house, which offers accommodations for five. Guests will find these apartments the perfect base for exploring the beauty of Umbria as well as the northern cities of Tuscany. Contact: British Travel Associates, P. O. Box 299, Elkton, VA 22827. Call 1-800-327-8097 (in Virginia, 703-298-2232). Ref. IU3, IU4.

Children: Y Pets: N Smoking: Y Handicap Access: N Payment: All

Assisi

IL FARO *Rates: moderate-expensive*
Open: year-round *Minimum Stay: one week*

Just 500 meters from Assisi, this newly built villa offers guests a special intimacy with the town of St. Francis, where medieval architecture and Giotto's cathedral frescoes attract art lovers and pilgrims from all over the world. The house stands in a large garden shaded by tall majestic trees and also features a courtyard and a barbecue. The house sleeps seven to nine guests in three bedrooms as well as a double convertible sofa bed in the large living/dining room, which also includes a fireplace. Auto excursions to nearby Perugia and Spoleto afford the best in art, architecture and fine dining. Contact: British Travel Associates, P. O. Box 299, Elkton, VA 22827. Call 1-800-327-8097 (in Virginia, 703-298-2232). Ref. IU31.

Children: Y Pets: N Smoking: Y Handicap Access: N Payment: All

Castiglione del Lago

COTTAGE BONAZZOLI *Rates: budget-inexpensive*
Open: year-round *Minimum Stay: one week*

One of four lovingly converted farm houses, this cottage is hidden away in the gently rolling countryside just a few minutes from Lake Trasimeno. With accommodations for four, this home features furniture both elegant and rustic, and in keeping with its country nature, offers an especially charming kitchen with an original stone sink, open fireplace and large dining table. A studio with a grand piano, a light-filled sitting room and a large living room with a TV and picture window promise the best of leisure and relaxation. From this idyllic spot, you can visit a lake for water sports or travel the beautiful Umbrian hills to Perugia and Cortona. Contact: British Travel Associates, P. O. Box 299, Elkton, VA 22827. Call 1-800-327-8097 (in Virginia, 703-298-2232). Ref. IU13

Children: Y   Pets: N   Smoking: Y   Handicap Access: N   Payment: All

Cenerente

MACINA DELL'OSCANO   *Rates: budget-moderate*
Open: year-round   *Minimum Stay: one week*

In the shadow of the romantic Castel dell'Oscano and built into a gently sloping hill, Macina dell'Oscano, once a lively olive mill, has been converted into spacious and comfortable apartments. Just outside the charming village of Cenerente, the grounds offer a swimming pool, barbecue facilities and, on the ground floor of the mill, a TV/game room. A car is essential for touring the plush countryside and ancient towns—including nearby Perugia (five and a half miles), Assisi and Spoleto. The Oscano one-bedroom apartments, on the ground and first floors, accommodate up to three, while the Mullino apartments accommodate up to five in two bedrooms and a living room. Contact: Hometours International, Inc., 1170 Broadway, New York, NY 10001. Call: 212-689-0851 or 1-800-367-4668. Ref. 3290/3, 3290/4.

Children: Y   Pets: N   Smoking: Y   Handicap Access: N   Payment: C, P, T

Collelungo

IL FIENILE   *Rates: moderate-deluxe*
Open: year-round   *Minimum Stay: one week*

Originally a 19th-century stone stable, this meticulously converted holiday home still displays many of the building's original features, including panoramic picture windows affording fine views of the Umbrian hills. Enter this spacious property by a flight of exterior stairs leading to the second floor, where accommodations for four to six include one double and one twin bedroom as well as a large sitting/dining room. The cozy kitchen looks out onto a courtyard. The swimming pool on the front lawn offers the ultimate in convenience, but you will want to try the waters at nearby Lake Trasimeno for swimming, sailing and windsurfing. Contact: British Travel Associates, P.O. Box 299, Elkton, VA 22827. Call 1-800-327-8097 (in Virginia, 703-298-2232). Ref. IU6.

Children: Y   Pets: N   Smoking: Y   Handicap Access: N   Payment: All

Collumbella

LA GIOFRA   *Rates: inexpensive-moderate*
Open: year-round   *Minimum Stay: one week*

The hardest choice you'll have to make when you stay here will be whether to drive to Perugia or Assisi, both within minutes of these two apartments in a newly renovated old farmhouse. Fenced for privacy and surrounded by a large park shaded by a variety of mature trees, both apartments remain rustically charming and inviting. A charming, spacious two-story apartment sleeps six and offers a large open living room with fireplace and a kitchen with dining area that opens onto a terrace. A cozy second-floor apartment has a private entrance and sleeps four. Contact: British Travel Associates, P. O. Box 299, Elkton, VA 22827. Call 1-800-327-8097 (in Virginia, 703-298-2232). Ref. IU34, IU35.

Children: Y   Pets: N   Smoking: Y   Handicap Access: N   Payment: All

Lake Trasimeno

TRE PINI   *Rates: budget-inexpensive*
Open: year-round   *Minimum Stay: one week*

This restored farmhouse in the hills north of Lake Trasimeno is surrounded by a big fenced-in yard with a large above-ground pool. The house is divided into three apartments, one for the owner on the ground floor, two for guests on the mezzanine. Both apartments are cozy and have a rustic atmosphere. There is a studio with double sofa bed, a cooking area with a small oven and a bath with a shower. The larger apartment sleeps four in a twin and a double bedroom. It also has a living/dining room with a fireplace and cooking corner and a bath with a shower. Located near Perugia, these apartments offer access to all of central Italy—if touring is on your agenda. If not, swim in the pool, relax in the yard and take advantage of the tennis and horseback riding facilities nearby. Contact: Europa-Let, PO Box 3537, Ashland, OR 97520. Call 1-800-462-4486 or 503-482-1442. Ref. Solemar 4.01.

Children: Y   Pets: N   Smoking: Y   Handicap Access: N   Payment: C, P, T

Passignano Trasimeno

SANT AGNESE   *Rates: moderate-expensive*
Open: year-round   *Minimum Stay: one week*

At the edge of a cool woods on a sunny hillside, this charming old stone house overlooks the blue waters of Lake Trasimeno, a magnet for Italian anglers. The roomy house greets up to ten guests with attractive modern furnishings; a TV, a dishwasher, a washing machine and central heating further contribute to the comfort. Garden furniture is provided out on the picturesque patio and a large garden tempts you to walk its fragrant pathways. The lake and its sandy beaches are a short walk away; there are plenty of facilities in town for enjoying all your favorite aquatic activities. Contact: Interhome Inc., 124 Little Falls Rd., Fairfield, NJ 07004. Call 201-882-6864. Ref. I5512/1.

Children: Y   Pets: Y   Smoking: Y   Handicap Access: N   Payment: P, V, M

Perugia

18TH-CENTURY VILLA   *Rates: moderate-expensive*
Open: year-round   *Minimum Stay: one week*

Set amid a grand garden of gravel terraces, clipped yews, baroque walls and lemon trees planted in enormous terra cotta pots, one of Umbria's finest villas looks much as it did in the 18th century. Much restoration has been done since its occupation by the German and British armies in WW II and the villa, with its elaborate rococo and neoclassical painted rooms and beautiful furniture, has been featured in *Country Life* magazine. Two apartments are available, one for four, one for up to eight people and a baby. Furnished mainly with antiques, the units feature country comforts, such as open fireplaces, and modern conveniences that co-exist delightfully. Contact: B & D de Vogue International, Inc., 1830 S. Mooney Blvd. Ste. 203, Visalia, CA 93277. Call 209-733-7119 or 1-800-727-4748. Ref. IT 104, 105.

Children: Y Pets: N Smoking: Y Handicap Access: N Payment: P, A, V, M

Petrignano

PALAZZO VECCHIO   *Rates: expensive-deluxe*
Open: year-round   *Minimum Stay: one week*

Built in the 17th century on what is today a large, shady acre of garden, this spacious villa commands a view of the magical, mystical city of Assisi. Beautifully restored by its owners, the large house boasts an impressive collection of fine antique furniture, paintings and painted ceilings. A rambling home with a large kitchen, sitting room, formal dining room with a large open fireplace and library, the villa sleeps seven adults and two children in four bedrooms. Two additional bedrooms and an additional bath can be made available to larger parties. You can dream your time away with a nap under one of the tall trees in the garden, invigorate yourself with a swim in the pool in nearby Assisi or take a quick ride to Lake Trasimeno for an afternoon of sailing. Contact: British Travel Associates, P. O. Box 299, Elkton, VA 22827. Call 1-800-327-8097 (in Virginia, 703-298-2232). Ref. IU30.

Children: Y Pets: N Smoking: Y Handicap Access: N Payment: All

Spoleto

LA LICINA   *Rates: inexpensive*
Open: year-round   *Minimum Stay: one week*

Nestled in the hills outside of Spoleto, this lovely cottage sleeps four in one double and one twin bedroom. The rustic charm of stone and whitewashed walls enriches the large open living/dining room. From this cozy retreat, vacationers can easily visit the beautiful medieval town of Spoleto, which lies an easy ten-minute drive through the unspoiled countryside of Umbria. Here, the celebrated festivals of music and dance have created an artistic mecca for the world, and some of Italy's best restaurants await hungry gourmands. Contact: British Travel Associates, P. O. Box 299, Elkton, VA 22827. Call 1-800-327-8097 (in Virginia, 703-298-2232). Ref. IU9.

Children: Y Pets: N Smoking: Y Handicap Access: N Payment: All

Umbertide

MONTONE   *Rates: inexpensive-moderate*
Open: year-round   *Minimum Stay: one week*

Views from the windows of these two vacation rentals in the small, unspoiled village of Montone offer an incomparable Umbrian panorama over the tiled rooftops of the village. Situated only a short drive away from art-filled Perugia and recreational Lake Trasimeno, the two properties adjoin. A second-floor flat sleeps four and features a terrace overlooking the narrow street that winds downhill through the village. A three-story house, also for four, boasts undoubtedly the best terrace in the village for an "al fresco meal" or viewing a sunset over the Tiber valley. This unit is only available during the summer months. Contact: British Travel Associates, P. O. Box 299, Elkton, VA 22827. Call 1-800-327-8097 (in Virginia, 703-298-2232). Ref. IU40, IU41.

Children: Y   Pets: N   Smoking: Y   Handicap Access: N   Payment: All

Villastrada

LE QUERCE *Rates: inexpensive-moderate*
Open: year-round *Minimum Stay: one week*

A pair of old oak trees give this restored Umbrian farmhouse its name and offer sweet shade to the garden. Sweeping views from the house encompass the medieval hilltowns of Paciano and Panicale. Set very nearly on the border of Tuscany, the ground floor apartment for four to six is a stone's throw away from the pleasures of Lake Trasimeno. Features of this attractive home include a large living room with exposed beams and an archway leading to the charming dining room. One double and one twin bedroom open onto the terrace, and larger parties may rent an adjoining studio for two. Central heating and access to a washing machine add comfort and convenience to this hundred-year-old home. Contact: British Travel Associates, P. O. Box 299, Elkton, VA 22827. Call 1-800-327-8097 (in Virginia, 703-298-2232). Ref. IU14.

Children: Y   Pets: N   Smoking: Y   Handicap Access: N   Payment: All

VALLE D'AOSTA

Cervinia

L'ESCARGOT *Rates: budget-expensive*
Open: year-round *Minimum Stay: one week*

The magnificent and mysterious Matterhorn looms overhead as you walk the bustling streets of the famous alpine resort, Cervinia. A modern residence on a sunny hillside above town, L'Escargot offers its guests the use of a large lounge, a ski room and its own ski lift. The several four-person apartments are compact but intelligently laid out; some rooms have balconies. Cervinia's famous winter amusements include downhill and cross-country skiing, ice-skating, curling and bob-sledding. In the summer there is still plenty to do, with golf and tennis, fishing, swimming, cable-car rides and even summer skiing on Plateau Rosa. Contact: Interhome Inc., 124 Little Falls Rd., Fairfield, NJ 07004. Call 201-882-6864. Ref. I3070/10B, /10C, /10D, /10I, /11I.

Children: Y   Pets: N   Smoking: Y   Handicap Access: N   Payment: P, V, M

St. Pierre

PLEIN SOLEIL   *Rates: budget*
Open: year-round   *Minimum Stay: one week*

The Plein Soleil lives up to its name, situated on a sunny alpine slope and surrounded by a grove of fragrant fruit trees. Enjoy your barbecued meals out on the patio, or pass the sunny days with a time-honored game of bocce. Up to six guests can lodge in the two- and four-room apartments. All are complete with kitchenettes and private baths and several have balconies affording splendid views of the valley. St. Pierre itself is a charming village just a few miles west of Aosta. It welcomes guests with restaurants, shops, mountaineering opportunities and lovely nature walks in the reserve. Contact: Interhome Inc., 124 Little Falls Rd., Fairfield, NJ 07004. Call 201-882-6864. Ref. I3015/50A, /50B, /50C, /51A.

Children: **Y**   Pets: **Y**   Smoking: **Y**   Handicap Access: **N**   Payment: **P, V, M**

VENETIA

Brenzone

CAVENETA   *Rates: budget-inexpensive*
Open: May-November   *Minimum Stay: one week*

Nestled between Lake Garda and the slopes of Monte Baldo, Brenzone annually entrances visitors who seek the solace of country jaunts amid the fragrant olive groves. The Caveneta, located only a few feet from the water's edge, enjoys open views of the splendid lake. The four-person apartment consists of a living room with a divan bed, a full kitchen and two bedrooms; the six-person apartment has two additional bedrooms. Both apartments feature charming balconies with deck chairs and simple yet tasteful furnishings. After enjoying the lake's clear waters and the pretty countryside, perhaps you'd enjoy an outing to nearby Verona. Contact: Interhome Inc., 124 Little Falls Rd., Fairfield, NJ 07004. Call 201-882-6864. Ref. I2880/100M, /105M.

Children: **Y**   Pets: **Y**   Smoking: **Y**   Handicap Access: **N**   Payment: **P, V, M**

Padua/Venice

MIRTILLO   *Rates: budget-expensive*
Open: year-round   *Minimum Stay: two weeks*

A small and rustic villa, and second home a few feet away, provide beautiful views of the Euganean hills and a peaceful retreat only minutes from both Padua and Venice. The villa appointments include a large fireplace in the living/dining room, a balcony, a lovely furnished arbor and sleeping accommodations for six. The nearby villa "annex" sleeps three and has a covered terrace. You will find tennis and a swimming pool a short drive away. From here, you can easily pop into Padua for a look at one of Italy's liveliest university towns and a visit to an open market. Or instead, catch the vaporetto to glorious Venice for Carnival, the Regata Lunga or a general exploration of one of the great cities of Europe. Contact: Posarelli Vacations (Cuendet Italia),

180 Kinderamack Road, Park Ridge, NJ 07656. Call 201-573-9558. Ref. 4.01.01-02.

Children: **Y**　Pets: **N**　Smoking: **Y**　Handicap Access: **N**　Payment: **C, P, T**

Torcello

SAN GIOVANNI

Rates: deluxe

Open: June 30-September 1

Minimum Stay: one week

San Giovanni, built in the 17th century and named for the romanesque church whose ruins lie in its gardens, stands in Torcello, a lagoon community that long ago was a rival of Venice. Settled between the 5th and 7th centuries, Torcello had palaces and churches, shipyards and docks, its own nobility and its own laws. There's still a dock, from which a boat and driver will take villa guests to the nearby islands of Burano and Murano—or all the way to Venice. With vast grounds including a swimming pool set on a hill overlooking lavish gardens, the house is overseen by a maid, gardener and butler/boatman. It includes sitting rooms and a library, two suites and three additional bedrooms, a kitchen and dining room, plus a large veranda and delightful roof terrace with marvelous views. Contact: Villas and Apartments Abroad Ltd, 420 Madison Ave, New York, NY 10017. Call 212-759-1025 or 1-800-433-3020.

Children: **Y**　Pets: **Y**　Smoking: **Y**　Handicap Access: **N**　Payment: **C, P, T**

Torri del Benaco

SUNNY APARTMENT HOUSE

Rates: budget

Open: April-November

Minimum Stay: one week

The small, friendly village of Torri lies on the eastern shore of Lake Garda. If you've never had the chance before, the school here makes this an ideal place to learn the ropes of wind surfing. A shingle beach, water-sport center and small harbor will please other aquatic enthusiasts. The apartment building is well placed in a sunny nook on the outskirts of town. The cozy three-room apartment is located on the third floor and includes a handy kitchenette, a living and dining room with two convertible beds and a separate bedroom. There is also a balcony for enjoying the warm, sunny days and cool, breezy evenings on the lake. Contact: Interhome Inc., 124 Little Falls Rd., Fairfield, NJ 07004. Call 201-882-6864. Ref. I2892/1C.

Children: **Y**　Pets: **Y**　Smoking: **Y**　Handicap Access: **N**　Payment: **P, V, M**

Venice

CA BADOER DEI BARBACANI

Rates: deluxe

Open: June 1-September 30

Minimum Stay: one week

Built in the 1400s on the original site of the 10th-century Ca Badoer, this architecturally unique house has an intriguing mix of medieval and Renaissance features. The residence is a self-contained flat on the fourth floor, reachable by elevator, that offers excellent views of the bell tower and the spires of the Frari Church. Featuring high ceilings and exposed beams, the apartment contains an entrance hall, large kitchen/breakfast room, two bedrooms and a living room graced by a Renaissance doorway that leads to a south-facing balcony. Ca Badoer is in a quiet location between Campo Frari and Campo San Stin, within easy reach of both the Accademia and Rialto. Contact: Villas and Apartments Abroad Ltd, 420 Madison Ave, New York, NY 10017. Call 212-759-1025 or 1-800-433-3020.

Children: Y   Pets: Y   Smoking: Y   Handicap Access: N   Payment: C, P, T

Venice

CANNAREGIO   *Rates: moderate*
Open: year-round   *Minimum Stay: one week*

Visitors learn their way around the city of Venice not by car or train, but by foot and boat. From these two simply furnished flats in an old artisan area of the city, a short walk brings you to the Grand Canal. From there, you choose your route to the Lido beach or to Piazza San Marco. Renaissance and Gothic architecture, museums and historic sights jostle for your attention. These apartments, located on the second and third floors, sleep four to five and offer views over a courtyard. A nearby street market and the welcome absence of tourists in the neighborhood lure those who want to meet the Venetians themselves. Contact: British Travel Associates, P. O. Box 299, Elkton, VA 22827. Call 1-800-327-8097 (in Virginia, 703-298-2232). Ref. IV1, IV2.

Children: Y   Pets: N   Smoking: Y   Handicap Access: N   Payment: All

Venice

CASA GESUITI   *Rates: inexpensive-moderate*
Open: year-round   *Minimum Stay: one week*

This charming one-bedroom, one-bathroom, ground-floor apartment with wonderful canal views offers both the privacy of a house and the convenience of an urban apartment. Conveniently situated only a 10-minute walk from St. Mark's square, it provides a perfect base from which to tour the magnificent city. A spacious, landscaped and furnished patio/yard offers a comfortable retreat ideal for al fresco dining—just the thing after a summer afternoon at Lido beach. The bedroom has a double bed; a sitting area contains two single beds; and a California-style kitchen opens onto a dining room. Contact: Hometours International, Inc., 1170 Broadway, New York, NY 10001. Call: 212-689-0851 or 1-800-367-4668. Ref. 3280/2.

Children: Y   Pets: N   Smoking: Y   Handicap Access: N   Payment: C, P, T

Venice

LIDO APARTMENT   *Rates: inexpensive-moderate*
Open: year-round   *Minimum Stay: one week*

The Lido di Venezia is a long, sandy beach that frames the floating labyrinth of Venice and entices elegant visitors with its casino and other amusements. After exploring the mysterious canals and winding streets of the city, you'll be able to retreat from most of the tourist hubbub to the worldly romance of the Lido. The apartment enjoys a sunny location, and its two balconies offer beautiful sea views. The four-room apartment can easily accommodate six people in its living and dining room, kitchenette and two comfortable bedrooms. Restaurants and shops are nearby, as are vaporetti (ferries) back to the islands of Venice. Contact: Interhome Inc., 124 Little Falls Rd., Fairfield, NJ 07004. Call 201-882-6864. Ref. I4200/20C.

Children: Y   Pets: Y   Smoking: Y   Handicap Access: N   Payment: P, V, M

Venice

PALAZZO CORNER-SPENELLI   *Rates: expensive*
Open: June 1-September 30   *Minimum Stay: one week*
Built between 1490 and 1510, the gorgeous Palazzo CornerSpenelli—named for two of its colorful former owners—is ideally situated at San Angelo right on the Grand Canal. This self-contained ground-floor flat makes a quiet and restful Venician residence, containing a well-equipped kitchen, living room/dining area and two bedrooms. Access to the flat is through the palazzo's opulent entrance, transformed in 1542 into a classical Roman-style hall. Contact: Villas and Apartments Abroad Ltd, 420 Madison Ave, New York, NY 10017. Call 212-759-1025 or 1-800-433-3020.

Children: Y   Pets: Y   Smoking: Y   Handicap Access: N   Payment: C, P, T

Venice

PALAZZO QUERINI   *Rates: expensive-deluxe*
Open: June 1-September 30   Minimum Stay: one week; two weeks for Flat 1
Three lovely, self-contained flats are available for rent in the splendid Palazzo Querini, a converted 18th-century Venetian house that also houses the British Consulate. Flat 1 is a bright second-floor apartment looking out on the Grand Canal and Accademia Square, containing a large living room with a marble fireplace, dining room, study and two bedrooms. The one-bedroom, ground-floor Flat 2 offers a private garden and sunny living room overlooking the canal. French windows provide a view of an exquisite little courtyard adorned with rare statues, marble wells, a fountain and an ancient column. Flat 3 is a cozy, fully equipped studio hideaway, also on the first floor, that has a fine view of the canal as well. Contact: Villas and Apartments Abroad Ltd, 420 Madison Ave, New York, NY 10017. Call 212-759-1025 or 1-800-433-3020.

Children: Y   Pets: Y   Smoking: Y   Handicap Access: N   Payment: C, P, T

Venice

S. EUFEMIA   *Rates: inexpensive*
Open: year-round   *Minimum Stay: one week*
Tucked away on a quiet, sun-filled canal in Venice is the lovely residence S. Eufemia. Enjoy a stroll through the large, pretty garden as the waters gently lap against the building's foundation in true Venetian style. There are shops and quaint restaurants nearby, or hop on a vaporetto to be picturesquely ferried into the center of town. The three-room and four-room apartments can both comfortably accommodate four guests and both are centrally heated. The furnishings are

simple but attractive. And so that you can fully enjoy the serenades of passing gondoliers, the larger apartment features a window in the living room that opens onto the canal. Contact: Interhome Inc., 124 Little Falls Rd., Fairfield, NJ 07004. Call 201-882-6864. Ref. I4200/ 30A, /30C.

Children: Y   Pets: Y   Smoking: Y   Handicap Access: N   Payment: P, V, M

Venice

SAN POLO   *Rates: deluxe*
Open: June 1-September 30   *Minimum Stay: one week*

A splendid apartment is available on the second floor of a quintessential old Venetian house. Offering a captivating view of San Rocco and situated close to Santa Maria Glorios Dei Frari, one of the loveliest churches in Venice, the residence makes a glorious, atmospheric home base for indulging in the manifold pleasures of this picturebook city. It contains a huge living room with decorative French windows, a fully equipped kitchen/dining area and two extremely comfortable bedrooms. Contact: Villas and Apartments Abroad Ltd, 420 Madison Ave, New York, NY 10017. Call 212-759-1025 or 1-800-433-3020.

Children: Y   Pets: Y   Smoking: Y   Handicap Access: N   Payment: C, P, T

Verona

CASA BUTIRRI   *Rates: moderate*
Open: June 1-September 30   *Minimum Stay: one week*

Casa Butirri is a charming converted old farmhouse that stands in the courtyard of a grand country estate. The two-story residence has its own large garden and veranda and contains a comfortable sitting room, kitchen and dining area opening onto the garden, plus three bedrooms upstairs. With the slopes of the Lessini mountains visible in the distance, the house is superbly situated for visits to Verona and to Lake Garda, both less than 20 minutes away. Contact: Villas and Apartments Abroad Ltd, 420 Madison Ave, New York, NY 10017. Call 212-759-1025 or 1-800-433-3020.

Children: Y   Pets: Y   Smoking: Y   Handicap Access: N   Payment: C, P, T

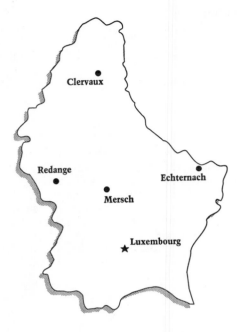

Luxembourg

NATIONAL TOURIST OFFICE
Open: year-round

Rates: budget-deluxe
Minimum Stay: varies

The Luxembourg National Tourist Office publishes a newsletter listing of hundreds of privately owned vacation rental properties throughout this charming country. From the capital city of Luxembourg to the smaller towns and provinces, the offerings represent virtually every type of accommodation (from modern condominium to mountainside chalet), price and level of luxury. The information—provided by the respective owners, who are responsible for their accuracy—is compiled, but not endorsed by, the Tourist Office, which takes no responsibility for their accuracy. All rental arrangements are to be made exclusively between the owner and prospective tenant and details regarding children, pets, smoking, access for the handicapped, payment, etc., vary with each property. While the Tourist Office does not handle bookings, they are happy to provide, in addition to the newsletter, information about the country or any particular areas you are interested in or considering for your visit. Contact: Luxembourg National Tourist Office, 801 Second Avenue, New York, NY 10017. Call: 212-370-9850.

Netherlands

NORTH HOLLAND

Amsterdam

CENTRAAL APARTMENT   *Rates: budget*
Open: July-August   *Minimum Stay: two weeks*

The magical canals, quaint streets and thriving nightlife of Amsterdam will all be at your doorstep in this marvelously located apartment for three. The lodgings include a comfortably furnished living room and a cozy bedroom. There's also a TV for relaxation and a piano for the musically adept. After a day full of seeing the sights and sampling the lifestyle of Amsterdam, the rooftop terrace is a splendid place to unwind with a glass of Dutch beer and survey the twinkling lights of the town. Contact: Binkhuysen Home Holidays, P.O. Box 279, 1900 AG Castricum, The Netherlands. Call 31-2518-57953. Ref. NL2-1354.

Children: **Y**   Pets: **Y**   Smoking: **Y**   Handicap Access: **N**   Payment: C, EC

Amsterdam

DE LANTAERNE   *Rates: budget-inexpensive*
Open: year-round   *Minimum Stay: none*

This attractive apartment hotel is located on not one, but two sparg canals near the center of the city. It's also wonderfully convenient to the Rijksmuseum, the Stedelijkmuseum and the Van Gogh Museum, three treasure troves bearing witness to the Netherlands' artistic wealth, both past and present. After seeing the sights and absorbing the ambience of Amsterdam, you'll return to a cozy suite in De Lantaerne, where you can relax for awhile in front of the TV before heading out for a night on the town. Contact: De Lantaerne, Leidsegracht 111, 1017 ND Amsterdam, The Netherlands. Call 31-20-23-22-21.

Children: **Y**   Pets: **Y**   Smoking: **Y**   Handicap Access: **N**   Payment: **C, V**

Amsterdam
GOLDEN TULIP BARBIZON PALACE   *Rates: moderate-deluxe*
Open: year-round   *Minimum Stay: none*
This large handsome hotel near the center of Amsterdam can provide you with luxurious accommodations during your stay in the city. The apartments are spacious and tastefully furnished; from the window of your suite you can watch the bustle and hum of lovely Amsterdam. The hotel stands on Prins Hendrikkade, a thriving thoroughfare that runs along the graceful Ij River. From this central position, the quaint canals spread out and wend their ways through the town; there's no better way to view the narrow houses and intricate facades of Amsterdam than from a seat on a little boat chugging along these watery highways. Contact: Golden Tulip Barbizon Palace, Prins Hendrikkade 59-72, 1012 AD Amsterdam, The Netherlands. Call 31-20-5564564.

Children: **Y**   Pets: **N**   Smoking: **Y**   Handicap Access: **N**   Payment: **C, V**

Amsterdam
PULITZER HOTEL   *Rates: expensive*
Open: year-round   *Minimum Stay: none*
The elegant Pulitzer overlooks the Prinsengracht, one of Amsterdam's most lovely canals. Just down the street, at Prinsengracht 263, you'll find the Anne Frank house, a poignant memorial to the courageous young girl and a tribute to the brave people who hid Anne and her family during World War II. To all the wonders and charm of Amsterdam, the Pulitzer adds the comforts and conveniences of a luxury hotel. The apartments are large and inviting; the excellent restaurant and other amenities will help make your stay worry-free. Contact: Pulitzer Hotel, Prinsengracht 315-331, 1016 GZ Amsterdam, The Netherlands. Call 31-20-5235235.

Children: **Y**   Pets: **Y**   Smoking: **Y**   Handicap Access: **N**   Payment: **C, V**

Huizen
HOLIDAY VILLA   *Rates: budget*
Open: July 7-August 4   *Minimum Stay: two weeks*
This pleasant villa sits by the woods outside of Huizen, a renowned pleasure port on the edge of the Ijsselmeer. The comfortably furnished interior includes a spacious living room, an eat-in kitchen and three comfy bedrooms; the TV and washing machine will add convenience

to your stay. Outside you'll find a large garden and a terrace with a view of the lovely park across the way. There are bikes available for gentle rides through the country. If you peddle over to the water's edge you can look across the narrow inlet and see the newly minted fields and towns of Flevoland, a large island that was reclaimed from the waters of the Ijsselmeer less than 30 years ago. Contact: Binkhuysen Home Holidays, P.O. Box 279, 1900 AG Castricum, The Netherlands. Call 31-2518-57953. Ref. NL3-1355.

Children: Y   Pets: Y   Smoking: Y   Handicap Access: N   Payment: C, EC

Opmeer

POLDER COTTAGES   *Rates: budget-inexpensive*
Open: year-round   *Minimum Stay: one week*

Opmeer is a pretty village on one of Holland's famous polders, the land reclaimed from the sea by back-breaking labor and ingenious technology. This is the land of windmills and flat, dike-rimmed fields—the perfect place for a bike ride. Here, a tidy little vacation village contains a collection of comfortable houses clustered near a swimming pool, tennis courts, miniature golf course and a small restaurant. The houses for six are airy and filled with light. There are two bedrooms downstairs; a circular stairway leads up to the mezzanine, where you'll find another secluded bedroom. Wind surfing on the Ijsselmeer is only eight miles away and the sandy beaches of the North Sea are just a bit further. Opmeer is conveniently close to Amsterdam. Contact: Interhome Inc., 124 Little Falls Rd., Fairfield, NJ 07004. Call 201-882-6864. Ref. N2700/1, /10.

Children: Y   Pets: Y   Smoking: Y   Handicap Access: N   Payment: P, V, M

Schellingwoude

DUTCH TREAT   *Rates: budget*
Open: July 21-August 11   *Minimum Stay: two weeks*

This historic home occupies a quiet corner in the town of Schellingwoude, just outside of Amsterdam. Here is a wonderful chance to sample the tranquil pace of yesteryear: After you feed the chickens and water the plants, perhaps you can use some of the eggs and vegetables you've gathered to prepare a hearty Dutch repast. The large flowering garden is a delightful place to pass a warm afternoon while you enjoy splendid views of the lake. Off the large living room inside you'll find three comfortable bedrooms for up to six people. The center of Amsterdam is just a couple of miles away; cheese connoisseurs will want to visit nearby Edam. Contact: Binkhuysen Home Holidays, P.O. Box 279, 1900 AG Castricum, The Netherlands. Call 31-2518-57953.

Children: Y   Pets: Y   Smoking: Y   Handicap Access: N   Payment: C, EC

Texel

DE COCKSDORP APARTMENTS   *Rates: budget*
Open: year-round   *Minimum Stay: one week*

The first of the graceful West Frisian Islands that arch from northern Holland up to the colder waters off Germany, lovely Texel offers sandy beaches and pretty forests. This charming country house in the traditional style has been converted into five private apartments for up to four people. The tastefully decorated rooms are centrally heated, and there are deck chairs available for enjoying the tranquil scenery outside. Watersports enthusiasts will enjoy Texel's ample facilities and sightseers should investigate the castle at the center of the island. Tennis, horseback riding and bicycling are also popular with visitors. Contact: Interhome Inc., 124 Little Falls Rd., Fairfield, NJ 07004. Call 201-882-6864. Ref. N1100/1A, /2M, /3M.

Children: Y   Pets: Y   Smoking: Y   Handicap Access: N   Payment: P, V, M

SOUTH HOLLAND

Katwijk

TERRACE HOUSE   *Rates: budget-inexpensive*
Open: year-round   *Minimum Stay: one week*

The pleasant resort of Katwijk will charm you with its tidy streets and beautiful scenery. The beaches here on the North Sea are wide and inviting, and the flatness of the land virtually demands a bike ride or outing on horseback. The attractively furnished rooms of this townhouse include a living room with a TV, a convenient kitchenette complete with washing machine and three comfy bedrooms sleeping six. The house is found on a sunny street near the center of town; the hearty fare at the local restaurants and the warm sands of the shore are both just a short walk away. Contact: Interhome Inc., 124 Little Falls Rd., Fairfield, NJ 07004. Call 201-882-6864. N3300/25.

Children: Y   Pets: Y   Smoking: Y   Handicap Access: N   Payment: P, V, M

Noordwijk

DUNE VILLAGE   *Rates: budget-inexpensive*
Open: year-round   *Minimum Stay: one week*

Noordwijk is a friendly holiday resort on the North Sea between Amsterdam and The Hague. It attracts visitors with its wide sandy beaches, rolling dunes and abundant bicycle and horseback trails. This holiday village is just north of Noordwijk, sheltered by pleasant dunes and overlooking some delightful flowering fields. The houses and apartments here come in a variety of sizes and shapes. They can accommodate either five or six people, and all are comfortably furnished. The beach is less than two miles away and the restaurants, shops and cinemas of town are just a bit further. Contact: Interhome Inc., 124 Little Falls Rd., Fairfield, NJ 07004. Call 201-882-6864. Ref. N3200/1, /5, /8, /9.

Children: Y   Pets: Y   Smoking: Y   Handicap Access: N   Payment: P, V, M

Oegstgeest

TUIN HOUSE   *Rates: budget*
Open: July-August   *Minimum Stay: two weeks*

Surrounded by a large garden with a swing and a pretty little pond, this charming house for five is a splendid base for enjoying the countryside as well as the exciting cities nearby. The three cozy bedrooms and the piano in the living room will make you feel right at home. Modern amenities include a TV, dishwasher, washer and dryer. Swimming, tennis and horseback riding can be enjoyed in the neighborhood and the sandy beaches of the North Sea are just five miles away. Leiden is practically next door, and the stately boulevards of The Hague are within a short drive. Contact: Binkhuysen Home Holidays, P.O. Box 279, 1900 AG Castricum, The Netherlands. Call 31-2518-57953. Ref. NL1-1353.

Children: Y   Pets: Y   Smoking: Y   Handicap Access: N   Payment: C, EC

Rotterdam

PAX HOTEL   *Rates: budget-inexpensive*
Open: year-round   *Minimum Stay: none*

Rotterdam is a thriving modern harbor town with an exuberant social life. The Pax Hotel is a favorite base for those who come to enjoy the city's cafes, nightclubs, discos and cinemas, not to mention the sleek modern sculpture and the impressive port. Cozy and inviting, the apartments feature kitchenettes and refrigerators in addition to TVs and full bathrooms. Everything is close by in the compact Netherlands: Delft's porcelain and Gouda's cheese are right next door, and the cool breezes of the North Sea are about half an hour away. Contact: Hotel Pax, Schiedkade 658, 3032 AK Rotterdam, The Netherlands. Call 31-104663344.

Children: Y   Pets: N   Smoking: Y   Handicap Access: N   Payment: C, V

Scheveningen

CARLTON-BEACH APARTHOTEL   *Rates: inexpensive-moderate*
Open: year-round   *Minimum Stay: one week*

Scheveningen is a large, modern resort town with splendid beaches and abundant recreational facilities. Surfing, sailing, tennis and bicycling are all available in the area, in addition to the traditional swimming and sunning. The Carlton-Beach boasts marvelous facilities of its own: After working out in the gym and relaxing in the sauna, stop by the beauty salon before meeting your companions in the restaurant for dinner. The studio apartments vary in size and can accommodate either two or four guests; all have color TVs and sunny balconies. The complex has both a swimming pool and its own private stretch of sand along the shore. Audacious souls may want to check out the naturist beach just a bit to the north. Contact: Interhome Inc., 124 Little Falls Rd., Fairfield, NJ 07004. Call 201-882-6864. Ref. N3500/10M, 21M.

Children: Y   Pets: Y   Smoking: Y   Handicap Access: N   Payment: P, V, M

UTRECHT

Bilthoven

BIJ BOSSEN   *Rates: budget*
Open: July-August   *Minimum Stay: three weeks*

Here's a charming country home complete with fragrant gardens and a friendly kitty. The open hearth in the commodious living room and the cheerful eat-in kitchen create an atmosphere of warmth and hospitality. The five comfortable bedrooms welcome up to eight guests. You'll look forward to coming home after a day spent biking through the countryside, counting windmills or exploring the neighboring cities of Utrecht and Amsterdam. The nearby woods offer shady walks; just a short ride will bring you to the gorgeous Veluwe National Park with its lovely lakeside beaches. Contact: Binkhuysen Home Holidays, P.O. Box 279, 1900 AG Castricum, The Netherlands. Call 31-2518-57953. Ref. NL31356.

Children: Y   Pets: N   Smoking: Y   Handicap Access: N   Payment: C, EC

ZEELAND

Breskens

MARITIME BUNGALOW   *Rates: budget-inexpensive*
Open: year-round   *Minimum Stay: one week*

Breskens was once a bustling fishing port, and the rich legacy of this past is found in the town's excellent seafood restaurants. Today the area caters to visitors who come to enjoy the lovely sand beaches and unspoiled countryside. The bungalow is part of a well-equipped holiday center just a short walk from the dunes. If somehow you manage to tire of the sea, the complex can amuse you with indoor and outdoor pools, tennis courts, Ping-Pong tables and bowling. After sampling all of this, perhaps you'll feel like relaxing in the bar or grabbing a bite in the restaurant. The bungalow has a full kitchen if you'd rather cook for yourself. There are also three generous double bedrooms, a living/dining room with TV and a bath. Contact: Interhome Inc., 124 Little Falls Rd., Fairfield, NJ 07004. Call 201-882-6864. Ref. N4350/100.

Children: Y   Pets: Y   Smoking: Y   Handicap Access: N   Payment: P, V, M

Goes

RUSTIG GELEGEN   *Rates: budget*
Open: February 23-March 2, July 7-28   *Minimum Stay: one week*

Located on a brave peninsula flanked by the wide waters of the Eastern and Western Scheldt, lovely Goes offers fields covered with flowers, medieval ruins and water all around. This house is a pleasant retreat on the edge of town. Here you'll find all the comforts of home: three generous bedrooms, a cheery fireplace in the living room, a piano, bikes, books and some tender plants that need you to water them. Outside is a delightful garden with some comfy furniture; excellent public transportation can take you right into town. The calm waters of the lake are just three miles from here and the bracing breezes of the North Sea are a bike ride away. Contact: Binkhuysen Home Holidays, P.O. Box 279, 1900 AG Castricum, The Netherlands. Call 31-2518-57953. Ref. NL1-1352.

Children: Y   Pets: N   Smoking: Y   Handicap Access: N   Payment: C, EC

Arctic Ocean

Norwegian Sea

Atlantic Ocean

MORE OG ROMSDAL
SOGN OG FJORDANE
Trondheim
Balestrand
HORDALAND
Bergen
Oslo
ROGALAND
North Sea

Norway

HORDALAND

Bergen

NATLANDS APARTMENT   *Rates: budget*
Open: May 1–December 1   *Minimum Stay: one week*

An attractive house located in a tranquil Bergen suburb contains this comfortable, self-contained cellar apartment available as a vacation residence. Only 10 minutes away from the hub of western Norway's major urban center, the residence is equally close to the woods and mountains. Great views of Bergen and the surrounding fjords and mountains can be savored from the lovely garden, which contains a barbecue and patio furniture amid dramatic scenery. A private entrance leads to the flat, which consists of a bedroom, kitchen, bath with washing machine and a sitting room with a sofa bed, to provide accommodations for up to four. Contact: Fjordhytter, Jon Smorgst, 11, 5011 Bergen. Call 011-47-5-232080. Ref. F-2808.

Children: **Y**   Pets: **N**   Smoking: **Y**   Handicap Access: **N**   Payment: **EC**

Eidesvik

SKIPPER HUS
Open: *May 1-December 1*

Rates: moderate-expensive
Minimum Stay: one week

This captivating restored "skipper hus" with a large terrace and garden area rests on the gorgeous tiny island of Espevaer, five minutes by boat from Eidesvik on the south end of Bomlo. The well-equipped residence, containing three bedrooms, sitting room and dining room, features such handy amenities as automatic washer/dryer and dishwasher, plus a TV/VCR and stereo. For outdoor pleasures, the house comes with a motorboat plus nets, crab pots and other fishing equipment to take advantage of the fine sea angling, while the island offers wonderful water recreation opportunities like diving, as well as fascinating seal and whale-watching expeditions. Contact: Fjordhytter, Jon Smorgst, 11, 5011 Bergen. Call 011-47-5-232080. Ref. F-2751.

Children: **Y** Pets: **N** Smoking: **Y** Handicap Access: **N** Payment: **EC**

Flatraker

TYSES FARMHOUSE
Open: *May 1-December 1*

Rates: budget
Minimum Stay: one week

Situated on a secluded working farm on the island of Tyses, which is connected to the mainland by a bridge, this restored 19th-century farmhouse accommodates a party of up to six. The house contains two sitting rooms plus a wood-burning stove on the first floor, with three bedrooms upstairs. The countryside surrounding the farm has many trails for bracing woodland hikes; a lake, where the farm offers a private rowboat, is also nearby. Less than 200 yards from the fjord, where another boat is available, and close to a clear, flowing river, this residence is graced by a bounty of fishing options. Contact: Fjordhytter, Jon Smorgst, 11, 5011 Bergen. Call 011-47-5-232080. Ref. F-2331.

Children: **Y** Pets: **N** Smoking: **Y** Handicap Access: **N** Payment: **EC**

Gjermundshamn

GJERMUNDSHAMN COTTAGE
Open: *May 1-December 1*

Rates: budget
Minimum Stay: one week

Built in 1885, this fully renovated cottage rests peacefully by the fjord at Gjermundshamn. Its quiet, graceful garden has a grand view of the fjord harbor, where a dinghy that comes with the property is available. A nearby lake offers the adventurous fisher the chance at an uncommon quarry—eel—as well as the more conventional, but still delicious, trout. Guests can also enjoy walking along the miles of scenic woodland and mountain trails in the area. The house features a new kitchen and bathroom and two comfortable bedrooms to sleep four. Contact: Fjordhytter, Jon Smorgst, 11, 5011 Bergen. Call 011-47-5-232080. Ref. F-2704.

Children: **Y** Pets: **N** Smoking: **Y** Handicap Access: **N** Payment: **EC**

Jondal

NEDRE KROSSDALEN   *Rates: budget*
Open: May 1-December 1   *Minimum Stay: one week*

Set beside the bracing waters of Eidevatnet Lake, this spacious house has panoramic views of the mountains gently rising from the shore. The two-story gabled residence includes a living room, dining room and four bedrooms, each with picture windows to take full advantage of the rustic setting. Guests also have access to a rowboat on the lake for fishing. An excursion through inner Hardanger, where some of Europe's most celebrated hiking trails are located, makes a memorable adventure. The two and a half-hour ferry ride from nearby Jondal to the cosmopolitan city of Bergen offers an unforgettable way to behold the spectacular fjord region. Contact: Fjordhytter, Jon Smorgst, 11, 5011 Bergen. Call 011-47-5-232080. Ref. F-2574.

Children: Y   Pets: N   Smoking: Y   Handicap Access: N   Payment: EC

Olensvag

OLEN HOUSE   *Rates: budget-inexpensive*
Open: May 1-December 1   *Minimum Stay: one week*

The upper two floors of this large house contain a quality residence that can accommodate a party of up to eight. The tastefully furnished apartment includes four bedrooms, sitting room with fireplace and fully equipped kitchen. Located in the little village of Kata less than three miles north of the picturesque town of Olensvag, the residence, featuring a large terrace with garden furniture, sits 100 yards from the water. A rowboat is included with the property and motor boats can be rented nearby. Back on shore, guests may arrange to enjoy the solarium and game room over at the owner's farm. Contact: Fjordhytter, Jon Smorgst, 11, 5011 Bergen. Call 011-47-5-232080. Ref. F-2724.

Children: Y   Pets: N   Smoking: Y   Handicap Access: N   Payment: EC

Osteroy

HOSANGER COTTAGE GROUP   *Rates: inexpensive-expensive*
Open: May 1-December 1   *Minimum Stay: one week*

This unusual holiday residence, perfect for two or three families vacationing together, consists of two cottages plus a converted boat house, all standing right by the fjord on the scenic island of Osteroy. The units contain a total of six bedrooms, three sitting rooms and two kitchens and the grounds feature a floating pier with rowboat, an enormous stone terrace overlooking the water, a charming garden with barbecue and an exquisite panorama. The location offers an array of attractions to suit the group's diverse tastes—swimming, fishing and hiking are available right at the property, the metropolitan enticements of Bergen are an hour away and renowned historic landmarks, like the exceptional monastery ruins on the island of Halsnoy, are close as well. Contact: Fjordhytter, Jon Smorgst, 11, 5011 Bergen. Call 011-47-5-232080. Ref. F-2950.

Children: Y   Pets: N   Smoking: Y   Handicap Access: N   Payment: EC

Skanevik
SKANEVIKSTRAND   *Rates: budget*
Open: May 1-December 1   *Minimum Stay: one week*
Sitting off a traffic-free cul-de-sac 100 yards from the fjord, this tranquil, renovated 19th-century house offers seclusion while also being convenient to active Hordaland town areas. The residence contains two bedrooms for two, a kitchen and a sitting room with panoramic views of the water. From here, guests can enjoy leisurely or vigorous walks through the surrounding fields and woods or along the fjord and can take motor trips to other scenic attractions of the region. Contact: Fjordhytter, Jon Smorgst, 11, 5011 Bergen. Call 011-47-5-232080. Ref. F-2974.
Children: Y   Pets: N   Smoking: Y   Handicap Access: N   Payment: EC

Skanevik
THE FARMHOUSE   *Rates: budget*
Open: May 1-December 1   *Minimum Stay: one week*
This traditional farmhouse on extensive grounds contains a comfortable first-floor budget flat that makes an excellent vacation residence for families with small children. The friendly owner lives in the upstairs quarters, yet the two-bedroom apartment, featuring a sitting room and fully equipped kitchen, offers total privacy. Marked paths over the fields and through the woods provide ample opportunities for terrific hikes of varying degrees of difficulty, while rowboats for cruising on the fjord can be rented less than a mile away. Contact: Fjordhytter, Jon Smorgst, 11, 5011 Bergen. Call 011-47-5-232080. Ref. F-2641.
Children: Y   Pets: N   Smoking: Y   Handicap Access: N   Payment: EC

MORE OG ROMSDAL

Storholmen
FRAENA FLAT   *Rates: budget-inexpensive*
Open: June 1-December 1   *Minimum Stay: one week*
Two comfortable, well-equipped flats are contained in a converted waterside boathouse at Storholmen. Offering panoramic views of sheer mountain cliffs plunging almost vertically into the sea, the units each contain a sitting room with kitchenette and two bedrooms; the bathroom is shared. Enjoy fishing right from the quay or from the motor boat that comes with the property, or take an exhilarating walk along the breakwater as the crashing waves of the North Sea pound against it. Drives to the scenic island of Averoy, the limestone cave Trollkyrkja and the quaint fishing village of Bud all make terrific day trips. Contact: Fjordhytter, Jon Smorgst, 11, 5011 Bergen. Call 011-47-5-232080. Ref. F-2530.
Children: Y   Pets: N   Smoking: Y   Handicap Access: N   Payment: EC

Tresfjord
HESTESENTER COTTAGES   *Rates: budget*
Open: June 1-December 1   *Minimum Stay: one week*

For a horse lover's ideal holiday, these well-equipped camping cabins are located right by the paddock at the Tresfjord Hestesenter. Featuring Icelandic ponies, the riding center offers lessons and horses for hire, as well as both day and overnight pack trips into the gorgeous surrounding mountains and forest. The area also provides fine opportunities for anglers, with the fjord only 300 yards away and a river running right by the cabins. These units each contain a small kitchenette and a bedroom with four bunks, while showers and toilets are steps away at the center. Contact: Fjordhytter, Jon Smorgst, 11, 5011 Bergen. Call 011-47-5-232080. Ref. F-2954.

Children: Y   Pets: N   Smoking: Y   Handicap Access: N   Payment: EC

ROGALAND

Havn

SKJOLDAFJORDEN HOUSE   *Rates: budget-inexpensive*
Open: May 1-December 1   *Minimum Stay: three weeks*

Resting next to the water on over an acre of quiet grounds, this roomy cottage features its own boathouse, with a choice of either a rowboat with outboard motor or a sailing dinghy. The cottage contains three bedrooms that sleep six or more, a spacious living room and fully equipped kitchen, plus a large, sunny veranda delivering an elegant, panoramic view. The area offers terrific water recreation facilities, as well as captivating fishing hamlets to explore along bewitching Boknfjord. Contact: Fjordhytter, Jon Smorgst, 11, 5011 Bergen. Call 011-47-5-232080. Ref. F-2003.

Children: Y   Pets: N   Smoking: Y   Handicap Access: N   Payment: EC

Rennesoy

OSTHUSVIK COTTAGE   *Rates: budget*
Open: May 1-December 1   *Minimum Stay: one week*

This charming cottage sits serenely on the east side of Rennesoy, a large and lush Boknfjord island. The idyllic setting offers peace and tranquility but is also only a short ferry ride away from the animated city of Stavanger. Less than 100 yards from the shore and featuring lovely views of the fjord, where guests can swim and fish, the three-bedroom residence includes a fully equipped kitchen, sitting room with wood-burning stove and a sunny garden area with barbecue for cooking up the catch of the day fresh out of the water. Contact: Fjordhytter, Jon Smorgst, 11, 5011 Bergen. Call 011-47-5-232080. Ref. F-2882.

Children: Y   Pets: N   Smoking: Y   Handicap Access: N   Payment: EC

Skudeneshavn

THE BOATHOUSE   *Rates: budget*
Open: May 1-December 1   *Minimum Stay: one week*

An authentic old boathouse on Skudeneshavn's calm harbor has been converted to a distinctive and comfortable two-bedroom flat. Graced with panoramic views of the boat traffic and neighboring dock huts and houses, the apartment comes with a dinghy of its own, while motor boats, crab pots and other equipment can be borrowed or rented to take full opportunity of the area's exceptional fishing opportunities. The unit includes a large sitting room and a spacious kitchen, plus a small garden area, and sleeps four. Contact: Fjordhytter, Jon Smorgst, 11, 5011 Bergen. Call 011-47-5-232080. Ref. F-2911.

Children: Y   Pets: N   Smoking: Y   Handicap Access: N   Payment: EC

SOGN OG FJORDANE

Fjaerland

HAMRUM FARM COTTAGE   *Rates: budget*
Open: May 1-December 1   *Minimum Stay: one week*

This beguiling cottage situated on a farm and featuring far-reaching views of the fjord toward stunning Jostedal Glacier, contains two bedrooms, kitchen and living room with fireplace, plus a loft with two additional beds. An excellent base for fishing, hikes into the mountains and treks to the glacier, the residence is near the lovely and beguiling village of Fjaerland, itself a top visitor attraction. There the famous long tunnel to Skei commences, providing easy access to other notable landmarks and sights of the region. Contact: Fjordhytter, Jon Smorgst, 11, 5011 Bergen. Call 011-47-5-232080. Ref. F-2179.

Children: Y   Pets: N   Smoking: Y   Handicap Access: N   Payment: EC

Fresvik

FRESVIK COTTAGE   *Rates: budget*
Open: May 1-December 1   *Minimum Stay: one week*

Complete with a white picket fence, this charming little house sits in a shady orchard in the picturesque hamlet of Fresvik. The fjord is less than a third of a mile down the road, and a lake and rivers are close by as well to provide a variety of recreational activities. The area also offers excellent forest and mountain trails, one of which leads hikers to the sublime Fresvikbreen Glacier. Featuring a private garden area excellent for sunbathing, the two-story cottage contains two bedrooms, a living room and a nicely appointed kitchen. Contact: Fjordhytter, Jon Smorgst, 11, 5011 Bergen. Call 011-47-5-232080. Ref. F-2650.

Children: Y   Pets: N   Smoking: Y   Handicap Access: N   Payment: EC

Gaular

FOREST CABIN   *Rates: budget*
Open: June 1-December 1   *Minimum Stay: one week*

For a truly secluded, back-to-nature holiday, this bewitching cabin in the woods can hardly be beat. The totally private house—only a couple of other cottages are even remotely nearby—is enveloped by forest, mountains and lakes. A sportsperson couldn't ask for better fishing and hiking, or closer encounters with the local wildlife. There may be no running water in the cabin, but there is outside—crystal-clear water from melting snow and glaciers flows in the creek 100 yards from the front door. For such an isolated, rugged location, the cabin is surprisingly comfortable, featuring three bedrooms, kitchenette and a spacious living room, with a fireplace that will be much appreciated and a large veranda that offers an all-encompassing view of the idyllic setting. Contact: Fjordhytter, Jon Smorgst, 11, 5011 Bergen. Call 011-47-5-232080. Ref. F-2684.

Children: Y   Pets: N   Smoking: Y   Handicap Access: N   Payment: EC

Haukas

HAUKAS CABINS   *Rates: budget*
Open: June 1-December 1   *Minimum Stay: one week*

These two comfortable cabins of distinction are located by the woods at Haukas. Embellished with such uncommon features as tree-trunk columns, a turf roof and original wood furniture, the residences both contain a sitting room/dining area, modern kitchenette, wood-burning stove and two bedrooms, plus two lofts with additional beds. The cabins are surrounded by plenty of open space and the woods just off the grounds offer numerous unspoiled trails for hiking and—when there's snow—cross-country skiing. Contact: Fjordhytter, Jon Smorgst, 11, 5011 Bergen. Call 011-47-5-232080. Ref. F-2197/8.

Children: Y   Pets: N   Smoking: Y   Handicap Access: N   Payment: EC

Lavik

HOYANGER HOUSE   *Rates: Inexpensive-moderate*
Open: May 1-December 1   *Minimum Stay: one week*

Facing south overlooking the majestic Sognefjord and steps away from the water, this sheltered home is a superb base for journeys throughout the Sogn district. The wood-paneled house for six is handsomely decorated with authentic Norwegian pine furniture and contains three bedrooms, a modern kitchen area and a sitting room with fireplace. The sitting room leads to the residence's choicest feature, a delightful roofed terrace that offers a sweeping view of the fjord and includes a fireplace of its own, bringing warmth on brisk mornings and late afternoons as you revel in the changing colors of sunrise and sunset. Contact: Fjordhytter, Jon Smorgst, 11, 5011 Bergen. Call 011-47-5-232080. Ref. F-2746.

Children: Y   Pets: N   Smoking: Y   Handicap Access: N   Payment: EC

Luster

HOYHEIMSVIK HOLIDAY FLATS   *Rates: budget*
Open: June 1-December 1   *Minimum Stay: one week*

Located in the beautiful rural district of Luster, this group of holiday flats is superbly situated in the scenic center of Norway near the landmarks, sights and attractions that visitors from around the world come to visit. Natural wonders like Nigardsbreen Glacier and historic buildings like the stave churches—or "Stavkirkene"—of Urne are within easy reach. Built right on the water's edge, the residence offers a quay and rowboats; each apartment has a marvelous view of the Sognefjord and the surrounding mountains and waterfalls, and contains a spacious living room/kitchen area, double bedroom and roomy loft with three extra beds. A game room is featured in the grounds basement. Contact: Fjordhytter, Jon Smorgst, 11, 5011 Bergen. Call 011-47-5-232080. Ref. F-2730-35.

Children: Y   Pets: N   Smoking: Y   Handicap Access: N   Payment: EC

Olden

THE CHALET   *Rates: budget*

Open: June 1-December 1   *Minimum Stay: one week*

This simple, wood-heated house is a no-frills yet engaging residence in one of Norway's most scenic areas, and can accommodate even tight holiday budgets. Perched on a pretty hillside in the Oldedalen valley, it is well-situated for journeys up to Briksdal and Kjenndal glaciers and the summer ski resort at Strynefjellen, or along the deep fjord. The chalet features grand views toward Floen Lake and the valley and contains a sitting room/kitchen area and a small bedroom. The toilet is outside and water can be carried by car from the owner's farm. Contact: Fjordhytter, Jon Smorgst, 11, 5011 Bergen. Call 011-47-5-232080. Ref. F-2295.

Children: Y   Pets: N   Smoking: Y   Handicap Access: N   Payment: EC

Stardalen

STARDALEN COTTAGE   *Rates: budget-inexpensive*

Open: June 1-December 1   *Minimum Stay: one week*

Located in a picturesque setting, this engaging two-story house sits beside a river and next to a vast field amid countryside rich with serene farmland, hills and forest. The river and nearby Jolstervatn Lake—well-known for its enormous trout—offer excellent fishing, and there are many trails that wind through the woods and up into the glaciers and mountains. While the accommodations are very comfortable, with two sitting rooms, kitchen and bedroom on the ground floor and two additional bedrooms upstairs, guests will want to spend as much time as possible outdoors enjoying the idyllic setting. Contact: Fjordhytter, Jon Smorgst, 11, 5011 Bergen. Call 011-47-5-232080. Ref. F-2864.

Children: Y   Pets: N   Smoking: Y   Handicap Access: N   Payment: EC

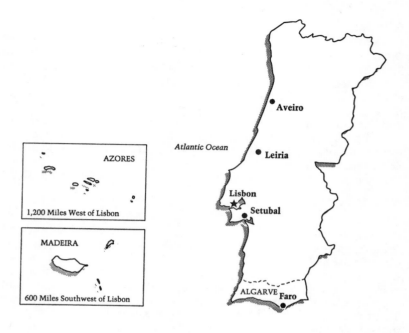

Portugal

ALGARVE

Albufeira

ALBUFEIRA TERRACE HOUSE   *Rates: budget-expensive*
Open: year-round   *Minimum Stay: one week*

A lovely kidney-shaped pool takes center stage in this holiday retreat, where sunbathing is a priority at the pool bar and children's pool. Each garden apartment has a balcony affording scenic views of bustling Albufeira and the coast below, and a covered terrace provides access to a small garden. Three bedrooms on two floors provide sleeping arrangements for six, as well as privacy and quiet. Work out in the gym and then relax in the sauna. A ten-minute walk to the bathing resorts in Albufeira reveals the rocky cliffs and colorful architecture of this former fishing village. Contact: Interhome Inc., 124 Little Falls Road, Fairfield, NJ 07004. Call 201-882-6864. Ref. P1610/275.

Children: **Y**   Pets: **N**   Smoking: **Y**   Handicap Access: **N**   Payment: **C, P, T**

Albufeira

VILLA GUIA   *Rates: budget-moderate*
Open: year-round   *Minimum Stay: one week*

Stylishly comfortable furnishings and views of the sea and valley enrich this four-room apartment in a private villa. The views will make outdoor barbecues on the covered terrace delightful, while a cozy fireplace takes the chill off the night breezes. Two bedrooms, a sofa bed and two and a half baths accommodate six comfortably. During the day, the owners invite you to share their swimming pool. Contact: Interhome Inc., 124 Little Falls Road, Fairfield, NJ 07004. Call 201-882-6864. Ref. P1610/265A.

Children: Y   Pets: N   Smoking: Y   Handicap Access: N   Payment: C, P, T

Albufeira

VILLA SERENA   *Rates: inexpensive-moderate*
Open: April-November   *Minimum Stay: two weeks*

Albufeira's lively port, with its Moorish-style architecture, is just a five-minute walk from Villa Serena. A garden wall ensures privacy and seclusion, while the lovely outdoor patio and terrace provide panoramic views of the sea. The two-story villa sleeps six in three double bedrooms, and an attractive modern kitchen adds to your comfort. Taste the superb, locally grown fruits and vegetables at the public market, and don't forget to bring home fresh flowers. For golfers, six championship courses are all within forty-five minutes by car. Casinos, shops, English-style pubs and many restaurants are all nearby. Daily maid service is provided and babysitting is available, but the owners will only accept children over four. Contact: David and Jane Harrison, P.O. Box 6865, Providence, RI 02940. Call 401-273-1063.

Children: Y   Pets: N   Smoking: Y   Handicap Access: N   Payment: C, P

Caldas de Monchique

CASA CHILDS   *Rates: deluxe*
Open: year-round   *Minimum Stay: one week*

The spas at Caldas de Monchique still sparkle with the therapeutic mineral waters that have soothed aches and pains since the Romans occupied these hills. A few minutes' walk from the spa, Casa Childs clings to the hills of Monchique three thousand feet above the coast. Sheltered by flowering shrubs and many mature trees, visitors enjoy lovely views from the large terrace overlooking the sea. Seven to nine can sleep comfortably in six bedrooms, and maid service will leave you free to enjoy the spas. A private tennis court and swimming pool provide exercise and relaxation. Contact: Villas International, 71 West 23rd Street, New York, NY 10010. Call 1-800-221-2260 (in New York, 212-929-7585).

Children: Y   Pets: N   Smoking: Y   Handicap Access: N   Payment: C, P, T

Carvoeiro

MOORISH VILLA   *Rates: expensive-deluxe*
Open: year-round   *Minimum Stay: one week; two weeks in summer*

Let the sunny southern coast of Portugal become your personal playground as you vacation in comfort and style in this Moorish villa. Set on one and a half acres, this house has room for ten guests in four bedrooms plus a sofa bed, and amenities to please the pickiest of travelers. Leonilde, the housekeeper and cook, will whip up a delicious breakfast and lunch in the modern kitchen, and you can barbecue dinner as you lounge by the large swimming pool and sip cocktails at the outdoor bar. Golfers can enjoy two good courses within a half-hour drive, and two more are planned for Carvoeiro. Several nearby hotels provide nightclubs and casinos. Babysitting can be arranged for children over six. Contact: At Home Abroad, Inc., 405 East 56th Street, 6-H, New York, NY 10022. Call 212-421-9165. Ref. 9448.

Children: Y   Pets: N   Smoking: Y   Handicap Access: N   Payment: C, P, T

Lago

QUINTA DO LAGO   *Rates: inexpensive-deluxe*
Open: year-round   *Minimum Stay: one week*

The airy and spacious white stucco villas of Lago Village blend harmoniously with the natural beauty of the Algarvean coast. Three-bedroom villas for six guests and a variety of apartments for two to four are luxuriously furnished and feature terraces and balconies. The villas have their own private swimming pools and small gardens. Lago Village sports two tennis courts on the grounds, and for golfing enthusiasts, a twenty-seven-hole championship course and an eighteen-hole course are nearby. At night, the clubs and casinos of the Algarve beckon visitors with their lights and music. Contact: Villas International, 71 West 23rd Street, New York, NY 10010. Call 1-800-221-2260 (in New York, 212-929-7585).

Children: Y   Pets: N   Smoking: Y   Handicap Access: N   Payment: C, P, T

Porto dos Mos

PORTO TOWNHOUSE 1   *Rates: expensive-deluxe*
Open: year-round   *Minimum Stay: one week; two weeks in summer*

The white-sand beach of Porto dos Mos is just a short downhill walk from this townhouse. You can swim and then eat at beachside restaurants, or travel by car or bus to visit the many shops and eateries in nearby Lagos. Four adults and two children can be comfortably accommodated in three bedrooms, and those in the master bedroom will have a fine view of the sea. Tropical gardens and high walls between the four townhouses in this block provide tranquility and privacy. Maid service, provided five days a week in summer, ensures everyone's life of leisure. Contact: At Home Abroad, Inc., 405 East 56th Street, 6-H, New York, NY 10022. Call 212-421-9165. Ref. 8021.

Children: Y   Pets: N   Smoking: Y   Handicap Access: N   Payment: C, P, T

Porto dos Mos

PORTO TOWNHOUSE 3   *Rates: expensive-deluxe*
Open: year-round   *Minimum Stay: one week; two weeks in summer*

Comfort and tranquility for four are to be found in this three-floor townhouse, one of four units overlooking the sea. A barbecue, garden and patio make a lovely setting for outdoor entertaining. Inside, there's a garden-level kitchen, dining room and bath, while twin bedrooms with patios that afford panoramic vistas of the sea are found on the second and third floors. A short walk down the hillside takes you to the beach at Porto dos Mos, and there are other attractions such as restaurants, shops, golf courses and the casino at Praia Da Rocha—all within a short drive. Maid service is included. Contact: At Home Abroad, Inc., 405 East 56th Street, 6-H, New York, NY 10022. Call 212-421-9165. Ref. 8021.

Children: Y   Pets: N   Smoking: Y   Handicap Access: N   Payment: C, P, T

Praia do Carvoeiro

ALGAR SECO PARQUE RESIDENCIAL   *Rates: budget-deluxe*
Open: year-round   *Minimum Stay: three nights*

The lovely bungalows and apartments of the Algar Seco Parque Residencial overlook the open waters of the Atlantic as far as distant Sagres. Inside you'll find splendidly furnished rooms featuring painted tiles, embroidered carpets, handcrafted furniture and charming pottery. The accommodations range from comfortable studios for two to generous three-bedroom apartments for six. All have cheerful fireplaces for a touch of old world charm, as well as electric heating to keep you warm during the occasional chilly night. The large swimming pool with diving board and the smaller children's wading pool are at your disposal, and the fine golden beaches of the Algarve are only a few minutes away. Contact: Hometours International, 1170 Broadway, New York, NY 10001. Call 1-800-367-4668 (in New York, 212-689-0851).

Children: Y   Pets: N   Smoking: Y   Handicap Access: Y   Payment: C, P

Praia do Carvoeiro

VALE DE LOBO   *Rates: inexpensive-deluxe*
Open: year-round   *Minimum Stay: one week*

The sunny Algarvean coast lies only a few feet from this waterfront resort, an upscale "adult" playground with enough surf and sand to tempt even the most sedentary of vacationers. Tastefully decorated, the one- and two-bedroom village houses have covered patios and modern kitchens and use of a common swimming pool, while guests at the larger three- and four-bedroom villas can take a dip in their own private pools. Golfers will find two championship courses nearby at Penina and Palmares, and the Carvoeiro Golf Club and Country Club is planned for completion in 1991. Catamaran sailing, dinghies, water skiing and wind surfing will satisfy even the most enthusiastic of sportsmen, while those who like to fish will find plenty of billfish, tuna and sea bass off the coast. Contact: Villas International, 71 West 23rd Street, New York, NY 10010. Call 1-800-221-2260 (in New York, 212-929-7585).

Children: Y   Pets: N   Smoking: Y   Handicap Access: N   Payment: C, P, T

Quarteira

QUARTEIRA-CAVACOS APARTMENTS   *Rates: budget-inexpensive*
Open: year-round   *Minimum Stay: one week*
This former fishing village has been developed into a popular bathing resort near the picturesque eighteen-hole golf course at Vale de Lobo, along with six other golf courses, fine restaurants, casinos and plenty of night spots. Cozy garden apartments for six feature a fireplace, modern kitchen, two bedrooms and a sofa bed. The swimming pool is solar heated, allowing for relaxing dips even on chilly days. For access to the beach or shops, bus service is provided. Contact: Interhome Inc., 124 Little Falls Road, Fairfield, NJ 07004. Call 201-882-6864.
Children: **Y**   Pets: **N**   Smoking: **Y**   Handicap Access: **N**   Payment: **C, P, T**

Quinta do Lago

VILLAR DO GOLF VILLAGE   *Rates: moderate-expensive*
Open: year-round   *Minimum Stay: one week*
Set among the pine groves on a gently sloping hill above the sea, and surrounded by a golf course, Quinta do Lago is the perfect place for a healthful and relaxing vacation. If golf isn't your idea of fun, use the swimming pools and squash and tennis courts in the complex, then relax on the sun terrace or in the sauna. Free bus service will take you to the ocean for windsurfing lessons, horseback riding or a nearby sandy beach. The tastefully furnished garden apartments sleep from four to six people and are cleaned daily. There's a supermarket, boutique and restaurant in the reception area. Visitors receive a 25 percent discount on greens fees. Contact: Interhome Inc., 124 Little Falls Road, Fairfield, NJ 07004. Call 201-882-6864.
Children: **Y**   Pets: **N**   Smoking: **Y**   Handicap Access: **N**   Payment: **C, P, T**

Vilamoura

ALDEIA DO MAR APARTMENTS   *Rates: budget-moderate*
Open: year-round   *Minimum Stay: one week*
Aldeia do Mar's vacation complex is surrounded by a pine forest, close to a sandy beach, less than a mile from the harbor, and even offers diving lessons in the pool or the ocean. Guests share many recreational facilities, including tennis, miniature golf, a playground for children, videos and a TV room. Several different apartments sleep two to four and feature a kitchenette and balcony. A change of linen three times a week and daily cleaning are on the house, and babysitting can be arranged. Contact: Interhome Inc., 124 Little Falls Road, Fairfield, NJ 07004. Call 201-882-6864.
Children: **Y**   Pets: **N**   Smoking: **Y**   Handicap Access: **N**   Payment: **C, P, T**

AVEIRO

Mealhada

SOLAR DA VACARICA   *Rates: deluxe*
Open: year-round   *Minimum Stay: one week*
This gracious mansion offers you the best of Portuguese hospitality in

pleasant surroundings. After passing through the flower-clad entrance gate, you'll be charmed by the simple elegance of the main house, which dates back to the 18th century. In addition to the spacious sleeping quarters for 12 people (some rooms with en suite baths), there are formal and informal living rooms, a beautiful dining room, an impressive library and a modern kitchen. There are also two annex apartments that can accommodate another eight guests. The manor's swimming pool, tennis court and bucolic surroundings make it perfect for large family reunions. And the sophisticated excitement of Lisbon is less than two hours away. Contact: Rent a Home International, 7200 34th Ave. N.W., Seattle, WA 98117. Call 206-545-6963.

Children: Y Pets: N Smoking: Y Handicap Access: N Payment: C, P, V, M

Ovar

PRAIADO FURADOURO   *Rates: budget*
Open: year-round   *Minimum Stay: one week*

Just a few feet from the glistening sands and lapping waves of the sea is this apartment for four people. Located in the town of Ovar on the Costa de Prata, the accommodations include a fully equipped kitchen, a living/dining room, two bedrooms and a darling little balcony. Local restaurants serve up hearty portions of delicious seafood dishes; there are several neighborhood taverns where you can quench your thirst for a Sagres or another fine Portuguese beer. The town of Porto, famous for the unique elixir that bears its name, is just a few miles to the north and well worth a visit. Contact: Rent a Home International, 7200 34th Ave. N.W., Seattle, WA 98117. Call 206-545-6963.

Children: Y Pets: N Smoking: Y Handicap Access: N Payment: C, P, V, M

AZORES

Caloura

GARDEN VILLA   *Rates: inexpensive*
Open: year-round   *Minimum Stay: two weeks*

This elegant villa on the island of Sao Miguel commands exquisite views of the blue Atlantic. Flanked by a sunny terrace and a beautiful formal garden, the house features a sophisticated blend of antique and contemporary furnishings. The two cozy bedrooms can easily accommodate up to four guests. The surrounding countryside is dotted with ancient churches, quaint hamlets and places of breathtaking natural beauty. May brings the lively Feast of Santa Christa, one of the many colorful festivals that fill the calendar here. Swimming is just a short walk away and golf, boating and fishing can all be enjoyed in the neighborhood. Contact: Villas International, 71 W. 23rd St., New York, NY 10010. Call 212-929-7585.

Children: N Pets: N Smoking: Y Handicap Access: N Payment: C, P, T

FARO

Praia da Luz

CASA MONTE PORCO   *Rates: budget-moderate*
Open: year-round   *Minimum Stay: one week*

This lovely townhouse is practically on the beach, yet its secluded patio and flower-filled garden help preserve the sense of privacy and serenity. Off the handsome entryway downstairs you'll find three twin bedrooms, two of which open onto the garden. Follow the spiral stairway up to the second floor and you'll discover a compact but well equipped kitchen and a spacious living room opening onto a large balcony with marvelous views of the ocean. A barbecue, frequent maid service and a parking space are some of the other holiday amenities here. The seaside town of Praia da Luz offers fishing, wind surfing and water skiing in addition to the ever-popular pursuits of swimming and sunning; horseback riding and golf can also be enjoyed in the area. Contact: Rent a Home International, 7200 34th Ave. N.W., Seattle, WA 98117. Call 206-545-6963.

Children: **Y** Pets: **N** Smoking: **Y** Handicap Access: **N** Payment: **C, P, V, M**

Praia da Luz

VIVENDA DAS ROCHAS   *Rates: deluxe*
Open: year-round   *Minimum Stay: one week*

This elegant villa is magnificently situated amidst rolling green lawns and flowering gardens. Commanding splendid views of the sea and Praia da Luz, it watches sheep and goats graze on the slopes below. The Moorish-style interior features rich colors and handsome antiques. The sunken living room glows in mellow tones of gold and blue; the kitchen is fully equipped with every modern convenience. Each of the five bedrooms (sleeping 10) has its own marble-tiled bathroom and opens onto the terrace. Outside you'll find a large swimming pool with a diving board, a barbecue and plenty of comfortable garden furniture. The maid, who is also an excellent cook, rides up to the house daily on her motor bike. Contact: Rent a Home International, 7200 34th Ave. N.W., Seattle, WA 98117. Call 206-545-6963.

Children: **Y** Pets: **N** Smoking: **Y** Handicap Access: **N** Payment: **C, P, V, M**

LEIRIA

Foz do Arelho

CASINHAS   *Rates: budget-deluxe*
Open: year-round   *Minimum Stay: one week*

The rustic Costa da Prata is a pleasant area of warm beaches, wildflower-covered hillsides and quaint villages. It's still largely untouched by resort developers, so the predominant rhythms are those of the farm and the sea. This is just the place to soak up the local atmosphere at a weekly market, enjoy a tranquil picnic on the beach or practice your haggling skills while buying some of the colorful local pottery. Casinhas offers a variety of holiday accommodations, from four-person apartments to larger villas for eight. All are comfortably furnished and enjoy marvelous views of the sea; many feature cheerful open fireplaces in the living rooms. Contact: B & D de Vogue International Inc., 1830 S. Mooney Blvd. Ste. 230, Visalia, CA 93277. Call 1-800-727-4748 (in California, 209-733-7119). Ref. PL12, PL14, PL15, PL21, PL24.

Children: Y Pets: Y Smoking: Y Handicap Access: N Payment: P, A, V, M

Sitio

MOREIRA   *Rates: budget-inexpensive*
Open: year-round   *Minimum Stay: one week*

This lovely house stands in a quiet residential quarter of Sitio, a town near Nazare on the Estoril Coast. A splendid base for relaxing at the beach, exploring the hilly countryside, or visiting nearby Lisbon, the house features comfy modern furnishings, a delightful garden and several balconies where you can catch a cool evening breeze or loll in the morning sun. The residence is part of a two-family home, but the separate entrance ensures complete privacy. Inside you'll find a spacious living room, three bedrooms for six, two baths and a modern kitchen. Local shops and neighborhood restaurants are just around the corner, and a cable car will bring you to Nazare and the sea. Contact: Rent a Home International, 7200 34th Ave. N.W., Seattle, WA 98117. Call 206-545-6963.

Children: Y Pets: N Smoking: Y Handicap Access: N Payment: C, P, V, M

LISBON

Almocageme

VIVENDA ISABEL   *Rates: budget*
Open: year-round   *Minimum Stay: one week*

You'll feel right at home in this pleasant family residence outside the small town of Almocageme. A living/dining room, three cheery bedrooms (the house sleeps up to seven), a breakfast nook and a kitchen are found inside the cozy house. After a stroll through the delightful garden, perhaps you'd like to bask in the warm Portuguese sun on one of the terraces. If you decide to visit the weekly market in the nearby village of Colares, or to spend an afternoon at the Cafe Adraga (just around the corner), the friendly owner, who lives next door, will be glad to watch the children. The warm waters and golden sands of the sea are scarcely a couple of miles away. Contact: Rent a Home International, 7200 34th Ave. N.W., Seattle, WA 98117. Call 206-545-6963.

Children: Y Pets: N Smoking: Y Handicap Access: N Payment: C, P, V, M

Cascais

APARTHOTEL   *Rates: budget*
Open: year-round   *Minimum Stay: one week*

Only in friendly Portugal could you get so much for so little. The Aparthotel in Cascais is affordable for every traveler but offers all the amenities of a luxurious resort. The game room, swimming pool, separate children's pool, sauna and TV will keep you busy during the day; the fine restaurants and energetic nightclubs will fill your evenings with fun. There's child care available, and a shuttle bus can whisk you to the center of Cascais for browsing in its boutiques. Finally, the spectacular views of the mountains and sea are second to none and the warm beaches of the coast are only a few minutes away. Contact: Rent a Home International, 7200 34th Ave. N.W., Seattle, WA 98117. Call 206-545-6963.

Children: Y Pets: N Smoking: Y Handicap Access: N Payment: C, P, V, M

Charneca de Caparica

HOUSE SILCENTRO   *Rates: budget*
Open: year-round   *Minimum Stay: one week*

With over 15 miles of fine sandy beaches, it's no surprise that this pleasant fishing village is a popular weekend destination for the residents of nearby Lisbon. During the week, though, you'll have the narrow streets, golden sands and warms waters pretty much to yourself; trains will connect you with other seaside villages if you'd like to do a bit of sightseeing. The apartments in House Silcentro are ideal bases for families or couples. The rooms are tastefully furnished with modern decor and can sleep up to four people. There's even an airy balcony where you can enjoy the peaceful surroundings while sipping a glass of rich Portuguese wine. Contact: Rent a Home International, 7200 34th Ave. N.W., Seattle, WA 98117. Call 206-545-6963.

Children: Y Pets: N Smoking: Y Handicap Access: N Payment: C, P, V, M

Ericeira

DINHO DO OUTERIO   *Rates: budget*
Open: year-round   *Minimum Stay: one week*

The village of Ericeira is an old fishing town that still follows ancestral traditions and the customs of the sea. You'll want to walk around the old harbor with its colorful boats and salty characters and watch the fishmongers as they divvy up the daily catch. The cottage, which sleeps five, and windmill, which sleeps three, are just outside town on a quiet, sunny perch overlooking the deep blue waters of the Atlantic. Both are charming traditional structures in the local style, but they've been fully renovated to offer modern conveniences and comfortable accommodations to their guests. Contact: Rent a Home International, 7200 34th Ave. N.W., Seattle, WA 98117. Call 206-545-6963.

Children: Y Pets: N Smoking: Y Handicap Access: N Payment: C, P, V, M

Estoril

VILLA RITA   *Rates: deluxe*
Open: year-round   *Minimum Stay: one week*

On a quiet hillside outside of Sao Pedro de Estoril sits this magnificent mansion. Its elegantly furnished rooms feature antique pieces and beautiful oil paintings. The main rooms downstairs include a formal living room with a handsome fireplace, a library with TV, an impressive dining room and a large, modern kitchen; each of these rooms opens through French doors to the delightful garden that surround the house. A private swimming pool and patio are also found outside. Upstairs are four spacious bedrooms (one with an en suite bath), two additional bathrooms and a large terrace with splendid views of the sea. Maid service is available and the large garage can hold two cars. Contact: Rent a Home International, 7200 34th Ave. N.W., Seattle, WA 98117. Call 206-545-6963.

Children: Y Pets: N Smoking: Y Handicap Access: N Payment: C, P, V, M

Fonte da Teiha
VILLA QUINTA DA AROEIRA   *Rates: moderate*
Open: year-round   *Minimum Stay: one week*

The sweet scent of pine pervades the air at Quinta da Aroeira, which is nestled in a pine forest only minutes from the beach. Enjoy long walks around the trees and cozy up to the charming stone fireplace at night. Two bedrooms and a sofa bed sleep five in comfort. Beginners and pros will want to try the nearby championship eighteen-hole golf course designed by Frank Pennink, and tennis courts and horseback riding are available for those who want a little more activity. Contact: Villas International, 71 West 23rd Street, New York, NY 10010. Call 1-800-221-2260 (in New York, 212-929-7585).

Children: Y Pets: N Smoking: Y Handicap Access: N Payment: C, P, T

Sintra
QUINTAL DOS PINTOS   *Rates: inexpensive*
Open: year-round   *Minimum Stay: one week*

The Quintal dos Pintos ("House of the Little Children") is a lovely old country house dating back to the 1730s. It is picturesquely situated on a mountain slope at the edge of a national forest; the views of the Atlantic, the wooded hillsides and the gentle valley are simply spectacular. Despite these incredibly bucolic surroundings, Lisbon is less than 20 miles away; the beaches are practically within walking distance. The rooms feature rustic antiques, hardwood floors and richly colored rugs. Both a cheery fireplace and a TV can be enjoyed in the living room; a modern kitchen and two spacious bedrooms are also found inside. The second story of the house is a separate apartment, which can also be rented. Contact: Rent a Home International, 7200 34th Ave. N.W., Seattle, WA 98117. Call 206-545-6963.

Children: Y Pets: N Smoking: Y Handicap Access: N Payment: C, P, V, M

Sintra
VILLA QUINTA DO BIESTER   *Rates: deluxe*
Open: year-round   *Minimum Stay: one week*

Portugal's royal family used to vacation in the exclusive resort town of Sintra, and it's still luxurious enough for royalty or pleasure-seeking guests. Quinta do Biester is a spacious, exquisitely decorated villa, built in 1893 and filled with fine wood carvings, frescoes and oil paintings. Surrounded by twenty acres of walled gardens with a waterfall, orchid house and artificial lake on the grounds, the house contains a music room with a Steinway piano. A staff of ten (including a cook and a maid) will take care of up to ten adults and four children in eight bedrooms. Contact: Villas International, 71 West 23rd Street, New York, NY 10010. Call 1-800-221-2260 (in New York, 212-929-7585).

Children: **Y**   Pets: **N**   Smoking: **Y**   Handicap Access: **N**   Payment: **C, P, T**

MADEIRA

Funchal

SEAVIEW HIGHRISE   *Rates: budget*
Open: year-round   *Minimum Stay: one week*

On a quiet residential street just outside of town you'll find this fabulously equipped apartment building catering to holiday visitors. Each of the comfortably furnished apartments has a stunning sea view from its own private balcony. The building's heated swimming pool is filled with fresh saltwater. After a refreshing swim, stop by the bar and restaurant where you can enjoy a delicious meal before hopping on the shuttle bus that will take you downtown to interesting boutiques. Once back at your hotel, perhaps you'd like to relax in the sauna or challenge a friend to some tennis before a moonlit stroll on the palm-lined promenade. Contact: Rent a Home International, 7200 34th Ave. N.W., Seattle, WA 98117. Call 206-545-6963.

Children: **Y**   Pets: **N**   Smoking: **Y**   Handicap Access: **N**   Payment: **C, P, V, M**

SETUBAL

Sesimbra

OCEAN OVERLOOK   *Rates: budget*
Open: year-round   *Minimum Stay: one week*

Charming Sesimbra is an old fishing village perched on the water's edge and sheltered by steep hills. The life of the town still revolves around the timeless rhythm of the sea, as the rugged fishers, lively fishmongers and excellent seafood restaurants will remind you. These four-person apartments enjoy splendid views of the ocean from their hillside position. Each boasts an airy balcony in addition to the bedroom, living room, kitchenette and bathroom. To make your holiday in sunny Portugal even more convenient, daily maid service is provided. Contact: Rent a Home International, 7200 34th Ave. N.W., Seattle, WA 98117. Call 206-545-6963.

Children: **Y**   Pets: **N**   Smoking: **Y**   Handicap Access: **N**   Payment: **C, P, V, M**

Scotland

BORDERS

Ashkirk, by Selkirk

SCOTT APARTMENT
Open: year-round

Rates: budget-inexpensive
Minimum Stay: one week

This lovely apartment for four occupies the ground floor of an historic country house set high above the Ale Valley. Quiet and self-contained, the apartment has its own entrance and garden and boasts breathtaking views. A sunny sitting room overlooks the lawns and the spacious kitchen has a dining alcove; a double bedroom (with two extra singles) and a twin bedroom provide sleeping comfort. The forty-acre grounds include many walking trails and an archery range. Home to many historic sites and country houses, the area also offers fishing, golf and tennis facilities. Contact: British Travel Associates, P.O. Box 299, Elkton, VA 22827. Call 1-800-327-6097 (in Virginia, 703-298-2232).

Children: Y Pets: N Smoking: Y Handicap Access: N Payment: C, P, A, V, M

Duns

ABBEY ST. BATHANS ESTATE *Rates: budget-moderate*
Open: year-round *Minimum Stay: one week*

This private country estate lies in a secluded valley offering an abundance of recreational activities, from hiking and riding to fishing and game hunting. Short trips can also be planned to Edinburgh, the majestic shores of the North Sea's Berwickshire Coast, or the salmon-filled River Tweed. Accommodations on the estate include three traditional, comfortable cottages and a luxury apartment in the mansion house, sleeping four to ten. All are provided with kitchen, central heating, TV and washer/dryer or linen service. Contact: Mrs. J.J. Dobie, Abbey St. Bathans Estate, Abbey St. Bathans, Duns, Berwickshire TD11 3TX. Call (036 14) 242.

Children: Y   Pets: N   Smoking: Y   Handicap Access: N   Payment: EC

Duns

ELBA WATERFALL COTTAGE *Rates: budget*
Open: year-round *Minimum Stay: one week*

Hidden away on the 4,000-acre private estate of Abbey St. Bathans, this cottage stands 100 yards from the River Whiteadder. Here the river make a sharp bend and tumbles from shallows to deep pools in which you can swim. Guests park 150 yards from the house and reach the cottage via a suspension footbridge above the falls. (Because of this and the rather dramatic rocky banks, this is not a good choice for parents of young, adventurous children!) The cottage includes three bedrooms, a sitting/dining room with a TV, a kitchen and one bath. Trout fishing is available, as are Fell ponies for experienced riders. Nearby St. Abbs Head is a favorite for bird watchers and skin divers. Contact: Castles, Cottages & Flats, Box 261, Westwood, MA 02090. Call 617-329-4680.

Children: Y   Pets: N   Smoking: Y   Handicap Access: N   Payment: P

Duns

LOCHSIDE COTTAGE *Rates: budget*
Open: year-round *Minimum Stay: one week*

This roomy cottage for eight is situated on the banks of Whiteadder Reservoir in the beautiful, rolling Lammermuir Hills. Bedrooms include one double, two rooms with bunk beds and one twin. There is an extra bed in one of the bunk rooms as well. A compact kitchen adjoins the dining/living area, which has a working fireplace. You can fish for trout in the reservoir (with permit) or enjoy a walk in the lovely countryside. The cottage makes a good base for touring, and numerous golf courses can be easily reached. Contact: Blakes Vacations, 4918 Dempster Street, Skokie, IL 60077. Call 1-800-628-8118.

Children: Y   Pets: N   Smoking: Y   Handicap Access: N   Payment: T, V, M

Ettrick Bridge

FAIRHOLM   *Rates: moderate-luxury*
Open: year-round   *Minimum Stay: one week*

This spacious two-story house is located in the cozy village of Ettrick
Bridge, six miles west of Selkirk. Completely renovated in 1988, the
modern residence features four large bedrooms to comfortably sleep
eight, a game room, a stately fireplace and wall-to-wall carpeting. A
porch out back opens onto a generous, meticulously kept garden,
hedged in except for the back, which looks out upon a gently flowing
creek adorned with a footbridge. Along with plentiful opportunities for
hiking and driving in the hills and valley of the Ettrick Waters, a full
variety of aquatic sports facilities are available at nearby St. Mary's
Loch. Contact: Castles, Cottages & Flats, Box 261, Westwood, MA
02090. Call 617-329-4680.

Children: Y   Pets: N   Smoking: Y   Handicap Access: N   Payment: P

Jedburgh

ABBEY BRIDGE END   *Rates: budget*
Open: year-round   *Minimum Stay: one week*

This beautifully renovated 200-year-old stone house stands on the
banks of the winding River Jed and overlooks the ruins of the 12th-
century Abbey. Recently converted into eleven one- and two-bedroom
flats (two of which are completely self-contained), Abbey Bridge also
has a small communal garden. A five-minute stroll takes you into the
charming town of Jedburgh, which offers a delightful array of shops,
pubs, small hotels and restaurants. This lodging is ideal for those who
enjoy the quiet life. Contact: Castles, Cottages & Flats, Box 261, Westwood, MA 02090. Call 617-329-4680.

Children: Y   Pets: N   Smoking: Y   Handicap Access: N   Payment: P

Kelso

HEITON MILL   *Rates: moderate-deluxe*
Open: year-round   *Minimum Stay: one week*

Hidden on the banks of the River Teviot, Heiton Mill sits amid four
acres of private garden-filled grounds, with a picturesque old watermill
nearby. The scenic Abbey and market town of Kelso are four miles
away, but when guests want to remain on the property, they can enjoy
free trout fishing on the owner's private stretch of the river. The two-
story house, with completely modern facilities as well as central heating and air conditioning, features a sun porch and three bedrooms,
sleeping six. Each room has an exquisite view across the river. Contact: Castles, Cottages & Flats, Box 261, Westwood, MA 02090. Call
617-329-4680.

Children: Y   Pets: N   Smoking: Y   Handicap Access: N   Payment: P

Langholm

BURNGRAINS COTTAGE   *Rates: moderate*
Open: year-round   *Minimum Stay: one week*

Drive one mile down hard farm track to reach a very private, newly renovated old stone croft in a truly picturesque setting. Backed by a gently sloping 1,500-foot hill, the rustic cottage sits at the foot of a shady glen from which a small creek quietly cascades. Containing three bedrooms with room for nine, the two-story cottage is heated by an open fireplace and electricity and faces the lovely Meikledale Valley. Contact: Castles, Cottages & Flats, Box 261, Westwood, MA 02090. Call 617-329-4680.

Children: Y   Pets: N   Smoking: Y   Handicap Access: Y   Payment: P

Langholm

GARDENER'S COTTAGE   *Rates: inexpensive*
Open: year-round   *Minimum Stay: one week*

Resting in the hills of a country estate near the English-Scottish border, this secluded stone cottage overlooks the undisturbed valley of the River Esk. The single-story house, easily accessible by car via country road, has two bedrooms plus a double-bed settee in the living room, offering sleeping space for up to six persons. A cool grove of trees reaches to the cottage door, and the grounds also boast a sunny garden. Recreational activities include hiking and easy climbing through the inviting hills, as well as exceptional fishing and bird watching. Contact: Castles, Cottages & Flats, Box 261, Westwood, MA 02090. Call 617-329-4680.

Children: Y   Pets: N   Smoking: Y   Handicap Access: N   Payment: P

Longtown

KIRKANDREWS-ON-ESK   *Rates: budget-inexpensive*
Open: year-round   *Minimum Stay: one week*

Steeped in history, this fortified 16th-century house remains in wonderful condition. The imposing structure stands near the River Esk and offers impressive views over parkland. A living room, eat-in kitchen, playroom with washing machine and two bedrooms provide abundant space and comfort. Logs are supplied for the open fireplaces in the living room and kitchen, which along with the three-foot-thick sandstone walls will keep you warm and secure on damp Scottish days. Outside, there's a garden with a barbecue and garden chairs for relaxing. A good base for touring the Lake District and the Solway coast, this house accommodates four to five people. Contact: British Travel Associates, P.O. Box 299, Elkton, VA 22827. Call 1-800-327-6097 (in Virginia, 703-298-2232).

Children: Y Pets: N Smoking: Y Handicap Access: N Payment: C, P, A, V, M

Melrose

ST. KIERANS   *Rates: budget*
Open: year-round   *Minimum Stay: one week*

This unusual and attractive three-bedroom Edwardian cottage is situated on its own quiet lane overlooking the grounds of the old Priory and Cloisters of the famous Melrose Abbey. Recently renovated and redecorated, this snug getaway has its own patio with garden furniture, leading onto a grassy area and enclosed orchard. Up to six can enjoy the sitting room with its color TV, the kitchen/dining room with a washing machine and the modern bath. Only a short walk takes you to shops, hotels and restaurants. There is ample heating supplied by Dimplex heaters throughout the house. Contact: Castles, Cottages & Flats, Box 261, Westwood, MA 02090. Call 617-329-4680.

Children: **Y**   Pets: **N**   Smoking: **Y**   Handicap Access: **N**   Payment: **P**

Peebles

LANGHAUGH FARMHOUSE/NORTH WING   *Rates: budget*
Open: year-round   *Minimum Stay: one week*

Nestled in a peaceful, scenic glen, this self-contained wing of a large country farmhouse sleeps eight. The spacious living room has an open fire, and the oak-lined hall/dining room boasts an ornamental fireplace. Modern and fully equipped, the kitchen is a pleasure to use. The second-floor sleeping accommodations comprise three bedrooms: two doubles and one with two twins and a double. Two bathrooms and a shower complete this floor. A neatly kept garden with magnificent hill and country views and free trout fishing on the nearby river make this cottage an ideal country reatreat. Contact: Blakes Vacations, 4918 Dempster Street, Skokie, IL 60077. Call 1-800-628-8118.

Children: **Y**   Pets: **N**   Smoking: **Y**   Handicap Access: **N**   Payment: **T, V, M**

Selkirk

HAINING LOCH APARTMENTS   *Rates: budget-inexpensive*
Open: year-round   *Minimum Stay: one week*

Down a private wooded drive half a mile from the center of the town of Selkirk—world famous for its tweed—this residence is on the first floor of a converted traditional coach house. The two-bedroom, fully equipped flat overlooks Haining Loch (where superb coarse fishing is available), a wild garden and the parklands of a stately country mansion. This apartment offers a rich combination of wooded seclusion and the enticements of one of Scotland's most charming towns. Contact: Castles, Cottages & Flats, Box 261, Westwood, MA 02090. Call 617-329-4680.

Children: **Y**   Smoking: **Y**   Pets: **N**   Handicap Access: **N**   Payment: **P**

Whitmuir, Selkirk

WHITMUIR ESTATE   *Rates: budget*
Open: year-round   *Minimum Stay: one week*

A private loch with boats is but one feature gracing this estate situated in the gentle Borders countryside. Guests enjoy the lush gardens and wooded areas located on the estate grounds, as well as sporting activities like riding and fishing. The mansion house, Whitmuir Hall, has been converted into nine spacious apartments; seven homey cottages are available as well, making the estate suitable for parties of two to seven. All guests have access to sauna, games room and laundry. Contact: Mrs. Hilary Dunlop, Whitmuir Estate, Whitmuir, Selkirk TD7 4PZ. Call (0750) 21728.

Children: **Y**   Pets: **N**   Smoking: **Y**   Handicap Access: **N**   Payment: **EC**

CENTRAL

Stirling

STIRLING UNIVERSITY CHALETS *Rates: budget*
Open: mid-June to mid-September *Minimum Stay: one week*
Five-bedroom Scandinavian chalets and student flats sleeping two to seven persons are situated on the wooded grounds of a modern university campus. Snuggled into the hills, the campus affords access to fishing and swimming on a private loch and includes a golf course, theater, movie house, public bar, supermarket and a self-service restaurant. This is an excellent center from which to visit Edinburgh, Glasgow, The Trossachs, St. Andrews and all the southern Highlands. Contact: Castles, Cottages & Flats, Box 261, Westwood, MA 02090. Call 617-329-4680.
Children: **Y**   Pets: **N**   Smoking: **Y**   Handicap Access: **N**   Payment: **P**

DUMFRIES AND GALLOWAY

Dumfries

SANQUHAR BUNGALOW *Rates: budget*
Open: year-round *Minimum Stay: one week*
Stay on a working farm in this spacious bungalow for six or seven, where in March and April you can watch the lambing and feed the pet lambs. Roomy enough for the whole family, the bungalow includes a dining/living room, a kitchen and three bedrooms (one double, one twin and one double-plus-single). Color TV, a microwave, a washer/dryer and a barbecue complete the comforts of home; babysitting services are available as well. The living room has an open fireplace, with logs and coal provided. In the surrounding area, guests can visit Drumlanrig Castle, the beaches at Ayr and several golf courses. The countryside is excellent for walking tours. Contact: British Travel Associates, P.O. Box 299, Elkton, VA 22827. Call 1-800-327-6097 (in Virginia, 703-298-2232).
Children: **Y** Pets: **N** Smoking: **Y** Handicap Access: **N** Payment: **C, P, A, V, M**

Kirkcudbright

BARNCROSH FARM *Rates: budget*
Open: year-round *Minimum Stay: one week*
These apartments and cottages are tucked away on a 500-acre dairy farm with twenty acres of private woodlands, four miles west of Castle Douglas and five miles from the Galloway shore. Enjoy a peaceful vacation either in a family house or in a smaller apartment in the converted stables. Accommodations range in size from one to three bedrooms. Relax and take in the spectacular scenery or make use of the nearby tennis, riding, bowling, squash and water sports facilties. Contact: Castles, Cottages & Flats, Box 261, Westwood, MA 02090. Call 617-329-4680.
Children: **Y**   Pets: **N**   Smoking: **Y**   Handicap Access: **N**   Payment: **P**

FIFE

Kingsbarn, by St. Andrews

ATTIC APARTMENT

Rates: budget

Open: year-round

Minimum Stay: one week

The magnificent Cambo Estate, near famous St. Andrews, sweeps from soft fields and wooded groves gently down to the gleaming sands of the North Sea shore. This apartment on the top floor of Cambo House, an exquisite neo-Georgian country mansion, offers full use of the estate's bountiful facilities. Indoor activities include a game room featuring billiards and table tennis, a sauna and a library overflowing with books. Outdoor offerings range from beaches, tennis courts (with practice equipment), picnic grounds and playground to a working farm with rare animals on display. The comfortable apartment contains three bedrooms—one double and two twins—with room for up to six, along with a kitchen and full amenities. Contact: Castles, Cottages & Flats, Box 261, Westwood, MA 02090. Call 617-329-4680.

Children: Y   Smoking: Y   Pets: N   Handicap Access: N   Payment: P

Kingsbarn, by St. Andrews

PARK VIEW APARTMENT

Rates: budget

Open: year-round

Minimum Stay: one week

A second-floor apartment in Cambo House, this flat offers panoramic vistas of the majestic 1,600-acre Cambo Estate. On the grounds, the path along the Cambo Burn leads down to the seashore with its pristine sandy beach and rock pools. Winding nature trails offer sightings of exotic woodland wildlife, including roe deer and herons in their natural habitat. Farm roads ideal for cycling beckon as well. The apartment includes two bedrooms, each with twin beds, plus a double-bed settee in the living room, providing room for up to six. Contact: Castles, Cottages & Flats, Box 261, Westwood, MA 02090. Call 617-329-4680.

Children: Y   Smoking: Y   Pets: N   Handicap Access: N   Payment: P

St. Andrews

DRON COURT

Rates: budget

Open: year-round

Minimum Stay: one week

Overlooking the picturesque valley of the River Eden, a 17th-century farmstead has been converted into nine vacation homes, each individually and luxuriously styled within the original three-foot-thick stone walls. The one-, two-, three- and four-bedroom cottages are built around an old courtyard that features one of the original wells, a fountain and a recreational clubhouse that guests can use. Each house has either a patio or a private patch of the two-acre garden. Contact: Castles, Cottages & Flats, Box 261, Westwood, MA 02090. Call 617-329-4680.

Children: Y   Pets: N   Smoking: Y   Handicap Access: N   Payment: P

St. Andrews

STRAVITHIE COUNTRY ESTATE *Rates: inexpensive*
Open: March-January *Minimum Stay: one week*

Set in the heart of the world's finest golf country, this gracious estate features stone-built houses, a barn, cottages and quality studio flats of singular character, sleeping two to eight people. When not on the St. Andrews golf links or using the grounds' putting greens and practice net, guests can ride along nature trails on horses from the estate's private stables or enjoy trout fishing, badminton or table tennis. Nearby, too, are the enticing sandy beaches that distinguish this region. Contact: Mr. J. Chalmers, Stravithie Country Estate, Stravithie, St. Andrews KY16 8LR. Call Boarhills (033 488) 251.

Children: Y   Pets: N   Smoking: Y   Handicap Access: N   Payment: EC

St. Andrews

WEST SANDS APARTMENT *Rates: inexpensive*
Open: year-round *Minimum Stay: one week*

The attic of an elegant 19th-century Victorian townhouse in St. Andrews has been converted into a quality flat for up to six persons. This splendidly located residence is minutes away from what visitors come to St. Andrews for: It's just across from the first tee, 100 yards from the Old Course, 100 yards from the beach and 200 yards from the nearest shops and pub. The fully equipped apartment contains three bedrooms with twin beds (two with showers, one with a full bath), and also features color TV with VCR. Contact: Castles, Cottages & Flats, Box 261, Westwood, MA 02090. Call 617-329-4680.

Children: Y   Pets: N   Smoking: Y   Handicap Access: N   Payment: P

St. Monans

FISHER'S COTTAGE *Rates: budget*
Open: year-round *Minimum Stay: one week*

This converted fisher's cottage dating from the 17th century has been restored to provide comfortable accommodations for four. The open-plan upper level includes a living area, a kitchen, a dining area and a bedroom; a wooden staircase leads down to the master bedroom and bath on the ground floor. The village flourishes as a boat-building center, and several local beaches are safe for children. Within a 15-mile radius visitors can find several golf courses, including the world-famous St. Andrews. Contact: British Travel Associates, P.O. Box 299, Elkton, VA 22827. Call 1-800-327-6097 (in Virginia, 703-298-2232).

Children: Y Pets: N Smoking: Y Handicap Access: N Payment: C, P, A, V, M

GRAMPIAN

Ballater, Deeside

MONALTRIE HOUSE/EAST WING *Rates: inexpensive*
Open: year-round *Minimum Stay: one week*

This self-contained wing of an 18th-century mansion sleeps six. Elegant accommodations include a large, luxurious kitchen/dining room and a spacious living room with fireplace and views of the six-acre grounds. In addition, there's a large bedroom with two double beds and two adjoining twin-bedded rooms. The surrounding scenery blends wooded moorland, lochs, nature reserves and broad rivers. Enjoy the shared gardens on the grounds or trek to nearby places of interest, such as Balmoral Castle. Contact: British Travel Associates, P.O. Box 299, Elkton, VA 22827. Call 1-800-327-6097 (in Virginia, 703-298-2232).

Children: Y Pets: N Smoking: Y Handicap Access: N Payment: C, P, A, V, M

Druminnor

LAUNDRY COTTAGE   *Rates: budget-inexpensive*

Open: year-round   *Minimum Stay: one week*

Surrounded by its own garden, this stone cottage for five is set on the lovely 40-acre grounds of a 15th-century castle. Secluded and idyllic, the cottage overlooks a small lake. Inside, the cottage has been recently refurbished and includes a sitting room with a dining area and an open fire, and a well-equipped kitchen with a breakfast nook. Upstairs are the two twin bedrooms and one single bedroom. Rich with castles, moors, rivers and mountains, the area offers golf, fishing and skiing as well. Contact: British Travel Associates, P.O. Box 299, Elkton, VA 22827. Call 1-800-327-6097 (in Virginia, 703-298-2232).

Children: Y Pets: N Smoking: Y Handicap Access: N Payment: C, P, A, V, M

Dufftown

KININVIE HOUSE   *Rates: budget-inexpensive*

Open: year-round   *Minimum Stay: one week*

You'll find this 15th-century mansion in the heart of whiskey country. The self-contained lower wing of the house, accesible from a small courtyard, can house up to four. Recently renovated and set on extensive grounds, the flat includes a living room, eat-in kitchen and two bedrooms. An open fireplace and color TV complete the cozy accommodations. The estate grounds are perfect for peaceful walks and private fishing—you even have your own garden with garden chairs. Golf courses, pony trekking, cross-country skiing and clay-pigeon shooting are all available nearby. Contact: British Travel Associates, P.O. Box 299, Elkton, VA 22827. Call 1-800-327-6097 (in Virginia, 703-298-2232).

Children: Y Pets: N Smoking: N Handicap Access: N Payment: C, P, A, V, M

Glass, by Huntly

BELDORNEY CASTLE COTTAGE   *Rates: budget*

Open: year-round   *Minimum Stay: one week*

This private one-story annex to a picturesque pinnacled castle provides lodging for four. Surrounded by the castle grounds on the banks of the Deveron River, the cottage offers views over the river of surrounding hills and glens. With a sitting room, farmhouse-style kitchen/dining area, twin bedroom and small bedroom with bunk beds, the cottage makes a cozy retreat. Riding, shooting, fishing and golf are all nearby, as are the beaches of the Moray coast. Contact: British Travel Associates, P.O. Box 299, Elkton, VA 22827. Call 1-800-327-6097 (in Virginia, 703-298-2232).

Children: Y Pets: N Smoking: Y Handicap Access: Y Payment: C, P, A, V, M

Glen Deveron, by Huntly

ASWANLEY ESTATE/EASTER FARM *Rates: budget-inexpensive*
Open: year-round *Minimum Stay: one week*

This peaceful, secluded farmhouse has been completely redecorated and furnished in period style. The roomy accommodations for six include a large kitchen/dining room, a sitting room with two sofa beds, an open fire and a piano and a second sitting room also with an open fire. Two rooms with twin beds and one large double bedroom comprise the upper level. In front of the house, a completely private garden commands unrestricted views across meadows to the town and river. This picturesque and unspoiled region offers a wide range of attractions, including walking, fishing, historic sites, riding, shopping and dining. Contact: British Travel Associates, P.O. Box 299, Elkton, VA 22827. Call 1-800-327-6097 (in Virginia, 703-2982232).

Children: Y Pets: N Smoking: Y Handicap Access: Y Payment: C, P, A, V, M

Keith

ISLA BANK HOUSE *Rates: deluxe*
Open: year-round *Minimum Stay: one week*

This truly opulent baronial mansion house, furnished with painstakingly selected antique pieces, accommodates parties of up to twelve in consummate luxury. The ground floor features a drawing room, a music room, a library and a billiards room (with a full-sized snooker table), while the upper floor contains five regal bedrooms and two baths. The fastidiously kept mansion grounds situated right on the outskirts of the historic town of Keith (on the famous and colorful Whiskey Trail) feature gardens with a barbecue and picnic facilities. A resident staff tends the house and estate daily and will, by arrangement, also prepare and serve meals. Contact: Blakes Vacations, 4918 Dempster Street, Skokie, IL 60077. Call 1-800-628-8118.

Children: Y Smoking: Y Pets: N Handicap Access: N Payment: T, V, M

Keith

LOCHPARK, DRUMMUIR CASTLE ESTATE *Rates: budget-inexpensive*
Open: year-round *Minimum Stay: one week*

Nestled in a secluded garden on the edge of a private loch, this lovely cottage sleeps seven. Lochpark features a spacious, modern kitchen/dining room, a sitting room with granite fireplace and loch views, one double bedroom with a bath, two twins and a single. acre Drummuir Castle Estate, the cottage has a sma can use for trout fishing. The location, directly on t is ideal for walking and bird watching, with ridin available nearby. Contact: British Travel Associat Elkton, VA 22827. Call 1-800-327-6097 (in Virgin

Children: Y Pets: N Smoking: Y Handicap Access: N Pay

Portsoy

CORNHILL
Open: year-round

Rates: budget-moderate
Minimum Stay: one week

A restored 13th-century castle houses this luxury apartment for five to seven people. Featuring a stone tower and minstrel gallery, Cornhill is a fine example of ancient Scottish baronial architecture. The large, gracious rooms have been fitted with period furnishings, creating an elegant yet comfortable family atmosphere. You can dine either in the paneled drawing room or in the kitchen. Guests also enjoy a library, two bathrooms, a sauna and three bedrooms. The naturally landscaped grounds boast a croquet lawn. In the surrounding area, you will find numerous castles, excellent whiskey, heritage trails, golf, fishing, water sports and riding. Contact: British Travel Associates, P.O. Box 299, Elkton, VA 22827. Call 1-800-327-6097 (in Virginia, 703-298-2232).

Children: Y Pets: N Smoking: Y Handicap Access: N Payment: C, P, A, V, M

Tomintoul

THE CLOCKHOUSE
Open: year-round

Rates: budget
Minimum Stay: one week

A newly renovated and refurbished two-bedroom apartment with carpeting, barbecue grill and microwave is available on the upper floor of this elegant period building, located in the middle of the lovely village of Tomintoul. The town is a popular fishing center, with superb trout and salmon angling and horseback riding available. The nearby Cairngorm Mountains offer splendid touring in the summer and skiing in the winter. Those seeking more far-reaching excursions can look to Inverness or Loch Ness to the west, or Aberdeen and the North Sea coast to the east. Contact: Blakes Vacations, 4918 Dempster Street, Skokie, IL 60077. Call 1-800-628-8118.

Children: Y Pets: N Smoking: Y Handicap Access: N Payment: T, V, M

Turriff

IVY COTTAGE AT FORGLEN ESTATE
Open: year-round

Rates: inexpensive
Minimum Stay: weekend

This cottage, located on the grounds of the thousand-acre Forglen Estate, brings guests to a beautiful stretch of the Deveron Valley, where the forests are ablaze with color in both spring and autumn. Hike down the many winding trails to enjoy wildlife, woodlands and waterfalls. Excellent fishing is available in the river that flows along the edge of the estate-salmon in spring and brown trout all year. Many of Scotland's most famous tourist destinations and loveliest scenic spots are within easy reach, including Royal Deeside, the Aviemore Mountains, the Spey Valley and its Whiskey Trails and castles galore. The cottage contains three bedrooms with room for six and features a shady porch and garden. Contact: Castles, Cottages & Flats, Box 261, stwood, MA 02090. Call 617-329-4680.

n: Y Pets: N Smoking: Y Handicap Access: N Payment: P

HIGHLAND

Applecross

CRUARY COTTAGE *Rates: moderate*
Open: year-round *Minimum Stay: one week*

A stone-built shepherd's cottage, newly refurbished to accommodate four people, Cruary is perched on a bluff overlooking two miles of golden sand and the endless turquoise-blue sea. The living room and dining room both have open fireplaces, while the compact kitchen is fitted with modern conveniences. Upstairs, two charming twin bedrooms with electric blankets and duvets make for warm nights. Salmon, otters and seals cavort near the shore side of the cottage; on the inland side, your view is of the mountains, moorlands and forests of Wester Ross in the distance. The royal yacht Brittania visits the quiet little village of Applecross—when you stay here, you'll see why. Contact: British Travel Associates, P.O. Box 299, Elkton, VA 22827. Call 1-800-327-6097 (in Virginia, 703-298-2232).

Children: Y Pets: N Smoking: Y Handicap Access: N Payment: C, P, A, V, M

Badachro, by Gairloch

HEATHERLEA *Rates: budget-moderate*
Open: year-round *Minimum Stay: one week*

This superb and substantial house is set on a rocky promontory overlooking Badachro Bay. Delightful, landscaped gardens run right to the water's edge, where you'll find a private jetty. Tastefully modernized, the house has two sitting rooms, both with open fireplaces. The enormous pine kitchen has a spacious dining area, and a sun lounge runs the full width of the house, overlooking the garden. Upstairs, two double bedrooms, a twin and a single bedroom sleep seven. A perfect location to enjoy water sports as well as wildlife, Heatherlea enjoys weather mild enough for palm trees and other exotic vegetation. Sandy swimming beaches lie within a few miles. Contact: British Travel Associates, P.O. Box 299, Elkton, VA 22827. Call 1-800-327-6097 (in Virginia, 703-298-2232).

Children: Y Pets: N Smoking: N Handicap Access: N Payment: C, P, A, V, M

Beauly

OLD STABLE *Rates: budget*
Open: year-round *Minimum Stay: one week*

Explore 400 acres of farmland while staying in this converted stable apartment for four. Simple but comfortable, the groundfloor apartment offers a spacious living/dining room with a well-equipped kitchen area. One double bedroom and one twin bedroom round out the accommodations. Guests can make use of a shared garden and a game room with table tennis, darts and pool. Set in the courtyard of a farmhouse, the apartment enjoys views of the scenic Beauly River valley. The immediate area, with its abundance of bird, plant and animal life, is perfect for walking tours. Beaches are within a few

minutes drive. Contact: British Travel Associates, P.O. Box 299, Elkton, VA 22827. Call 1-800-327-6097 (in Virginia, 703-298-2232).
Children: Y Pets: N Smoking: Y Handicap Access: N Payment: C, P, A, V, M

Boat of Garten

TYNDRUM
Open: year-round

Rates: budget
Minimum Stay: one week

A house of distinction and character awaits your visit in the charming village of Boat of Garten. The centrally located two-story house sleeps five in its three upstairs bedrooms, one double, one twin and one single. Well appointed, with a modern kitchen and dining area, the house also features two downstairs sitting rooms. Maid service is available at an extra charge. Minutes from a golf course and tennis courts, the house also offers easy access to the scenic six-mile steam railway, which connects Aviemore with Aviemore Center. Within a few miles, visitors can spot the reindeer herd at Glenmore, tour the Highland Wildlife Park at Kincraig and stop in at the Clan Tartan Centre. This house makes a great home base for an interesting vacation. Contact: Blakes Vacations, 4918 Dempster Street, Skokie, IL 60077. Call 1-800-628-8118.
Children: Y Pets: N Smoking: Y Handicap Access: N Payment: T, V, M

Bridge of Gaur

GILLIES APARTMENT
Open: year-round

Rates: inexpensive
Minimum Stay: one week

The self-contained three-bedroom wing of a splendid Victorian house built from local stone can accommodate up to four people. Perched on a serene hillside overlooking Loch Rannoch, with lofty mountain views, the house features a fine garden with patio furniture and barbecue that guests may share with the owner. Ample fishing and game hunting is available nearby. Contact: Castles, Cottages & Flats, Box 261, Westwood, MA 02090. Call 617-329-4680.
Children: Y Pets: N Smoking: Y Handicap Access: N Payment: P

Callander

MOOREND COTTAGES
Open: year-round

Rates: budget
Minimum Stay: one week

These two cottages, located on a large, privately owned estate, lie on the southern shore of Loch Venachar in the spectacular countryside of the Trossachs. Each cottage boasts French doors opening onto a sunny terrace, which faces south across woodland and bracken to the nearby Menteith Hills. Sightseers enjoy scenic drives to Oban, Fort William and Pitlochry, while the more energetic guests appreciate the nearby fishing, boating, golfing and hiking. In the evening, try Callander's fine restaurants or relax in front of your cottage's open fireplace. Contact: Castles, Cottages & Flats, Box 261, Westwood, MA 02090. Call 617-329-4680.
Children: Y Pets: N Smoking: Y Handicap Access: N Payment: P

Carrbridge

LYNPHAIL　　　　　　　　　　　　　　　　　*Rates: expensive*
Open: year-round　　　　　　　　　*Minimum Stay: one week*

This roomy house lies on an acre of private meadowlands just outside the captivating village of Carrbridge and ten miles away from the Cairngorm Mountains ski resort of Aviemore. The comfortable two-story, four bedroom (one master suite, two twin, one single) residence boasts a sauna and two bright patios. Looking out on the gardens and the rolling stream that borders the property, the patios catch both the morning and afternoon sun. Contact: Castles, Cottages & Flats, Box 261, Westwood, MA 02090. Call 617-329-4680.

Children: Y　　Smoking: Y　　Pets: N　　Handicap Access: Y　　Payment: P

Coli of Lochalsh

TORR GHRINN　　　　　　　　　　　　　　　　*Rates: budget*
Open: year-round　　　　　　　　　*Minimum Stay: one week*

Meaning "sunny knoll," Torr Ghrinn lives up to its name, an appealing house overlooking lovingly kept grounds. This roomy, graciously appointed and furnished residence has a separate living room and dining room and comfortably sleeps up to five adults and two children. It is also graced with its own exquisite garden. The town of Coli of Lochalsh is a quick walk away, where a memorable visit to the Isle of Skye—or other island spots—can be launched. Contact: Blakes Vacations, 4918 Dempster Street, Skokie, IL 60077. Call 1-800-628-8118.

Children: Y　　Pets: N　　Smoking: Y　　Handicap Access: N　　Payment: T, V, M

Invergordon

KINDEACE HOUSE　　　　　　　　　　*Rates: budget-inexpensive*
Open: year-round　　　　　　　　　*Minimum Stay: one week*

This country house stands in a large, secluded woodland garden with a pond and tennis court. Up to seven or eight guests can stay in a wing that encompasses three floors and includes a large kitchen, two bathrooms, a dining room, a living room and four bedrooms: one double, two twins and a single. Well decorated and comfortably furnished, it also includes central heating and a log fireplace. The location is ideal for walking, sailing, bird watching and fishing; excellent wind surfing, pony trekking and golf are easily accessible. Contact: British Travel Associates, P.O. Box 299, Elkton, VA 22827. Call 1-800-327-6097 (in Virginia, 703-298-2232).

Children: Y　　Pets: N　　Smoking: Y　　Handicap Access: N　　Payment: C, P, A, V, M

Isle of Oronsay

EVE COTTAGE　　　　　　　　　　　　　　　　*Rates: moderate*
Open: year-round　　　　　　　　　*Minimum Stay: one week*

For a vacation that truly lives up to the term "getaway," this fetching cottage is located on the remote island of Oronsay, which boasts a permanent population of four souls. Oronsay is reachable only via the larger island of Colonsay, to which it is linked during low tide by a mile-long path of sand. Thrice-weekly ferries transport visitors from the port of Oban on the mainland to Colonsay. Once on sublimely isolated Oronsay, swimmers, hikers, and nature lovers find plenty to do. You may wish to simply lounge around the three-bedroom cottage, with its spectacular view, open fireplace, and cozy walled garden. For a change of pace, guests can cross over to Colonsay and enjoy the isle's social activities—tide permitting, that is. Contact: Castles, Cottages & Flats, Box 261, Westwood, MA 02090. Call 617-329-4680.

Children: Y   Pets: N   Smoking: Y   Handicap Access: N   Payment: P

Isle of Tiree
TRAIGH MHOR   *Rates: inexpensive*
Open: year-round   *Minimum Stay: one week*

Located on the Isle of Tiree, westernmost of the Inner Hebrides and accessible by ferry from Oban, Traigh Mhor is perched on a grassy slope overlooking Gott Bay, a three-mile stretch of sand just 100 yards below. Seemingly endless expanses of Tiree's coastline are covered by deserted silver beaches, all with sweeping views of the neighboring islands. The house is a spacious and superbly outfitted two-story, four-bedroom residence with room for nine. A pub and nine-hole golf course are minutes away by foot and the island's main village, Scaranish, is two miles down the road. Contact: Castles, Cottages & Flats, Box 261, Westwood, MA 02090. Call 617-329-4680.

Children: Y   Pets: N   Smoking: Y   Handicap Access: N   Payment: P

Kinross
KINROSS FARMHOUSE   *Rates: inexpensive*
Open: year-round   *Minimum Stay: one week*

A spacious 18th-century farmhouse sits in a sunny garden near Loch Leven, where you and your group of six to eight can make yourselves right at home. The living room with a dining area, kitchen, sun room and three bedrooms (two doubles, one with four singles) allow plenty of space. Among the house's conveniences are a color TV with VCR, a washing machine, a microwave and babysitting services. A garden is equipped with chairs and a barbecue. Fishing, golf, gliding and water sports are available nearby. Contact: British Travel Associates, P.O. Box 299, Elkton, VA 22827. Call 1-800-327-6097 (in Virginia, 703-298-2232).

Children: Y Pets: N Smoking: Y Handicap Access: N Payment: C, P, A, V, M

Kirremuir
GLEN COVA COTTAGE   *Rates: budget-inexpensive*
Open: year-round   *Minimum Stay: one week*

This charming cottage for four boasts a lovely setting on two acres of garden and woodlands near a quiet glen road. Its original open beams and paneling lend warmth to the decor, while the living room with a dining area includes an inglenook hearth. The master bedroom features a Victorian fireplace. A twin bedroom and bath complete the unit. An excellent touring base, the area offers hiking, alpine flowers, pony trekking, wildlife, fishing and magnificent scenery. Contact: British Travel Associates, P.O. Box 299, Elkton, VA 22827. Call 1-800-327-6097 (in Virginia, 703-298-2232).

Children: Y Pets: N Smoking: Y Handicap Access: N Payment: C, P, A, V, M

Laggan Bridge, by Newtonmore

STRATHMASHIE HOUSE *Rates: inexpensive*
Open: year-round *Minimum Stay: one week*

The entire upper floor of Strathmashie House's former kitchen wing has been converted into a modern, self-contained two-bedroom flat for up to four. Located in a sedate farmland area three miles from Loch Laggan, the house offers imposing views of the Highland hills and mountains. Guests may arrange for full access to the nearby Ardverikie Estate, where they can enjoy sandy lakeside beaches, nature trails, sheep farms and throngs of wild red deer. Contact: Castles, Cottages & Flats, Box 261, Westwood, MA 02090. Call 617-329-4680.

Children: Y   Smoking: Y   Pets: N   Handicap Access: N   Payment: P

Loch Ness, Foyers Hotel

THE COACH HOUSE *Rates: budget*
Open: year-round *Minimum Stay: one week*

Perched high above Loch Ness with magnificent views across the water from its large picture window, this modern chalet has been constructed using the original walls of the old coach house. Accommodations for six lie on the upper floor and include one double and two twin bedrooms, plus an open-style kitchen/dining/living room. Beach and boat access to the loch are nearby, and guests can arrange through the hotel to fish for salmon and trout. The immediate countryside offers beautiful forest walks, while the city of Inverness is only 25 minutes away. Contact: Blakes Vacations, 4918 Dempster Street, Skokie, IL 60077. Call 1-800-628-8118.

Children: Y   Pets: N   Smoking: Y   Handicap Access: N   Payment: T, V, M

Lochcarron

THE WHITE HOUSE *Rates: budget*
Open: year-round *Minimum Stay: one week*

On the shore of one of northern Scotland's most striking inlets, the three-story White House is the tallest building in the small West Highland village of Lochcarron. The ground floor houses a craft shop; the upper floors contain two fully equipped two-bedroom flats, each with a separate entrance. Both apartments offer marvelous panoramic views of the inlet and the majestic surrounding Highland mountains. These lodgings make a fine base for excursions along the rugged coast or to Kyle of Lochalsh; the ferry to the Isle of Skye is easily accessible. Contact: Castles, Cottages & Flats, Box 261, Westwood, MA 02090. Call 617-329-4680.

Children: Y   Pets: N   Smoking: Y   Handicap Access: N   Payment: P

Lonbain, by Applecross

THE OLD SCHOOL HOUSE

Open: year-round

Rates: budget-moderate

Minimum Stay: one week

Set in a scenic, sunny spot twenty yards from the sea, this converted schoolhouse sleeps five. From the picture windows in the sitting room, you glimpse a spectacular view across the water of the Isle of Skye. The living room with its open fireplace also affords such a view. Also on the ground floor you'll find a well-appointed kitchen with a dining area and a fuel-burning stove; upstairs is a single and two twin bedrooms. Seashore wildlife abounds, and a sandy beach is just three miles away. There's also a garden patio with furniture and views of the sea. Contact: British Travel Associates, P.O. Box 299, Elkton, VA 22827. Call 1-800-327-6097 (in Virginia, 703-298-2232).

Children: Y Pets: N Smoking: Y Handicap Access: N Payment: C, P, A, V, M

Lonbain, by Applecross

TIGH RUARAIDH

Open: year-round

Rates: moderate

Minimum Stay: one week

Seals bask on the rocks just outside your door at this warm, roomy cottage for five on the seashore. The cottage includes a large modern kitchen, a dining area and a spacious living room with a wood-burning stove and windows overlooking the sea. Upstairs are one double bedroom, one twin and one with full-size pine stacking beds. Pine furnishings and fitted carpets complete the interior. You can fish from your doorstep or at a sandy beach just three miles away. You'll see seals, otters, deer and golden eagles outside. Contact: British Travel Associates, P.O. Box 299, Elkton, VA 22827. Call 1-800-327-6097 (in Virginia, 703-298-2232).

Children: Y Pets: N Smoking: Y Handicap Access: N Payment: C, P, A, V, M

Lyth, by Wick

BARROCK HOUSE

Open: year-round

Rates: budget-expensive

Minimum Stay: one week

Stay in a unspoiled mansion with many of its original furnishings, paintings and ornaments intact. Ancestral home to the clan Sinclair, Barrock House offers comfortable, well-appointed and spacious accommodation in grand style. The large entrance hall with its imposing staircase opens to a library with an open fire and a bow window overlooking the 70-acre grounds. A drawing room, card room, dining room, pantry and kitchen with modern fittings also occupy the ground floor. Upstairs, off a large landing, three suites of bedrooms—two with their own bath—provide sleeping space for up to ten. The location is ideal for exploring northernmost Scotland and the Orkney Islands, or for game fishing in the nearby lochs, rivers and sea. Contact: British Travel Associates, P.O. Box 299, Elkton, VA 22827. Call 1-800-327-6097 (in Virginia, 703-298-2232).

Children: Y Pets: N Smoking: Y Handicap Access: N Payment: C, P, A, V, M

Nairn

LAVENDER COTTAGE   *Rates: budget*
Open: year-round   *Minimum Stay: one week*

This 17th-century "Crook House" has been cleverly modernized as a cottage for two, yet it retains great character. Located on the Cawdor Castle estate in one of the most beautiful and varied regions of Scotland, the cottage offers a modern, fully equipped kitchen with a dining area, a double bedroom and a living room with a sleeper couch. Outside, enjoy a private garden or one of the many nature trails. Golf courses and beaches are within easy reach and Cawdor Castle is open to the public from May to September. Contact: British Travel Associates, P.O. Box 299, Elkton, VA 22827. Call 1-800-327-6097 (in Virginia, 703-298-2232).

Children: **Y** Pets: **N** Smoking: **Y** Handicap Access: **N** Payment: **C, P, A, V, M**

Newtonmore

GLEN BANCHOR ESTATE   *Rates: budget*
Open: year-round   *Minimum Stay: one week*

Deep in the Highland on the Glen Banchor Estate lie three delightful cottages. One mile from Newtonmore (the last 500 yards by farm track) and just back from the Calder River, two-bedroom Calder Cottage is an old shepherd's croft renovated into a cozy south-facing hideaway with its own garden. Riseley Cottage, the most far-flung house in Newtonmore, offers two bedrooms with only the hills and heathery moorlands beyond. With a traditional crofthouse exterior, three-bedroom Baillid Beg Cottage looks across the Spey River to the Cairngorm Mountains. It does not have electricity; heating, lighting and cooking are by gas. Visitors to the area can enjoy every form of outdoor recreation, from hiking to golf and from canoeing to skiing in winter. Contact: Castles, Cottages & Flats, Box 261, Westwood, MA 02090. Call 617-329-4680.

Children: **Y** Pets: **N** Smoking: **Y** Handicap Access: **N** Payment: **P**

Newtonmore

NORTH DRUMOCHTER LODGE   *Rates: luxury*
Open: year-round   *Minimum Stay: one week*

This spacious two-story, six-bedroom house, accommodating ten in style, makes a splendid Highland vacation residence for large parties. Once a popular hunting lodge, the house features huge rooms offering plenty of space for entertaining or playing, while its fireplaces provide opportunities for cozy, intimate evenings as well. Many of the region's top attractions—like Loch Ness to the north or Balmoral to the east—are a leisurely drive away. Guests can enjoy free trout- and salmon-fishing privileges. Contact: Castles, Cottages & Flats, Box 261, Westwood, MA 02090. Call 617-329-4680.

Children: **Y** Smoking: **Y** Pets: **N** Handicap Access: **N** Payment: **P**

Rumbling Bridge

PAVILION COTTAGE *Rates: moderate*
Open: year-round *Minimum Stay: one week*

Designed as a teahouse, this fascinating cottage offers very comfortable accommodations for four. Furnished mainly in pine and set in an attractive garden, the cottage includes a living/dining room with an open fireplace and doors leading out to the garden. The kitchen features a spiral staircase leading up to the sitting room, which was originally the tearoom. One twin bedroom and one double occupy the ground floor. The surrounding area offers golf, fishing and riding as well as touring. Contact: British Travel Associates, P.O. Box 299, Elkton, VA 22827. Call 1-800-327-6097 (in Virginia, 703-298-2232).

Children: N Pets: N Smoking: N Handicap Access: N Payment: C, P, A, V, M

St. Fillans

DUNDURN *Rates: moderate*
Open: year-round *Minimum Stay: one week*

This 14th-century house, furnished with antiques, sits on four acres of garden and woodland on the banks of the Earn River. Accommodations for six include a sitting room with an open fireplace, a study, dining room and a fully equipped kitchen. There's one twin bedroom and a bath on the second floor and two twin bedrooms with washbasins on the third. Each morning housekeeping service is provided, and you can make arrangements to use the property's Landrover if you like. Outdoors, stroll the landscaped river walk and go fishing, or observe the red deer that inhabit the surrounding forest. Golf and water sports are within easy reach. Contact: British Travel Associates, P.O. Box 299, Elkton, VA 22827. Call 1-800-327-6097 (in Virginia, 703-2982232).

Children: N Pets: N Smoking: Y Handicap Access: N Payment: C, P, A, V, M

Strathcarron

CRAIGELLACHIE *Rates: moderate*
Open: year-round *Minimum Stay: one week*

An expansive two-story house resting on the placid shore of Loch Kishorn, Craigellachie is a luxurious residence for those yearning to explore the windswept mountains, craggy shores, pristine lochs, and castle ruins of the Western Highlands. The unforgettable Isle of Skye, too, is only a short drive away. Craigellachie is located in a charming village that provides shopping and pubs for a day's—and evening's—entertainment. Eight to ten people can sleep comfortably in the four-bedroom house, which also features a striking garden on the loch, complete with a barbecue ready for a relaxing cookout upon your return from Highland adventures. Contact: Castles, Cottages & Flats, Box 261, Westwood, MA 02090. Call 617-329-4680.

Children: Y Pets: N Smoking: Y Handicap Access: N Payment: P

Strontian

ARDERY COTTAGE

Rates: budget

Open: year-round

Minimum Stay: one week

Ardery Cottage sits in a beautifully isolated location on a working croft, overlooking wooded countryside and Loch Sunart. The ground floor features a well-equipped, modern kitchen, a separate dining area, a living room and a room with bunk beds. Upstairs, you'll find a double bedroom, a twin bedroom and the bath. Garden chairs and a barbecue will enhance your enjoyment of the fresh air and rustic surroundings. Visitors reach the cottage via a well-maintained, mile-long forestry track, guaranteeing bucolic privacy. The village of Strontian is five miles away. Contact: Blakes Vacations, 4918 Dempster Street, Skokie, IL 60077. Call 1-800-628-8118.

Children: Y   Pets: N   Smoking: Y   Handicap Access: N   Payment: T, V, M

Tarbert

DOLLS HOUSE, KILLEAN ESTATE

Rates: inexpensive

Open: year-round

Minimum Stay: one week

Outside the windows of Killean Estate's Dolls House, the island of Gigha beckons. And the nearby town of Tayinloan helps guests answer the call, with regular ferry service. After memorable hikes and explorations on the island, side trips to the charming fishing villages of Campbeltown and Tarbert offer more urban pleasures. Dolls House is a picturebook two-story, two-bedroom residence with accommodations for four, seconds from the estate's private beach. Contact: Castles, Cottages & Flats, Box 261, Westwood, MA 02090. Call 617-329-4680.

Children: Y   Pets: N   Smoking: Y   Handicap Access: N   Payment: P

Tarbert

KILLEAN LODGE

Rates: inexpensive

Open: year-round

Minimum Stay: one week

A handsome two-story, three-bedroom cottage overlooking the sea, Killean Lodge is the gatehouse to the towering 16th-century Killean Mansion. Sylvan trails both on and off the grounds lead to a wondrous variety of gentle wildlife, including deer and golden eagles, while walks along the shore will often bring guests in contact with a native seal or two. Local hikes offer riches of historical interest, such as abandoned fortresses, castle ruins, old churches and ancient battlefields—all accessible by foot. Contact: Castles, Cottages & Flats, Box 261, Westwood, MA 02090. Call 617-329-4680.

Children: Y   Pets: N   Smoking: Y   Handicap Access: N   Payment: P

Tarbert

THE DUNMORE ESTATE

Rates: expensive

Open: year-round

Minimum Stay: one week

The 1,200-acre Dunmore Estate, situated on the north shore of the inlet of West Loch Tarbert, offers an assortment of nine high-quality cottages, ranging from two to five bedrooms and sleeping from five to ten people. Each is equipped with full modern amenities, several have fireplaces and some provide breathtaking views down the loch all the way to the Atlantic. The weather here is so mild that exotic species of subtropical plants abound; the estate grounds have been cited by the Scottish Nature Conservatory Council. Guests can use a wide selection of recreational facilities, including a four-hole golf course and loch and sea fishing with boats and dinghies for hire. A nine-hole course is minutes away and excursions to the easily reached islands of Islay, Gigha and Arran make for excellent day-trip options. Contact: Castles, Cottages & Flats, Box 261, Westwood, MA 02090. Call 617-329-4680.

Children: Y   Smoking: Y   Pets: N   Handicap Access: P   Payment: P

Taynuilt

BONAWE HOUSE/EDWARDIAN APARTMENT   *Rates: moderate*
Open: year-round   *Minimum Stay: one week*

This elegant two-story apartment comprises one wing of an 18th-century Georgian house surrounded by gardens. The enormous oak-paneled drawing room features a magnificent fireplace, period furniture and bay windows overlooking the grounds. A private entrance, a spacious kitchen with modern fittings and two large rooms containing twin beds provide the ultimate in comfort. Great care has been taken to offer the finest accommodation while retaining the historical character of this fine old house. The property overlooks Loch Etive, one of Scotland's longest tidal lochs, and is well situated for sightseeing and outdoor activities. Contact: British Travel Associates, P.O. Box 299, Elkton, VA 22827. Call 1-800-327-6097 (in Virginia, 703-298-2232).

Children: N Pets: N Smoking: Y Handicap Access: N Payment: C, P, A, V, M

Whitebridge

ARDOCHY COTTAGE   *Rates: budget*
Open: year-round   *Minimum Stay: one week*

Set in a rural area east of Loch Ness, this country cottage has room for six. Three bedrooms (two double and one twin), a living/dining room with a fireplace and a well-equipped kitchen offer roomy comfort. The cottage is conveniently located for day trips to the Highland or the Isle of Skye. Fishing and boating are available nearby, and the surrounding countryside is ideal for walking or bird watching. Contact: Blakes Vacations, 4918 Dempster Street, Skokie, IL 60077. Call 1-800-628-8118.

Children: Y   Pets: N   Smoking: Y   Handicap Access: N   Payment: T, V, M

HIGHLANDS

Isle of Eigg

CROWS NEST   *Rates: budget-moderate*
Open: year-round   *Minimum Stay: one week*

Enjoy a holiday on a rustic Scottish island with no cars and countless birds, from eagles to puffins. Reached by ferry, the Isle of Eigg offers complete tranquility. Crows Nest offers simple yet comfortable accommodation for six, including private access to the beach. A living room with an open fireplace, a dining room, a farmhouse kitchen, a bath and one double, one twin and one bunk-style bedroom comprise the cottage, which is set in its own private garden. A walker's paradise, Eigg has wooded lowlands, craggy hilltops and vast stretches of deserted beach. There is also good fishing, canoeing and sailing. Contact: British Travel Associates, P.O. Box 299, Elkton, VA 22827. Call 1-800-327-6097 (in Virginia, 703-298-2232).

Children: Y Pets: N Smoking: Y Handicap Access: N Payment: C, P, A, V, M

LOTHIAN

Beattock

DETACHED COTTAGE   *Rates: budget*
Open: year-round   *Minimum Stay: one week*

This newly renovated cottage for four or five enjoys lovely views from all sides. Situated on a working farm in the midst of pastoral countryside, the unit includes two bedrooms, a living room, a brand-new bath and a dining room. A color TV and washing machine are among the cottage's creature comforts, in addition to a garden with garden furniture. In the region, walkers may explore miles of hilly countryside or tour to Edinburgh, the coast at Ayr, or the historic Borders country by car. Contact: British Travel Associates, P.O. Box 299, Elkton, VA 22827. Call 1-800-327-6097 (in Virginia, 703-298-2232).

Children: Y Pets: N Smoking: Y Handicap Access: N Payment: C, P, A, V, M

Edinburgh

1A SCOTLAND STREET   *Rates: inexpensive-expensive*
Open: year-round   *Minimum Stay: one week*

This elegantly furnished two-floor garden flat is tucked away on a quiet street, yet places you right in Edinburgh's city center. Princes Street, Holyrood Palace and the Royal Mile are all a short walk away. The three-bedroom (one double, one twin, one single) apartment sleeps six and features a sunny patio area; guests also have access to a nearby private garden. Plus, the house's owner plays a mean set of bagpipes, and will never turn down a request for a tune made at a reasonable hour. Contact: Castles, Cottages & Flats, Box 261, Westwood, MA 02090. Call 617-329-4680.

Children: Y   Smoking: Y   Pets: N   Handicap Access: N   Payment: P

Edinburgh

LADY STAIR'S CLOSE   *Rates: budget*
Open: year-round   *Minimum Stay: one week*

Two elegant apartments (a one-bedroom and a studio) occupy the first floor of an historic building in the heart of Edinburgh. Looking out onto the Royal Mile that leads up to the castle, both flats come equipped with telephones, audio/cassettes, microwave ovens, coffee makers, food mixers, hair dryers, electric blankets and electric central heating. Guests can walk to the well-known gardens and shops of

Princes Street as well as to the many monuments, theaters, pubs and restaurants of Scotland's greatest city. Contact: Castles, Cottages & Flats, Box 261, Westwood, MA 02090. Call 617-329-4680.

Children: Y   Pets: N   Smoking: Y   Handicap Access: N   Payment: P

Edinburgh
LINDEN COURT APARTMENTS   *Rates: budget-inexpensive*
Open: year-round   *Minimum Stay: one day*
Scotland's regal capital city surrounds Linden Court, located one mile from the city center. The best of Edinburgh's galleries, shopping and cultural events, as well as its historical sites, are within a leisurely stroll down some of the city's loveliest streets. Units in this charming, ideally situated four-story apartment building range from bedroom/ sitting room suites sleeping two to full four-room flats for seven, all equipped with linen, TV and telephone, and tended by daily maid service. Contact: Linden Court Apartments, Murieston Road, Edinburgh EH11 2JJ. Call 031-337-4040.

Children: Y   Pets: N   Smoking: Y   Handicap Access: Y   Payment: EC

Edinburgh
LINTON COURT APARTMENTS   *Rates: budget-inexpensive*
Open: year-round   *Minimum Stay: one week*
This handsome building contains 45 apartments, each accommodating two to seven people, and every single one of them is a wonderful base for exploring the city. After a hectic day at the castles and museums, you'll be glad to return to this home away from home, where the elevator whisks you to a flat in which everything is provided for your comfort. The convenient facilities include color TVs, washers and dryers, complete kitchens, and frequent maid service. There are even baby-sitters available for looking after the wee bairns while you check out the local pubs. Contact: Mrs. L. J. Marr, Linton Court Apartments, Murieston Rd., Edinburgh, Scotland EH112JJ. Call 44031-337-4040.

Children: Y   Pets: N   Smoking: Y   Handicap Access: N   Payment: EC

Edinburgh
WEST END APARTMENTS   *Rates: budget-inexpensive*
Open: year-round   *Minimum Stay: one week*
Conveniently located near Princes Street, this elegant Victorian edifice contains welcoming accommodations for Edinburgh's guests. The lodgings range from studios to two-bedroom flats; the largest can sleep six people. The tasteful furnishings are comfortable and complete; modern kitchens, color TVs, and laundry facilities are available in each apartment. Baby-sitters are also available. If you've brought a car you'll rejoice at the unrestricted parking; those who are hoofing it will appreciate the frequent bus service near the building. Contact: Mr. Brian Mathieson, 2 Learmonth Terrace, Edinburgh, Scotland, EH4 1PQ. Call 44-031-332-0717.

Children: Y   Pets: N   Smoking: Y   Handicap Access: N   Payment: EC

Pathhead

CRICHTON HOUSE *Rates: budget-moderate*
Open: year-round *Minimum Stay: one week*

This historic 17th-century mansion has been converted into two apartments, one of which is available to guests. Resting amid placid Scottish farmland with sweeping rustic views, the house is only 15 miles away from both Edinburgh and the shore—ideally situated for touring the citadels and abbeys of the southern uplands, including the haunting ruins of Crichton Castle. A spiral staircase leads from the house entrance to the two-bedroom flat, which also features an extra alcove with a double bed to provide accommodations for up to six. The unit comes with a complete kitchen, but overseas guests may arrange evening meal service. Contact: Castles, Cottages & Flats, Box 261, Westwood, MA 02090. Call 617-329-4680.

Children: Y Pets: N Smoking: Y Handicap Access: N Payment: P

STRATHCLYDE

Appin

LAICH COTTAGE *Rates: budget*
Open: year-round *Minimum Stay: one week*

Laich Cottage is nestled on the expansive grounds of Kinlochlaich House, located along the shores of narrow Loch Linnhe, midway between the towns of Oban and Fort William. Both the Highland Mountains and Inner Hebrides-dotted sea are a short journey away; bicycles can be rented for local jaunts. The house is the estate's lone cottage, a comfortable single-story, two-bedroom residence, with an extra bed to accommodate five persons. Contact: Castles, Cottages & Flats, Box 261, Westwood, MA 02090. Call 617-329-4680.

Children: Y Pets: N Smoking: Y Handicap Access: N Payment: P

Appin

LINNHE FLATS *Rates: budget*
Open: year-round *Minimum Stay: one week*

Four cozy, modern one-bedroom flats are available within the walls of stately Kinlochlaich House, a noteworthy 18th-century mansion. Guests can enjoy all the amenities of the estate grounds. One seasonal highlight not to be missed is a course in gardening offered by Kinlochlaich's owner during April and May. A stroll to Appin Village, whose friendly residents make visitors feel right at home, is always amply rewarded—particularly when it includes a visit to the markets and grocery stands to procure fresh-picked local produce. Contact: Castles, Cottages & Flats, Box 261, Westwood, MA 02090. Call 617-329-4680.

Children: Y Pets: N Smoking: Y Handicap Access: N Payment: P

Campbeltown

ANGUS COTTAGE *Rates: budget*
Open: year-round *Minimum Stay: one week*

This cozy two-floor cottage forms the main part of the 17th-century

Old Byre of Kilchrist on the grounds of Kilchrist Castle. Fable has it that Billeonie, the Kilchrist brownie, frequents the wishing well at the Old Byre. Accommodations for six include an open-plan living/dining/kitchen area on the ground floor, with a fully modern bath, a double bedroom and bedroom with twin bunks upstairs. Fresh air, peace and tranquility abound; golf and water sports are nearby. Children are welcome and have plenty of romping room. Contact: Blakes Vacations, 4918 Dempster Street, Skokie, IL 60077. Call 1-800-628-8118.
Children: Y   Pets: N   Smoking: Y   Handicap Access: N   Payment: T, V, M

Campbeltown

TORRISDALE CASTLE   *Rates: inexpensive*
Open: year-round   *Minimum Stay: one week*

This vast estate set in the heart of the hills of Argyll offers inspiring seaward views. Three two-bedroom apartments on the grand castle's ground floor have full modern amenities; four very private, gracefully furnished one- and two-story cottages (one with a darling bedroom loft), range from two to four bedrooms; the one-bedroom South Lodge is a cozy hideaway. Guests can fish for free on the River Carradale or enjoy other highlights of the grounds, which include wooded paths for bird and deer watching and the estate's own little sandy bay, where fishing off a mackerel boat is available. Only three miles away is the town of Carradale, a quaint fishing village that has exceptional facilities for golf, riding, wind surfing and squash. Contact: Castles, Cottages & Flats, Box 261, Westwood, MA 02090. Call 617-329-4680.
Children: Y   Smoking: Y   Pets: N   Handicap Access: N   Payment: P

Isle of Bute

SHALUNT FARM FLAT   *Rates: budget*
Open: year-round   *Minimum Stay: one week*

This attractive self-contained flat forms part of a working farmhouse on the scenic Isle of Bute. Located on the ground floor, it features two twin bedrooms, a full-size kitchen/dining area and a living room with a fold-out couch, allowing for a total of six lodgers. Shalunt Farm itself overlooks the waters of the Isle of Bute and lies within easy reach of unspoiled beaches. Cycling and boating are available on the property; fishing, golfing and pony trekking can all be enjoyed on the isle. A spacious indoor gaming area next door to the flat provides further amusement for farm guests. Contact: Blakes Vacations, 4918 Dempster Street, Skokie, IL 60077. Call 1-800-628-8118.
Children: Y   Pets: N   Smoking: Y   Handicap Access: N   Payment: T, V, M

Kilkenzie, Campbeltown

TANGY LODGE   *Rates: budget*
Open: year-round   *Minimum Stay: one week*

A magnificent Atlantic panorama is yours from this ideal family house for seven. Perched above the seashore near a sandy beach, Tangy Lodge comes fully equipped. From the spacious living room with fireplace, look out sliding-glass doors to the sea. Two twin bedrooms and one double with a single make up the sleeping accommodations. A full kitchen and separate dining area complete the layout. The entire cottage has been recently refurbished and expanded. Boat trips, golf, and loch and sea fishing are among the attractions to the surrounding area. Contact: Blakes Vacations, 4918 Dempster Street, Skokie, IL 60077. Call 1-800-628-8118.

Children: Y Pets: N Smoking: Y Handicap Access: N Payment: T, V, M

Kimmelford, by Oban

SPIRRUCH COTTAGE   *Rates: budget*
Open: year-round   *Minimum Stay: one week*

This traditional shepherd's cottage sits on a hill overlooking Loch Melfort. A warm and comfortable place, it has been expanded to provide lodging for four in peace and privacy. The kitchen/dining room has full modern facilities, while the sitting room has a wood-burning stove. There's one double bedroom and one small room with full-sized bunks. Nearby, the bustling port of Oban makes a delightful destination. The cottage is centrally located for exploring County Argyll and the Western Isles. Fishing, riding and water sports are readily available. Contact: British Travel Associates, P.O. Box 299, Elkton, VA 22827. Call 1-800-327-6097 (in Virginia, 703-298-2232).

Children: Y Pets: N Smoking: Y Handicap Access: Y Payment: C, P, A, V, M

Loch Awe, by Taynuilt

LARACH BHAN   *Rates: budget-expensive*
Open: year-round   *Minimum Stay: one week*

This splendid country house, set on a 30-acre private estate, commands glorious views of picturesque Loch Awe. Originally dating from the 14th-century, the now largely Victorian house has been restored to provide elegant lodging for seven. A spacious drawing room with a large fireplace and a baby grand piano overlooks the loch. Featuring a tower alcove and picture windows with loch views, the huge kitchen incorporates a dining area. A single bedroom with a bath completes the ground floor. Above, a master bedroom suite with tower alcove and two twin bedrooms provide comfortable sleeping accommodations. The extensive wooded grounds include a sunken garden, bountiful plant and wildlife, and a private beach with boat-launching facilities. The house is well situated for touring and other activities as well. Contact: British Travel Associates, P.O. Box 299, Elkton, VA 22827. Call 1-800-327-6097 (in Virginia, 703-298-2232).

Children: Y Pets: N Smoking: Y Handicap Access: Y Payment: C, P, A, V, M

Lochgilphead

ISLAY COTTAGE   *Rates: budget*
Open: year-round   *Minimum Stay: one week*

Situated close to the water at Craobh Haven, this cottage for four, though modern, is steeped in traditional character. The ground-floor sitting room overlooks the sea and features a cozy open fireplace; adjoining it is a modern eat-in kitchen. Up a winding, exposed staircase lie the two bedrooms, one double and one twin. Furnished to award-winning standards, Islay offers an unspoiled view of the Western Isles and beautiful sunsets. A superb marina just outside your door provides the best in boating facilities. Babysitting service is available. Contact: Blakes Vacations, 4918 Dempster Street, Skokie, IL 60077. Call 1-800-628-8118.

Children: Y   Pets: N   Smoking: Y   Handicap Access: N   Payment: T, V, M

Oban

THE STABLES AT ARDMADDY CASTLE   *Rates: budget-moderate*
Open: year-round   *Minimum Stay: one week*

The former stables to Ardmaddy Castle have been sensitively converted to a cottage for seven. Overlooking Ardmaddy Bay, the cottage sits in a private and quiet location. The spacious open-plan living area is fitted and furnished extensively in pine. A modern, comprehensively equipped kitchen adjoins a dining area, while the sitting room features an open fireplace and views to the sea. The four bedrooms are furnished in pine also: one double, two twins and one with full-sized bunks. Above, the former granary has been converted into a game room. The 3,000-acre estate offers a wealth of attractions, among them sailing, hiking and tennis. Contact: British Travel Associates, P.O. Box 299, Elkton, VA 22827. Call 1-800-327-6097 (in Virginia, 703-298-2232).

Children: Y Pets: N Smoking: Y Handicap Access: N Payment: C, P, A, V, M

Taynuilt

DUNARD COTTAGE   *Rates: budget*
Open: year-round   *Minimum Stay: one week*

A traditional Highland home for two, Dunard is situated in the picturesque village of Taynuilt near the shores of Loch Etive. Roomy, with a kitchen/dining area, a sitting room with a fireplace and a double bedroom, the cottage also has a pleasant little garden outside. Whether you prefer peaceful walks in the village, tours of the magnificent mountains of Glencoe or a cruise from Oban to the Western Isles, this cottage makes an excellent base. Contact: Blakes Vacations, 4918 Dempster Street, Skokie, IL 60077. Call 1-800-628-8118.

Children: Y   Pets: N   Smoking: Y   Handicap Access: N   Payment: T, V, M

TAYSIDE

Aberfeldy

CUILALUINN   *Rates: budget-expensive*
Open: year-round   *Minimum Stay: one week*

A magnificent house in a wooded setting, Cuilaluinn provides spacious accommodation for nine. Both house and garden enjoy views of the River Tay. A spacious living room with open fire has a bay window overlooking the garden, and the luxury kitchen leads to a breakfast room with a wood-burning stove. One twin bedroom is on the ground floor; three double bedrooms and one single are upstairs, featuring fireplaces, period furniture and lovely views. Guests can explore the delightful town of Aberfeldy and take part in water sports and golf. The spectacular highland scenery makes for wonderful touring. Contact: British Travel Associates, P.O. Box 299, Elkton, VA 22827. Call 1-800-327-6097 (in Virginia, 703-298-2232).

Children: Y Pets: N Smoking: Y Handicap Access: Y Payment: C, P, A, V, M

Abernethy

GLENFOOT *Rates: budget*
Open: year-round *Minimum Stay: one week*

This converted old stone cottage for four has panoramic views over the Tay River to the hills beyond Perth. In addition to the two bedrooms—one double, one twin—you'll find a living room, a kitchen, a bathroom with shower and a washing machine. Stroll the quiet country lane, walk the hills outside your front door or explore the area's many historic monuments and resort towns. Nearby, you can enjoy boating, canoeing and fishing on the river, or you can stay home instead and barbecue on your patio. Contact: British Travel Associates, P.O. Box 299, Elkton, VA 22827. Call 1-800-327-6097 (in Virginia, 703-298-2232).

Children: Y Pets: N Smoking: Y Handicap Access: N Payment: C, P, A, V, M

Arbroath

KELLY CASTLE *Rates: inexpensive*
Open: year-round *Minimum Stay: one week*

This private, utterly modern apartment in a 14th-century castle allows you to indulge in a flamboyant medieval fantasy without sacrificing up-to-date conveniences. Through the imperial courtyard entrance, climb the grand main staircase to reach your quarters, a two-level, sumptuously furnished unit on the third and fourth floors. An oak-paneled living room, dining room and two bedrooms (with a third available to provide accommodations for up to six) await. Guests can enjoy the picturesque castle grounds—sorry, no moat, but there is a lovely garden with barbecue—and all the pleasures of the surrounding Angus region. Contact: Blakes Vacations, 4918 Dempster Street, Skokie, IL 60077. Call 1-800-628-8118.

Children: N Pets: N Smoking: Y Handicap Access: N Payment: T, V, M

Blairgowrie

BLAIRGOWRIE HOUSE *Rates: budget-inexpensive*
Open: year-round *Minimum Stay: one week*

One wing of an Edwardian country house can be your Scottish vacation home, where you can relax on the banks of the Ericht River in a peaceful woodland setting. First-class ground-floor accommodations feature a large living room with a gas fire, large eat-in kitchen, two double bedrooms and one double bed-settee. Guests can fish on the grounds or play golf on the excellent course at the nearby Rosemount Club. If you feel like walking, you're in the ideal setting, or you can amuse yourself at the town's numerous recreational facilities. Get a taste of local life at the pub only 100 yards away. Contact: British Travel Associates, P.O. Box 299, Elkton, VA 22827. Call 1-800-327-6097 (in Virginia, 703-298-2232).

Children: Y Pets: N Smoking: Y Handicap Access: N Payment: C, P, A, V, M

Brechin

COACHMAN'S COTTAGE   *Rates: budget*
Open: year-round   *Minimum Stay: one week*

As its name suggests, the Coachman's Cottage was once servants' quarters for Balhall Lodge. Now it has been meticulously renovated and handsomely furnished with comfort in mind. The two-story cottage contains three bedrooms, to sleep five comfortably, and includes a well-equipped kitchen. The lodge grounds feature a private garden, a game room and a small riding school. Glenshee, Stonehaven, the Angus Glens, a host of golf courses and medieval castles and the splendid beaches at Montrose are all only a short trip away. Contact: Blakes Vacations, 4918 Dempster Street, Skokie, IL 60077. Call 1-800-628-8118.

Children: Y Pets: N Smoking: Y Handicap Access: N Payment: T, V, M

Carnoustie

THE WING, PANBRIDE HOUSE   *Rates: budget*
Open: year-round   *Minimum Stay: one week*

This self-contained, fully equipped and tastefully decorated studio apartment for two, with separate kitchen and private entrance, is available in the wing of Panbride House. The first tee of Carnoustie Golf Course is minutes away, not to mention the beach and other glories of the region. Guests are also free to enjoy the grounds of this country manor estate. Note: The Stables Cottage is not far from The Wing, and both units can be rented together at a 10 percent reduced price. Contact: Blakes Vacations, 4918 Dempster Street, Skokie, IL 60077. Call 1-800-628-8118.

Children: N Pets: N Smoking: Y Handicap Access: N Payment: T, V, M

Gleneagles

CALLIUVAR COTTAGE   *Rates: budget*
Open: year-round   *Minimum Stay: one week*

Set in a well-groomed garden, Calliuvar has a magnificent view toward Crieff and the mountains beyond. This cottage for four lies just a five-minute walk from Auchterarder Golf Course; Gleneagles Hotel and the Mark Philips Riding School are also nearby. Tastefully furnished, the lodgings include a kitchen with dishwasher and microwave, a living room with a dining area and a gas fire, one double bedroom and one twin. A color TV with VCR, a washer/drier, garden furniture and a barbecue add to this rental's comfort. Contact: Blakes Vacations, 4918 Dempster Street, Skokie, IL 60077. Call 1-800-628-8118.

Children: Y Pets: N Smoking: Y Handicap Access: N Payment: T, V, M

Glenshee, by Blairgowrie

DALNAGAR CASTLE AND COTTAGES   *Rates: luxury*
Open: year-round   *Minimum Stay: one week*

The east wing of this august Victorian mansion provides truly palatial accommodations for a group of up to forty. The house features such dramatic architectural highlights as circular stair turrets, crow-stepped gables, and battlement towers, and the wing itself includes twelve bedrooms, five baths, a music room, a drawing room, a dining room and a conservatory, with all modern conveniences, including central heating and air conditioning, plus maid service. When not strolling the estate grounds or enjoying the area's recreational opportunities, guests can pay a visit to nearby Birnam Wood, the legendary forest of Shakespeare's "Macbeth." Contact: Castles, Cottages & Flats, Box 261, Westwood, MA 02090. Call 617-329-4680.

Children: Y   Pets: N   Smoking: Y   Handicap Access: N   Payment: P

Glenshee, by Blairgowrie

KEEPER'S COTTAGE   *Rates: inexpensive*
Open: year-round   *Minimum Stay: one week*

This comfortable four-bedroom house is located on the stately grounds of Dalnagar Castle in the heart of pastoral Glenshee. Sleeping seven, equipped with modern amenities and tended by maid service, the cottage offers guests a restful residence from which to enjoy the area's rich scenic pleasures and sporting facilities; superb skiing and golf and some of Scotland's finest river and lake fishing are all nearby. Contact: Castles, Cottages, & Flats, Box 261, Westwood, MA 02090. Call 617-329-4680.

Children: Y   Pets: N   Smoking: Y   Handicap Access: N   Payment: P

Perth

ST. MADOES   *Rates: budget-moderate*
Open: year-round   *Minimum Stay: one week*

A magnificent flat on the first floor of a 16th-century castle offers the opportunity to sample the grandeur of a bygone age amidst some of Perthshire's finest scenery. Many of the original features, such as intricate plaster ceilings, arched windows and massive wooden doors, are still intact. The library, circular music room with grand piano, dining room, kitchen, master bedroom and loft living room all have views of the countryside. An open fireplace warms the music room, while the dining table converts into a billiard table. No expense has been spared in furnishing this flat with period pieces as well as modern conveniences, such as a stereo, a dishwasher and a color TV. Convenient to numerous golf courses and fishing on nearby River Tay, the flat sleeps six to eight. Contact: British Travel Associates, P.O. Box 299, Elkton, VA 22827. Call 1-800-327-6097 (in Virginia, 703-298-2232).

Children: Y Pets: N Smoking: N Handicap Access: N Payment: C, P, A, V, M

Pitlochry

TUMMEL BRIDGE COTTAGE *Rates: budget-inexpensive*
Open: year-round *Minimum Stay: one week*

Set just yards from the loch in a 17th-century farm courtyard, this cottage for four to six has plenty of character. An eat-in kitchen, bath and bedroom occupy the lower level; a central spiral staircase leads to a spacious gallery (with folding bed) and double bedroom above. Newly renovated and tastefully decorated, the cottage also features a living room with an open fireplace. The beautiful surroundings will delight hikers and bird watchers, and there's salmon fishing on the loch. Golfers can try the nearby courses, or make the hour's drive to the famous Gleneagles course. Pitlochry, meanwhile, offers an abundance of shops and the Festival Theatre. Contact: British Travel Associates, P.O. Box 299, Elkton, VA 22827. Call 1-800-327-6097 (in Virginia, 703-298-2232).

Children: Y Pets: N Smoking: Y Handicap Access: N Payment: C, P, A, V, M

Spittal of Glenshee

GATE LODGE SOUTH *Rates: budget*
Open: year-round *Minimum Stay: one week*

Forming a part of the main gate lodge at the private Dalmunzie sporting estate, this compact apartment sleeps four. The combination living room/dining area fits into the gatekeeper's corner turret, while the twin and double bedrooms comprise the rest of the apartment. On the 6,000-acre estate, guests can enjoy golf, tennis, trout fishing and pony trekking. In the winter, nearby Glenshee offers skiing. The Dalmunzie House Hotel, also on the grounds, features food and drink in elegant surroundings, should you decide to treat yourself to a night out. Contact: Blakes Vacations, 4918 Dempster Street, Skokie, IL 60077. Call 1-800-628-8118.

Children: Y Pets: N Smoking: Y Handicap Access: N Payment: T, V, M

WESTERN ISLES

Isle of Berneray

WESTER RHUMHOR *Rates: budget*
Open: year-round *Minimum Stay: one week*

The Isle of Berneray has few roadways, almost no cars and no bustling cities. But it has incomparable white sandy beaches, beautiful serene countryside and a friendly bilingual Gaelic/English community that has changed remarkably little over the last hundred or so years. This spacious and completely modern two-story, five-bedroom house accommodates six. With wall-to-wall carpeting, fully equipped kitchen and a cozy fireplace in the living room, it is a superb spot for those who seek a secluded vacation to be enjoyed in total comfort. Contact: Blakes Vacations, 4918 Dempster Street, Skokie, IL 60077. Call 1-800-628-8118.

Children: Y Pets: N Smoking: Y Handicap Access: N Payment: T, V, M

Spain

Andalusia

El Pinar

VILLA LAS CAPUCHINAS   *Rates: expensive-deluxe*
Open: year-round   *Minimum Stay: one week*

Villa Las Capuchinas is nearly hidden from view amid a lush tropical garden filled with large swaying palms and other greenery native to this hot southern climate. Trees help shade the interior from a sometimes searing sun; first-floor air conditioning makes sure the house stays cool. Stylishly furnished, six bedrooms provide plenty of space for two children. The large dining table seats eight and opens onto the terrace for long, leisurely meals. A swimming pool, game room and laundry room add to your comfort; maid service is provided. Contact: Villas International, 71 West 23rd Street, New York, NY 10010. Call 1-800-221-2260 (in New York, 212-929-7585).

Children: Y   Pets: N   Smoking: Y   Handicap Access: N   Payment: C, P, T

Estepona

CALLE MARGARITA

Open: year-round

Rates: moderate-deluxe

Minimum Stay: one week

A walled garden and plenty of shrubbery ensure your privacy in this tasteful villa and a built-in barbecue and swimming pool complete a fine setting for outdoor entertaining. Bring the party inside and you'll find a spacious lounge/dining area, which opens via patio doors to a terrace and garden. Three double bedrooms (one with a bathroom) provide accommodations for six people. A large, fitted kitchen makes for convenient meal preparation and maid service is provided. Children over 12 years old are welcome. Contact: Villas International, 71 West 23rd Street, New York, NY 10010. Call 1-800-221-2260 (in New York, 212-929-7585).

Children: Y   Pets: N   Smoking: Y   Handicap Access: N   Payment: C, P, T

Marbella

SEASIDE FLOWERS

Open: year-round

Rates: deluxe

Minimum Stay: two weeks

Surrounded by flowering gardens, these lovely terrace houses stand near the sea and the town. As they are individually owned and furnished, each has its own character and style. All feature marble floors and fireplaces in the spacious living and dining rooms. The modern kitchens are well equipped with dishwashers and washing machines, and four bedrooms and three full baths round out the accommodations. There is a large pool and patio for the shared use of the guests, and each house has its own sunny rooftop terrace with a barbecue. To make your jaunts through the countryside more convenient, the use of a car is included in the rental; maid and laundry service is available for those seeking a truly carefree holiday. Contact: At Home Abroad Inc., 405 E. 56th St., 6H, New York, NY 10022. Call 212-421-9165. Ref. 9666.

Children: Y   Pets: N   Smoking: Y   Handicap Access: N   Payment: C, P, T

Mijas

SHANGRI-LA

Open: year-round

Rates: deluxe

Minimum Stay: one week

Secluded in the hills above the Costa del Sol, this large rambling villa offers magnificent views of the surrounding countryside. Simple yet highly stylized Scandanavian furniture creates a light, airy feel throughout. The open plan living/dining room leads outside to the shaded outdoor dining area, barbecue and very large, pretty swimming pool. Maid service three times a week and a spacious modern kitchen add to your comfort. Four carpeted bedrooms easily accommodate up to eight guests and a small indoor sun room makes for relaxing days. Contact: Villas International, 71 West 23rd Street, New York, NY 10010. Call 1-800-221-2260 (in New York, 212-929-7585).

Children: Y   Pets: N   Smoking: Y   Handicap Access: N   Payment: C, P, T

Nerja

CASA SANDRA   *Rates: inexpensive-moderate*
Open: April 7-November 20   *Minimum Stay: one week*
Several decorative railed walkways thread through the grounds of Casa Sandra, a lovely villa on a private road at the entrance of the resort at Nerja. Divided into a main house for six and a small separate annex for two, the villa sports comfortable furnishings and modern kitchens. A garden and large terraces allow for outdoor lounging, and the villa's elevated position affords good views. Stroll through the old village center for a taste of a simpler life, or explore the famous limestone caves. Sample the fresh fruits, vegetables and fruits of the sea on Tuesday, the town's market day. Contact: Interhome Inc., 124 Little Falls Road, Fairfield, NJ 07004. Call 201-882-6864.
Children: Y   Pets: N   Smoking: Y   Handicap Access: N   Payment: P, V, M

Puerto Banus

JARDINES RESIDENCE   *Rates: moderate-deluxe*
Open: year-round   *Minimum Stay: one week*
Lush tropical gardens dotted with graceful palm trees and beautiful fountains surround the modern low-rise apartments at Jardines Residence. Expansive windows throughout create a cool and airy ambience, so relaxing in the warm Spanish climate. Studio apartments and one-, two- and three-bedroom units are all air conditioned and stylishly furnished with modern kitchens. Enjoy exercising in the complex's gymnasium, tennis and squash courts and then relax in the swimming pool, jacuzzi or sauna. Contact: Villas International, 71 West 23rd Street, New York, NY 10010. Call 1-800-221-2260 (in New York, 212-929-7585).
Children: Y   Pets: N   Smoking: Y   Handicap Access: N   Payment: C, P, T

San Pedro de Alcantara

CASA DE LOS ABETOS   *Rates: moderate-deluxe*
Open: year-round   *Minimum Stay: one week*
The terrace views from Casa de los Abetos are stunning, with the village of San Pedro stretched out below. Hedges along the split-level garden ensure privacy, while a kidney-shaped pool provides recreation and refreshment. A fireplace inside the lounge/dining room keeps the atmosphere cosy at night. Three upstairs bedrooms sleep six and the kitchen, separate laundry and maid service provide for all your needs. Contact: Villas International, 71 West 23rd Street, New York, NY 10010. Call 1-800-221-2260 (in New York, 212-929-7585).
Children: Y   Pets: N   Smoking: Y   Handicap Access: N   Payment: C, P, T

Santa Rosa

CASA CASTANA   *Rates: deluxe*
Open: year-round   *Minimum Stay: one week*
Casa Castana is nestled on a tree-covered hillside below the village of Mijas and offers outstanding views of the surrounding countryside and

sea. Graceful curved archways punctuate a long tile-roofed terrace running along the top floor of the villa. Sunbathe on one of the uncovered terraces or lounge around the long, narrow pool, refreshing for adults but unsafe for children because it has no shallow end. The kitchen's older style is quaintly reminiscent of an earlier age, yet is still fully functional. Three twin bedrooms provide nicely for six guests and a maid makes cleaning unnecessary. Contact: Villas International, 71 West 23rd Street, New York, NY 10010. Call 1-800-221-2260 (in New York, 212-929-7585).

Children: **Y** Pets: **N** Smoking: **Y** Handicap Access: **N** Payment: **C, P, T**

Seville

SANTA CRUZ RESIDENCE   *Rates: inexpensive-moderate*
Open: year-round   *Minimum Stay: one week*

These traditional Spanish apartments with wrought-iron terraces overlook a cobblestone street in the heart of the old quarter, a place alive with the strains of the flamenco and the delightful fragrance of Andalusian cuisine. One- and two-bedroom apartments sleep four to six in comfort and style, with air conditioning providing welcome cool in this steamy city. The apartments' central location provides a good base for historical sightseeing, such as a trip to the world's largest Gothic church, final resting place of Christopher Columbus. Also worth exploring is The Alcazar, the ruins of a Moorish palace. Contact: Villas International, 71 West 23rd Street, New York, NY 10010. Call 1-800-221-2260 (in New York, 212-929-7585).

Children: **Y** Pets: **N** Smoking: **Y** Handicap Access: **N** Payment: **C, P, T**

CATALONIA

Ametlla de Mar

EL CARRETE   *Rates: budget-moderate*
Open: year-round   *Minimum Stay: one week*

Ametlla de Mar is a charming little village on the Costa Dorada, blessed with winding streets and a bustling fishing harbor. There is plenty to amuse visitors here: Once you've explored the town and the wooded hillsides beyond, there's wind surfing, sailing, and fishing as well as the inevitable bronzing and bathing. Sunny El Carrete sits in a quiet spot near the woods and enjoys pleasant views of both the mountains and the sea. The delightfully large garden features an outdoor shower, and there is a pleasant terrace as well. El Carrete has three bedrooms and accommodates up to eight guests. The fireplace in the living room makes this house cheerful and inviting; the washing machine and oven make it convenient. Contact: Rent a Home International, 7200 34th Ave. N.W., Seattle, WA 98117. Call 206-545-6963. Ref. E9587/500.

Children: **Y** Pets: **Y** Smoking: **N** Handicap Access: **N** Payment: **C, P, V, M**

Ampuriabrava

BAHIA TERRACE HOUSE   *Rates: budget-inexpensive*
Open: year-round   *Minimum Stay: one week*

The pretty town of Ampuriabrava enjoys a splendid setting on the coast, with one of the loveliest beaches on the Costa Brava. The sparkling sea-water canals that wind through the town add to its unique charm. This attractive terrace house for four is located in a quiet cul-de-sac only a few feet from the beach. The accommodations include an open kitchen with an oven, a large living and dining room and two bedrooms. There is a pretty garden where you can sit and pass the time of day, or try the view from the terrace. Contact: Interhome Inc., 124 Little Falls Rd., Fairfield, NJ 07004. Call 201-882-6864. Ref. E9420/35.

Children: Y   Pets: Y   Smoking: Y   Handicap Access: N   Payment: P, V, M

Ampuriabrava

EBRE HOUSE   *Rates: expensive-deluxe*
Open: year-round   *Minimum Stay: one week*

You'll find this lovely house in a quiet, sunny spot near the canal. It's a wonderful abode for those who enjoy relaxing in privacy at home as well as joining the convivial throngs of the town and beach. A handsome fireplace serves as the focal point of the living and dining room; the kitchen includes modern amenities such as an oven, a dishwasher and a washing machine. There is also a large bedroom with bunk beds on this floor, which opens to the terrace. Upstairs is a twin bedroom with its own fireplace; the house can accommodate up to 10. Graceful archways lead to the terrace, which features a barbecue and a lusciously inviting pool. A motor boat is also available for hire. Contact: Interhome Inc., 124 Little Falls Rd., Fairfield, NJ 07004. Call 201-882-6864. Ref. E9421/265.

Children: Y   Pets: N   Smoking: Y   Handicap Access: N   Payment: P, V, M

Barcelona

CENTRAL APARTMENTS   *Rates: inexpensive*
Open: year-round   *Minimum Stay: one week*

This studio for two boasts an excellent location for touring Barcelona's Gothic Square, its numerous art museums, and the many bohemian cafes and night spots. After a long day or night of sightseeing, relax by the pool or enjoy a light meal from the snack bar while sunning in the solarium. The self-contained apartment features a dining and living area with a double bed, and a full bath and kitchen. Maid service and daily change of linens are included. Contact: Overseas Connections, 70 West 71st Street, #1C, New York, NY 10023. Call 212-769-1170.

Children: Y   Pets: N   Smoking: Y   Handicap Access: N   Payment: C, P

Barcelona

HERREROS RESIDENCE   *Rates: budget-inexpensive*
Open: year-round   *Minimum Stay: one week*

Herreros Residence is tucked into a quiet neighborhood close to Barcelona's thriving central business district. These small but well de-signed apartments for two to four people are equipped with modern kitchens, color TVs and air conditioning for comfort. Among the hotel services is a 24-hour concierge desk to attend to all your needs. Sample the fresh fruits, vegetables, rich olive oil and hearty local wines at Barcelona's bustling street markets. Contact: Villas International, 71 West 23rd Street, New York, NY 10010. Call 1-800-221-2260 (in New York, 212-929-7585).

Children: Y   Pets: N   Smoking: Y   Handicap Access: N   Payment: C, P, T

Barcelona
PENTHOUSE APARTMENT   *Rates: budget*
Open: year-round   *Minimum Stay: one week*

Beauteous Barcelona, capital of ancient Catalonia, lures visitors from around the world with its rich history, venerable cathedrals and pal-aces, monumental artistic achievements and energetic cultural life. This sunny apartment is located right in the center of town but away from the street noise, a perfect base for exploring the city. The com-fortably furnished accommodations include a living room, a full kitchen and two bedrooms (sleeping up to four guests). There is also a small balcony, where you can gaze at the city and plan your next exciting day. Contact: Interhome Inc., 124 Little Falls Rd., Fairfield, NJ 07004. Call 201-882-6864. Ref. E9510/105G.

Children: Y   Pets: N   Smoking: Y   Handicap Access: N   Payment: P, V, M

Begur
POLADO TIPICO LA BORNA III   *Rates: budget-moderate*
Open: year-round   *Minimum Stay: one week*

The quaint village of Begur clusters around a tall hill that is crowned by a 17th-century castle. Not only sightseers make this place part of their itinerary, though: the cloudless beaches and warm, clear waters are among the best on the Costa Brava. The Poblado Tipico is a group of terrace houses set on a sunny hillside and surrounded by cool wood-lands. The two- and three-bedroom houses can accommodate up to six people; all boast open fireplaces and include ovens in the kitchens. The complex includes a swimming pool and a convenient grocery store, and there are beautiful views toward the sea. Contact: Inter-home Inc., 124 Little Falls Rd., Fairfield, NJ 07004. Call 201-882-6864. Ref. E9440/80, /91, /101B.

Children: Y   Pets: Y   Smoking: Y   Handicap Access: N   Payment: P, V, M

Calonge
LARGE MAS CABANYES HOUSE   *Rates: moderate-deluxe*
Open: year-round   *Minimum Stay: one week*

Larger parties dedicated to enjoying the Spanish sun together will appreciate the pleasant accommodations offered by this lovely house for 12. Sitting on a quiet hillside outside of town, the house commands wonderful views of the sea and surrounding countryside. When you're not at the nearby beach or sampling the social life of Calonge, you can take a dip in the pool, wander through the fragrant garden, or brush up on your bocce skills. The simply furnished interior includes a comfy living and dining room, a kitchen and four bedrooms on the first floor; these rooms open onto a pretty terrace. Downstairs you'll find two more bedrooms—one with a cozy open fireplace—and access to another terrace. Contact: Interhome Inc., 124 Little Falls Rd., Fairfield, NJ 07004. Call 201-882-6864. Ref. E9456/654.

Children: Y   Pets: Y   Smoking: Y   Handicap Access: N   Payment: P, V, M

Calonge

VAL REPOS   *Rates: budget-moderate*
Open: year-round   *Minimum Stay: one week*

Tucked away in a quiet corner near the woods, this stately Spanish villa enjoys panoramic views of the rugged mountains that surround it. The charming uncultivated garden, small patio and furnished terrace make this a wonderful place to bask in the sun in solitude. There's also a barbecue outside. When you've had your fill of the quiet countryside, the nearby tennis courts and swimming pool can offer a healthy dose of conviviality. Inside the house you'll find a large living and dining room with a fireplace and a modern kitchen complete with an oven and a washing machine. There are two twin bedrooms and one double bedroom on the first floor and the twin bedroom upstairs boasts its own bathroom. Contact: Interhome Inc., 124 Little Falls Rd., Fairfield, NJ 07004. Call 201-882-6864. Ref. E9456/801.

Children: Y   Pets: Y   Smoking: Y   Handicap Access: N   Payment: P, V, M

Calonge

VIZCONDADO DE CABANYES APARTMENT   *Rates: budget*
Open: year-round   *Minimum Stay: one week*

This apartment for three is part of a handsome two-family house sitting on a sunny slope outside of town. Its splendid location allows panoramic views of the rolling hillside. The first-floor apartment includes a nice living and dining area with a divan bed, a convenient little kitchenette and a twin bedroom. The apartment has its own large terrace and the house features a private swimming pool in the garden for when the crowds at the beach get to be too much. Those who hunger for sand and saltwater won't be disappointed, though—there's a pleasant sandy beach scarcely a couple of miles away. Contact: Interhome Inc., 124 Little Falls Rd., Fairfield, NJ 07004. Call 201-882-6864. Ref. E9456/622A.

Children: Y   Pets: Y   Smoking: Y   Handicap Access: N   Payment: P, V, M

Cambrils

CASA NURY   *Rates: budget-moderate*
Open: year-round   *Minimum Stay: one week*

The interesting details are what make Casa Nury special. Spiraled columns support the tile roof over the shaded terrace; an outside shower conveniently lets you rinse off after a dip in the pool or cool off after basking in the sun. The rooms inside are simply but comfortably furnished. Two cozy bedrooms and a divan bed in the living room sleep up to five guests. The renowned restaurants and plentiful boutiques of Cambrils are a pleasant stroll away and the sandy beach is just down the road. In addition to water sports and sun worshiping, horseback riding and tennis can be enjoyed in the area. Contact: Interhome Inc., 124 Little Falls Rd., Fairfield, NJ 07004. Call 201-882-6864. Ref. E9582/115.

Children: Y   Pets: Y   Smoking: Y   Handicap Access: N   Payment: P, V, M

Cambrils

FILADELFIA   *Rates: budget-inexpensive*
Open: year-round   *Minimum Stay: one week*

This cheery apartment house is the perfect base for connoisseurs of the sun and surf. Located in a sun-drenched spot right at the water's edge, the building boasts panoramic views of the sea. Guests enjoy use of the swimming pool and tennis court, and there is a friendly restaurant just a few feet away. The apartment for five people is furnished with tasteful modern pieces and is located on the fourth floor. The airy rooms include a combined living and dining area, an open kitchen complete with an oven and two bedrooms. A splendid balcony with garden furniture provides a place to relax outside in privacy after a day at the beach. Contact: Interhome Inc., 124 Little Falls Rd., Fairfield, NJ 07004. Call 201-882-6864. Ref. E9582/175D.

Children: Y   Pets: Y   Smoking: Y   Handicap Access: N   Payment: P, V, M

Cubelles

CASA VINADOR   *Rates: budget-inexpensive*
Open: year-round   *Minimum Stay: one week*

This fine old house occupies a sunny spot in the center of Cubellas, a quiet town that offers not only the holiday pleasures of beaches, sports and nightspots but also the timeless delights of a rural Spanish village. Entering the house through a patio with graceful arches and leafy plantings, you'll be charmed by the airy open spaces and rustic furnishings. The very large living and dining room features a handsome open fireplace and both this room and the kitchen enjoy access to the balcony. Up to seven guests will find comfortable sleeping quarters in the three bedrooms. Contact: Interhome Inc., 124 Little Falls Rd., Fairfield, NJ 07004. Call 201-882-6864. Ref. E9524/1.

Children: Y   Pets: Y   Smoking: Y   Handicap Access: N   Payment: P, V, M

Deltebre la Cava

RIOMAR   *Rates: budget-inexpensive*
Open: April 7-November 20   *Minimum Stay: one week*

A nature reserve surrounded by rice fields makes an unusual and attractive setting for this three-room terrace house. Fine views of the sea and close proximity to a sandy beach helps guests enjoy long days in the sun and surf. Inside, rustic furniture creates a natural ambience for five. The fishing's great here, whether deep sea or freshwater. Bed linens and bath towels aren't provided but can be rented locally. Contact: Interhome Inc., 124 Little Falls Road, Fairfield, NJ 07004. Call 201-882-6864. Ref. E9588/100.

Children: Y   Pets: N   Smoking: Y   Handicap Access: N   Payment: P, V, M

Deltebre la Cava

RIOMAR   *Rates: budget-inexpensive*
Open: April 7-November 20   *Minimum Stay: one week*

Tucked in a residential neighborhood just a few hundred yards from a fine sandy beach, this sunny terrace house provides a quiet base for the many sports activities along the river Ebro. The three-room unit sleeps five in two bedrooms including a sofa bed and it also has a kitchenette and washing machine. Share the swimming pool with your neighbors and grill a casual barbecue dinner on the furnished patio. Hire a boat and sail on the river, where you can also find good angling. Contact: Interhome Inc., 124 Little Falls Road, Fairfield, NJ 07004. Call 201-882-6864. Ref. E9588/132.

Children: Y   Pets: N   Smoking: Y   Handicap Access: N   Payment: P, V, M

L'Escala

LAKOUBA   *Rates: inexpensive*
Open: July-August   *Minimum Stay: one week*

Explore the old town of L'Escala, and you'll find a traditional fishing harbor (famous for its anchovies) still alive and working beneath the tourist bustle. Venture a bit inland and you'll be rewarded with unspoiled villages and pleasant rural haunts. Though most people come here for the warm, sunny beaches, and they aren't disappointed. Lakouba is a lovely villa for six about half a mile from the golden sands. The elegant rooms feature ceramic tile floors and rustic furnishings; the living/dining room opens through French doors to a covered terrace adjacent to a delightful walled garden. The garden dining area is conveniently close to the kitchen, but you may prefer to do most of your holiday cooking outdoors on the barbecue. Contact: Blakes Holidays, Wroxham, Norwich, England NR12 8DH. Call 44-603-784141. Ref. EAD.

Children: Y   Pets: N   Smoking: Y   Handicap Access: N   Payment: P, T, V, M

L'Escala

SUPER-BRANCS HOUSE   *Rates: budget-moderate*
Open: year-round   *Minimum Stay: one week*

This semi-detached house is pleasantly shaded by some tall, leafy trees. The dining room features a cheery open fireplace and opens onto a cool, covered terrace; the kitchen also opens onto the terrace. There are two comfy bedrooms on this first floor and four more bedrooms upstairs, one of which has its own pleasant balcony. The picturesque town of L'Escala is marvelously situated in the Gulf of Roses on the Costa Brava. Its long, wide, sandy beaches are separated by rocky reefs. In town there are some charming boutiques, fine restaurants and energetic clubs; a baby-sitting service is available for those who want to sightsee or visit the nightspots without the kids in tow. Contact:

Interhome Inc., 124 Little Falls Rd., Fairfield, NJ 07004. Call 201-882-6864. Ref. E9425/28.

Children: Y   Pets: Y   Smoking: Y   Handicap Access: N   Payment: P, V, M

L'Escala

TAMARINDO   *Rates: budget-inexpensive*
Open: May-September   *Minimum Stay: one week*

Only a short stroll from the sandy beach of Platja del Riells stands this pretty villa for up to eight guests. The floors covered with handsome ceramic tiles and the pretty fireplace in the airy living and dining room add a touch of Spanish cheer. In addition to the convertible bed in the living area, there are three cozy bedrooms. Outside you'll find a pleasant patio partially shaded by leafy trees and a nice little garden with furniture and a barbecue. The villa is convenient not only to the beach but also to the shops and restaurants of L'Escala. The area also offers sailing, horseback riding, golf and tennis. Contact: Blakes Holidays, Wroxham, Norwich, England NR12 8DH. Call 44-603-784141. Ref. EAF.

Children: Y   Pets: N   Smoking: Y   Handicap Access: N   Payment: P, T, V, M

Llanssa

CASA CAN MANEL   *Rates: budget-moderate*
Open: year-round   *Minimum Stay: one week*

This attractive house, with its stone gateway and pretty tiled roof, is tucked away on a quiet side street just a few feet from the waters' edge. In addition to a large terrace with views of the neighboring mountains, there is a pleasant garden to relax in. The three comfortable bedrooms can sleep up to four adults and two children, and there is a cozy fireplace in the large living and dining room. Best of all, it's marvelously convenient both to the quaint medieval sights of the old town and to the swimming, surfing and boating of the sunny beaches. Contact: Interhome Inc., 124 Little Falls Rd., Fairfield, NJ 07004. Call 201-882-6864. Ref. E9401/720.

Children: Y   Pets: Y   Smoking: Y   Handicap Access: N   Payment: P, V, M

Llanssa

CATALUNYA   *Rates: budget*
Open: year-round   *Minimum Stay: one week*

Nestled between the Pyrenees and the warm waters of the Mediterranean, the charming village of Llanssa is a pleasant spot for a holiday. The Catalunya is well situated in a quiet neighborhood not far from the shingle beach and its water-sport opportunities. Inside you'll find a living and dining room with a convertible bed, an additional twin bedroom and a kitchen complete with an oven. After a day of frolicking in the surf, relax in a chair out on the balcony and enjoy the marvelous sea view. And the grapevine-covered hills outside of town are splendid for private picnics or tranquil walks. Contact: Interhome

Inc., 124 Little Falls Rd., Fairfield, NJ 07004. Call 201-882-6864. Ref. E9401/224B.

Children: Y   Pets: Y   Smoking: Y   Handicap Access: N   Payment: P, V, M

Miami Platja
KASBAH   *Rates: budget-moderate*
Open: year-round   *Minimum Stay: one week*

The Kasbah lives up to its name with exotic palm trees and colorful tiles around the shared swimming pool. The airy rooms are decorated in a charming rustic manner. The living room features a handsome fireplace and the kitchenette is fully equipped with an oven; a dining room, three bedrooms and two bathrooms round out the accommodations. In addition to the shared garden of the complex, the house has its own delightful garden with furniture and a barbecue. The supermarket around the corner and the washing machine in the building help make your stay convenient as well as pleasurable; the complex even has its own disco. If you do venture beyond the immediate area, you'll find the sandy beaches and magnificent cliffs of the sea less than two miles away. Contact: Interhome Inc., 124 Little Falls Rd., Fairfield, NJ 07004. Call 201-882-6864. Ref. E9584/195.

Children: Y   Pets: Y   Smoking: Y   Handicap Access: N   Payment: P, V, M

Miami Platja
RUSTICAL MONTROIG VILLA   *Rates: budget-moderate*
Open: year-round   *Minimum Stay: one week*

This gracious house occupies a sunny spot on a private road not far from the glistening sands of the seashore. The spacious rooms feature rustic furnishings. There is a nice fireplace in the large living and dining room (the house is fully heated) and the four comfy bedrooms can sleep up to eight guests. The lovely swimming pool and separate children's wading pool are found in back by the elegant terrace, and the whole area is surrounded by a high cypress hedge. The house is convenient to some interesting shops and charming restaurants and town with its windsurfing and riding facilities is less than two miles away. Contact: Interhome Inc., 124 Little Falls Rd., Fairfield, NJ 07004. Call 201-882-6864. Ref. E9584/281.

Children: Y   Pets: Y   Smoking: Y   Handicap Access: N   Payment: P, V, M

Miami Platja
VIA MARINA TERRACE HOUSE   *Rates: budget-inexpensive*
Open: year-round   *Minimum Stay: one week*

The Via Marina complex offers its guests a wide array of holiday diversions: Tennis courts, a large swimming pool, friendly restaurants and lively discos all conspire to fill your days and nights with fun. The lovely sea and its many aquatic activities are near, as well: A pleasant stroll will bring you to the wide, golden beaches and recreational facilities. The simply furnished terrace house can sleep up to five people beneath its cheerfully tiled roof. It features both a nice little terrace where you can catch a cooling breeze and a large, leafy garden for quiet strolls. Contact: Interhome Inc., 124 Little Falls Rd., Fairfield, NJ 07004. Call 201-882-6864. Ref. E9584/130.

Children: Y   Pets: Y   Smoking: Y   Handicap Access: N   Payment: P, V, M

Palamos

L'EMPORDA   *Rates: budget-inexpensive*
Open: year-round   *Minimum Stay: one week*

Palamos is a bustling harbor town situated at the heart of the Costa Brava. Despite its busy facade, it still finds time to cater to its many visitors: tennis, yachting, water-skiing, angling and sailing opportunities abound here, not to mention the sunning and swimming that are ubiquitous along the coast. The town enjoys a rather sophisticated social life and you'll probably want to sample some of the fine restaurants and chic cafes. L'Emporda sits on the beach right in the center of town, a marvelously convenient place for enjoying all that Palamos has to offer. The three-room apartment comfortably accommodates four guests and features a nice balcony for viewing the scenery. Contact: Interhome Inc., 124 Little Falls Rd., Fairfield, NJ 07004. Call 201-882-6864. Ref. E9454/230E.

Children: Y   Pets: Y   Smoking: Y   Handicap Access: N   Payment: P, V, M

Platja d'Aro

MANAURE   *Rates: budget-inexpensive*
Open: year-round   *Minimum Stay: one week*

Platja d'Aro is a popular resort with an energetic social life. Here you can join other sun-worshipers as they make their rounds in the many beachside cafes, interesting boutiques, genial restaurants and lively discos. Needless to say, the long and wonderfully wide beach is the reason for all this excitement. The Manaure apartment house occupies a sunny slope about a mile from the center of town and features its own swimming pool. The accommodations for four include a living and dining room with a fireplace, a kitchenette and two bedrooms. The balcony outside enjoys wonderful views of rolling hills stretched out beneath an endless azure sky. Contact: Interhome Inc., 124 Little Falls Rd., Fairfield, NJ 07004. Call 201-882-6864. Ref. E9460/410C.

Children: Y   Pets: Y   Smoking: Y   Handicap Access: N   Payment: P, V, M

Roses

MAS BUSCA HOUSE   *Rates: budget-inexpensive*
Open: year-round   *Minimum Stay: one week*

This well-furnished house is a wonderful base for enjoying the beaches, water sports and scenery of Roses. During the summer there is a friendly restaurant just down the street. The sandy beaches, available year-round for sunning, splashing or quiet walks, are just a couple of miles away. If you prefer to paddle in privacy, the house has its own sparkling swimming pool out by the sunny terrace. There are one double bedroom and two twin bedrooms inside, and the pleasant living and dining room boasts a handsome fireplace. A garage and TV add to the comfort. Contact: Interhome Inc., 124 Little Falls Rd., Fairfield, NJ 07004. Call 201-882-6864. Ref. E9410/506.

Children: Y   Pets: Y   Smoking: Y   Handicap Access: N   Payment: P, V, M

S'Agaro

CASA ROCHA   *Rates: budget-moderate*
Open: year-round   *Minimum Stay: one week*

The Casa Rocha sits on a sunny side road on the outskirts of S'Agaro, a pleasant holiday town. Off of the handsome entrance are a charming living room with an open fireplace and a separate dining room. There are two cozy bedrooms on this floor and two downstairs; the house can accommodate up to eight guests. Wander outside and you'll find a lovely garden and terrace; comfortable garden furniture invites you to stretch out and relax while a friend fixes supper on the barbecue. There's also another terrace up on the roof. The house is near both restaurants and stores and there is a sandy beach just a short walk away. Contact: Interhome Inc., 124 Little Falls Rd., Fairfield, NJ 07004. Call 201-882-6864. Ref. E9462/101.

Children: Y   Pets: Y   Smoking: Y   Handicap Access: N   Payment: P, V, M

Salou

CASA M'CINTA   *Rates: budget-expensive*
Open: year-round   *Minimum Stay: one week*

The Casa M'Cinta is located in a quiet suburb not too far from the beach. The elegant pool out back is a lovely way to cool off after a game or two of tennis at the nearby courts. Inside you'll find a living and dining room, a kitchen, four bedrooms and two bathrooms. There's also a pleasant balcony; the garage and washing machine help to make your stay even more convenient. The town of Pineda is about a mile away and the restaurants, discos and bars of Salou are close as well. Riding, miniature golf, water-skiing and sailing can all be enjoyed in the area. Contact: Interhome Inc., 124 Little Falls Rd., Fairfield, NJ 07004. Call 201-882-6864. Ref. E9580/400.

Children: Y   Pets: Y   Smoking: Y   Handicap Access: N   Payment: P, V, M

Salou

HELIOS   *Rates: budget-inexpensive*
Open: year-round   *Minimum Stay: one week*

One of the best-loved family vacation spots on the Costa Daurada, Salou features lifeguards on its splendidly wide beaches and a stately parade of yachts and sailboats in its harbor. The Helios apartment building is so close to the beach that you can taste the salt air; needless to say, it offers splendid sea views. The apartment for six is located on the fifth floor and includes a pleasant balcony. The rustic furnishings add a touch of charm to the rooms, which include a living and dining area, a full kitchen and three bedrooms. There is parking provided and the center of town is just a short walk away. Contact: Interhome Inc.,

124 Little Falls Rd., Fairfield, NJ 07004. Call 201-882-6864. Ref. E9580/220F.

Children: Y   Pets: Y   Smoking: Y   Handicap Access: N   Payment: P, V, M

Santa Margarita

SALINES TERRACE HOUSE   *Rates: budget-inexpensive*
Open: year-round   *Minimum Stay: one week*

This charming terrace house provides privacy and comfort during your stay in Santa Margarita. Off of the cool, spacious entrance hall are a pleasant living and dining room and an open kitchen complete with an oven; the three twin bedrooms offer cozy sleeping quarters for up to six guests. The house also has a large terrace where you can relax during the midday siesta. The house is very conveniently located, near shops and restaurants, and a very short stroll will bring you to the gentle waters and wide beaches of the shore. Contact: Interhome Inc., 124 Little Falls Rd., Fairfield, NJ 07004. Call 201-882-6864. Ref. E9415/160.

Children: Y   Pets: Y   Smoking: Y   Handicap Access: N   Payment: P, V, M

Sitges

CUMBRE   *Rates: budget-inexpensive*
Open: year-round   *Minimum Stay: one week*

Sitges is a cheerful old town with colorful streets, interesting historic sights, golden beaches and plentiful recreational facilities—what more could you ask? In case you asked for a quiet, sunny abode with a splendid view of the sea, check out the Cumbre. Only half a mile away from the beach, this large apartment will comfortably sleep up to eight guests. In addition to a living and dining room with a divan and a kitchen complete with oven, there are three additional bedrooms and two bathrooms. Best of all, the two large balconies give you wonderful views of the luxuriant countryside and endless blue waters. Contact: Interhome Inc., 124 Little Falls Rd., Fairfield, NJ 07004. Call 201-882-6864. Ref. E9519/120D.

Children: Y   Pets: Y   Smoking: Y   Handicap Access: N   Payment: P, V, M

St. Antoni de Calonge

IBIZA   *Rates: budget-moderate*
Open: year-round   *Minimum Stay: one week*

This pleasant terrace house boasts a wonderfully convenient location in the popular resort of St. Antoni. The wide, sloping beaches are a short walk away and the main road nearby puts the restaurants, shops and nightspots of the town at your disposal. You may prefer to stay at home, though, basking in the warm afternoon sun after a refreshing swim, enjoying a home-cooked barbecue for dinner and later curling up in front of the cheery open fire when the evening grows a bit chilly. The house comfortably accommodates five people with a divan bed in the living and dining room and two additional bedrooms upstairs.

Contact: Interhome Inc., 124 Little Falls Rd., Fairfield, NJ 07004. Call 201-882-6864. Ref. E9458/610.

Children: **Y** Pets: **Y** Smoking: **Y** Handicap Access: **N** Payment: **P, V, M**

St. Antoni de Calonge

PAGEILLS
Rates: budget-inexpensive
Open: year-round
Minimum Stay: one week

The gleaming white walls of the Pageills, with their unique arches and striking stairways, are well situated only a few yards from fine sandy beaches. The residence offers a large swimming pool for the use of its guests, and there is a friendly restaurant right around the corner. There are two apartments available, both for four people. The larger one has a living and dining room, a kitchenette with an oven and a twin bedroom downstairs; upstairs there is another bedroom with its own balcony and a stairway leading to the terrace. The other apartment shares a similar layout and has a nice little terrace. Contact: Interhome Inc., 124 Little Falls Rd., Fairfield, NJ 07004. Call 201-882-6864. Ref. E9458/290B, /291B.

Children: **Y** Pets: **Y** Smoking: **Y** Handicap Access: **N** Payment: **P, V, M**

Tamariu

EL MADRONO
Rates: inexpensive-expensive
Open: year-round
Minimum Stay: one week

Swathed in pine trees and overlooking the azure sea, this lovely house is a charming and convenient home away from home. The large living room and handsome dining room on the first floor open onto a peaceful covered terrace. Upstairs are three bedrooms, sleeping up to six, and the door to another terrace—this one opens to the golden magic of the sun. Outside you'll find a fragrant garden with a barbecue and another large covered terrace on the lower level. Tamariu is a small fishing village surrounded by some lovely hills, which are sure to entice dedicated hikers. The bay welcomes bathers with fine, sandy beaches and more rugged waters nearby will delight divers and water-skiers. Contact: Interhome Inc., 124 Little Falls Rd., Fairfield, NJ 07004. Call 201-882-6864. Ref. E9466/102.

Children: **Y** Pets: **Y** Smoking: **Y** Handicap Access: **N** Payment: **P, V, M**

Tossa de Mar

VILA VELLA HOUSE
Rates: budget-moderate
Open: year-round
Minimum Stay: one week

The picturesque town of Tossa de Mar dates back to Roman times and features a well-preserved medieval quarter. Nonetheless, it also offers all the amenities you'd expect at a popular modern resort—riding, tennis, sailing, water-skiing, diving and fishing, to name a few. This house for six in the lovely medieval section of town enchants guests with its charming rustic furnishings and antique surroundings. After returning from the sandy beach through narrow, winding streets, relax in the pleasant living room (with a fireplace for chillier evenings) or pop into the complete kitchen to whip up some Mediterranean delight. For those who'd rather eat out, there are some genial restaurants nearby. Contact: Interhome Inc., 124 Little Falls Rd., Fairfield, NJ 07004. Call 201-882-6864. Ref. E9465/100.

Children: Y   Pets: Y   Smoking: Y   Handicap Access: N   Payment: P, V, M

IBIZA

Ibiza

CASA SA FONT   *Rates: expensive-deluxe*
Open: April-October   *Minimum Stay: two weeks*

This elegant, Phoenician-style villa commands magnificent views from its perch atop a lushly wooded hill. In one direction you see quaint whitewashed villages dwarfed by jagged mountains; in the other, the blue sea studded with countless gem-like islands. There is a lovely fireplace in the enormous living and dining room of this luxury home; sleeping quarters for ten and a modern kitchen are also found in the main part of the house. A separate guest apartment accommodating four additional people includes its own kitchen and living room. Sun-drenched terraces and an ample swimming pool await you outside. Other activities available in the area include tennis, sailing, snorkeling and golf, while a few miles away the ancient town of Ibiza is renowned for its traditional cuisine and exciting nightlife. Contact: Villas International, 71 West 23rd St., New York, NY 10010. Call 212-929-7585.

Children: Y   Pets: Y   Smoking: Y   Handicap Access: N   Payment: C, P, T

MADRID

Madrid

MURALTA APARTMENTS   *Rates: moderate-deluxe*
Open: year-round   *Minimum Stay: one week*

Ideally situated for those seeking a Madrid holiday, this modern apartment building is located in a residential section in the center of town, near the Princesa-Gran Via development and within easy reach of many of the capital city's top sights and attractions. Studio, one- and two-bedroom units are all available, each self-contained with full kitchen facilities. Only a short walk away from a number of renowned restaurants and clubs serving up the finest in Spanish cuisine and entertainment, the building itself offers an excellent restaurant, as well as parking facilities for guests. Contact: Villas International, 71 West 23rd Street, New York, NY 10010. Call 212-929-7585.

Children: Y   Pets: N   Smoking: Y   Handicap Access: N   Payment: C, P, T

MAJORCA

Cala d'Or

VILLA ES FORTI   *Rates: deluxe*
Open: year-round   *Minimum Stay: one week*

Overlooking the Mediterranean, this handsome villa located near the heart of Cala d'Or has a private path leading down to the beach and a sparkling, L-shaped swimming pool. On the first floor, the house contains a spacious living room/dining area, fully equipped kitchen and three bedrooms, one with a separate entrance from the courtyard, while upstairs is a twin master suite with a balcony offering striking sea views. The pool area features lounge chairs and an open shower. Contact: Villas International, 71 West 23rd Street, New York, NY 10010. Call 212-929-7585.

Children: Y   Pets: N   Smoking: Y   Handicap Access: N   Payment: C, P, T

Cala d'Or

VILLA ESTERLICIA   *Rates: deluxe*
Open: year-round   *Minimum Stay: one week*
This recently built, tastefully furnished villa stands in a quiet residential section of Cala d'Or, only yards from the nearest beach and close to the shops, bars, restaurants and clubs that have made the tree-lined resort world renowned. The grounds feature a pool with a covered terrace to the side and a barbecue for pleasant outdoor repasts, plus an additional sun terrace on the roof. Inside, the house contains a living room with a comfy fireplace and French doors that open onto the terrace, a kitchen and three bedrooms, one of which is an upstairs suite reachable by an exterior staircase. Contact: Villas International, 71 West 23rd Street, New York, NY 10010. Call 212-929-7585.

Children: Y   Pets: N   Smoking: Y   Handicap Access: N   Payment: C, P, T

Cala Ratjada

CASA LA CASITA   *Rates: budget-inexpensive*
Open: year-round   *Minimum Stay: one week*
A delightful Majorcan hideaway for two, La Casita is a self-contained annex to a grand villa, with a separate entrance for complete privacy. This is a quiet and secluded spot less than a mile from Cala Ratjada on the northern coast of the island, an area abounding with unspoiled beaches and magnificent views. The unit contains a split-level living room, fully equipped kitchen, bedroom and a small patio and garden area. Guests have direct access to a bathing terrace on the bay only steps away and may also use the villa's swimming pool. Contact: Villas International, 71 West 23rd Street, New York, NY 10010. Call 212-929-7585.

Children: Y   Pets: N   Smoking: Y   Handicap Access: N   Payment: C, P, T

Pollensa

CASA LA VINA II   *Rates: expensive-deluxe*
Open: year-round   *Minimum Stay: one week*
This charming, converted farmhouse is superbly situated less than three miles from the walled medieval town of Pollensa—one of Majorca's premiere historic attractions—and five miles from the resort beaches and shops of Puerto Pollensa. The house contains three bedrooms to accommodate up to seven guests, as well as a full kitchen and lounge/dining room. Set in a lovely garden, the residence includes

a pool with outdoor shower, surrounded by bright terraces next to a shady porch area. Contact: Villas International, 71 West 23rd Street, New York, NY 10010. Call 212-929-7585.

Children: Y Pets: N Smoking: Y Handicap Access: N Payment: C, P, T

Pollensa

CASA LA VINA   *Rates: expensive-deluxe*
Open: year-round   *Minimum Stay: one week*

Set amid lush gardens in an isolated area, La Vina is a traditional single-story Spanish house close to miles of gleaming sandy beaches and the colorful resort of Puerto Pollensa. The house includes three bedrooms, two with double beds, a kitchen and a sitting room/dining area that leads out to a shady terrace and pool. An open staircase leads to the roof, where a large and sunny second terrace is located, offering sweeping views of the countryside. Contact: Villas International, 71 West 23rd Street, New York, NY 10010. Call 212-929-7585.

Children: Y Pets: N Smoking: Y Handicap Access: N Payment: C, P, T

Pollensa

VILLA L'HORT C'AN SUREDA   *Rates: expensive-deluxe*
Open: year-round   *Minimum Stay: one week*

This simple, restored farmhouse is situated in the picturesque rural area of Ternellas, on the north side of Majorca near the historic town of Pollensa. The two-story residence includes an entrance hall, lounge, well-equipped modern kitchen and three bedrooms sleeping five, with a swimming pool and built-in barbecue outside. Among the neighbors is the owner's pet donkey, who loves to take children for rides. The Cape of Formentor with its awesome rock formations is within easy reach and shouldn't be missed. Contact: Villas International, 71 West 23rd Street, New York, NY 10010. Call 212-929-7585.

Children: Y Pets: N Smoking: Y Handicap Access: N Payment: C, P, T

Pollensa

VILLA L'HORT DE CAN BOTA   *Rates: expensive-deluxe*
Open: year-round   *Minimum Stay: one week*

Set in a large, cultivated garden, this restored stone farmhouse stays cool even when the Mediterranean sun is at its most fierce, and a pool is out back for a refreshing dip whenever you so wish. It's swimming weather year-round at this holiday residence, located in the serene rural area of Ternellas, not far from Cala San Vicente and Puerto Pollensa. With a barbecue next to the pool and an additional terrace on the roof, the two-story house contains a sitting room, dining room, kitchen and three comfortable bedrooms. Contact: Villas International, 71 West 23rd Street, New York, NY 10010. Call 212-929-7585.

Children: Y Pets: N Smoking: Y Handicap Access: N Payment: C, P, T

Pollensa

VILLA VISTA HERMOSA   *Rates: deluxe*
Open: year-round   *Minimum Stay: one week*

This enchanting villa is located in the residential area of Huerta de la Font within easy reach of Cala San Vicente and Puerto Pollensa. The residence contains a sitting room, dining room, fully equipped kitchen, master suite with a king-size bed and two other bedrooms. French windows open onto a sumptuous covered terrace, with commanding mountain views that extend the entire length of the villa. From the house, steps lead down to the pool area, enveloped by flowering shrubs and trees and featuring a changing room and showers, a barbecue and a bar for outdoor entertaining in high style. Contact: Villas International, 71 West 23rd Street, New York, NY 10010. Call 212-929-7585.

Children: Y   Pets: N   Smoking: Y   Handicap Access: N   Payment: C, P, T

Porto Petro

CASA SON DURI   *Rates: expensive-deluxe*
Open: year-round   *Minimum Stay: one week*

Casa Son Duri is built on two levels featuring two sunny terraces—one on the roof, the other offering a small pool, garden and barbecue area. Located in the Porto Petro, a tranquil residential area graced with lovely gardens and whitewashed walls, it is on the road to Cala Mondrago, one mile from the beach. The house contains a kitchen, living room/dining area and two bedrooms on the first floor, with an additional bedroom and bath upstairs. Contact: Villas International, 71 West 23rd Street, New York, NY 10010. Call 212-929-7585.

Children: Y   Pets: N   Smoking: Y   Handicap Access: N   Payment: C, P, T

Porto Petro

CASA TENIS   *Rates: expensive-deluxe*
Open: year-round   *Minimum Stay: one week*

Surrounded by a quiet pine forest, this lovely Spanish-style villa stands over the beautiful Bay of Es Calo de Sa Torre, offering terrific views of the Mediterranean from the covered terrace. The nearby waters provide splendid opportunities for swimming and snorkeling; the closest beach, immaculate and uncrowded, is a short distance away. Featuring a private swimming pool, Casa Tenis contains a fully equipped kitchen, living room/dining area and three bedrooms that sleep six comfortably. It is within a mile of exceptional shopping and dining. Contact: Villas International, 71 West 23rd Street, New York, NY 10010. Call 212-929-7585.

Children: Y   Pets: N   Smoking: Y   Handicap Access: N   Payment: C, P, T

S'Horta

VILLA FINCA C'AN JERONI   *Rates: deluxe*
Open: year-round   *Minimum Stay: one week*

Ten minutes from the exciting and exotic resort of Cala d'Or, this elegant villa rests in a quiet and secluded location with panoramic views to the coast over acres of orchards. The house contains a master suite and three additional bedrooms, large kitchen and pantry area and a living room/dining area with an open fireplace and a door leading out onto the villa's covered terrace. The property also includes a pool with poolside shower and spacious patio area and a built-in barbecue to make tempting Mediterranean meals al fresco. Contact: Villas International, 71 West 23rd Street, New York, NY 10010. Call 212-929-7585.

Children: **Y**   Pets: **N**   Smoking: **Y**   Handicap Access: **N**   Payment: **C, P, T**

Santanyi
CASA PONS   *Rates: deluxe*
Open: year-round   *Minimum Stay: one week*

Within five hundred yards of the beach and near the charming market town of Santanyi, Casa Pons consists of two entirely self-contained floors, each with separate entrance, making this an ideal holiday home for two families vacationing together. The first floor of the large and well-furnished villa contains a kitchen, living room/dining area and three bedrooms, while the second floor offers its own kitchen with breakfast bar, a spacious bedroom and additional sleeping accommodations in the living room. Casa Pons comes with a private swimming pool and features fabulous views of the Majorcan countryside. Contact: Villas International, 71 West 23rd Street, New York, NY 10010. Call 212-929-7585.

Children: **Y**   Pets: **N**   Smoking: **Y**   Handicap Access: **N**   Payment: **C, P, T**

VALENCIA

Altea
ALFAZ DEL PI   *Rates: budget-inexpensive*
Open: April 7-Nov. 20   *Minimum Stay: one week*

This three-room apartment on the ground floor of a luxurious house looks out over the old fishing villages of Benidorm and Altea to the sea. Shops, a post office and restaurants are within three miles and a rocky beach and a sandy beach are both a short drive away. The living/dining room has a fireplace and opens onto the terrace and swimming pool, which is shared with other residents. Two double bedrooms sleep four, one of them opening out onto the terrace. You must bring bed linens and bath towels with you. Contact: Interhome Inc., 124 Little Falls Road, Fairfield, NJ 07004. Call 201-882-6864. Ref. E9740/110A.

Children: **Y**   Pets: **N**   Smoking: **Y**   Handicap Access: **N**   Payment: **P, V, M**

Benidorm
MIRA MAR   *Rates: budget*
Open: April 7-Nov. 20   *Minimum Stay: one week*

You needn't go far to find recreation at the Mira Mar apartment complex, which features a private swimming pool, children's playground, supermarket and bar. If you must venture out, you'll find restaurants and a sandy beach within walking distance. This ninth-floor apartment for two features a living/dining room with a divan bed, a kitchen and a double bedroom. From the balcony you'll have a good view of the sea. Riding, tennis, go-cart track, parachuting, waterskiing, surfing, diving and fishing are all available nearby. Bed linens and bath towels aren't provided, but they can be rented locally. Contact: Interhome Inc., 124 Little Falls Road, Fairfield, NJ 07004. Call 201-882-6864. Ref. E9742/60J.

Children: Y   Pets: N   Smoking: Y   Handicap Access: N   Payment: P, V, M

Benissa

CASA BENISSA   *Rates: moderate*
Open: April 7-Nov. 20   *Minimum Stay: one week*

Awake to an inspiring view of the sea or an invigorating dip in your own pool at this lovely house featuring sunny terraces, covered terraces and a pretty furnished garden. Large families or groups of friends will find comfort in two living areas with two separate entrances for privacy. One part of the house features six rooms for four to five guests and has a living/dining room with fireplace, kitchen and two twin bedrooms. The smaller part of the house has a living/dining room with fireplace and divan, kitchen and two more twin bedrooms for four. You'll find a fine sandy beach at Moraira only three miles away and a market, restaurants, bars, bays and tennis within two miles. Contact: Interhome Inc., 124 Little Falls Road, Fairfield, NJ 07004. Call 201-882-6864. Ref. E9734/10.

Children: Y   Pets: N   Smoking: Y   Handicap Access: N   Payment: P, V, M

Benissa

MONTEMAR   *Rates: budget-inexpensive*
Open: April 7-Nov. 20   *Minimum Stay: one week*

This spacious, comfortable house sits on a slope at the top of Montemar, offering fine views of the sea from Calpe to Penon de Ifach. A swimming pool, sun terrace, patio with furniture and a barbecue will add to your vacation pleasure. One floor is unused and remains locked, but six guests have access to the living/dining room, kitchen and two bedrooms. If it gets too hot to play outside, you'll find a market, restaurants, a swimming pool and tennis courts within a mile. There are no bed linens or bath towels here, but they can be rented locally. Contact: Interhome Inc., 124 Little Falls Road, Fairfield, NJ 07004. Call 201-882-6864. Ref. E9735/6.

Children: Y   Pets: N   Smoking: Y   Handicap Access: N   Payment: P, V, M

Benissa

VILLA CHAPPARAL   *Rates: moderate-expensive*
Open: April 7-Nov. 20   *Minimum Stay: one week*

Benissa is about five miles inland, but Villa Chapparal boasts a sea view. A short flight of stone stairs takes you up to this house, which features a garden, swimming pool, two terraces (one covered and one open), a barbecue house and deck chairs. Inside, five rooms accommodate six on two floors, with a separate entrance on each floor. A kitchen with a dishwasher and deep freeze adds to your comfort. For the kids, you'll find a children's playground within walking distance, as well as restaurants, bars, a market and tennis courts. Contact: Interhome Inc.,

124 Little Falls Road, Fairfield, NJ 07004. Call 201-882-6864. Ref. E9735/14.

Children: Y   Pets: N   Smoking: Y   Handicap Access: N   Payment: P, V, M

Calpe

APOLO IV   *Rates: budget*
Open: April 7-Nov. 20   *Minimum Stay: one week*

Sun lovers will appreciate Costa Blanca's mild climate as they experience the beach, swimming pool, tennis court and sun terrace at the Apolo IV apartments. In town, walk the main shopping street filled with restaurants and discotheques. This fifth-floor apartment sleeps four and features two bedrooms, a living/dining room, kitchenette and a furnished balcony with a sea view. Bed linens and bath towels aren't provided but can be rented locally. Contact: Interhome Inc., 124 Little Falls Road, Fairfield, NJ 07004. Call 201-882-6864. Ref. E9733/330F.

Children: Y   Pets: N   Smoking: Y   Handicap Access: N   Payment: P, V, M

Calpe

CASA MARYVILLA   *Rates: moderate-deluxe*
Open: April 7-Nov. 20   *Minimum Stay: one week*

The living is easy in this charming Spanish-style house in a quiet residential neighborhood close to the sea. A terraced garden, swimming pool and several furnished sun terraces add to your ease. There's even a water tank for those infrequent water shortages in very dry, hot periods. Five bedrooms accommodate ten and two entrances make coming and going convenient. There's plenty to do in the area, with a restaurant, bar, market, swimming pool, tennis courts, fishing, parachuting and water-skiing facilities all nearby. Contact: Interhome Inc., 124 Little Falls Road, Fairfield, NJ 07004. Call 201-882-6864. Ref. E9730/13.

Children: Y   Pets: N   Smoking: Y   Handicap Access: N   Payment: P, V, M

Calpe

CASA O   *Rates: exxpensive-deluxe*
Open: April 7-Nov. 20   *Minimum Stay: one week*

Casa O stands on the coast road in La Fustrera, only a short walk from the sea and a short drive from a sandy bathing beach. But you don't need to leave the house to have fun, as a swimming pool, children's playground, Ping-Pong table, barbecue and bread-baking oven are all on its grounds. Eight rooms are spread over two floors, all comfortably furnished and providing ample room for 11 guests. On the upper floor, a large living/dining room with fireplace, kitchen, one twin and two double bedrooms accommodate six. On the ground floor, which has a separate entrance and simpler furnishings, there's also a large living/dining room, kitchen, one single and two twin bedrooms. Bed linens and bath towels are not provided but can be rented locally. Contact: Interhome Inc., 124 Little Falls Road, Fairfield, NJ 07004. Call 201-882-6864. Ref. E9370/144.

Children: Y   Pets: N   Smoking: Y   Handicap Access: N   Payment: P, V, M

Calpe

EMPEDROLA   *Rates: expensive-deluxe*
Open: April 7-Nov. 20   *Minimum Stay: one week*

This 17th-century manor house was renovated in 1982, and a number of extras were added to make its eight rooms luxurious and comfortable. The view to the sea is good and you can swim in an indoor pool, even though the weather is almost always fair here. A ground-floor living/dining room with a fireplace is a soothing place to relax with friends. A total of four double bedrooms on the two upper floors provide sleeping comfort for up to eight guests. Sports enthusiasts will love the fishing, diving and water-skiing opportunities nearby, while those who want to take it easier can relax at the beach, shop or dine without traveling far. Contact: Interhome Inc., 124 Little Falls Road, Fairfield, NJ 07004. Call 201-882-6864. Ref. E9730/121.

Children: **Y**   Pets: **N**   Smoking: **Y**   Handicap Access: **N**   Payment: **P, V, M**

Calpe

OCEANIC   *Rates: budget*
Open: April 7-Nov. 20   *Minimum Stay: one week*

Stylish and modern, the Oceanic apartment building is set on the beach promenade, offering guests instant access to the sea. This first-floor apartment sleeps three and commands views of the water from the balcony. Nearby, you'll find the harbor and many cafes, restaurants and shops. The building also has its own restaurants and cafes on the ground floor. Bed linens and bath towels must be brought with you or rented locally. Contact: Interhome Inc., 124 Little Falls Road, Fairfield, NJ 07004. Call 201-882-6864. Ref. E9731/101B.

Children: **Y**   Pets: **N**   Smoking: **Y**   Handicap Access: **N**   Payment: **P, V, M**

Calpe

SAN BERNARDO   *Rates: expensive-deluxe*
Open: April 7-Nov. 20   *Minimum Stay: one week*

There's room to stretch out in this luxury house in the residential Maryvilla section of Calpe. A swimming pool, tennis court and panoramic views might make it hard to leave, but the sea and yacht harbor in La Canuta, beckon the adventurous to do some sailboarding. Opportunities to sky dive, ride, dance, dine and take in some films also abound nearby. The house sleeps six on two floors in three twin bedrooms, all with direct access to the peaceful garden. Contact: Interhome Inc., 124 Little Falls Road, Fairfield, NJ 07004. Call 201-882-6864. Ref. E9730/14.

Children: **Y**   Pets: **N**   Smoking: **Y**   Handicap Access: **N**   Payment: **P, V, M**

Calpe

SEAVIEW   *Rates: inexpensive-moderate*
Open: April 7-Nov. 20   *Minimum Stay: one week*

The stairs leading to it are rather steep, but once you reach this house nestled into a hillside overlooking the sea, you'll agree the view is worth the trip. The house's tranquil garden is furnished, and the living/

dining room with fireplace bring warmth to the interior, which sleeps nine. Swim, play tennis or take the kids to the playground a short hop away, then sample the flavor of a local restaurant or bar. Water lovers will enjoy the coast and the scenic sandy beach at Calpe. No bed linens or bath towels are provided, but they can be rented locally. Contact: Interhome Inc., 124 Little Falls Road, Fairfield, NJ 07004. Call 201-882-6864. Ref. E9730/67.

Children: Y   Pets: N   Smoking: Y   Handicap Access: N   Payment: P, V, M

Denia

ALMADRAVA PARK   *Rates: expensive*
Open: April 7-Nov. 20   *Minimum Stay: one week*

Large families will find privacy in this villa, which is divided into two separate wings. The larger wing sleeps eight in three bedrooms and has a full kitchen with a dishwasher. Tanning's a breeze on the sunroof, accessible by a spiral staircase from one of the bedrooms. Four can stay in the second wing's two double bedrooms and kitchenette. Bed linens and bath towels aren't provided but can be rented locally. Contact: Interhome Inc., 124 Little Falls Road, Fairfield, NJ 07004. Call 201-882-6864. Ref. E9704/1.

Children: Y   Pets: N   Smoking: Y   Handicap Access: N   Payment: P, V, M

Denia

L'ALQUERIA SERRA   *Rates: moderate-expensive*
Open: April 7-Nov. 20   *Minimum Stay: one week*

Perfect for families, this eight-person house even has a straw hut on its grounds for the kids to play in. In addition to its swimming pool (open April through October), it offers a barbecue house with running cold water. A sitting area with garden furniture, a fish pond, a covered terrace and a glazed terrace with a bar area add to the entertainment options. Inside, the master bedroom features a sunken bath. Two other double bedrooms and an open gallery with a double divan bed complete the sleeping arrangements. When you want to branch out, hop over to the nearby markets, boutiques, restaurants and nightclubs or try yachting. No bed linens or bath towels are provided, but they can be rented locally. Contact: Interhome Inc., 124 Little Falls Road, Fairfield, NJ 07004. Call 201-882-6864. Ref. E9705/290.

Children: Y   Pets: N   Smoking: Y   Handicap Access: N   Payment: P, V, M

Denia

MARQUESA V   *Rates: budget-inexpensive*
Open: April 7-Nov. 20   *Minimum Stay: one week*

Scan the sea for incoming ships from this house's circular watchtower, or relax in its swimming pool, sun terrace and garden. A sandy beach lies invitingly three miles away; the center of Denia, gateway to Costa Blanca, is even closer. The small house for four offers two double bedrooms, an open kitchen and a living/dining room with fireplace. The tower room holds an extra divan bed and hand basin. Markets, nightclubs, boating and tennis await, a short trip away. Bed linens and bath towels aren't provided but can be rented locally. Contact: Interhome Inc., 124 Little Falls Road, Fairfield, NJ 07004. Call 201-882-6864. Ref. E9705/430.

Children: Y   Pets: N   Smoking: Y   Handicap Access: N   Payment: P, V, M

Denia

VIEUSAN VILLA   *Rates: inexpensive-deluxe*
Open: April 7-Nov. 20   *Minimum Stay: one week*

Set on a stretch of land studded with old trees, this large, rambling villa features a panoramic view of the sea and its rocky coastline. Spend sunny days on a flagstone terrace around the swimming pool, then enjoy cocktails with your barbecued dinner. There's even an outdoor refrigerator and bathroom with shower. Adults will feel at ease while children wade in the paddling pool. Inside, the villa for eight has many extras, including a bar in the living room, a TV and a writing desk. Contact: Interhome Inc., 124 Little Falls Road, Fairfield, NJ 07004. Call 201-882-6864. Ref. E9703/50.

Children: Y   Pets: N   Smoking: Y   Handicap Access: N   Payment: P, V, M

Javea

BALCON AL MAR   *Rates: budget-inexpensive*
Open: April 7-June 30; mid-August-Nov. 20   *Minimum Stay: one week*

Sea lovers will delight in the view from this three-room apartment in a house in Balcon al Mar. Swim in the pool next door, walk down to the water (taking care on the steep, rocky path), or drive to the nearby sandy beach. Also withing walking distance is a public swimming pool with a bar. An iron gate ensures privacy in the terraced garden with patio furniture, or you can relax around the barbecue. Two double bedrooms—one with a sea view—a kitchen and a living/dining room accommodate four people. Contact: Interhome Inc., 124 Little Falls Road, Fairfield, NJ 07004. Call 201-882-6864. Ref. E9711/94B.

Children: Y   Pets: N   Smoking: Y   Handicap Access: N   Payment: P, V, M

Javea

HALCON TERRACE HOUSE   *Rates: budget*
Open: April 7-Nov. 20   *Minimum Stay: one week*

This garden apartment for four in Halcon has a south-facing balcony with furniture and a panoramic view of the sea. Visit the scenic bay of Granadella five miles away or swim on a sandy beach seven and a half miles away. The apartment's living/dining room features a divan bed and access to the balcony. The kitchenette's breakfast bar makes for convenient, casual dining and the comfortable double bedroom promises a good night's sleep. A swimming pool, various Spanish restaurants and the center of Balcon al Mar all lie within walking distance. Contact: Interhome Inc., 124 Little Falls Road, Fairfield, NJ 07004. Call 201-882-6864. Ref. E9711/200.

Children: Y   Pets: N   Smoking: Y   Handicap Access: N   Payment: P, V, M

Javea

TARRAULA   *Rates: moderate-deluxe*
Open: April 7-Nov. 20   *Minimum Stay: one week*

An athlete's paradise, this spacious house boasts a Tartan tennis court to go with a lovely view of the surrounding mountains and valleys. Try your swing at a golf course less than a mile away, or explore the center of nearby Benitachell or Javea. The house's amenities also include a sun terrace, covered terrace, grill house, outdoor shower and bathroom. Lounge in the large living/dining room with fireplace, or savor the evening breeze on the partially covered terrace. Six can sleep in three double bedrooms, one with a full bath. Contact: Interhome Inc., 124 Little Falls Road, Fairfield, NJ 07004. Call 201-882-6864. Ref. E9710/846.

Children: Y   Pets: N   Smoking: Y   Handicap Access: N   Payment: P, V, M

Javea

VILLA JAVEA   *Rates: inexpensive-moderate*
Open: April 7-Nov. 20   *Minimum Stay: one week*

This villa sits on a hillside in Balcon al Mar overlooking the sea. A kidney-shaped pool, sun terrace and outdoor grill provide an opportunity for relaxing near the resorts of the Costa Blanca. Venturing out, you can make the short drive to nearby beaches. There's room for four people here in two double bedrooms on the ground floor. The second floor features a living/dining room with a fireplace, a balcony, an open kitchen with microwave and grill and a washing machine in the storeroom. Restaurants, shops, boutiques and recreational facilities provide activities nearby. Contact: Interhome Inc., 124 Little Falls Road, Fairfield, NJ 07004. Call 201-882-6864. Ref. E9710/636.

Children: Y   Pets: N   Smoking: Y   Handicap Access: N   Payment: P, V, M

Moraira

ARIES   *Rates: budget*
Open: April 7-Nov. 20   *Minimum Stay: one week*

You'll find this three-room ground-floor garden apartment in a Spanish-style building with whitewashed exterior and tiled roof lovely. Four people will have plenty of room in two bedrooms, a modern kitchen and a living/dining room with a fireplace, plus a terrace. Apartment residents share the common swimming pool and can walk to a market, restaurants and a shopping center. The sandy beach at Moraira is a mile and a half away and riding stables and a nine-hole golf course are nearby. No bed linens or bath towels are provided, but they can be rented locally. Contact: Interhome Inc., 124 Little Falls Road, Fairfield, NJ 07004. Call 201-882-6864. Ref. E9738/220A.

Children: Y   Pets: N   Smoking: Y   Handicap Access: N   Payment: P, V, M

Moraira

LA FINCA   *Rates: moderate*
Open: April 7-Nov. 20   *Minimum Stay: one week*

The Moraira landscape is lush with green forests, fertile fields and plantations. La Finca has a view past the vineyards to the sea as well as a footpath to the bathing beach of El Portet. Four people can stay comfortably in this three-room house, which features a living/dining room with fireplace, kitchen with breakfast bar, two twin bedrooms and a covered terrace and garden. You'll find a public swimming pool within walking distance and a sandy beach a little over a mile away. The usually mild climate on the Costa Blanca gives way to very hot, dry periods, so be prepared. There are no bed linens or bath towels provided, but they can be rented locally. Contact: Interhome Inc., 124 Little Falls Road, Fairfield, NJ 07004. Call 201-882-6864. Ref. E9738/2.

Children: Y   Pets: N   Smoking: Y   Handicap Access: N   Payment: P, V, M

Moraira

MONTEPARK   *Rates: expensive-deluxe*
Open: April 7-Nov. 20   *Minimum Stay: one week*

This eight-room villa divided into three separate units provides luxurious accommodations for nine people, plus a spectacular view of the surrounding countryside and sea. The property has large, enclosed grounds and includes a swimming pool and a private tennis court with a separate practice wall. There's plenty of room for sunbathing or partying on the furnished roof-terrace. The upper floor features a double and a twin bedroom, one and a half baths, a kitchen and a living/dining room with a fireplace and access to the terrace and swimming pool. On the ground floor, a double bedroom opens onto a terrace. The third living area offers a living room with open fireplace, a kitchen, one double and one single bedroom and a bath. Contact: Interhome Inc., 124 Little Falls Road, Fairfield, NJ 07004. Call 201-882-6864. Ref. E9738/516.

Children: Y   Pets: N   Smoking: Y   Handicap Access: N   Payment: P, V, M

Oliva

EL PANORAMA   *Rates: budget*
Open: April 7-Nov. 20   *Minimum Stay: one week*

Set amid orange and lemon groves, Oliva reflects the cultural and architectural influence of the Moors, who ruled here until 1492. Overlooking the sea, this house provides a fine base for exploring the beauties of the area. There's an uncultivated garden to enjoy at home and a sandy beach five miles away. Five guests can choose from three bedrooms. Spend the day exploring the many places of historical interest, or visit some folklore festivals. Bed linen and baths towels aren't provided but can be rented locally. Contact: Interhome Inc., 124 Little Falls Road, Fairfield, NJ 07004. Call 201-882-6864. Ref. E9696/10.

Children: Y   Pets: N   Smoking: Y   Handicap Access: N   Payment: P, V, M

Peniscola

BASTIDA   *Rates: budget-inexpensive*
Open: April 7-Nov. 20   *Minimum Stay: one week*

Four-room Bastida offers solitude with a sea view from its lawn terrace, a barbecue on a covered terrace and its own swimming pool. But
it also lies close to conveniences like a post office, grocers, sandy
beach, tennis courts and even a riding school. You can spend your days
here exploring the rocks or beach along Peniscola's coastline, or pop in
and out of the shops and restaurants lining its narrow streets. The
house sleeps seven in three double bedrooms and a folding bed. Bed
linens and bath towels aren't provided. Contact: Interhome Inc., 124
Little Falls Road, Fairfield, NJ 07004. Call 201-882-6864. Ref. E9640/
251.

Children: Y   Pets: N   Smoking: Y   Handicap Access: N   Payment: P, V, M

San Jaime

PEPITA   *Rates: budget*
Open: April 7-Nov. 20   *Minimum Stay: one week*

Pepita lies in quiet San Jaime between the bustling resorts of Moraira
and Calpe, and offers inspiring views of the mountains. Perfect for a
first or second honeymoon, this two-room semi-detached house features a living room with fireplace, open kitchen with breakfast bar,
one double bedroom, a covered terrace and a garden. You can play a
quick nine holes of golf or visit the tennis courts within miles. If the
resort towns seem too hectic, you'll find a market and restaurants
within walking distance. Bed linens and bath towels are not provided,
but they can be rented locally. Contact: Interhome Inc., 124 Little
Falls Road, Fairfield, NJ 07004. Call 201-882-6864. Ref. E9738/20.

Children: Y   Pets: N   Smoking: Y   Handicap Access: N   Payment: P, V, M

San Juan

ALTAMIRA   *Rates: moderate-expensive*
Open: April 7-Nov. 20   *Minimum Stay: one week*

Traditional Spanish architectural elements are apparent throughout
these three-story garden apartments built of white stucco and accented
with lovely archways. Comfortably furnished and large enough for
eight, the apartments feature a modern kitchen complete with a grill
for indoor barbecuing. Guests have the use of a large swimming pool
(May to September) and a tennis court. Here, you can experience Spain
through its native foods: Many nearby restaurants serve up fine paella
and fish dishes, with plenty of Sangria on hand. Contact: Interhome
Inc., 124 Little Falls Road, Fairfield, NJ 07004. Call 201-882-6864. Ref.
E9748/121.

Children: Y   Pets: N   Smoking: Y   Handicap Access: N   Payment: P, V, M

San Juan

CASA REMESK   *Rates: inexpensive-moderate*
Open: April 7-Nov. 20   *Minimum Stay: one week*

This vacation spot on the Playa Alicante is less than five miles north
of Alicante, a popular winter resort with ferries to Marseilles, Oran,

Ibiza and Palma de Mallorca. Casa Remesk offers the convenience of a large kitchen with a washing machine and freezer, plus sleeping accommodations for six. The furnishings are comfortable and you can swim in the private pool or lounge on the furnished patio. Alicante offers an historic castle, church and mosque, as well as many restaurants and shops. Contact: Interhome Inc., 124 Little Falls Road, Fairfield, NJ 07004. Call 201-882-6864. Ref. E9748/1.

Children: Y   Pets: N   Smoking: Y   Handicap Access: N   Payment: P, V, M

San Juan

LAS SIRENAS   *Rates: budget-moderate*
Open: April 7-Nov. 20   *Minimum Stay: one week*
This towering apartment building offers inspiring views of the sand, sun and fun of the Playa Alicante. Smooth sandy beaches, tennis courts, a swimming pool and a children's playground will fill your days, while four-room apartments sleep six at night. Sightseers will warm to Alicante, where the main promenade is studded with marble and lined with palms. In June, take part in the festival of St. John, when Alicante lights up the streets with parades and fireworks. Contact: Interhome Inc., 124 Little Falls Road, Fairfield, NJ 07004. Call 201-882-6864.

Children: Y   Pets: N   Smoking: Y   Handicap Access: N   Payment: P, V, M

Torrevieja

CASA TORREVIEJA   *Rates: budget-moderate*
Open: April 7-Nov. 20   *Minimum Stay: one week*
This charming white stucco house is set in a quiet sunny street just a short walk from a sandy beach and the center of town. Modern in design, the house is very comfortable and includes such unique features as a wide open solarium for indoor sunbathing. Six people can share this three-bedroom house with a large furnished terrace for outdoor sunbathing. Learn to waterski and windsurf, or rent a boat and compete with the locals for the catch of the day. Contact: Interhome Inc., 124 Little Falls Road, Fairfield, NJ 07004. Call 201-882-6864. Ref. E9755/166.

Children: Y   Pets: N   Smoking: Y   Handicap Access: N   Payment: P, V, M

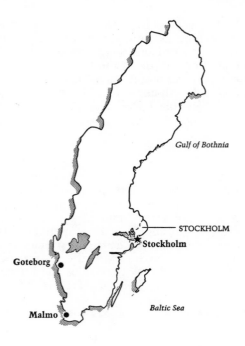

Gulf of Bothnia

STOCKHOLM

Stockholm

Goteborg

Malmo

Baltic Sea

Sweden

STOCKHOLM

Ingmarso
HOLIDAY COTTAGES   *Rates: budget*
Open: year-round   *Minimum Stay: one week*

The fragrant woods of little Ingmarso are interspersed with fertile farms and tranquil shores. The island boasts a permanent population of only a hundred steadfast souls, but many others have discovered its welcoming demeanor: In the summer, the population swells to over a thousand. The holiday village lures visitors with modern cottages and recreational opportunities. Sandy shores, rocky beaches and placid lakes tempt sunbathers and swimmers of all ages. Rowboats and bikes are available for rent; there's even a sauna. And in the late summer, to everyone's delight, the countryside is covered with tasty berries ripe for the picking. Cozy and comfortable, the four-person cottages feature open fireplaces (there's also electric heating), TV and radio. Contact: Ljustero Stuguthyrning, Lillstrom, 180 23 Ljustero, Sweden. Call 46-764-401-56 or 46-8-789-20-00.

Children: **Y**   Pets: **Y**   Smoking: **Y**   Handicap Access: **N**   Payment: **T**

Ljustero

VASBY STRAND HOUSE *Rates: inexpensive*
Open: year-round *Minimum Stay: one week*

Ljustero is the largest member of the Stockholm archipelago, a magnificently wooded island only an hour from Sweden's capital. This rustic country house is shaded by a grove of trees right on the water's edge; there's even a rowboat in case you want to paddle up the coast a bit. Surrounded by the quiet countryside, you're sure to get a good night's sleep in one of the cozy bedrooms (the house sleeps five). The sunny kitchen features an electric range in addition to the traditional wood stove; a TV and telephone are the other modern amenities you'll find in this comfy little get-away. Contact: Ljustero Stuguthyrning, Lillstrom, 180 23 Ljustero, Sweden. Call 46-764-401-56 or 46-8789-20-00. Ref. AS170106.

Children: **Y**   Pets: **Y**   Smoking: **Y**   Handicap Access: **N**   Payment: **T**

Norrhamnen

VAXHOLM HOUSE *Rates: budget*
Open: year-round *Minimum Stay: one week*

A pretty little picket fence surrounds this fine country-style residence with just a hint of half-timbering in the front. The four-room house can sleep up to four people in its cozy bedrooms. A short walk will take you to the refreshing waters of the beach, and there are some interesting shops and convivial restaurants nearby. Whether you prefer the rustic pleasures of the countryside or the cosmopolitan delights of nearby Stockholm, this house makes an excellent base for a family holiday. Contact: Ljustero Stuguthyrning, Lillstrom, 180 23 Ljustero, Sweden. Call 46-764-401-56 or 46-8-789-20-00. Ref. AL870328.

Children: **Y**   Pets: **Y**   Smoking: **Y**   Handicap Access: **N**   Payment: **T**

Varmdo

ALVSALA HOUSE *Rates: inexpensive*
Open: year-round *Minimum Stay: one week*

The history of Varmdo dates back to the 14th century, when the district was first mentioned as a parish. Since then it has developed a reputation as a producer of fine porcelain; the bone china factory in Gustavberg is open for tours daily in the summer. This large house complete with a small boat is ideal for a party of anglers who've come here to enjoy the clear waters of these northern shores. The house is comfortably furnished and sleeps up to ten people in its cozy rooms. Although the house has electric heating, the open fireplace in the living room is the perfect spot to stretch out and recount the tale of the one that got away. Contact: Ljustero Stuguthyrning, Lillstrom, 180 23 Ljustero, Sweden. Call 46-764-401-56 or 46-8-789-20-00. Ref. AS220322.

Children: **Y**   Pets: **Y**   Smoking: **Y**   Handicap Access: **N**   Payment: **T**

Varmdo

VASTRA SKAGGA HOUSE   *Rates: expensive*
Open: year-round   *Minimum Stay: one week*

Splendidly perched on the rocky shore and shaded by magnificent trees, this elegant house is a wonderful place for a family get-together or a group retreat. The luxurious rooms can accommodate up to nine people. There's a handsome fireplace in the living room and a microwave, dishwasher and freezer are found in the well-equipped kitchen. Outside, you can relax on the breezy summer lawn or take a ride in the little rowboat. A short drive will bring you to several local restaurants and some interesting shops; the vigor of Stockholm is never far away. Contact: Ljustero Stuguthyrning, Lillstrom, 180 23 Ljustero, Sweden. Call 46-764-401-56 or 46-8-789-20-00. Ref. AS221501.

Children: **Y**   Pets: **Y**   Smoking: **Y**   Handicap Access: **N**   Payment: **T**

Vaxholm

VAXHOLMS RESIDENCE   *Rates: budget*
Open: year-round   *Minimum Stay: one week*

This elegant old building has been recently renovated to provide pleasant accommodations for up to four people. The large windows let in plenty of the friendly northern sun; the airy living and dining room, kitchen and bedroom are comfortably furnished and filled with light. A pleasant stroll along the streets of this old town will bring you to the sandy beach and some good local restaurants. Perhaps as you walk along the shore, you'll catch a glimpse of the graceful sailing ships that ply these waters during the warm summer months. Contact: Ljustero Stuguthyrning, Lillstrom, 180 23 Ljustero, Sweden. Call 46-764-401-56 or 46-8-789-20-00. Ref. AL870330.

Children: **Y**   Pets: **Y**   Smoking: **Y**   Handicap Access: **N**   Payment: **T**

Switzerland

BERN

Adelboden

CHALET BOIS   *Rates: budget*
Open: April 7-November 20   *Minimum Stay: one week*

Located at the edge of the woods, a short walk from the lovely mountain resort of Adelboden, this pleasant chalet houses quality three-bedroom apartments that accommodate up to six, each containing a kitchenette and sitting room/dining area. The residence offers a cordial terrace and garden with deck chairs. Sports like swimming, hiking, skiing and tennis, plus a cornucopia of entertainment activities, are all available at Adelboden, which enjoys a commanding view of the hypnotically beautiful valley of Engstligen. Contact: Interhome Inc., 124 Little Falls Road, Fairfield, NJ 07004. Call 201-882-6864. Ref. C3715/45A.

Children: Y   Pets: N   Smoking: Y   Handicap Access: N   Payment: P, V, M

Aeschiried

AESCHI CHALET *Rates: moderate*
Open: April 7-November 20 *Minimum Stay: one week*

Set on a slope far from the traffic and overlooking Lake Thun and the surrounding mountains, this attractive chalet is located in the small farming village of Aeschiried. The residence is near ski lifts and cross-country trails, as well as a multitude of paths for novice and experienced mountain trekkers alike. Surrounded by a lawn garden and patio area, the three-floor house contains three bedrooms, a living room/dining area with a tiled stove and a well-equipped kitchen, and is highlighted by its enchanting closed arbor with an open fireplace. Contact: Interhome Inc., 124 Little Falls Road, Fairfield, NJ 07004. Call 201-882-6864. Ref. C3703/10.

Children: Y Pets: N Smoking: Y Handicap Access: N Payment: P, V, M

Brienz

SCHWANDEN GLYSSEN APARTMENT *Rates: budget*
Open: April 7 - November 20 *Minimum Stay: one week*

This warm chalet contains a pleasant two-bedroom apartment on the upper ground floor, which is superb for a family of up to five. It is located in Schwanden, a farming village in an elevated position near the town of Brienz on the upper end of Brienz lake. The area is best known for its unusual steam-powered rack railway that climbs up the Brienz Rothorn. It is also a splendid region for mountain hiking, and the lake offers swimming, boating and waterskiing. Featuring a cool, covered veranda, the residence is surrounded by a sunny lawn where guests and their children can lounge or romp in the crisp Alpine air. Contact: Interhome Inc., 124 Little Falls Road, Fairfield, NJ, 07004. Call 201-882-1742. Ref. C3855/2A.

Children: Y Pets: Y Smoking: Y Handicap Access: N Payment: P, V, M

Chateau d'Oex

CHALET MIETTE *Rates: expensive*
Open: year-round *Minimum Stay: two weeks*

This superb chalet combines spacious, attractive lodgings with an ideal location. The tastefully furnished rooms feature some lovely Swiss antiques and exposed-beam ceilings, and there is an imposing fireplace in the living room. Four cozy bedrooms, two bathrooms, and a modern kitchen with laundry facilities round out the accommodations. Both the sunny garden and the large terrace upstairs command fine views of the valley and neighboring mountains. The village of Chateau d'Oex offers its visitors splendid sports facilities year-round, as well as fine restaurants and charming avenues. Contact: Villas International, 71 W. 23rd St., New York, NY 10010. Call 212-929-7585.

Children: Y Pets: N Smoking: Y Handicap Access: N Payment: C, P, T

Grinderwald

MISLIN FLAT *Rates: budget*
Open: April 7 - November 20 *Minimum Stay: one week*

Ski runs pass right by Mislin, a handsome chalet that commands beautiful views and holds several well kept, self-contained apartments, including this first-floor studio. Featuring a spacious main room, a kitchen area and private patio, the flat is a comfortable and affordable residence for visitors to Grinderwald, a breathtaking glacier village surrounded by pine forests and mountain pastures dominated by the ice-capped peaks and stunning north wall of the Eiger. A wealth of recreational facilities are offered here, including riding, swimming, mountaineering, tennis and, of course, enough year-round skiing to satisfy any athlete's appetite. Contact: Interhome Inc., 124 Little Falls Road, Fairfield, NJ, 07004. Call 201-882-1742. Ref. C3818/7A.

Children: **Y** Pets: **Y** Smoking: **Y** Handicap Access: **N** Payment: **P, V, M**

Gstaad

EDITH   *Rates: budget*
Open: April 7 - November 20   *Minimum Stay: one week*

Set beside a stream close to Gstaad, this congenial chalet contains a homey and private three-bedroom apartment that can accommodate a party of four. The flat itself is quite comfortable, with a sitting room, fully equipped kitchen and small balcony; guests are welcome to use the chalet's pleasant garden area. But it's Gstaad itself—and its countless recreational and other holiday attractions—that's the main attraction, and this highly affordable residence allows visitors to partake of all the rich opportunities the illustrious resort has to offer. Contact: Interhome Inc., 124 Little Falls Road, Fairfield, NJ, 07004. Call 201-882-1742. Ref. C3780/3B.

Children: **Y** Pets: **Y** Smoking: **Y** Handicap Access: **N** Payment: **P, V, M**

Gstaad

IN DER RUETTI   *Rates: budget-inexpensive*
Open: April 7 - November 20   *Minimum Stay: one week*

An economical residence for couples craving an exciting Gstaad holiday, this apartment house offers several self-contained budget studio flats. Each unit provides quiet and privacy and includes a kitchenette and a balcony with a view. Several ski lifts, plus tennis and swimming, are available right next to the building. Most of the area's top recreational opportunities, highlighted by Gstaad's unparalleled summer skiing and mountaineering as well as golf and riding, are within easy reach. Contact: Interhome Inc., 124 Little Falls Road, Fairfield, NJ, 07004. Call 201-882-1742. Ref. C3779/100B.

Children: **Y** Pets: **Y** Smoking: **Y** Handicap Access: **N** Payment: **P, V, M**

Gstaad

KABINE APARTMENTS   *Rates: inexpensive-moderate*
Open: year-round   *Minimum Stay: one week*

These homey apartments are set on a sunny slope conveniently close to Gstaad's many sports facilities. They are ideal bases for anyone who relishes the chance to ski, hike or go riding in the sparkling air in the glorious mountains of Switzerland, or who wishes to play golf or tennis. The apartments range from cozy studios to luxurious four-bedroom duplexes. Most apartments have cheerful open fires, and many have terraces overlooking the beautiful scenery. After a day skiing or hiking, you'll appreciate the spa facilities of the complex: indoor and outdoor pools, spring baths, and water massages. Contact: Villas International, 71 W. 23rd St., New York, NY 10010. Call 212-929-7585.

Children: Y   Pets: N   Smoking: Y   Handicap Access: N   Payment: C, P, T

Interlaken

MATTEN FLAT   *Rates: budget*
Open: April 7 - November 20   *Minimum Stay: one week*

A cozy, private and very economical studio apartment for two is available in this two-family home surrounded by a pleasant lawn in the Matten quarter of Interlaken. Superbly located, the residence is a short walk from the ice rink, tennis courts and indoor pool of the resort, as well as cross-country ski trails and the lido on the lake. The fascinating Beautus caves in the area are well worth visiting, and vacationers will also want to catch a performance at the delightful open-air Tell theater. Contact: Interhome Inc., 124 Little Falls Road, Fairfield, NJ, 07004. Call 201-882-1742. Ref. C3800/10A.

Children: Y   Pets: Y   Smoking: Y   Handicap Access: N   Payment: P, V, M

Kandergrund

ARVLI   *Rates: budget*
Open: April 21 - November 20   *Minimum Stay: one week*

Seven miles from the renowned resort of Kandersteg, Arvli lies on a quiet slope right by Kandergrund, a friendly Bernese hamlet nestled in a flat, sweeping valley. The gently rising hills surrounding the town offer outstanding opportunities for hiking, while swimming and other recreational activities are available nearby. The chalet features a living room/dining area, kitchen and two bedrooms that can accommodate up to five, with a pleasant garden outside. Contact: Interhome Inc., 124 Little Falls Road, Fairfield, NJ, 07004. Call 201-882-1742. Ref. C3716/3.

Children: Y   Pets: Y   Smoking: Y   Handicap Access: N   Payment: P, V, M

Krattigen

CHALET LUNA   *Rates: budget*
Open: April 7-November 20   *Minimum Stay: one week*

A comfortable two-room apartment is available on the first floor of Chalet Luna, located on a steep slope in Krattigen, an enormously friendly village above Lake Thun. Containing a double bedroom, open kitchen and combined parlor/dining room with a huge window giving a view of the entire lake, the flat also features a private patio and small lawn. A swimming pool is not far away, but visitors may want to opt for the quiet, picturesque beach one and a half miles away, where excellent boating facilities are also available. Contact: Interhome Inc.,

124 Little Falls Road, Fairfield, NJ 07004. Call 201-882-6864. Ref. C3704/2A.

Children: **Y**   Pets: **N**   Smoking: **Y**   Handicap Access: **N**   Payment: **P, V, M**

Lauenen

TROGLI   *Rates: inexpensive-moderate*
Open: April 7 - November 20   *Minimum Stay: one week*

Located in a small village less than 5 miles from Gstaad, Trogli is a sunny and very private chalet only steps from the nearest cross-country ski trail, in a region that offers miles of scenic mountain tours. The two-story house furnished with some fine antique pieces, includes four bedrooms, kitchen, gallery and a living room/dining area with fireplace. There, a door leads out to a terrace, which overlooks a quiet lawn area equipped with garden furniture. Contact: Interhome Inc., 124 Little Falls Road, Fairfield, NJ, 07004. Call 201-882-1742. Ref. C3781/2.

Children: **Y**   Pets: **Y**   Smoking: **Y**   Handicap Access: **N**   Payment: **P, V, M**

Lenk

LENKERBOEDELI   *Rates: inexpensive-moderate*
Open: April 7 - November 20   *Minimum Stay: one week*

A comfortable apartment is available in this multi-family house that stands on a sunny slope in the Simmen Valley. A mile away is the engaging, uncrowded holiday village of Lenk, one of the region's best kept secrets, which is graced with mineral baths and beautiful scenery as well as fine skiing, hiking and tennis. Featuring a balcony that commands a wide-reaching mountain and valley view, the apartment takes up two floors and contains a kitchen, drawing room and three bedrooms. Contact: Interhome Inc., 124 Little Falls Road, Fairfield, NJ, 07004. Call 1-201-882-1742. Ref. C3775/16B.

Children: **Y**   Pets: **Y**   Smoking: **Y**   Handicap Access: **N**   Payment: **P, V, M**

Oberried

EDELWEISS FLAT   *Rates: budget*
Open: April 7 - November 20   *Minimum Stay: one week*

Located in the friendly mountainside town of Oberried, a quality apartment is offered on the ground floor of this handsome chalet perched 200 yards above picturesque Lake Brienz. The flat contains a living room, kitchen with dining corner and two double bedrooms. Guests also have shared use of the chalet's covered terrace and garden area, which features deck chairs and other patio furniture for enjoying the blissful setting. Take a refreshing swim in the lake or an invigorating hike in the sedate Bernese countryside, and be sure to visit the famous open-air museum of Ballenberg. Contact: Interhome Inc., 124 Little Falls Road, Fairfield, NJ, 07004. Call 201-882-1742. Ref. C3854/16A.

Children: **Y**   Pets: **Y**   Smoking: **Y**   Handicap Access: **N**   Payment: **P, V, M**

Tschingel

KRINDENHOF HOUSE
Open: April 21-November 20

Rates: budget
Minimum Stay: one week

A pleasant and private flat is available on the second floor of this house over a fine restaurant in the quiet hamlet of Tschingel, which rests on a sunny slope above refreshing Lake Thun. The area features great hiking trails offering gorgeous and unusual views of the Bernese Alps, while lakeside lidos and the brine baths of Sigriswil are only a short distance away. With two balconies, the large apartment includes a living room, two bedrooms and a fully equipped kitchen and accommodates up to seven. Contact: Interhome Inc., 124 Little Falls Road, Fairfield, NJ 07004. Call 201-882-6864. Ref. C3656/1A.

Children: Y   Pets: N   Smoking: Y   Handicap Access: N   Payment: P, V, M

GENEVA

Villette

VILLETTE RESIDENCE
Open: year-round

Rates: inexpensive
Minimum Stay: one week

Located in a peaceful suburb outside Switzerland's most cosmopolitan city, these apartments are wonderful bases for exploring both Geneva and the surrounding countryside. The one-bedroom apartments sleep up to four people; their sunny, open rooms are quiet and comfortable. The surrounding area is splendid for tranquil walks and brisk hikes. Filled with impressive museums and unique history, the clean, stately streets of Geneva are less than five miles away, and stunning Lake Geneva lies just beyond. Contact: Villas International, 71 W. 23rd St., New York, NY 10010. Call 212-929-7585.

Children: Y   Pets: N   Smoking: Y   Handicap Access: N   Payment: C, P, T

GRAUBUNDEN

Davos-Dorf

PROMENADE APARTMENTS
Open: year-round

Rates: inexpensive-moderate
Minimum Stay: one week

Fans of The Magic Mountain can follow the footsteps of Hans Castorp to the lovely resort of Davos; like him, they may decide to stay a little longer than they had planned. In addition to its wonderful ski opportunities and intoxicating alpine scenery, Davos offers some interesting shops and a very sophisticated night life. There are also extensive tennis facilities and an ice rink, which makes it a year-round magnet for athletic sorts. The studio and one-bedroom apartments at the Promenade are comfortable and well equipped; the furnishings are lean and modern. There is a private balcony off of every apartment for enjoying the local scenery. Contact: Villas International, 71 W. 23rd St., New York, NY 10010. Call 212-929-7585.

Children: Y   Pets: N   Smoking: Y   Handicap Access: N   Payment: C, P, T

Ober-Urmein

DANIS CHALET   *Rates: budget*
Open: April 7 - November 20   *Minimum Stay: one week*

This economical chalet is located in Ober-Urmein, a small town perched on the bright slopes of the Heinzberg seven miles from the town of Thusis. The house is made up of a living room/ dining area with a door leading out to a southeast-facing balcony, a well-equipped open kitchen and two bedrooms, one with a double bed and the other containing bunks. The fenced grounds offer deck chairs and other garden furniture. With fine skiing and hiking available locally, the residence is also superbly situated for adventures throughout eastern Switzerland, not to mention journeys over to Austria or the tiny principality of Liechtenstein. Contact: Interhome Inc., 124 Little Falls Road, Fairfield, NJ, 07004. Call 201-882-1742. Ref. C7431/502.

Children: Y   Pets: Y   Smoking: Y   Handicap Access: N   Payment: P, V, M

Schmitten

ALBULA   *Rates: budget-inexpensive*
Open: April 7 - November 20   *Minimum Stay: one week*

This chalet is perched on a slope near Schmitten, a secluded village tucked away in the narrow gorges of the Landwasseer river valley. The area offers tranquility and relaxation, breathtaking scenery, superb skiing and some of the best hiking in Switzerland. Featuring a large, partially covered terrace with barbecue and garden furniture, the two-floor house contains a spacious living room/dining area with fireplace, kitchenette, gallery and four bedrooms, with a balcony that provides sweeping mountain and valley views. Contact: Interhome Inc., 124 Little Falls Road, Fairfield, NJ, 07004. Call 201-882-1742. Ref. C7499/300.

Children: Y   Pets: Y   Smoking: Y   Handicap Access: N   Payment: P, V, M

Segnes

PEISEL HOUSE   *Rates: budget*
Open: April 7 - November 20   *Minimum Stay: one week*

This quality house is one of several modern, well-kept residences in a quiet holiday community 350 yards above the scenic mountain hamlet of Segnes. Comprising a foyer, kitchen, three bedrooms and spacious living room/dining area with large picture windows to take full advantage of the panoromic view, the house also features a covered patio with garden furniture. A ski run passes right by and the woods contain an elaborate network of trails for hiking. The peaks, which pose a rigorous challenge to any climber, are only steps away from the front door. Contact: Interhome Inc., 124 Little Falls Road, Fairfield, NJ, 07004. Call 201-882-1742. Ref. C7181/16.

Children: Y   Pets: Y   Smoking: Y   Handicap Access: N   Payment: P, V, M

Silvaplana

MODERN APARTMENT

Rates: inexpensive

Open: year-round

Minimum Stay: one week

Silvaplana vaunts the perfect Swiss setting: A pretty little village sits on a shining lake surrounded by majestic, ice-capped mountains. Thanks to the glaciers, there is skiing year-round; summer visitors can also amuse themselves with golf, tennis, or sailing, not to mention walks through the spectacular mountain scenery. The apartment is nicely situated on a pleasant street overlooking the lake. The three double bedrooms are comfortably furnished, and the modern kitchen is well equipped. There are laundry facilities available in the building, and the shops and restaurants of the town are just around the corner. Contact: Villas International, 71 W. 23rd St., New York, NY 10010. Call 212-929-7585.

Children: Y   Pets: N   Smoking: Y   Handicap Access: N   Payment: C, P, T

St. Moritz

CHAMPFER APARTMENTS

Rates: moderate-expensive

Open: April 7 - November 20

Minimum Stay: one week

A cross-country ski track passes in front of this attractive, traditional Engadine-style apartment house located in Champfer, a town near the world-famous resort of St. Moritz. Among the elegant, self-contained units available here is a two-bedroom flat on the second floor, luxuriously decorated with country furnishings. It includes a parlor/dining room, very contemporary and well-equipped kitchen and a balcony with a view of the lake. The residence accommodates four guests in style as they enjoy all the matchless recreational and cultural opportunities of St. Moritz: its museums and concert performances, golfing and tennis, spas and saunas, every popular water sport and, of course, its celebrated skiing. Contact: Interhome Inc., 124 Little Falls Road, Fairfield, NJ, 07004. Call 201-882-1742. Ref. C7501/330B.

Children: Y   Pets: Y   Smoking: Y   Handicap Access: N   Payment: P, V, M

St. Moritz

CHESA BELLARIA

Rates: expensive

Open: year-round

Minimum Stay: one week

Located near the exclusive resort of St. Moritz, this spacious villa offers luxurious accommodations while retaining the character of a traditional rustic chalet. The commodious living and dining room features charming furnishings and a cheerful open fireplace; the modern kitchen includes a dishwasher, a microwave and laundry facilities. Five large double bedrooms are located on the second floor, and an additional three beds suitable for children are on the top floor. The house is set on a splendid hillside and enjoys unspoiled, panoramic views of the mountains and valleys. The slopes of Corvatsch and Furtschellas are a few minutes away by car, and summer visitors will appreciate the golf course at nearby Samaden. Contact: Villas International, 71 W. 23rd St., New York, NY 10010. Call 212-929-7585.

Children: Y   Pets: N   Smoking: Y   Handicap Access: N   Payment: C, P, T

LUCERNE

Alpnach

ALPNACH FARMHOUSE FLAT *Rates: budget-moderate*
Open: April 7 - November 20 *Minimum Stay: one week*

This well-appointed four-bedroom apartment, perfect for a large family, is contained in an engaging farmhouse that sits in a spacious grassy area above the quiet hamlet of Alpnach. The flat, built on two floors, features an old-fashioned parlor and large eat-in kitchen, with one bedroom on the first floor and the other three upstairs. About a mile from Alpnach, which is on an especially beautiful arm of Lake Lucerne frequently visited by sightseeing boats, the residence is in an area offering bounteous scenic pleasures and an abundance of recreational activities. Contact: Interhome Inc., 124 Little Falls Road, Fairfield, NJ, 07004. Call 201-882-1742. Ref. C6055/10B.

Children: **Y** Pets: **Y** Smoking: **Y** Handicap Access: **N** Payment: **P, V, M**

Brunnen

BRUNNEN FLAT *Rates: budget*
Open: April 7-November 20 *Minimum Stay: one week*

This handsome country house set in a large tree-filled park on the outskirts of the Lake Lucerne resort of Brunnen contains a comfortable and private apartment available for guests. Located on the second floor, the flat features a sitting room, spacious eat-in kitchen and three bedrooms that sleep up to five, and has shared access to the airy garden patio. All watersports are offered nearby, including boating excursions on the lake, where some fascinating destinations are within easy reach. The historic hamlet of Treib, a key site during the founding of Switzerland, is a mere seven minutes away by water. Contact: Interhome Inc., 124 Little Falls Road, Fairfield, NJ, 07004. Call 201-882-6864. Ref. C6440/10B.

Children: **Y** Pets: **Y** Smoking: **Y** Handicap Access: **N** Payment: **P, V, M**

Dallenwil

AM RAENKLI *Rates: budget*
Open: April 7 - November 20 *Minimum Stay: one week*

Poised at an altitude of 4,000 feet in Dallenwil, an affable village ten miles from Lucerne, this captivatingly secluded house is reachable at some times of the year only by cable car and footpath. Nevertheless, it is very convenient to the grocery, a restaurant, fishing facilities and, needless to say, some exceptional skiing. The house makes a fine vacation residence for families, with a lawn and patio area outside offering garden furniture, a barbecue and swing set, while the interior contains a comfortable sitting room, kitchenette and two bedrooms. Contact: Interhome Inc., 124 Little Falls Road, Fairfield, NJ, 07004. Call 201-882-1742. Ref. C6383/100.

Children: **Y** Pets: **Y** Smoking: **Y** Handicap Access: **N** Payment: **P, V, M**

Engelberg
HAHNENFUSS

Rates: budget

Open: April 7 - November 20

Minimum Stay: one week

Positioned at wood's edge in a prime hiking area, this peaceful chalet stands one and a half miles from the major ski lifts of Engelberg, one of central Switzerland's most desirable resort areas. In addition to the allure of the slopes and the trails, indoor and outdoor tennis, swimming and a horde of other recreational and amusement opportunities are available here. The two-story house features a combined living room/dining area with a tiled stove, kitchenette with breakfast bar and two bedrooms—one with a sloping roof—along with an outside deck. Contact: Interhome Inc., 124 Little Falls Road, Fairfield, NJ, 07004. Call 201-882-1742. Ref. C6390/21.

Children: Y   Pets: Y   Smoking: Y   Handicap Access: N   Payment: P, V, M

Engelberg
OASE

Rates: budget

Open: April 7 - November 20

Minimum Stay: one week

Oase, a small holiday complex in the Langacher district outside Engelberg, provides homey, self-contained apartments. A one-bedroom unit on the first floor of the lodge includes a living/dining room with additional sleeping accommodations for two, a kitchenette and a private terrace, while the second floor of the building features a two-bedroom flat built on two levels and containing a sitting room with fireplace, kitchenette, gallery with two more beds, plus a balcony. Most of the area's notable sports facilities are within a mile. With nightclubs, discos and a movie house in town, as well as the concert festivals and folklore programs offered, the nights at Engelberg hold as many opportunities for fun and excitement as the days. Contact: Interhome Inc., 124 Little Falls Road, Fairfield, NJ, 07004. Call 201-882-1742. Ref. C6390/132A (1 bedroom), C6390133B (2 bedrooms).

Children: Y   Pets: Y   Smoking: Y   Handicap Access: N   Payment: P, V, M

Fluehli
AUF HAHNENWEIDI

Rates: budget

Open: April 7 - November 20

Minimum Stay: one week

Auf Hahnenweidi is an inviting chalet that stands beneath tall pines outside the small woodland village of Fluehli. Offering sweeping views of the surrounding forests and open countryside, the house features a living/dining room, fully equipped kitchen with gas- and wood-fired stove, master bedroom and two other bedrooms, with a large sun terrace and appealing lawn area. The residence is centrally located for excursions to the nearby sport retreat of Sorenberg. Lake Lucerne lies less than a 45-minute drive away and, not much further, is Switzerland's enchanting capital city of Bern. Contact: Interhome Inc., 124 Little Falls Road, Fairfield, NJ, 07004. Call 201-882-1742. Ref. C6173/5.

Children: Y   Pets: Y   Smoking: Y   Handicap Access: N   Payment: P, V, M

Luzern

GUETSCHBAHN APARTMENTS *Rates: budget-moderate*
Open: April 7 - November 20 *Minimum Stay: one week*
For a memorable holiday in Luzern, one of Switzerland's premiere travel destinations, the studio, one- and two-bedroom flats of this gracious apartment house make terrific vacation residences. Only a few minutes from the old town and the lake, each self-contained unit features a well equipped kitchen and its own balcony. The building grounds, right by the entrance of a top nature reserve, include a large sun terrace and grocery. The surrounding town is bursting with life any time of year, with a host of recreational opportunities, renowned landmarks and exciting seasonal events, like the International Music Festival, nocturnal lake festival and folklore carnival. Contact: Interhome Inc., 124 Little Falls Road, Fairfield, NJ, 07004. Call 201-882-1742. Ref. C6000/102E (studio), C6000/122D (1 bedroom), C6000/140E (2 bedroom).
Children: Y   Pets: Y   Smoking: Y   Handicap Access: N   Payment: P, V, M

Vitznau

LAKE APARTMENTS *Rates: inexpensive-expensive*
Open: mid-June-mid-September *Minimum Stay: one week*
Lake Lucerne is one of Switzerland's prettiest and longest lakes, its shores dotted with many resorts as it winds its way through the Alps. For winter visitors, excellent cross-country and downhill skiing is, of course, plentiful in the nearby slopes. Several different apartments are comfortably furnished with bedrooms for two to six guests, a living/dining area, kitchen, bathroom and balcony. All visitors share the use of a swimming pool, sauna, fitness room and two restaurants on the premises. Contact: Villas International, 71 West 23rd Street, New York, NY 10010. Call 1-800-221-2260 (in New York, 212-929-7585).
Children: Y   Pets: N   Smoking: Y   Handicap Access: N   Payment: C, P, T

Weggis

VIERWALD RESIDENCE *Rates: expensive-deluxe*
Open: year-round *Minimum Stay: one week*
Palm trees in Switzerland? Some delightful quirk of nature has given Lake Lucerne a surprisingly mild climate in addition to its lovely waters and splendid setting. The area offers lovely mountain walks and water sports during the summer and, of course, excellent skiing in the winter. The two-, three-, and four-room apartments in the handsome Vierwald Residence feature wonderful views of the surrounding countryside. The sunny rooms are charmingly furnished in the traditional Swiss style, with exposed-beam ceilings and rustic furniture. The residence is set right on the lake, so swimming in its clear waters is popular during the summer; there is also an indoor swimming pool. Daily maid service and color TV are additional advantages. Contact: Villas International, 71 W. 23rd St., New York, NY 10010. Call 212-929-7585.
Children: Y   Pets: N   Smoking: Y   Handicap Access: N   Payment: C, P, T

TICINO

Brissago

BRISSAGO VILLA   *Rates: deluxe*
Open: March 5-November 25   *Minimum Stay: one week*

You'll find this luxurious villa on a sunny hillside not far from the majestic southern border, where people speak the Italian dialect they've spoken since before the region became part of Switzerland in 1803. The villa offers fine views of the Alps and Lake Maggiore, and a beautiful yard dotted with flowers and palm trees. A private road leads up to the villa, which boasts a private swimming pool, large terrace and partially covered balcony with a grill for outdoor dining. Four bedrooms are roomy enough for seven and a modern kitchen, fireplace, radio and color TV add to your comfort. Contact: Hilde Freeman, Rent A Home International, Inc., 7200 34th Avenue N.W., Seattle, WA 98117. Call 206-545-6963.

Children: **Y** Pets: **N** Smoking: **Y** Handicap Access: **N** Payment: **C, P, V, M**

Cadro

PANORAMICA RESIDENCE   *Rates: inexpensive-deluxe*
Open: July-August   *Minimum Stay: one week*

This popular Alpine retreat sits high up in the mountains, affording scenic views of Lake Lugano and the surrounding hills. You can hike, swim, ski or participate in a variety of water sports during the day, and then relax in the sauna, take in a game of tennis or have a leisurely dinner at the restaurant. There are several apartments available, sleeping up to eight people, and each features a living/dining room, fully equipped kitchen, one or more baths, and a terrace or balcony. The resort is near the snow-capped peaks that are mirrored in lovely Lake Como and not far from the year-round festivities in St. Moritz and Milan. Contact: Villas International, 71 West 23rd Street, New York, NY 10010. Call 1-800-221-2260 (in New York, 212-929-7585).

Children: **Y** Pets: **N** Smoking: **Y** Handicap Access: **N** Payment: **C, P, T**

Caminada

OR FU FING   *Rates: budget-inexpensive*
Open: April 7 - November 20   *Minimum Stay: one week*

Situated below Ponte Valentine in the quiet village of Caminada deep in the Valle di Blenio, Or Fu Fing is a charming chalet superb for a family seeking a holiday in one of Switzerland's most fascinating regions. Good roads and a bus service run the length of the verdant valley, offering visitors the chance to enjoy its picturesque hamlets, lush plant life and historic Roman churches. Making a tranquil home base for these adventures, the two-floor house contains a combined living/dining room with fireplace and large kitchen opening onto a pleasant garden area. A wooden stairway leads to two double bedrooms and a balcony that overlooks the surrounding vineyards. Contact: Interhome Inc., 124 Little Falls Road, Fairfield, NJ, 07004. Call 201-882-1742. Ref. C6711/11.

Children: **Y** Pets: **Y** Smoking: **Y** Handicap Access: **N** Payment: **P, V, M**

Locarno

LOCARNO TERRACE HOUSE
Open: April 7 - November 20

Rates: budget-inexpensive
Minimum Stay: one week

Less than a mile from the center of the dynamic resort town of Locarno, this rustic residence is a fine example of a characteristic Ticinese terrace house. It's decorated with contemporary furniture and contains a parlor, kitchenette, gallery stairway and double bedroom. Meandering down the town's quaint old streets and along the countryside lanes, visitors to Locarno will find such diverse attractions as a lively flea market, tennis, golf, skiing, water sports on the river Maggia and Lake Maggiore and, in the summer, a renowned international film festival. Contact: Interhome Inc., 124 Little Falls Road, Fairfield, NJ, 07004. Call 201-882-1742. Ref. C6600/201.

Children: Y   Pets: Y   Smoking: Y   Handicap Access: N   Payment: P, V, M

Locarno

MINUSIO VILLAS AND APARTMENTS
Open: July-August

Rates: inexpensive-expensive
Minimum Stay: two weeks

These well-equipped, comfortably furnished villas and apartments are located on Lake Maggiore, one of the sunniest places in all of Switzerland, where panoramic views of the mountains, mild winters and hot summers make for great vacations. Follow the lake south as it spills into Italy, visit the historic city of Milan or drive northeast to the resorts in St. Moritz. Choose a two-bedroom villa or apartment for two to seven people, all featuring a living/dining room, kitchen and one or more baths. Some of the apartments offer a terrace, balcony or garden. Guests have the use of a heated swimming pool in the complex. Contact: Villas International, 71 West 23rd Street, New York, NY 10010. Call 1-800-221-2260 (in New York, 212-929-7585).

Children: Y   Pets: N   Smoking: Y   Handicap Access: N   Payment: C, P, T

Ponte Valentino

CASA DI CAMILLA
Open: April 7 - November 20

Rates: budget-moderate
Minimum Stay: one week

Casa di Camilla is an august 200-year-old country house recently renovated to provide completely modern facilities along with authentic 18th-century atmosphere. Surrounded by grounds made up of a vineyard, lawn and garden and featuring a covered patio area offering a grill and outdoor furniture, the residence is just outside Ponte Valentino in the heart of the Valle di Blenio. With a trout-filled river flowing right by, the two-story house includes a living room with fireplace and wooden ceilings and a kitchen plus dining corner. Four guests can sleep in two double bedrooms, one opening onto a balcony that commands a terrific view of the countryside. Contact: Interhome Inc., 124 Little Falls Road, Fairfield, NJ 07004. Call 201-882-1742. Ref. C6711/14.

Children: Y   Pets: Y   Smoking: Y   Handicap Access: N   Payment: P, V, M

San Nazzaro

CASA BECK

Open: April 7 - November 20

Rates: budget-inexpensive

Minimum Stay: one week

Holding two separate, comfortable apartments, Casa Beck is an inviting house built on an elevated site overlooking Lake Maggiore and the surrounding mountains in San Nazzaro. The studio flat is located on the first floor and contains a kitchenette and a small private patio, while the two-bedroom unit on the second floor features a parlor with fireplace, a kitchen and a large balcony. The lake provides numerous recreational activities, from swimming to boating to windsurfing; nearby Locarno offers more sport and entertainment attractions. Contact: Interhome Inc., 124 Little Falls Road, Fairfield, NJ 07004. Call 201-882-1742. Ref. C6575/5A (studio), C6575-5B (2 bedroom).

Children: Y Pets: Y Smoking: Y Handicap Access: N Payment: P, V, M

Scaiano

LA TORTUE

Open: April 7 - November 20

Rates: budget-inexpensive

Minimum Stay: one week

This two-story terrace house stands on the outskirts of Scaiano, a lovely village set on a gentle slope near the Swiss/Italian border. Lake Maggiore is less than a mile away, while excursions to Locarno and market trips to Luino, Italy, allow visitors the chance to enjoy the charms of both countries at their leisure. Containing a living room with fireplace, a large and well-equipped kitchen/dining room and bedroom on the first floor, plus three more bedrooms upstairs, the residence accommodates up to seven comfortably and features a sunny patio with deck chairs. Contact: Interhome Inc., 124 Little Falls Road, Fairfield, NJ, 07004. Call 201-882-1742. Ref. C6578/1.

Children: Y Pets: Y Smoking: Y Handicap Access: N Payment: P, V, M

Vira-Gambarogno

VIRAMONTE

Open: March 3-November 20

Rates: budget-moderate

Minimum Stay: one week

Located in the quaint town of Vira-Gambarogno, this complex of six residential buildings on a beautiful estate overlooking Lake Maggiore provides a number of studio, one- and two-bedroom flats. Each unit, furnished warmly in traditional Swiss-Italian style, includes a well-equipped kitchenette and either a private patio, garden or balcony, most with gorgeous views of the lake. The grounds offer a swimming pool, a lawn with a play area and a breakfast cafe. Whether you stroll down the town's narrow streets to visit its exquisite old churches, hike along the roads and footpaths on Monte-Gambarogno or enjoy water sports on Lake Maggiore, there's a remarkable variety of holiday pleasures available in the region. Contact: Interhome Inc., 124 Little Falls Road, Fairfield, NJ 07004. Call 201-882-6864. Ref. C6573/102B,121B,127A (studios), C6573/131C,140D,150C (1 bedrooms), C6573/160C (2 bedrooms).

Children: Y Pets: Y Smoking: Y Handicap Access: N Payment: P, V, M

VALAIS

Crans-Montana

BELLA YOUVA CHALET *Rates: budget-expensive*
Open: April 7-November 20 *Minimum Stay: one week*

This spacious chalet is located on the outskirts of CransMontana, one of the most elegant resorts of the Valasian Alps. Offering majestic views, the two-story house contains a parlor/dining room with open fireplace, well-equipped kitchen and four bedrooms sleeping seven, and features a balcony and restful garden with table and deck chairs for enjoying refreshing outdoor meals. Spend the day skiing or pursuing other recreational activities in the area, then join the other visitors at Montana's lively casino in the evening. Contact: Interhome Inc., 124 Little Falls Road, Fairfield, NJ 07004. Call 201-882-6864. Ref. C3962/6.

Children: **Y** Pets: **N** Smoking: **Y** Handicap Access: **N** Payment: **P, V, M**

Crans-Montana

MATOU BLANC ROUGE *Rates: budget-expensive*
Open: April 7 - November 20 *Minimum Stay: one week*

This chalet in the outskirts of Montana commands sensational views of the Alps and the Rhone Valley from the terrace that wraps around three sides of the building. Inside, the two-story residence offers a large living room/dining area with fireplace and a well-equipped kitchen and gallery, with three bedrooms downstairs. A lawn with garden furniture provides a quiet spot to enjoy a break from all the recreational and entertainment activities available nearby. Contact: Interhome Inc., 124 Little Falls Road, Fairfield, NJ 07004. Call 201-882-1742. Ref. C3962/50.

Children: **Y** Pets: **Y** Smoking: **Y** Handicap Access: **N** Payment: **P, V, M**

Ernen

ARAGON APARTMENTS *Rates: budget*
Open: April 7-November 20 *Minimum Stay: one week*

Aragon, a friendly holiday complex near the ancient village of Ernen, offers an assortment of quality apartments, all with their own balconies commanding majestic views of the nearby peaks that soar more than ten thousand feet above sea level. The two-room flats contain a double bedroom, kitchenette and living room with extra beds, making comfortable and economical Alpine holiday residences for couples or small families. Hiking, mountaineering and skiing are the main activities in this area dominated by the majestic Aletsch glacier. The residence itself features outdoor Ping-Pong and chess, a picnic area with barbecues and a playground. Contact: Interhome Inc., 124 Little Falls Road, Fairfield, NJ 07004. Call 201-882-6864. Ref. C3979/123B.

Children: **Y** Pets: **N** Smoking: **Y** Handicap Access: **N** Payment: **P, V, M**

Grone

PETITE FLEUR CHALET *Rates: budget*
Open: April 7-November 20 *Minimum Stay: one week*

A short footpath leads to this isolated chalet located in Loye, a tiny mountain village above the picturesque resort of Grone. With a beautiful view across the Rhone Valley, the house contains a living room with fireplace and gallery, a well-equipped kitchen and two comfy bedrooms, and features a delightful garden with a barbecue and patio furniture. The residence is a fine starting point for either leisurely or rigorous hikes in the mountains and through the valleys. The area also offers tennis, downhill and cross-country skiing and other excellent recreational opportunities. Contact: Interhome Inc., 124 Little Falls Road, Fairfield, NJ 07004. Call 201-882-6864. Ref. C1974/40.

Children: **Y**   Pets: **N**   Smoking: **Y**   Handicap Access: **N**   Payment: **P, V, M**

Nendaz

BERLIZE CHALET   *Rates: budget-moderate*
Open: April 7-November 20   *Minimum Stay: one week*

Commanding a sensational view of the Rhone valley below, this two-story chalet is located in the small hamlet of Sornard less than two miles from the holiday center of Nendaz. The house is surrounded by lawns and contains three bedrooms, a kitchenette and a drawing room/dining area with an open fireplace, plus a balcony and a garden area to provide guests with the maximum opportunity to enjoy the awesome scenery. A wonderful vacation choice for families: Rebates are given during the summer, and most of the facilities at Nendaz, including its tennis courts, ski lifts and restaurants, offer discounts or free entry for children. Contact: Interhome Inc., 124 Little Falls Road, Fairfield, NJ 07004. Call 201-882-6864. Ref. C1961/13.

Children: **Y**   Pets: **N**   Smoking: **Y**   Handicap Access: **N**   Payment: **P, V, M**

Ovronnaz

L'ALPAGE CHALET   *Rates: budget-inexpensive*
Open: April 7-November 20   *Minimum Stay: one week*

Set back from the main road in a bright and tranquil location, this attractive chalet lies on the outskirts of Ovronnaz, a well-known health resort between the larger towns of Martigny and Sion. The three-floor house includes three bedrooms, kitchen with dishwasher, balcony overlooking the lawn, parlor/dining room with fireplace and a basement family room with access to the terrace. The area offers numerous recreational opportunities, featuring full ski facilities—including a ski school—tennis courts, a fitness course and miles of woodland hiking trails. Contact: Interhome Inc., 124 Little Falls Road, Fairfield, NJ 07004. Call 201-882-6864. Ref. C1912/13.

Children: **Y**   Pets: **N**   Smoking: **Y**   Handicap Access: **N**   Payment: **P, V, M**

Saas Fee

CASANOU CHALET   *Rates: inexpensive-expensive*
Open: March 31-November 20   *Minimum Stay: one week*

A spacious Saas Fee chalet ideal for families vacationing together, Casanou has a playground out front and is a short walk from the sports center. The three-level house features two bedrooms and a ski-storage alcove on the ground floor, a big living room/dining area with fireplace, well-equipped kitchen, double bedroom and large balcony upstairs, plus a loft containing two more double bedrooms. Cars are not allowed in the hub of the resort area, so children can venture out on their own in total safety while the grown-ups enjoy a Jacuzzi, massage and Turkish bath. The whole gang can meet up to try some cross-country or summer skiing, play a bit of tennis or a round of miniature golf, frolic in the pool or take a refreshing mountain hike. Contact: Interhome Inc., 124 Little Falls Road, Fairfield, NJ 07004. Call 201-882-6864. Ref. C3906/15.

Children: Y   Pets: N   Smoking: Y   Handicap Access: N   Payment: P, V, M

Saas Fee

CHATEAU MIGNON   *Rates: budget-inexpensive*
Open: March 31-November 20   *Minimum Stay: one week*

Chateau Mignon is a cozy, secluded residence resting in an open field in the Saas Valley. While this is the largest and best-known sports community in the Valais region, the resort, enclosed by a luminous, semi-circular glacier, retains an enchanting traditional Alpine village character. The house contains a bedroom with bunk beds, kitchenette and a large living room/dining area with two fold-out beds and a door to the balcony. A ski lift and leisure center, which features the sport of curling, are steps away, and the extraordinary recreational facilities of Saas Fee are all within easy reach. Contact: Interhome Inc., 124 Little Falls Road, Fairfield, NJ 07004. Call 201-882-6864. Ref. C3906/13.

Children: Y   Pets: N   Smoking: Y   Handicap Access: N   Payment: P, V, M

Tasch

MATTERTAL APARTMENTS   *Rates: inexpensive-moderate*
Open: year-round   *Minimum Stay: one week*

Tasch is a pretty alpine village with weathered wooden chalets nestled amongst the larches and pines. A shuttle leaves every half hour and will bring you to the slopes at Zermatt within ten minutes. With marvelous views of the Little Matterhorn, the Mattertal apartments offer comfortable accommodations in a peaceful area. The one- and two-bedroom apartments can sleep up to seven people. Some boast handsome open fireplaces and all feature roomy balconies where you can breathe deeply of the clear, cold air and watch the last glimmers of twilight play across the sparkling snows. Contact: Villas International, 71 W. 23rd St., New York, NY 10010. Call 212-929-7585.

Children: Y   Pets: N   Smoking: Y   Handicap Access: N   Payment: C, P, T

Verbier

LARA HOUSE   *Rates: budget-expensive*
Open: April 7-November 20   *Minimum Stay: one week*

Containing two guest apartments, this comfortable house is located in Verbier, a renowned holiday community lying on a scenic plateau in the Val de Bagnes. Verbier offers exceptional indoor and outdoor sports facilities, including a golf course, thirteen tennis courts, ski runs and lifts and a modern recreation center with a pool, saunas, squash courts and ice-skating rink. A flat on the third floor holds three bedrooms, drawing room and kitchen, while the fourth-floor unit also features a balcony and small extra bedroom across the hall. Contact: Interhome Inc., 124 Little Falls Road, Fairfield, NJ 07004. Call 201-882-6864. Ref. C1935/12C (3rd floor), C1935/12D (4th floor).

Children: Y   Pets: N   Smoking: Y   Handicap Access: N   Payment: P, V, M

Verbier

MITSOUKO CHALET   *Rates: budget-moderate*
Open: April 7-November 20   *Minimum Stay: one week*

A self-contained two-bedroom apartment with a kitchenette, living room/dining area and private terrace is one of two units housed in this traditional Swiss chalet located near the center of Verbier. Right by the aerial cableway and children's ski lift, the residence is convenient to all of the amenities of the fashionable resort. Traverse over a hundred miles of exhilarating hiking trails or enjoy the summer skiing at nearby Mount Font. Evenings on the town offer a choice of fifty fine restaurants, followed by a visit to one of Verbier's four flashy discotheques. Contact: Interhome Inc., 124 Little Falls Road, Fairfield, NJ 07004. Call 201-882-6864. Ref. C1935/47A.

Children: Y   Pets: N   Smoking: Y   Handicap Access: N   Payment: P, V, M

Zermatt

BAZZIT HOUSE   *Rates: budget-inexpensive*
Open: April 7-November 20   *Minimum Stay: one week*

A self-contained apartment is available on the second floor of this pleasant house, which enjoys a sunny and tranquil location. Reached by a steep footpath, the residence offers captivating mountain views and includes a bedroom, kitchen, living room/dining area containing two additional beds, plus a corner balcony with patio furniture from which to savor the view of the Matterhorn. The shuttle train takes visitors into nearby Zermatt, the world-famous resort, which offers exceptional tennis, swimming, hiking, summer skiing, miniature golf and exciting opportunities for robust late-night adventures. Contact: Interhome Inc., 124 Little Falls Road, Fairfield, NJ 07004. Call 201-882-6864. Ref. C3920/329B.

Children: Y   Pets: N   Smoking: Y   Handicap Access: N   Payment: P, V, M

Zermatt

CHALET TALISMAN   *Rates: deluxe*
Open: year-round   *Minimum Stay: one week*

Imagine a horse-drawn sleigh bringing you to your cozy chalet after a fabulous day of skiing in the magnificent Alps. As you sip a warm toddy in front of the blazing fire, you remember the gleaming white snow, the endless blue sky and the crisp air—and you realize that all this can be yours again tomorrow. The spacious Chalet Talisman boasts comfortable furnishings, an open fireplace in the living room, a separate dining room, a fully equipped kitchen, and five large bedrooms. For your amusement during those few hours off the slopes, there is a TV and a VCR. The skiing here is year-round, and you can even ski across the border into Italy. Contact: Villas International, 71 W. 23rd St., New York, NY 10010. Call 212-929-7585.

Children: Y   Pets: N   Smoking: Y   Handicap Access: N   Payment: C, P, T

Zermatt

LE GROS CAILLOU CHALET   *Rates: budget-moderate*
Open: April 7-November 20   *Minimum Stay: one week*

Resting in a secluded forest clearing with a marvelous view of the Matterhorn, this likeable chalet in the Oberhaeusern quarter is next to the skier's paradise of Zermatt. Motor cars are banned at the resort, preserving its traditional Alpine village atmosphere, but horse-drawn carriages and electric taxis are available to take visitors from the bustling main street, with its restaurants, taverns, dance clubs and movie theater, to the ski area and all the other choice recreational facilities. The two-story house contains a living room, kitchenette, three bedrooms and large balcony. Just outside, trails lead into the surrounding woods for exhilarating Alpine hikes. Contact: Interhome Inc., 124 Little Falls Road, Fairfield, NJ 07004. Call 201-882-6864. Ref. C3920/5.

Children: Y   Pets: N   Smoking: Y   Handicap Access: N   Payment: P, V, M

VAUD

Alpe-des-Chaux

COMBE DU SCEX CHALET   *Rates: budget*
Open: April 7-November 20   *Minimum Stay: one week*

A short walk from the nearest ski run, this comfortable chalet is just outside the sunny and picturesque family resort of Alpedes-Chaux, five miles north of Villars. The residence can accommodate up to six and contains a living room/dining area with open fireplace, kitchenette and two bedrooms. Tennis is available nearby and the immediate area also features many terrific Alpine trails that offer hikers either leisurely strolls or challenging treks. Contact: Interhome Inc., 124 Little Falls Road, Fairfield, NJ 07004. Call 201-882-6864. Ref. C1882/19.

Children: Y   Pets: N   Smoking: Y   Handicap Access: N   Payment: P, V, M

Chateau d'Oex

SWISS CHALET   *Rates: expensive-deluxe*
Open: year-round   *Minimum Stay: one week*

This sunny chalet nestled in the Gstaad valley offers superb views of the majestic mountains. The large rooms spread over three floors, and doubled glazed windows and central heating keeps the chalet toasty warm. Three bedrooms—two double and one with bunk beds—and a wide, sunny balcony that doubles as a third double bedroom, sleep six to eight, and there's a large TV in one of two living rooms. A ten-minute walk takes you to the center of Chateau d'Oex, where you'll find a variety of restaurants and shops. It's worth a trip to Bern (75 miles) to visit the Kunstmuseum, which has the largest collection in the world of works by Paul Klee. Contact: Hilde Freeman, Rent A Home International, Inc., 7200 34th Avenue N.W., Seattle, WA 98117.

Call 206-545-6963.

Children: Y Pets: N Smoking: Y Handicap Access: N Payment: C, P, V, M

Savigny

ZENTNER HOUSE

Rates: inexpensive

Open: April 7-November 20

Minimum Stay: one week

Set on a quiet slope with panoramic views of Lake Geneva and the Savoyen Alps, Zentner is two miles from the small resort of Sauvigny and ten miles from Lausanne. The spacious residence, built on four floors, contains a large living room/dining area with fireplace, a kitchen and four bedrooms. Outside is a pleasant garden area with a patio, well-manicured lawn and table and chairs for enjoying the sunny afternoons. The area immediately around the house offers many paths for bracing woodland hikes and cross-country skiing in season, while golf and tennis near town, and water sports on the lake, are all only minutes away. Contact: Interhome Inc., 124 Little Falls Road, Fairfield, NJ 07004. Call 201-882-6864. Ref. C1073/1.

Children: Y Pets: N Smoking: Y Handicap Access: N Payment: P, V, M

Ste. Croix

LES PETITES ROCHES CHALET

Rates: budget

Open: April 7-November 20

Minimum Stay: one week

Resting on a sunny slope, this three-floor chalet stands two miles outside Ste. Croix, the Jura mountain resort near the French border. The house contains four bedrooms, a kitchenette, living room/dining area with a fireplace and additional beds to sleep a total of ten, plus a small balcony and, for an extra charge, a sauna. The area offers over a hundred miles of superb hiking trails, including the Jura highland route dotted with over a dozen courtesy cabins serving refreshments. Also within easy reach are skiing facilities, a swimming pool and an ice-skating rink, while the town features a number of interesting activities, including a renowned juke box museum and a weekly farmer's market. Contact: Interhome Inc., 124 Little Falls Road, Fairfield, NJ 07004. Call 201-882-6864. Ref. C3979/123B.

Children: Y Pets: N Smoking: Y Handicap Access: N Payment: P, V, M

Vevey

MODERN CHALET

Rates: expensive

Open: year-round

Minimum Stay: two weeks

Vevey lies on Lake Geneva, between Lausanne, which is the home of the International Olympic Committee, and Montreux, known as the center of the Vaud Riviera because of its mild climate. Fig, cypress, palm and walnut trees grow around the lakes and in the hills, and some of Switzerland's finest cheeses and wines are produced here. This luxurious new chalet boasts splendid views of the lake and offers many amenities, including a grand piano in the living room and maid service by arrangement. Six guests can be accommodated in two bedrooms and a loft. Open-air theater, concerts, sporting and recreational activities are available throughout the area. Contact: Villas International, 71 West 23rd Street, New York, NY 10010. Call 1-800-221-2260 (in New York, 212-929-7585).

Children: Y Pets: N Smoking: Y Handicap Access: N Payment: C, P, T

Villars

AGATE APARTMENTS *Rates: budget*
Open: April 7-November 20 *Minimum Stay: one week*

This homey chalet-style apartment house enjoys a sunny position above Villars, half a mile from the center of town. Comfortable, self-contained studio, one- and two-bedroom flats are available on the second floor, each with a kitchenette and a south-facing balcony offering panoramic mountain views. Surrounded by a pretty lawn, the building is next to skiing, tennis and squash facilities; the plentiful recreational and entertainment opportunities of Villars are only minutes away. Contact: Interhome Inc., 124 Little Falls Road, Fairfield, NJ 07004. Call 201-882-6864. Ref. C1884/415B (studio), C1884/414B (one bedroom), C1884/417B (two bedrooms).

Children: Y Pets: N Smoking: Y Handicap Access: N Payment: P, V, M

Villars

CHALET EAU VIVE *Rates: budget-inexpensive*
Open: April 7-November 20 *Minimum Stay: one week*

Resting in an elevated, sunny location, Chalet Eau Vive is less than half a mile from the resort of Villars. The house includes a combined living room/dining area with an open fireplace, kitchen and bedroom on the first floor and three additional bedrooms upstairs. A balcony and pleasant garden allow guests to enjoy the lovely surroundings. Along with the exceptional facilities and attractions available in town, Lake Geneva is a mere fifteen miles away, and there's an exhilarating cable railway nearby that takes visitors to a gorgeous mountaintop vista. Contact: Interhome Inc., 124 Little Falls Road, Fairfield, NJ 07004. Call 201-882-6864. Ref. C1885/2.

Children: Y Pets: N Smoking: Y Handicap Access: N Payment: P, V, M

ZURICH

Zurich

RESIDENCE VOLKMAR *Rates: moderate-expensive*
Open: year-round *Minimum Stay: four nights*

On a quaint, sloping street above the River Limmat stands the Residence Volkmar with its comfortably furnished guest quarters. A studio apartment for two includes a kitchen, a living/dining area with a convertible bed and a full bathroom. The three-room apartment for up to four guests also includes a cozy bedroom. A convenient tram will take you directly to the center of Zurich, a city rich in historic buildings, fine museums and elegant stores. The serene waters of Lake Zurich, on whose northern shore the city is built, is a lovely place for a boat ride, and skiing opportunities abound in the surrounding mountains. Contact: Villas International, 71 W. 23rd St., New York, NY 10010. Call 212-929-7585.

Children: Y Pets: N Smoking: Y Handicap Access: N Payment: C, P, T

Wales

CLWYD

Colwyn Bay

THE FARMHOUSE
Open: year-round

Rates: budget-inexpensive
Minimum Stay: one week

Located on a working farm on the coast of Northern Wales, this enchanting, renovated house built around 1500 still contains many of its original features. The living room offers a splendid inglenook fireplace, with ceiling beams of old wood in this uncommon, elegantly furnished two-story residence. A steep and narrow spiral staircase leads to the two second-floor bedrooms. Sheep and cattle roam the grounds of this seventy-acre farm, which also includes a well-tended garden for the guests' private use. Don't miss the ruins of an ancient Roman road that runs right through the farmyard. Contact: Interhome Inc., 124 Little Falls Road, Fairfield, NJ 07004. Call 201-882-6864. Ref. G6001/100.

Children: Y   Pets: N   Smoking: Y   Handicap Access: N   Payment: P, V, M

Llangar

PLAS UCHAF
Open: year-round

Rates: budget-inexpensive
Minimum Stay: one week

This 14th-century hall house is the ancestral home of the family of Hugh of Gwerclas. Craggy stone walls support the ceiling's heavy oaken beams, darkened by the hearth fires of generations. The magnificent fireplace was added in the 16th century and now provides a handsome focal point for the ancient hall. Plas Uchaf has been comfortably furnished and welcomes guests who will savor its venerable heritage and tranquil location. Set in a pleasant valley of the river Dee, the house is near Ruthin and Chirk Castles. Pretty Bala Lake beckons to the west, while beautiful Mount Snowdon awaits you in the north. Contact: The Landmark Trust, Shottesbrooke, Maidenhead, Berkshire, England SL6 3SW. Call 44-0628-82-5925.

Children: Y   Pets: N   Smoking: Y   Handicap Access: N   Payment: V, M, EC

Llangollen

ERW GERRIG COTTAGES
Open: year-round

Rates: budget-inexpensive
Minimum Stay: one week

The dramatic, steep-sided landscape of Ceirog Valley forms the backdrop for Erw Gerrig ("stony acre" in Gaelic), two peaceful cottages surrounded by the unspoiled beauty of the North Welsh countryside. Guests can wander the fourteen acres of untamed land to search for wildlife and fish in the owner's trout lake. Converted stone farm buildings, the two cottages are simply but comfortably furnished to sleep two to six, and have modern kitchens and color TV. Explore the highest waterfall in Wales at Pistyll Rhaeadr and the 14th-century stone bridge at Llangollen, both within six miles. Castles, mansions and other historic sites lie a short drive from the cottages. Contact: Blakes Vacations, 4918 Dempster Street, Skokie, IL 60077. Call 1-800-628-8118.

Children: Y   Pets: N   Smoking: Y   Handicap Access: N   Payment: V, M

St. Asaph

WIGFAIR HALL
Open: year-round

Rates: expensive-deluxe
Minimum Stay: one week

This elegant 19th-century house has 23 acres of terraced gardens and parkland that overlook the River Elwy Valley and the Clwydian mountain range. Large stone mullion windows throughout provide plenty of light and gorgeous views of the magnificent Welsh countryside. Inside, antiques and fine oil paintings punctuate the well-furnished rooms, including an oak-paneled dining room and a large drawing room with ornate molded ceilings and a grand piano. A game room offers table tennis and pool table. There's room enough for thirteen guests, with four double bedrooms, two twins and a cot. The area is a golfer's paradise, with six courses nearby. Beaches, mountains and castles are also within easy reach. Contact: British Travel Associates, P.O. Box

299, Elkton, VA 22827. Call 1-800-327-6097 (in Virginia, 703-298-2232). Ref. JBY.

Children: Y   Pets: N   Smoking: Y   Handicap Access: N   Payment: All

DYFED

Cardigan

ST. MARY'S COTTAGE   *Rates: budget-inexpensive*
Open: year-round   *Minimum Stay: one week*

Located near the center of Cardigan, a quiet market town on the River Teifi, St. Mary's Cottage is a charming residence that features a lovely garden with rose trellises, patio and a lawn. The delightfully decorated house contains a living room adorned with a ship's piano, grandfather clock and large, hand-carved chess set, a dining room with fine oak furniture, a modern kitchen opening onto the garden and three comfortable bedrooms. An abundance of recreational opportunities are within easy reach: A splendid sports facility with an indoor swimming pool is two hundred yards away; superb trout and salmon fishing, as well as river cruises, are available on the Teifi; and a golf course and the sandy beaches of Cardigan Bay are nearby. Contact: British Travel Associates, P.O. Box 299, Elkton, VA 22827. Call 1-800-327-6097 (703-298-2232 in Virginia).

Children: Y   Pets: N   Smoking: Y   Handicap Access: N   Payment: All

Glandwr

ABERELWYN GRANARY   *Rates: budget*
Open: year-round   *Minimum Stay: one week*

This cozy, converted granary surrounded by a hilly paddock on the grounds of Aberelwyn Mill in the heart of rural Wales makes an uncommon and charming holiday home for two. Overlooking the old mill, a dairy farm and wooded area, the residence is close to the small village of Glandwr and within easy reach of the stunning Pembrokeshire coast. The granary contains a kitchen with whitewashed open stone walls and wood-burning stove on the first floor. A steep stone staircase leads to a sitting room that features a pitched, beamed ceiling and a bedroom that opens onto a balcony above the tranquil mill stream. Contact: British Travel Associates, P.O. Box 299, Elkton, VA 22827. Call 1-800-327-6097 (703-298-2232 in Virginia).

Children: Y   Pets: N   Smoking: Y   Handicap Access: N   Payment: All

Llanarthney

TOWER HILL LODGE   *Rates: budget-inexpensive*
Open: year-round   *Minimum Stay: one week*

This charming old cottage, with its picturesque flagstone courtyard and twin chimneys, dates to the beginning of the 19th century. Set high on a hillside, it enjoys fine views of the surrounding countryside to the south. A bit higher on the hill is Paxton's Tower, a crenelated curiosity built as a scenic focal point around the same time. Up here the views are even lovelier. To the west you look down the verdant valley of the river of Tywi, bending and coursing past castles and mountains. The cottage features a fully modernized interior and it is conveniently located near the waters of Carmarthen Bay. Contact: The Landmark Trust, Shottesbrooke, Maidenhead, Berkshire, England SL6 3SW. Call 44-0628-82-5925.

Children: Y Pets: N Smoking: Y Handicap Access: N Payment: V, M, EC

Llandissilio

AERONDEG HOUSE   *Rates: budget*
Open: year-round   *Minimum Stay: one week*

This large and modernized house offers a good base for exploring the "blue stones" of the nearby Preseli Mountains and the wonderful Welsh countryside of old castles and working sheep and cattle farms. Four adults and one child can sleep comfortably in three bedrooms, and the large modern kitchen features a dishwasher and a washing machine. The house stands within walking distance of the owner's motel, which has a restaurant, bar and shop. Also nearby is Pembrokeshire National Park, with its outstanding views of the coast. Contact: Blakes Vacations, 4918 Dempster Street, Skokie, IL 60077. Call 1-800-628-8118. Ref. UAR.

Children: Y Pets: N Smoking: Y Handicap Access: N Payment: V, M

Llwyncelyn

CELYN VILLA   *Rates: budget-inexpensive*
Open: year-round   *Minimum Stay: one week*

Celyn Villa is an attractive village cottage that was once the residence of a respected Welsh sea captain. His descendants now own the house as well as a nearby horsebreeding farm, where guests are invited to visit and children may be given a free ride. Close to several picturesque harbor villages and sandy beaches, the area offers excellent opportunities for fishing, boating and pub-crawling. The house features a pleasant garden overlooking the surrounding farmland and contains a living room/dining area with open fireplace, a kitchen with French doors leading to the garden and two handsomely decorated bedrooms upstairs. Contact: British Travel Associates, P.O. Box 299, Elkton, VA 22827. Call 1-800-327-6097 (703-298-2232 in Virginia).

Children: Y Pets: N Smoking: Y Handicap Access: N Payment: All

Pembrokeshire National Park

ROCH CASTLE   *Rates: budget-expensive*
Open: year-round   *Minimum Stay: one week*

The Norman invaders traveled no further into Wales than Roch Castle, which was built in the 13th century and marks the northern limits of the conquest. Enter the main castle's large hall to mount the curved stone staircase and climb to the living room and baronial dining area, then climb one more flight to the modern kitchen. Children will especially love to explore the castle's secret dungeon passage. Ten can sleep in the main wing, while the self-contained west wing sleeps six in three bedrooms and has a modern kitchen as well as a living room and dining room. The castle lies within Pembrokeshire National Park,

which boasts a long stretch of coastline with magnificent views of craggy cliffs and sandy beaches. Contact: Blakes Vacations, 4918 Dempster Street, Skokie, IL 60077. Call 1-800-628-8118. Ref. UAR.
Children: Y   Pets: N   Smoking: Y   Handicap Access: N   Payment: V, M

St. Davids

15 TOWER HILL   *Rates: budget-inexpensive*
Open: year-round   *Minimum Stay: one week*

On a pleasant peninsula flanking St. Brides Bay is the charming town of St. Davids, with its impressive cathedral and quiet streets. The modern cottage at 15 Tower Hill enjoys a striking view of the cathedral's tower, perched as it is on a tall hillside nearby. With a view of the tower from one window and cheerful sunlight streaming in through another, the cottage's living room is a pleasant place to relax after a day at the seaside, scarcely a mile away. The coastal pathway follows along the edge of the peninsula and there are fishing and sailing opportunities over in the bay. Contact: The Landmark Trust, Shottesbrooke, Maidenhead, Berkshire, England SL6 3SW. Call 440628-82-5925.
Children: Y   Pets: N   Smoking: Y   Handicap Access: N   Payment: V, M, EC

GWENT

Abergavenny

CLYTHA CASTLE   *Rates: inexpensive-moderate*
Open: year-round   *Minimum Stay: one week*

This extravagant crenelated castle, with its frivolous towers and merrily arching battlements, was built by William Jones of Clytha House in 1790 as a memorial to his late wife Elizabeth. Whether she would have appreciated the gesture is unknown, but visitors today treasure the unique architecture and marvelous setting. The castle is situated at the top of a gentle hill and overlooks a pleasant green lawn and a grove of old chestnut trees. The rooms are handsome and comfortable. The friendly market town of Abergavenny and the pleasant river Usk are nearby, and Wordsworth's famous Tintern Abbey is a few minutes' drive away. Contact: The Landmark Trust, Shottesbrooke, Maidenhead, Berkshire, England SL6 3SW. Call 44-0628-82-5925.
Children: Y   Pets: N   Smoking: Y   Handicap Access: N   Payment: V, M, EC

Chepstow

FALLS HOUSE   *Rates: budget*
Open: year-round   *Minimum Stay: one week*

An enchanting apartment is available on the top floor of this handsome 18th-century house on the banks of the River Wye. Highlighted by magnificent coursing waterfalls, the grounds offer a grand view of the river down to Tintern Abbey and include a charming garden area where afternoon tea and evening meals are available. The apartment, reached by a separate entrance from the garden, contains two bedrooms, a kitchen and living room featuring a window seat that overlooks the river. A dining room with French doors opens onto a private pa. complete with outdoor furniture and a barbecue. Contact: British Travel Associates, P.O. Box 299, Elkton, VA 22827. Call 1-800-327-6097 (703-298-2232 in Virginia).

Children: Y   Pets: N   Smoking: Y   Handicap Access: N   Payment: All

Monmouth

THE STABLE COURT   *Rates: budget-inexpensive*
Open: year-round   *Minimum Stay: one week*

Dingestow, a regal thousand-acre estate dating from the 15th century, offers a cleverly converted gate house that retains its authentic Welsh charm while providing modern comfort. Reached by a covered staircase, the house contains a small but well-equipped kitchen and three bedrooms and is highlighted by its huge living room/dining area with high-pitched ceilings, exposed beams, mullion windows and a wood-burning fireplace. Guests have access to much of the estate grounds, including gardens, tennis court and fishing lake where a boat is available. Such scenic attractions as the Wye Valley and the Forest of Dean and Brecon Beacons are within easy reach. Contact: British Travel Associates, P.O. Box 299, Elkton, VA 22827. Call 1-800-327-6097 (703-298-2232 in Virginia).

Children: Y   Pets: N   Smoking: Y   Handicap Access: N   Payment: All

GWYNEDD

Aberdovey

ABERDOVEY HILLSIDE VILLAGE   *Rates: budget-inexpensive*
Open: year-round   *Minimum Stay: one week*

These splendid holiday houses tucked between the sea and the hills offer pleasant accommodations for four to nine guests. All have balconies or patios with gorgeous views of the sea, and the sandy beach is only a few feet away. Well-tended gardens offer picturesque pathways for sedate perambulations, while the rugged hills beyond tempt more intrepid wanderers. One of the most important advantages of these peaceful lodgings is their friendly, efficient managers, who live nearby. Contact: Mr. & Mrs. M. Fowler, Aberdovey Hillside Village, Aberdovey, Wales LL35 OND. Call 44-065-472-5222.

Children: Y   Pets: N   Smoking: Y   Handicap Access: N   Payment: EC

Beaumaris, Anglesey

WERN MEWS MANSION   *Rates: budget-inexpensive*
Open: year-round   *Minimum Stay: one week*

This august country mansion, resting peacefully amid acres of lawns and orchards at the end of a quiet lane, offers a comfortable and private second-floor apartment for refreshing Anglesey holidays. Overlooking the estate's colorful gardens and lake, the flat includes a spacious sitting room/dining area with a large bay window, a small den with fireplace, kitchen and breakfast room and two bedrooms. The house is within a mile of an uncrowded sandy beach and three miles from the

n of Beaumaris, a popular yachting center that's also the
⌐ enthralling 13th-century castle. Contact: British Travel
⌐s, P.O. Box 299, Elkton, VA 22827. Call 1-800-327-6097 (703-
⌐2 in Virginia).

⌐ ⌐n: **Y**   Pets: **N**   Smoking: **Y**   Handicap Access: **N**   Payment: All

Beaumaris
HENLLYS FARMHOUSE APARTMENTS   *Rates: budget*
Open: year-round   *Minimum Stay: one week*

These handsome old stables have been converted into luxurious cottage apartments for up to six guests. They are surrounded by 40 acres
of pasture and woodland, yet water fanatics need not fear—the sandy
beaches with their swimming, sailing and angling opportunities are
only a mile away. Riding and golf are also available in the area. Guests
enjoy the use of a heated swimming pool, a tennis court, a gymnasium,
a sauna and a jacuzzi; an excellent restaurant and two bars are found
next door. Contact: Mr. & Mrs. Minors, Dinlle Park, Dinan Dinlle,
Caernarvon, Gwynedd, Wales LL545TW. Call 44-0248-811303.

Children: **Y**   Pets: **N**   Smoking: **Y**   Handicap Access: **N**   Payment: EC

Caernarvon
BRYN BRAS CASTLE   *Rates: budget-inexpensive*
Open: year-round   *Minimum Stay: one week*

Amidst verdant woodland, rolling green lawns and tranquil gardens
sits a picturesque turreted castle; inside are warm, comfortable guest
accommodations equipped with color TVs, dishwashers and microwaves. And all of this is available for surprisingly little money. Sound
too good to be true? Visit Bryn Bras Castle and you'll be pleasantly
surprised. The lodgings can sleep from two to six people and are charmingly decorated. Set in the rolling foothills of Snowdonia, the estate
features many pleasant pathways and magnificent views of the mountains and sea. The sandy beach is only a short ride away. Contact: Mrs.
Marita Gray-Parry, Bryn Bras Castle, Llanrug, Caernarvon, Wales LL55
4RE. Call 44-0286-870210.

Children: **Y**   Pets: **N**   Smoking: **Y**   Handicap Access: **N**   Payment: EC

Caernarvon
THE BATH TOWER   *Rates: budget-inexpensive*
Open: year-round   *Minimum Stay: one week*

This ancient stone tower is part of the castle and town wall built by
Edward I of England in 1283 to impress the Welsh. From the majestic
windows in the living room you can look across the splendid Menai
Strait—the perfect private sea view. In the other direction you'll see a
stretch of the old wall and the venerable castle itself. Follow a spiral
stairway down from the living room and you'll find a spacious room
where several people can sleep. Additional sleeping accommodations
are found above, at the secluded top of the castellated tower. Never
was there a more splendid spot for enjoying the history and heritage of

Caernarvon. Contact: The Landmark Trust, Shottesbrooke, Maidenhead, Berkshire, England SL6 3SW. Call 44-0628-82-5925.

Children: Y   Pets: N   Smoking: Y   Handicap Access: N   Payment: V, M, EC

Conwy

ROSE COTTAGE

Rates: budget-inexpensive

Open: year-round

Minimum Stay: one week

This delightful little cottage is located in the center of the historic coastal resort of Conwy on the edge of the Snowdonia National Park. Decorated with exquisite stained-glass windows of intricate rose design, the beautifully furnished two-story house has a beamed living room/dining area with an open fireplace, a modern kitchen and two comfortable bedrooms. A cozy enclosed patio garden comes with a barbecue and outdoor furniture. A fascinating hamlet dominated by its town walls and the ancient castle of Edward I, Conwy offers sandy beaches and a charming harbor with opportunities for fishing and sailing. Contact: British Travel Associates, P.O. Box 299, Elkton, VA 22827. Call 1-800-327-6097 (703-298-2232 in Virginia).

Children: Y   Pets: N   Smoking: Y   Handicap Access: N   Payment: All

Dolgellau

BRYNYGWIN ISAF

Rates: budget

Open: year-round

Minimum Stay: one week

This handsome stone country house flanked by two charming cottages is located within lovely Snowdonia National Park. Serene mountains studded with ancient castles provide a peaceful setting, and the beautiful sandy beaches are only a few miles away. Brynygwin Isaf welcomes up to nine guests and features pleasant, comfortable accommodations. A large, pretty garden is the perfect spot for a quiet stroll. Those who prefer nature in its untamed state will find plenty of mountains to climb and forests to traverse; the beautiful Mawddach Estuary is nearby and Mount Snowdon itself is within easy reach. Contact: Mrs. H. Gauntlett, Brynygwin Isaf, Dolgellau, Wales LL40 1YA. Call 440341-422214 or 44-0341-423481.

Children: Y   Pets: N   Smoking: Y   Handicap Access: N   Payment: EC

Moelfre, Anglesey

BOLDON COTTAGE

Rates: budget-inexpensive

Open: year-round

Minimum Stay: one week

Located on Anglesey, an island right off the northern Wales coast, this 150-year-old gray stone cottage sits on the waterfront in the picturesque fishing village of Moelfre. Guests can look across the bay to the majestic Snowdonian Mountains on the mainland. The house features beamed ceilings throughout and contains a kitchen/dining area overlooking the beach, three bedrooms and a sunny sitting room with coal-burning stove and stunning sea views. A pebble beach where boats are available for hire is steps away and miles of sandy beaches for swimming are nearby, while invigorating cliff walks offer a magnificent opportunity to explore the rocky bay. Contact: British Travel

Associates, P.O. Box 299, Elkton, VA 22827. Call 1-800-327-6097 (703-298-2232 in Virginia).

Children: Y   Pets: N   Smoking: Y   Handicap Access: N   Payment: All

Penisa'rwaen

CAPEL-Y-WAEN CHAPEL   *Rates: budget*
Open: year-round   *Minimum Stay: one week*
Take life slowly at Capel-y-Waen and and experience the simple joys of a small Welsh town. Enter this former chapel through the old porch, and you'll find much of the original pine used for interior furnishings, including the supports for a pair of Victorian washbasins. Seven can sleep in four bedrooms, and a pine sauna off the master bedroom adds a luxurious touch. A sightseeing trip on the Snowdon Mountain Railway takes you around the lake where you can wind surf or row a boat. The famous Caernarfon's Castle is worth exploring, and you can meander through an assortment of village shops only five miles away. Contact: Castles, Cottages & Flats, Box 261, Westwood, MA, 02090. Call 617-329-4680.

Children: N   Pets: N   Smoking: Y   Handicap Access: N   Payment: V, M

Penmaenpool

PENMAENUCHA FARM   *Rates: budget*
Open: year-round   *Minimum Stay: one week*
Set on a five-hundred-acre sheep and cattle farm, this traditional stone farmhouse offers guests an opportunity to get involved in the farm's daily operation and learn about livestock management. The house sleeps seven in three bedrooms and a sofa bed, and features a modern kitchen and color TV. Splendid views of the beautiful Mawddach estuary and surrounding hills can be had from many parts of the farm. The farm is also close to the market town of Dolgellau, sandy beaches and resorts and the beautiful mountains and lakes of Snowdonia National Park. Contact: Blakes Vacations, 4918 Dempster Street, Skokie, IL 60077. Call 1-800-628-8118. Ref. UGP.

Children: Y   Pets: N   Smoking: Y   Handicap Access: N   Payment: V, M

Rhiwddolion

TY CAPEL AND TY COCH   *Rates: budget-inexpensive*
Open: year-round   *Minimum Stay: one week*
Once the home of productive slate quarry, tiny Rhiwddolion has become the tranquil domain of grazing sheep. There are only five houses left in the settlement and two of these are open to guests. The robust stone building of Ty Capel once served as the school and chapel for the stonemasons' families. It sits beside a gentle stream that flows through the valley and gazes out at rolling pastures. The older Ty Coch is perched a bit higher on the hillside, next to the waterfall. It features a flagstone living room and a large open fireplace. Neither house is accessible by car; you must reach them by following a pathway of half-buried stones. However, once you reach your destination, you'll be richly rewarded with the serene grace of a silent, wooded valley.

Contact: The Landmark Trust, Shottesbrooke, Maidenhead, Berkshire, England SL6 3SW. Call 44-0628-82-5925.

Children: Y   Pets: N   Smoking: Y   Handicap Access: N   Payment: V, M, EC

Sling

BODFEURIG FARM COTTAGE   *Rates: budget*
Open: year-round   *Minimum Stay: one week*

Nestled high in the foothills of Snowdonia National Park, Bodfeurig Farm Cottage rewards visitors with outstanding views of the Carneddau Mountains and the sea. Down a rough and gated track above the village, the cottage for five is built of granite in the Welsh tradition. A pot-bellied stove in the kitchen/living room adds warmth to the original slate flooring. Night storage heaters, a microwave oven and TV bring the amenities up to date. The heaters can also be used in the three bedrooms. There's plenty to see and do in the park, which is graced by lakes, mountains and reservoirs. Contact: Castles, Cottages & Flats, Box 261, Westwood, MA 02090. Call 617-329-4680.

Children: Y   Pets: N   Smoking: Y   Handicap Access: N   Payment: V, M

MID GLAMORGAN

Llangeinor

PENNY CROFT COTTAGE   *Rates: budget*
Open: year-round   *Minimum Stay: one week*

A splendid residence for couples yearning to explore the south Wales coast and its serene sandy beaches, Penny Croft is a pretty and very well-equipped cottage containing a spacious living room with gas fire, a nicely outfitted kitchen/dining area and comfy bedroom. The cottage commands superb views and is within easy reach not only of the shore but also the bewitching green valleys and mining museums inland. After a bit of touring, hiking or fishing, guests may relax in the lovely garden shared with the friendly owners, or stop in at their beguiling traditional Welsh pub and restaurant a hundred yards down the road. Contact: British Travel Associates, P.O. Box 299, Elkton, VA 22827. Call 1-800-327-6097 (703-298-2232 in Virginia).

Children: Y   Pets: N   Smoking: Y   Handicap Access: N   Payment: All

POWYS

Carreghofa

THE LOCKS HOUSE   *Rates: budget-inexpensive*
Open: year-round   *Minimum Stay: one week*

Bounded by the Montgomery canal on one side and a tributary of the River Tanat on the other, this former lock-keeper's house is a lovely and truly distinctive vacation residence. The old toll office has been converted into a quiet study, and fascinating canal artifacts are placed throughout the house. Three bedrooms, a beamed sitting room with a log stove and a kitchen with dining alcove and a splendid view across the lush surrounding countryside make this house comfy for travelers.

There's a lawn outside with patio furniture, and footpaths, including a trail along Offa's Dyke, offer a more active way of enjoying the canal area and its wildlife. Contact: British Travel Associates, P.O. Box 299, Elkton, VA 22827. Call 1-800-327-6097 (703-298-2232 in Virginia).

Children: **Y**   Pets: **N**   Smoking: **Y**   Handicap Access: **N**   Payment: **All**

Cwmdu

18TH-CENTURY WATERMILL   *Rates: budget*
Open: year-round   *Minimum Stay: one week*

This charming converted watermill is found in Cwmdu ("Black Valley"), a picturesque area within the Black Mountains. It is an ideal spot for enjoying the bucolic beauty of Wales: The stream that flows by the mill teems with trout, while the lovely countryside beyond can be enjoyed by car, foot or horseback. After a day spent exploring some of the nearby castles and gardens, you'll return to a clean, comfortable house for five with modern conveniences such as a color TV, a washing machine and central heating. The pretty patio outside features stone and wooden seats by the river. Babysitting service can be arranged if you want to take a moonlight stroll or drop in on the local pub. Contact: British Travel Associates, P.O. Box 299, Elkton, VA 22827. Call 1-800-327-6097 (in Virginia, 703-298-2232). Ref. A1248.

Children: **Y**   Pets: **N**   Smoking: **Y**   Handicap Access: **N**   Payment: **All**

Glasbury-on-Wye

MAESYRONEN CHAPEL   *Rates: budget-inexpensive*
Open: year-round   *Minimum Stay: one week*

Perched high on a hillside above the lovely valley of the Wye sits this remote and austere building, a monument to the simple rural faith that consecrated it. The chapel itself was converted from an old barn at the end of the 17th century; the adjoining cottage was added later, at the end of the 18th century. Both parts of the building have preserved their simple character and strength, although the little cottage is now pleasantly furnished to accommodate a few guests. Glasbury-on-Wye is a fine base for exploring central Wales and the English countryside around Hereford. The magnificent Brecon Beacons and the Black Mountains lie to the south and charming villages are scattered throughout. Contact: The Landmark Trust, Shottesbrooke, Maidenhead, Berkshire, England SL6 3SW. Call 44-0628-82-5925.

Children: **Y**   Pets: **N**   Smoking: **Y**   Handicap Access: **N**   Payment: **V, M, EC**

Radnor

HIGHBROOK COTTAGE   *Rates: budget-inexpensive*
Open: year-round   *Minimum Stay: one week*

Tranquil and secluded, Highbrook Cottage rests by a quiet stream between Radnor Forest and Offa's Dyke path, a richly scenic area rife with hiking and nature trails. A good farm track on the side of a fertile field leads to the traditionally furnished two-story house. The house features a living room with a stone hearth and panoramic views, a well-equipped kitchen, two comfortable bedrooms and a fetching garden by the water. Horseback riding, golf and private fishing are available nearby, and the popular inland resort of Llandrindod Wells, once a celebrated spa, is fifteen minutes away by car. Contact: British Travel Associates, P.O. Box 299, Elkton, VA 22827. Call 1-800-327-6097 (703-298-2232 in Virginia).

Children: Y   Pets: N   Smoking: Y   Handicap Access: N   Payment: All

Welshpool

POULTRY COTTAGE   *Rates: budget-inexpensive*
Open: year-round   *Minimum Stay: one week*

This fascinating cottage is part of a model farm built by a wealthy Liverpool banker in the middle of the 19th century. Part economic experiment, part whimsy, the Poultry Yard features individually designed quarters for each species of fowl; keeping them all together willy-nilly simply wouldn't do. The poultry keeper's cottage, a charming gothic revival curiosity, has been converted into a guest house. After you've investigated the farm and the lush forests surrounding it, you may want to visit nearby Powis Castle, just across the scenic Severn valley. Or take a pop into England and visit the medieval town of Shrewsbury. Contact: The Landmark Trust, Shottesbrooke, Maidenhead, Berkshire, England SL6 3SW. Call 44-0628-82-5925.

Children: Y   Pets: N   Smoking: Y   Handicap Access: N   Payment: V, M, EC

WEST GLAMORGAN

Oxwich

THE NOOK   *Rates: budget-inexpensive*
Open: year-round   *Minimum Stay: one week*

Located on the breathtaking Gower peninsula, this renovated 14th-century cottage, which still features its original beams and inglenook fireplace, is a site of historic significance, once used by John Wesley. The two-story house contains a living room/dining area, small modern kitchen overlooking the private terrace and garden to the rear and a steep staircase leading up to a landing (with twin beds) and master bedroom. Depending on your mood, a church and a pub are both nearby. The residence is within walking distance of the glorious sandy beaches and sweeping dunes of Oxwich, offering superb opportunities for swimming, sailing, wind surfing and water skiing. Contact: British Travel Associates, P.O. Box 299, Elkton, VA 22827. Call 1-800-327-6097 (703-298-2232 in Virginia).

Children: Y   Pets: N   Smoking: Y   Handicap Access: N   Payment: All

Yugoslavia

Bosnia and Herzegovina

Split

FJORD CRUISER   *Rates: moderate-deluxe*
Open: March-October   *Minimum Stay: one week*

Skippers with some boating experience will delight in cruising along a thousand miles of sunny Adriatic coast, exploring tiny inlets, uninhabited islands and picturesque ports in luxurious private vessels that sleep four or six. Setting off from the ancient Romanesque port of Split, you have free mooring privileges at any one of two dozen Adriatic Club Marinas from the Istrian peninsula in the north to the southern island of Hvar. Fully equipped cruisers include full-sized berths, well-equipped galleys with modern refrigerators and cooking facilities and a bathroom with a hot shower. Bedding, kitchenware and all navigational and safety equipment are included. Contact: Blakes Vacations, 4819 Dempster Street, Skokie, IL 60077. Call: 1-800-628-8118.

Children: Y   Pets: N   Smoking: Y   Handicap Access: N   Payment: T, V, M

Vodice

LASAN HOUSE *Rates: budget*
Open: April-November *Minimum Stay: one week*

The ground floor of the Lasan house offers a three-room apartment that can sleep a family of five, featuring a living room/dining room/kitchenette and one bedroom with twin beds and a bath. The second-floor six-room apartment can sleep nine in four bedrooms, and offers a beautiful terrace and garden. For guests in the small harbor port of Vodice, the mode of transportation that offers the best way to take in the varied coastline, grassy peninsula, fragrant pine forests and local cafes and vineyards is a simple bicycle. Of course, rental cars are available, too; and those who are more daring might try a small boat for an intimate tour of the wide, emerald-green bay waters and serenely beautiful coves. Contact: Interhome, Inc., 124 Little Falls Road, Fairfield, NJ 07006. Ref. Y5400/100A/B. Call: 201-882-6864.

Children: Y   Pets: N   Smoking: Y   Handicap Access: N   Payment: P, V, M

SLOVENIA

Istria

NOVIGRAD APARTMENTS *Rates: budget-inexpensive*
Open: April-November *Minimum Stay: one week*

In this two-thousand-year-old fishing village, you'll enjoy watching the local fisherman bring in their catch of the day. And later that evening, you can prepare the fresh fish on the outdoor grill in the garden outside your spacious apartment by the sea. These four-room units, which include a living room/dining room/kitchenette, one double and two twin bedrooms, bath and private patio can comfortably accommodate a family of six. Go boating on the calm bay; take a short walk to the ocean breakers; and explore the famous deep caverns of Limfjord and Postojna, nearby. And don't forget the quaint cafes where you can sample all the traditional fish dishes. Contact: Interhome, Inc., 124 Little Falls Road, Fairfield, NJ 07006. Ref. Y/1350/100A. Call: 201-882-6864.

Children: Y   Pets: N   Smoking: Y   Handicap Access: N   Payment: P, V, M

Istria

PORTOREZ APARTMENTS *Rates: budget-moderate*
Open: April-November *Minimum Stay: one week*

A popular vacation area for Europeans, this sunny Adriatic resort is surrounded by local vineyards, wooded hills and flower-lined promenades in addition to its many bathing beaches. Enjoy the breathtaking view from the terrace of this two-bedroom apartment/villa, which sleeps up to seven and also features a living/dining room, full kitchen and bath. In the immediate area there's easy access to tennis, bowling, surfing and waterskiing; or venture a few miles away to tiny Piran, a medieval village with narrow, winding streets where local artisans will demonstrate their traditional crafts. Contact: Interhome Inc., 124

Little Falls Road, Fairfield, NJ 07006. Ref. Y1200/60W. Call: 201-882-6864.

Children: **Y** Pets: **Y** Smoking: **Y** Handicap Access: **N** Payment: **P, V, M**

Istria

UMAG RESORT HOUSES   *Rates: budget-inexpensive*
Open: April-November   *Minimum Stay: one week*

In this newly developed resort area on the Istrian peninsula, you'll find a sparkling complex of one- to three-bedroom modern apartments situated just a few hundred yards from the long, rocky beaches of Umag. Each apartment, accommodating from three to five people, has a comfortably furnished living/dining room, kitchen, bath and individual terrace or garden/patio area. You can settle in and laze around town or hop on a bicycle to tour the nearby historic villages of Koper, Pula and the magnificent caves of Adelsberg. Contact: Interhome, Inc., 124 Little Falls Road, Fairfield, New Jersey 07006. Ref. Y1300/100-140W. Call: 201-882-6864.

Children: **Y** Pets: **N** Smoking: **Y** Handicap Access: **Y** Payment: **P, V, M**

Opatija

ZIGANTO HOUSE   *Rates: budget*
Open: April-November   *Minimum Stay: one week*

This ground-floor, one-bedroom oceanfront apartment in an airy country house provides an ideal romantic getaway for two and comes complete with a living room, kitchenette, well-tendered garden and shared terrace. Located on the serene Opatija Riviera at the base of the gentle Ucka Mountains, this is the perfect base from which to enjoy walks along the winding beach paths and woodland hikes through the slopes above. Cultural activities abound here all year, and guests will enjoy art exhibitions, outdoor concerts and operas, sailing regattas, carnivals and tennis tournments. The location and low rental make the Ziganto a real vacation bargain. Contact: Interhome, Inc., 124 Little Falls Road, Fairfield, NJ 07006. Ref. Y2100/101A. Call: 201-882-6864.

Children: **Y** Pets: **Y** Smoking: **Y** Handicap Access: **N** Payment: **P, V, M**

Rovinj

PAVACIC HOUSE   *Rates: budget-inexpensive*
Open: April-November   *Minimum Stay: one week*

For a romantic getaway, plan a stop in this tiny town of steep, winding alleys and secluded cafes, where picturesque squares are decorated with flowers and cozy wine parlors. This is the view from the covered terrace of this charming, furnished apartment with a living/dining room, two twin bedrooms, a kitchenette, one bath and an outside garden. A stroll down the streets where the aristocratic families have lived for centuries reveals stately palaces — some of which you can visit — and patrician houses of notable architecture. The restaurants, active nightlife and discotheques may lure you away from the seaside activities on the nearby Istrian peninsula. Contact: Interhome, Inc.,

124 Little Falls Road, Fairfield, NJ 07006. Ref. Y1500/100B. Call: 201-882-6864.

Children: Y   Pets: N   Smoking: Y   Handicap Access: N   Payment: P, V, M

Rovinj

SAINA HOUSE   *Rates: budget-inexpensive*
Open: April-November   *Minimum Stay: one week*

For those who want to vacation close to the Adriatic coast, this four-room apartment in a house with a private garden is a perfect alternative. Situated above a string of crystal-clear bays surrounded by rocky and sandy beaches, it also offers easy access to many offshore islands. (Red Island is only fifteen minutes away by boat.) The first floor of this duplex apartment is a spacious living and dining room with one double divan and a kitchenette; and the second floor has three twin bedrooms and a furnished, covered terrace from which to enjoy the sea view. This area has numerous nudist beaches (if you're so inclined) and local sports include wind surfing, sailing, tennis and scuba diving. Contact: Interhome, Inc., 124 Little Falls Road, Fairfield, NJ 07006. Ref. Y1500/110B. Call: 201-882-6864.

Children: Y   Pets: N   Smoking: Y   Handicap Access: N   Payment: P, V, M

Tourist Offices

Austrian National Tourist Office
  500 Fifth Avenue
  New York, NY 10110
  212-944-6880

  500 North Michigan Avenue
  Chicago, IL 60611
  312-644-5556

  11601 Wilshire Boulevard
  Los Angeles, CA 90025-1760
  213-477-3332

Belgian Tourist Office
  745 Fifth Avenue
  New York, NY 10151
  212-758-8130

British Tourist Authority
(England, Northern Ireland, Scotland, Wales)
  40 West 57th Street
  New York, NY 10019
  212-581-4700

  875 North Michigan Avenue
  Chicago, IL 60611
  312-787-0490

  350 South Figueroa Street
  Los Angeles, CA 90071
  213-628-3525

Cyprus Tourism Organization
  13 East 40th Street
  New York, NY 10016
  212-683-5280

French Government Tourist Office
  610 Fifth Avenue
  New York, NY 10020
  212-757-1125

  645 North Michigan Avenue
  Chicago, IL 60611
  312-337-6301

  9454 Wilshire Boulevard
  Beverly Hills, CA 90212
  213-271-6665

German National Tourist Office
747 Third Avenue
New York, NY 10017
212-308-3300

444 South Flower Street
Los Angeles, CA 90071
213-688-7332

Greek National Tourist Organization
645 Fifth Avenue
New York, NY 10022
212-421-5777

Hungarian Travel Bureau
1603 Second Avenue
New York, NY 10028
212-249-9342

Irish Tourist Board
757 Third Avenue
New York, NY 10017
212-418-0800

Italian Government Travel Office
630 Fifth Avenue
New York, NY 10111
212-245-4822

500 North Michigan Avenue
Chicago, IL 60611
312-644-0990

360 Post Street
San Francisco, CA 94108
415-392-5266

Luxembourg National Tourist Office
801 Second Avenue
New York, NY 10017
212-370-9850

Netherlands Board of Tourism
355 Lexington Avenue
New York, NY 10017
212-370-7360

Portuguese National Tourist Office
590 Fifth Avenue
New York, NY 10036
212-354-4403

Scandinavian Tourist Boards
(Denmark, Finland, Norway, Sweden)
   655 Third Avenue
   New York, NY 10017
   212-949-2333

   8929 Wilshire Boulevard
   Beverly Hills, CA 90211
   213-657-4808

Spain, National Tourist Office
   665 Fifth Avenue
   New York, NY 10022
   212-759-8822

   845 North Michigan Avenue
   Chicago, IL 60611
   312-642-1992

   8383 Wilshire Boulevard
   Beverly Hills, CA 90211
   213-658-7188

Swiss National Tourist Office
   608 Fifth Avenue
   New York, NY 10020
   212-757-5944

   150 South Michigan Avenue
   Chicago, IL 60601
   312-630-5840

   260 Stockton Street
   San Francisco, CA 94108
   415-362-2260

Yugoslavian National Tourist Office
   630 Fifth Avenue
   New York, NY 10111
   212-757-2801